W9-ALU-610

# HANDBOOK OF ELECTRONIC DESIGN AND ANALYSIS PROCEDURES USING PROGRAMMABLE CALCULATORS

Van Nostrand Reinhold
Electrical/Computer Science and Engineering Series

HANDBOOK OF ELECTRONIC DESIGN AND ANALYSIS PROCEDURES USING PROGRAMMABLE CALCULATORS, by Bruce K. Murdock

COMPILER DESIGN AND CONSTRUCTION, by Arthur Pyster

# HANDBOOK OF ELECTRONIC DESIGN AND ANALYSIS PROCEDURES USING PROGRAMMABLE CALCULATORS

BRUCE K. MURDOCK

VAN NOSTRAND REINHOLD
ELECTRICAL/COMPUTER SCIENCE AND ENGINEERING SERIES

VNR VAN NOSTRAND REINHOLD COMPANY
NEW YORK CINCINNATI ATLANTA DALLAS SAN FRANCISCO
LONDON TORONTO MELBOURNE

**Although every effort has been made to ensure the correctness of each program in this book, the author and the publisher are not responsible for any errors that may appear during execution of these programs by the reader. Furthermore, neither the author nor the publisher shall be liable for incidental or consequential damages in connection with or arising out of the furnishing, use, or performance of the program materials herein. If any errors are found by the readers, or program improvements noted, the author would would welcome correspondence to bring them to his attention.**

Van Nostrand Reinhold Company Regional Offices:
New York Cincinnati Atlanta Dallas San Francisco

Van Nostrand Reinhold Company International Offices:
London Toronto Melbourne



Library of Congress Catalog Card Number: 79-15122
ISBN 0-442-26137-3

Published by Van Nostrand Reinhold Company
135 West 50th Street, New York, N.Y. 10020

Published simultaneously in Canada by Van Nostrand Reinhold Ltd.

15 14 13 12 11 10 9 8 7 6 5 4 3 2 1

Library of Congress Cataloging in Publication Data

Murdock, Bruce K
Handbook of electronic design and analysis procedures using programmable calculators.

(Van Nostrand Reinhold Electrical/computer science and engineering series)
Bibliography: p. 513
Includes index.
1. Electronics--Data Processing. 2. Electronics--Computer Programs. 3. Programmable calculators. I. Title.
TK7835.M84 621.381'028'54 79-15122
ISBN 0-442-26137-3

# PREFACE

This book provides programs for programmable calculators enabling solutions to problems in network analysis, active and passive filter design, electromagnetic component design, high frequency amplifier design, and engineering mathematics.

These programs are meant to serve at least two purposes. The first, which is immediate, is to provide to the working engineer or scientist a library of programs for his or her fully programmable calculator. Fully programmable calculators such as the Hewlett-Packard HP-67/97 and the Texas Instruments TI-59 have substantial computing power and program memory. One noticeable difference between programmable calculators and larger computers is the speed of operation. Programmable calculators are slower because most have bit serial architecture and low clock speed. This speed sacrifice is offset by one big advantage; the programmable calculator is dedicated to its owner. The length of time from problem conception to problem solution is generally shorter using a calculator rather than using a remote centralized computer or time sharing terminal. Because the calculator is immediately at the disposal of its owner, no waiting is involved to use it. Errors in programming or data can be rapidly corrected in an interactive manner. Even though the actual program execution time may be longer, the beginning-to-end solution time is generally shorter, which, in the final analysis, is what is important.

The second purpose of these programs is to provide, by way of example, programming tips and algorithms to enhance the usefulness of programmable calculators in the HP-67/97 family. This statement does not imply that the programs described in this book are necessarily better, only that they may be different. One way to gain programming proficiency is to study how others attack and program a particular problem.

In my opinion, the latter purpose may be more important than the first, although not as immediate. Because today's fully programmable calculator has the ability to call subroutines, make conditional and unconditional branches, and to iterate, the user may, in the solitude of his own office or study, investigate those areas of engineering and applied mathematics that have previously been reserved for the users of large computers. An example might be the quantitative study into the behavior of a system described by a set of nonlinear differential equations.

When one owns the instrument, and does not have to pay for computing time by the minute, a newly found freedom is experienced. No longer must the need to run a particular program be justified; programs can be run for fun. All sorts of "what if" investigations can be made, no matter how trivial. In this respect, I like to quote R.W. Hamming, "The purpose of computing is insight, not numbers."

This collection of programs is by no means exhaustive, but can serve as a nucleus around which to build. Many programs in the sets have duplicate subroutines. As programmable calculators grow both in memory size and program storage capacity, existing programs may be combined to take advantage of common subroutines. Because future members of the Hewlett-Packard family of fully programmable calculators are planned to be upwardly compatible from the HP-67/97, the above expansion and combination may be easily achieved.

The author is indebted to Professor S.K. Mitra for his encouragement to write this book and his advice and comments, Dr. K. Mondal for his thorough proofreading of the manuscript and correction of numerous errors, and to the reviewers, Dr. Sidney Darlington and P.R. Geffe, for their most thorough and critical reviews. The working environment and wide range of engineering assignments at Delco Electronics provided the experience and background that helped make this book possible.

The author also wishes to thank R. Junk and W. Ware for their TI-59 translations of Programs 1-3 and 1-4.

My special appreciation goes to my wife and daughter, Bonnie and Marline, for bearing with me while preparing the manuscript.

# CONTENTS

# INTRODUCTION

## *INTRODUCTION*

This book provides programming techniques and programs to make the fully programmable calculator a valuable design tool for the working engineer. This book is not specifically intended to be a textbook on calculator programming, although documented programs can serve this purpose. Three books can be recommended for programming methods and algorithms: Jon M. Smith, "Scientific Analysis on the Pocket Calculator," Wiley 1975, John Ball, "Algorithms for RPN Calculators," Wiley 1978, and Richard W. Hamming, "Numerical Methods for Scientists and Engineers," McGraw-Hill 1973.

Many programs in this book are meant to be used in sets, i.e., the output of one program becomes the input for another through common storage register allocations. The description of each program is meant to stand alone, and consists of the following parts:

1) Problem description with pertinent equations,
2) Program operating instructions,
3) One or more program examples,
4) Equation and method derivation, or references,
5) Annotated program listing, which is its own flowchart.

Part 4 is not present in every program.

This program ordering was chosen so the variable definitions and operating instructions are immediately available to the experienced user. Should the user wish more information or background on the program and equations, or the details of the program operation, this material is also available, but is placed after the operating instructions.

Although the program language, and resulting program flow is tailored to the Hewlett-Packard (HP) fully programmable calculators, the HP-67/97, the annotated program listing/flowchart can be used as a basis for generating programs in other languages.

The language of the Texas Instruments (TI) fully programmable calculator, the TI-59, is not very different from the HP-67/97 language when considered on a gross scale, therefore, the HP-67/97 programs may be easily translated into the language of the TI-59. While it is easy to write a program from equations and flowcharts, the new program must still be debugged. Translating a program that has already been tested and debugged can lead to a new program that has no bugs at all. The TI program translation will also closely follow the flow of the original HP program.

The differences between the HP and TI languages are mainly in format and not in form. Because the TI-59 has few merged keycodes, must use parentheses to set hierarchy, and must branch to a label or line number as the result of a true conditional test, the TI-59 program will be longer than the mating HP-67/97 program. This increased program length is generally not a detriment as it is accommodated by the larger program memory available in the TI-59. Because the TI-59 always starts label searches from the top of the program, the program execution time can also be longer unless direct addressing is used, or the labeled subroutines are placed at the beginning of the program.

Since the TI-59 does not have a stack to hold the results of an equals operation, a set of scratchpad registers must be set aside to hold those intermediate results normally retained in the HP-67/97 stack. Results residing in the TI-59 display register after the equals operation will permanently disappear unless stored before subsequent operations are performed.

The arithmetic hierarchy of the Algebraic Operating System (AOS) can sometimes be a problem which becomes particularly apparent when calling subroutines. If an equals operation does not precede the subroutine call, the subroutine hierarchy will be dependent on the hierarchy set up in the main program. To make the subroutine hierarchy independent of the main program, the subroutine should always start with an open parenthesis and terminate with a close parenthesis. This rule can be extended to the "go to" command also. The last statement prior to the unconditional jump should be an equals to terminate all pending operations. It will cause no harm to have an open parenthesis as the first statement after the label that is the jump destination. The TI-59 has enough program memory so that, whenever in doubt, parenthesis can be inserted to establish unconditional arithmetic hierarchy.

The TI-59 does not have the equivalent of the HP-67/97 flag 3 function where flag 3 is automatically set whenever numeric data is entered from the keyboard. Because of this difference, the convenience feature existing in most of the HP-67/97 programs herein where the execution of a user definable key such as "A" without numeric entry results in the currently stored parameter value being displayed cannot be translated to the TI-59 program.

None of the TI-59 flags are test cleared, while flags 2 and 3 of the HP-67/97 are test cleared, thus, clear flag statements may be required in the TI-59 program and subroutines involving the use of flags 2 and 3.

The HP-67/97 and the TI-59 both have user definable labels A through E, and a through e (the latter are designated A' through E' on the TI-59). Executing these keys from the keyboard acts like a subroutine call on either machine: the program pointer jumps to the designated label, and program execution begins. The HP-67/97 and the TI-59 are different in the labels called "common labels" by TI, i.e., labels other than the user definable ones. HP uses the label designators 0 through 9, and a given label may be used more than once as label searches start from the present place in program memory, hence a "local label" such as label 6 in Program 2-4 is used many times within the program. The TI-59 cannot use numeric labels, but uses other function keys as labels, e.g., "sin," "fix," etc. There are 62 such keys available for labels. The TI-59 always starts label searches from the top of the program, hence, a given label can only be used once within the program.

The TI-59 is internally set up to be most efficient, time wise, when jumps and branches are made to line numbers rather than to labels. The HP-67/97 appears to be as fast in a label search as the TI-59 is in a line number search. The HP-67/97 cannot go to a specified line number under program control, hence, it is restricted to label searches only. There is a simple program trick shown on page IV-98 of the TI-59 owner's manual where a program is initially written with labels, and the label calls have "NOP" statements following so the program can easily be modified for line number addressing after the program is debugged and complete.

Care should be exercised when translating program coding containing rectangular-to-polar (→P) and polar-to-rectangular (→R) conversions as the TI-59 and HP-67/97 operate on the variables in opposite manner. The HP-67/97 takes the x and y coordinates from the x and y registers and places the magnitude and angle equivalents back into the x and y registers respectively for the →P conversion, and vice-versa for the →R conversion. The TI-59 uses the t and x registers for the two variables, and takes the x and y coordinates from the t and x registers and places the equivalent magnitude and angle back into the t and x registers respectively for the →P conversion, and vice-versa for the →R conversion. Both machines display the contents of the x register, so the TI-59 will display angle or y coordinate whereas the HP-67/97 will display magnitude or x coordinate after respective →P or →R conversions.

To guide the reader in this translation, several programs in this book have been translated into the TI-59 language. These programs have user instructions, examples, and program coding in both languages. Program 1-1 has been flowcharted in addition to provide a common point of reference between the two program listings.

The preceding paragraphs mention anomalies in the TI-59 language. The HP-67/97 language has its idiosyncracies also. Reading the program listings, one will notice some "non-standard" program coding. The prime consideration was to fit the algorithm into the program memory. Within this constraint, the program coding was selected to minimize program execution time whenever possible. Numeric entries within the body of the program are to be avoided, and should be recalled from register storage. Entry of each numeric digit requires 72 milliseconds to execute while a register recall only requires 35 milliseconds typically. Numeric entries such as "10," "100," or any other power of 10 should be entered as a power of ten through the "EEX" key. The number "1" should be entered as "EEX" alone and requires only 48 milliseconds to execute. Similarly, the "CLX" function will result in a zero in the display, and only requires 30 milliseconds to execute. Multiplication of a number by two (2, x) requires 179 milliseconds to execute, while addition of a number to itself (ENT ↑, +) requires 82 milliseconds execution time and yields the same result. Register arithmetic is executed faster than stack arithmetic when the register recalls are considered, and register arithmetic can save program steps. Whenever the algorithm allows, subroutine calls should be minimized as they typically require 240 milliseconds for the label search and return. Likewise unconditional jumps such as GTOA require 160 milliseconds for the label search typically. By paying attention to small details such as these, the program execution time can be shortened considerably expecially when iteration or looping is required. For more information on execution times and programming hints with the HP-67/97, see "Better Programming on the HP-67/97" edited by William Kolb, John Kennedy, and Richard Nelson, and available from the PPC Club (new name for the HP-65 Users Club), 2541 W. Camden Place, Santa Ana, Calif. 92704.

Even though the program coding has been chosen for minimum execution time, the program LNAP may require more than a minute of computation time before output is provided when the number of branches is large. Likewise, the same time requirement may exist for the filter programs when the filter order is large.

An attempt has been made to choose self-explanatory label descriptions for the user definable keys; hence, once familiar with a particular program, the user need only refer to the magnetic card label markings to run the program.

To restate a point made in the preface of this book, it is not possible to include programs and descriptions covering all areas of engineering analysis and design. The programs herein are only representative of areas in networks and circuits (the terms "networks" and "circuits" may be used interchangeably). The 39 programs contained in this book have been selected from the author's library, and have proved to be quite useful to the author; hopefully, they will prove equally useful to the reader.

The program description not only shows the equations used by the program, but gives a reference, or has a derivation of the equations so these programs may serve as a base for the generation of other related programs as may be needed by the reader for his or her particular application.

Because the programs herein cover several different disciplines in electrical engineering, a problem with nomenclature arises. To the control systems oriented engineer, the term "transfer function" implies system output divided by system input. On the other hand, to the filter design engineer, "transfer function" implies system input divided by system output, or the reciprocal of the control system engineer's definition. To avoid confusion, the term "transmission function" is used to mean system output divided by input and "transfer function" is used to mean system input divided by output. This convention will be followed throughout the book.

The appendix has a list of a list of abbreviations used, along with the bibliography give the reader an easily found place to go should confusion or uncertainty to variable or abbreviation meaning arise.

# HANDBOOK OF ELECTRONIC DESIGN AND ANALYSIS PROCEDURES USING PROGRAMMABLE CALCULATORS

# Part 1
# NETWORK ANALYSIS

## PROGRAM 1-1 LOSSY TRANSMISSION LINE INPUT IMPEDANCE.

Program Description and Equations Used

This program uses Eq. (1-1.1) to determine the complex input impedance, $Z_s$, of a lossy transmission line of length $\ell$, loaded with a complex impedance $Z_r$, and having a characteristic impedance $Z_o$, an attenuation constant $\alpha_{dB}$ in dB per unit length, and a phase constant $\beta$ in radians per unit length (or velocity of propagation $C_m$). For solid dielectric cables, $C_m$ is typically 1/2 to 2/3 the free-space speed of light, and is approximated by Eq. (1-1.9) for low loss coaxial cables, or calculated from Eqs. (1-1.5) and (1-1.6) if the cable impedance and admittance per unit length are known at the operating frequency. The unit of length has purposely not been given because it is to be selected by the user. As long as the same length unit is used throughout, length will cancel out of Eq. (1-1.1). Figure 1-1.1 shows the general circuit topology.

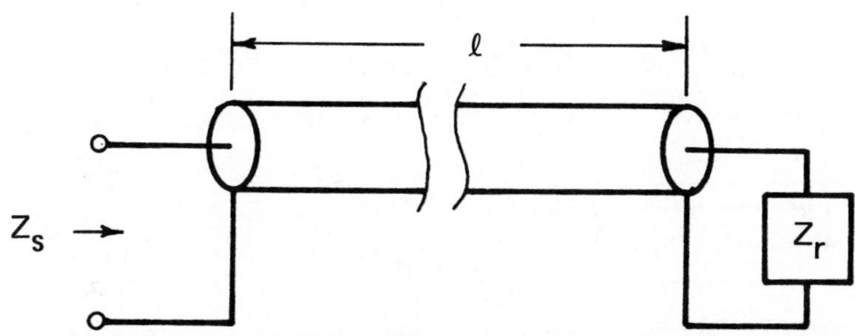


Figure 1-1.1 Transmission line setup.

The equation that describes the problem is:

$$Z_s = Z_o \frac{1 + \rho e^{-2\gamma\ell}}{1 - \rho e^{-2\gamma\ell}} \tag{1-1.1}$$

where $\rho$ is the reflection coefficient and $\gamma$ is the propagation function. These quantities are given by the following equations:

$$\rho = \frac{Z_r/Z_o - 1}{Z_r/Z_o + 1} \tag{1-1.2}$$

$$\gamma = \alpha + j\beta \tag{1-1.3}$$

$$\alpha = (\alpha_{db})/(20 \log e) \tag{1-1.4}$$

$$\beta = \frac{2\pi}{\lambda} = \frac{2\pi f}{C_m} \tag{1-1.5}$$

If the per unit length series impedance, $\bar{R} + j\omega\bar{L}$, and shunt admittance, $\bar{G} + j\omega\bar{C}$, are available at the frequency of operation, then the propagation function is given by:

$$\gamma = \sqrt{(\bar{R} + j\omega\bar{L})(\bar{G} + j\omega\bar{C})} \tag{1-1.6}$$

If $Z_r$ is desired in terms of $Z_s$, $Z_r$ is replaced by $Z_s$ in Eq. (1-1.1), $Z_s$ is replaced by $Z_r$ in Eq. (1-1.2), and $\ell$ is replaced by $-\ell$ in Eq. (1-1.1).

This quasi-symmetrical property allows the use of the same program to calculate the transmission line input impedance with a complex load by using a positive line length, or to calculate the complex load that will provide a specified input impedance by using a negative line length.

A duality also exists with Eq. (1-1.1) and Eq. (1-1.2). The same equation form holds for the transmission line input or output admittance providing each Z is replaced by the corresponding Y, i.e., $Y_s = 1/Z_s$, $Y_r = 1/Z_r$, and $Y_o = 1/Z_o$. The admittance forms of Eqs. (1-1.1) and (1-1.2) are as follows:

$$Y_s = Y_o \frac{1 + \rho' e^{-2\gamma\ell}}{1 - \rho' e^{-2\gamma\ell}} \tag{1-1.7}$$

where

$$\rho' = \frac{Y_r/Y_o - 1}{Y_r/Y_o + 1} \qquad (1\text{-}1.8)$$

$$(\rho' = -\rho)$$

Because the equation form is the same, the program will work with admittances as well as impedances.

In this HP-67/97 program, keys "A" through "E" and "a" through "c" on the calculator have a dual function role. Execution of these keys following a data entry from the keyboard is interpreted as data input by the program, and the numeric entry is stored. Execution of these keys following a nonnumeric entry, or following the "e" (clear) key is interpreted as an output request, and the currently stored values are printed (HP-97 only) and displayed. This feature cannot be translated into the TI-59 program.

The data required by the program is entered in either cartesian (real and imaginary) or polar (magnitude and angle) form through keys "b" and "c," or "B" and "C" respectively. On large coax cables such as underwater telephone cable, both the cable attenuation and phase constants are provided as a function of frequency by the manufacturer, and are loaded into the program using the units of dB per unit length and radians per unit length respectively. If $\beta$ is unknown, it can be calculated from the velocity of propagation in the transmission line. If the transmission line has less than 1 dB loss in the length being used, and is of coaxial construction, the velocity in the medium (phase velocity) may be approximated by

$$C_m \simeq \frac{\text{speed of light in free space}}{\sqrt{\varepsilon_r \mu_r}} \qquad (1\text{-}1.9)$$

where $\varepsilon_r$ and $\mu_r$ are the relative dielectric constant and relative permeability of the cable dielectric and conductors respectively. For cables constructed of nonmagnetic parts, or for cables with a steel strength member within the center conductor of the cable and operating at frequencies where the skin effect keeps currents from flowing within the strength member, the relative permeability, $\mu_r$ becomes unity.

# User Instructions

HP-67/97 PROGRAM

| LOSSY TRANSMISSION LINE INPUT IMPEDANCE | | | | |
|---|---|---|---|---|
| $f \uparrow C_m$ | $\mathrm{Re}\ Z_o \uparrow \mathrm{Im}\ Z_o$ | $\mathrm{Re}\ Z_r \uparrow \mathrm{Im}\ Z_r$ | compute $\lvert Z_s \rvert, \measuredangle Z_s$ | clear entry mode |
| $\alpha_{dB} \uparrow \beta \uparrow f$ | $\lvert Z_o \rvert \uparrow \measuredangle Z_o$ | $\lvert Z_r \rvert \uparrow \measuredangle Z_r$ | $\lvert \rho \rvert, \measuredangle \rho$ | $\ell$ |

| STEP | INSTRUCTIONS | INPUT DATA/UNITS | KEYS | OUTPUT DATA/UNITS |
|---|---|---|---|---|
| 1 | Load both sides of program card | | | |
| 2 | Enter transmission line parameters | | | |
| | line loss in dB/unit length | $\alpha_{dB}$ | ↑ | |
| | phase constant in radians/unit length | $\beta$ | ↑ | |
| | frequency in hertz | f | A | $C_m$ |
| | If velocity of propogation is known instead of phase constant, enter dummy value of 1 for phase constant in step 3 above, then | | | |
| | Enter frequency in hertz | f | ↑ | |
| | Enter propagation velocity* | $C_m$ | f A | $\beta$ |
| | * note: | | | |
| | The units of length must be consistent throughout the data, i.e., all in meters, or feet, or miles, etc. | | | |
| 3 | Enter the transmission line characteristics at the chosen analysis frequency | | | |
| | magnitude of $Z_o$ in ohms | $\lvert Z_o \rvert$ | ↑ | |
| | phase angle of $Z_o$ in degrees | $\measuredangle Z_o$ | B | |
| | OR | | | |
| | real part of $Z_o$ in ohms | $\mathrm{Re}\ Z_o$ | ↑ | |
| | imaginary part of $Z_o$ in ohms | $\mathrm{Im}\ Z_o$ | f B | |
| 4 | Enter load impedance | | | |
| | magnitude of load impedance in ohms | $\lvert Z_r \rvert$ | ↑ | |
| | phase angle of load impedance in degrees | $\measuredangle Z_r$ | C | |
| | OR | | | |
| | real part of load impedance in ohms | $\mathrm{Re}\ Z_r$ | ↑ | |
| | imaginary part of load impedance in Ω | $\mathrm{Im}\ Z_r$ | f C | |

# User Instructions

LOSSY TRANSMISSION LINE INPUT IMPEDANCE
HP-67/97
CONTINUED

1 2

| STEP | INSTRUCTIONS | INPUT DATA/UNITS | KEYS | | OUTPUT DATA/UNITS |
|---|---|---|---|---|---|
| 5 | Enter transmission line length | $\pm \ell$ | E | | |
| | $+\ell$ to calculate $Z_s$ given $Z_r$ | | | | |
| | $-\ell$ to calculate $Z_r$ given $Z_s$ | | | | |
| 6 | Optional, printout or enter refl coef | | | | |
| | $\rho$ entry | $\lvert\rho\rvert \uparrow \measuredangle \rho^\circ$ | D | | |
| | $\rho$ printout | | D | | $\lvert\rho\rvert, \measuredangle \rho^\circ$ |
| | Of the three variables $Z_o, Z_r$, & $\rho$ | | | | |
| | either $Z_o$ & $Z_r$ or $Z_o$ & $\rho$ | | | | |
| | are required. | | | | |
| 7 | Compute $\lvert Z_s\rvert, \measuredangle Z_s$ ( length positive ) | | f | D | $\lvert Z\rvert, \measuredangle Z^\circ$ |
| | $\lvert Z_r\rvert, \measuredangle Z_r$ ( length negative ) | | | | |
| 8 | To clear input mode and initialize program | | f | E | |
| 9 | To review input data | | f | E | |
| | | | f | A | f , $C_m$ |
| | | | A | | $\alpha_{dB}, \beta, f$ |
| | | | f | B | $ReZ_o, ImZ_o$ |
| | | | B | | $\lvert Z_o\rvert, \measuredangle Z_o^\circ$ |
| | | | f | C | $ReZ_r, ImZ_r$ |
| | | | C | | $\lvert Z_r\rvert, \measuredangle Z_r^\circ$ |
| | | | D | | $\lvert\rho\rvert, \measuredangle \rho^\circ$ |
| | | | E | | $\ell$ |

NOTE:
The angular mode of the program is degrees. All angular data input and output is in degrees with the exception of $\beta$. The angular mode should not be changed as program malfunction will occur because of R→D and D→R conversions that are used.

# User Instructions

TI-59 TRANSLATION

| LOSSY TRANSMISSION LINE INPUT IMPEDANCE (TI-59) | | | | |
|---|---|---|---|---|
| $C_m$ | $ReZ_o$, $ImZ_o$ | $ReZ_r$, $ImZ_r$ | calculate $\|Z_r\|$, $\measuredangle Z_r$ | |
| $\alpha_{dB}$, $\beta$, f | $\|Z_o\|$, $\measuredangle Z_o$ | $\|Z_r\|$, $\measuredangle Z_r$ | output $\|\rho\|$, $\measuredangle \rho$ | $\ell$ |

TI-59 TRANSLATION

| STEP | INSTRUCTIONS | INPUT DATA/UNITS | KEYS | OUTPUT DATA/UNITS |
|---|---|---|---|---|
| 1 | Load both sides of magnetic card | | | |
| 2 | Load line loss in dB/unit length | $\alpha_{dB}$ | A | |
| | Load line phase constant in rad / unit length | $\beta$ | R/S | |
| | If $C_m$, the velocity in the medium, is known instead, load dummy $\beta$ of 1 | | | |
| | Load analysis frequency in hertz | f | R/S | |
| 3 | If $C_m$ is known instead of $\beta$, load $C_m$ | $C_m$ | 2nd A | |
| 4 | Enter $Z_o$, the transmission line characteristic impedance in polar or rectangular co-ords | | | |
| | polar co-ordinates: magnitude | $\|Z_o\|$, Ω | B | |
| | phase angle | $\measuredangle Z_o$, ° | R/S | |
| | rectangular co-ordinates: real part | Re $Z_o$, Ω | 2nd B | |
| | imaginary part | Im $Z_o$, Ω | R/S | |
| 5 | Enter load impedance at the analysis freq as either polar or rectangular data | | | |
| | polar co-ordinates: | $\|Z_r\|$, Ω | C | |
| | | $\measuredangle Z_r$, ° | R/S | |
| | rectangular co-ordinates: | Re $Z_r$, Ω | 2nd C | |
| | | Im $Z_r$, Ω | R/S | |
| 6 | Load transmission line length | $\pm\ell$ | E | |
| | $+\ell$ to calculate $Z_s$ given $Z_r$ | | | |
| | $-\ell$ to calculate $Z_r$ given $Z_s$ | | | |
| 7 | Optional: output reflection coefficient | | D | $\|\rho\|$ |
| | | | R/S* | $\measuredangle \rho$° |
| 8 | To calculate $Z_s$ (or $Z_r$ given negative length) | | 2nd D | $\|Z\|$, Ω |
| | | | R/S* | $\measuredangle Z$° |
| | * If the TI-59 is attached to the PC-100A printer, the second value will be printed without the R/S command. | | | |

<u>Example 1-1.1</u>

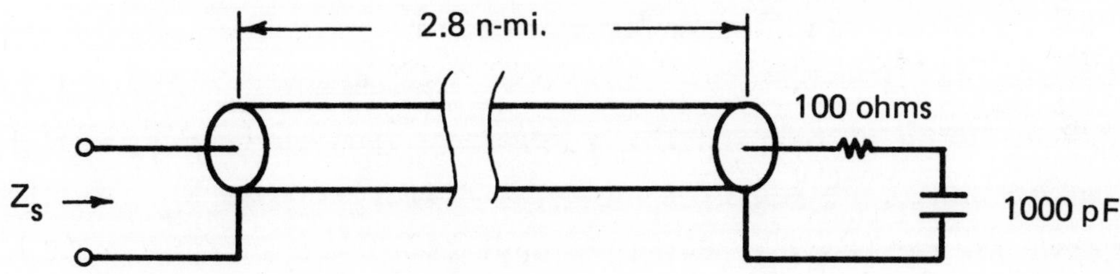


Figure 1-1.2 SD coaxial cable circuit for Ex. 1-1.1.

Type SD underwater telephone coax is to be used at 0.72 MHz. The cable section is 2.8 nautical miles (n-mi.) long and is loaded by a series RC network of 100 ohms and 1000 pF as shown in Fig. 1-1.2. Find the cable input impedance, $Z_s$, at this frequency.

At 0.72 MHz the electrical parameters of SD coax are:

$$\alpha_{dB} = 2.070 \text{ dB/n-mi.}$$

$$\beta = 42.511 \text{ radians/n-mi.}$$

$$Z_o = 44.625 \text{ ohms at } -0.315 \text{ degree}$$

The RC load impedance is:

$$\text{Re } Z_r = 100 \text{ ohms}$$

$$\text{Im } Z_r = -j/(2\pi fC) = -j221 \text{ ohms}$$

The input impedance of the loaded coax is 66.902 + j11.167 ohms as obtained from using the program and shown in the printout below:

| PROGRAM INPUT | | | PROGRAM OUTPUT | | |
|---|---|---|---|---|---|
| 2.070 | ENT↑ | $\alpha_{dB}$, dB/n-mi. | | GSBd | calculate $Z_s$ |
| 42.511 | ENT↑ | β, rad/n-mi. | 67.827 | *** | $\|Z_s\|$, ohms |
| .72+06 | GSBA | frequency, Hz | 9.476 | *** | ∡ $Z_s$ , degrees |
| 44.265 | ENT↑ | $\|Z_o\|$, ohms | | X⇄Y<br>→R | convert to rect |
| -.315 | GSBB | ∡ $Z_o$, degrees | 66.902 | *** | Re $Z_s$, ohms |
| 100.000 | ENT↑ | Re $Z_r$, ohms | 11.167 | *** | Im $Z_s$, " |
| -221.000 | GSBc | Im $Z_r$, " | | GSBa | calculate $C_m$ |
| 2.800 | GSBE | length, n-mi. | 720000.000 | *** | frequency, Hz |
| | | | 106417.008 | *** | $C_m$, n-mi./sec |

Example 1-1.2

Using the type SD underwater telephone coax of Example 1-1.1, find the load impedance at 0.72 MHz that will result in an input impedance of 60 + j0 ohms. The length of the coax is 2.8 n-mi. as in the previous example.

When using a lossy cable, a negative real part in $Z_r$ will be required to obtain values of $Z_s$ greatly different than $Z_o$. Furthermore, if $\alpha\ell$ is greater than 30 dB, the input impedance will be nearly $Z_o$, independent of the load impedance.

In this example, a negative line length is loaded to use the quasi-symmetric properties of Eqs. (1-1.1) and (1-1.2) for calculating $Z_r$ given $Z_s$.

The HP-97 printout reproduced next shows a load impedance of 67.396 - j73.338 ohms is required. The equivalent load network is also shown.

| PROGRAM INPUT | | PROGRAM OUTPUT | | |
|---|---|---|---|---|
| 2.070 ENT↑ | $\alpha_{dB}$, dB/n-mi. | | GSBa | calculate load $Z_r$ |
| 42.511 ENT↑ | β, rad/n-mi. | 99.603 | *** | $\|Z_r\|$, ohms |
| .72+06 GSBA | frequency, Hz | -47.418 | *** | $\measuredangle Z_r$, degrees |
| 44.265 ENT↑ | $\|Z_o\|$, ohms | | X⇄Y | convert to rect |
| -.315 GSBB | $\measuredangle Z_o$, degrees | | →R | |
| 60.000 ENT↑ | Re $Z_s$, ohms | 67.396 | *** | Re $Z_r$, ohms |
| 0.000 GSBc | Im $Z_s$, " | -73.338 | *** | Im $Z_r$, " |
| -2.800 GSBE | | 2.000 | Pi | |
| | | | × | calculate |
| | | .72+06 | × | equivalent |
| | | | × | capacitor |
| | | | 1/X | |
| | | 3.014-09 | *** | C, farad |

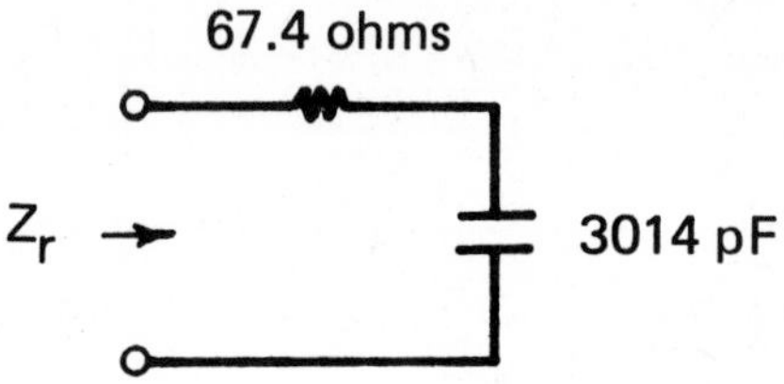


Figure 1-1.3 Equivalent load network.

Example 1-1.3, TI-59 Program Example

This example is the same as Example 1-1.2 where the problem is to determine load impedance, $Z_r$, that results in an input impedance, $Z_s$, of 60 + j0 ohms. The line length is 2.8 n-mi. Because $Z_r$ is to be calculated given $Z_s$, a negative line length is used. The PC-100A printer output is shown below.

**PROGRAM INPUT**

| | |
|---:|---|
| 2.07 | $\alpha_{dB}$, dB/n-mi. |
| 42.511 | $\beta$, rad/n-mi. |
| 7.2 05 | frequency, Hz |
| 106417.0079 | $C_m$ (output), n-mi./sec |
| 44.265 | $\lvert Z_o \rvert$, ohms |
| -0.315 | $\measuredangle Z_o$, degrees |
| 60. | Re $Z_s$, ohms |
| 0. | Im $Z_s$, " |
| -2.8 | line length, n-mi. |

**PROGRAM OUTPUT**

| | |
|---:|---|
| .1509385583 | $\lvert \rho \rvert$, dimensionless |
| 1.019762234 | $\measuredangle \rho$, degrees |
| 99.60303649 | $\lvert Z_r \rvert$, ohms |
| -47.41754913 | $\measuredangle Z_r$, degrees |

Note: the PC-100A printer will not print the mnemonic representing the input key. The HP-97 does this automatically when in the "norm" mode.

## PROGRAM FLOW DIAGRAM

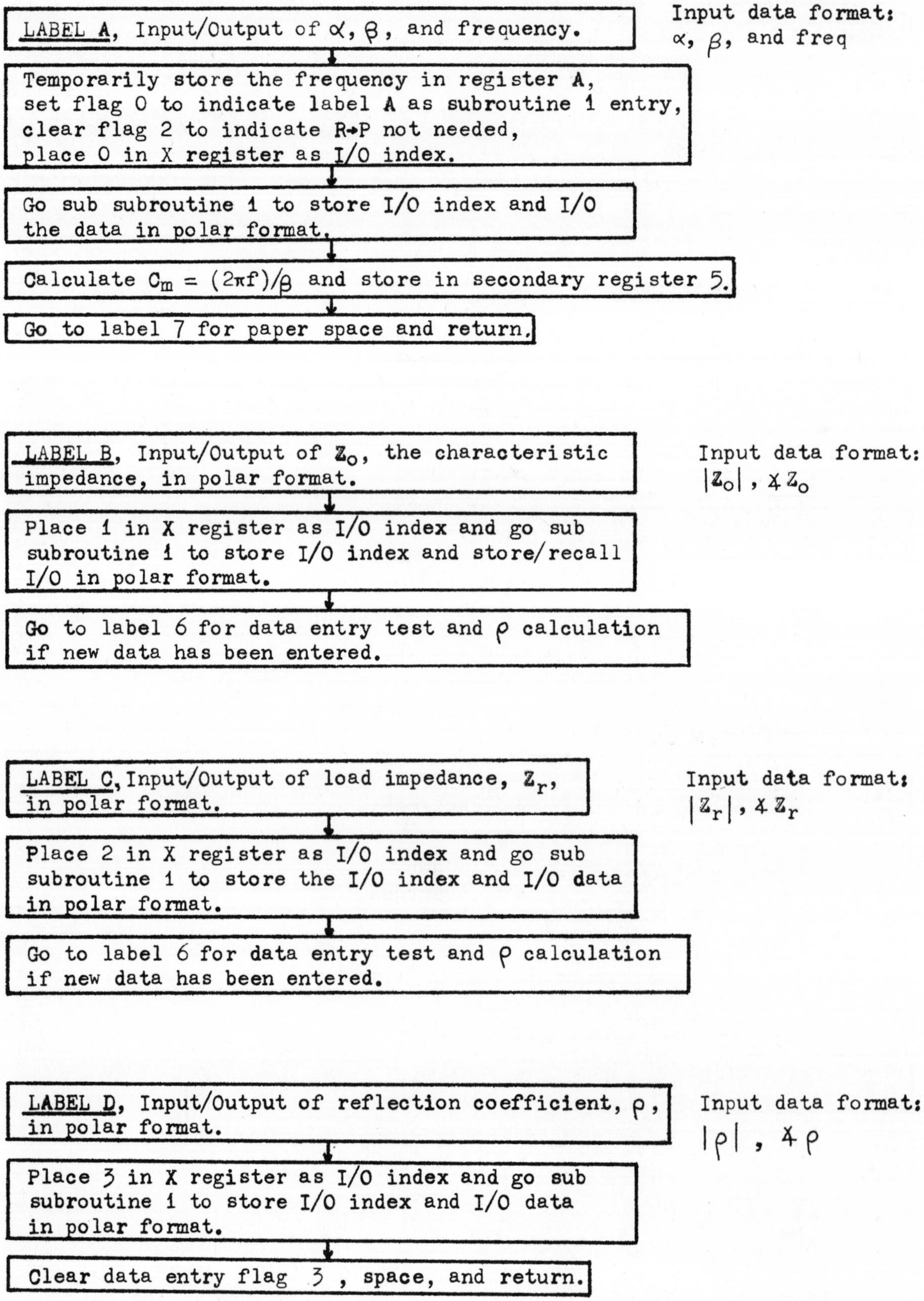

LABEL A, Input/Output of $\alpha$, $\beta$, and frequency.

Input data format: $\alpha$, $\beta$, and freq

↓

Temporarily store the frequency in register A, set flag 0 to indicate label A as subroutine 1 entry, clear flag 2 to indicate R→P not needed, place 0 in X register as I/O index.

↓

Go sub subroutine 1 to store I/O index and I/O the data in polar format.

↓

Calculate $C_m = (2\pi f)/\beta$ and store in secondary register 5.

↓

Go to label 7 for paper space and return.

---

LABEL B, Input/Output of $Z_o$, the characteristic impedance, in polar format.

Input data format: $|Z_o|$, $\measuredangle Z_o$

↓

Place 1 in X register as I/O index and go sub subroutine 1 to store I/O index and store/recall I/O in polar format.

↓

Go to label 6 for data entry test and $\rho$ calculation if new data has been entered.

---

LABEL C, Input/Output of load impedance, $Z_r$, in polar format.

Input data format: $|Z_r|$, $\measuredangle Z_r$

↓

Place 2 in X register as I/O index and go sub subroutine 1 to store the I/O index and I/O data in polar format.

↓

Go to label 6 for data entry test and $\rho$ calculation if new data has been entered.

---

LABEL D, Input/Output of reflection coefficient, $\rho$, in polar format.

Input data format: $|\rho|$, $\measuredangle \rho$

↓

Place 3 in X register as I/O index and go sub subroutine 1 to store I/O index and I/O data in polar format.

↓

Clear data entry flag 3, space, and return.

## PROGRAM FLOW DIAGRAM

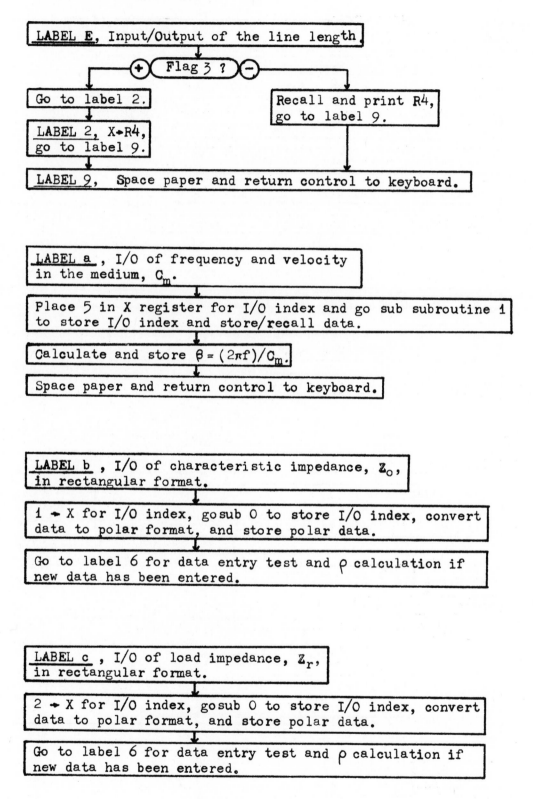

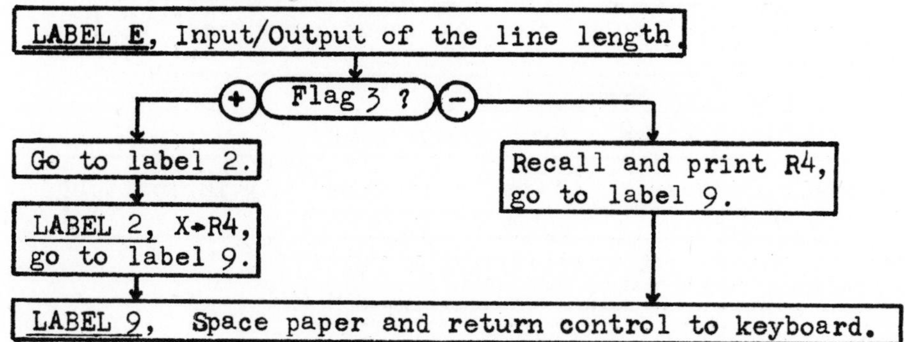


LABEL a, I/O of frequency and velocity in the medium, $C_m$.

↓

Place 5 in X register for I/O index and go sub subroutine 1 to store I/O index and store/recall data.

↓

Calculate and store $\beta = (2\pi f)/C_m$.

↓

Space paper and return control to keyboard.

LABEL b, I/O of characteristic impedance, $Z_o$, in rectangular format.

↓

1 → X for I/O index, gosub 0 to store I/O index, convert data to polar format, and store polar data.

↓

Go to label 6 for data entry test and $\rho$ calculation if new data has been entered.

LABEL c, I/O of load impedance, $Z_r$, in rectangular format.

↓

2 → X for I/O index, gosub 0 to store I/O index, convert data to polar format, and store polar data.

↓

Go to label 6 for data entry test and $\rho$ calculation if new data has been entered.

PROGRAM FLOW DIAGRAM

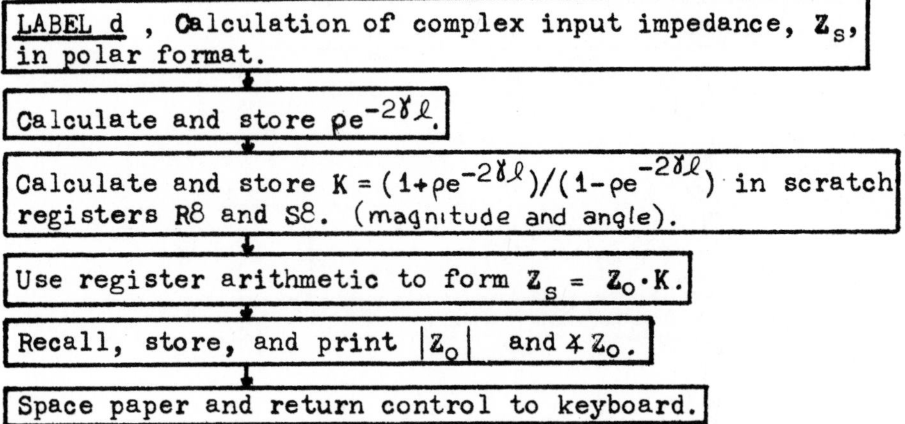

LABEL d , Calculation of complex input impedance, $Z_s$, in polar format.
Calculate and store $\rho e^{-2\gamma\ell}$.
Calculate and store $K = (1+\rho e^{-2\gamma\ell})/(1-\rho e^{-2\gamma\ell})$ in scratch registers R8 and S8. (magnitude and angle).
Use register arithmetic to form $Z_s = Z_o \cdot K$.
Recall, store, and print $|Z_o|$ and $\measuredangle Z_o$.
Space paper and return control to keyboard.


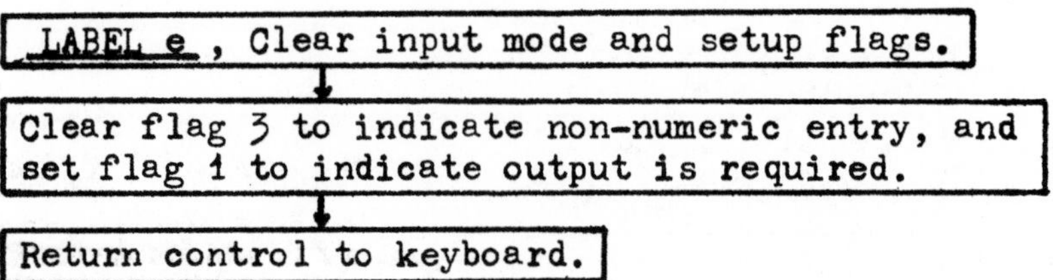

LABEL e , Clear input mode and setup flags.
Clear flag 3 to indicate non-numeric entry, and set flag 1 to indicate output is required.
Return control to keyboard.


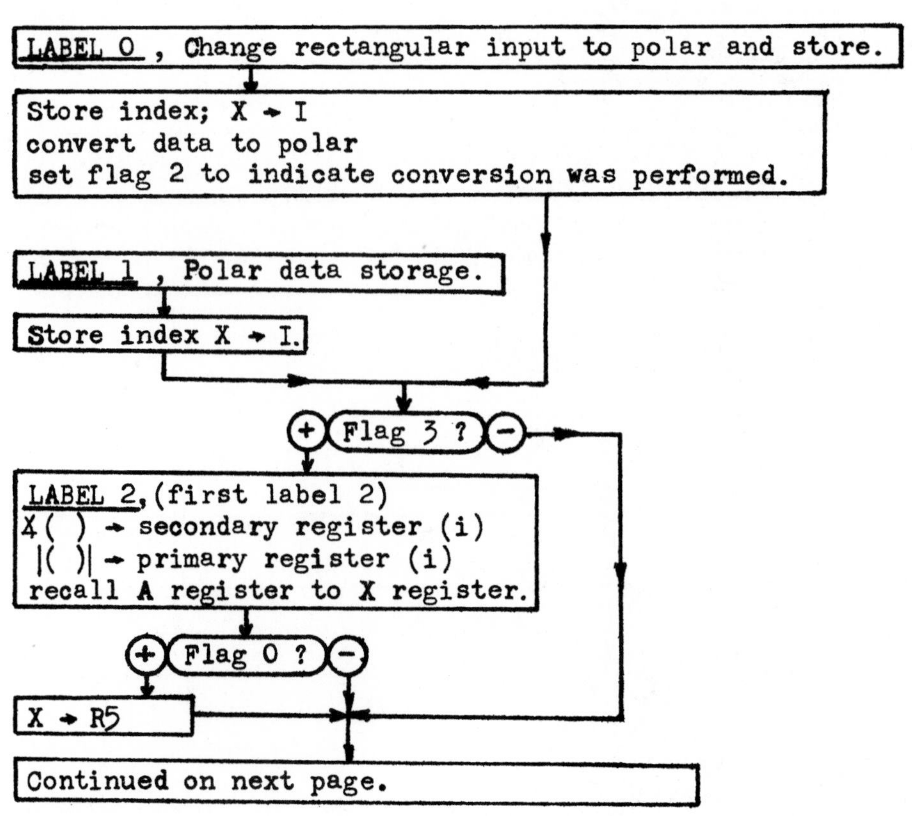

## PROGRAM FLOW DIAGRAM

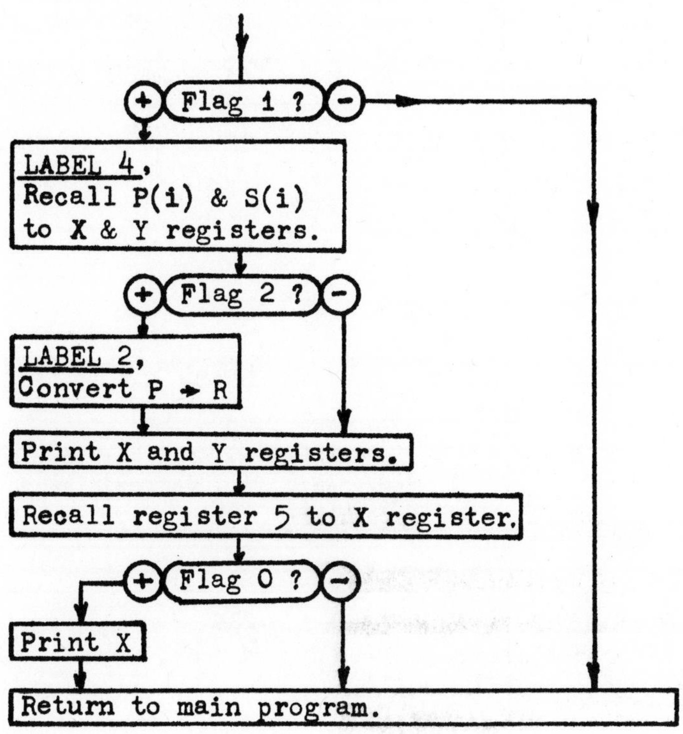


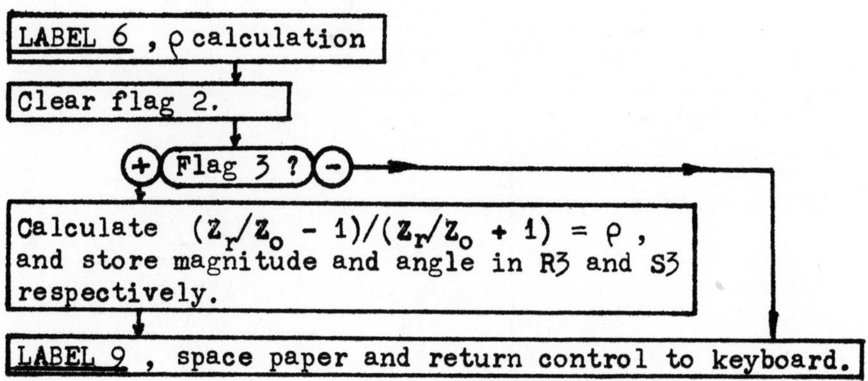

# Program Listing I

| Step | Key | Comment |
|---|---|---|
| 001 | *LBLA | I/O OF $\alpha_{dB}$, $\beta$, AND FREQ |
| 002 | STOA | |
| 003 | R↓ | |
| 004 | SF0 | |
| 005 | CF2 | |
| 006 | 0 | |
| 007 | GSB1 | |
| 008 | CF0 | |
| 009 | CF3 | |
| 010 | Pi | |
| 011 | Pi | |
| 012 | + | |
| 013 | RCL5 | |
| 014 | × | |
| 015 | P⇄S | |
| 016 | RCL0 | |
| 017 | ÷ | |
| 018 | STO5 | |
| 019 | GTO7 | |
| 020 | *LBLB | I/O OF $\lvert Z_o\rvert$, $\measuredangle Z_o$, THE CHARACTERISTIC IMPEDANCE IN POLAR CO-ORDINATES |
| 021 | EEX | |
| 022 | GSB1 | |
| 023 | GTO6 | |
| 024 | *LBLC | I/O OF $\lvert Z_r\rvert$, $\measuredangle Z_r$, THE LOAD IMPEDANCE IN POLAR CO-ORDINATES |
| 025 | 2 | |
| 026 | GSB1 | |
| 027 | GTO6 | |
| 028 | *LBLD | I/O OF $\lvert\rho\rvert$, $\measuredangle\rho$, THE COMPLEX REFLECTION COEF IN POLAR CO-ORDINATES |
| 029 | 3 | |
| 030 | GSB1 | |
| 031 | CF3 | |
| 032 | GTO9 | |
| 033 | *LBLE | I/O OF THE LINE LENGTH |
| 034 | F3? | |
| 035 | GTO2 | (→ 038) |
| 036 | RCL4 | |
| 037 | GTO8 | |
| 038 | *LBL2 | |
| 039 | STO4 | |
| 040 | GTO9 | |
| 041 | *LBLa | I/O OF FREQUENCY AND VELOCITY IN THE MEDIUM, $C_m$ |
| 042 | 5 | |
| 043 | GSB1 | |
| 044 | CF3 | |
| 045 | RCL5 | |
| 046 | ENT↑ | |
| 047 | + | |
| 048 | Pi | |
| 049 | × | |
| 050 | P⇄S | |
| 051 | RCL5 | |
| 052 | ÷ | |
| 053 | STO0 | |
| 054 | GTO7 | |
| 055 | *LBLb | I/O OF Re $Z_o$, Im $Z_o$, THE CHARACTERISTIC IMPEDANCE IN CARTESIAN CO-ORDINATES |
| 056 | EEX | |
| 057 | GSB0 | |
| 058 | GTO6 | |
| 059 | *LBLc | I/O OF Re $Z_r$, Im $Z_r$, THE LOAD IMPEDANCE IN CARTESIAN CO-ORDINATES |
| 060 | 2 | |
| 061 | GSB0 | |
| 062 | GTO6 | |
| 063 | *LBLd | CALCULATION OF $\lvert Z_s\rvert$, $\measuredangle Z_s$, THE COMPLEX INPUT IMPEDANCE |
| 064 | RCL3 | |
| 065 | RCL0 | |
| 066 | RCL4 | |
| 067 | × | |
| 068 | EEX | |
| 069 | 1 | |
| 070 | ÷ | |
| 071 | CHS | |
| 072 | 10^x | $e^{-2\alpha\ell}$ |
| 073 | × | |
| 074 | STOA | $\lvert\rho\rvert\cdot e^{-2\alpha\ell} = \lvert\rho e^{-2\gamma\ell}\rvert$ |
| 075 | P⇄S | |
| 076 | RCL3 | $\measuredangle\rho$ |
| 077 | RCL0 | $\beta$, radians/length |
| 078 | R→D | $\beta$, degrees/length |
| 079 | P⇄S | |
| 080 | RCL4 | $\ell$ |
| 081 | × | |
| 082 | ENT↑ | |
| 083 | + | $2\beta\ell$ |
| 084 | − | $\measuredangle\rho - 2\beta\ell = \measuredangle(\rho e^{-2\gamma\ell})$ |
| 085 | RCLA | |
| 086 | →R | |
| 087 | STOA | $Re(\rho e^{-2\gamma\ell})$ |
| 088 | EEX | |
| 089 | + | $1 + Re(\rho e^{-2\gamma\ell})$ |
| 090 | X⇄Y | |
| 091 | STOB | $Im(\rho e^{-2\gamma\ell})$ |
| 092 | X⇄Y | |
| 093 | →P | |
| 094 | STO7 | $\lvert 1 + \rho e^{-2\gamma\ell}\rvert$ |
| 095 | X⇄Y | |
| 096 | STO9 | $\measuredangle(1 + \rho e^{-2\gamma\ell})$ |
| 097 | RCLB | |
| 098 | CHS | $Im(1 - \rho e^{-2\gamma\ell})$ |
| 099 | EEX | |
| 100 | RCLA | |
| 101 | − | $Re(1 - \rho e^{-2\gamma\ell})$ |
| 102 | →P | |
| 103 | ST÷7 | |
| 104 | X⇄Y | |
| 105 | ST−9 | |
| 106 | RCL1 | $\lvert Z_o\rvert$ |
| 107 | ST×7 | |
| 108 | P⇄S | |
| 109 | RCL1 | $\measuredangle Z_o$ |
| 110 | P⇄S | |
| 111 | ST+9 | |
| 112 | RCL9 | $\measuredangle Z_s$ |

**REGISTERS**

| 0 | 1 | 2 | 3 | 4 | 5 | 6 | 7 | 8 | 9 |
|---|---|---|---|---|---|---|---|---|---|
| $\alpha$, dB/$\ell$ | $\lvert Z_o\rvert$ | $\lvert Z_r\rvert$ | $\lvert\rho\rvert$ | $\ell$ | freq | $\measuredangle\rho$, scratch | $\pi\lvert Z\rvert$ | $\lvert Z\rvert$ | $\Sigma\measuredangle Z$ |

| S0 | S1 | S2 | S3 | S4 | S5 | S6 | S7 | S8 | S9 |
|---|---|---|---|---|---|---|---|---|---|
| $\beta$, rad/$\ell$ | $\measuredangle Z_o$ | $\measuredangle Z_r$ | $\measuredangle\rho$ | | $C_m$ | | | $\measuredangle Z$ | |

| A | B | C | D | E | I |
|---|---|---|---|---|---|
| scratchpad | scratchpad | scratchpad | | | index |

# Program Listing II

| | | |
|---|---|---|
| 113 | RCL7 | $\|Z_s\|$ |
| 114 | →R | eliminates neg magnitude |
| 115 | →P | |
| 116 | ST08 | $\|Z_s\|$ |
| 117 | PRTX | |
| 118 | X⇄Y | |
| 119 | P⇄S | |
| 120 | ST08 | ∡ $Z_s$ |
| 121 | P⇄S | |
| 122 | GSB8 | |
| 123 | GT09 | |
| 124 | *LBLe | CLEAR INPUT MODE |
| 125 | CF3 | initialize and set flags |
| 126 | SF1 | |
| 127 | RTN | |
| 128 | *LBL0 | change rectangular input |
| 129 | STOI | to polar format |
| 130 | R↓ | |
| 131 | X⇄Y | |
| 132 | →P | |
| 133 | X⇄Y | |
| 134 | SF2 | |
| 135 | GT02 | |
| 136 | *LBL1 | data I/O in polar mode |
| 137 | STOI | |
| 138 | R↓ | |
| 139 | *LBL2 | |
| 140 | F3? | test for input |
| 141 | GSB2 | goto input routine |
| 142 | F1? | test for output |
| 143 | GSB4 | goto output routine |
| 144 | SF1 | |
| 145 | RTN | |
| 146 | *LBL2 | input data storage routine |
| 147 | SF3 | (data stored in polar form) |
| 148 | P⇄S | |
| 149 | STOi | |
| 150 | P⇄S | |
| 151 | R↓ | |
| 152 | STOi | |
| 153 | RCLA | |
| 154 | F0? | |
| 155 | ST05 | |
| 156 | CF1 | |
| 157 | RTN | |
| 158 | *LBL4 | data output routine |
| 159 | P⇄S | |
| 160 | RCLi | |
| 161 | P⇄S | |
| 162 | RCLi | |
| 163 | F2? | P → R required ? |
| 164 | GT02 | |
| 165 | PRTX | |
| 166 | R↓ | |
| 167 | PRTX | |
| 168 | RCL5 | recall frequency |
| 169 | F0? | print required ? |
| 170 | PRTX | print frequency |
| 171 | RTN | |
| 172 | *LBL2 | convert polar data to rectangular format and |
| 173 | →R | |
| 174 | PRTX | print results |
| 175 | R↓ | |
| 176 | *LBL8 | print and space subroutine |
| 177 | PRTX | |
| 178 | GT09 | goto space subroutine |
| 179 | *LBL6 | ρ calculation |
| 180 | CF2 | |
| 181 | F3? | ρ calculation needed ? |
| 182 | F3? | |
| 183 | GT09 | goto space and return subr |
| 184 | P⇄S | |
| 185 | RCL2 | ∡ $Z_r$ |
| 186 | RCL1 | ∡ $Z_o$ |
| 187 | - | ∡ $(Z_r - Z_o)$ |
| 188 | P⇄S | |
| 189 | RCL2 | $\|Z_r\|$ |
| 190 | RCL1 | $\|Z_o\|$ |
| 191 | X=0? | exit if $\|Z_o\|$ is zero |
| 192 | GT09 | |
| 193 | ÷ | $\|Z_r/Z_o\|$ |
| 194 | →R | |
| 195 | STOA | $Re(Z_r/Z_o)$ |
| 196 | EEX | |
| 197 | - | $Re(Z_r/Z_o - 1)$ |
| 198 | X⇄Y | |
| 199 | STOB | $Im(Z_r/Z_o - 1)$ |
| 200 | X⇄Y | |
| 201 | →P | |
| 202 | ST03 | $\|Z_r/Z_o - 1\|$ |
| 203 | X⇄Y | |
| 204 | ST06 | ∡ $(Z_r/Z_o - 1)$ |
| 205 | RCLB | $Im(Z_r/Z_o)$ |
| 206 | RCLA | $Re(Z_r/Z_o)$ |
| 207 | EEX | |
| 208 | + | $Re(Z_r/Z_o + 1)$ |
| 209 | →P | |
| 210 | ST÷3 | $\|\rho\|$ |
| 211 | X⇄Y | |
| 212 | ST-6 | ∡ ρ |
| 213 | RCL6 | |
| 214 | P⇄S | |
| 215 | ST03 | |
| 216 | *LBL7 | P⇄S & space subroutine |
| 217 | P⇄S | |
| 218 | *LBL9 | space and return subr |
| 219 | SPC | |
| 220 | RTN | |

**LABELS**

| A | B | C | D | E |
|---|---|---|---|---|
| I/O: $\alpha_{dB}$, β, f | I/O: \|\|, ∡ $Z_o$ | I/O: \|\|, ∡ $Z_r$ | I/O: \|\|, ∡ ρ | I/O: length |
| a I/O: f, $C_m$ | b I/O: ReImZo | c I/O: ReImZr | d calc. $Z_s$ | e clear input mode |
| 0 P → R | 1 I/O index | 2 local lbl | 3 | 4 print in polar |
| 5 | 6 calc ρ | 7 p⇄s, spc, rt | 8 prt, spc, rt | 9 spc, rtn |

**FLAGS**

| | | ON/OFF |
|---|---|---|
| 0 | label A ? | OFF |
| 1 | input or output | ON |
| 2 | cartesian data fmt | OFF |
| 3 | data entry | OFF |

**SET STATUS**

| TRIG | DISP |
|---|---|
| DEG ■ | FIX ■ |
| GRAD | SCI |
| RAD | ENG |
| | n 3 |

## 1-1 TI-59 PROGRAM LISTING

| Step | Code | Key | Comment |
|---|---|---|---|
| 000 | 76 | LBL | LOAD $\alpha_{dB}$ |
| 001 | 11 | A | |
| 002 | 42 | STO | store and print $\alpha$ dB |
| 003 | 00 | 00 | |
| 004 | 99 | PRT | |
| 005 | 91 | R/S | LOAD $\beta$ |
| 006 | 42 | STO | store and print $\beta$ |
| 007 | 10 | 10 | |
| 008 | 99 | PRT | |
| 009 | 91 | R/S | LOAD FREQUENCY |
| 010 | 42 | STO | store and print frequency |
| 011 | 05 | 05 | |
| 012 | 99 | PRT | |
| 013 | 65 | × | calculate and store $2\pi f$ |
| 014 | 02 | 2 | |
| 015 | 65 | × | |
| 016 | 89 | π | |
| 017 | 95 | = | |
| 018 | 42 | STO | |
| 019 | 26 | 26 | |
| 020 | 55 | ÷ | calculate and store $C_m$ |
| 021 | 43 | RCL | |
| 022 | 10 | 10 | $C_m = \frac{2\pi f}{\beta}$ |
| 023 | 95 | = | |
| 024 | 42 | STO | |
| 025 | 15 | 15 | |
| 026 | 02 | 2 | set flag 7 if calculator attached to printer |
| 027 | 00 | 0 | |
| 028 | 69 | OP | |
| 029 | 07 | 07 | |
| 030 | 69 | OP | |
| 031 | 19 | 19 | |
| 032 | 25 | CLR | |
| 033 | 43 | RCL | recall $C_m$ and go to R/S or print routine |
| 034 | 15 | 15 | |
| 035 | 71 | SBR | |
| 036 | 68 | NOP | |
| 037 | 98 | ADV | |
| 038 | 92 | RTN | |
| 039 | 76 | LBL | LOAD $C_m$ |
| 040 | 16 | A' | |
| 041 | 42 | STO | store and print $C_m$ |
| 042 | 15 | 15 | |
| 043 | 99 | PRT | |
| 044 | 35 | 1/X | calculate and store $\beta$ |
| 045 | 65 | × | |
| 046 | 43 | RCL | $\beta = \frac{2\pi f}{C_m}$ |
| 047 | 26 | 26 | |
| 048 | 95 | = | |
| 049 | 42 | STO | |
| 050 | 10 | 10 | |
| 051 | 71 | SBR | go to print or R/S routine |
| 052 | 68 | NOP | |
| 053 | 98 | ADV | |
| 054 | 92 | RTN | |
| 055 | 76 | LBL | LOAD $\lvert Z_o \rvert$ |
| 056 | 12 | B | |
| 057 | 42 | STO | store and print $\lvert Z_o \rvert$ |
| 058 | 01 | 01 | |
| 059 | 99 | PRT | |
| 060 | 91 | R/S | LOAD $\angle Z_o$ |
| 061 | 42 | STO | store and print $\angle Z_o$ |
| 062 | 11 | 11 | |
| 063 | 99 | PRT | |
| 064 | 98 | ADV | |
| 065 | 61 | GTO | goto $\rho$ calculation subroutine |
| 066 | 70 | RAD | |
| 067 | 76 | LBL | LOAD Re $Z_o$ |
| 068 | 17 | B' | |
| 069 | 99 | PRT | print and store Re$Z_o$ |
| 070 | 32 | X:T | |
| 071 | 91 | R/S | LOAD Im $Z_o$ |
| 072 | 22 | INV | convert to polar |
| 073 | 37 | P/R | |
| 074 | 42 | STO | store $\angle Z_o$ |
| 075 | 11 | 11 | |
| 076 | 32 | X:T | recall and store $\lvert Z_o \rvert$ |
| 077 | 42 | STO | |
| 078 | 01 | 01 | |
| 079 | 98 | ADV | go to $\rho$ calculation subroutine |
| 080 | 61 | GTO | |
| 081 | 70 | RAD | |
| 082 | 76 | LBL | LOAD $\lvert Z_r \rvert$ |
| 083 | 13 | C | |
| 084 | 42 | STO | store and print $\lvert Z_r \rvert$ |
| 085 | 02 | 02 | |
| 086 | 99 | PRT | |
| 087 | 91 | R/S | LOAD $\angle Z_r$ |
| 088 | 42 | STO | store and print $\angle Z_r$ |
| 089 | 12 | 12 | |
| 090 | 99 | PRT | |
| 091 | 98 | ADV | |
| 092 | 61 | GTO | goto $\rho$ calculation subroutine |
| 093 | 70 | RAD | |
| 094 | 76 | LBL | LOAD Re $Z_r$ |
| 095 | 18 | C' | |
| 096 | 99 | PRT | store and print Re $Z_r$ |
| 097 | 32 | X:T | |
| 098 | 91 | R/S | LOAD Im $Z_r$ |
| 099 | 99 | PRT | print Im $Z_r$ |

NOTE: The register assignments are the same as the HP-97 program. Read S0 as $R_{10}$, and RA as $R_{20}$, etc. $R_{26}$ - $R_{28}$ are scratchpads

1-1

## TI-59 PROGRAM LISTING

| Step | Code | Key | Comment |
|---|---|---|---|
| 100 | 98 | ADV | |
| 101 | 22 | INV | convert to polar |
| 102 | 37 | P/R | |
| 103 | 42 | STO | store $\measuredangle Z_r$ |
| 104 | 12 | 12 | |
| 105 | 32 | X:T | store $\lvert Z_r \rvert$ |
| 106 | 42 | STO | |
| 107 | 02 | 02 | |
| 108 | 76 | LBL | $\rho$ calculation |
| 109 | 70 | RAD | |
| 110 | 43 | RCL | calculate & store: $\measuredangle(Z_r - Z_o)$ |
| 111 | 12 | 12 | |
| 112 | 75 | − | |
| 113 | 43 | RCL | |
| 114 | 11 | 11 | |
| 115 | 95 | = | |
| 116 | 32 | X:T | |
| 117 | 43 | RCL | calculate & store: $\lvert Z_r / Z_o \rvert$ |
| 118 | 02 | 02 | |
| 119 | 55 | ÷ | |
| 120 | 43 | RCL | |
| 121 | 01 | 01 | |
| 122 | 95 | = | |
| 123 | 32 | X:T | |
| 124 | 37 | P/R | convert to rect |
| 125 | 42 | STO | store $Im(Z_r/Z_o)$ |
| 126 | 27 | 27 | |
| 127 | 32 | X:T | store $Re(Z_r/Z_o)$ |
| 128 | 42 | STO | |
| 129 | 28 | 28 | |
| 130 | 75 | − | calculate & store: $Z_r/Z_o - 1$ |
| 131 | 01 | 1 | |
| 132 | 95 | = | |
| 133 | 32 | X:T | |
| 134 | 22 | INV | convert to polar |
| 135 | 37 | P/R | |
| 136 | 42 | STO | store $\measuredangle(Z_r/Z_o - 1)$ |
| 137 | 13 | 13 | |
| 138 | 43 | RCL | recall & store: $Im(Z_r/Z_o + 1)$ |
| 139 | 27 | 27 | |
| 140 | 32 | X:T | store $\lvert Z_r/Z_o - 1 \rvert$ |
| 141 | 42 | STO | |
| 142 | 03 | 03 | |
| 143 | 43 | RCL | form $Z_r/Z_o + 1$ |
| 144 | 28 | 28 | |
| 145 | 85 | + | |
| 146 | 01 | 1 | |
| 147 | 95 | = | |
| 148 | 32 | X:T | |
| 149 | 22 | INV | convert to polar |

| Step | Code | Key | Comment |
|---|---|---|---|
| 150 | 37 | P/R | |
| 151 | 22 | INV | use register arithmetic to form: $\measuredangle\rho$ |
| 152 | 44 | SUM | |
| 153 | 13 | 13 | |
| 154 | 32 | X:T | use register arithmetic to form: $\lvert\rho\rvert$ |
| 155 | 22 | INV | |
| 156 | 49 | PRD | |
| 157 | 03 | 03 | |
| 158 | 92 | RTN | rtn to main pgm |
| 159 | 76 | LBL | $\rho$ OUTPUT ROUTINE |
| 160 | 14 | D | |
| 161 | 43 | RCL | recall $\lvert\rho\rvert$ |
| 162 | 03 | 03 | |
| 163 | 71 | SBR | goto print or R/S |
| 164 | 68 | NOP | |
| 165 | 43 | RCL | recall $\measuredangle\rho$ |
| 166 | 13 | 13 | |
| 167 | 71 | SBR | goto print or R/S |
| 168 | 68 | NOP | |
| 169 | 98 | ADV | space and return |
| 170 | 92 | RTN | |
| 171 | 76 | LBL | CALCULATE $Z_s$ |
| 172 | 19 | D' | |
| 173 | 43 | RCL | form $\alpha\ell$ in dB |
| 174 | 00 | 00 | |
| 175 | 65 | × | |
| 176 | 43 | RCL | |
| 177 | 04 | 04 | |
| 178 | 55 | ÷ | convert to nepers |
| 179 | 53 | ( | |
| 180 | 01 | 1 | |
| 181 | 22 | INV | |
| 182 | 23 | LNX | |
| 183 | 28 | LOG | |
| 184 | 65 | × | |
| 185 | 01 | 1 | |
| 186 | 00 | 0 | |
| 187 | 54 | ) | |
| 188 | 95 | = | |
| 189 | 94 | +/- | calculate: $e^{-2\alpha\ell}$ |
| 190 | 22 | INV | |
| 191 | 23 | LNX | |
| 192 | 65 | × | calculate & store: $\lvert\vec{\rho} e^{-2\gamma\ell}\rvert$ |
| 193 | 43 | RCL | |
| 194 | 03 | 03 | |
| 195 | 95 | = | |
| 196 | 32 | X:T | |
| 197 | 43 | RCL | recall $\measuredangle\rho$ |
| 198 | 13 | 13 | |
| 199 | 75 | − | |

| | | | |
|---|---|---|---|
| 200 | 53 | ( | form $\beta\ell$ in radians |
| 201 | 43 | RCL | |
| 202 | 10 | 10 | |
| 203 | 65 | $\times$ | |
| 204 | 43 | RCL | |
| 205 | 04 | 04 | |
| 206 | 65 | $\times$ | |
| 207 | 03 | 3 | form $2\beta\ell$ in degrees |
| 208 | 06 | 6 | |
| 209 | 00 | 0 | |
| 210 | 55 | $\div$ | |
| 211 | 89 | $\pi$ | |
| 212 | 54 | ) | |
| 213 | 95 | = | form $\angle\rho - 2\beta\ell$ |
| 214 | 37 | P/R | convert to rect |
| 215 | 42 | STO | store $Im(\rho e^{-2\delta\ell})$ |
| 216 | 21 | 21 | |
| 217 | 32 | X:T | store $Re(\rho e^{-2\delta\ell})$ |
| 218 | 42 | STO | |
| 219 | 20 | 20 | |
| 220 | 85 | + | form: $1 + \rho e^{-2\delta\ell}$ |
| 221 | 01 | 1 | |
| 222 | 95 | = | |
| 223 | 32 | X:T | convert to polar |
| 224 | 22 | INV | |
| 225 | 37 | P/R | |
| 226 | 42 | STO | store $\angle(1 + \rho e^{-2\delta\ell})$ |
| 227 | 09 | 09 | |
| 228 | 32 | X:T | store $\mid 1 + \rho e^{-2\delta\ell}\mid$ |
| 229 | 42 | STO | |
| 230 | 07 | 07 | |
| 231 | 01 | 1 | form and store: |
| 232 | 75 | - | $Re(1 - \rho e^{-2\delta\ell})$ |
| 233 | 43 | RCL | |
| 234 | 20 | 20 | |
| 235 | 95 | = | |
| 236 | 32 | X:T | |
| 237 | 43 | RCL | form: $Im(1 - \rho e^{-2\delta\ell})$ |
| 238 | 21 | 21 | |
| 239 | 94 | +/- | |
| 240 | 22 | INV | convert to polar |
| 241 | 37 | P/R | |
| 242 | 22 | INV | divide to memory |
| 243 | 44 | SUM | |
| 244 | 09 | 09 | |
| 245 | 32 | X:T | subtract from memory |
| 246 | 22 | INV | |
| 247 | 49 | PRD | |
| 248 | 07 | 07 | |
| 249 | 43 | RCL | recall $\mid Z_o\mid$ |
| 250 | 01 | 01 | use register arith to form $\mid Z_r\mid$ |
| 251 | 49 | PRD | |
| 252 | 07 | 07 | |
| 253 | 43 | RCL | use register arith to form $\angle Z_r$ |
| 254 | 11 | 11 | |
| 255 | 44 | SUM | |
| 256 | 09 | 09 | |
| 257 | 43 | RCL | recall $\mid Z_r\mid$ |
| 258 | 07 | 07 | |
| 259 | 32 | X:T | |
| 260 | 43 | RCL | recall $\angle Z_r$ |
| 261 | 09 | 09 | |
| 262 | 37 | P/R | eliminate negative magnitude |
| 263 | 22 | INV | |
| 264 | 37 | P/R | |
| 265 | 42 | STO | store $\angle Z$ |
| 266 | 18 | 18 | |
| 267 | 32 | X:T | store $\mid Z\mid$ |
| 268 | 42 | STO | |
| 269 | 08 | 08 | |
| 270 | 71 | SBR | goto print or R/S |
| 271 | 68 | NOP | |
| 272 | 43 | RCL | recall $\angle Z$ |
| 273 | 18 | 18 | |
| 274 | 71 | SBR | goto print or R/S |
| 275 | 68 | NOP | |
| 276 | 98 | ADV | space & return |
| 277 | 92 | RTN | |
| 278 | 76 | LBL | print or R/S |
| 279 | 68 | NOP | subroutine |
| 280 | 87 | IFF | jump if flag 7 set |
| 281 | 07 | 07 | |
| 282 | 38 | SIN | |
| 283 | 91 | R/S | stop & await start |
| 284 | 92 | RTN | return to main pgm |
| 285 | 76 | LBL | |
| 286 | 38 | SIN | |
| 287 | 99 | PRT | print |
| 288 | 92 | RTN | rtn to main program |
| 289 | 76 | LBL | **LOAD LINE LENGTH** |
| 290 | 15 | E | |
| 291 | 42 | STO | store line length |
| 292 | 04 | 04 | |
| 293 | 99 | PRT | print line length |
| 294 | 98 | ADV | |
| 295 | 92 | RTN | rtn to keyboard |

## PROGRAM 1-2 VOLTAGE ALONG A LOSSY LOADED TRANSMISSION LINE.

### Program Description and Equations Used

This program calculates the voltage V(x) in dBV, at any distance, x, along a doubly loaded transmission line (a line with terminating Y's or Z's at both ends). Both the source and load impedances are allowed to be complex quantities. This program is parasitic to Program 1-1, and that program must be run first to properly load the registers for this program. The same line length and units must be used with both programs.

Given a section of transmission line of length $\ell$ (Fig. 1-2.1) which may be a coax as shown, or open wire line, stripline, microstrip, or other, the input impedance, $Z_s$, can be expressed in terms of the load impedance, $Z_r$, and the cable parameters as given by Eqs. (1-1.1) and (1-1.2). With the input impedance, $Z_s$ known, and given the transmitter source impedance, $Z_t$, the voltage at the input of the transmission line, $V_s$, is given by:

$$V_s = V_t \left[ \frac{Z_s}{Z_s + Z_t} \right] \tag{1-2.1}$$

where $Z_s$ is given by Eq. (1-1.1).

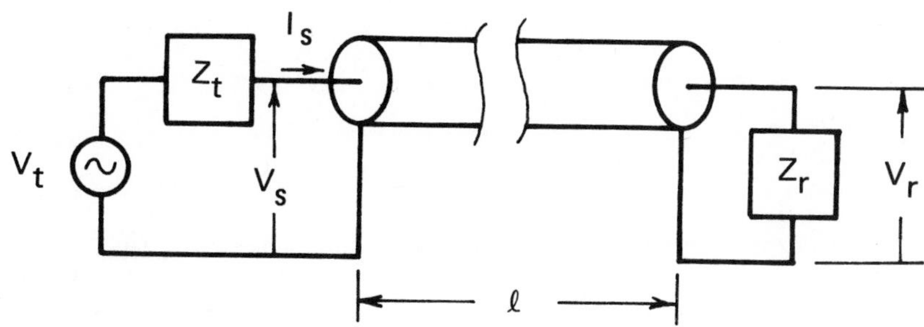


Figure 1-2.1 Transmission line circuit topology.

The voltage and current distribution of the transmission line can be written in terms of the voltage and current at any point along the transmission line as the reference. Most commonly, the voltage at the receiving end is taken as the reference, but for this problem, the voltage and current at the transmitting end are more convenient references. The voltage at any distance, x, from the transmitting end is given by Eq. (1-2.2), where the reflection coefficient at the transmitter is designated $\rho_t$ and is defined by Eq. (1-2.3). The derivation of Eq. (1-2.2) is given later.

$$V(x) = \frac{V_s}{1 + \rho_t} \cdot \left[ e^{-\gamma x} + \rho_t e^{\gamma x} \right] \tag{1-2.2}$$

$$\rho_t = \frac{Z_s/Z_o - 1}{Z_s/Z_o + 1} \tag{1-2.3}$$

In Eq. (1-2.2), $\gamma$ is as defined in Eq. (1-1.3). With these equations in mind, the program operation is now described (Program 1-1 has already calculated and stored $Z_s$ using Eq. (1-1.1)).

The routines under labels "A," "a," and "B" provide for data entry and storage. All impedances are stored in polar form; hence, impedances entered in cartesian form (real and imaginary) under label "a" are converted to polar form and stored using the routine under label "A," which is the polar impedance entry and storage routine. The routine under label "B" causes the source voltage strength in volts to be stored.

Label "E" is the start of the data output routine. On the first execution of label "E" after program loading and data entry, $\rho_t$ is calculated and stored. Flag 2 is tested on each execution of label "E" to determine if the reflection coefficient calculation is needed ($\rho_t$). Since flag 2 is test cleared, and is only set by card loading, the $\rho_t$ calculation is skipped after the first execution of label "E."

Following the $\rho_t$ calculation decision, is a routine to evaluate Eq. (1-2.2) without the $V_s$ term (lines 050 and 096 in the program listing). $V_s$ is calculated using Eq. (1-2.1) in lines 097 through 118 and combined with the results of Eq. (1-2.2) in lines 119 to 125. The output is provided as magnitude (in dBV) of V(x) and its angle.

Label 9 is a space and return subroutine used by labels "a," "A," "B," and "E."

# User Instructions

| VOLTAGE ALONG A LOSSY LOADED TRANSMISSION LINE | | | | |
|---|---|---|---|---|
| load $ReZ_t \uparrow ImZ_t$ / load $\|Z_t\| \uparrow \measuredangle Z_t$ | load source voltage | | | load dist from xmit & calc: $\|V(x)\|_{dB}$, $\measuredangle V(x)$ |

| STEP | INSTRUCTIONS | INPUT DATA/UNITS | KEYS | OUTPUT DATA/UNITS |
|---|---|---|---|---|
| | This program is to be used in conjunction with Program 1-1. Run that program first using the frequency, cable parameters, and total line length which are germane to this program | | | |
| 1 | Load and run Program 1-1 | | | |
| 2 | Load both sides of Program 1-2 magnetic card | | | |
| 3 | Load transmitter output impedance | | | |
| | a) If data is in cartesian coordinates: | | | |
| | real part of impedance in ohms | $Re\ Z_t$ | ENT | |
| | imaginary part of impedance in ohms | $Im\ Z_t$ | A | |
| | or | | | |
| | b) If data is in polar coordinates: | | | |
| | magnitude of impedance in ohms | $\|Z_t\|$ | ENT | |
| | angle of impedance in degrees | $\measuredangle Z_t$ | f A | |
| 4 | Load source voltage of transmitter in volts | $V_t$ | B | |
| 5 | Load length between transmitter and analysis point using the same units as used with Program 1-1 | x | E | $20 \log \|V(x)\|$<br>$\measuredangle V(x)°$ |
| 6 | Go back to step 5 for another case | | | |

Example 1-2.1

Given the coax cable with source and load impedances as shown in Fig. 1-2.2, find the voltages on the cable at the transmitting end, the receiving end, and 1 n-mi. from the transmitting end.

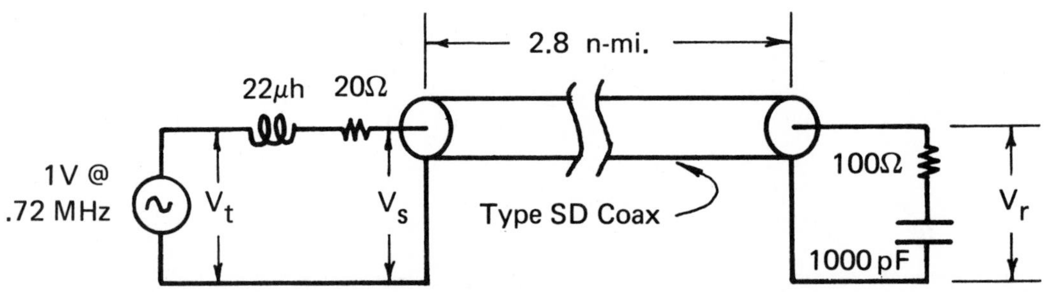


Figure 1-2.2 Doubly loaded coaxial cable for Ex. 1-2.1.

At 0.72 MHz, the characteristics of the SD coax cable are:

$$\alpha_{dB} = 2.070 \text{ dB/n-mi.}$$
$$\beta = 42.511 \text{ radians/n-mi.}$$
$$Z_o = 44.265\ \Omega\ @\ -0.315 \text{ degree}$$

At the same frequency, the complex source and load impedances are:

$$\text{Re } Z_t = 20 \text{ ohms}$$
$$\text{Im } Z_t = j2\pi fL = j99.53 \text{ ohms}$$

$$\text{Re } Z_r = 100 \text{ ohms}$$
$$\text{Im } Z_r = -j/(2\pi fC) = -j221 \text{ ohms}$$

Since this program is parasitic to Program 1-1, that program is run first with the line length required here (2.8 n-mi.). The print-out from that program is included here for clarity.

<u>HP-97 printout for Example 1-2.1</u>

First, Program 1-1 is run to calculate and store $Z_s$ and to load the registers.

2.070 ENT↑ load $\alpha_{dB}$ in dB/n-mi.
42.511 ENT↑ load $\beta$ in radians/n-mi.
.72+06 GSBA load frequency in hertz

44.265 ENT↑ load $|Z_o|$ in ohms
-.315 GSBB load $\measuredangle Z_o$ in degrees

100.000 ENT↑ load Re $Z_r$ in ohms
-221.000 GSBc load Im $Z_r$ in ohms

2.800 GSBE load line length in nautical miles

GSBd calculate $Z_s$ (will be automatically stored)
67.827 *** $|Z_s|$, ohms
9.476 *** $\measuredangle Z_s$, degrees

Second, load and run this program.

20.00 ENT↑ load Re $Z_t$
99.53 GSBc load Im $Z_t$

1.00 GSBE load source voltage in volts

0.00 GSBE load line length to transmitting end and start
-6.34 *** 20 log $|V_s|$, dBV
-42.39 *** $\measuredangle V_s$, degrees

2.80 GSBE load line length to receiving end and start
-8.54 *** 20 log $|V_r|$, dBV
-34.96 *** $\measuredangle V_r$, degrees

1.00 GSBE load line length to 1 n-mi. from xmit end and start
-12.96 *** 20 log $|V(x)|$, dBV
22.18 *** $\measuredangle V(x)$, degrees

## Derivation of Equations Used

A transmission line provides a conduit for the propagation of electrical power. If the transmission line is not terminated in the characteristic impedance of the line, $Z_o$, then not all of the power that propagates down the line is absorbed in the termination, and thus some is reflected into the line and propagates back to the source. The "reflection coefficient," $\rho$, is a measure of the amount of power that is reflected. A reflection coefficient of zero ($\rho = 0$) implies no power is reflected, and all of it is absorbed by the load. When $\rho = \pm 1$, all the power is reflected. The reflection coefficient in terms of the characteristic impedance ($Z_o$) and the load impedance ($Z_r$) is given by Eq. (1-1.2).

If the transmission line is doubly terminated, then there will be a reflection coefficient for both ends, and Eq. (1-1.2) is used with $Z_r$ replaced by $Z_s$, the cable input impedance at the transmitter end. This is the transmitter reflection coefficient and is designated $\rho_t$. The receiver reflection coefficient is left unsubscripted.

The power propagates along the transmission line as a voltage wave and a current wave. Considering both the voltage wave from the transmitter directly, and the reflected wave from the receiver, there exist points along the cable where these waves are in phase, and constructively add together; while there are other points where the waves are 180° out of phase and produce a voltage null.

Reference [43] (chapters 8 and 9) contains the solution to the wave equation for voltage and current waves traveling along a transmission line. The voltage and current along the transmission line can conveniently be expressed in terms of hyperbolic functions and a reference voltage and current taken at any point on the line. If x represents the distance from the transmitter (or source) to the point under observation, then the voltage and current (V(x) and I(x)) at this point are:

$$\begin{bmatrix} V(x) \\ I(x) \end{bmatrix} = \begin{bmatrix} \{\text{Cosh}\ (\gamma x)\} & \{-Z_o\ \text{Sinh}\ (\gamma x)\} \\ \{\frac{-1}{Z_o}\ \text{Sinh}\ (\gamma x)\} & \{\text{Cosh}\ (\gamma x)\} \end{bmatrix} \cdot \begin{bmatrix} V_s \\ I_s \end{bmatrix} \qquad (1\text{-}2.4)$$

where the hyperbolic functions are defined by:

$$\text{Sinh }(\gamma x) = \frac{e^{\gamma x} - e^{-\gamma x}}{2} \qquad (1\text{-}2.5)$$

$$\text{Cosh }(\gamma x) = \frac{e^{\gamma x} + e^{-\gamma x}}{2} \qquad (1\text{-}2.6)$$

Remembering that $I_s = V_s/Z_s$, and using the transmitter reflection coefficient defined by:

$$\rho_t = \frac{Z_s/Z_o - 1}{Z_s/Z_o + 1} \qquad (1\text{-}2.3)$$

Equation (1-2.4) may be solved for V(x) yielding:

$$V(x) = \frac{V_s}{1 + \rho_t} \cdot \left[ e^{-\gamma x} + \rho_t \, e^{\gamma x} \right] \qquad (1\text{-}2.2)$$

# Program Listing I

| | | |
|---|---|---|
| 001 | *LBL$_a$ | LOAD transmitter output Z |
| 002 | X⇄Y | in cartesian coordinates |
| 003 | →P | |
| 004 | X⇄Y | |
| 005 | *LBLA | LOAD transmitter output Z |
| 006 | P⇄S | in polar coordinates |
| 007 | ST07 | |
| 008 | X⇄Y | |
| 009 | ST06 | |
| 010 | P⇄S | |
| 011 | GT09 | goto space and return subr |
| 012 | *LBLB | LOAD source voltage in volts |
| 013 | P⇄S | |
| 014 | ST09 | |
| 015 | P⇄S | |
| 016 | GT09 | goto space and return subr |
| 017 | *LBLE | LOAD distance, x, from |
| 018 | ST04 | xmit and calculate V(x) |
| 019 | F2? | calculate $\rho_t$ on the first |
| 020 | F2? | execution of label E |
| 021 | GT01 | goto V(x) calculation |
| 022 | P⇄S | $\rho_t$ calculation routine |
| 023 | RCL8 | ∡ $Z_s$ |
| 024 | RCL1 | ∡ $Z_o$ |
| 025 | P⇄S | |
| 026 | - | |
| 027 | RCL8 | $|Z_s|$ |
| 028 | RCL1 | $|Z_o|$ |
| 029 | ÷ | |
| 030 | →R | |
| 031 | STOA | $Re(Z_s/Z_o)$ |
| 032 | EEX | |
| 033 | - | $Re(Z_s/Z_o - 1)$ |
| 034 | X⇄Y | |
| 035 | STOB | $Im(Z_s/Z_o) = Im(Z_s/Z_o - 1)$ |
| 036 | X⇄Y | |
| 037 | →P | |
| 038 | ST03 | $|Z_s/Z_o - 1|$ |
| 039 | X⇄Y | |
| 040 | ST06 | ∡$(Z_s/Z_o - 1)$ |
| 041 | RCLB | $Im(Z_s/Z_o) = Im(Z_s/Z_o + 1)$ |
| 042 | RCLA | $Re(Z_s/Z_o)$ |
| 043 | EEX | |
| 044 | + | $Re(Z_s/Z_o + 1)$ |
| 045 | →P | |
| 046 | ST÷3 | $|\rho_t|$ |
| 047 | X⇄Y | |
| 048 | ST-6 | ∡ $\rho_t$ |
| 049 | *LBL1 | V(x) calculation routine |
| 050 | RCL4 | $\ell$ |
| 051 | RCL0 | $\alpha_{dB}$ |
| 052 | x | |
| 053 | 2 | |
| 054 | 0 | |
| 055 | ÷ | $\alpha\ell/\ln 10$ , nepers |
| 056 | 10$^x$ | $e^{\alpha\ell}$ |
| 057 | STOA | |
| 058 | RCL3 | |
| 059 | x | $|\rho_t e^{\gamma\ell}|$ |
| 060 | RCL6 | ∡ $\rho_t$ |
| 061 | P⇄S | |
| 062 | RCL0 | $\beta$, radians/length |
| 063 | P⇄S | |
| 064 | R→D | $\beta$, degrees/length |
| 065 | RCL4 | |
| 066 | x | |
| 067 | STOB | $\beta\ell$, degrees |
| 068 | + | $\beta\ell + $ ∡ $\rho_t$, degrees |
| 069 | X⇄Y | |
| 070 | →R | |
| 071 | ST07 | $Re(\rho_t e^{\gamma\ell})$ |
| 072 | X⇄Y | |
| 073 | ST09 | $Im(\rho_t e^{\gamma\ell})$ |
| 074 | RCLB | calculate $e^{-\gamma\ell}$ in real and |
| 075 | CHS | imaginary parts |
| 076 | RCLA | |
| 077 | 1/X | |
| 078 | →R | |
| 079 | ST+7 | continue numerator calc of |
| 080 | X⇄Y | (1-2.4) using reg arith |
| 081 | ST+9 | |
| 082 | RCL9 | convert numerator to polar |
| 083 | RCL7 | coordinates |
| 084 | →P | |
| 085 | ST07 | $|e^{-\gamma\ell} + \rho_t e^{\gamma\ell}|$ |
| 086 | X⇄Y | |
| 087 | ST09 | ∡$(e^{-\gamma\ell} + \rho_t e^{\gamma\ell})$ |
| 088 | RCL6 | calculate $1 + \rho_t$ in polar |
| 089 | RCL3 | coordinates |
| 090 | →R | |
| 091 | EEX | |
| 092 | + | |
| 093 | →P | |
| 094 | ST÷7 | divide $1 + \rho_t$ into |
| 095 | X⇄Y | numerator |
| 096 | ST-9 | |
| 097 | P⇄S | calculate $V_s$ from $V_t$ |
| 098 | RCL8 | ∡ $Z_s$ |
| 099 | P⇄S | |
| 100 | ST+9 | |
| 101 | RCL8 | $|Z_s|$ |
| 102 | STx7 | |
| 103 | →R | |
| 104 | STOA | $Re\ Z_s$ |
| 105 | X⇄Y | |
| 106 | STOB | $Im\ Z_s$ |
| 107 | P⇄S | |
| 108 | RCL7 | form $Z_s + Z_t$ |
| 109 | RCL6 | |
| 110 | P⇄S | |

| REGISTERS | | | | | | | | | |
|---|---|---|---|---|---|---|---|---|---|
| 0 $\alpha_{dB}$ | 1 $|Z_o|$ | 2 $|Z_r|$ | 3 $|\rho_t|$ | 4 $\ell$ | 5 freq | 6 ∡$\rho_t$ | 7 scratch | 8 $|Z_s|$ | 9 scratch |
| S0 $\beta$ | S1 ∡$Z_o$ | S2 ∡$Z_r$ | S3 ∡$\rho$ | S4 | S5 $O_m$ | S6 $|Z_t|$ | S7 ∡$Z_t$ | S8 ∡$Z_s$ | S9 $V_t$ |
| A scratchpad | B scratchpad | C scratchpad | D 20log e | E 2$\pi$ | I index | | | | |

# Program Listing II

NOTE FLAG SET STATUS

```
 →R
 RCLA
 +        Re(Zs + Zt)
 X⇄Y
 RCLB
 +        Im(Zs + Zt)
 X⇄Y
 →P
 ST÷7     |Zs + Zt|
 X⇄Y
 ST-9     ∡(Zs + Zt)
 P⇄S
 RCL9     Vt
 P⇄S
 ST×7     complete |V(x)| calculation
 RCL7
 LOG
 2
 0
 ×
 PRTX     20 log V(x)
 RCL9
 PRTX     ∡ V(x)
 ----------------------------------------
 *LBL9    space and return subroutine
 SPC
 RTN
```

NOTE FLAG SET STATUS

| LABELS | | | | | FLAGS |
|---|---|---|---|---|---|
| A $\lvert Z_t \rvert \uparrow \measuredangle Z_t$ | B source voltage | C | D | E calc V(x) | 0 |
| a $ReZ_t \uparrow ImZ_t$ | b | c | d | e | 1 |
| 0 | 1 ρ calc jump | 2 | 3 | 4 | 2 ρ calc ? |
| 5 | 6 | 7 | 8 | 9 spc & rtn | 3 |

| SET STATUS | | |
|---|---|---|
| FLAGS | TRIG | DISP |
| ON OFF<br>0<br>1<br>2 ■<br>3 | DEG ■<br>GRAD<br>RAD | FIX ■<br>SCI<br>ENG<br>n 2 |

## PROGRAM 1-3 SECOND ORDER ACTIVE NETWORK TRANSMISSION FUNCTION.

Program Description and Equations Used

This program provides the coefficients of the numerator and denominator polynomials of the transmission function T(s) = N(s)/D(s), of the generalized second order active network shown in Fig. 1-3.1. A second part of the program provides the polynomial roots. If a real (non-ideal) operational amplifier (op-amp) is used, the amplifier will have both finite gain and bandwidth. The compensation pole of the op-amp will introduce a parasitic pole causing D(s) to become third order even though the RC network is set up to provide second order response. This program accepts the gain and 3 dB bandwidth of the amplifier and calculates the resulting third order transmission function.

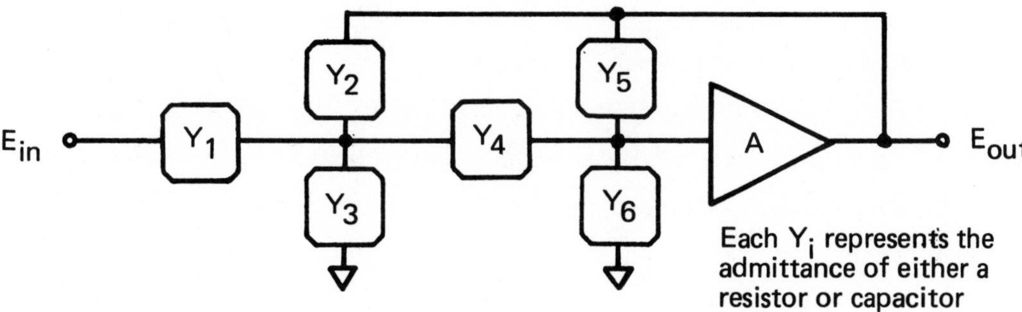


Figure 1-3.1 Generalized second order circuit.

If the natural frequencies of the response governed by the RC network alone are many decades removed from the amplifier unity gain crossover frequency, then the transmission function T(s), will be practically equal to the transmission function of the second order network with an ideal infinite bandwidth amplifier. The component values dictated by many active filter references assume ideal operational amplifier characteristics.

When the natural frequencies are within a decade or two of the amplifier unity gain crossover frequency, then the parasitic pole will cause a noticeable shift in the natural frequencies governed by the RC network alone. The network can be predistorted so the natural frequencies shift to the desired positions (see Program 2-11).

The transmission function is determined by writing the nodal equations for the network, and solving for $E_{out}$ in terms of $E_{in}$. This derivation is done later and provides:

$$E_{out} = \frac{A_0 Y_1 Y_4}{D(s)} \tag{1-3.1}$$

where

$$D(s) = (Y_1 + Y_2 + Y_3)\Big[(Y_4 + Y_6)(1 + \tau s) + Y_5 (1 - A_0 + \tau s)\Big] + Y_4\Big[Y_6 + (1 + \tau s) + Y_5 (1 - A_0 + \tau s) - A_0 Y_2\Big]$$

and where a one-pole model of the amplifier is assumed:

$$A = \frac{A_0}{1 + \tau s} \tag{1-3.2}$$

The sign of $A_0$ may be either positive or negative depending upon the amplifier characteristics (see examples). The first program uses Eq. (1-3.1) to form the numerator and denominator polynomials, and the second program finds the zeros of these polynomials (polynomial roots).

When the element values are loaded, capacitors are signified by a negative mantissa. The subroutine under label 8 tests the sign of the entry; if it is negative, the absolute value is stored; if it is positive, it is a resistor, and the reciprocal is taken to convert to conductance, and then multiplied by $10^{50}$ before storage.

The magnitude of the stored element value is used to signal whether the element is a resistor or a capacitor. Other programs use the sign of the stored value to differentiate between resistors and capacitors, but that indicator cannot be used in this program because algebraic operations are performed on the element values in the main program before the element type subroutine is entered and the resistor/capacitor test is done, i.e., the term $Y_5(1 - A_0)$ can have either sign depending upon the magnitude and sign of $A_0$, and $Y_5$ can legitimately represent the admittance of either a resistor or a capacitor.

The magnitude test is done in the summing routine under label 0.

If the absolute value of the coefficient is greater than $10^{30}$, it is assumed to be a conductance ($s^0$ term), the value is divided by $10^{50}$ to undo the original storage operation, and the summation is done in the stack. If the absolute value of the coefficient is less than $10^{30}$, it is assumed to be a capacitance ($s^1$ term), and the summation is done in the designated i register.

Some terms in the denominator of Eq. (1-3.1) contain the factor $\tau s$. These terms generate $s^1$ and $s^2$ coefficients. Subroutine 3 is used to perform multiplication by $\tau s$ and to append the $s^1$ and $s^2$ terms to the presently stored $s^0$ and $s^1$ terms to form the complete admittance sum set for the denominator segment being evaluated.

After each set of admittance sums ($s^0$, $s^1$, & $s^2$) are calculated and stored, polynomial multiplication is done to generate the coefficients of the various powers of s in the denominator polynomial. This multiplication is accomplished by the routine under label 6. If flag 0 is set, the polynomial coefficient registers are cleared before multiplication. This condition exists for the first product-of-sums. Flag 0 is cleared for the second product-of-sums to indicate continued summation into the polynomial coefficient registers.

After the denominator has been calculated, the polynomial coefficients are normalized by dividing by the $s^0$ polynomial coefficient. The numerator coefficient is likewise normalized, and the polynomial coefficients are provided as output. This normalization process can cause the program to halt displaying "ERROR" for certain classes of degenerate networks, e.g., a differentiator constructed with capacitors in locations 1 and 4, no elements in locations 2, 3, and 6, and feedback resistor in location 5. The series capacitors should be combined into a single capacitor in location 1 or 4 with the feedback resistor in location 2 or 5 and no elements in locations 3 and 6. The unspecified series elements can be 1 ohm resistors.

The second program finds the zeros of the denominator polynomial (poles of the transmission function). The numerator polynomial will be either a constant, a single zero at the origin, or a double zero at the origin depending on whether the filter is lowpass, bandpass, or highpass, respectively. The second program also indicates the degree of the zero, and the gain constant of the second order pair, K, after the third order root has been removed (if any), i.e.:

Lowpass: $$T(s) = K \frac{1}{\frac{s^2}{\omega_n^2} + \frac{s}{\omega_n Q} + 1} \qquad (1\text{-}3.3)$$

Bandpass: $$T(s) = K \frac{\frac{s}{\omega_n Q}}{\frac{s^2}{\omega_n^2} + \frac{s}{\omega_n Q} + 1} \qquad (1\text{-}3.4)$$

Highpass: $$T(s) = K \frac{\frac{s^2}{\omega_n^2}}{\frac{s^2}{\omega_n^2} + \frac{s}{\omega_n Q} + 1} \qquad (1\text{-}3.5)$$

If the denominator polynomial is second order, the quadratic formula is used to find the zeros. If it is third order, a Newton-Raphson iterative technique is used to find the real third order zero (there will be at least one), then the third order polynomial is deflated to second order, and the quadratic formula is used to find the remaining zeros of the polynomial. If the zeros of the denominator polynomial are complex, the program will also calculate the natural frequency, $f_n = \omega_n/2\pi$, and the Q, or quality factor of the complex pair (see the equation derivation part of this description for equations and details).

# User Instructions

| SECOND ORDER ACTIVE NETWORK TRANSMISSION FUNCTION | | | | |
|---|---|---|---|---|
| element 6 | $e_{in}$ o-1—2—4—5—A—o $e_o$ | | $A_o \uparrow f_o$ | start analysis |
| element 1 | element 2 | element 3 | element 4 | element 5 |

| STEP | INSTRUCTIONS | INPUT DATA/UNITS | KEYS | OUTPUT DATA/UNITS |
|---|---|---|---|---|
| 1 | Load both sides of program card | | | |
| 2 | Enter element 1 | | | |
| | a) if resistor (value ≠ 0) | R, ohms | [A] | |
| | b) if capacitor, enter negative value | C, farad | [chs] [A] | |
| 3 | Enter element 2 | | | |
| | a) if resistor | R, ohms | [B] | |
| | b) if capacitor | C, farad | [chs] [B] | |
| | c) if no element present | zero | [B] | |
| 4 | Enter element 3 | | | |
| | a) if resistor | R, ohms | [C] | |
| | b) if capacitor | C, farad | [chs] [C] | |
| | c) if no element present | zero | [C] | |
| 5 | Enter element 4 | | | |
| | a) if resistor (value ≠ 0) | R, ohms | [D] | |
| | b) if capacitor | C, farad | [chs] [D] | |
| 6 | Enter element 5 | | | |
| | a) if resistor | R, ohms | [E] | |
| | b) if capacitor | C, farad | [chs] [E] | |
| | c) if no element present | zero | [E] | |
| 7 | Enter element 6 | | | |
| | a) if resistor | R, ohms | [f] [A] | |
| | b) if capacitor | C, farad | [chs] [f] [A] | |
| | c) if no element present | zero | [f] [A] | |
| 8 | Enter operational amplifier parameters | $A_o$ | [↑] | |
| | | $f_o$, Hz | [f] [D] | |
| 9 | Start analysis | | [f] [E] | Den coefs |
| | | | | Num coefs |
| 10 | Go back and change any element then rerun step 9, or load second card to find denominator pole locations, $f_n$, and Q | | | |

# User Instructions

SECOND AND THIRD ORDER ROOT FINDER PROGRAM
USE AFTER TRANSMISSION FUNCTION PROGRAM

1 | | | | | START | 2

| STEP | INSTRUCTIONS | INPUT DATA/UNITS | KEYS | OUTPUT DATA/UNITS |
|---|---|---|---|---|
| 1 | Load both sides of program card when display | | | |
| | flashes, program execution begins unaided | | | |
| 2 | Program output | | | |
| 2a | If three real roots, (s+a)(s+b)(s+c) | | | -a |
| | | | | -b |
| | | | | -c |
| 2b | If one real root and a complex conjugate pair, (s+a)(s+α+jβ)(s+α-jβ) | | | -a |
| | | | | β |
| | | | | -α |
| | | | | -β |
| | | | | -α |
| | | | of second order pair | $f_n$ (Hz) |
| | | | | Q |
| | | | | midband gain |
| | | | | num zero locations |
| 2c | If two real roots: (s+a)(s+b) | | | -a |
| | | | | -b |
| 2c | A complex conjugate pair, (s+α+jβ)(s+α-jβ) | | | β |
| | | | | -α |
| | | | | -β |
| | | | | -α |
| | | | of second order pair | $f_n$ (Hz) |
| | | | | Q |
| | | | | midband gain |
| | | | | num zero locations |

# User Instructions

TI-59 TRANSLATION

| SECOND ORDER ACTIVE NETWORK TRANSMISSION FUNCTION | | | | |
|---|---|---|---|---|
| init | | | | start analysis |
| k | $R_k$ | $C_k$ | $A_o$ | $f_{-3}$ dB |

TI-59 TRANSLATION

| STEP | INSTRUCTIONS | INPUT DATA/UNITS | KEYS | OUTPUT DATA/UNITS |
|---|---|---|---|---|
| 1 | Load both sides of program card one | | | |
| 2 | Initialize and clear registers | | 2nd A | 0 |
| 3 | Load elements | | | |
| | a) load element number (1 to 6) | k | A | k |
| | b) load element values: | | | |
| | if resistor | $R_k$, ohms | B | $R_k$ |
| | if capcitor | $C_k$, F | C | $C_k$ |
| | if no element present | 0 | C | 0 |
| | Repeat step 3 until all elements have been entered. | | | |
| 4 | Load amplifier dc gain (load negative gain for inverting op-amp) | $A_o$ | D | $A_o$ |
| 5 | Load -3 dB rolloff frequency of amplifier | $f_{-3}$ dB, Hz | E | $f_{-3}$ dB |
| 6 | Start analysis | | 2nd E | den coefs |
| | | | | $b_3$ |
| | | | R/S* | $b_2$ |
| | | | R/S* | $b_1$ |
| | | | R/S* | 1 |
| | | | | num coefs |
| | | | R/S* | $a_2$ |
| | | | R/S* | $a_1$ |
| | | | R/S* | $a_o$ |
| | * "R/S" not necessary if the TI-59 is attached to the PC-100A printer. All results will be printed automatically after the program is started. | | | |

# User Instructions

TI-59 TRANSLATION

| SECOND AND THIRD ORDER ROOT FINDER PROGRAM use with 1-3 | | | | |
|---|---|---|---|---|
| | | | | |
| | | | | start |

2

TI-59 TRANSLATION

| STEP | INSTRUCTIONS | INPUT DATA/UNITS | KEYS | OUTPUT DATA/UNITS |
|---|---|---|---|---|
| 7 | Load both sides of program card 2 | | | |
| 8 | Start second program | | E | |
| | a) If three real roots: | | | -a |
| | (s+a)(s+b)(s+b) | | R/S* | -b |
| | | | R/S* | -c |
| | b) If one real root and a complex conjugate | | | -a |
| | pair: $(s+a)(s+\alpha+j\beta)(s+\alpha-j\beta)$ | | | |
| | | | R/S* | $\beta$ |
| | | | R/S* | $-\alpha$ |
| | | | R/S* | $-\beta$ |
| | | | R/S* | $-\alpha$ |
| | | | R/S* | $f_n$, Hz |
| | | | R/S* | Q |
| | | | R/S* | midband gain |
| | c) If two real roots: (s+a)(s+b) | | | -a |
| | | | R/S* | -b |
| | d) If a complex conjugate pair: | | | $\beta$ |
| | $(s+\alpha+j\beta)(s+\alpha-j\beta)$ | | R/S* | $-\alpha$ |
| | | | R/S* | $-\beta$ |
| | | | R/S* | $-\alpha$ |
| | | | R/S* | $f_n$, Hz |
| | | | R/S* | Q |
| | | | R/S* | midband gain |
| | * "R/S" not necessary if the TI-59 is attached to the PC-100A printer. All results will be automatically printed after the program is started. | | | |

Example 1-3.1

The schematic in Fig. 1-3.2 represents a second order active band-pass filter using the infinite gain, multiple feedback topology. The filter element values were designed assuming the op-amp to be ideal, i.e., having infinite gain and bandwidth. The type 741 op-amp is not ideal in that it has both finite gain and bandwidth. This example will use the program to show that the element values provide the desired specification when the op-amp has very large gain ($-10^9$) and infinite bandwidth ($\tau = 0$). The program will then be run with the gain and bandwidth values for the 741 type op-amp to show that both the pole natural frequency and "Q" have shifted away from the desired values. The 741 has a typical gain of -100,000, and open loop break frequency of 5 Hz.

The design specifications for the filter are:

| | |
|---|---|
| center frequency: | 10 kHz |
| midband gain: | 10 |
| quality factor, Q: | 10 |
| capacitor value: | 1000 pF |

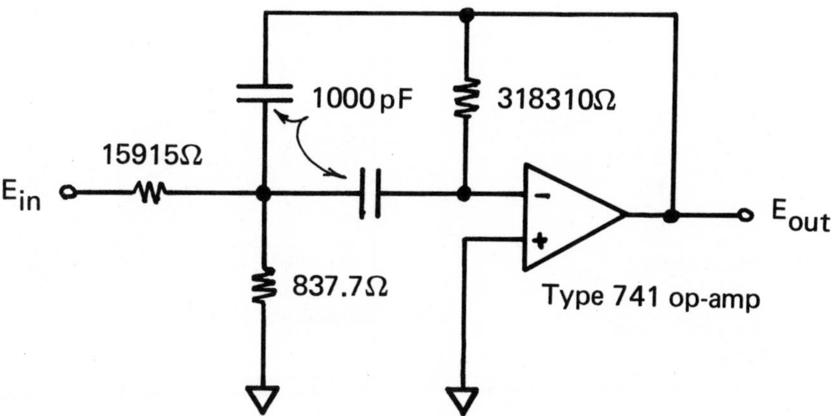


Figure 1-3.2 Second order bandpass active filter, infinite gain-multiple feedback topology.

## HP-97 PRINTOUT FOR EXAMPLE 1-3.1

load first program and
enter element values

| | | |
|---|---|---|
| 15915. | GSBA | element 1, resistor |
| -1.-09 | GSBB | element 2, cap |
| 837.7 | GSBC | element 3, resistor |
| -1.-09 | GSBD | element 4, cap |
| 318310. | GSBE | element 5, resistor |
| 0. | GSBa | element 6, missing |
| -1.+09 | ST00 | enter infinite gain app |
| 0. | ST07 | set $\tau$ to zero (BW=$\infty$) |
| | GSBe | start analysis |
| 0.000+00 | *** | $s^3$ denominator coef |
| 253.3-12 | *** | $s^2$ " " |
| 1.592-06 | *** | $s^1$ " " |
| 1.000+00 | *** | $s^0$ " " |
| 0.000+00 | *** | $s^2$ numerator coef |
| -15.92-06 | *** | $s^1$ " " |
| 0.000+00 | *** | $s^0$ " " |
| | | load second card and start analysis |
| 62.75+03 | *** | imag } complex conjugate poles |
| -3.142+03 | *** | real } complex conjugate poles |
| -62.75+03 | *** | imag } complex conjugate poles |
| -3.142+03 | *** | real } complex conjugate poles |
| 10.00+03 | *** | $f_n$ } of second order pole pair |
| 10.00+00 | *** | Q } of second order pole pair |
| -10.00+00 | *** | midband gain |
| 0.000+00 | *** | numerator zero location |

reload first card

| | | |
|---|---|---|
| -100000. | ENT↑ | 741 dc gain |
| 5. | GSBd | 741 break freq |
| | GSBe | start analysis |
| 80.63-18 | *** | $s^3$ |
| 355.1-12 | *** | $s^2$ |
| 1.913-06 | *** | $s^1$ |
| 1.000+00 | *** | $s^0$ |
| 0.000+00 | *** | $s^2$ |
| -15.92-06 | *** | $s^1$ |
| 0.000+00 | *** | $s^0$ |
| | | load second card & start analysis |
| -4.400+06 | *** | real pole location |
| 53.04+03 | *** | imag } complex conjugate poles |
| -2.376+03 | *** | real } complex conjugate poles |
| -53.04+03 | *** | imag } complex conjugate poles |
| -2.376+03 | *** | real } complex conjugate poles |
| 8.450+03 | *** | $f_n$ } of second order pole pair |
| 11.17+00 | *** | Q } of second order pole pair |
| -9.441+00 | *** | midband gain |
| 0.000+00 | *** | numerator zero location |

## TI-59 PRINTOUT FOR EXAMPLE 1-3.1

load first program and enter element values

| | | |
|---|---|---|
| 1. | | element # |
| 15915. | R | resistor |
| 2. | | element # |
| 1. -09 | C | capacitor |
| 3. | | element # |
| 837.7 | R | resistor |
| 4. | | element # |
| 1. -09 | C | capacitor |
| 5. | | element # |
| 318310. | R | resistor |
| -1. 09 | A | amplifier gain (ideal) |
| 1. 25 | F | amplifier BW (ideal) |
| 0.00 00 | | $s^3$ den coef |
| 253.31-12 | | $s^2$ " " |
| 1.59-06 | | $s^1$ " " |
| 1.00 00 | | $s^0$ " " |
| 0.00 00 | | $s^2$ num coef |
| -15.92-06 | | $s^1$ " " |
| 0.00 00 | | $s^0$ " " |

load second card

| | | |
|---|---|---|
| 62.75 03 | imag | complex conj. pole pair |
| -3.14 03 | real | |
| -62.75 03 | imag | |
| -3.14 03 | real | |
| 10.00 03 | $f_n$ | |
| 10.00 00 | Q | |
| -10.00 00 | midband gain | |

reload first card

| | | |
|---|---|---|
| -100. 03 | A | 741 dc gain |
| 5. 00 | F | 741 break freq |
| 80.63-18 | | $s^3$ den coef |
| 355.14-12 | | $s^2$ " " |
| 1.91-06 | | $s^1$ " " |
| 1.00 00 | | $s^0$ " " |
| 0.00 00 | | $s^2$ num coef |
| -15.92-06 | | $s^1$ " " |
| 0.00 00 | | $s^0$ " " |

load second card

| | | |
|---|---|---|
| -4.3997 06 | real pole location | |
| 53.03 03 | imag | complex conj. pole pair |
| -2.3760 03 | real | |
| -53.03 03 | imag | |
| -2.3760 03 | real | |
| 8.4499 03 | $f_n$ | |
| 11.17 00 | Q | |
| -9.4414 00 | midband gain | |

Example 1-3.2

Figure 1-3.3 is the schematic of a second order highpass filter using the Sallen and Key controlled source topology. An operational amplifier is connected in the voltage follower configuration to provide the unity gain non-inverting buffer amplifier required. The design procedure assumes infinite bandwidth in this buffer, but physical op-amps, such as the 741 type have finite bandwidth (BW). This example will show how this finite bandwidth affects the filter performance. The design specifications are:

| | |
|---|---|
| natural frequency, $f_o$: | 10000 Hz |
| quality factor, Q: | $1/\sqrt{2} = 0.707$ |
| capacitor value, $C_1$, $C_4$: | 1 nF |
| asymptotic high frequency gain: | unity |

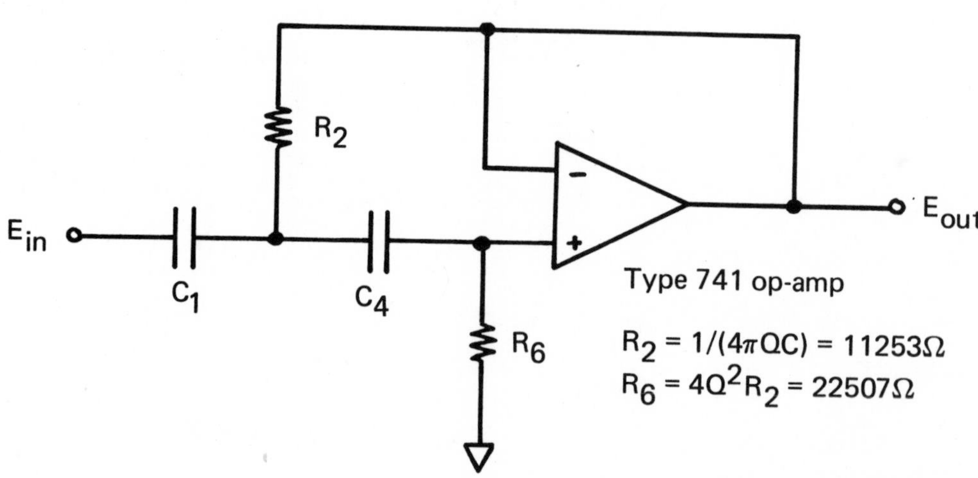


Figure 1-3.3 Sallen and Key type second order highpass filter.

The HP-97 printout is shown on the next page. Again, two runs were made; first the amplifier was assumed to be ideal, and the program output verifies the design specifications; second, the finite gain and bandwidth characteristics of the 741 operational amplifier were used. The program output for the second case shows the non-ideal (finite) characteristics of the 741 have caused the second order pole positions to shift away from the desired positions, and a real pole has also been introduced.

## HP-97 PRINTOUT FOR EXAMPLE 1-3.2

**load first program and enter element values**

| | | |
|---|---|---|
| -1.-09 | GSBA | element 1, capacitor |
| 11253. | GSBB | element 2, resistor |
| 0. | GSBC | element 3, missing |
| -1.-09 | GSBD | element 4, capacitor |
| 0. | GSBE | element 5, missing |
| 22507. | GSBa | element 6, resistor |
| 1. | ST00 | set $A_0 = 1$ |
| 0. | ST07 | set $\tau = 0$ (BW $= \infty$) |
| | GSBe | start analysis |
| 0.000+00 | *** | $s^3$ |
| 253.3-12 | *** | $s^2$ |
| 22.51-06 | *** | $s^1$ |
| 1.000+00 | *** | $s^0$ |
| 253.3-12 | *** | $s^2$ |
| 0.000+00 | *** | $s^1$ |
| 0.000+00 | *** | $s^0$ |
| | | load second card & start analysis |
| 44.43+03 | *** | imag (complex conjugate poles) |
| -44.43+03 | *** | real (complex conjugate poles) |
| -44.43+03 | *** | imag (complex conjugate poles) |
| -44.43+03 | *** | real (complex conjugate poles) |
| 10.00+03 | *** | $f_n$ (of second order pole pair) |
| 707.1-03 | *** | Q (of second order pole pair) |
| 1.000+00 | *** | asymptotic gain |
| 0.000+00 | *** | numerator zero locations |
| 0.000+00 | *** | numerator zero locations |

**Reload first card and enter op-amp parameters**

| | | |
|---|---|---|
| 1. | ENT↑ | gain (type 741) |
| 500000. | GSBd | bandwidth (type 741) |
| | GSBe | start analysis |
| 80.62-18 | *** | $s^3$ denominator coef |
| 267.6-12 | *** | $s^2$ denominator coef |
| 22.82-06 | *** | $s^1$ denominator coef |
| 1.000+00 | *** | $s^0$ denominator coef |
| 253.3-12 | *** | $s^2$ numerator coef |
| 0.000+00 | *** | $s^1$ numerator coef |
| 0.000+00 | *** | $s^0$ numerator coef |
| | | load second card & start analysis |
| -3.233+06 | *** | real pole location |
| 44.40+03 | *** | imag (complex conjugate poles) |
| -43.19+03 | *** | real (complex conjugate poles) |
| -44.40+03 | *** | imag (complex conjugate poles) |
| -43.19+03 | *** | real (complex conjugate poles) |
| 9.858+03 | *** | $f_n$ (of second order pole pair) |
| 717.0-03 | *** | Q (of second order pole pair) |
| 971.7-03 | *** | asymptotic gain |
| 0.000+00 | *** | numerator zero locations |
| 0.000+00 | *** | numerator zero locations |

## TI-59 PRINTOUT FOR EXAMPLE 1-3.2

| | | | | | |
|---|---|---|---|---|---|
| load first program and enter element values | | | | | |
| 1. | | element # | | | |
| 1. -09 | C | capacitor | | | |
| 2. | | element # | | | |
| 11253. | R | resistor | | | |
| 4. | | element # | | | |
| 1. -09 | C | capacitor | reload first card | | |
| 6. | | element # | | | |
| 22507. | R | resistor | | | |
| 1. | A | amplifier gain (ideal) | 1. 00 | A | 741 gain |
| 1. 25 | F | amplifier BW (ideal) | 500. 03 | F | 741 BW |
| 0.00 00 | | $s^3$ den coef | 80.62-18 | | $s^3$ den coef |
| 253.27-12 | | $s^2$ " " | 267.60-12 | | $s^2$ " " |
| 22.51-06 | | $s^1$ " " | 22.82-06 | | $s^1$ " " |
| 1.00 00 | | $s^0$ " " | 1.00 00 | | $s^0$ " " |
| 253.27-12 | | $s^2$ num coef | 253.27-12 | | $s^2$ num coef |
| 0.00 00 | | $s^1$ " " | 0.00 00 | | $s^1$ " " |
| 0.00 00 | | $s^0$ " " | 0.00 00 | | $s^0$ " " |
| load second card | | | load second card | | |
| | | | -3.23 06 | | real pole location |
| 44.43 03 | | imag — complex conj. pole pair | 44.40 03 | | imag — complex conj. pole pair |
| -44.43 03 | | real — complex conj. pole pair | -43.19 03 | | real — complex conj. pole pair |
| -44.43 03 | | imag — complex conj. pole pair | -44.40 03 | | imag — complex conj. pole pair |
| -44.43 03 | | real — complex conj. pole pair | -43.19 03 | | real — complex conj. pole pair |
| 10.00 03 | | $f_n$ of second order pole pair | 9.86 03 | | $f_n$ of second order pole pair |
| 707.12-03 | | Q of second order pole pair | 717.04-03 | | Q of second order pole pair |
| 1.00 00 | | asymptotic gain | 971.75-03 | | asymptotic gain |

Derivation of Equations and Algorithms Used

Active network transfer function: The schematic of the generalized second order active network is shown in Fig. 1-3.1. Let the junction of $Y_1$, $Y_2$, $Y_3$, and $Y_4$ be designated node 1. Furthermore, let the junction of $Y_4$, $Y_5$, and $Y_6$ be designated as node 2. The nodal equations for this circuit may be written in matrix form in terms of the voltages at node 1 ($E_1$), and at node 2 ($E_2$):

$$\begin{bmatrix} \{Y_1 + Y_2 + Y_3 + Y_4\} & \{-Y_4\} \\ \{-Y_4\} & \{Y_4 + Y_5 + Y_6\} \end{bmatrix} \cdot \begin{bmatrix} E_1 \\ E_2 \end{bmatrix} = \begin{bmatrix} Y_1 & Y_2 \\ 0 & Y_5 \end{bmatrix} \cdot \begin{bmatrix} E_{in} \\ E_{out} \end{bmatrix} \qquad (1\text{-}3.6)$$

Since $E_2 = E_{out}/A$, this expression is substituted into Eq. (1-3.6), and the dependent variables brought to the left hand side.

$$\begin{bmatrix} \{Y_1 + Y_2 + Y_3 + Y_4\} & \left\{\dfrac{Y_4}{A} - Y_2\right\} \\ \{-Y_4\} & \left\{\dfrac{Y_4 + Y_5 + Y_6}{A} - Y_5\right\} \end{bmatrix} \cdot \begin{bmatrix} E_1 \\ E_{out} \end{bmatrix} = \begin{bmatrix} Y_1 \\ 0 \end{bmatrix} (E_{in}) \qquad (1\text{-}3.7)$$

$T(s) = E_{out}/E_{in}$ may be obtained from Eq. (1-3.7) using Cramer's rule. To this end, the determinant of the coefficient matrix ($\Delta$) is needed:

$$\Delta = (Y_1 + Y_2 + Y_3 + Y_4) \cdot \left[\frac{Y_4 + Y_5 + Y_6}{A} - Y_5\right] - Y_4\left[\frac{Y_4}{A} - Y_2\right] \qquad (1\text{-}3.8)$$

After clearing fractions and eliminating term subtraction,

$$A \cdot \Delta = (Y_1 + Y_2 + Y_3)[Y_4 + Y_6 + Y_5(1 - A)] + Y_4\,[Y_5(1 - A) - AY_2 + Y_6] \qquad (1\text{-}3.9)$$

Substituting $A = A_0/(1 + \tau s)$ as the amplifier gain, and clearing fractions, Eq. (1-3.9) becomes:

$$A_0 \cdot \Delta = (Y_1 + Y_2 + Y_3)[(Y_4 + Y_5)(1 + \tau s) + Y_5(1 - A_0 + \tau s)] + Y_4\,[Y_6(1 + \tau s) + Y_5(1 - A_0 + \tau s) - A_0 \cdot Y_2] \qquad (1.3.10)$$

Using Cramer's rule, the transmission function becomes:

$$T(s) = E_{out}/E_{in} = (Y_1 \cdot Y_4)/\Delta \quad (1\text{-}3.11)$$

Newton-Raphson solution for finding real zeros of third order polynomials: The Newton-Raphson solution is an iterative procedure for finding the values of x where f(x) becomes zero, hence, these values of x are called the zeros of f(x). If the mathematical operations are restricted to real numbers, then the procedure will only find the real zeros of the function, f(x). All odd ordered polynomials with real coefficients have at least one real zero. The third order polynomial generated by this program falls into this class, therefore real arithmetic is used to extract the real zero.

Given the function f(x) = 0, the Newton-Raphson solution provides a new estimate, $x_{i+1}$, based on the present estimate, $x_i$, and the tangent to $f(x_i)$. The value of $x_{i+1}$ is determined by calculating the intercept of the tangent, $f'(x_i)$ on the x axis as shown in Fig. 1-3.2.

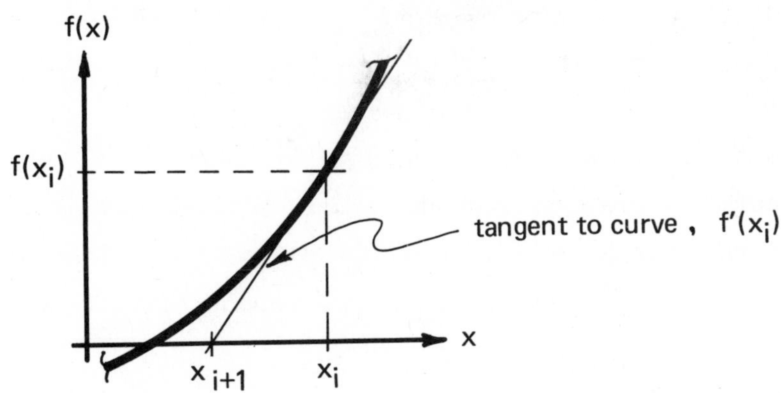


Figure 1-3.2 Newton-Raphson solution method.

$$f'(x_i) = \Delta f(x_i)/\Delta x_i = (f(x_i)-0)/(x_i - x_{i+1})$$

Solving for $x_{i+1}$:

$$x_{i+1} = x_i - f(x_i)/f'(x_i)$$

The iteration is stopped when the absolute value of the correction term, $f(x_i)/f'(x_i)$ becomes smaller than the desired error limit, $x_i \cdot 10^{-8}$.

Once the real zero of the third order polynomial has been found, a polynomial division is done to deflate the polynomial to second order. The quadratic equation is used to obtain the zeros of the second order polynomial, and these zeros may be complex. If s = a is a zero of f(s), then s-a must be a factor of f(s), and can be removed:

$$\begin{array}{l} \qquad b_3s^2 + (ab_3 + b_2)s + (a(ab_3 + b_2) + b_1) \\ s-a\overline{)b_3s^3 + b_2s^2 + b_1s \quad + 1} \\ \quad -(b_3s^3 - ab_3s^2) \\ \qquad (ab_3 + b_2)s^2 + b_1s + 1 \\ \qquad -[(ab_3 + b_2)s^2 - a(ab_3 + b_2)s] \\ \qquad\qquad a(ab_3 + b_2)s + b_1s + 1 \\ \qquad\qquad -\{a(ab_3 + b_2)s + b_1s - a[a(ab_3 + b_2) + b_1]\} \\ \qquad\qquad\qquad 0^* \end{array} \tag{1-3.14}$$

The third order polynomial is evaluated in nested form, i.e.:

$$D(s) = (((b_3)s + b_2)s + b_1)s + 1 \tag{1-3.15}$$

When s = a, the intermediate products in D(s) are the same as the second order polynomial coefficients in Eq. (1-3.14). These intermediate products are stored at lines 027 and 031 of the program on the second card. The numbers stored only have value in the last iteration loop before loop exit, at which time s = a, and f(s) = 0, the desired result.

The second order polynomial is normalized so $c_0 = 1$ (lines 064 to 066). This normalization places the second order polynomial in the same form as the third order polynomial was originally. The quadratic formula is now used to find the zeros of the second order polynomial, $c_2 s^2 + c_1 s + 1$.

$$s_{1,2} = -c_1/(2c_2) \pm \sqrt{(c_1/(2c_2))^2 - 1/c_2} \tag{1-3.16}$$

If the discriminant, $(c_1/(2c_2))^2 - 1/c_2$, is positive, then two real zeros exist, if it is zero, a double zero exists, and if it is negative, a complex conjugate pair of zeros exist. Steps 067 through 102 find the zeros of the second order polynomial.

---

* By definition since s = a is a zero of the polynomial.

If the zeros of the second order polynomial are complex conjugates, then the poles of the transmission function are also complex conjugates, and a natural frequency, $f_n$, and quality factor, Q, may be calculated:

$$f_n = 1/(2\pi\sqrt{c_2}) \tag{1-3.17}$$

$$Q = \sqrt{c_2}/c_1 \tag{1-3.18}$$

These calculations are performed by steps 103 through 113 of the program. Assuming the third order real pole of the transmission function (parasitic pole caused by the op-amp characteristics) to be large compared to the other poles, then the gain term, K, can be defined in terms of the numerator and denominator coefficients:

$$T(s) = \frac{a_2s^2 + a_1s + a_0}{(s/a + 1)(c_2s^2 + c_1s + 1)} \tag{1-3.19}$$

$$\text{lowpass case:} \quad K = a_0 \tag{1-3.20}$$

$$\text{bandpass case:} \quad K = a_1/c_1 \tag{1-3.21}$$

$$\text{highpass case:} \quad K = a_2/c_2 \tag{1-3.22}$$

The gain term is calculated by steps 114 through 137 of the program.

1-3 card 1

# Program Listing I

| Step | Key | Comment |
|---|---|---|
| 001 | *LBLA | LOAD ELEMENT 1 |
| 002 | EEX | |
| 003 | GTO8 | |
| 004 | *LBLB | LOAD ELEMENT 2 |
| 005 | 2 | |
| 006 | GTO8 | |
| 007 | *LBLC | LOAD ELEMENT 3 |
| 008 | 3 | |
| 009 | GTO8 | |
| 010 | *LBLD | LOAD ELEMENT 4 |
| 011 | 4 | |
| 012 | GTO8 | |
| 013 | *LBLE | LOAD ELEMENT 5 |
| 014 | 5 | |
| 015 | GTO8 | |
| 016 | *LBLa | LOAD ELEMENT 6 |
| 017 | 6 | |
| 018 | *LBL8 | element load subroutine |
| 019 | STOI | store register index |
| 020 | R↓ | recover and store |
| 021 | STO9 | element value |
| 022 | X>0? | test for resistor |
| 023 | GTO8 | |
| 024 | CHS | |
| 025 | GTO7 | store capacitor value |
| 026 | *LBL8 | |
| 027 | 1/X | calculate conductance, |
| 028 | EEX | multiply by $10^{50}$, and store |
| 029 | 5 | |
| 030 | 0 | |
| 031 | STO8 | store $10^{50}$ for later use |
| 032 | × | |
| 033 | *LBL7 | |
| 034 | STO(i) | store modified element value |
| 035 | RCL9 | recall original element to |
| 036 | RTN | display and return to keybd |
| 037 | *LBLd | LOAD $A_0$ AND $f_o$ OF AMPLIFIER |
| 038 | Pi | |
| 039 | × | |
| 040 | ENT↑ | calculate and store |
| 041 | + | $\tau = 1/(2\pi f_o)$ |
| 042 | 1/X | |
| 043 | STO7 | |
| 044 | R↓ | recover and store $A_0$ |
| 045 | STO0 | |
| 046 | RTN | return control to keyboard |
| 047 | *LBLe | START ANALYSIS |
| 048 | GSB1 | |
| 049 | RCL1 | calculate $s^0$ and $s^1$ terms |
| 050 | GSB0 | |
| 051 | RCL2 | of $Y_1 + Y_2 + Y_3$ |
| 052 | GSB0 | |
| 053 | RCL3 | |
| 054 | GSB2 | |
| 055 | RCL4 | |
| 056 | GSB0 | |
| 057 | RCL6 | |
| 058 | GSB0 | |
| 059 | RCL5 | calculate and store $s^0$ and |
| 060 | EEX | |
| 061 | RCL0 | $s^1$ terms of: |
| 062 | − | |
| 063 | × | $Y_4 + Y_6 + Y_5(1 - A_0)$ |
| 064 | STO9 | |
| 065 | GSB2 | |
| 066 | RCL4 | |
| 067 | GSB0 | calculate and store $s^1$ and |
| 068 | RCL5 | |
| 069 | GSB0 | $s^2$ terms of: |
| 070 | RCL6 | |
| 071 | GSB0 | $\tau s(Y_4 + Y_5 + Y_6)$ |
| 072 | GSB3 | |
| 073 | SF0 | calculate and store: |
| 074 | GSB6 | $(Y_1+Y_2+Y_3)\{(Y_4+Y_6)(1+\tau s) + Y_5(1-A_0+\tau s)\}$ |
| 075 | GSB1 | initialize index counter |
| 076 | RCL4 | calculate and store $Y_4$ |
| 077 | GSB2 | |
| 078 | RCL6 | |
| 079 | GSB0 | calculate $s^0$ and $s^1$ terms |
| 080 | RCL9 | of: |
| 081 | GSB0 | $Y_6 + Y_5(1 - A_o) - A_oY_2$ |
| 082 | RCL2 | |
| 083 | RCL0 | |
| 084 | × | |
| 085 | CHS | |
| 086 | GSB2 | |
| 087 | RCL6 | |
| 088 | GSB0 | calculate and store $s^1$ and |
| 089 | RCL5 | |
| 090 | GSB0 | $s^2$ terms of $\tau s(Y_5 + Y_6)$ |
| 091 | GSB3 | |
| 092 | CF0 | clear flag 0 to indicate |
| 093 | GSB6 | additional summing and |
| 094 | P⇄S | calculate and store: |
| 095 | RCL0 | $Y_4\{Y_6(1+\tau s) + Y_5(1-A_0+\tau s) - A_0 Y_2\}$ |
| 096 | STOA | normalize denominator terms: |
| 097 | ST÷1 | |
| 098 | ST÷2 | $\frac{a_3}{a_o}s^3 + \frac{a_2}{a_o}s^2 + \frac{a_1}{a_o}s + 1$ |
| 099 | ST÷3 | |
| 100 | RCL3 | recall, store, and print |
| 101 | PRTX | normalized denominator terms |
| 102 | STOD | |
| 103 | RCL2 | |
| 104 | PRTX | $a_3/a_o \to R_D$ |
| 105 | STOC | |
| 106 | RCL1 | $a_2/a_o \to R_C$ |
| 107 | P⇄S | |
| 108 | PRTX | $a_1/a_o \to R_B$ |
| 109 | STOB | |
| 110 | EEX | |
| 111 | ENT↑ | |
| 112 | PRTX | |

REGISTERS

| 0 | 1 | 2 | 3 | 4 | 5 | 6 | 7 | 8 | 9 |
|---|---|---|---|---|---|---|---|---|---|
| $A_o$ | $Y_1$ | $Y_2$ | $Y_3$ | $Y_4$ | $Y_5$ | $Y_6$ | $\tau$ | $10^{50}$ | scratch |

| S0 | S1 | S2 | S3 | S4 | S5 | S6 | S7 | S8 | S9 |
|---|---|---|---|---|---|---|---|---|---|
| $\Sigma s^0$ terms | $\Sigma s^1$ terms | $\Sigma s^2$ terms | $\Sigma s^3$ terms | | $s_1^2$ | $s_1^0$ | $s_1^1$ | $s_2^0$ | $s_2^1$ |

| A | B | C | D | E | I |
|---|---|---|---|---|---|
| $b_o$ | $D_1$ | $D_2$ | $D_3$ | scratchpad | index |

1-3 card 1

# Program Listing II

| Step | Key | Comments |
|---|---|---|
| 113 | SPC | |
| 114 | SF0 | indicate summing register clr |
| 115 | GSB1 | initialize registers and index |
| 116 | RCL1 | calculate and store $Y_1$ |
| 117 | GSB2 | |
| 118 | RCL4 | calculate and store $Y_4$ |
| 119 | GSB2 | |
| 120 | CLX | set $s^2$ term of $Y_4$ to zero |
| 121 | STO i | |
| 122 | GSB6 | calculate and store $Y_1 \cdot Y_4$ |
| 123 | RCL0 | normalize numerator terms |
| 124 | P⇄S | |
| 125 | RCLA | |
| 126 | ÷ | |
| 127 | ST×2 | |
| 128 | ST×1 | |
| 129 | ST×0 | |
| 130 | RCL2 | recall and print numerator terms |
| 131 | PRTX | |
| 132 | RCL1 | |
| 133 | PRTX | |
| 134 | RCL0 | |
| 135 | P⇄S | |
| 136 | PRTX | |
| 137 | SPC | |
| 138 | *LBLb | wait loop for 2nd card read |
| 139 | PSE | |
| 140 | GTOb | |
| 141 | *LBL0 | subroutine to determine whether recalled Y element is a conductance or a capacitance. If a conductance, perform summation in the stack, otherwise, element is a susceptance, and summation is done in the designated i register. |
| 142 | ENT↑ | |
| 143 | ABS | |
| 144 | EEX | |
| 145 | 3 | |
| 146 | 0 | |
| 147 | X>Y? | |
| 148 | GTO9 | |
| 149 | R↓ | |
| 150 | R↓ | |
| 151 | RCL8 | |
| 152 | ÷ | |
| 153 | + | |
| 154 | RTN | |
| 155 | *LBL9 | susceptance summation in R(i) |
| 156 | R↓ | |
| 157 | R↓ | |
| 158 | ST+i | |
| 159 | R↓ | |
| 160 | RTN | |
| 161 | *LBL1 | register and index initialization |
| 162 | 1 | |
| 163 | 9 | |
| 164 | STOI | $19 \rightarrow R_I$ |
| 165 | CLX | |
| 166 | STO i | $0 \rightarrow R_{19}$ |
| 167 | RTN | |
| 168 | *LBL2 | finish Y element summation, store stack summation, and initialize next susceptance summation register |
| 169 | GSB0 | |
| 170 | DSZI | |
| 171 | STO i | |
| 172 | DSZI | |
| 173 | CLX | |
| 174 | STO i | |
| 175 | RTN | |
| 176 | *LBL3 | multiply by $\tau s$ to form $s^2$ and additional $s^1$ terms, and add to presently stored terms |
| 177 | RCL7 | |
| 178 | P⇄S | |
| 179 | ST×5 | |
| 180 | × | |
| 181 | ST+7 | |
| 182 | P⇄S | |
| 183 | RTN | |
| 184 | *LBL6 | polynomial multiplication |
| 185 | P⇄S | |
| 186 | CLX | $s^0$ term calculation |
| 187 | GSB5 | |
| 188 | RCL6 | |
| 189 | RCL8 | |
| 190 | GSB4 | |
| 191 | EEX | $s^1$ term calculation |
| 192 | GSB5 | |
| 193 | RCL7 | |
| 194 | RCL8 | |
| 195 | GSB4 | |
| 196 | RCL6 | |
| 197 | RCL9 | |
| 198 | GSB4 | |
| 199 | 2 | $s^2$ term calculation |
| 200 | GSB5 | |
| 201 | RCL7 | |
| 202 | RCL9 | |
| 203 | GSB4 | |
| 204 | RCL5 | |
| 205 | RCL8 | |
| 206 | GSB4 | |
| 207 | 3 | $s^3$ term calculation |
| 208 | GSB5 | |
| 209 | RCL5 | |
| 210 | RCL9 | |
| 211 | GSB4 | |
| 212 | P⇄S | |
| 213 | RTN | |
| 214 | *LBL4 | polynomial multiplication subroutine |
| 215 | × | |
| 216 | ST+i | |
| 217 | RTN | |
| 218 | *LBL5 | initialization subroutine used with polynomial multiplication subroutine |
| 219 | STOI | |
| 220 | CLX | |
| 221 | F0? | |
| 222 | STO i | |
| 223 | RTN | |

**LABELS**

| A load $Y_1$ | B load $Y_2$ | C load $Y_3$ | D load $Y_4$ | E load $Y_5$ |
|---|---|---|---|---|
| a load $Y_6$ | b second card wait loop | c | d load $A_0$ ↑ $f_0$ | e start analysis |
| 0 sum R & sC | 1 initialize | 2 loop terminate | 3 calculate $s^0$ & $s^1$ | 4 summation subroutine |
| 5 summation initialize | 6 polynomial multiplication | 7 input routine | 8 input routine | 9 recall subroutine |

**FLAGS**

| | |
|---|---|
| 0 | continued summation |
| 1 | |
| 2 | |
| 3 | |

**SET STATUS**

| FLAGS | ON | OFF | TRIG | DISP |
|---|---|---|---|---|
| 0 | | ■ | USERS CHOICE | |
| 1 | | | DEG | FIX |
| 2 | | | GRAD | SCI |
| 3 | | | RAD | ENG |
| | | | | n ___ |

# Program Listing I

| | | |
|---|---|---|
| 001 | *LBLE | START ANALYSIS |
| 002 | SPC | |
| 003 | P⇄S | |
| 004 | RCLD | if $s^3$ coefficient is not |
| 005 | X≠0? | zero go to 3rd order soln |
| 006 | GT00 | otherwise store remaining |
| 007 | RCLC | second order coefficients |
| 008 | ST09 | and go to second order |
| 009 | RCLB | solution |
| 010 | ST08 | |
| 011 | GT02 | |
| 012 | *LBL0 | third order solution |
| 013 | RCLC | |
| 014 | X⇄Y | calculate initial guess |
| 015 | ÷ | for real 3rd order root |
| 016 | CHS | |
| 017 | ST06 | |
| 018 | *LBL1 | Newton-Raphson start |
| 019 | RCL6 | |
| 020 | ENT↑ | |
| 021 | ENT↑ | |
| 022 | ENT↑ | |
| 023 | RCLD | |
| 024 | x | |
| 025 | RCLC | |
| 026 | + | |
| 027 | ST08 | |
| 028 | x | |
| 029 | RCLB | calculate $f(x_i)$ |
| 030 | + | |
| 031 | ST07 | |
| 032 | x | |
| 033 | EEX | |
| 034 | + | |
| 035 | ST05 | |
| 036 | CLX | |

| | | |
|---|---|---|
| 037 | RCLD | |
| 038 | 3 | |
| 039 | x | |
| 040 | x | |
| 041 | RCLC | |
| 042 | ENT↑ | calculate $f'(x_i)$ |
| 043 | + | |
| 044 | + | |
| 045 | x | |
| 046 | RCLB | |
| 047 | + | |
| 048 | X≠0? | $f'(x_i) = 0$ escape |
| 049 | ST÷5 | calc $f(x_i)/f'(x_i)$ |
| 050 | RCL5 | apply correction to $x_i$ |
| 051 | ST-6 | |
| 052 | ABS | |
| 053 | RCL6 | |
| 054 | EEX | |
| 055 | 8 | |
| 056 | ÷ | test for loop exit |
| 057 | ABS | |
| 058 | X≤Y? | |
| 059 | GT01 | |
| 060 | RCL6 | print real root |
| 061 | GSB9 | |
| 062 | RCLD | |
| 063 | ST09 | normalize remaining |
| 064 | RCL7 | second order coefficients |
| 065 | ST÷8 | |
| 066 | ST÷9 | |

## REGISTERS

| 0 $A_0$ | 1 $Y_1$ | 2 $Y_2$ | 3 $Y_3$ | 4 $Y_4$ | 5 $Y_5$ | 6 $Y_6$ | 7 $\tau$ | 8 scratch | 9 scratch |
|---|---|---|---|---|---|---|---|---|---|
| S0 $\sum s_n^0$ | S1 $\sum s_n^1$ | S2 $\sum s_n^2$ | S3 | S4 | S5 scratch | S6 $\sigma$ | S7 $c_0, 1/c_2$ | S8 $c_1, c_1/2c_2$ | S9 $c_2$ |
| A $b_0$ | B $D_1$ | C $D_2$ | D $D_3$ | | E | | I | | |

# Program Listing II

```
067  *LBL2   second order solution
068   RCL9   c2
069   ENT↑
070     +    2*c2
071   ST÷8 } c1/(2c2)
072   RCL8 }
073    X²
074   RCL9
075   1/X
076   STO7
077     -    (c1/(2c2))^2 - 1/c2
078   X<0?   if discriminant is negative,
079   GTO3   go to imaginary solution
080    √X
081   STO5
082   RCL8   calculate and print
083     -    one real root
084   GSB9
085   RCL5
086   RCL8   calculate and print
087     +    other real root
088   CHS
089   GTO0
090  *LBL3   imaginary solution routine
091   CHS
092    √X
093   STO5
094   PRTX   calculate and print
095   RCL8   one imaginary root
096   CHS
097   GSB9
098   RCL5
099   CHS    calculate and print
100   PRTX   other imaginary root
101   X⇄Y
102   GSB9
103   RCL7   ωn^2
104    √X
105     2
106     ÷
107   STO5   ωn/2
108    Pi
109     ÷
110   PRTX   fn, the natural frequency
111   RCL5
112   RCL8
113     ÷    Q, the quality factor
114  *LBL0
115   GSB9   print Q, or second real root
116   RCL9
117   ST×7   restore second order
118   ENT↑   coefficients
119     +
120   ST×8
121   SPC
122   RCL2 } is numerator second order?
123   X≠0? }
124   GTO0
125   RCL0 } is numerator a constant?
126   X≠0? }
127   GTO8
128   RCL1   numerator is first order
129   RCL8   calculate and print the
130     ÷    gain term, K
131   GSB9
132   CLX    print location of numerator
133   GTO8   zero and exit program
134  *LBL0   numerator is second order
135   RCL9
136     ÷    calculate and print the
137   GSB9   gain term, K
138   CLX    print location of the
139   PRTX   numerator zeros
140  *LBL8   program exit, restore
141   P⇄S    registers to original order
142  *LBL9   print and space subroutine
143   PRTX
144   SPC
145   RTN
```

| LABELS | | | | | FLAGS |
|---|---|---|---|---|---|
| A | B | C | D | E start analysis | 0 |
| a | b | c | d | e | 1 |
| 0 local label | 1 local label | 2 2nd order solution | 3 imag roots | 4 | 2 |
| 5 | 6 | 7 | 8 P⇄S, prt & space | 9 print & space | 3 |

| SET STATUS | | |
|---|---|---|
| FLAGS | TRIG | DISP |
| ON OFF<br>0<br>1<br>2<br>3 | DEG ■<br>GRAD<br>RAD | FIX<br>SCI<br>ENG ■<br>n 3 |

Suggested program changes for the HP-67: Program space does not allow the inclusion of a print, R/S toggle and associated output routine. To cause the program execution to stop at the data output points, replace the "print" statements with "R/S" statements at the following line numbers: 101, 104, 108, 112, 131, 133, and 136 in program one, and at lines 094, 100, 110, 139, and 143 in program two.

If these changes are made, the program will stop at each output point. To continue program execution, key a "R/S" command from the keyboard.

## TI-59 PROGRAM LISTING 1-3 card 1

| Step | Code | Key | Comment |
|---|---|---|---|
| 000 | 76 | LBL | subroutine to sum |
| 001 | 44 | SUM | conductance & susceptance |
| 002 | 42 | STO | store entry in scratchpad |
| 003 | 09 | 09 | |
| 004 | 50 | I×I | test for conductance: |
| 005 | 32 | X⇄T | If entry is smaller than |
| 006 | 01 | 1 | $10^{30}$, then it is a |
| 007 | 52 | EE | susceptance and program |
| 008 | 03 | 3 | execution jumps to |
| 009 | 00 | 0 | step 24. |
| 010 | 77 | GE | |
| 011 | 00 | 00 | |
| 012 | 24 | 24 | |
| 013 | 43 | RCL | recover entry |
| 014 | 09 | 09 | |
| 015 | 55 | ÷ | remove conductance |
| 016 | 01 | 1 | scaling |
| 017 | 52 | EE | |
| 018 | 05 | 5 | |
| 019 | 00 | 0 | |
| 020 | 95 | = | |
| 021 | 74 | SM* | sum conductance |
| 022 | 05 | 05 | |
| 023 | 92 | RTN | return to main program |
| 024 | 43 | RCL | recover entry |
| 025 | 09 | 09 | |
| 026 | 74 | SM* | sum susceptance |
| 027 | 04 | 04 | |
| 028 | 92 | RTN | return to main program |
| 029 | 76 | LBL | initialization |
| 030 | 59 | INT | subroutine |
| 031 | 02 | 2 | |
| 032 | 00 | 0 | initialize susceptance |
| 033 | 42 | STO | storage register index |
| 034 | 04 | 04 | |
| 035 | 02 | 2 | |
| 036 | 01 | 1 | initialize conductance |
| 037 | 42 | STO | storage register index |
| 038 | 05 | 05 | |
| 039 | 61 | GTO | jump to step 51 and |
| 040 | 00 | 00 | continue program |
| 041 | 51 | 51 | execution |
| 042 | 76 | LBL | subroutine to complete |
| 043 | 85 | + | summation |
| 044 | 71 | SBR | gosub subroutine "sum" |
| 045 | 44 | SUM | |
| 046 | 02 | 2 | |
| 047 | 44 | SUM | increment storage |
| 048 | 04 | 04 | register indices |
| 049 | 44 | SUM | |

| Step | Code | Key | Comment |
|---|---|---|---|
| 050 | 05 | 05 | |
| 051 | 00 | 0 | |
| 052 | 72 | ST* | clear next set of storage |
| 053 | 04 | 04 | registers |
| 054 | 72 | ST* | |
| 055 | 05 | 05 | |
| 056 | 92 | RTN | return to main program |
| 057 | 76 | LBL | LOAD ELEMENT INDEX |
| 058 | 11 | A | |
| 059 | 98 | ADV | space paper in printer |
| 060 | 22 | INV | |
| 061 | 52 | EE | set fix 0 format |
| 062 | 22 | INV | |
| 063 | 57 | ENG | |
| 064 | 99 | PRT | print element index |
| 065 | 85 | + | |
| 066 | 32 | X⇄T | save index entry |
| 067 | 01 | 1 | |
| 068 | 00 | 0 | calculate storage |
| 069 | 95 | = | register location |
| 070 | 42 | STO | |
| 071 | 04 | 04 | |
| 072 | 32 | X⇄T | recover index to display |
| 073 | 91 | R/S | stop program execution |
| 074 | 76 | LBL | LOAD RESISTOR VALUE |
| 075 | 12 | B | |
| 076 | 35 | 1/X | form conductance |
| 077 | 65 | × | |
| 078 | 32 | X⇄T | save conductance |
| 079 | 01 | 1 | |
| 080 | 52 | EE | multiply conductance by |
| 081 | 05 | 5 | $10^{50}$ and indirectly store |
| 082 | 00 | 0 | |
| 083 | 95 | = | |
| 084 | 72 | ST* | |
| 085 | 04 | 04 | |
| 086 | 03 | 3 | setup to print "R" as |
| 087 | 05 | 5 | annotation on right |
| 088 | 69 | OP | hand edge of printout |
| 089 | 04 | 04 | |
| 090 | 32 | X⇄T | |
| 091 | 35 | 1/X | recover resistor entry |
| 092 | 22 | INV | and print annotated |
| 093 | 52 | EE | value |
| 094 | 69 | OP | |
| 095 | 06 | 06 | |
| 096 | 91 | R/S | stop program execution |
| 097 | 76 | LBL | LOAD CAPACITOR VALUE |
| 098 | 13 | C | |
| 099 | 72 | ST* | |

Note: This translation was provided by Mr. Roger Junk.

## TI - 59 PROGRAM LISTING 1-3 card 1

| | | | |
|---|---|---|---|
| 100 | 04 | 04 | indirectly store cap |
| 101 | 32 | X:T | save entry |
| 102 | 01 | 1 | |
| 103 | 05 | 5 | setup to print "C" on |
| 104 | 69 | OP | right hand edge of paper |
| 105 | 04 | 04 | |
| 106 | 32 | X:T | |
| 107 | 57 | ENG | print capacitor value in |
| 108 | 69 | OP | engineering format along |
| 109 | 06 | 06 | with annotation |
| 110 | 91 | R/S | stop program execution |
| 111 | 76 | LBL | LOAD OP-AMP DC GAIN, $A_o$ |
| 112 | 14 | D | |
| 113 | 42 | STO | store $A_o$ |
| 114 | 10 | 10 | |
| 115 | 32 | X:T | save entry |
| 116 | 01 | 1 | |
| 117 | 03 | 3 | setup to print "A" on |
| 118 | 69 | OP | right hand edge of paper |
| 119 | 04 | 04 | |
| 120 | 32 | X:T | recover entry, |
| 121 | 98 | ADV | space paper, and |
| 122 | 69 | OP | print entry and notation |
| 123 | 06 | 06 | |
| 124 | 91 | R/S | stop program execution |
| 125 | 76 | LBL | LOAD OP-AMP BREAK |
| 126 | 15 | E | FREQUENCY (-3 dB point) |
| 127 | 65 | × | |
| 128 | 32 | X:T | save entry |
| 129 | 02 | 2 | |
| 130 | 65 | × | |
| 131 | 89 | π | form and store: |
| 132 | 95 | = | $\tau = \frac{1}{2\pi f_{-3\ dB}}$ |
| 133 | 35 | 1/X | |
| 134 | 42 | STO | |
| 135 | 17 | 17 | |
| 136 | 01 | 1 | |
| 137 | 52 | EE | if entry is larger than |
| 138 | 02 | 2 | $10^{20}$ set $\tau$ to zero |
| 139 | 00 | 0 | |
| 140 | 77 | GE | |
| 141 | 01 | 01 | |
| 142 | 46 | 46 | |
| 143 | 00 | 0 | |
| 144 | 42 | STO | |
| 145 | 17 | 17 | |
| 146 | 02 | 2 | |
| 147 | 01 | 1 | setup to print "F" on |
| 148 | 69 | OP | right hand edge of paper |
| 149 | 04 | 04 | |
| 150 | 32 | X:T | recover entry |
| 151 | 98 | ADV | space paper and |
| 152 | 69 | OP | print annotated entry |
| 153 | 06 | 06 | |
| 154 | 91 | R/S | stop program execution |
| 155 | 76 | LBL | INITIALIZE |
| 156 | 16 | A' | |
| 157 | 00 | 0 | |
| 158 | 42 | STO | zero elements 2, 3, 5, & 6 |
| 159 | 12 | 12 | |
| 160 | 42 | STO | |
| 161 | 13 | 13 | |
| 162 | 42 | STO | |
| 163 | 15 | 15 | |
| 164 | 42 | STO | |
| 165 | 16 | 16 | |
| 166 | 91 | R/S | stop program execution |
| 167 | 76 | LBL | START ANALYSIS |
| 168 | 10 | E' | |
| 169 | 71 | SBR | test for printer attached |
| 170 | 04 | 04 | to calculator |
| 171 | 75 | 75 | |
| 172 | 71 | SBR | initialize counters and |
| 173 | 59 | INT | registers |
| 174 | 43 | RCL | |
| 175 | 11 | 11 | |
| 176 | 71 | SBR | |
| 177 | 44 | SUM | |
| 178 | 43 | RCL | calculate and store |
| 179 | 12 | 12 | $s^0$ and $s^1$ terms of: |
| 180 | 71 | SBR | |
| 181 | 44 | SUM | $Y_1 + Y_2 + Y_3$ |
| 182 | 43 | RCL | |
| 183 | 13 | 13 | |
| 184 | 71 | SBR | |
| 185 | 85 | + | |
| 186 | 43 | RCL | |
| 187 | 14 | 14 | |
| 188 | 71 | SBR | |
| 189 | 44 | SUM | calculate and store |
| 190 | 43 | RCL | $s^0$ and $s^1$ terms of: |
| 191 | 16 | 16 | |
| 192 | 71 | SBR | $Y_4 + Y_6 + Y_5(1 - A_0)$ |
| 193 | 44 | SUM | |
| 194 | 01 | 1 | |
| 195 | 75 | - | |
| 196 | 43 | RCL | |
| 197 | 10 | 10 | |
| 198 | 95 | = | |
| 199 | 65 | × | |

## TI-59 PROGRAM LISTING 1-3 card 1

| | | | |
|---|---|---|---|
| 200 | 43 | RCL | |
| 201 | 15 | 15 | |
| 202 | 95 | = | |
| 203 | 42 | STO | |
| 204 | 19 | 19 | |
| 205 | 71 | SBR | |
| 206 | 85 | + | |
| 207 | 43 | RCL | calculate and store $s^1$ and $s^2$ terms of: $\tau s(Y_4 + Y_5 + Y_6)$ |
| 208 | 14 | 14 | |
| 209 | 71 | SBR | |
| 210 | 44 | SUM | |
| 211 | 43 | RCL | |
| 212 | 15 | 15 | |
| 213 | 71 | SBR | |
| 214 | 44 | SUM | |
| 215 | 43 | RCL | |
| 216 | 16 | 16 | |
| 217 | 71 | SBR | |
| 218 | 44 | SUM | |
| 219 | 71 | SBR | |
| 220 | 49 | PRD | |
| 221 | 86 | STF | calculate and store: $(Y_1+Y_2+Y_3)\{(Y_4+Y_6)(1+\tau s)+Y_5(1-A_0+\tau s)\} = D_1$ |
| 222 | 00 | 00 | |
| 223 | 71 | SBR | |
| 224 | 65 | × | |
| 225 | 71 | SBR | initialize indices |
| 226 | 59 | INT | |
| 227 | 43 | RCL | calculate and store $s^0$ and $s^1$ terms of $Y_4$ |
| 228 | 14 | 14 | |
| 229 | 71 | SBR | |
| 230 | 85 | + | |
| 231 | 43 | RCL | calculate and store $s^0$ and $s^1$ terms of: $Y_6 + Y_5(1 - A_o) + A_oY_2$ |
| 232 | 16 | 16 | |
| 233 | 71 | SBR | |
| 234 | 44 | SUM | |
| 235 | 43 | RCL | |
| 236 | 19 | 19 | |
| 237 | 71 | SBR | |
| 238 | 44 | SUM | |
| 239 | 43 | RCL | |
| 240 | 12 | 12 | |
| 241 | 65 | × | |
| 242 | 43 | RCL | |
| 243 | 10 | 10 | |
| 244 | 95 | = | |
| 245 | 94 | +/- | |
| 246 | 71 | SBR | |
| 247 | 85 | + | |
| 248 | 43 | RCL | |
| 249 | 16 | 16 | |

| | | | |
|---|---|---|---|
| 250 | 71 | SBR | calculate and store $s^1$ and $s^2$ terms of: $\tau s(Y_5 + Y_6)$ |
| 251 | 44 | SUM | |
| 252 | 43 | RCL | |
| 253 | 15 | 15 | |
| 254 | 71 | SBR | |
| 255 | 44 | SUM | |
| 256 | 71 | SBR | |
| 257 | 49 | PRD | |
| 258 | 22 | INV | calculate and store: $D_1 + Y_4\{Y_6(1+\tau s) + Y_5(1-A_o+\tau_s) - A_oY_2\}$ |
| 259 | 86 | STF | |
| 260 | 00 | 00 | |
| 261 | 71 | SBR | |
| 262 | 65 | × | |
| 263 | 29 | CP | test for non-zero denominator coefs |
| 264 | 43 | RCL | |
| 265 | 00 | 00 | |
| 266 | 22 | INV | |
| 267 | 67 | EQ | |
| 268 | 02 | 02 | |
| 269 | 78 | 78 | |
| 270 | 43 | RCL | non-zero test continued |
| 271 | 01 | 01 | |
| 272 | 22 | INV | |
| 273 | 67 | EQ | |
| 274 | 02 | 02 | |
| 275 | 78 | 78 | |
| 276 | 43 | RCL | non-zero test concluded |
| 277 | 02 | 02 | |
| 278 | 42 | STO | |
| 279 | 18 | 18 | |
| 280 | 35 | 1/X | normalize denominator terms |
| 281 | 49 | PRD | |
| 282 | 00 | 00 | |
| 283 | 49 | PRD | |
| 284 | 01 | 01 | |
| 285 | 49 | PRD | |
| 286 | 02 | 02 | |
| 287 | 49 | PRD | |
| 288 | 03 | 03 | |
| 289 | 43 | RCL | recall and print $s^3$ denominator coefficient (program will stop if printer is not attached) |
| 290 | 03 | 03 | |
| 291 | 71 | SBR | |
| 292 | 98 | ADV | |
| 293 | 42 | STO | |
| 294 | 29 | 29 | |
| 295 | 43 | RCL | recall and print $s^2$ denominator coefficient |
| 296 | 02 | 02 | |
| 297 | 71 | SBR | |
| 298 | 04 | 04 | |
| 299 | 64 | 64 | |

## TI-59 PROGRAM LISTING 1-3 card 1

| Step | Code | Key | Comment |
|---|---|---|---|
| 300 | 42 | STO | |
| 301 | 28 | 28 | |
| 302 | 43 | RCL | recall and print $s^1$ denominator coefficient |
| 303 | 01 | 01 | |
| 304 | 71 | SBR | |
| 305 | 99 | PRT | |
| 306 | 42 | STO | |
| 307 | 27 | 27 | |
| 308 | 43 | RCL | recall and print $s^0$ denominator coefficient |
| 309 | 00 | 00 | |
| 310 | 71 | SBR | |
| 311 | 99 | PRT | |
| 312 | 42 | STO | |
| 313 | 26 | 26 | |
| 314 | 86 | STF | indicate first product of sums |
| 315 | 00 | 00 | |
| 316 | 71 | SBR | initialize indices |
| 317 | 59 | INT | |
| 318 | 43 | RCL | calculate and store $s^0$, $s^1$, and $s^2$ terms of $Y_1 \cdot Y_4$ |
| 319 | 11 | 11 | |
| 320 | 71 | SBR | |
| 321 | 85 | + | |
| 322 | 43 | RCL | |
| 323 | 14 | 14 | |
| 324 | 71 | SBR | |
| 325 | 85 | + | |
| 326 | 00 | 0 | |
| 327 | 72 | ST* | |
| 328 | 04 | 04 | |
| 329 | 71 | SBR | |
| 330 | 65 | × | |
| 331 | 43 | RCL | normalize numerator coefficients |
| 332 | 10 | 10 | |
| 333 | 55 | ÷ | |
| 334 | 43 | RCL | |
| 335 | 18 | 18 | |
| 336 | 95 | = | |
| 337 | 49 | PRD | |
| 338 | 02 | 02 | |
| 339 | 49 | PRD | |
| 340 | 01 | 01 | |
| 341 | 49 | PRD | |
| 342 | 00 | 00 | |
| 343 | 43 | RCL | recall and print $s^2$ numerator coefficient |
| 344 | 02 | 02 | |
| 345 | 71 | SBR | |
| 346 | 98 | ADV | |
| 347 | 43 | RCL | recall and print $s^1$ numerator coefficient |
| 348 | 01 | 01 | |
| 349 | 71 | SBR | |
| 350 | 04 | 04 | |
| 351 | 64 | 64 | |
| 352 | 43 | RCL | recall and print $s^0$ numerator coefficient |
| 353 | 00 | 00 | |
| 354 | 71 | SBR | |
| 355 | 04 | 04 | |
| 356 | 64 | 64 | |
| 357 | 91 | R/S | stop program execution |
| 358 | 00 | 0 | unused program memory |
| 359 | 00 | 0 | |
| 360 | 00 | 0 | |
| 361 | 00 | 0 | |
| 362 | 00 | 0 | |
| 363 | 00 | 0 | |
| 364 | 00 | 0 | |
| 365 | 00 | 0 | |
| 366 | 00 | 0 | |
| 367 | 00 | 0 | |
| 368 | 76 | LBL | subroutine to multiply by $\gamma s$ to form $s^2$ and additional $s^1$ terms, and add to presently stored terms |
| 369 | 49 | PRD | |
| 370 | 43 | RCL | |
| 371 | 17 | 17 | |
| 372 | 49 | PRD | |
| 373 | 24 | 24 | |
| 374 | 65 | × | |
| 375 | 43 | RCL | |
| 376 | 25 | 25 | |
| 377 | 95 | = | |
| 378 | 44 | SUM | |
| 379 | 22 | 22 | |
| 380 | 92 | RTN | |
| 381 | 76 | LBL | polynomial multiplication subroutine |
| 382 | 65 | × | |
| 383 | 00 | 0 | $s^0$ term calculation |
| 384 | 71 | SBR | |
| 385 | 04 | 04 | |
| 386 | 48 | 48 | |
| 387 | 43 | RCL | |
| 388 | 23 | 23 | |
| 389 | 65 | × | |
| 390 | 43 | RCL | |
| 391 | 21 | 21 | |
| 392 | 95 | = | |
| 393 | 74 | SM* | |
| 394 | 05 | 05 | |
| 395 | 01 | 1 | $s^1$ term calculation |
| 396 | 71 | SBR | |
| 397 | 04 | 04 | |
| 398 | 48 | 48 | |
| 399 | 43 | RCL | |

## TI-59 PROGRAM LISTING 1-3 card 1

| Step | Code | Key | Comments |
|---|---|---|---|
| 400 | 22 | 22 | $s^1$ term calculation continued |
| 401 | 65 | × | |
| 402 | 43 | RCL | |
| 403 | 21 | 21 | |
| 404 | 95 | = | |
| 405 | 74 | SM* | |
| 406 | 05 | 05 | |
| 407 | 43 | RCL | |
| 408 | 23 | 23 | |
| 409 | 65 | × | |
| 410 | 43 | RCL | |
| 411 | 20 | 20 | |
| 412 | 95 | = | |
| 413 | 74 | SM* | |
| 414 | 05 | 05 | |
| 415 | 02 | 2 | $s^2$ term calculation |
| 416 | 71 | SBR | |
| 417 | 04 | 04 | |
| 418 | 48 | 48 | |
| 419 | 43 | RCL | |
| 420 | 22 | 22 | |
| 421 | 65 | × | |
| 422 | 43 | RCL | |
| 423 | 20 | 20 | |
| 424 | 95 | = | |
| 425 | 74 | SM* | |
| 426 | 05 | 05 | |
| 427 | 43 | RCL | |
| 428 | 24 | 24 | |
| 429 | 65 | × | |
| 430 | 43 | RCL | |
| 431 | 21 | 21 | |
| 432 | 95 | = | |
| 433 | 74 | SM* | |
| 434 | 05 | 05 | |
| 435 | 03 | 3 | $s^3$ term calculation |
| 436 | 71 | SBR | |
| 437 | 04 | 04 | |
| 438 | 48 | 48 | |
| 439 | 43 | RCL | |
| 440 | 24 | 24 | |
| 441 | 65 | × | |
| 442 | 43 | RCL | |
| 443 | 20 | 20 | |
| 444 | 95 | = | |
| 445 | 74 | SM* | |
| 446 | 05 | 05 | |
| 447 | 92 | RTN | |
| 448 | 42 | STO | polynomial multiplication storage subroutine |
| 449 | 05 | 05 | |

| Step | Code | Key | Comments |
|---|---|---|---|
| 450 | 22 | INV | |
| 451 | 87 | IFF | |
| 452 | 00 | 00 | |
| 453 | 04 | 04 | |
| 454 | 58 | 58 | |
| 455 | 00 | 0 | |
| 456 | 72 | ST* | |
| 457 | 05 | 05 | |
| 458 | 92 | RTN | |
| 459 | 76 | LBL | subroutine to print and continue if calculator attached to PC-100A printer, or else to stop program execution and display answer |
| 460 | 98 | ADV | |
| 461 | 98 | ADV | |
| 462 | 76 | LBL | |
| 463 | 99 | PRT | |
| 464 | 57 | ENG | |
| 465 | 99 | PRT | |
| 466 | 22 | INV | |
| 467 | 87 | IFF | |
| 468 | 01 | 01 | |
| 469 | 04 | 04 | |
| 470 | 74 | 74 | |
| 471 | 91 | R/S | |
| 472 | 22 | INV | |
| 473 | 57 | ENG | |
| 474 | 92 | RTN | |
| 475 | 69 | OP | subroutine to sense PC-100A printer is attached to calculator |
| 476 | 08 | 08 | |
| 477 | 86 | STF | |
| 478 | 01 | 01 | |
| 479 | 92 | RTN | |

## REGISTER ALLOCATIONS FOR TI-59 1-3 card 1

| register number | contents |
|---|---|
| 0 | sum of $s^0$ terms |
| 1 | sum of $s^1$ terms |
| 2 | sum of $s^2$ terms |
| 3 | sum of $s^3$ terms |
| 4 | indirect storage register index |
| 5 | indirect storage register index |
| 6 | |
| 7 | |
| 8 | |
| 9 | |
| 10 | $A_0$, the op-amp dc gain |
| 11 | $Y_1$ |
| 12 | $Y_2$ |
| 13 | $Y_3$ |
| 14 | $Y_4$ |
| 15 | $Y_5$ |
| 16 | $Y_6$ |
| 17 | $\tau$ |
| 18 | $b_0$ |
| 19 | $Y_5(1-A_0)$ |
| 20 | ---------$s_2{}^1$ |
| 21 | ------------$s_2{}^0$ |
| 22 | ---------------$s_1{}^1$ |
| 23 | ------------------$s_1{}^0$ |
| 24 | ---------------------$s_1{}^2$ |
| 25 | |
| 26 | $D_0$ |
| 27 | $D_1$ |
| 28 | $D_2$ |
| 29 | $D_3$ |
| 30 | |

## TI-59 PROGRAM LISTING 1-3 card 2

| Step | Code | Key | Comment |
|---|---|---|---|
| 000 | 76 | LBL | START |
| 001 | 15 | E | |
| 002 | 71 | SBR | test for PC-100A printer attached to calculator |
| 003 | 04 | 04 | |
| 004 | 75 | 75 | |
| 005 | 43 | RCL | if $s^3$ coefficient is zero, go to second order solution routine |
| 006 | 29 | 29 | |
| 007 | 29 | CP | |
| 008 | 67 | EQ | |
| 009 | 01 | 01 | |
| 010 | 19 | 19 | |
| 011 | 55 | ÷ | calculate initial guess for real third order root $x_o = D_2/D_3$ |
| 012 | 43 | RCL | |
| 013 | 28 | 28 | |
| 014 | 95 | = | |
| 015 | 35 | 1/X | |
| 016 | 94 | +/- | |
| 017 | 42 | STO | |
| 018 | 23 | 23 | |
| 019 | 43 | RCL | Newton-Raphson start; calculate $f(x_i)$ |
| 020 | 23 | 23 | |
| 021 | 65 | × | |
| 022 | 43 | RCL | |
| 023 | 29 | 29 | |
| 024 | 85 | + | |
| 025 | 43 | RCL | |
| 026 | 28 | 28 | |
| 027 | 95 | = | |
| 028 | 42 | STO | |
| 029 | 21 | 21 | |
| 030 | 65 | × | |
| 031 | 43 | RCL | |
| 032 | 23 | 23 | |
| 033 | 85 | + | |
| 034 | 43 | RCL | |
| 035 | 27 | 27 | |
| 036 | 95 | = | |
| 037 | 42 | STO | |
| 038 | 22 | 22 | |
| 039 | 65 | × | |
| 040 | 43 | RCL | |
| 041 | 23 | 23 | |
| 042 | 85 | + | |
| 043 | 43 | RCL | |
| 044 | 26 | 26 | |
| 045 | 95 | = | |
| 046 | 42 | STO | |
| 047 | 25 | 25 | |
| 048 | 03 | 3 | calculate $f'(x_i)$ |
| 049 | 65 | × | |
| 050 | 43 | RCL | |
| 051 | 29 | 29 | |
| 052 | 65 | × | |
| 053 | 43 | RCL | |
| 054 | 23 | 23 | |
| 055 | 85 | + | |
| 056 | 02 | 2 | |
| 057 | 65 | × | |
| 058 | 43 | RCL | |
| 059 | 28 | 28 | |
| 060 | 95 | = | |
| 061 | 65 | × | |
| 062 | 43 | RCL | |
| 063 | 23 | 23 | |
| 064 | 85 | + | |
| 065 | 43 | RCL | |
| 066 | 27 | 27 | |
| 067 | 95 | = | |
| 068 | 29 | CP | $f'(x_i) = 0$ escape |
| 069 | 67 | EQ | |
| 070 | 00 | 00 | |
| 071 | 75 | 75 | |
| 072 | 35 | 1/X | calc $f(x_i)/f'(x_i)$ |
| 073 | 49 | PRD | |
| 074 | 25 | 25 | |
| 075 | 43 | RCL | apply correction to $x_i$ |
| 076 | 25 | 25 | |
| 077 | 94 | +/- | |
| 078 | 44 | SUM | |
| 079 | 23 | 23 | |
| 080 | 50 | I×I | test for loop exit |
| 081 | 32 | X↕T | |
| 082 | 43 | RCL | |
| 083 | 23 | 23 | |
| 084 | 55 | ÷ | |
| 085 | 01 | 1 | |
| 086 | 52 | EE | |
| 087 | 08 | 8 | |
| 088 | 95 | = | |
| 089 | 50 | I×I | |
| 090 | 22 | INV | |
| 091 | 77 | GE | |
| 092 | 00 | 00 | |
| 093 | 19 | 19 | |
| 094 | 43 | RCL | print real root |
| 095 | 23 | 23 | |
| 096 | 71 | SBR | |
| 097 | 04 | 04 | |
| 098 | 65 | 65 | |
| 099 | 43 | RCL | |

## TI-59 PROGRAM LISTING 1-3 card 2

| Loc | Code | Key | Comments |
|---|---|---|---|
| 100 | 29 | 29 | |
| 101 | 42 | STO | |
| 102 | 20 | 20 | |
| 103 | 43 | RCL | |
| 104 | 22 | 22 | |
| 105 | 29 | CP | |
| 106 | 67 | EQ | normalize second order |
| 107 | 01 | 01 | coefficients |
| 108 | 31 | 31 | |
| 109 | 35 | 1/X | |
| 110 | 49 | PRD | |
| 111 | 20 | 20 | |
| 112 | 49 | PRD | |
| 113 | 21 | 21 | |
| 114 | 49 | PRD | |
| 115 | 22 | 22 | |
| 116 | 61 | GTO | |
| 117 | 01 | 01 | |
| 118 | 31 | 31 | |
| 119 | 43 | RCL | |
| 120 | 28 | 28 | |
| 121 | 42 | STO | store second order |
| 122 | 20 | 20 | coefficients |
| 123 | 43 | RCL | |
| 124 | 27 | 27 | |
| 125 | 42 | STO | |
| 126 | 21 | 21 | |
| 127 | 43 | RCL | |
| 128 | 26 | 26 | |
| 129 | 42 | STO | |
| 130 | 22 | 22 | |
| 131 | 43 | RCL | second order solution: |
| 132 | 20 | 20 | |
| 133 | 35 | 1/X | |
| 134 | 49 | PRD | |
| 135 | 22 | 22 | |
| 136 | 55 | ÷ | |
| 137 | 02 | 2 | |
| 138 | 95 | = | calculate discriminant, |
| 139 | 49 | PRD | |
| 140 | 21 | 21 | $b^2 - 4ac$ |
| 141 | 43 | RCL | |
| 142 | 21 | 21 | |
| 143 | 33 | X² | |
| 144 | 75 | - | |
| 145 | 43 | RCL | |
| 146 | 22 | 22 | |
| 147 | 95 | = | |
| 148 | 29 | CP | test for negative |
| 149 | 22 | INV | discriminant |
| 150 | 77 | GE | |
| 151 | 01 | 01 | |
| 152 | 75 | 75 | |
| 153 | 34 | √X | |
| 154 | 42 | STO | |
| 155 | 25 | 25 | |
| 156 | 75 | - | |
| 157 | 43 | RCL | calculate and print |
| 158 | 21 | 21 | one real root |
| 159 | 95 | = | |
| 160 | 71 | SBR | |
| 161 | 04 | 04 | |
| 162 | 65 | 65 | |
| 163 | 43 | RCL | |
| 164 | 25 | 25 | |
| 165 | 85 | + | |
| 166 | 43 | RCL | |
| 167 | 08 | 08 | calculate and print |
| 168 | 94 | +/- | other real root |
| 169 | 71 | SBR | |
| 170 | 04 | 04 | |
| 171 | 65 | 65 | |
| 172 | 61 | GTO | |
| 173 | 02 | 02 | |
| 174 | 25 | 25 | |
| 175 | 94 | +/- | imaginary solution: |
| 176 | 34 | √X | |
| 177 | 42 | STO | |
| 178 | 25 | 25 | |
| 179 | 71 | SBR | |
| 180 | 04 | 04 | |
| 181 | 65 | 65 | calculate and print |
| 182 | 43 | RCL | one complex root |
| 183 | 21 | 21 | |
| 184 | 94 | +/- | |
| 185 | 71 | SBR | |
| 186 | 04 | 04 | |
| 187 | 66 | 66 | |
| 188 | 43 | RCL | |
| 189 | 25 | 25 | |
| 190 | 94 | +/- | |
| 191 | 71 | SBR | |
| 192 | 04 | 04 | |
| 193 | 65 | 65 | |
| 194 | 43 | RCL | calculate and print |
| 195 | 21 | 21 | the other complex root |
| 196 | 94 | +/- | |
| 197 | 71 | SBR | |
| 198 | 04 | 04 | |
| 199 | 66 | 66 | |

## TI-59 PROGRAM LISTING 1-3 card 2

| Step | Code | Key | Comment |
|---|---|---|---|
| 200 | 68 | NOP | |
| 201 | 68 | NOP | |
| 202 | 43 | RCL | |
| 203 | 22 | 22 | |
| 204 | 34 | √X | |
| 205 | 55 | ÷ | |
| 206 | 02 | 2 | |
| 207 | 95 | = | |
| 208 | 42 | STO | calculate and print $f_n$, the natural frequency |
| 209 | 25 | 25 | |
| 210 | 55 | ÷ | |
| 211 | 89 | π | |
| 212 | 95 | = | |
| 213 | 71 | SBR | |
| 214 | 04 | 04 | |
| 215 | 65 | 65 | |
| 216 | 43 | RCL | |
| 217 | 25 | 25 | |
| 218 | 55 | ÷ | |
| 219 | 43 | RCL | |
| 220 | 21 | 21 | calculate and print **Q** |
| 221 | 95 | = | |
| 222 | 71 | SBR | |
| 223 | 04 | 04 | |
| 224 | 66 | 66 | |
| 225 | 43 | RCL | |
| 226 | 20 | 20 | |
| 227 | 49 | PRD | |
| 228 | 22 | 22 | restore second order coefficients |
| 229 | 65 | × | |
| 230 | 02 | 2 | |
| 231 | 95 | = | |
| 232 | 49 | PRD | |
| 233 | 21 | 21 | |
| 234 | 43 | RCL | |
| 235 | 02 | 02 | |
| 236 | 22 | INV | |
| 237 | 67 | EQ | is numerator second order |
| 238 | 02 | 02 | |
| 239 | 55 | 55 | |
| 240 | 43 | RCL | |
| 241 | 00 | 00 | |
| 242 | 22 | INV | |
| 243 | 67 | EQ | is numerator a constant? |
| 244 | 02 | 02 | |
| 245 | 59 | 59 | |
| 246 | 43 | RCL | |
| 247 | 01 | 01 | |
| 248 | 55 | ÷ | |
| 249 | 43 | RCL | |

| Step | Code | Key | Comment |
|---|---|---|---|
| 250 | 21 | 21 | |
| 251 | 95 | = | |
| 252 | 61 | GTO | |
| 253 | 02 | 02 | |
| 254 | 59 | 59 | |
| 255 | 55 | ÷ | calculate and print the gain term, K |
| 256 | 43 | RCL | |
| 257 | 20 | 20 | |
| 258 | 95 | = | |
| 259 | 71 | SBR | |
| 260 | 04 | 04 | |
| 261 | 65 | 65 | |
| 262 | 61 | GTO | |
| 263 | 91 | R/S | |
| 264 | 00 | 0 | |
| 265 | 00 | 0 | |
| 266 | 00 | 0 | |
| 267 | 00 | 0 | |
| 268 | 00 | 0 | |
| 269 | 00 | 0 | |
| 270 | 00 | 0 | |
| 457 | 00 | 0 | |
| 458 | 00 | 0 | |
| 459 | 00 | 0 | |
| 460 | 76 | LBL | subroutine to lock up "R/S" command-prevents further program execution via the "R/S" command |
| 461 | 91 | R/S | |
| 462 | 61 | GTO | |
| 463 | 04 | 04 | |
| 464 | 61 | 61 | |
| 465 | 98 | ADV | |
| 466 | 99 | PRT | |
| 467 | 68 | NOP | print or display subroutine |
| 468 | 22 | INV | |
| 469 | 87 | IFF | |
| 470 | 01 | 01 | |
| 471 | 04 | 04 | |
| 472 | 74 | 74 | |
| 473 | 91 | R/S | |
| 474 | 92 | RTN | |
| 475 | 69 | OP | |
| 476 | 08 | 08 | PC-100A sense routine |
| 477 | 86 | STF | |
| 478 | 01 | 01 | |
| 479 | 92 | RTN | |

## REGISTER ALLOCATIONS FOR TI-59 1-3 card 2

| register number | contents |
|---|---|
| 0 | $N_0$ |
| 1 | $N_1$ |
| 2 | $N_2$ |
| 3 | |
| 4 | |
| 5 | |
| 6 | |
| 7 | |
| 8 | |
| 9 | |
| 10 | $A_0$ |
| 11 | $Y_1$ |
| 12 | $Y_2$ |
| 13 | $Y_3$ |
| 14 | $Y_4$ |
| 15 | $Y_5$ |
| 16 | $Y_6$ |
| 17 | $\tau$ |
| 18 | $b_0$ |
| 19 | |
| 20 | $c_2$ |
| 21 | $c_1$, $c_1/2c_2$ |
| 22 | $c_0$, $1/c_2$ |
| 23 | $x_i$ |
| 24 | |
| 25 | $f(x_i)/f'(x_i)$ |
| 26 | $D_0$ |
| 27 | $D_1$ |
| 28 | $D_2$ |
| 29 | $D_3$ |

## PROGRAM 1-4 L N A P, LADDER NETWORK ANALYSIS PROGRAM.

Program Description and Equations Used

This program evaluates the frequency response and input impedance of a RLC ladder network containing up to 4 nodes and 8 branches using a sweep of discrete evaluation frequencies. The frequency response is provided as magnitude (dB) and phase (degrees, radians, or grads), and the input impedance is provided as real and imaginary parts (ohms). The evaluation frequency may be incremented in a linear manner using an additive increment or in a logarithmic manner using a multiplicative increment.

Each branch of the ladder may contain a resistor (R), a capacitor (C), an inductor (L), a series RC, a parallel RC, a series RL, or a parallel RL network. All element values are stored, and may be reviewed at any time to check or correct the component values and interconnection.

Because of the number of available storage registers in the HP-67/97, the number of nodes cannot exceed four, while the TI-59 can accommodate the data for ten nodes. Elements that inhibit signal flow through the network are not allowed, and will cause the program execution to halt displaying "Error." Examples of these inhibiting elements are a shunt resistor or a shunt inductor having zero value, or series capacitors in series branches having zero values.

The algorithm used by this program assumes 1 volt at the output of the ladder network (see Fig. 1-4.1). From the knowledge of the last branch admittance, the complex branch current may be determined. Since no current flows out of the last node, the last shunt branch current must also flow through the preceding series branch. The complex voltage drop across this branch may be determined by multiplying the branch impedance and the branch current. By adding the series branch voltage to the last node voltage, the next lower node voltage may be obtained. This node voltage times the shunt node admittance will yield the shunt node current. Adding this shunt node current to the previous series branch current will yield the next lower series branch current.

This loop is repeated until the input voltage source is reached (node 0). The frequency response is found from Eq. (1-4.1) and the input impedance from Eq. (1-4.2), i.e.:

$$T(j\omega) = E_{out}/E_{in} = 1/E_0 \tag{1-4.1}$$

$$Z_{in}(j\omega) = E_0/I_0 \tag{1-4.2}$$

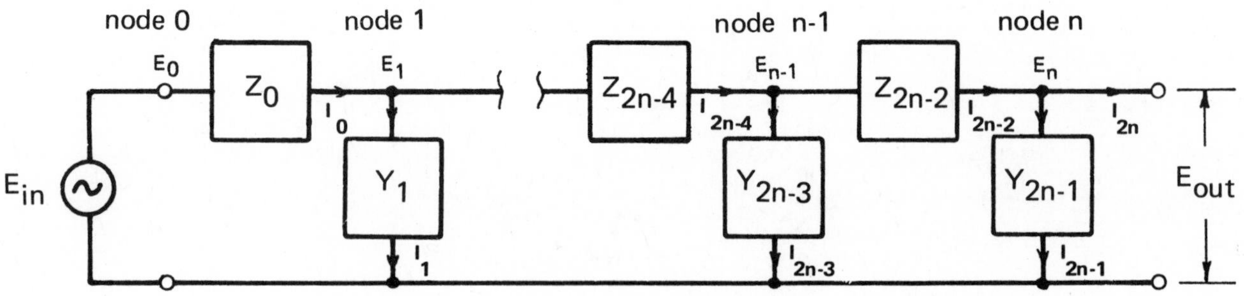


Figure 1-4.1 General ladder network topology.

The preceding algorithm may be expressed in mathematical shorthand using indices:

$$I_{2k-2} = (E_k)(Y_{2k-1}) + I_{2k} \tag{1-4.3}$$

$$E_{k-1} = (I_{2k-2})(Z_{2k-2}) + E_k \tag{1-4.5}$$

where k = n, n-1, n-2, ... , 1, and n is the highest numbered node. The initial conditions for the n-th node are given by:

$$I_{2n} = 0 \tag{1-4.5}$$

$$E_n = 1 + j0 \tag{1-4.6}$$

Equation (1-4.3) is evaluated for $I_{2k-2}$ and substituted into Eq. (1-4.4) to obtain the next lower numbered node voltage. The index, k, is decremented by one, and Eqs. (1-4.3) and (1-4.4) are again evaluated. This process is continued until the voltage at node 0 is obtained. Equation (1-4.1) is used to find the frequency response, $T(j\omega)$, from the node 0 voltage, and Eq. (1-4.2) is used to find the input impedance.

# User Instructions

| L N A P, LADDER NETWORK ANALYSIS PROGRAM | | | | |
|---|---|---|---|---|
| # of nodes | linear sweep | log sweep | data review | start analysis |
| load R | load L | load C | load start freq | load freq increment |

| STEP | INSTRUCTIONS | INPUT DATA/UNITS | KEYS | OUTPUT DATA/UNITS |
|---|---|---|---|---|
| 1 | Load both sides of the magnetic card | | | |
| 2 | Load the number of nodes in the network | | | |
| | The number of nodes cannot exceed four | # nodes | [f] [A] | # branches |
| 3 | Enter data starting with the highest numbered node: | | | |
| | a) If parallel RC or RL: | | | |
| | key in resistance and change sign* | R, ohms | [chs*] [A] | branch # |
| | key in inductance | L, henry | [B] | br # - 1 |
| | OR key in capacitance | C, farad | [C] | br # - 1 |
| | b) If series RC or RL: | | | |
| | key in resistance | R, ohms | [A] | branch # |
| | key in inductance | L, henry | [B] | br # - 1 |
| | OR key in capacitance | C, farad | [C] | br # - 1 |

For resistance, inductance, or capacitance alone in one branch, use step 3b with zero resistance for L or C entry, or use zero inductance for resistance entry. A zero or positive resistance is interpreted as a series branch indication.

Alternately, step 3a may be used to enter single inductors or capacitors by entering a very large negative resistance like $-10^{20}$ ohms.

Fastest program execution will result if the zero resistance method with step 3b is used for series branches, and the large negative resistance method with step 3a is used for shunt branches.
By observing this convention, the program will not use the series to parallel conversion subroutine which requires about 2 seconds to execute each time it is called.

Repeat step 3 until all branches including branch 0 have been entered.

* The sign change must affect the mantissa and not the exponent on numbers entered using scientific notation.

# User Instructions

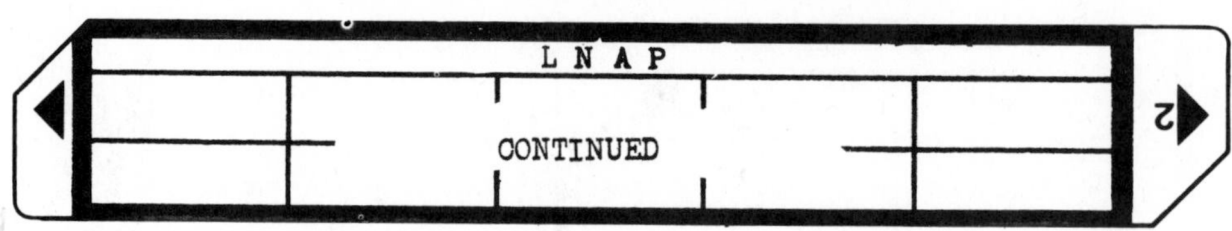


| STEP | INSTRUCTIONS | INPUT DATA/UNITS | KEYS | OUTPUT DATA/UNITS |
|---|---|---|---|---|
| 4 | To review stored element values | | [f] [D] | branch # |
| | | | | $R_n$* |
| | * A negative resistance value indicates | | | $L_n$ or $C_n$** |
| | a parallel connection of elements | | | space |
| | | | | $R_{n-1}$* |
| | ** A negative value for the reactive | | | L C ** |
| | element indicates the element is a | | | ⋮ |
| | capacitor. The capacitance value is | | | |
| | the absolute value of the number given. | | | $R_0$* |
| | | | | $L_0$ or $C_0$** |
| 5 | To change the value of a stored element: | | | |
| | a) Key in branch number to be changed | branch # | [STO] [I] | |
| | b) Key in correct resistance | R | [A] | |
| | c) Key in correct reactive element value | L OR | [B] OR | |
| | | C | [C] | |
| | Repeat step 4 or 5 if desired. | | | |
| 6 | To run analysis: | | | |
| | a) Load start frequency in hertz | $f_{start}$ | [D] | |
| | b) Load frequency increment | $f_{incr}$ | [E] | |
| | (for linear sweep, the new frequency | | | |
| | will be the old frequency plus the | | | |
| | increment, and for log sweep, the new | | | |
| | frequency will be the old frequency | | | |
| | times the increment) | | | |
| | c) Select linear or logarithmic sweep | | | |
| | For linear sweep | | [f] [B] | "0" |
| | For logarithmic sweep | | [f] [C] | "1" |
| | Steps 6a, 6b, and 6c may be executed in | | | |
| | any order. | | | |
| | d) Start analysis run | | [f] [E] | see Ex. |
| | | | | (1-4.1) |

# User Instructions

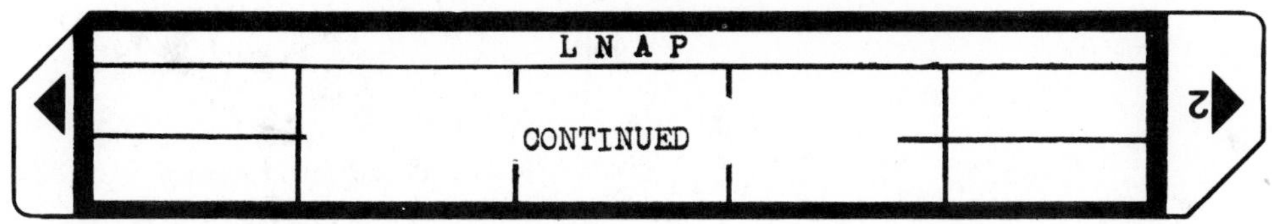


| STEP | INSTRUCTIONS | INPUT DATA/UNITS | KEYS | OUTPUT DATA/UNITS |
|---|---|---|---|---|
| 7 | To stop the analysis: | | | |
| | Wait until the pause that occurs after the imaginary $Z_{in}$ is printed, then key R/S | | R/S | |
| | If the program execution is halted without waiting for the pause, the primary and secondary registers may be left interchanged. | | | |
| | If a register interchange is suspected, recall register 0 and check to see that branch 0 resistance is stored there. | | | |
| | If the branch 0 reactive element is found in register 0, an interchange has occurred, and a P≷S operation is required. | | P≷S | |

Example 1-4.1

Figure 1-4.2 is the schematic of a predistorted 8th order Butterworth lowpass filter with a -3 dB cutoff frequency of 1000 Hz, and a design impedance level of 1000 ohms. Determine the frequency response and input impedance of this filter over a frequency range of 100 Hz to 10 kHz using a logarithmic sweep with 10 points per decade.

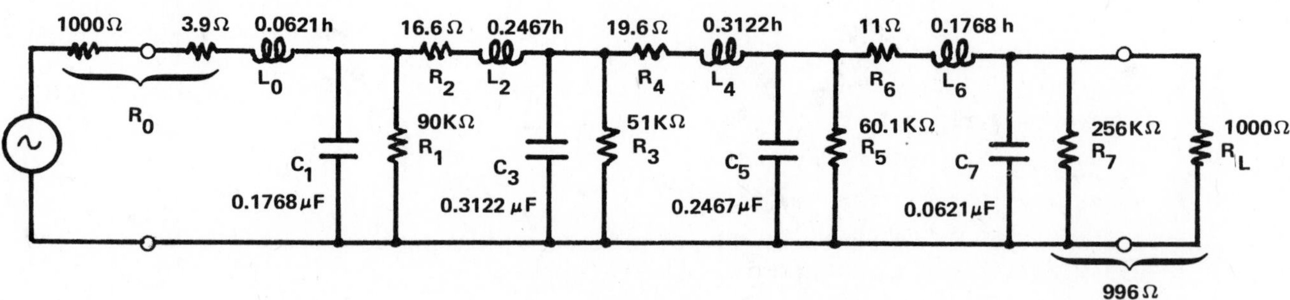


Figure 1-4.2 Predistorted 8th order Butterworth LP filter.

## HP-97 PRINTOUT FOR EXAMPLE 1-4.1

| PROGRAM INPUT | | DATA REVIEW | |
|---|---|---|---|
| 4.00 GSBa | load # of nodes | | |
| | | GSBd | start data review |
| -996. GSBA | $R_7$* | 7.000+00 *** | branch number |
| .0621-06 GSBC | $C_7$ | -996.0+00 *** | resistive part* |
| 11. GSBA | $R_6$ | -62.10-09 *** | reactive part** |
| .1768 GSBB | $L_6$ | | |
| -60100. GSBA | $R_5$ | 6.000+00 *** | |
| .2647-06 GSBC | $C_5$ | 11.00+00 *** | |
| | | 176.8-03 *** | |
| 19.6 GSBA | $R_4$ | 5.000+00 *** | |
| .3122 GSBB | $L_4$ | -60.10+03 *** | |
| | | -264.7-09 *** | |
| -51000. GSBA | $R_3$ | 4.000+00 *** | |
| .3122-06 GSBC | $C_3$ | 19.60+00 *** | |
| | | 312.2-03 *** | |
| 16.6 GSBA | $R_2$ | 3.000+00 *** | |
| .2647 GSBB | $L_2$ | -51.00+03 *** | |
| | | -312.2-09 *** | |
| -90000. GSBA | $R_1$ | 2.000+00 *** | |
| .1768-06 GSBC | $C_1$ | 16.60+00 *** | |
| | | 264.7-03 *** | |
| 1003.9 GSBA | $R_0$ | 1.000+00 *** | |
| .0621 GSBB | $C_0$ | -90.00+03 *** | |
| | | -176.8-09 *** | |
| | | 0.000+00 *** | |
| | | 1.004+03 *** | |
| | | 62.10-03 *** | |

* A negative sign indicates a parallel connection of elements.

** A negative sign indicates a capacitor as the reactive element.

## HP-97 PRINTOUT FOR EXAMPLE 1-4.1

| | | |
|---|---|---|
| | GSBc | **select log sweep** |
| 100. | GSBD | **load start frequency** |
| .1 | 10ˣ | **calculate freq increment for 10 points per decade** |
| 1.259+00 | *** | **multiplicative increment (manual print command)** |
| | GSBE | **load multiplicative increment** |
| | GSBe | **start analysis** |

### PROGRAM OUTPUT

| | | | | |
|---|---|---|---|---|
| 100.0+00 | **freq, Hz** | 316.2+00 | 1.000+03 | 3.162+03 |
| -6.467+00 | **gain, dB** | -6.482+00 | -9.816+00 | -86.07+00 |
| -29.40+00 | **phase, °** | -94.00+00 | 2.263+00 | 95.46+00 |
| 2.000+03 | **Re $Z_{in}$, Ω** | 2.000+03 | 5.622+03 | 1.005+03 |
| 208.2-03 | **Im $Z_{in}$, Ω** | 115.0-03 | -415.8+00 | 932.4+00 |
| | | | | |
| 125.9+00 | | 398.1+00 | 1.259+03 | 3.981+03 |
| -6.468+00 | | -6.493+00 | -22.54+00 | -102.0+00 |
| -37.04+00 | | -119.2+00 | -98.07+00 | 75.48+00 |
| 2.000+03 | | 2.000+03 | 1.049+03 | 1.005+03 |
| 250.4-03 | | -723.8-03 | -813.0+00 | 1.319+03 |
| | | | | |
| 158.5+00 | | 501.2+00 | 1.585+03 | 5.012+03 |
| -6.470+00 | | -6.513+00 | -38.24+00 | -118.0+00 |
| -46.68+00 | | -152.0+00 | -161.3+00 | 59.79+00 |
| 2.000+03 | | 1.993+03 | 1.013+03 | 1.004+03 |
| 292.3-03 | | -2.388+00 | -139.0+00 | 1.772+03 |
| | | | | |
| 199.5+00 | | 631.0+00 | 1.995+03 | 6.310+03 |
| -6.472+00 | | -6.557+00 | -54.14+00 | -134.0+00 |
| -58.87+00 | | 164.2+00 | 154.3+00 | 47.41+00 |
| 2.000+03 | | 1.957+03 | 1.008+03 | 1.004+03 |
| 322.3-03 | | 17.75+00 | 248.9+00 | 2.317+03 |
| | | | | |
| 251.2+00 | | 794.3+00 | 2.512+03 | 7.943+03 |
| -6.476+00 | | -6.770+00 | -70.09+00 | -150.0+00 |
| -74.33+00 | | 101.8+00 | 121.1+00 | 37.62+00 |
| 2.000+03 | | 1.931+03 | 1.006+03 | 1.004+03 |
| 305.9-03 | | 275.6+00 | 586.1+00 | 2.985+03 |
| | | | | |
| | | | | 10.00+03 |
| | | | | -166.0+00 |
| | | | | 29.86+00 |
| | | | | 1.004+03 |
| | | | | 3.811+03 |

Example 1-4.2

Over a frequency range of 8 Hz to 12 Hz using a linear sweep with 0.2 Hz steps, evaluate the transmission function and input impedance of the network shown in Fig. 1-4.3.

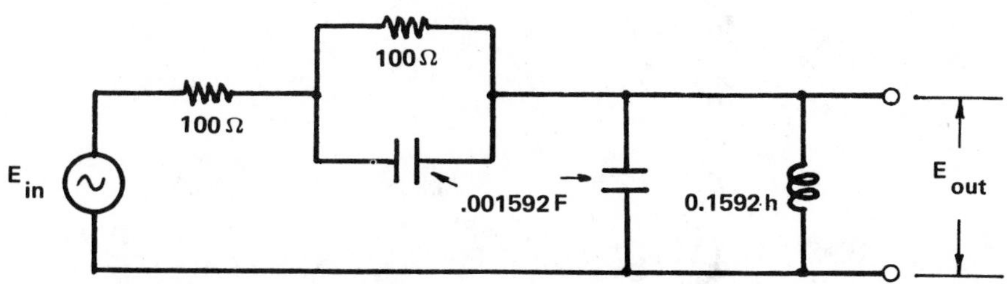


Figure 1-4.3 Network for Example 1-4.2.

The network must be redrawn with the insertion of dummy elements to place it in the ladder format meeting the program input requirements, i.e., only parallel RC or RL networks can be accommodated, not parallel LC networks. The redrawn network is shown in Fig. 1-4.4.

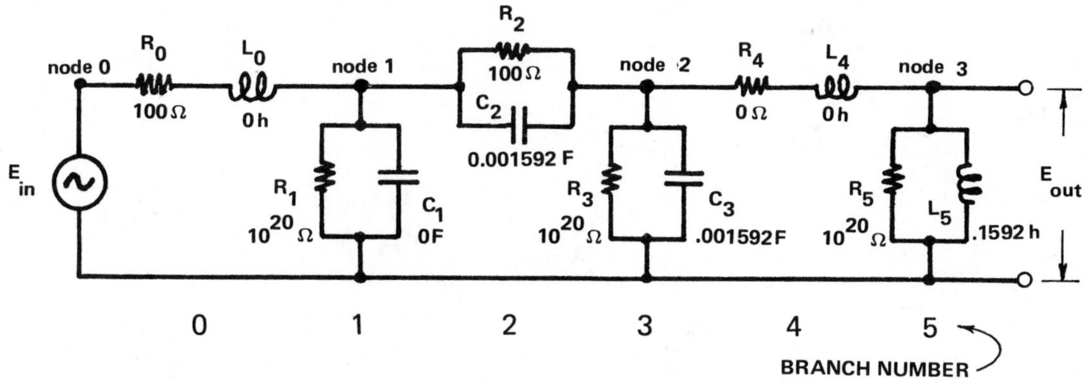


Figure 1-4.4 Network of Fig. 1-4.3 redrawn with dummy elements.

## HP-97 PRINTOUT FOR EXAMPLE 1-4.2

| PROGRAM INPUT | | DATA REVIEW | |
|---|---|---|---|
| 3.00 GSBa | enter # of nodes | | |
| | | GSBd | start data review |
| -1.+20 GSBA | $R_5$ * | | |
| .159155 GSBB | $L_5$ | 5.000+00 *** | branch number |
| | | -100.0+18 *** | resistive part * |
| 0. GSBA | $R_4$ | 159.2-03 *** | reactive part ** |
| 0. GSBB | $L_4$ | | |
| | | 4.000+00 *** | |
| -1.+20 GSBA | $R_3$ | 0.000+00 *** | |
| 1.59155-03 GSBC | $C_3$ | 0.000+00 *** | |
| -100. GSBA | $R_2$ | 3.000+00 *** | |
| 1.59155-03 GSBC | $C_2$ | -100.0+18 *** | |
| | | -1.592-03 *** | |
| -1.+20 GSBA | $R_1$ | | |
| 0. GSBC | $C_1$ | 2.000+00 *** | |
| | | -100.0+00 *** | |
| 100. GSBA | $R_0$ | -1.592-03 *** | |
| 0. GSBB | $L_0$ | | |
| | | 1.000+00 *** | |
| | | -100.0+18 *** | |
| | | 0.000+00 *** | |
| | | 0.000+00 *** | |
| | | 100.0+00 *** | |
| | | 0.000+00 *** | |

*  A negative sign indicates parallel connection of elements.

**  A negative sign indicates a capacitor.

| | | |
|---|---|---|
| 8. GSBD | **start frequency** | **Analysis Particulars** |
| .2 GSBE | **frequency increment** | |
| GSBb | **select linear sweep** | |
| GSBe | **start analysis** | |

## PROGRAM OUTPUT

| | | | | |
|---|---|---|---|---|
| 8.000+00 | **freq, Hz** | 9.000+00 | 10.00+00 | 11.00+00 |
| -13.24+00 | **gain, dB** | -7.123+06 | -6.158-06 | -7.057+00 |
| 84.42+00 | **phase, °** | 70.22+00 | -414.3-06 | -58.65+00 |
| 101.5+00 | **Re $Z_{in}$, Ω** | 101.2+00 | 101.0+00 | 100.8+00 |
| 9.915+00 | **Im $Z_{in}$, Ω** | 36.39+00 | -13.97+06 | -61.40+00 |
| | | | | |
| 8.200+00 | | 9.200+00 | 10.20+00 | 11.20+00 |
| -12.23+00 | | -5.473+00 | -928.2-03 | -8.251+00 |
| 82.69+00 | | 64.09+00 | -21.06+00 | -62.31+00 |
| 101.5+00 | | 101.2+00 | 101.0+00 | 100.8+00 |
| 13.01+00 | | 49.15+00 | -262.2+00 | -52.88+00 |
| | | | | |
| 8.400+00 | | 9.400+00 | 10.40+00 | 11.40+00 |
| -11.13+00 | | -3.663+00 | -2.509+00 | -9.306+00 |
| 80.60+00 | | 55.[illegible]2+00 | -36.38+00 | -65.11+00 |
| 101.4+00 | | 101.1+00 | 100.9+00 | 100.8+00 |
| 16.79+00 | | 70.24+00 | -137.0+00 | -46.76+00 |
| | | | | |
| 8.600+00 | | 9.600+00 | 10.60+00 | 11.60+00 |
| -9.930+00 | | -1.819+00 | -4.173+00 | -10.25+00 |
| 77.99+00 | | 42.03+00 | -46.69+00 | -67.31+00 |
| 101.3+00 | | 101.1+00 | 100.9+00 | 100.7+00 |
| 21.55+00 | | 112.1+00 | -95.11+00 | -42.12+00 |
| | | | | |
| 8.800+00 | | 9.800+00 | 10.80+00 | 11.80+00 |
| -8.602+00 | | -361.1-03 | -5.702+00 | -11.09+00 |
| 74.66+00 | | 23.05+00 | -53.70+00 | -69.09+00 |
| 101.3+00 | | 101.0+00 | 100.9+00 | 100.7+00 |
| 27.79+00 | | 237.4+00 | -74.08+00 | -38.49+00 |
| | | | | |
| | | | | 12.00+00 |
| | | | | -11.86+00 |
| | | | | -70.55+00 |
| | | | | 100.7+00 |
| | | | | -35.55+00 |

## TI-59 PRINTOUT FOR EXAMPLE 1-4.2

### DATA REVIEW

| | |
|---|---|
| 5. | **branch #** |
| -1. 20 | **resistive part *** |
| 0.159155 | **reactive part **** |
| | |
| 4. | |
| 0. | |
| 0. | |
| | |
| 3. | |
| -1. 20 | |
| -0.00159155 | |
| | |
| 2. | |
| -100. | |
| -0.00159155 | |
| | |
| 1. | |
| -1. 20 | |
| 0. | |
| | |
| 0. | |
| 100. | |
| 0. | |

### PROGRAM OUTPUT

| | |
|---|---|
| 0.10 | **freq, Hz** |
| -267.18 | **phase, °** |
| -65.99 | **gain, dB** |
| 199.01 | **Re $Z_{in}$, Ω** |
| -9.80 | **Im $Z_{in}$, Ω** |
| | |
| 0.13 | |
| -266.46 | |
| -63.97 | |
| 198.44 | |
| -12.27 | |
| | |
| 0.16 | |
| -265.57 | |
| -61.94 | |
| 197.55 | |
| -15.30 | |
| | |
| 0.20 | |
| -264.47 | |
| -59.89 | |
| 196.17 | |
| -18.99 | |
| | |
| 0.25 | |
| -263.13 | |
| -57.82 | |
| 194.06 | |
| -23.38 | |
| | |
| 0.32 | |
| -261.53 | |
| -55.70 | |
| 190.91 | |
| -28.43 | |

## References and Equation Derivation

The algorithm is completely described in the program description section. This particular analysis method is widely referenced. The earliest reference known to the author is T.R. Bashkow [ 4 ].

# Program Listing I

| | | | | | | |
|---|---|---|---|---|---|---|
| 001 | *LBLA | LOAD RESISTOR VALUE | | 056 | *LBLd | INPUT DATA REVIEW |
| 002 | GSB5 | odd or even branch? | | 057 | GSB4 | initialize |
| 003 | F0? | | | 058 | *LBL8 | review loop start |
| 004 | 1/X | if odd numbered branch, | | 059 | GSB5 | odd numbered branch? |
| 005 | F0? | form G = -1/R | | 060 | RCLI | recall and print branch # |
| 006 | CHS | | | 061 | PRTX | |
| 007 | STOi | store value | | 062 | RCLi | recall branch R or G |
| 008 | RCLI | recall branch # to display | | 063 | F0? | |
| 009 | RTN | return control to keyboard | | 064 | 1/X | if odd branch (flag 0 set) |
| 010 | *LBLC | LOAD CAPACITOR VALUE | | 065 | F0? | form $-1/R(i)$ |
| 011 | CHS | change sign of entry | | 066 | CHS | |
| 012 | *LBLE | LOAD INDUCTOR VALUE | | 067 | PRTX | print branch resistance |
| 013 | GSB5 | odd numbered branch? | | 068 | P≠S | |
| 014 | F0? | change sign of entry if | | 069 | RCLi | recall branch L or C |
| 015 | CHS | branch number is odd | | 070 | P≠S | |
| 016 | P≠S | | | 071 | F0? | change sign if branch odd |
| 017 | STOi | indirectly store reactive | | 072 | CHS | |
| 018 | P≠S | element values | | 073 | PRTX | print L or -C |
| 019 | DSZI | decrement branch number | | 074 | SPC | |
| 020 | CF3 | clr flag 3 (a NOP statement) | | 075 | F3? | test for loop exit |
| 021 | RCLI | recall branch number | | 076 | RTN | |
| 022 | GTO7 | goto space and return | | 077 | SF3 | decrement index register |
| 023 | *LBLD | LOAD START FREQUENCY | | 078 | DSZI | and SF3 if index is zero |
| 024 | STO8 | | | 079 | CF3 | |
| 025 | GTO7 | | | 080 | GTO8 | |
| 026 | *LBLE | LOAD FREQUENCY INCREMENT | | 081 | *LBLe | LNAP ANALYSIS START |
| 027 | STO9 | | | 082 | GSB4 | goto initialization |
| 028 | GTO7 | | | 083 | *LBL9 | analysis loop start |
| 029 | *LBLa | LOAD NUMBER OF NODES | | 084 | GSB3 | recall shunt branch elements |
| 030 | STOE | store number of nodes | | 085 | RCLB | recall complex node voltages |
| 031 | *LBL4 | initialization routine | | 086 | RCLA | and execute complex multiply |
| 032 | EEX | | | 087 | GSB1 | |
| 033 | STOA | $E_n = 1 + j0$ | | 088 | RCLD | recall previous complex |
| 034 | CLX | | | 089 | RCLC | branch current and perform |
| 035 | STOB | | | 090 | GSB2 | complex addition |
| 036 | STOC | | | 091 | STOC | store complex branch |
| 037 | STOD | $I_{2n} = 0 + j0$ | | 092 | X≠Y | currents for present branch |
| 038 | RCLE | | | 093 | STOD | |
| 039 | ENT↑ | calculate and store | | 094 | X≠Y | |
| 040 | + | highest branch number | | 095 | CF0 | decrement index register |
| 041 | EEX | | | 096 | DSZI | & SF0 if index is zero |
| 042 | - | Br# = 2(# nodes) - 1 | | 097 | SF0 | |
| 043 | STOI | | | 098 | GSB3 | recall series branch elts |
| 044 | CF3 | clear data entry flag and | | 099 | GSB1 | execute complex multiply |
| 045 | GTO7 | goto space and return | | 100 | RCLB | recall complex node voltage |
| 046 | *LBLb | SET LINEAR SWEEP | | 101 | RCLA | and add to branch voltage |
| 047 | CF1 | | | 102 | GSB2 | |
| 048 | CLX | place "zero" in display | | 103 | X≠Y | store new complex node |
| 049 | GTO7 | goto space and return | | 104 | STOB | voltage |
| 050 | *LBLc | SET LOGARITHMIC SWEEP | | 105 | X≠Y | |
| 051 | SF1 | | | 106 | STOA | |
| 052 | EEX | | | 107 | DSZI | decrement branch number and |
| 053 | *LBL7 | space and return subroutine | | 108 | F0? | test for loop exit |
| 054 | SPC | | | 109 | GTO9 | |
| 055 | RTN | | | 110 | →P | convert to magnitude & angle |

| REGISTERS | | | | | | | | | |
|---|---|---|---|---|---|---|---|---|---|
| 0 $R_0$ | 1 $G_1$ | 2 $R_2$ | 3 $G_3$ | 4 $R_4$ | 5 $G_5$ | 6 $R_6$ | 7 $G_7$ | 8 start frequency | 9 freq increment |
| S0 $-C_0$ or $L_0$ | S1 $C_1$ or $-L_1$ | S2 $-C_2$ or $L_2$ | S3 $C_3$ or $-L_3$ | S4 $-C_4$ or $L_4$ | S5 $C_5$ or $-L_5$ | S6 $-C_6$ or $L_6$ | S7 $C_7$ or $-L_7$ | S8 cmplx multiply | S9 cmplx multiply |
| A $Re\ E_k$ | | B $Im\ E_k$ | | C $Re\ I_k$ | | D $Im\ I_k$ | | E number of nodes | I index |

# Program Listing II

| Step | Key | Comment |
|---|---|---|
| 111 | STOA | temporarily store \|Ein\| |
| 112 | LOG | |
| 113 | 2 | convert to dB |
| 114 | 0 | |
| 115 | × | |
| 116 | RCL8 | |
| 117 | RND | recall and print present |
| 118 | PRTX | analysis frequency |
| 119 | R↓ | |
| 120 | CHS | recover and print -dB |
| 121 | RND | |
| 122 | PRTX | |
| 123 | R↓ | recover phase angle |
| 124 | STOB | temporarily store ∡ $E_{in}$ |
| 125 | CHS | |
| 126 | RND | print -(phase angle) |
| 127 | PRTX | |
| 128 | RCLD | recall $I_0$ |
| 129 | RCLC | |
| 130 | →P | |
| 131 | RCLA | |
| 132 | X⇄Y | |
| 133 | ÷ | |
| 134 | X⇄Y | perform complex division: |
| 135 | RCLB | |
| 136 | X⇄Y | $Z_{in} = E_{in}/I_0$ |
| 137 | - | |
| 138 | X⇄Y | |
| 139 | →R | |
| 140 | PRTX | print Re $Z_{in}$ |
| 141 | X⇄Y | |
| 142 | PRTX | print Im $Z_{in}$ |
| 143 | PSE | |
| 144 | RCL9 | recall frequency increment |
| 145 | F1? | |
| 146 | ST×8 | use multiplicative increment |
| 147 | F1? | if logarithmic sweep selected |
| 148 | GTOe | |
| 149 | ST+8 | use additive increment if |
| 150 | GTOe | linear sweep selected |
| 151 | *LBL1 | complex multiplication |
| 152 | P⇄S | $(a+jb)(c+jd) = e+jf$ |
| 153 | STO8 | a |
| 154 | STO9 | a |
| 155 | R↓ | |
| 156 | ENT↑ | |
| 157 | R↓ | |
| 158 | R↓ | c |
| 159 | ST×8 | ac in register 8 |
| 160 | R↓ | d |
| 161 | ST×9 | ad in register 9 |
| 162 | × | bd in stack |
| 163 | ST-8 | ac - bd in register 8 |
| 164 | R↓ | |
| 165 | × | bc in stack |
| 166 | ST+9 | ad + bc in register 9 |
| 167 | RCL9 | rcl f = ac + bc |
| 168 | RCL8 | rcl e, ac - bd = e |
| 169 | P⇄S | restore register order |
| 170 | RTN | return to main program |
| 171 | *LBL2 | complex add subroutine |
| 172 | X⇄Y | |
| 173 | R↓ | |
| 174 | + | |
| 175 | R↓ | |
| 176 | + | |
| 177 | R↑ | |
| 178 | RTN | return to main program |
| 179 | *LBL3 | complex recall subroutine |
| 180 | RCL8 | calculate $\omega = 2\pi f$ |
| 181 | Pi | |
| 182 | × | |
| 183 | ENT↑ | |
| 184 | + | |
| 185 | P⇄S | |
| 186 | RCLi | recall reactive branch |
| 187 | P⇄S | element, $b_x$, and form |
| 188 | × | $2\pi f b_x$ |
| 189 | X<0? | |
| 190 | 1/X | form reciprocal if $b_x < 0$ |
| 191 | RCLi | recall resistive element |
| 192 | X<0? | if <0, perform parallel |
| 193 | GTO3 | series conversion |
| 194 | RTN | return to main program |
| 195 | *LBL3 | parallel series conversion |
| 196 | ABS | |
| 197 | 1/X | conductance⇄resistance |
| 198 | X⇄Y | |
| 199 | 1/X | susceptance⇄reactance |
| 200 | X⇄Y | |
| 201 | →P | |
| 202 | 1/X | calculate complex inverse |
| 203 | →R | |
| 204 | RTN | return to main program |
| 205 | *LBL5 | odd or even branch subr |
| 206 | RCLI | |
| 207 | 2 | form 0 if branch even |
| 208 | ÷ | or 0.5 if branch odd |
| 209 | FRC | |
| 210 | SF0 | |
| 211 | X=0? | set flag 0 if branch is odd |
| 212 | CF0 | |
| 213 | R↓ | restore x register in stack |
| 214 | RTN | return to main program |

| LABELS | | | | | FLAGS |
|---|---|---|---|---|---|
| A load R | B load L | C load C | D load start freq | E load freq increment | 0 odd branch |
| a load # of nodes | b set linear sweep | c set log sweep | d start data revu | e start analysis | 1 log/lin |
| 0 | 1 complex multiply | 2 complex add | 3 complex recall | 4 initialize | 2 |
| 5 odd/even branch | 6 series⇄parallel | 7 log sweep | 8 | 9 | 3 data entry |

SET STATUS

| FLAGS | ON | OFF | TRIG | | DISP | |
|---|---|---|---|---|---|---|
| 0 | | ■ | DEG | ■ | FIX | |
| 1 | | ■ | GRAD | | SCI | |
| 2 | | | RAD | | ENG | ■ |
| 3 | | ■ | | | n 3 | |

## 1-4 TI-59 PROGRAM LISTING

| Step | Code | Key | Comment |
|---|---|---|---|
| 000 | 76 | LBL | **LOAD RESISTOR VALUE** |
| 001 | 11 | A | |
| 002 | 42 | STO | temporarily store |
| 003 | 57 | 57 | |
| 004 | 71 | SBR | set flag 0 if branch number is odd |
| 005 | 04 | 04 | |
| 006 | 18 | 18 | |
| 007 | 43 | RCL | recall entry |
| 008 | 57 | 57 | |
| 009 | 87 | IFF | if odd branch, form G = -1/R |
| 010 | 00 | 00 | |
| 011 | 00 | 00 | |
| 012 | 18 | 18 | |
| 013 | 72 | ST* | store R or G |
| 014 | 59 | 59 | |
| 015 | 43 | RCL | recall resistor value to display |
| 016 | 57 | 57 | |
| 017 | 92 | RTN | |
| 018 | 94 | +/- | routine for G = -1/R |
| 019 | 35 | 1/X | |
| 020 | 61 | GTO | |
| 021 | 00 | 00 | |
| 022 | 13 | 13 | |
| 023 | 76 | LBL | **LOAD CAPACITOR VALUE** |
| 024 | 13 | C | |
| 025 | 54 | ) | |
| 026 | 94 | +/- | change sign and temporarily store |
| 027 | 42 | STO | |
| 028 | 58 | 58 | |
| 029 | 76 | LBL | **LOAD INDUCTOR VALUE** |
| 030 | 12 | B | |
| 031 | 42 | STO | |
| 032 | 58 | 58 | |
| 033 | 71 | SBR | set flag 0 if branch number is odd |
| 034 | 04 | 04 | |
| 035 | 18 | 18 | |
| 036 | 43 | RCL | recall entry |
| 037 | 58 | 58 | |
| 038 | 22 | INV | if branch number is odd, change the sign of the entry |
| 039 | 87 | IFF | |
| 040 | 00 | 00 | |
| 041 | 00 | 00 | |
| 042 | 44 | 44 | |
| 043 | 94 | +/- | |
| 044 | 72 | ST* | store reactive element |
| 045 | 56 | 56 | |
| 046 | 01 | 1 | decrement index of resistive and reactive storage registers |
| 047 | 94 | +/- | |
| 048 | 44 | SUM | |
| 049 | 59 | 59 | |
| 050 | 44 | SUM | |
| 051 | 56 | 56 | |
| 052 | 43 | RCL | recall reactive element to display |
| 053 | 58 | 58 | |
| 054 | 92 | RTN | |
| 055 | 76 | LBL | **LOAD SWEEP STARTING FREQ** |
| 056 | 14 | D | |
| 057 | 42 | STO | |
| 058 | 55 | 55 | |
| 059 | 92 | RTN | |
| 060 | 76 | LBL | **LOAD FREQ INCREMENT** |
| 061 | 15 | E | |
| 062 | 42 | STO | |
| 063 | 54 | 54 | |
| 064 | 92 | RTN | |
| 065 | 76 | LBL | **SELECT LINEAR SWEEP** |
| 066 | 17 | B' | |
| 067 | 22 | INV | |
| 068 | 86 | STF | |
| 069 | 01 | 01 | |
| 070 | 00 | 0 | display 0 |
| 071 | 92 | RTN | |
| 072 | 76 | LBL | **SELECT LOG SWEEP** |
| 073 | 18 | C' | |
| 074 | 86 | STF | |
| 075 | 01 | 01 | |
| 076 | 01 | 1 | display 1 |
| 077 | 92 | RTN | |
| 078 | 76 | LBL | **INPUT DATA REVIEW** |
| 079 | 19 | D' | |
| 080 | 71 | SBR | initialize |
| 081 | 03 | 03 | |
| 082 | 80 | 80 | |
| 083 | 71 | SBR | set flag 0 if branch number is odd |
| 084 | 04 | 04 | |
| 085 | 18 | 18 | |
| 086 | 53 | ( | recall branch number |
| 087 | 43 | RCL | |
| 088 | 59 | 59 | |
| 089 | 75 | - | |
| 090 | 01 | 1 | |
| 091 | 00 | 0 | |
| 092 | 54 | ) | |
| 093 | 98 | ADV | |
| 094 | 71 | SBR | print or display branch number |
| 095 | 04 | 04 | |
| 096 | 66 | 66 | |
| 097 | 73 | RC* | recall resistive element |
| 098 | 59 | 59 | |
| 099 | 22 | INV | |

**This translation was provided by Mr. Walter Ware**

**1-4** TI-59 PROGRAM LISTING

| Step | Code | Key | Comment |
|---|---|---|---|
| 100 | 87 | IFF | if odd branch, form R = -1/G |
| 101 | 00 | 00 | |
| 102 | 01 | 01 | |
| 103 | 06 | 06 | |
| 104 | 35 | 1/X | |
| 105 | 94 | +/- | |
| 106 | 71 | SBR | display or print resistance |
| 107 | 04 | 04 | |
| 108 | 66 | 66 | |
| 109 | 73 | RC* | recall reactive element |
| 110 | 56 | 56 | |
| 111 | 22 | INV | if odd branch, change sign |
| 112 | 87 | IFF | |
| 113 | 00 | 00 | |
| 114 | 01 | 01 | |
| 115 | 17 | 17 | |
| 116 | 94 | +/- | |
| 117 | 71 | SBR | print or display L or C |
| 118 | 04 | 04 | |
| 119 | 66 | 66 | |
| 120 | 87 | IFF | test for loop exit |
| 121 | 03 | 03 | |
| 122 | 01 | 01 | |
| 123 | 47 | 47 | |
| 124 | 86 | STF | decrement indirect storage register indices |
| 125 | 03 | 03 | |
| 126 | 01 | 1 | |
| 127 | 94 | +/- | |
| 128 | 44 | SUM | |
| 129 | 56 | 56 | |
| 130 | 44 | SUM | |
| 131 | 59 | 59 | |
| 132 | 43 | RCL | set t = 10 |
| 133 | 09 | 09 | |
| 134 | 85 | + | |
| 135 | 01 | 1 | |
| 136 | 95 | = | |
| 137 | 32 | X:T | |
| 138 | 43 | RCL | recall register index |
| 139 | 59 | 59 | |
| 140 | 22 | INV | if index = 10, execute one more loop |
| 141 | 67 | EQ | |
| 142 | 01 | 01 | |
| 143 | 48 | 48 | |
| 144 | 61 | GTO | |
| 145 | 00 | 00 | |
| 146 | 83 | 83 | |
| 147 | 92 | RTN | |
| 148 | 22 | INV | clear flag 3 |
| 149 | 86 | STF | |
| 150 | 03 | 03 | |
| 151 | 68 | NOP | |
| 152 | 68 | NOP | |
| 153 | 68 | NOP | |
| 154 | 61 | GTO | goto loop start |
| 155 | 00 | 00 | |
| 156 | 83 | 83 | |
| 157 | 29 | CP | complex recall subr |
| 158 | 53 | ( | |
| 159 | 43 | RCL | calculate $\omega = 2\pi f$ |
| 160 | 55 | 55 | |
| 161 | 65 | × | |
| 162 | 89 | π | |
| 163 | 65 | × | |
| 164 | 02 | 2 | |
| 165 | 65 | × | recall reactive branch element value and form branch immittance |
| 166 | 73 | RC* | |
| 167 | 56 | 56 | |
| 168 | 54 | ) | |
| 169 | 77 | GE | if immittance is negative, form reciprocal |
| 170 | 01 | 01 | |
| 171 | 73 | 73 | |
| 172 | 35 | 1/X | |
| 173 | 42 | STO | store immittance |
| 174 | 58 | 58 | |
| 175 | 73 | RC* | recall branch resistance and store |
| 176 | 59 | 59 | |
| 177 | 42 | STO | |
| 178 | 57 | 57 | |
| 179 | 22 | INV | if resistance negative, perform series⇄parallel conversion |
| 180 | 77 | GE | |
| 181 | 01 | 01 | |
| 182 | 84 | 84 | |
| 183 | 92 | RTN | |
| 184 | 43 | RCL | series⇄parallel conversion subroutine |
| 185 | 57 | 57 | |
| 186 | 50 | I×I | conductance⇄resistance |
| 187 | 35 | 1/X | |
| 188 | 32 | X:T | |
| 189 | 43 | RCL | susceptance⇄reactance |
| 190 | 58 | 58 | |
| 191 | 35 | 1/X | |
| 192 | 94 | +/- | |
| 193 | 22 | INV | calculate complex inverse |
| 194 | 37 | P/R | |
| 195 | 94 | +/- | |
| 196 | 32 | X:T | |
| 197 | 35 | 1/X | |
| 198 | 32 | X:T | |
| 199 | 37 | P/R | |

## 1-4 TI-59 PROGRAM LISTING

| | | | |
|---|---|---|---|
| 200 | 42 | STO | temporarily store immittance |
| 201 | 58 | 58 | |
| 202 | 32 | X:T | temporarily store resistance or cond |
| 203 | 42 | STO | |
| 204 | 57 | 57 | |
| 205 | 92 | RTN | return to main program |
| 206 | 76 | LBL | LNAP ANALYSIS START |
| 207 | 10 | E' | |
| 208 | 58 | FIX | set display mode |
| 209 | 02 | 02 | |
| 210 | 98 | ADV | advance paper |
| 211 | 98 | ADV | |
| 212 | 71 | SBR | initialize |
| 213 | 03 | 03 | |
| 214 | 83 | 83 | |
| 215 | 71 | SBR | recall shunt branch |
| 216 | 01 | 01 | |
| 217 | 57 | 57 | |
| 218 | 43 | RCL | recall complex node voltage and execute complex multiply to obtain complex branch current |
| 219 | 57 | 57 | |
| 220 | 42 | STO | |
| 221 | 01 | 01 | |
| 222 | 43 | RCL | |
| 223 | 58 | 58 | |
| 224 | 42 | STO | |
| 225 | 02 | 02 | |
| 226 | 43 | RCL | |
| 227 | 49 | 49 | |
| 228 | 42 | STO | |
| 229 | 03 | 03 | |
| 230 | 43 | RCL | |
| 231 | 50 | 50 | |
| 232 | 42 | STO | |
| 233 | 04 | 04 | |
| 234 | 36 | PGM | |
| 235 | 04 | 04 | |
| 236 | 13 | C | |
| 237 | 43 | RCL | recall previous complex branch current, perform complex add and store result |
| 238 | 01 | 01 | |
| 239 | 44 | SUM | |
| 240 | 51 | 51 | |
| 241 | 43 | RCL | |
| 242 | 02 | 02 | |
| 243 | 44 | SUM | |
| 244 | 52 | 52 | |
| 245 | 01 | 1 | decrement indirect recall indices |
| 246 | 94 | +/- | |
| 247 | 44 | SUM | |
| 248 | 56 | 56 | |
| 249 | 44 | SUM | |
| 250 | 59 | 59 | |
| 251 | 71 | SBR | recall series branch elements |
| 252 | 01 | 01 | |
| 253 | 57 | 57 | |
| 254 | 43 | RCL | multiply series impedance by complex branch current to obtain series branch voltage drop |
| 255 | 57 | 57 | |
| 256 | 42 | STO | |
| 257 | 01 | 01 | |
| 258 | 43 | RCL | |
| 259 | 58 | 58 | |
| 260 | 42 | STO | |
| 261 | 02 | 02 | |
| 262 | 43 | RCL | |
| 263 | 51 | 51 | |
| 264 | 42 | STO | |
| 265 | 03 | 03 | |
| 266 | 43 | RCL | |
| 267 | 52 | 52 | |
| 268 | 42 | STO | |
| 269 | 04 | 04 | |
| 270 | 36 | PGM | |
| 271 | 04 | 04 | |
| 272 | 13 | C | |
| 273 | 43 | RCL | add complex series voltage drop to previous node voltage to obtain next node voltage and store result |
| 274 | 01 | 01 | |
| 275 | 44 | SUM | |
| 276 | 49 | 49 | |
| 277 | 43 | RCL | |
| 278 | 02 | 02 | |
| 279 | 44 | SUM | |
| 280 | 50 | 50 | |
| 281 | 01 | 1 | decrement indirect recall indices |
| 282 | 94 | +/- | |
| 283 | 44 | SUM | |
| 284 | 56 | 56 | |
| 285 | 44 | SUM | |
| 286 | 59 | 59 | |
| 287 | 43 | RCL | test for loop exit |
| 288 | 09 | 09 | |
| 289 | 32 | X:T | |
| 290 | 43 | RCL | |
| 291 | 59 | 59 | |
| 292 | 67 | EQ | |
| 293 | 02 | 02 | |
| 294 | 98 | 98 | |
| 295 | 61 | GTO | repeat loop |
| 296 | 02 | 02 | |
| 297 | 15 | 15 | |
| 298 | 43 | RCL | recall present freq |
| 299 | 55 | 55 | |

1-4 TI-59 PROGRAM LISTING

| Step | Code | Key | Comment |
|---|---|---|---|
| 300 | 71 | SBR | print or display frequency |
| 301 | 04 | 04 | |
| 302 | 66 | 66 | |
| 303 | 43 | RCL | recall complex input voltage |
| 304 | 49 | 49 | |
| 305 | 32 | X:T | |
| 306 | 43 | RCL | |
| 307 | 50 | 50 | |
| 308 | 22 | INV | convert to polar |
| 309 | 37 | P/R | |
| 310 | 94 | +/- | change sign of angle and store |
| 311 | 42 | STO | |
| 312 | 05 | 05 | |
| 313 | 71 | SBR | print or display angle of network transmission function |
| 314 | 04 | 04 | |
| 315 | 66 | 66 | |
| 316 | 32 | X:T | calculate 20 log of network transmission function magnitude |
| 317 | 28 | LOG | |
| 318 | 94 | +/- | |
| 319 | 65 | × | |
| 320 | 02 | 2 | |
| 321 | 00 | 0 | |
| 322 | 95 | = | |
| 323 | 42 | STO | |
| 324 | 06 | 06 | |
| 325 | 71 | SBR | print or display dB response |
| 326 | 04 | 04 | |
| 327 | 66 | 66 | |
| 328 | 43 | RCL | recall complex network input voltage |
| 329 | 49 | 49 | |
| 330 | 42 | STO | |
| 331 | 01 | 01 | |
| 332 | 43 | RCL | |
| 333 | 50 | 50 | |
| 334 | 42 | STO | |
| 335 | 02 | 02 | |
| 336 | 43 | RCL | recall complex network input current |
| 337 | 51 | 51 | |
| 338 | 42 | STO | |
| 339 | 03 | 03 | |
| 340 | 43 | RCL | |
| 341 | 52 | 52 | |
| 342 | 42 | STO | |
| 343 | 04 | 04 | |
| 344 | 36 | PGM | perform complex division |
| 345 | 04 | 04 | |
| 346 | 18 | C' | |
| 347 | 43 | RCL | print or display Re $Z_{in}$ |
| 348 | 01 | 01 | |
| 349 | 71 | SBR | |
| 350 | 04 | 04 | |
| 351 | 66 | 66 | |
| 352 | 43 | RCL | print or display Im $Z_{in}$ |
| 353 | 02 | 02 | |
| 354 | 71 | SBR | |
| 355 | 04 | 04 | |
| 356 | 66 | 66 | |
| 357 | 43 | RCL | recall frequency increment |
| 358 | 54 | 54 | |
| 359 | 87 | IFF | jump if log sweep selected |
| 360 | 01 | 01 | |
| 361 | 03 | 03 | |
| 362 | 68 | 68 | |
| 363 | 44 | SUM | add frequency increment for linear sweep |
| 364 | 55 | 55 | |
| 365 | 61 | GTO | |
| 366 | 02 | 02 | |
| 367 | 06 | 06 | |
| 368 | 49 | PRD | multiply by frequency increment for log sweep |
| 369 | 55 | 55 | |
| 370 | 61 | GTO | |
| 371 | 02 | 02 | |
| 372 | 06 | 06 | |
| 373 | 76 | LBL | LOAD NUMBER OF NODES |
| 374 | 16 | A' | |
| 375 | 71 | SBR | test for printer |
| 376 | 04 | 04 | |
| 377 | 75 | 75 | |
| 378 | 42 | STO | store number of nodes |
| 379 | 53 | 53 | |
| 380 | 09 | 9 | initialization subr |
| 381 | 42 | STO | set minimum loop counter value allowed |
| 382 | 09 | 09 | |
| 383 | 53 | ( | calculate highest branch number storage index for real immittance storage |
| 384 | 43 | RCL | |
| 385 | 53 | 53 | |
| 386 | 65 | × | |
| 387 | 02 | 2 | |
| 388 | 75 | - | |
| 389 | 01 | 1 | |
| 390 | 85 | + | |
| 391 | 01 | 1 | |
| 392 | 00 | 0 | |
| 393 | 54 | ) | |
| 394 | 42 | STO | |
| 395 | 59 | 59 | |
| 396 | 85 | + | calculate highest branch number storage index for imaginary immitance storage |
| 397 | 01 | 1 | |
| 398 | 00 | 0 | |
| 399 | 54 | ) | |

## 1-4 TI-59 PROGRAM LISTING

| Step | Code | Key | Comments |
|---|---|---|---|
| 400 | 42 | STO | |
| 401 | 56 | 56 | |
| 402 | 01 | 1 | initialize node voltage of highest node: |
| 403 | 42 | STO | |
| 404 | 49 | 49 | |
| 405 | 00 | 0 | $E_n = 1 + j0$ |
| 406 | 42 | STO | |
| 407 | 50 | 50 | |
| 408 | 42 | STO | initialize $I_{2n} = 0 + j0$ |
| 409 | 51 | 51 | |
| 410 | 42 | STO | |
| 411 | 52 | 52 | |
| 412 | 22 | INV | clear flag 3 |
| 413 | 86 | STF | |
| 414 | 03 | 03 | |
| 415 | 43 | RCL | recall number of nodes |
| 416 | 53 | 53 | |
| 417 | 92 | RTN | return to main program |
| 418 | 29 | CP | odd or even branch subr |
| 419 | 22 | INV | |
| 420 | 86 | STF | clear flag 0 |
| 421 | 00 | 00 | |
| 422 | 43 | RCL | |
| 423 | 59 | 59 | |
| 424 | 55 | ÷ | |
| 425 | 02 | 2 | |
| 426 | 54 | ) | |
| 427 | 22 | INV | |
| 428 | 59 | INT | |
| 429 | 67 | EQ | |
| 430 | 04 | 04 | |
| 431 | 34 | 34 | |
| 432 | 86 | STF | set flag 0 if branch number is odd |
| 433 | 00 | 00 | |
| 434 | 92 | RTN | |
| 435 | 00 | 0 | unused program memory |
| 436 | 00 | 0 | |
| 437 | 00 | 0 | |
| 438 | 00 | 0 | |
| 439 | 00 | 0 | |
| 440 | 00 | 0 | |
| 441 | 00 | 0 | |
| 442 | 00 | 0 | |
| 443 | 00 | 0 | |
| 444 | 00 | 0 | |
| 445 | 00 | 0 | |
| 446 | 00 | 0 | |
| 447 | 00 | 0 | |
| 448 | 00 | 0 | |
| 449 | 00 | 0 | |
| 450 | 00 | 0 | |
| 451 | 00 | 0 | |
| 452 | 00 | 0 | |
| 453 | 00 | 0 | |
| 454 | 00 | 0 | |
| 455 | 00 | 0 | |
| 456 | 00 | 0 | |
| 457 | 00 | 0 | |
| 458 | 00 | 0 | |
| 459 | 00 | 0 | |
| 460 | 00 | 0 | |
| 461 | 00 | 0 | |
| 462 | 00 | 0 | |
| 463 | 00 | 0 | |
| 464 | 00 | 0 | |
| 465 | 00 | 0 | |
| 466 | 22 | INV | print or R/S routine |
| 467 | 87 | IFF | |
| 468 | 05 | 05 | |
| 469 | 04 | 04 | |
| 470 | 73 | 73 | |
| 471 | 91 | R/S | |
| 472 | 92 | RTN | |
| 473 | 99 | PRT | |
| 474 | 92 | RTN | |
| 475 | 69 | OP | printer sense routine |
| 476 | 08 | 08 | |
| 477 | 86 | STF | |
| 478 | 05 | 05 | |
| 479 | 92 | RTN | |

## REGISTER ALLOCATIONS FOR TI-59

| register number | contents | register number | contents |
|---|---|---|---|
| 0 | | 40 | |
| 1 | Re } complx arith temp storage | 41 | |
| 2 | Im } complx arith temp storage | 42 | |
| 3 | Re } complx arith temp storage | 43 | |
| 4 | Im } complx arith temp storage | 44 | |
| 5 | | 45 | |
| 6 | xmsn fcn magnitude | 46 | |
| 7 | | 47 | |
| 8 | | 48 | |
| 9 | loop counter | 49 | Re node V sum |
| 10–19 | real immittance storage | 50 | Im node V sum |
| | | 51 | Re branch I |
| | | 52 | Im branch I |
| | | 53 | # of nodes |
| | | 54 | freq increment |
| | | 55 | start freq |
| | | 56 | Im storage index |
| | | 57 | temp store |
| | | 58 | temp store |
| | | 59 | Re storage index |
| 20–29 | imaginary immittance storage | | |
| 30 | | | |
| 31 | | | |
| 32 | | | |
| 33 | | | |
| 34 | | | |
| 35 | | | |
| 36 | | | |
| 37 | | | |
| 38 | | | |
| 39 | | | |
| 40 | | | |

## PROGRAM 1-5 LC - L N A P, LC LADDER NETWORK ANALYSIS PROGRAM.

### Program Description and Equations Used

This program evaluates the frequency response and input impedance of a resistively terminated lossless (LC) ladder network having up to seven branches. The frequency response is provided as magnitude (dB) and phase (degrees, radians, or grads), and the input impedance is provided as real and imaginary parts.

The input impedance is the impedance seen by the voltage generator in the source. It is more common to calculate the input impedance at the input terminals of the lossless ladder network, but this way was not implemented because program steps are not available for the coding to recall the source resistor value and subtract it from the real part of the input impedance. If the program feature of allowing the number of branches to be entered via a user definable key (key "a") is sacrificed, and the number of branches is stored into register E, then the additional coding for calculating the network input impedance can be added to the program by deleting steps 028 and 029 and adding "RCLØ," "-" after step Ø97 (Ø99 before deletions).

The frequency response and input impedance evaluation frequency can be incremented in either a linear manner using an additive increment, or a logarithmic manner using a multiplicative increment. Each branch of the network may contain an inductor (L), a capacitor (C), a series LC network, or a parallel LC network. All element values and interconnection topology are stored, and can be reviewed at any time to check or correct the component values or interconnection.

Because of the available number of HP-67/97 registers, the number of branches cannot exceed seven. The TI-59 can accommodate data for 20 branches. Elements that inhibit signal flow through the network are not allowed, and will cause the program execution to halt displaying "Error." Examples of elements that inhibit signal flow are single shunt resistors or inductors that have zero value, or series capacitors in series branches that have zero value.

The algorithm used by this program is the same as used in Program 1-4 where 1 volt is assumed at the network output, and the required input voltage is calculated. In this program, the branch immittances (impedances or admittances) are purely imaginary, and the branch numbers start with branch #1 instead of branch #0. This changes all indices by +1. The difference is necessary to let the DSZ instruction operation allow the source resistance to be added to branch #1 with minimum coding. The load resistance is combined with the last branch immittance. If the number of branches is odd, the last branch consists of the load resistor alone.

# User Instructions

| LC-LNAP, LC LADDER NETWORK ANALYSIS PROGRAM | | | | |
|---|---|---|---|---|
| load # of branches | linear sweep? | log sweep? | review input data | start analysis |
| load $R_L \uparrow R_S$ | load br C | load br L | load start frequency | load freq increment |

| STEP | INSTRUCTIONS | INPUT DATA/UNITS | KEYS | OUTPUT DATA/UNITS |
|---|---|---|---|---|
| 1 | Load both sides of magnetic card | | | |
| 2 | Load the number of branches in the network | # branches | [f] [A] | |
| 3 | Enter the load and source resistances | $R_L$ | [ENT↑] | |
| | in ohms | $R_S$ | [A] | |
| 4 | Load branch capacitance: | | | |
| | If a parallel tank in a series branch, | | | |
| | or a series tank in a shunt branch, | | | |
| | change the sign of the mantissa in | | | |
| | the capacitor value | $\pm C_{branch}$ | [B] | |
| | | (farads) | | |
| | Start loading network capacitors | | | |
| | (and inductors) from the highest | | | |
| | numbered branch (load resistor end) | | | |
| 5 | Load branch inductance: | | | |
| | If a parallel tank in a series branch, | | | |
| | or a series tank in a shunt branch, | | | |
| | change the sign of the mantissa in | | | |
| | the inductor value | $\pm L_{branch}$ | [C] | |
| | | (henries) | | |
| 6 | Input data review (optional) | | [f] [D] | $R_{load}$ |
| | | | | space |
| | Negative element values indicate series | | | highest branch # |
| | tanks in shunt branches, or parallel | | | $\pm C$ |
| | tanks in series branches | | | $\pm L$ |
| | | | | space |
| | | | | : |
| | | | | $R_{source}$ |
| 7 | Select frequency sweep mode: | | | |
| | a) linear sweep | | [f] [B] | |
| | b) logarithmic sweep | | [f] [C] | |
| 8 | Load start frequency for sweep in hertz | $f_{start}$ | [D] | |

# User Instructions

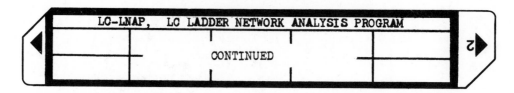

LC-LNAP, LC LADDER NETWORK ANALYSIS PROGRAM

CONTINUED

| STEP | INSTRUCTIONS | INPUT DATA/UNITS | KEYS | OUTPUT DATA/UNITS |
|---|---|---|---|---|
| 9 | Load frequency increment | $f_{incr}$ | [E] | |
| | If linear sweep, the increment is added to the present frequency to obtain the next frequency. | | | |
| | If logarithmic sweep, the increment is multiplied by the present frequency to obtain the next frequency. | | | |
| 10 | Start analysis | | [f] [E] | freq (Hz) |
| | | | | gain (dB) |
| | * The phase units will be in whatever trig mode the calculator is set. The trig mode is at the discretion of the user. | | | phase*( ) |
| | | | | Re $Z_{in}$, Ω |
| | | | | Im $Z_{in}$, Ω |
| | | | | space |
| | | | | ⋮ |
| 11 | Stop analysis: Press R/S when the printer starts to print. | | | |
| | Pressing R/S at other times may leave the registers interchanged. To determine if an interchange has occurred, goto step 6 and review input data. If L and C values are reversed, execute a P⇄S instruction from the keyboard. | | | |

Example 1-5.1

Bartlett's bisection theorem [53], [56], [57] has been applied to an equally terminated (1000 ohm) third order Butterworth bandpass filter with 10 kHz center frequency and 1 kHz bandwidth to produce the unequally terminated LC filter shown in Fig. 1-5.1. The source resistance is 1000 ohms and the load resistance is 10000 ohms. Determine the frequency response and input impedance of this LC network over a frequency range of 9000 Hz to 10900 Hz using a linear sweep with 100 Hz steps.

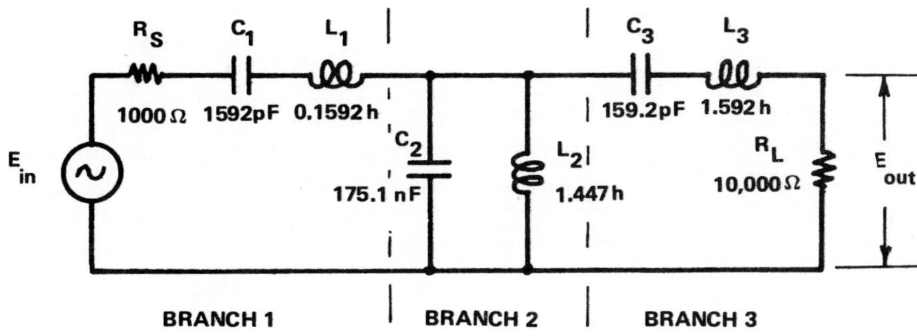


Figure 1-5.2 Network for Example 1-5.1.

| PROGRAM INPUT | | | DATA REVIEW | | |
|---|---|---|---|---|---|
| 3.00 | GSBa | number of branches | | GSBd | start review |
| | | | 10.00+03 | *** | load resistance |
| 10000. | ENT↑ | $R_L$ | | | |
| 1000. | GSBA | $R_S$ | 3.000+00 | *** | branch number |
| | | | 159.2-12 | *** | C |
| 159.2-12 | GSBB | $C_3$ | 1.592+00 | *** | L |
| 1.592 | GSBC | $L_3$ | | | |
| | | | 2.000+00 | *** | branch number |
| .1751-06 | GSBB | $C_2$ | 175.1-09 | *** | C |
| 1.447-03 | GSBC | $L_2$ | 1.447-03 | *** | L |
| 1592.-12 | GSBB | $C_1$ | 1.000+00 | *** | branch number |
| .1592 | GSBC | $L_1$ | 1.592-09 | *** | C |
| | | | 159.2-03 | *** | L |
| | GSBb | linear sweep | 1.000+03 | *** | source resistance |
| 9000.00 | GSBD | start freq, Hz | | | |
| 100.00 | GSBE | freq incr, Hz | | | |

## HP-97 PRINTOUT FOR EXAMPLE 1-5.1

GSBe **start analysis**

### PROGRAM OUTPUT

| freq, Hz | gain, dB | phase, ° | Re $Z_{in}$, Ω | Im $Z_{in}$, Ω |
|---|---|---|---|---|
| 9000.00 | -20.29 | -146.92 | 1003.54 | -1666.97 |
| 9100.00 | -17.44 | -154.43 | 1005.32 | -1391.66 |
| 9200.00 | -14.32 | -164.23 | 1008.28 | -1105.20 |
| 9300.00 | -10.93 | -177.51 | 1013.48 | -801.44 |
| 9400.00 | -7.40 | 163.89 | 1023.10 | -470.17 |
| 9500.00 | -4.14 | 136.09 | 1042.21 | -93.28 |
| 9600.00 | -1.93 | 106.39 | 1083.75 | 364.31 |
| 9700.00 | -1.04 | 74.86 | 1186.21 | 979.39 |
| 9800.00 | -0.85 | 47.27 | 1498.05 | 1951.68 |
| 9900.00 | -0.83 | 22.71 | 2964.18 | 3870.77 |
| 10000.00 | -0.83 | -0.48 | 10994.89 | -227.42 |
| 10100.00 | -0.83 | -23.45 | 2916.29 | -3831.85 |
| 10200.00 | -0.84 | -47.28 | 1504.60 | -1965.91 |
| 10300.00 | -1.01 | -73.45 | 1195.73 | -1020.61 |
| 10400.00 | -1.76 | -102.68 | 1091.62 | -426.27 |
| 10500.00 | -3.58 | -132.20 | 1048.16 | 10.31 |
| 10600.00 | -6.35 | -157.06 | 1027.54 | 363.73 |
| 10700.00 | -9.45 | -175.59 | 1016.80 | 668.16 |
| 10800.00 | -12.47 | 170.95 | 1010.80 | 941.35 |
| 10900.00 | -15.27 | 160.95 | 1007.25 | 1193.23 |

Example 1-5.2

The filter shown in Fig. 1-5.3 is a 5th order, 30° modular angle, 50% reflection coefficient elliptic filter designed for 10 kHz cutoff frequency and 1000 ohm impedance level. This example shows how dummy elements are inserted to place the filter in proper ladder format for this program. The frequency response and input impedance are calculated with the analysis frequency being logarithmically swept from 1 kHz to 100 kHz using 10 points per decade.

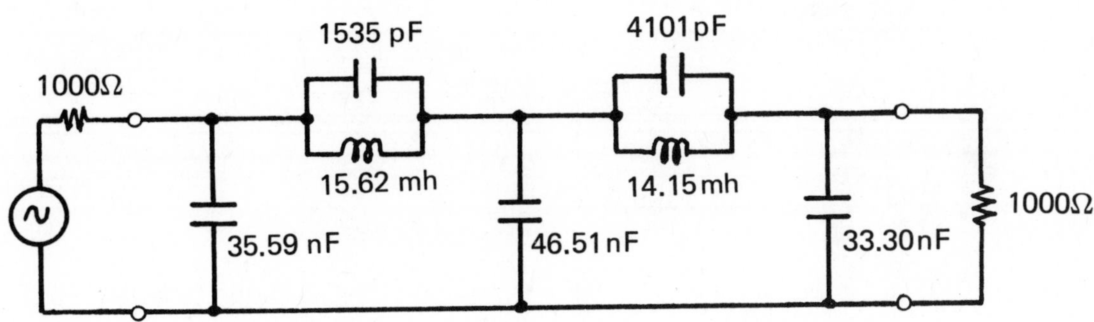


Figure 1-5.3 Elliptic filter for Example 1-5.2.

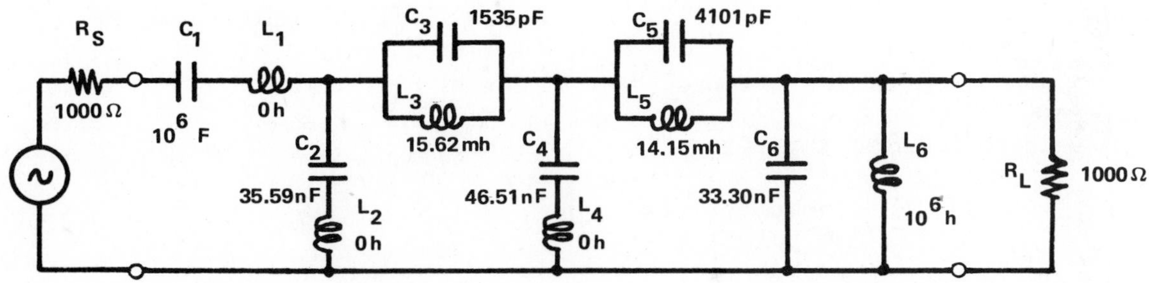


Figure 1-5.4 Network of Fig. 1-5.3 redrawn with dummy elements to place in proper ladder format for program input.

## HP-97 PRINTOUT FOR EXAMPLE 1-5.2

| PROGRAM INPUT | | | DATA REVIEW | | |
|---|---|---|---|---|---|
| 6.00 | GSBa | # of branches | | GSBd | start review |
| | | | 1.000+03 | *** | load resistance |
| 1000. | ENT↑ | enter load R | | | |
| | GSBA | enter source R | 6.000+00 | *** | branch number |
| | | | 33.30-09 | *** | C |
| .03330-06 | GSBB | $C_6$ | 1.000+06 | *** | L |
| 1.+06 | GSBC | $L_6$ (dummy) | | | |
| | | | 5.000+00 | *** | branch number |
| -4101.-12 | GSBB | $C_5$ (note minus) | -4.101-09 | *** | C |
| -14.15-03 | GSBC | $L_5$ " " | -14.15-03 | *** | L |
| -.04651-06 | GSBB | $C_4$ | 4.000+00 | *** | branch number |
| 0. | GSBC | $L_4$ (dummy) | -46.51-09 | *** | C |
| | | | 0.000+00 | *** | L |
| -1535.-12 | GSBB | $C_3$ (note minus) | | | |
| -15.62-03 | GSBC | $L_3$ " " | 3.000+00 | *** | branch number |
| | | | -1.535-09 | *** | C |
| -.03559-06 | GSBB | $C_2$ | -15.62-03 | *** | L |
| 0. | GSBC | $L_2$ (dummy) | | | |
| | | | 2.000+00 | *** | branch number |
| 1.+06 | GSBB | $C_1$ (dummy) | -35.59-09 | *** | C |
| 0. | GSBC | $L_1$ (dummy) | 0.000+00 | *** | L |
| | | | 1.000+00 | *** | branch number |
| | | | 1.000+06 | *** | C |
| | GSBc | log sweep | 0.000+00 | *** | L |
| 1000. | GSBD | start freq | 1.000+03 | *** | source resistance |
| .10 | $10^x$ | increment for | | | |
| | GSBE | 10 points per decade | | | |

## HP-97 PRINTOUT FOR EXAMPLE 1-5.2

```
DSP3   set display format
GSBe   start analysis
```

### PROGRAM OUTPUT

| | | | | |
|---|---|---|---|---|
| 1000.000 | freq, Hz | 3162.278 | 10000.000 | 31622.777 |
| -6.304 | gain, dB | -7.265 | -7.275 | -95.872 |
| -25.492 | phase, ° | -71.409 | 46.462 | 106.137 |
| 1731.945 | Re $Z_{in}$, Ω | 1341.972 | 2425.429 | 1000.000 |
| -354.815 | Im $Z_{in}$, Ω | -144.944 | -1314.534 | -141.760 |
| | | | | |
| 1258.925 | | 3981.072 | 12589.254 | 39810.717 |
| -6.445 | | -7.140 | -29.301 | -80.704 |
| -31.679 | | -87.812 | -34.999 | -77.360 |
| 1641.443 | | 1354.476 | 1001.496 | 1000.000 |
| -367.449 | | -16.643 | -520.507 | -110.753 |
| | | | | |
| 1584.893 | | 5011.872 | 15848.932 | 50118.724 |
| -6.636 | | -6.543 | -48.256 | -77.037 |
| -39.149 | | -111.901 | -53.026 | -80.045 |
| 1545.329 | | 1510.069 | 1000.017 | 1000.000 |
| -354.383 | | 144.638 | -334.325 | -87.088 |
| | | | | |
| 1995.262 | | 6309.573 | 19952.623 | 63095.735 |
| -6.872 | | -6.035 | -75.897 | -76.495 |
| -48.061 | | -151.933 | -62.745 | -82.135 |
| 1455.184 | | 2050.032 | 1000.000 | 1000.000 |
| -312.318 | | -105.785 | -242.424 | -68.745 |
| | | | | |
| 2511.886 | | 7943.282 | 25118.864 | 79432.824 |
| -7.114 | | -7.176 | -76.839 | -77.128 |
| -58.642 | | 154.808 | 110.795 | -83.773 |
| 1383.210 | | 1466.092 | 1000.000 | 1000.000 |
| -242.073 | | -532.050 | -183.485 | -54.393 |
| | | | | |
| | | | | 100000.000 |
| | | | | -78.338 |
| | | | | -85.064 |
| | | | | 1000.000 |
| | | | | -43.101 |

# Program Listing I

| | | | | | | |
|---|---|---|---|---|---|---|
| 001 | *LBLA | LOAD $R_L$↓$R_s$ | 057 | GSB2 | add complex branch currents |
| 002 | STO0 | store $R_s$ | 058 | STOC | store next lower branch |
| 003 | R↓ | | 059 | X⇄Y | current (complex) |
| 004 | P⇄S | | 060 | STOD | |
| 005 | STO0 | store $R_L$ | 061 | DSZI | decrement branch number |
| 006 | P⇄S | | 062 | GSB3 | recall series branch Z |
| 007 | GTO7 | goto space and return | 063 | CLX | |
| 008 | *LBLC | LOAD BRANCH INDUCTANCE | 064 | RCL0 | |
| 009 | CHS | indicate inductance by chs | 065 | CF0 | |
| 010 | P⇄S | | 066 | DSZI | If branch 1, add |
| 011 | GSBB | interchange registers and | 067 | SF0 | source resistance to |
| 012 | P⇄S | goto capacitor load routine | 068 | F0? | branch impedance |
| 013 | DSZI | | 069 | CLX | |
| 014 | RCLI | decrement and recall branch | 070 | ENT↑ | |
| 015 | GTO7 | goto space and return | 071 | RCLD | recall present |
| 016 | *LBLB | LOAD BRANCH CAPACITANCE | 072 | RCLC | branch current |
| 017 | GSB5 | odd/even branch? | 073 | GSB1 | calculate branch voltage |
| 018 | F0? | change sign of entry if | 074 | RCLA | recall next higher |
| 019 | CHS | branch number is odd | 075 | RCLB | branch voltage |
| 020 | STOi | store entry | 076 | GSB2 | add branch voltages |
| 021 | RTN | return control to keyboard | 077 | STOA | |
| 022 | *LBLD | LOAD START FREQUENCY | 078 | X⇄Y | store next lower |
| 023 | STO8 | | 079 | STOB | node voltage |
| 024 | GTO7 | | 080 | F0? | test for loop exit |
| 025 | *LBLE | LOAD FREQUENCY INCREMENT | 081 | GTO9 | |
| 026 | STO9 | | 082 | X⇄Y | |
| 027 | GTO7 | | 083 | →P | convert to magnitude & angle |
| 028 | *LBLα | LOAD NUMBER OF BRANCHES | 084 | LOG | |
| 029 | STOE | | 085 | 2 | |
| 030 | *LBL4 | initialization routine | 086 | 0 | calculate magnitude in dB |
| 031 | EEX | | 087 | x | |
| 032 | STOA | $E_n = 1 + j0$ | 088 | RCL8 | recall present frequency |
| 033 | CLX | | 089 | SF0 | indicate sign change in p/o |
| 034 | STOB | | 090 | GSB0 | gosub printout (p/o) routine |
| 035 | STOC | | 091 | RCLD | |
| 036 | STOD | $I_{2n+1} = 0 + j0$ | 092 | CHS | |
| 037 | RCLE | set index to | 093 | RCLC | recall branch 1 current ($I_0$) |
| 038 | STOI | highest branch number | 094 | →P | and form complex inverse |
| 039 | SF2 | initialize flags | 095 | 1/X | |
| 040 | CF3 | | 096 | →R | |
| 041 | GTO7 | goto space and return | 097 | RCLB | recall node 0 voltage ($E_{in}$) |
| 042 | *LBLb | SELECT LINEAR SWEEP | 098 | RCLA | |
| 043 | CF1 | | 099 | GSB1 | perform complex multiply |
| 044 | GTO7 | | 100 | PRTX | print Re $Z_{in}$ |
| 045 | *LBLc | SELECT LOGARITHMIC SWEEP | 101 | X⇄Y | |
| 046 | SF1 | | 102 | PRTX | print Im $Z_{in}$ |
| 047 | GTO7 | | 103 | RCL9 | recall frequency increment |
| 048 | *LBLe | START ANALYSIS | 104 | F1? | |
| 049 | GSB4 | initialize | 105 | STx8 | multiply present frequency |
| 050 | *LBL9 | analysis loop start | 106 | F1? | by increment if log sweep |
| 051 | GSB3 | recall shunt branch Y | 107 | GTOe | |
| 052 | RCLB | recall complex node voltage | 108 | ST+8 | add increment to present |
| 053 | RCLA | | 109 | GTOe | frequency if linear sweep |
| 054 | GSB1 | calculate shunt branch I | 110 | *LBLd | INPUT DATA REVIEW |
| 055 | RCLC | recall next higher (series) | 111 | GSB4 | initialize registers & flags |
| 056 | RCLD | branch current | 112 | P⇄S | |

| REGISTERS | | | | | | | | | |
|---|---|---|---|---|---|---|---|---|---|
| 0 $R_s$ | 1 $C_1$ | 2 $C_2$ | 3 $C_3$ | 4 $C_4$ | 5 $C_5$ | 6 $C_6$ | 7 $C_7$ | 8 present frequency | 9 freq increment |
| S0 $R_L$ | S1 $L_1$ | S2 $L_2$ | S3 $L_3$ | S4 $L_4$ | S5 $L_5$ | S6 $L_6$ | S7 $L_7$ | S8 cmplx multiply | S9 cmplx multiply |
| A Re $E_k$ | B Im $E_k$ | C Re $I_j$ | D Im $I_j$ | E number of branches | | | | I index | |

# Program Listing II

| | | |
|---|---|---|
| 113 | RCL0 | |
| 114 | P⇄S | |
| 115 | PRTX | |
| 116 | *LBL8 | data review loop start |
| 117 | GSB5 | odd/even branch? |
| 118 | P⇄S | |
| 119 | RCLi | recall branch inductance |
| 120 | P⇄S | |
| 121 | CHS | |
| 122 | RCLi | recall branch capacitance |
| 123 | RCLI | recall branch number |
| 124 | SPC | |
| 125 | GSB0 | gosub printout routine |
| 126 | DSZI | decrement branch number |
| 127 | GTO8 | and exit at branch 0 |
| 128 | RCL0 | |
| 129 | SPC | recall and print |
| 130 | PRTX | source resistance |
| 131 | *LBL7 | space and return subroutine |
| 132 | SPC | |
| 133 | RTN | |
| 134 | *LBL0 | output subroutine |
| 135 | PRTX | print x register contents |
| 136 | GSB0 | print y register contents |
| 137 | *LBL0 | print z register contents |
| 138 | R↓ | |
| 139 | F0? | |
| 140 | CHS | if odd branch, change sign |
| 141 | PRTX | |
| 142 | RTN | return to subroutine call |
| 143 | *LBL1 | complex multiplication $(a+jb)(c+jd) = e+jf$ |
| 144 | P⇄S | |
| 145 | STO8 | a |
| 146 | STO9 | a |
| 147 | R↓ | b |
| 148 | ENT↑ | b |
| 149 | R↓ | b |
| 150 | R↓ | c |
| 151 | STX8 | ac |
| 152 | R↓ | d |
| 153 | STX9 | ad |
| 154 | x | bd |
| 155 | ST-8 | ac − bd = e |
| 156 | R↓ | b |
| 157 | x | bc |
| 158 | ST+9 | ad + bc = f |
| 159 | RCL9 | recall f |
| 160 | RCL8 | recall e |
| 161 | P⇄S | |
| 162 | RTN | return to subroutine call |
| 163 | *LBL2 | complex add: (b↑a↑c↑d) |
| 164 | R↓ | $(a+jb) + (c+jd) = e+jf$ |
| 165 | + | a + c = e |
| 166 | R↓ | |
| 167 | + | b + d = f |
| 168 | R↑ | |

| | | |
|---|---|---|
| 169 | RTN | |
| 170 | *LBL7 | branch immittance recall |
| 171 | GSB5 | odd/even branch? |
| 172 | RCL8 | |
| 173 | Pi | |
| 174 | x | form $\omega = 2\pi f$ present |
| 175 | ENT↑ | |
| 176 | + | |
| 177 | ENT↑ | |
| 178 | ENT↑ | |
| 179 | RCLi | recall $C_i$ |
| 180 | X<0? | |
| 181 | SF3 | set flag 3 if $C_i$ negative |
| 182 | x | form $\omega C_i$ |
| 183 | X<0? | |
| 184 | 1/X | if $C_i$ minus, take reciprocal |
| 185 | X⇄Y | |
| 186 | P⇄S | |
| 187 | RCLi | recall $L_i$ |
| 188 | P⇄S | |
| 189 | x | form $\omega L_i$ |
| 190 | X<0? | if $L_i$ minus, take reciprocal |
| 191 | 1/X | |
| 192 | + | form branch immittance |
| 193 | F0? | if odd branch (exclusive or) |
| 194 | F3? | sign of $C_i$ negative, form |
| 195 | F3? | −1/(immittance) |
| 196 | GSB3 | |
| 197 | F2? | add load resistance if |
| 198 | GTO0 | first time through loop |
| 199 | 0 | |
| 200 | RTN | return to subroutine call |
| 201 | *LBL3 | negative reciprocal routine |
| 202 | 1/X | |
| 203 | CHS | |
| 204 | RTN | |
| 205 | *LBL0 | load resistance addition subroutine |
| 206 | F0? | |
| 207 | 0 | if odd branch, reactive part |
| 208 | P⇄S | does not exist, |
| 209 | RCL0 | recall load resistance and |
| 210 | P⇄S | form load conductance |
| 211 | 1/X | |
| 212 | F0? | if odd branch, increment |
| 213 | ISZI | index register |
| 214 | RTN | return to subroutine call |
| 215 | *LBL5 | odd/even branch subroutine |
| 216 | RCLI | |
| 217 | 2 | form 0 if branch even or |
| 218 | ÷ | 0.5 if branch odd |
| 219 | FRC | |
| 220 | SF0 | |
| 221 | X=0? | set flag 0 if branch odd |
| 222 | CF0 | |
| 223 | R↓ | restore stack x register |
| 224 | RTN | return to subroutine call |

| LABELS | | | | |
|---|---|---|---|---|
| A load $R_L$↑$R_s$ | B load $C_i$ | C load $L_i$ | D load start freq | E load freq incr |
| a # of branches | b linear sweep | c log sweep | d data review | e start analysis |
| 0 multiple uses | 1 complex multiply | 2 complex add | 3 complex recall | 4 initialize |
| 5 odd/even branch | 6 | 7 space & return | 8 input data loop | 9 analysis loop |

| FLAGS | SET STATUS | | |
|---|---|---|---|
| 0 odd br | FLAGS | TRIG | DISP |
| 1 log swp | ON OFF | users choice | |
| 2 first time thru loop | 0 ▪ | DEG | FIX |
| 3 | 1 ▪ | GRAD | SCI |
| | 2 ▪ | RAD | ENG |
| | 3 | | n |

## PROGRAM 1-6 EQUIVALENT INPUT NOISE OF AN AMPLIFIER WITH GENERALIZED INPUT COUPLING NETWORK

Program Description and Equations Used

When low noise amplifiers are designed, the amplifier equivalent current and voltage noise densities (noise in a 1 Hz band), and the coupling network noise sources, response, and impedance behavior must be considered. This program calculates the total noise voltage density that is reflected to the amplifier input which is coupled to a sensor by means of a transformer (Fig. 1-6.1).

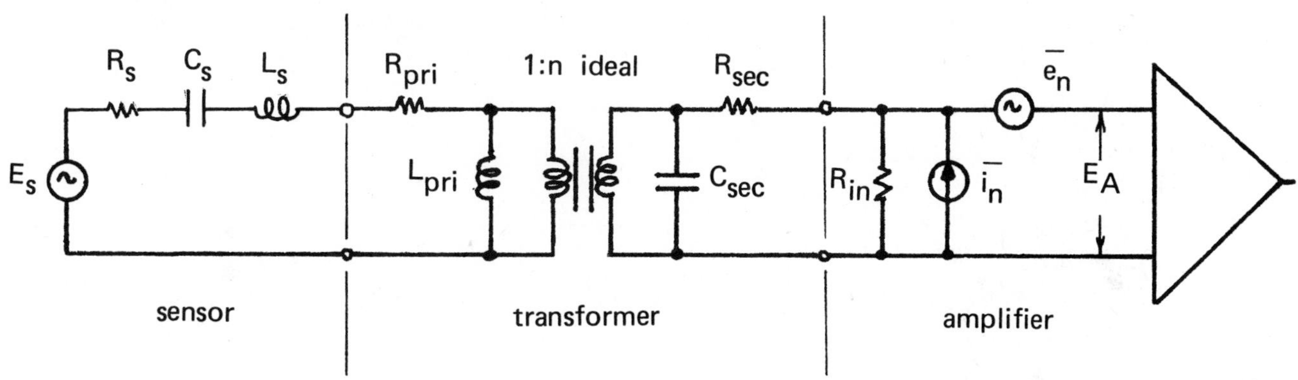


Figure 1-6.1 Generalized input coupling network.

The transformer model includes the turns ratio (1:n), the primary and secondary resistances ($R_{pri}$ and $R_{sec}$), the primary inductance ($L_{pri}$), and the secondary capacitance ($C_{sec}$). The coupling network noise sources include: the thermal noise densities (Johnson noise) of the transformer primary and secondary resistances and of the source resistance, the amplifier equivalent voltage noise density ($\bar{e}_n$), and the equivalent noise voltage density generated by the amplifier current noise density ($\bar{i}_n$) flowing through the coupling network impedance presented to the amplifier input.

The noise voltage density of each noise source is reflected to the amplifier input through the network gain (at the analysis frequency) from the noise source location to the amplifier input. The total noise reflected to the amplifier input is calculated from the root-sum-squared (RSS) values of the individual contributions.

The sensor is represented by a voltage source ($E_s$) and a series LRC network ($L_s$, $R_s$, and $C_s$). The inductance may be set to zero if not needed, and the capacitor may be set to $10^{50}$ farads to remove its contribution. The sensor resistance may be zero if the transformer primary resistance is not zero and vice-versa.

The equivalent circuit can be modified to reflect the transformer secondary capacitance to the primary if desired by deleting steps 059, 060, and 061 in the program. The primary capacitance is now loaded in step 2f of the users' instructions. This modification allows piezoelectric transducer elements to be modeled as the source. $R_{pri}$ is set to zero, and the transformer primary capacitance is used to represent the clamped capacity of the piezoelectric element.

If the transformer is not wanted in the circuit, the turns ratio should be set to one.

The equations are derived using nodal analysis, and the user is referred to the section following Example 1-6.2 for details.

# User Instructions

| AMPLIFIER EQUIVALENT INPUT NOISE | | | | |
|---|---|---|---|---|
| print ? / select dB output | select linear output | enter noise current density | enter noise voltage density | enter frequency & compute |

| STEP | INSTRUCTIONS | INPUT DATA/UNITS | KEYS | OUTPUT DATA/UNITS |
|---|---|---|---|---|
| 1 | Load both sides of the program card | | | |
| 2 | Load network element values | | | |
| | a) sensor resistance, ohms | $R_s$ | STO 0 | |
| | b) sensor capacitance, farads | $C_s$ | STO 1 | |
| | c) sensor inductance, henries | $L_s$ | STO 2 | |
| | d) transformer primary resistance, Ω | $R_{pri}$ | STO 3 | |
| | e) transformer primary inductance, h | $L_{pri}$ | STO 4 | |
| | f) xfmr secondary capacitance, farads | $C_{sec}$ | STO 5 | |
| | g) xfmr secondary resistance, ohms | $R_{sec}$ | STO 6 | |
| | h) amplifier input resistance, ohms | $R_{in}$ | STO 7 | |
| | i) transformer turns ratio | n | STO 8 | |
| 3 | Select output mode | | | |
| | a) for voltages in dBV and network gain in dB | | A | |
| | b) for voltages in volts, and network gain as a voltage ratio | | B | |
| 4 | Select print(1) / run-stop (0) option | | f A | 0,1 |
| 5 | Enter amplifier input noise current density | $\overline{i_n}$, $A/\sqrt{Hz}$ | C | |
| 6 | Enter amplifier input noise voltage density | $\overline{e_n}$, $V/\sqrt{Hz}$ | D | |
| 7 | Enter analysis frequency and compute output | f, Hz | E | gain |
| | | | | space |
| | Note: | | | $\overline{e_1}$ |
| | All noise voltages are reflected | | | $\overline{e_2}$ |
| | to the amplifier input, i.e., the | | | $\overline{e_3}$ |
| | gain of the network from the noise | | | $\overline{e_n}$, amp |
| | voltage source to the amplifier | | | $\overline{i_n * Z}$, amp |
| | input is taken into account. | | | space |
| | | | | RSS noise |
| | | | | space |
| | | | | space |
| 8 | For another case, go back to steps 2 thru 6 as required | | | |

Example 1-6.1

A type 2N4867A low-noise field effect transistor (FET) is to be used as a preamplifier for a piezoelectric hydrophone. A frequency range of 10 Hz to 1000 Hz is to be covered. The hydrophone is operating well below its self-resonant frequency, hence, its equivalent circuit is accurately represented by a 4000 pF capacitor in series with a 10 ohm resistor. To avoid preamplifier overload problems from cable flutter and other subsonic signals, the input resistance of the preamplifier is chosen to provide a 50 Hz low frequency break with the hydrophone capacity. The hydrophone will be coupled to the preamp without using a transformer, therefore a dummy turns ratio of 1:1 will be used in the program. The current and voltage noise densities for the 2N4867A are listed in Table 1-6.1.

Table 1-6.1 Current and voltage noise densities of 2N4867A operating at drain current $I_{dss}$.

| Frequency, Hz | $\bar{i}_n$, noise $A/\sqrt{Hz}$ | $\bar{e}_n$, noise $V/\sqrt{Hz}$ |
|---|---|---|
| 10 | $6 \times 10^{-16}$ | $7.0 \times 10^{-9}$ |
| 20 | $6 \times 10^{-16}$ | $5.3 \times 10^{-9}$ |
| 50 | $6 \times 10^{-16}$ | $4.1 \times 10^{-9}$ |
| 100 | $6 \times 10^{-16}$ | $3.6 \times 10^{-9}$ |
| 200 | $6.1 \times 10^{-16}$ | $3.2 \times 10^{-9}$ |
| 500 | $6.2 \times 10^{-16}$ | $2.8 \times 10^{-9}$ |
| 1000 | $6.3 \times 10^{-16}$ | $2.7 \times 10^{-9}$ |

The HP-97 printout is shown on the next page. Dummy values have been entered for unused components to remove their contribution.

HP-97 PRINTOUT FOR EXAMPLE 1-6.1

PROGRAM INPUT

```
     10.0 ST00  sensor resistance
    4.-09 ST01  sensor capacitance
      0.0 ST02  sensor inductance
      0.0 ST03  primary resistance
    1.+50 ST04  primary inductance
      0.0 ST05  secondary capacitance
      1.0 ST06  secondary resistance
          RCL1  }
     50.0    x  }
            Pi  }  calculate and store
             x  }  amplifier input
      2.0    x  }  resistance for
           1/X  }  50 Hz  breakpoint
 795774.7  ***  }
          ST07  }
      1.0 ST08  n, xfmr turns ratio

          GSBA  select dB/dBV output
```

PROGRAM OUTPUT

```
    6.-16 GSBC  in @ 10 Hz
    7.-09 GSBD  en @ 10 Hz
     10.0 GSBE  frequency

    -14.1  ***  Av, network gain, dB

   -202.1  ***  Rs+Rpri thermal noise, dBV
   -212.1  ***  Rsec  thermal noise, dBV
   -139.1  ***  Rin  thermal noise, dBV
   -163.1  ***  en, transistor
   -186.6  ***  in*Z equiv noise, dBV

   -139.1  ***  total noise (RSS), dBV
```

```
  5.3-09 GSBD  en @ 20 Hz  *
    20.0 GSBE  frequency

    -6.6  ***
                     * in is unchanged
  -196.5  ***          from the previous
  -206.5  ***          entry.
  -139.5  ***
  -165.5  ***
  -187.1  ***

  -139.5  ***  total noise at 20 Hz
```

```
  4.1-09 GSBD  en @ 50 Hz
    50.0 GSBE  frequency

    -3.0  ***

  -190.9  ***
  -200.9  ***
  -141.9  ***
  -167.7  ***
  -189.4  ***

  -141.9  ***  total noise at 50 Hz
```

```
  3.6-09 GSBD  en @ 100 Hz.
   100.0 GSBE  frequency

    -1.0  ***

  -188.9  ***
  -198.9  ***
  -145.9  ***
  -168.9  ***
  -193.4  ***

  -145.9  ***  total noise at 100 Hz
```

```
  6.1-16 GSBC  in @ 200 Hz
  3.2-09 GSBD  en @ 200 Hz
   200.0 GSBE  frequency

    -0.3  ***

  -188.2  ***
  -198.2  ***
  -151.2  ***
  -169.9  ***
  -198.6  ***

  -151.1  ***  total noise at 200 Hz
```

```
  6.2-16 GSBC  in @ 500 Hz
  2.8-09 GSBD  en @ 500 Hz
   500.0 GSBE  frequency

     0.0  ***

  -188.0  ***
  -198.0  ***
  -158.9  ***
  -171.1  ***
  -206.2  ***

  -158.7  ***  total noise at 500 Hz
```

```
  6.3-16 GSBC  in @ 1000 Hz
  2.7-09 GSBD  en @ 1000 Hz
  1000.0 GSBE  frequency

     0.0  ***

  -187.9  ***
  -197.9  ***
  -164.9  ***
  -171.4  ***
  -212.0  ***

  -164.0  ***  total noise at 1000 Hz
```

Example 1-6.1 continued

This example points up one of the problems associated with using the characteristics of the sensor impedance along with the amplifier input resistance to effect frequency shaping. It will be noticed that the dominant source of noise comes from the thermal noise of the input resistor. The low noise characteristics of the input transistor are buried by the input resistor noise contribution.

If the input resistor is made larger, the noise contribution of the input resistor will be less. Although this statement may seem backwards, the logic may be seen by looking at the input resistor and its noise generator as a Norton equivalent source instead of a Thevenin equivalent as is presently used. In this light, one can see that the injected noise current is proportional to $1/\sqrt{R}$. Since other circuit impedances are unchanged, lower injected noise current means lower input resistor noise contribution.

The input resistor noise contribution may also be reduced by lowering the sensor impedance to lower the noise voltage resulting from the input resistor noise current.

To illustrate the above point, the example is rerun using a larger input resistor; 100 megohms is used instead of 796 kilohms. The HP-97 printout for this case is shown on the next page. The noise contribution of the input resistor loses dominance above 500 Hz in this case.

Fortunately, the ocean self noise is greatest at low frequencies, and low noise performance is less critical here.

EXAMPLE 1-6.1 CONTINUED

**PROGRAM INPUT**

```
100.+06 STO7   store new Rin
        PREG   print registers to show
               currently stored values

10.00+00   0   sensor resistance
4.000-09   1   sensor capacitance
0.000+00   2   sensor inductance
0.000+00   3   primary resistance
100.0+48   4   primary inductance
0.000+00   5   secondary capacitance
1.000+00   6   secondary resistance
100.0+06   7   input resistance
1.000+00   8   xfmr turns ratio
```

**PROGRAM OUTPUT**

```
6.-16 GSBC   in @ 10 Hz
7.-09 GSBD   en @ 10 Hz
  10. GSBE   frequency

   0.0  ***  Av, network gain, dB

-187.9  ***  Rs+Rpri thermal noise, dBV
-197.9  ***  Rsec thermal noise, dBV
-145.9  ***  Rin thermal noise, dBV
-163.1  ***  en, transistor, dBV
-172.4  ***  in*Z equiv. noise, dBV

-145.6  ***  total noise (RSS), dBV
```

```
5.3-09 GSBD   en @ 20 Hz  *
  20.0 GSBE   frequency

   0.0  ***
                 *in is unchanged
-187.9  ***       from the last
-197.9  ***       entry.
-151.9  ***
-165.5  ***
-178.5  ***

-151.7  ***  total noise at 20 Hz
```

```
4.1-09 GSBD   en @ 50 Hz
  50.0 GSBE   frequency

   0.0  ***

-187.9  ***
-197.9  ***
-159.9  ***
-167.7  ***
-186.4  ***

-159.2  ***  total noise at 50 Hz
```

```
3.6-09 GSBD   en @ 100 Hz
 100.0 GSBE   frequency

   0.0  ***

-187.9  ***
-197.9  ***
-165.9  ***
-168.9  ***
-192.4  ***

-164.1  ***  total noise at 100 Hz
```

```
6.1-16 GSBC   in @ 200 Hz
3.2-09 GSBD   en @ 200 Hz
 200.0 GSBE   frequency

   0.0  ***

-187.9  ***
-197.9  ***
-171.9  ***
-169.9  ***
-198.3  ***

-167.7  ***  total noise at 200 Hz
```

```
6.2-16 GSBC   in @ 500 Hz
2.8-09 GSBD   en @ 500 Hz
 500.0 GSBE   frequency

   0.0  ***

-187.9  ***
-197.9  ***
-179.9  ***
-171.1  ***
-206.1  ***

-170.4  ***  total noise at 500 Hz
```

```
6.3-16 GSBC   in @ 1000 Hz
2.7-09 GSBD   en @ 1000 Hz
1000.0 GSBE   frequency

   0.0  ***

-187.9  ***
-197.9  ***
-185.9  ***
-171.4  ***
-212.0  ***

-171.1  ***  total noise at 1000 Hz
```

Example 1-6.2

A small hydrophone is to be matched to a low-noise preamplifier for optimum noise performance at 30 kHz. The hydrophone equivalent circuit is shown in Fig. 1-6.2. The amplifier input transistor will be a 2N4867A FET operating at a drain current of $I_{dss}$.

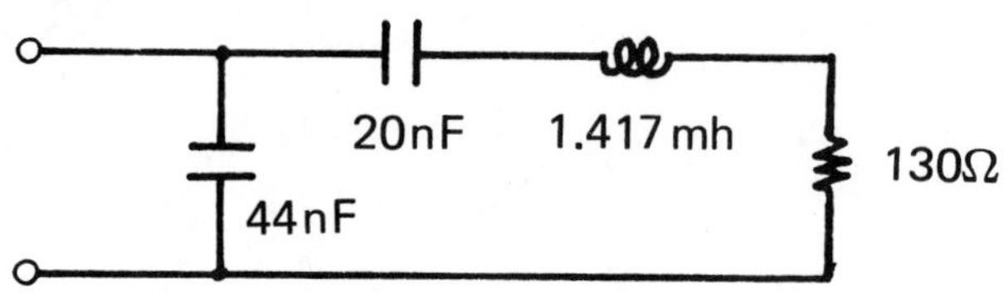


Figure 1-6.2 Hydrophone equivalent circuit.

Table 1-6.2 Current and voltage noise densities of 2N4867A operating at $I_{dss}$.

| Frequency, kHz | $\overline{i_n}$, A/$\sqrt{Hz}$ | $\overline{e_n}$, V/$\sqrt{Hz}$ |
|---|---|---|
| 10 | $8.0 \times 10^{-16}$ | $2.3 \times 10^{-9}$ |
| 15 | $1.0 \times 10^{-15}$ | |
| 20 | $1.2 \times 10^{-15}$ | |
| 25 | $1.4 \times 10^{-15}$ | |
| 30 | $1.6 \times 10^{-15}$ | $2.3 \times 10^{-9}$ |
| 35 | $1.75 \times 10^{-15}$ | $2.2 \times 10^{-9}$ |
| 40 | $1.9 \times 10^{-15}$ | |
| 45 | $2.15 \times 10^{-15}$ | |
| 50 | $2.4 \times 10^{-15}$ | |
| 55 | $2.7 \times 10^{-15}$ | |
| 60 | $3.0 \times 10^{-15}$ | $2.2 \times 10^{-9}$ |

Before the analysis is started, the transformer turns ratio, primary inductance, and amplifier input resistance must be chosen. The transformer ratio should be kept low to minimize the current noise contribution of the input transistor.

The parallel equivalent circuit of the hydrophone at 30 kHz is required. The capacitive part will be resonated by the transformer primary inductance, leaving only the resistive part. Figure 1-6.3 shows the parallel equivalent circuit before resonating, and Fig. 1-6.4 shows the HP-97 calculations used to obtain the parallel equivalent circuit.

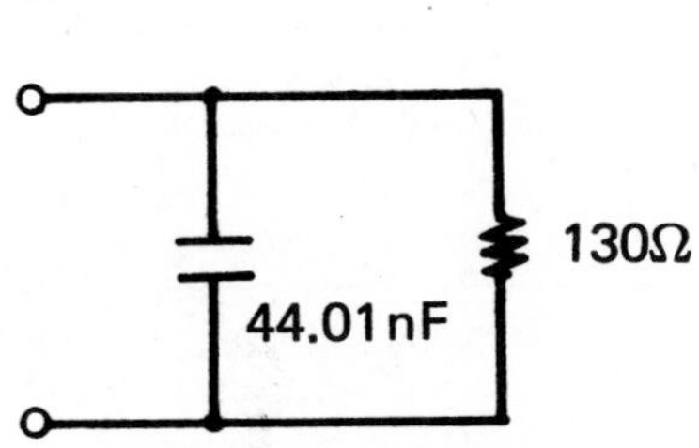


Figure 1-6.3 Parallel equivalent circuit of hydrophone at 30 kHz.

| | | |
|---|---|---|
| 30000. | PI | enter frequency and calculate and store $\omega = 2\pi f \Rightarrow R_E$ |
| | × | |
| 2. | × | |
| | STOE | |
| 1.407-03 | × | form $\omega L$ |
| | RCLE | form $1/(\omega C)$ |
| 20000.-12 | × | |
| | 1/X | |
| | - | form and print |
| -44.99-03 | *** | $\omega L - 1/(\omega C) = \text{Im } Z$ |
| 130. | →P | load Re Z |
| | 1/X | convert impedance to admittance |
| | X⇄Y | |
| | CHS | |
| | X⇄Y | |
| | →R | |
| | 1/X | $\frac{1}{\text{Re } Y}$ in ohms |
| 130.0+00 | *** | |
| | 1/X | Re Y back in mhos |
| | X⇄Y | Im Y |
| 44000.-12 | RCLE | add clamp capacity susceptance |
| | × | |
| | + | |
| | RCLE | convert total susceptance to capacitance & print |
| | ÷ | |
| 44.01-09 | *** | |

Figure 1-6.4 HP-97 printout showing calculations used to find the parallel equivalent circuit at 30 kHz.

The thermal noise of the equivalent parallel resistor in a one Hz band is:

$$\overline{e}_n\ (130\ \Omega) = \sqrt{4KT(130)} = 1.45 \times 10^{-9}\ \text{V}/\sqrt{\text{Hz}}$$

If the transformer raises this noise to 6 dB above the transistor noise, the RSS sum of both resistor and transistor noises will be 1 dB higher than the resistor noise alone. The transformer turns-ratio necessary to meet this condition is:

$$n = \frac{2(2.2 \times 10^{-9})}{1.45 \times 10^{-9}} = 3.03$$

The noise current contribution to the total noise voltage also may be calculated (only Re $Z_{in}$ is used as Im $Z_{in}$ is resonated out):

$$\overline{e_n} = \overline{i_n} \cdot n^2 \cdot |Z_{in}| = (1.6 \times 10^{-15})(10^2)(130) = 20.8 \times 10^{-12}\ \mathrm{V}/\sqrt{\mathrm{Hz}}$$

This contribution is insignificant compared to the voltage noise term, and the transformer ratio may be raised to make the dominant noise source that of the hydrophone resistance only. This will be the best noise performance obtainable.

With a transformer ratio of 10:1, the equivalent hydrophone resistor noise is $1.45 \times 10^{-8}$ V/$\sqrt{\mathrm{Hz}}$ at the transistor input, and the RSS of both the transistor and resistor noises is $1.467 \times 10^{-8}$. This RSS voltage is only 0.1 dB above the resistor noise alone!

To represent the equivalent hydrophone shunt capacity (44.01 nF), the transformer secondary capacitance term, $C_{sec}$ is used. This equivalent secondary capacity is the primary capacity (hydrophone capacity) divided by the square of the turns ratio:

$$C_{sec} = (44.01\ \mathrm{nF})/(10^2) = 440\ \mathrm{pF}$$

The primary inductance is chosen to parallel resonate with the equivalent hydrophone capacity, 44.01 nF, at the design frequency of 30 kHz. This primary inductance is:

$$L_{pri} = 1/((2\pi f)^2 C) = 1/((2\pi 30000)^2 \cdot 44.01 \times 10^{-9})$$

$$L_{pri} = 639.5\ \mu\mathrm{h}$$

The "Q" of the network is $R/(2\pi fL) = 1.078$, which means the approximate bandwidth of the network is 30000/1.078 = 27829 Hz. Additional broadbanding using the shunting effect of an amplifier input resistor is not necessary. This input resistor may be removed altogether as the transformer secondary provides the dc return for the transistor gate connection. The input resistor will be omitted by making its value $10^{50}$ ohms.

The HP-97 printout for this example is shown on the next page, and the equivalent circuit is shown in Fig. 1-6.5.

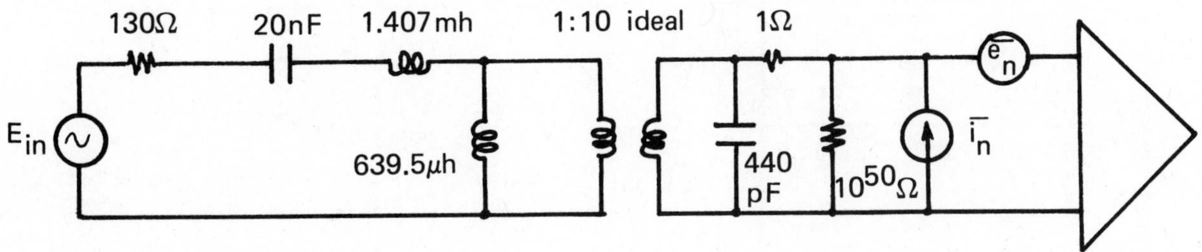


Figure 1-6.5 Equivalent circuit for hydrophone and amplifier.

HP-97 PRINTOUT FOR EXAMPLE 1-6.2

| | |
|---|---|
| 130.0 ST00 | $R_s$ |
| 20000.-12 ST01 | $C_s$ |
| 1.407-03 ST02 | $L_s$ |
| 0.0 ST03 | $R_{pri}$ |
| 639.5-06 ST04 | $L_{pri}$ |
| 440.-12 ST05 | $C_{sec}$ |
| 1.0 ST06 | $R_{sec}$ |
| 1.+50 ST07 | $R_{in}$ |
| 10.0 ST08 | $n_{transformer}$ |
| GSBA | select dB mode for p/c |

PROGRAM OUTPUT

| | |
|---|---|
| 8.-16 GSBC | load $\bar{i}_n$@10kHz |
| 2.3-09 GSBD | load $\bar{e}_n$@ " |
| 10000.0 GSBE | load freq & start |
| -3.5 *** | $A_v$ dB |
| -180.3 *** | |
| -197.9 *** | |
| -624.3 *** | |
| -172.8 *** | |
| -228.3 *** | |
| -172.0 *** | RSS of all noise $\bar{e}$'s, dBV |

| | |
|---|---|
| 1.-15 GSBC | $\bar{i}_n$ @ 15 kHz * |
| 15000.0 GSBE | freq & start (*$\bar{e}_n$ unchged) |
| 7.4 *** | |
| -169.4 *** | |
| -197.9 *** | |
| -618.1 *** | |
| -172.8 *** | |
| -220.2 *** | |
| -167.7 *** | $\bar{e}_n$ tot @ 15kHz |

| | |
|---|---|
| 1.2-15 GSBC | $\bar{i}_n$ @ 20 kHz |
| 20000.0 GSBE | freq & start |
| 19.6 *** | |
| -157.1 *** | |
| -197.9 *** | |
| -610.1 *** | |
| -172.8 *** | |
| -210.6 *** | |
| -157.0 *** | $\bar{e}_n$ tot @ 20kHz |

| | |
|---|---|
| 1.4-15 GSBC | $\bar{i}_n$ @ 25 kHz |
| 25000.0 GSBE | freq & start |
| 21.9 *** | |
| -154.9 *** | |
| -197.9 *** | |
| -611.8 *** | |
| -172.8 *** | |
| -211.0 *** | |
| -154.8 *** | $\bar{e}_n$ tot @ 25kHz |

| | |
|---|---|
| 1.6-15 GSBC | $\bar{i}_n$ @ 30 kHz |
| 30000.0 GSBE | freq & start |
| 20.0 *** | |
| -156.8 *** | |
| -197.9 *** | |
| -615.6 *** | |
| -172.8 *** | |
| -213.6 *** | |
| -156.7 *** | $\bar{e}_n$ tot @ 30kHz |

| | |
|---|---|
| 1.75-15 GSBC | $\bar{i}_n$ @ 35 kHz |
| 2.2-09 GSBD | $e_n$ @ " |
| 35000.0 GSBE | freq & start |
| 21.3 *** | |
| -155.4 *** | |
| -197.9 *** | |
| -612.8 *** | |
| -173.2 *** | |
| -210.1 *** | |
| -155.4 *** | $\bar{e}_n$ tot @ 35kHz |

| | |
|---|---|
| 1.9-15 GSBC | $\bar{i}_n$ @ 40 kHz |
| 40000.0 GSBE | freq & start |
| 23.4 *** | |
| -153.4 *** | |
| -197.9 *** | |
| -608.4 *** | |
| -173.2 *** | |
| -204.9 *** | |
| -153.3 *** | $\bar{e}_n$ tot @ 40kHz |

| | |
|---|---|
| 2.15-15 GSBC | $\bar{i}_n$ @ 45 kHz |
| 45000.0 GSBE | freq & start |
| 19.6 *** | |
| -157.1 *** | |
| -197.9 *** | |
| -610.1 *** | |
| -173.2 *** | |
| -205.5 *** | |
| -157.0 *** | $\bar{e}_n$ tot @ 45kHz |

| | |
|---|---|
| 2.4-15 GSBC | $\bar{i}_n$ @ 50 kHz |
| 50000.0 GSBE | freq & start |
| 14.5 *** | |
| -162.3 *** | |
| -197.9 *** | |
| -613.6 *** | |
| -173.2 *** | |
| -208.1 *** | |
| -162.0 *** | $\bar{e}_n$ tot @ 50kHz |

| | |
|---|---|
| 2.7-15 GSBC | $\bar{i}_n$ @ 55 kHz |
| 55000.0 GSBE | freq & start |
| 10.5 *** | |
| -166.3 *** | |
| -197.9 *** | |
| -616.2 *** | |
| -173.2 *** | |
| -209.6 *** | |
| -165.5 *** | $\bar{e}_n$ tot @ 55kHz |

| | |
|---|---|
| 3.-15 GSBC | $\bar{i}_n$ @ 60 kHz |
| 60000.0 GSBE | freq & start |
| 7.4 *** | |
| -169.4 *** | |
| -197.9 *** | |
| -618.1 *** | |
| -173.2 *** | |
| -210.6 *** | |
| -167.8 *** | $\bar{e}_n$ tot @ 60kHz |

Example 1-6.2 is meant to illustrate both the program functioning and to give some insight on hydrophone matching. The gain versus frequency response has two peaks, which is characteristic of doubly tuned networks.

The whole subject of optimum hydrophone matching is beyond the scope of this program and discussion. Equiripple passband response and optimum noise performance may be simultaneously obtained with higher order matching networks which represent bandpass filter like structures and include the hydrophone equivalent circuit in the filter structure. Typical broadbanding networks are fifth order and have Chebyshev responses. These networks are an extension of the work of Fano [23] and Matthaei [37].

## Derivation of Equations Used

The network shown in Fig. 1-6.1 is redrawn with the components on the secondary side of the transformer reflected to the primary side, and the thermal noise sources of the resistors added. This new network is shown in Fig. 1-6.6.

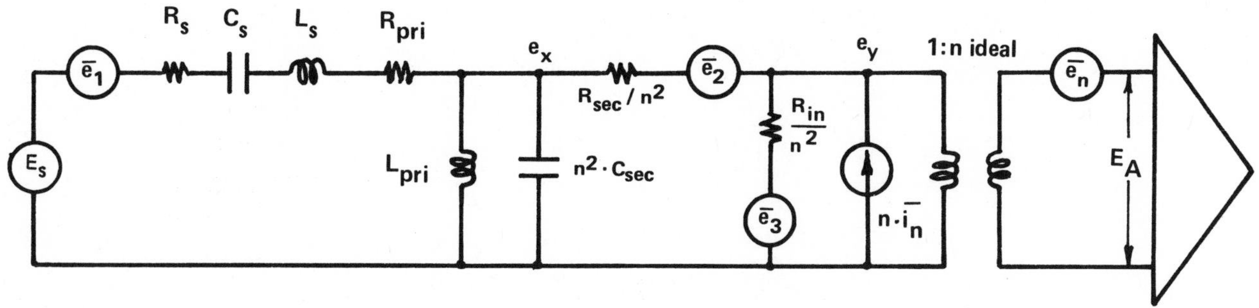


Fig. 1-6.6 Network of Fig. 1-6.1 redrawn with the transformer moved to the right side.

The network of Fig. 1-6.6 is shown in Fig. 1-6.7 with the individual element groups replaced by generalized admittance blocks. The noise voltage densities of the noise generators are defined by Eqs. (1-6.1) through (1-6.3), and the admittance blocks are defined by Eqs. (1-6.4) through (1-6.7).

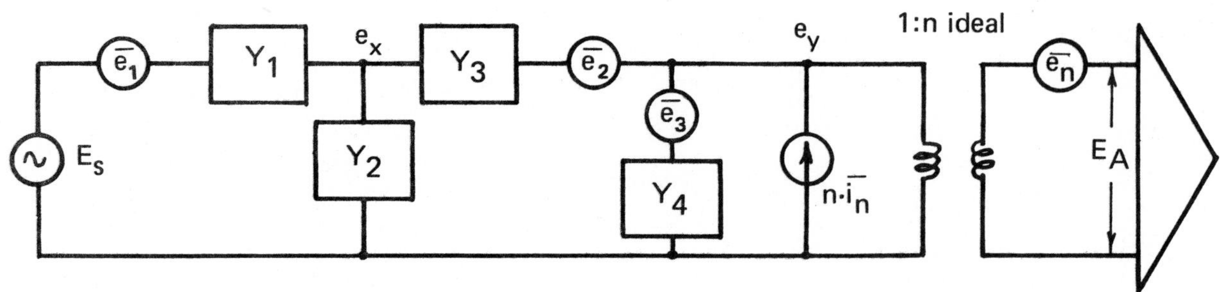


Figure 1-6.7 Network of Fig. 1-6.6 redrawn with generalized admittance blocks.

$$\bar{e}_1 = \sqrt{4KT(R_s + R_{pri})} \qquad (1\text{-}6.1)$$

$$\bar{e}_2 = (1/n)\sqrt{4KTR_{sec}} \qquad (1\text{-}6.2)$$

$$\bar{e}_3 = (1/n)\sqrt{4KTR_{in}} \qquad (1\text{-}6.3)$$

$$Y_1 = \frac{1}{R_s + R_{pri} + sL_s + 1/(sC_s)} = \frac{1}{R_s + R_{pri} + j(\omega L_s - 1/(\omega C_s))} \qquad (1\text{-}6.4)$$

$$Y_2 = s(n^2 \cdot C_{sec}) + 1/(sL_{pri}) = j(n^2\omega C_{sec} - 1/(\omega L_{pri})) \qquad (1\text{-}6.5)$$

$$Y_3 = n^2/R_{sec} \qquad s = j\omega \qquad (1\text{-}6.6)$$

$$Y_4 = n^2/R_{in}$$

Where K is Boltzmann's constant ($1.380 \times 10^{-23}$ Joules/K), and T is the temperature in Kelvin (290 K at room temperature).

The nodal equations are written from Fig. 1-6.7:

$$\begin{bmatrix} (Y_1 + Y_2 + Y_3) & (-Y_3) \\ (-Y_3) & (Y_3 + Y_4) \end{bmatrix} \cdot \begin{bmatrix} e_x \\ e_y \end{bmatrix} = \begin{bmatrix} Y_1(\bar{e}_1 + e_s) - Y_3\bar{e}_2 \\ Y_3\bar{e}_2 + Y_4\bar{e}_3 + n \cdot \bar{i}_n \end{bmatrix} \qquad (1\text{-}6.8)$$

The variable, $e_y$, is obtained using Cramer's rule. The determinant of the coefficient matrix is designated $\Delta$.

$$\Delta = (Y_1 + Y_2 + Y_3)(Y_3 + Y_4) - Y_3^2$$

which upon rearranging yields:

$$\Delta = (Y_1 + Y_2 + Y_3)(Y_4) + (Y_1 + Y_2)\ (Y_3) \tag{1-6.9}$$

Substituting the constant matrix (right hand side) into the second column of the coefficient matrix, and evaluating the determinant yields the following:

$$n\cdot e_y = (n/\Delta)\left[(Y_1+Y_2+Y_3)(Y_3\bar{e}_2+Y_4\bar{e}_3+n\cdot\bar{i}_n)+(Y_1Y_3)(\bar{e}_1+E_s)-(Y_3{}^2)(\bar{e}_2)\right] \tag{1-6.10}$$

Simplifying and removing term subtraction yields:

$$n\cdot e_y = (n/\Delta)\left[(Y_1+Y_2+Y_3)(Y_4\bar{e}_3+n\cdot\bar{i}_n)+(Y_1Y_3)(\bar{e}_1+E_s)+(Y_1-Y_2)(Y_3\bar{e}_2)\right] \tag{1-6.11}$$

The voltage gain of the network is: $n\dfrac{\partial e_y}{\partial E_s} = \dfrac{\partial e_A}{\partial E_s} = A_v$, or: (1-6.12)

$$A_v = (nY_1Y_3)/(\Delta), \tag{1-6.13}$$

In terms of magnitude only:

$$A_v = n\cdot|Y_1|\cdot|Y_3|/|\Delta| \tag{1-6.14}$$

Since the noise voltages $\bar{e}_2$, $\bar{e}_3$, and $\bar{e}_n$, and the current $\bar{i}_n$ are random in nature, their addition must be done in RSS fashion to obtain the overall RMS noise voltage at the amplifier input, $e_A$, i.e.,

$$\bar{e}_A{}^2 = \bar{e}_n{}^2 + n^2\cdot\bar{e}_y{}^2 \tag{1-6.15}$$

Upon expanding:

$$\bar{e}_A{}^2 = \bar{e}_n{}^2 + \frac{n^2}{|\Delta|^2}\left(|Y_1+Y_2+Y_3|^2\cdot(\bar{e}_3{}^2|Y_4|^2+n^2\bar{i}_n{}^2) + |Y_1Y_3|^2\cdot\bar{e}_1{}^2+|Y_1+Y_2|^2Y_3^2\,\bar{e}_2{}^2\right) \tag{1-6.16}$$

This program uses Eqs. (1-6.14) and (1-6.16) to calculate the overall noise voltage density.

# Program Listing I

| | | |
|---|---|---|
| 001 | *LBLA | SELECT OUTPUT IN dB & dBV |
| 002 | CF1 | |
| 003 | RTN | |
| 004 | *LBLB | SELECT OUTPUT IN RATIO |
| 005 | SF1 | AND VOLTS |
| 006 | RTN | |
| 007 | *LBLC | LOAD AMPLIFIER INPUT CURRENT |
| 008 | P⇄S | NOISE DENSITY IN $A/\sqrt{Hz}$ |
| 009 | F3? | if numeric entry, jump to |
| 010 | GTO0 | storage routine |
| 011 | RCL0 | recall presently stored value |
| 012 | P⇄S | jump to print and space |
| 013 | GTO2 | routine |
| 014 | *LBL0 | store entered value of $\overline{I}_n$, |
| 015 | ST00 | and return control to |
| 016 | P⇄S | keyboard |
| 017 | RTN | |
| 018 | *LBLD | LOAD AMPLIFIER INPUT VOLTAGE |
| 019 | F3? | NOISE DENSITY IN $V/\sqrt{Hz}$ |
| 020 | GTO0 | if numeric entry, jump |
| 021 | RCL9 | recall presently stored value |
| 022 | *LBL2 | print and space routine |
| 023 | PRTX | |
| 024 | SPC | |
| 025 | RTN | return control to keyboard |
| 026 | *LBL0 | store entered value of $\overline{e}_n$ |
| 027 | ST09 | |
| 028 | RTN | return control to keyboard |
| 029 | *LBLE | LOAD ANALYSIS FREQ & START |
| 030 | F3? | if numeric entry, store it |
| 031 | STOI | |
| 032 | RCLI | recall present stored freq |
| 033 | GSB3 | if flag 0, space |
| 034 | ENT↑ | |
| 035 | + | form and store $\omega = 2\pi f$ |
| 036 | Pi | |
| 037 | x | |
| 038 | STOE | |
| 039 | RCL2 | form $\omega L_{sens}$ |
| 040 | x | |
| 041 | RCLE | |
| 042 | RCL1 | form $1/(\omega C_{sens})$ |
| 043 | x | |
| 044 | 1/X | |
| 045 | − | $Im\ Z_1 = \omega L_s - 1/(\omega C_s)$ |
| 046 | RCL0 | |
| 047 | RCL3 | $Re\ Z_1 = R_s + R_{pri}$ |
| 048 | + | |
| 049 | →P | convert rectangular to polar |
| 050 | 1/X | form and store $|Y_1|$ |
| 051 | STOD | |
| 052 | X⇄Y | finish complex inverse, |
| 053 | CHS | and return output in |
| 054 | X⇄Y | rectangular co-ordinates |
| 055 | →R | |

| | | |
|---|---|---|
| 056 | STOA | store $Re(Y_1 + Y_2)$ $Re\ Y_2$ |
| 057 | X⇄Y | calculate and store |
| 058 | RCL5 | $Im(Y_1 + Y_2)$: |
| 059 | RCL8 | |
| 060 | X² | calculate $n^2 \omega C_{sec}$ |
| 061 | x | |
| 062 | RCLE | |
| 063 | x | |
| 064 | + | |
| 065 | RCLE | calculate $1/(\omega L_{pri})$ |
| 066 | RCL4 | |
| 067 | x | |
| 068 | 1/X | |
| 069 | − | form and store $Im(Y_1 + Y_2)$ |
| 070 | STOB | |
| 071 | RCLA | take $Y_1 + Y_2$ to polar |
| 072 | →P | |
| 073 | RCL8 | calculate and store: |
| 074 | X² | $Y_3 = n^2/R_{sec}$ |
| 075 | RCL6 | |
| 076 | ÷ | |
| 077 | STOC | |
| 078 | x | form and store $|Y_3| \cdot |Y_1 + Y_2|$ |
| 079 | P⇄S | |
| 080 | STO2 | |
| 081 | P⇄S | |
| 082 | RCLB | $Im(Y_1+Y_2+Y_3)$ $Im(Y_1+Y_2)$ |
| 083 | RCLA | calculate $Re(Y_1+Y_2+Y_3)$ |
| 084 | RCLC | |
| 085 | + | |
| 086 | →P | form and store $Y_1+Y_2+Y_3$ |
| 087 | STOE | |
| 088 | RCL8 | form $|Y_4| \cdot |Y_1+Y_2+Y_3|$ |
| 089 | X² | |
| 090 | x | |
| 091 | RCL7 | |
| 092 | ÷ | |
| 093 | →R | form Re&Im $(Y_4(Y_1+Y_2+Y_3))$ |
| 094 | RCLA | form $Re(Y_3(Y_1+Y_2))$ |
| 095 | RCLC | |
| 096 | x | |
| 097 | + | form $Re\ \Delta$ |
| 098 | X⇄Y | form $Im(Y_3(Y_1+Y_2))$ |
| 099 | RCLB | |
| 100 | RCLC | |
| 101 | x | |
| 102 | + | form $Im\ \Delta$ |
| 103 | →P | form $|\Delta|$ |
| 104 | RCL8 | form and store $n/|\Delta|$ |
| 105 | ÷ | |
| 106 | 1/X | |
| 107 | STOA | |
| 108 | RCLD | form $|Y_1 Y_3|$ |
| 109 | RCLC | |
| 110 | x | |

| REGISTERS | | | | | | | | | |
|---|---|---|---|---|---|---|---|---|---|
| $^0 R_s$ | $^1 C_s$ | $^2 L_s$ | $^3 R_{pri}$ | $^4 L_{pri}$ | $^5 C_{sec}$ | $^6 R_{sec}$ | $^7 R_{in}$ | $^8$ n | $^9 \overline{e}_{n_{amp}}$ |
| $^{S0} \overline{I}_{n_{amp}}$ | $^{S1} \sum v^2$ | $^{S2} |Y_3(Y_1+Y_2)|$ | S3 | S4 | S5 | S6 | S7 | S8 | S9 |
| $^A Re\ Y_1$ , $\dfrac{n}{|\Delta|}$ | | $^B Im(Y_1+Y_2)$, 4KT | | $^C |Y_3|$ , $|Y_1 Y_3|$ | | $^D |Y_1|$ , $|A_v|$ | | $^E 2\pi f$, $|Y_1+Y_2+Y_3|$ | $^I f$, the freq for analysis |

# Program Listing II

| Step | Key | Comment |
|---|---|---|
| 111 | STOC | calculate and store: |
| 112 | × | $\lvert A_v \rvert = n \cdot \lvert Y_1 Y_3 \rvert / \lvert \Delta \rvert$ |
| 113 | STOD | |
| 114 | GSB1 | print $A_v$ or $20 \cdot \log A_v$ |
| 115 | 0 | initialize $\Sigma V^2$ register |
| 116 | P⇄S | |
| 117 | STO1 | |
| 118 | P⇄S | |
| 119 | GSB3 | space if flag 0 is set |
| 120 | 1 | form and store 4KT |
| 121 | . | |
| 122 | 6 | |
| 123 | 1 | |
| 124 | 7 | |
| 125 | 3 | |
| 126 | 6 | |
| 127 | EEX | |
| 128 | CHS | |
| 129 | 2 | |
| 130 | 0 | |
| 131 | STOB | |
| 132 | RCL0 | calculate and output: |
| 133 | RCL3 | $A_v \cdot \sqrt{4KT(R_s + R_{pri})}$ |
| 134 | + | which is the transformer |
| 135 | × | primary resistance and |
| 136 | √X | sensor resistance thermal |
| 137 | RCLD | voltage noise density |
| 138 | × | |
| 139 | GSB1 | |
| 140 | RCLB | calculate and output: |
| 141 | RCL6 | $\lvert Y_3(Y_1+Y_2)/\Delta \rvert \cdot \sqrt{4KTR_{sec}}$ |
| 142 | × | which is the transformer |
| 143 | √X | secondary resistance thermal |
| 144 | RCL8 | voltage noise density |
| 145 | ÷ | |
| 146 | P⇄S | |
| 147 | RCL2 | |
| 148 | P⇄S | |
| 149 | × | |
| 150 | RCLA | |
| 151 | × | |
| 152 | GSB1 | |
| 153 | RCLB | calculate and output: |
| 154 | RCL7 | |
| 155 | ÷ | $\frac{n}{\lvert \Delta \rvert} \cdot \lvert Y_4(Y_1+Y_2+Y_3) \rvert \cdot \sqrt{4KTR_{in}}$ |
| 156 | √X | which is the thermal noise |
| 157 | RCL8 | voltage density due to the |
| 158 | × | amplifier input resistance |
| 159 | RCLA | |
| 160 | RCLE | |
| 161 | × | |
| 162 | STOE | |
| 163 | × | |
| 164 | GSB1 | |
| 165 | RCL9 | recall and output the amplifier noise voltage dens |
| 166 | GSB1 | |
| 167 | P⇄S | calculate and output the |
| 168 | RCL0 | voltage noise density |
| 169 | P⇄S | caused by the amplifier |
| 170 | RCL8 | input current noise density |
| 171 | × | acting on the equivalent |
| 172 | RCLE | circuit impedance |
| 173 | × | |
| 174 | GSB1 | |
| 175 | GSB3 | space if flag 0 is set |
| 176 | P⇄S | |
| 177 | RCL1 | recall and output the RSS |
| 178 | P⇄S | of all the above noise |
| 179 | √X | voltage densities |
| 180 | GSB1 | $(\sqrt{\Sigma V^2})$ |
| 181 | GSB3 | |
| 182 | GTO3 | |
| 183 | *LBL1 | output subroutine: |
| 184 | X² | store $\Sigma V^2$ |
| 185 | P⇄S | |
| 186 | ST+1 | |
| 187 | P⇄S | |
| 188 | LSTX | recall V |
| 189 | F1? | if flag 1, output voltage |
| 190 | GTO1 | in engineering format (→ 199) |
| 191 | FIX | flag 1 is cleared: output |
| 192 | DSP1 | 20 log V in fix 1 format |
| 193 | LOG | |
| 194 | 2 | |
| 195 | 0 | |
| 196 | × | |
| 197 | RND | |
| 198 | GTO2 | (→ 202) |
| 199 | *LBL1 | |
| 200 | ENG | |
| 201 | DSP3 | |
| 202 | *LBL2 | print-R/S subroutine |
| 203 | F0? | |
| 204 | PRTX | |
| 205 | F0? | |
| 206 | RTN | |
| 207 | R/S | |
| 208 | RTN | |
| 209 | *LBL3 | space if flag 0 subroutine |
| 210 | F0? | |
| 211 | SPC | |
| 212 | RTN | |
| 213 | *LBLa | print - R/S toggle |
| 214 | CF0 | |
| 215 | 0 | a "0" displayed indicates |
| 216 | RTN | R/S mode selected |
| 217 | *LBLa | |
| 218 | SF0 | |
| 219 | 1 | a "1" displayed indicates |
| 220 | RTN | print mode selected |

**LABELS**

| | | | | |
|---|---|---|---|---|
| A select dB | B select linear | C load $\bar{i}_n$ | D load $\bar{e}_n$ | E input freq & go |
| a | b | c | d | e |
| 0 local lbl | 1 output | 2 print R/S | 3 spc if F0 | 4 |
| 5 | 6 | 7 | 8 | 9 |

**FLAGS**

| | |
|---|---|
| 0 | R/S, prt |
| 1 | dB/ linear |
| 2 | |
| 3 | data entry |

**SET STATUS**

| FLAGS | ON | OFF | TRIG | DISP |
|---|---|---|---|---|
| 0 | ■ | | DEG ■ | FIX |
| 1 | | ■ | GRAD | SCI |
| 2 | | | RAD | ENG |
| 3 | | | | n ____ |

# Part 2
# FILTER DESIGN

## PROGRAM 2-1 BUTTERWORTH AND CHEBYSHEV FILTER ORDER CALCULATION.

Program Description and Equations Used

This program calculates the minimum filter order required to meet specifications for maximum passband attenuation ($Ap_{dB}$) and minimum stopband attenuation ($As_{dB}$) for the Butterworth or Chebyshev filter approximations. A second part of the program calculates the stopband-to-passband frequency ratio, $\lambda$, if the filter order and type are given. Furthermore, a third part of the program predicts the stopband attenuation if n, $\lambda$, $Ap_{dB}$, and the filter order are provided.

Figures 2-1.1 and 2-1.2 are nomographs adapted from Kawakami [34], and can prove useful to rough out the problem and provide tradeoffs. Once the desired parameters have been estimated, this program may be used to fine-tune the results.

Equation (2.1.1) is the analytic expression for the Butterworth amplitude response characteristic.

$$A_s^2 - 1 = (A_p^2 - 1)\, \lambda^{2n} \qquad (2\text{-}1.1)$$

where

$$A_s^2 = 10^{0.1 As_{dB}} \qquad (2\text{-}1.2)$$

and

$$A_p^2 = 10^{0.1 Ap_{dB}} \qquad (2\text{-}1.3)$$

The quantities $A_s$ and $A_p$ are ratios greater than one (it is the convention to express attenuation as positive decibels).

Equations (2-1.1), (2-1.2), and (2-1.3) can be used to find expressions for $As_{dB}$, $\lambda$, or n:

$$As_{dB} = 10 \cdot \log \left[ (A_p^{\,2} - 1)\, \lambda^{2n} + 1 \right] \tag{2.1-4}$$

$$\lambda = \left[ \frac{A_s^{\,2} - 1}{A_p^{\,2} - 1} \right]^{\frac{1}{2n}} = \left[ \sqrt{\frac{A_s^{\,2} - 1}{A_p^{\,2} - 1}} \right]^{\frac{1}{n}} \tag{2-1.5}$$

$$n = \frac{\ln \sqrt{\dfrac{A_s^{\,2} - 1}{A_p^{\,2} - 1}}}{\ln \lambda} \tag{2-1.6}$$

Equation (2-1.7) is the analytic expression for the Chebyshev amplitude characteristic where $A_s^2$ and $A_p^2$ are defined by Eqs. (2-1.2) and (2-1.3). Equation (2-1.7) can also yield expressions for $As_{dB}$, $\lambda$, or n:

$$A_s^{\,2} - 1 = (A_p^{\,2} - 1)\left[\cosh\,(n \cosh^{-1} \lambda)\right]^2 \tag{2-1.7}$$

$$As_{dB} = 10 \cdot \log \left[ (A_p^{\,2} - 1)(\cosh\,(n \cdot \cosh^{-1} \lambda)^2 + 1 \right]^2 \tag{2-1.8}$$

$$\lambda = \cosh \left( \frac{1}{n} \cosh^{-1} \sqrt{\frac{A_s^{\,2} - 1}{A_p^{\,2} - 1}} \right) \tag{2-1.9}$$

$$n = \frac{\cosh^{-1} \sqrt{\dfrac{A_s^{\,2} - 1}{A_p^{\,2} - 1}}}{\cosh^{-1} \lambda} \tag{2-1.10}$$

A certain degree of similarity can be noticed between the Butterworth and Chebyshev equations. Keeping in mind that ln and exp are complementary operations as are cosh and $\cosh^{-1}$, and noticing that $y^x$ can be expressed as exp $(x \cdot \ln y)$, then replacing ln with cosh and exp with $\cosh^{-1}$ will convert the Butterworth formulas to the Chebyshev formulas. This technique is used by this program where flag 1 indicates the function to be used (set for Butterworth).

A separate subprogram is also included to aid in the specification of bandpass or bandstop filters. The characteristics of these filters are symmetrical when plotted on logarithmic frequency scales (log paper). This characteristic implies geometric symmetry of the various defining frequencies (-3dB, etc.) about the filter center frequency, i.e., the center frequency is the square root of the product of similar response frequencies located above and below the center frequency.

To use the bandstop and bandpass programs in this section, the filter center frequency ($f_o$) and bandwidth (BW) are needed, however, when specifying the filter initially, the bandedge frequencies may be of greater interest. The separate subprogram provides the conversion between center frequency and bandwidth, and upper and lower bandedge frequencies ($f_{upr}$ and $f_{lwr}$), and vice-versa. The definition of "bandedge frequencies" in the present context means a pair of frequencies (one on either side of the center frequency) where the filter attenuation is the same, i.e., -0.01 dB, -3 dB, -60 dB, etc.

To convert from center frequency and bandwidth to upper and lower bandedge frequencies, Eqs. (2-1.11) and (2-1.12) apply.

$$f_{upr} = (BW/2) + \sqrt{(BW/2)^2 + f_o^{\,2}} \tag{2-1.11}$$

$$f_{lwr} = (f_o^{\,2})/f_{upr} \tag{2-1.12}$$

To do the reverse conversion, i.e., to go from upper and lower bandedge frequencies to center frequency and bandwidth, Eqs. (2-1.13) and (2-1.14) apply.

$$f_o = \sqrt{(f_{upr})(f_{lwr})} \tag{2-1.13}$$

$$BW = f_{upr} - f_{lwr} \tag{2-1.14}$$

In the case of a bandpass or bandstop filter, the stopband-to-passband frequency ratio, λ, still holds. The user should remember to use <u>bandwidths</u>, and not bandedge frequencies. This is an easy trap to fall into since bandedge frequencies and bandwidths can be one and the same for lowpass filters.

# User Instructions

| BUTTERWORTH AND CHEBYSHEV FILTER ORDER CALCULATION | | | | |
|---|---|---|---|---|
| Butter-worth | Chebyshev | print, R/S | BW↑$f_o$ → $f_{upr}$, $f_{lwr}$ | $f_{upr}$↑$f_{lwr}$ → $f_o$, BW |
| $Ap_{dB}$ | $As_{dB}$ | n→λ | λ→n | λ→ $As_{dB}$ |

| STEP | INSTRUCTIONS | INPUT DATA/UNITS | KEYS | OUTPUT DATA/UNITS |
|---|---|---|---|---|
| 1 | Load program card (either side) | | | |
| 2 | Select print (HP-97), or R/S (HP-67) option | | f C | 1 (print) |
| | | | f C | 0 (R/S) |
| | | | f C | 1 |
| | | | | ⋮ |
| 3 | Select filter type: | | | |
| | Butterworth | | f A | |
| | Chebyshev | | f B | |
| 4 | Load the maximum passband attenuation in dB | $Ap_{dB}$ | A | |
| 5 | Load the minimum stopband attenuation in dB | $As_{dB}$ | B | |
| 6 | To find filter order, n, given the frequency ratio, λ, load λ | λ | D | n |
| 7 | To find the frequency ratio, λ, given the filter order, n: load n (n must be integer) | n | C | λ |
| 8 | After finding n, to find As (dB) given λ | | | |
| | a) perform step 7 to store n | | | |
| | b) load λ | λ | E | $As_{dB}$ |
| | Step 8b may be repeated with other values of λ without having to repeat step 8a. | | | |
| 9 | A separate program section to aid with bandpass filter selection, enter bandwidth and center frequency and calculate the upper and lower bandedge frequencies, or vice-versa | | | |
| | load bandwidth (for any dB down points) | BW, Hz | ENT↑ | |
| | load center frequency | $f_o$, Hz | f D | $f_{upr}$, Hz |
| | | | | $f_{lwr}$, Hz |
| | load upper bandedge frequency | $f_{upr}$, Hz | ENT | |
| | load lower bandedge frequency | $f_{lwr}$, Hz | f E | $f_o$, Hz |
| | | | | BW, Hz |

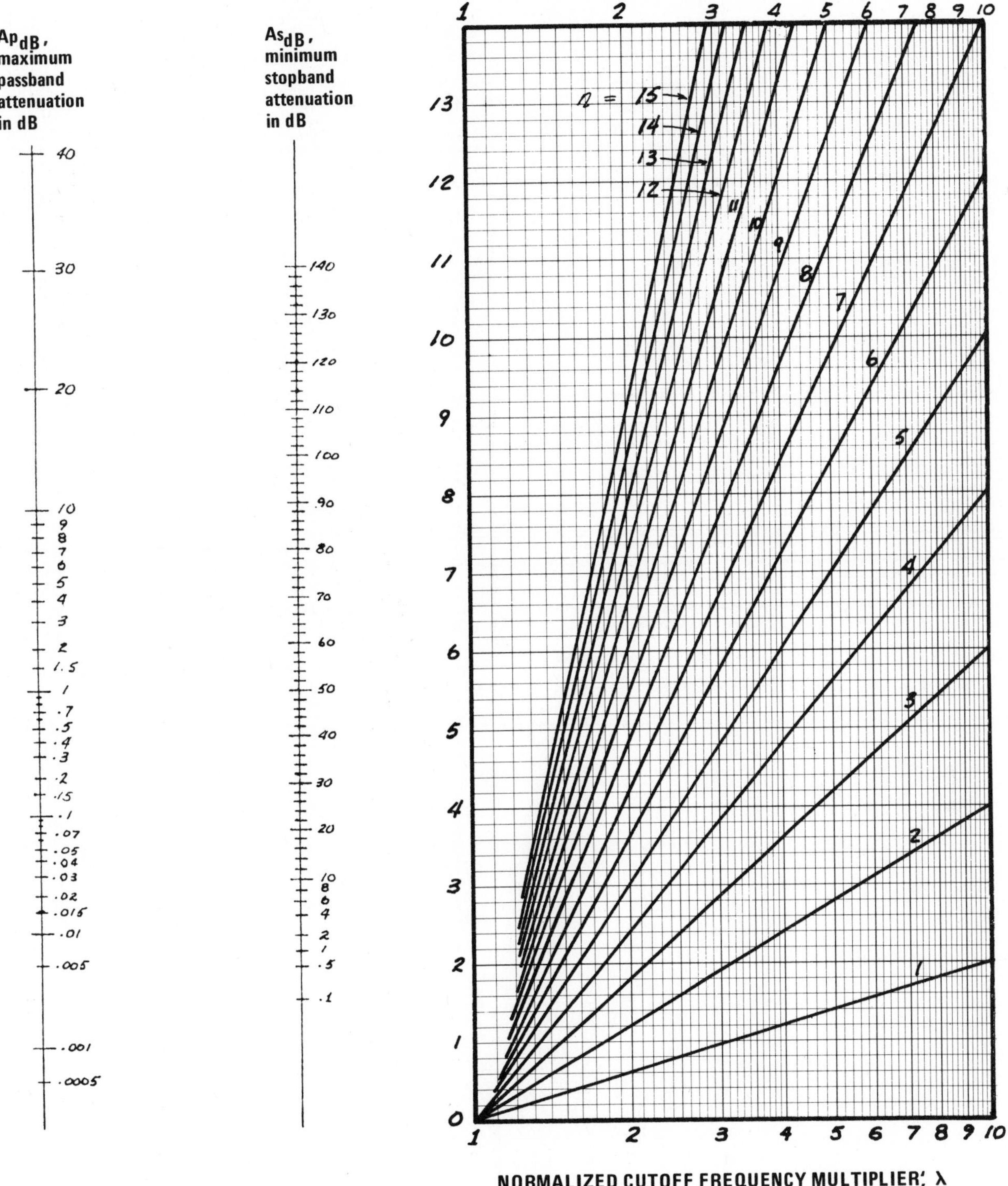


**Figure 2-1.1 Butterworth filter nomograph.**

$$A_s^2 - 1 = (A_p^2 - 1)\lambda^{2n}.$$

Adapted from Kawakami [34]

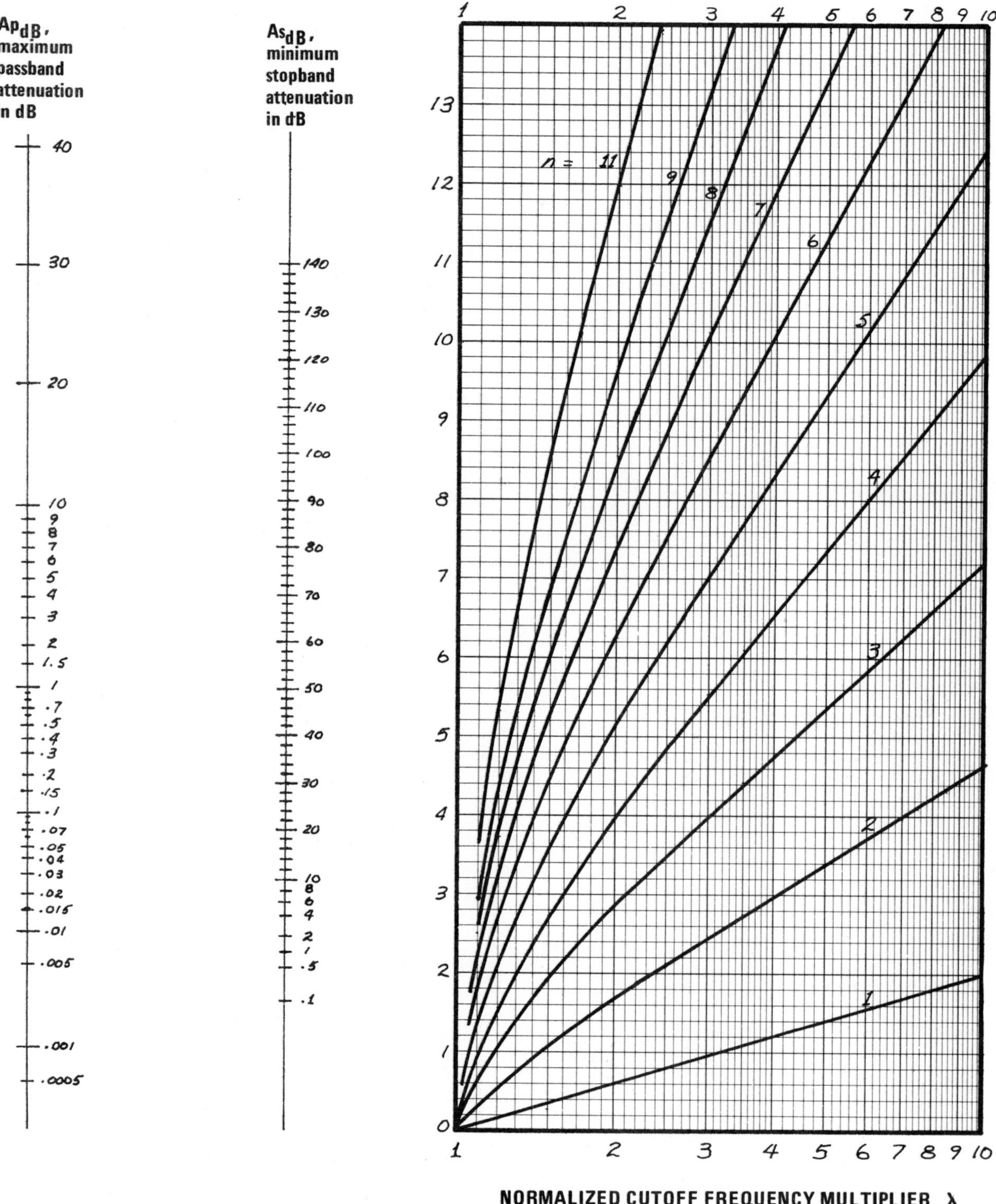


**Figure 2-1.2 Chebyshev filter nomograph.**

$$A_s^2 - 1 = (A_p^2 - 1)\{\cosh(n \cdot \cosh^{-1}\lambda)\}$$

Adapted from Kawakami [34]

## How to Use the Nomographs

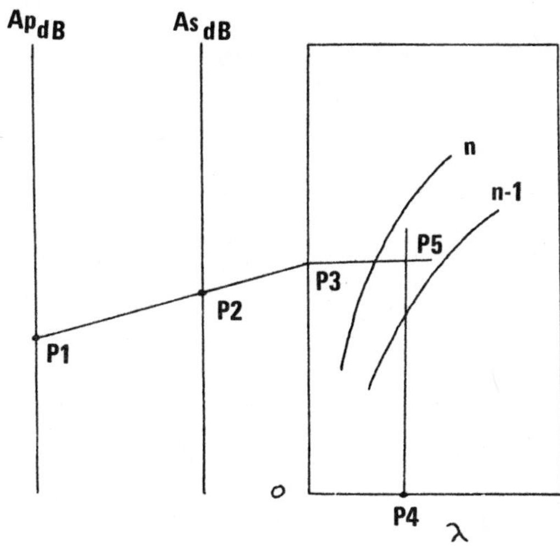


Figure 2-1.3 Nomograph use.

P1 and P2 are the required passband and stopband attenuation, P3 is a turning point, P4 represents the ratio between the frequencies where the stopband attenuation and the passband attenuation are specified, and P5 represents the required filter order, n.

Since n must be an integer, and P5 will generally lie between two integral numbers, always choose the larger of the two integers. Furthermore, if any of the narrowband approximations to bandpass filters are going to be generated, and Chebyshev response is specified, n must be an odd integer. This requirement occurs as even ordered Chebyshev filters have unequal termination resistances, and the narrowband bandpass approximations require equal termination resistances.

These nomographs are also contained in Zverev, however, the two vertical scales appear to be misregistered slightly, and in some applications will give inaccurate results.

These nomographs may also be used in other ways. If the filter order is known, then the filter response may be predicted. In this case, P5 would lie directly on one of the filter order lines, λ and P1, or P2 are the input variables, with P2, or P1 being the output quantity.

## Example 2-1.1 Highpass filter

A Butterworth filter is to pass 20 kHz and higher with 3 dB or less attenuation, and reject 10 kHz and lower with at least 40 dB of attenuation. Find the minimum filter order to meet these specifications.

| | | |
|---|---|---|
| | GSBa | select Butterworth |
| 3.00 | GSBA | load $Ap_{dB}$ |
| 40.00 | GSBB | load $As_{dB}$ |
| 2.00 | GSBD | load $\lambda$ = (20 kHz)/(10 kHz) = 2, & calculate n |
| 6.65 | *** | filter order, n (use n = 7) |

## Example 2-1.2 Bandpass filter

A Chebyshev bandpass filter is centered at 100 kHz (center frequency is not a parameter of the filter order calculation). Frequencies in a 20 kHz passband (geometrically centered about the center frequency) must be passed with 0.5 dB attenuation or less, and frequencies outside a 40 kHz bandwidth (again geometrically centered) must be rejected with at least 40 dB attenuation. Find the minimum filter order to meet these requirements.

| | | |
|---|---|---|
| | GSBb | select Chebyshev |
| .50 | GSBA | load passband ripple in dB ($Ap_{dB}$) |
| 40.00 | GSBB | load minimum stopband attenuation in dB ($As_{dB}$) |
| 2.00 | GSBD | load $\lambda$ = (40 kHz)/(20 kHz) = 2, and calculate n |
| 4.82 | *** | filter order, n (use n = 5 as smallest integer value to meet specs) |

## Example 2-1.3 Bandstop example

A maximally flat (Butterworth) bandstop filter is centered at 20 kHz. Frequencies lying outside a 10 kHz band geometrically centered on the center frequency should be attenuated by 3 dB or less. Frequencies inside a band of 1 kHz geometrically centered on the center frequency should be attenuated by at least 60 dB. Find the minimum filter order meeting these specifications.

```
        GSBa   select Butterworth
   3.00 GSBA   load Ap_dB
  60.00 GSBB   load As_dB
  10.00 GSBD   load λ = (10 kHz)/(1 kHz) = 10 & calculate n
   3.00  ***   filter order required

        DSP4   display 4 figures past the decimal point
 3.0010  ***   the filter order required is greater than 3

 3.0000 GSBC   enter filter order of exactly three & calc. λ
10.0079  ***   λ where filter is 60 dB down

10.0000 GSBE   enter λ and calculate As_dB
55.9794  ***   As_dB at λ = 10
```

This bandstop example shows other features of this program. Given n, the ratio, $\lambda$, where $A_s$ is met is calculated, and alternately, given $\lambda$, $A_s$ for this ratio is calculated.

As an aside, Butterworth filters are not exactly three dB down at the bandedge, but are $10 \cdot \log_{10} 2 = 3.010299957$ dB. If this number had been entered for $A_p$, the calculated filter order would have been three (to seven significant figures).

Example 2-1.4 Lowpass filter

Find the frequency where a 2 dB ripple, 7th order Chebyshev lowpass filter will be 60 dB down when the cutoff (-2dB) frequency is 1000 Hz.

```
        GSBb   select Chebyshev
   2.00 GSBA   load Ap_dB, the passband ripple
  60.00 GSBB   load As_dB, the minimum stopband rejection
   7.00 GSBC   load the filter order, n, and calculate λ
   1.70  ***   λ to meet above requirements

1000.00    ×   cutoff frequency of filter times λ
1701.27  ***   frequency where the filter is 60 dB down
```

# Program Listing I

| | | |
|---|---|---|
| 001 | *LBLA | LOAD $Ap_{dB}$ |
| 002 | GSB0 | |
| 003 | ST01 | store $A_p^2 - 1$ |
| 004 | RTN | |
| 005 | *LBLB | LOAD $As_{dB}$ |
| 006. | GSB0 | |
| 007 | ST02 | store $A_s^2 - 1$ |
| 008 | RTN | |
| 009 | *LBL0 | subroutine to convert dB to |
| 010 | EEX | $(magnitude)^2 - 1$ |
| 011 | 1 | |
| 012 | ÷ | |
| 013 | $10^x$ | |
| 014 | EEX | |
| 015 | - | |
| 016 | RTN | |
| 017 | *LBLC | LOAD n, THE FILTER ORDER |
| 018 | ST03 | AND CALCULATE $\lambda$ |
| 019 | RCL2 | |
| 020 | RCL1 | calculate $k = \sqrt{\dfrac{A_s^2 - 1}{A_p^2 - 1}}$ |
| 021 | ÷ | |
| 022 | $\sqrt{X}$ | |
| 023 | F1? | jump if Butterworth |
| 024 | GT03 | |
| 025 | GSB2 | calculate cosh k |
| 026 | RCL3 | |
| 027 | ÷ | |
| 028 | GSB1 | calc $\lambda = \cosh^{-1}(\frac{1}{n}\cosh k)$ |
| 029 | ST04 | |
| 030 | GT08 | goto the print/stop routine |
| 031 | *LBL3 | calculate $\lambda$ for Butterworth |
| 032 | RCL3 | |
| 033 | 1/X | |
| 034 | $Y^x$ | $\lambda = (k)^{\frac{1}{n}}$ |
| 035 | ST04 | |
| 036 | GT08 | |

| | | |
|---|---|---|
| 037 | *LBLD | LOAD $\lambda$ AND CALCULATE n |
| 038 | ST04 | |
| 039 | RCL2 | |
| 040 | RCL1 | calculate k |
| 041 | ÷ | |
| 042 | $\sqrt{X}$ | |
| 043 | F1? | jump if Butterworth |
| 044 | GT03 | |
| 045 | GSB2 | |
| 046 | RCL4 | for Chebyshev: |
| 047 | GSB2 | |
| 048 | ÷ | $n = \dfrac{\cosh^{-1} k}{\cosh^{-1} \lambda}$ |
| 049 | ST03 | |
| 050 | GT08 | |
| 051 | *LBL3 | |
| 052 | LN | for Butterworth: |
| 053 | RCL4 | |
| 054 | LN | $n = \dfrac{\ln k}{\ln \lambda}$ |
| 055 | ÷ | |
| 056 | ST03 | |
| 057 | GT08 | |
| 058 | *LBLE | LOAD $\lambda$ AND CALCULATE $As_{dB}$ |
| 059 | F1? | jump if Butterworth |
| 060 | GT03 | |
| 061 | GSB2 | for Chebyshev: |
| 062 | RCL3 | |
| 063 | x | |
| 064 | GSB1 | $q = \cosh(n \cdot \cosh^{-1} \lambda)$ |
| 065 | GT04 | |
| 066 | *LBL3 | for Butterworth: |
| 067 | RCL3 | $q = (\lambda)^n$ |
| 068 | $Y^x$ | |
| 069 | *LBL4 | common part for Buttr & Cheb |
| 070 | $X^2$ | |
| 071 | RCL1 | |
| 072 | x | $As_{dB} = 10 \cdot \log((A_p^2 - 1)q^2 + 1)$ |
| 073 | EEX | |
| 074 | + | |
| 075 | LOG | |
| 076 | EEX | |
| 077 | 1 | |
| 078 | x | |
| 079 | GT08 | |

| REGISTERS | | | | | | | | | |
|---|---|---|---|---|---|---|---|---|---|
| 0 | 1 $A_p^2 - 1$ | 2 $A_s^2 - 1$ | 3 $n$ | 4 $\lambda$ | 5 | 6 | 7 | 8 | 9 |
| S0 | S1 | S2 | S3 | S4 | S5 | S6 | S7 | S8 | S9 |
| A | | B | | C | | D | | E | I |

# Program Listing II

```
080  *LBL1   cosh x   subroutine
081     e^x
082    ENT↑
083     1/X           cosh x = (e^x + e^-x)/2
084      +
085      2
086      ÷
087    RTN
088  *LBL2   cosh^-1 x   subroutine
089    ENT↑
090     X²
091    EEX
092      -
093     √X            cosh^-1 x = ln(x + √(x² - 1))
094      +
095     LN
096    RTN
097  *LBLa   SELECT BUTTERWORTH
098    SF1
099    RTN
100  *LBLb   SELECT CHEBYSHEV
101    CF1
102    RTN
103  *LBLc   SELECT PRINT OR R/S
104    F0?     jump if flag 0 is set
105   GTO3
106    SF0     set flag 0 to indicate print
107      1
108    RTN
109  *LBL3
110    CF0     clear flag 1 to indicate R/S
111      0
112    RTN
```

```
113  *LBLd   BANDPASS: enter BW↑ f_o and
114     X²      calculate f_upr and f_lwr
115   STO5
116    X⇄Y
117      2
118      ÷
119   ENT↑
120     X²            f_upr = (BW/2) + √((BW/2)² + f_o²)
121   RCL5
122      +
123     √X
124      +
125   ENT↑            f_lwr = (f_o)²/f_upr
126   GSB9
127   RCL5
128    X⇄Y            f_lwr = (f_o)²/f_upr
129      ÷
130   GTO8
131  *LBLe   BANDPASS: enter f_upr & f_lwr
132   STO5    calculate f_o and BW
133    X⇄Y
134   STO6
135      x            f_o = ((f_upr)(f_lwr))^(1/2)
136     √X
137   GSB9
138   RCL6
139   RCL5            BW = f_upr - f_lwr
140      -
141  *LBL8   print or R/S subroutine
142   GSB9
143    F0?    if flag 0, space
144    SPC
145    RTN
146  *LBL9
147    F0?    if flag 0, go to print
148   GTO9
149    R/S    flag 0 not set, R/S
150    RTN
151  *LBL9
152   PRTX
153    RTN
```

| LABELS | | | | | FLAGS |
|---|---|---|---|---|---|
| A $A_p$ dB | B $A_s$ dB | C n→λ | D λ→n | E λ→$A_s$ dB | 0 print? |
| a set Buttr | b set Chebyshev | c print, no-print | d fo↑BW→ fu,fl | e | 1 Buttr |
| 0 dB→\|\|²-1 | 1 cosh x | 2 $\cosh^{-1}$ x | 3 | 4 | 2 |
| 5 | 6 | 7 | 8 print & space | 9 print | 3 |

| SET STATUS | | |
|---|---|---|
| FLAGS | TRIG | DISP |
| --USERS CHOICE-- | | |
| 0 | DEG | FIX |
| 1 | GRAD | SCI |
| 2 | RAD | ENG |
| 3 | | n ____ |

## PROGRAM 2-2 BUTTERWORTH AND CHEBYSHEV FILTER FREQUENCY RESPONSE AND GROUP DELAY.

### Program Description and Equations Used

This program calculates the frequency response (magnitude in dB and phase in degrees) and the un-normalized group delay in seconds for the Butterworth or Chebyshev all pole filter approximations. The response may be in lowpass, highpass, bandpass, or bandstop form (the lowpass and highpass responses are special cases of the bandpass and bandstop responses respectively in that the center frequency is zero). Both single frequency analysis and frequency sweeps may be done. The sweep can be linear using an additive increment, or logarithmic using a multiplicative increment.

The actual analysis routine that is buried within the program analyzes a normalized lowpass filter. The input data is normalized and transformed as required to place it in normalized lowpass form. The phase and gain response (frequency response) of the normalized lowpass filter is the same as the original filter type before transformation; hence, no reverse transformation is necessary for output. The group delay is the rate of change of phase with respect to frequency (derivative of the phase function) and is affected by the transformation to normalized lowpass form, therefore, an output transformation from the normalized lowpass group delay is required.

The logarithm of the normalized lowpass filter transmission function, $T(j\Omega)$ is composed of two components, the attenuation, a, and the phase, b. As a complex number, these two components represent the constant, g:

$$T(j\Omega) = \prod_k \frac{K}{\sigma_k + j\,(\omega_k - \Omega)} \qquad (2.2.1)$$

$$g = \ln(T(j\Omega)) = a + jb \qquad (2\text{-}2.2)$$

$$\Omega = F(\omega) \qquad (2\text{-}2.3)$$

$$\omega = 2\pi f \qquad (2\text{-}2.4)$$

where $F(\omega)$ represents the transformation to normalized lowpass, and $\sigma_k$ and $\omega_k$ are the pole locations of the Butterworth or Chebyshev normalized lowpass transfer function (see the equation derivation section following the examples for pole location details).

The group delay of the normalized lowpass filter is the derivative of the phase function, b, taken with respect to radian frequency:

$$b = \sum_{k=1}^{n} \tan^{-1}\left\{\frac{\omega_k - \Omega}{\sigma_k}\right\} \tag{2-2.5}$$

$$\tau_{g_{nor}} = \frac{db}{d\Omega} = \sum_{k=1}^{n} \frac{|\sigma_k|}{\sigma_k^{2} + (\omega_k - \Omega)^2} \tag{2-2.6}$$

The group delay is denormalized by multiplying the normalized group delay, Eq. (2-2.6), by the derivative of the transformation function, Eq. (2-2.3), taken with respect to the un-normalized radian frequency, $\omega$.

$$\tau_g = \tau_{g_{nor}} \cdot \frac{d\Omega}{d\omega} \tag{2-2.7}$$

The transform functions for the bandpass and lowpass cases are:

$$\Omega_{BP} = \left|\frac{1}{BW}\left\{f - \frac{f_o^{2}}{f}\right\}\right| \tag{2-2.8}$$

$$\frac{d\Omega_{BP}}{d\omega} = \frac{1}{2\pi BW}\left\{1 + \frac{f_o^{2}}{f^2}\right\} \tag{2-2.9}$$

where "BW" and "$f_o$" are the bandwidth and center frequency of the bandpass filter in hertz, and "f" is the frequency to be transformed (in hertz). The center frequency is zero for the lowpass case.

The transform functions for the bandstop and highpass cases are:

$$\Omega_{BS} = \frac{1}{\Omega_{BP}} = \left|\frac{BW}{f - \frac{f_o^{2}}{f}}\right| \tag{2.2.10}$$

$$\frac{d\Omega_{BS}}{d\omega} = \frac{BW}{2\pi}\left\{\frac{f^2 + f_o^{2}}{(f^2 - f_o^{2})^2}\right\} \tag{2-2.11}$$

The definitions of the terms are the same as above, and the highpass case has zero center frequency also.

The program uses Eqs. (2-2.8) and (2-2.10) to transform the input data to normalized lowpass, and then evaluates Eqs. (2-2.1) and (2-2.6) to obtain the frequency response and normalized lowpass group delay. The group delay is denormalized using Eqs. (2-2.9) or (2-2.11), and the frequency response and group delay are printed (HP-97 only) and displayed.

# User Instructions

| | | | | | |
|---|---|---|---|---|---|
| BUTTERWORTH AND CHEBYSHEV FILTER GROUP DELAY | | | | | |
| C: n↑DBR | HP: $f_o$ | BP: BW↑$f_o$ | lin: 0 log: 1 | $f_{start}$↑Δf | 2 |
| B: n | LP: $f_o$ | BS: BW↑$f_o$ | start sweep | single freq analysis | |

| STEP | INSTRUCTIONS | INPUT DATA/UNITS | KEYS | OUTPUT DATA/UNITS |
|---|---|---|---|---|
| 1 | Load both sides of magnetic card | | | |
| 2 | a) if Butterworth, enter filter order | n | [A] | |
| | b) if Chebyshev: | | | |
| | enter passband ripple in dB | DBR | [ENT↑] | |
| | enter filter order | n | [f] [A] | |
| 3 | Select filter type and enter characteristics | | | |
| | a) if lowpass: enter cutoff frequency* | BW, Hz | [B] | |
| | b) if highpass: enter cutoff frequency* | BW, Hz | [f] [B] | |
| | c) if bandstop: | | | |
| | enter bandwidth** | BW, Hz | [ENT↑] | |
| | enter center frequency | $f_o$, Hz | [C] | |
| | d) if bandpass: | | | |
| | enter bandwidth** | BW, Hz | [ENT↑] | |
| | enter center frequency | $f_o$, Hz | [f] [C] | |
| 4 | If sweep of frequencies is desired: | | | |
| | a) select linear or logarithmic sweep (toggle) | | [f] [D] | 0 |
| | | | [f] [D] | 1 |
| | | | [f] [D] | 0 |
| | | | | ⋮ |
| | b) enter sweep starting frequency in hertz | $f_{start}$ | [ENT↑] | |
| | c) enter frequency increment: | f | [f] [E] | |
| | if linear sweep, the increment is additive; if logarithmic, the increment is multiplicative. | | | |
| | d) start sweep | | [D] | f, Hz |
| | | | | loss, dB |
| | | | | phase, deg |
| | | | | group delay sec |
| 5 | for analysis at a single frequency | f, Hz | [E] | analysis above |
| | NOTE (* & **) The LP & HP cutoff frequency and the BP & BS bandwidth are defined as the -3dB point for Butterworth, and the -DBR point for Chebyshev | | | |

<u>**Example 2-2.1**</u>

**Calculate the amplitude, phase, and group delay characteristics of a third order, 1 dB ripple Chebyshev bandpass filter with 1000 Hz bandwidth and 10000 Hz center frequency. Calculate these characteristics from 8000 Hz to 12000 Hz in linear increments of 100 Hz.**

| PROGRAM INPUT | PROGRAM OUTPUT | | | | |
|---|---|---|---|---|---|
| | 8.000+03 | 9.000+03 | 10.00+03 | 11.00+03 | 12.00+03 |
| | -45.04+00 | -24.06+00 | 0.000+00 | -21.06+00 | -39.53+00 |
| | -257.1+00 | -240.1+00 | 0.000+00 | -235.9+00 | -254.0+00 |
| 3. ENT↑ n | 21.23-06 | 110.6-06 | 802.3-06 | 121.1-06 | 21.89-06 |
| 1. GSBa DBR | | | | | |
| 1000. ENT↑ BW | 8.100+03 | 9.100+03 | 10.10+03 | 11.10+03 | frequency |
| 10000. GSBc $f_o$ | -43.48+00 | -20.73+00 | -345.5-03 | -23.78+00 | $20 \log \lvert H(j\omega) \rvert$ |
| ← bandpass | -256.3+00 | -235.4+00 | -27.82+00 | -239.7+00 | $\measuredangle H(j\omega)$, deg |
| GSBd } linear | 23.69-06 | 151.2-06 | 723.6-06 | 92.14-06 | $\tau_g$, sec |
| 0.000+00 *** } sweep | | | | | |
| | 8.200+03 | 9.200+03 | 10.20+03 | 11.20+03 | |
| 8000. ENT↑ fstart | -41.85+00 | -16.90+00 | -894.2-03 | -26.20+00 | |
| | -255.4+00 | -228.8+00 | -51.87+00 | -242.6+00 | |
| 100. GSBe Δf | 26.62-06 | 223.1-06 | 624.7-06 | 72.90-06 | |
| | | | | | |
| GSBD start | 8.300+03 | 9.300+03 | 10.30+03 | 11.30+03 | |
| analysis | -40.13+00 | -12.35+00 | -906.8-03 | -28.38+00 | |
| | -254.4+00 | -218.5+00 | -74.49+00 | -245.0+00 | |
| | 30.17-06 | 371.0-06 | 667.2-06 | 59.38-06 | |
| | | | | | |
| | 8.400+03 | 9.400+03 | 10.40+03 | 11.40+03 | |
| | -38.31+00 | -6.901+00 | -195.5-03 | -30.36+00 | |
| | -253.3+00 | -199.6+00 | -103.5+00 | -247.0+00 | |
| | 34.53-06 | 731.4-06 | 1.006-03 | 49.47-06 | |
| | | | | | |
| | 8.500+03 | 9.500+03 | 10.50+03 | 11.50+03 | |
| | -36.37+00 | -1.466+00 | -654.3-03 | -32.17+00 | |
| | -251.9+00 | -160.9+00 | -148.3+00 | -248.6+00 | |
| | 39.96-06 | 1.430-03 | 1.371-03 | 41.94-06 | |
| | | | | | |
| | 8.600+03 | 9.600+03 | 10.60+03 | 11.60+03 | |
| | -34.30+00 | -82.00-03 | -4.904+00 | -33.85+00 | |
| | -250.4+00 | -109.8+00 | -189.4+00 | -250.0+00 | |
| | 46.88-06 | 1.189-03 | 844.2-06 | 36.08-06 | |
| | | | | | |
| | 8.700+03 | 9.700+03 | 10.70+03 | 11.70+03 | |
| | -32.07+00 | -865.9-03 | -9.967+00 | -35.42+00 | |
| | -248.5+00 | -76.75+00 | -211.4+00 | -251.2+00 | |
| | 55.92-06 | 726.3-06 | 432.4-06 | 31.41-06 | |
| | | | | | |
| | 8.800+03 | 9.800+03 | 10.80+03 | 11.80+03 | |
| | -29.66+00 | -909.1-03 | -14.30+00 | -36.87+00 | |
| | -246.3+00 | -52.79+00 | -223.3+00 | -252.3+00 | |
| | 68.11-06 | 648.4-06 | 253.9-06 | 27.62-06 | |
| | | | | | |
| | 8.900+03 | 9.900+03 | 10.90+03 | 11.90+03 | |
| | -27.01+00 | -351.4-03 | -17.94+00 | -38.24+00 | |
| | -243.6+00 | -28.08+00 | -230.8+00 | -253.2+00 | |
| | 85.24-06 | 737.1-06 | 168.4-06 | 24.50-06 | |

Equations Used and Pole Locations

Butterworth pole locations: The pole locations of a normalized lowpass Butterworth filter lie on a circle in the complex plane. Odd ordered filters have a real pole plus complex conjugate pairs. Even order filters have only complex conjugate pairs. No poles ever lie directly on the $j\omega$ axis. Figure 2-2.1 shows the pole locations for a 5th order normalized Butterworth lowpass filter, and Eqs. (2-2.12) and (2-2.13) show the generalized pole locations.

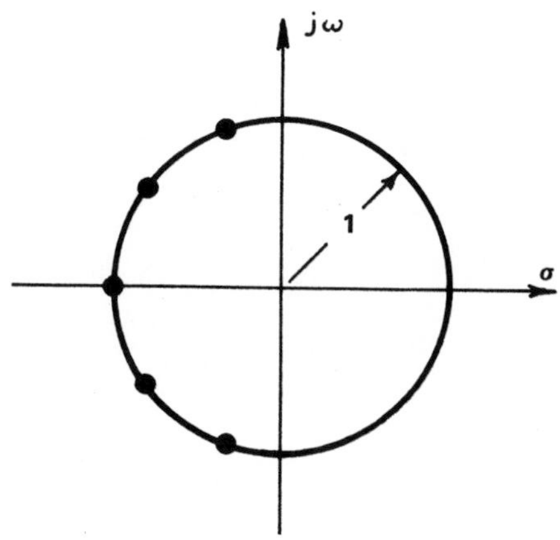


Figure 2-2.1 Butterworth pole locations.

Pole locations:

$$\text{Real part,} \quad \sigma_k = -\sin\left(\frac{2k-1}{2n}\pi\right) \tag{2-2.12}$$

$$\text{Imag part,} \quad \omega_k = \cos\left(\frac{2k-1}{2n}\pi\right) \tag{2-2.13}$$

$k = 1, 2, \ldots, n$

(trig argument is in radians)

The attenuation of the normalized Butterworth lowpass filter is 3 dB at $\omega = 1$. At other frequencies, the attenuation in dB is expressed by:

$$A_{dB} = 10 \log\left(1 + \omega^{2n}\right) \tag{2-2.14}$$

As shown by this equation, the attenuation monotonically increases as frequency increases. Figure 2-2.2 shows the general shape of the Butterworth response.

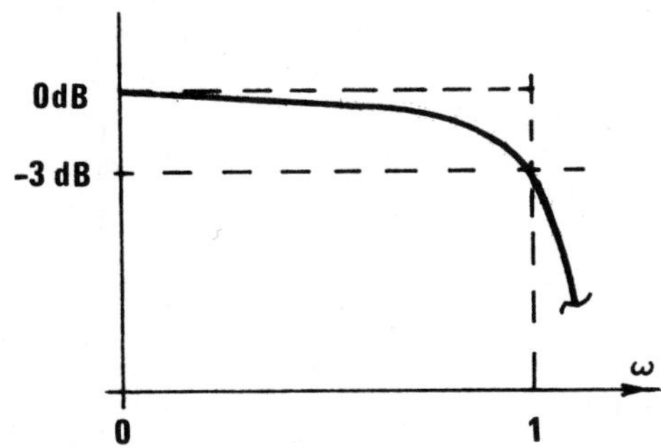


Figure 2-2.2 Normalized Butterworth amplitude response.

Chebyshev pole locations: The normalized lowpass pole locations of a Chebyshev lowpass filter lie on an ellipse with major axis dimension cosh a, and minor axis dimension sinh a where a is defined by:

$$a = 1/n \sinh^{-1}(1/\varepsilon) \tag{2-2.15}$$

The parameter $\varepsilon$ is related to the passband ripple in dB by:

$$\varepsilon = \left(10^{0.1\varepsilon dB} - 1\right)^{\frac{1}{2}} \tag{2-2.16}$$

Using these quantities, the real and imaginary parts of the pole locations are given by Eqs. (2-2.17) and (2-2.18). Figure 2-2.3 shows the pole locations for a fifth order Chebyshev filter.

$$\text{Real part, } \sigma_k = -(\sinh a)\left(\sin \frac{2k-1}{2n}\pi\right) \tag{2-2.17}$$

$$\text{Imag part, } \omega_k = (\cosh a)\left(\cos \frac{2k-1}{2n}\pi\right) \tag{2-2.18}$$

$$k = 1, 2, \ldots, n$$

(trig argument is in radians)

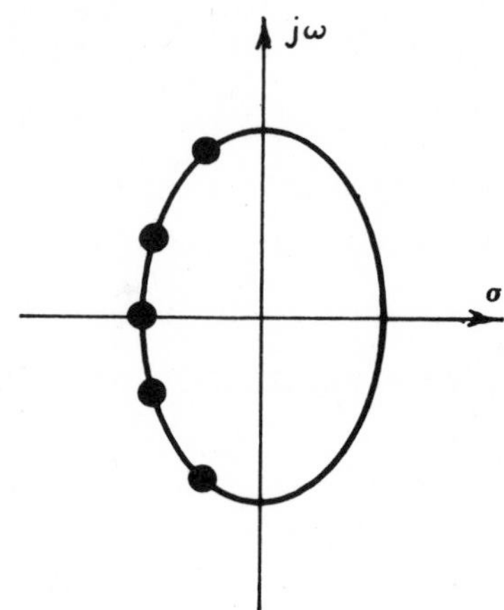


Figure 2-2.3 Chebyshev pole locations (5th order).

The passband edge of a Chebyshev filter is defined as the highest frequency where the response is $\varepsilon_{dB}$ down. Remember, the Chebyshev passband response oscillates within a band of $\varepsilon_{dB}$. Fourth and fifth order Chebyshev responses are shown in Fig. 2-2.4.

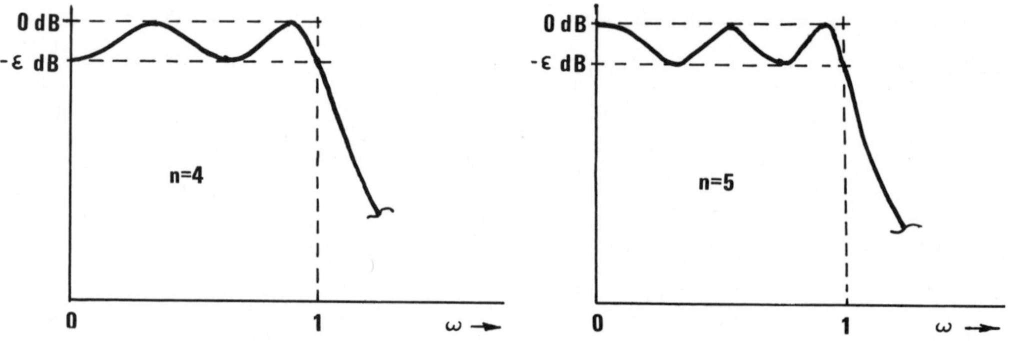


Figure 2-2.4 Chebyshev normalized lowpass filter responses.

The normalized frequency where the Chebyshev filter response is 3 dB down is given by the expression:

$$f_{-3dB} = \cosh\left\{ \frac{1}{n} \cosh^{-1}\left(\frac{1}{\varepsilon}\right) \right\} \tag{2-2.19}$$

Comparing the equations that define the pole locations for the Butterworth and Chebyshev filters, one will notice that the only difference is the Chebyshev poles are modified by hyperbolic functions. If the sinh a and cosh a functions are defined to be unity, then the

Chebyshev equations become the Butterworth equations. This technique is used in the program. Chebyshev poles are always calculated; however, if Butterworth response is selected, the hyperbolic functions are not calculated, but are set equal to one in register storage.

Another difference between Butterworth and Chebyshev filters lies in the definition of the bandedge. Butterworth response is 3 dB down at the bandedge, and Chebyshev response is $\varepsilon_{dB}$ down at the bandedge where $\varepsilon_{dB}$ is the passband ripple in dB. Flag 1 is used to indicate the filter type, and is set for Butterworth. When the pole locations are calculated, flag 1 is tested to see what equation, if any, is to be used to convert the given passband edge frequency into the appropriate frequency for the filter type being used.

# Program Listing I

| | | |
|---|---|---|
| 001 | *LBLA | LOAD BUTTERWORTH FILTER ORDER |
| 002 | STO1 | store n |
| 003 | EEX | |
| 004 | STO5 | cosh ≡ 1 for Butterworth |
| 005 | STO6 | sinh ≡ 1  "  " |
| 006 | RCL1 | recall n to display |
| 007 | RTN | |
| 008 | *LBLa | LOAD CHEB ORDER AND DB RIPPLE |
| 009 | STOC | store dB ripple |
| 010 | R↓ | |
| 011 | STO1 | store n |
| 012 | RCLC | calculate epsilon, $\varepsilon$ |
| 013 | EEX | |
| 014 | 1 | $\varepsilon = \sqrt{10^{0.1\,A_{max}} - 1}$ |
| 015 | ÷ | |
| 016 | 10ˣ | |
| 017 | EEX | |
| 018 | - | |
| 019 | √X̄ | |
| 020 | 1/X | calculate $\sinh^{-1}(1/\varepsilon)$ |
| 021 | ENT↑ | |
| 022 | X² | |
| 023 | EEX | |
| 024 | + | |
| 025 | √X̄ | |
| 026 | + | |
| 027 | RCL1 | calculate $\sinh\left(\frac{1}{n}\sinh^{-1}\left(\frac{1}{\varepsilon}\right)\right)$ |
| 028 | 1/X | |
| 029 | Yˣ | |
| 030 | ENT↑ | $\sinh^{-1} x = \ln\left(x + \sqrt{x^2 + 1}\right)$ |
| 031 | ENT↑ | |
| 032 | ENT↑ | $Y^{\frac{1}{n}x} \equiv e^{\frac{1}{n}\ln x}$ |
| 033 | 1/X | |
| 034 | - | $\sinh x = \dfrac{e^x - e^{-x}}{2}$ |
| 035 | STO6 | |
| 036 | R↓ | calculate $\cosh\left(\frac{1}{n}\sinh^{-1}\left(\frac{1}{\varepsilon}\right)\right)$ |
| 037 | 1/X | |
| 038 | + | $\cosh x = \dfrac{e^x + e^{-x}}{2}$ |
| 039 | STO5 | |
| 040 | 2 | |
| 041 | ST÷5 | |
| 042 | ST÷6 | |
| 043 | RTN | |
| 044 | *LBLB | LOAD $f_o$ FOR LOWPASS CASE |
| 045 | CF0 | |
| 046 | GTO1 | |
| 047 | *LBLb | LOAD $f_o$ FOR HIGHPASS CASE |
| 048 | SF0 | |
| 049 | *LBL1 | |
| 050 | STO3 | store $f_o$ |
| 051 | CLX | $f_o^2 \equiv 0$ for lowpass and |
| 052 | STO2 | highpass cases |
| 053 | RCL3 | |
| 054 | RTN | |

| | | |
|---|---|---|
| 055 | *LBLC | LOAD BW AND $f_o$ FOR BANDSTOP |
| 056 | SF0 | |
| 057 | GTO1 | |
| 058 | *LBLc | LOAD BW AND $f_o$ FOR BANDPASS |
| 059 | CF0 | |
| 060 | *LBL1 | |
| 061 | X² | calc & store $f_o^2$ |
| 062 | STO2 | |
| 063 | R↓ | |
| 064 | STO3 | store bandwidth |
| 065 | RTN | |
| 066 | *LBLD | START SWEEP |
| 067 | SPC | |
| 068 | *LBL7 | |
| 069 | RCL8 | |
| 070 | PRTX | |
| 071 | GSBE | |
| 072 | RCL9 | |
| 073 | F1? | |
| 074 | GTO1 | |
| 075 | ST+8 | linear sweep increment |
| 076 | GTO7 | |
| 077 | *LBL1 | |
| 078 | STx8 | log sweep increment |
| 079 | GTO7 | |
| 080 | *LBLd | SELECT LIN/LOG SWEEP |
| 081 | F1? | |
| 082 | GTO1 | |
| 083 | SF1 | |
| 084 | EEX | |
| 085 | RTN | |
| 086 | *LBL1 | |
| 087 | CF1 | |
| 088 | CLX | |
| 089 | RTN | |
| 090 | *LBLe | LOAD SWEEP $f_{start}$ AND $\Delta f$ |
| 091 | STO9 | |
| 092 | R↓ | |
| 093 | STO8 | |
| 094 | RTN | |

## REGISTERS

| 0 present frequency | 1 n | 2 $f_o^2$ | 3 bandwidth | 4 f | 5 cosh | 6 sinh | 7 $\sum$ delay | 8 $\pi\frac{\sigma^2 + \omega^2}{\sigma^2 + (\omega - \Omega)^2}$ | 9 $\sum$ phase |
|---|---|---|---|---|---|---|---|---|---|
| S0 | S1 | S2 | S3 | S4 | S5 | S6 | S7 | S8 | S9 |

| A $\sigma_R$ | B $\omega_R$ | C $A_{max}$ | D $\Delta f$ | E $\Omega$ | I index |
|---|---|---|---|---|---|

# Program Listing II

|  |  |
|---|---|
| *LBLE | LOAD ANALYSIS FREQUENCY |
| STO4<br>RCL2<br>RCL4<br>÷<br>-<br>RCL3<br>÷ | store frequency and form: $\Omega = \frac{1}{BW}\left\{f - \frac{f_o^2}{f}\right\}$ |
| F0?<br>1/X | if bandstop, $\frac{1}{\Omega} \rightarrow \Omega$ |
| ABS<br>STOE | store $\lvert\Omega\rvert$ |
| RCL1<br>STOI<br>CLX<br>STO7<br>STO9<br>EEX<br>STO8 | initialize loop:<br>$n \rightarrow RI$<br>$\Sigma_7 = 0$<br>$\Pi_8 = 1$<br>$\Sigma_9 = 0$ |
| *LBL0<br>RCLI<br>ENT↑<br>+<br>EEX<br>-<br>RCL1<br>÷<br>9<br>0<br>× | calculate angle: $\Theta_k = 90\left(\frac{2k-1}{n}\right)$ |
| EEX<br>→R | calculate sin $\Theta_k$ & cos $\Theta_k$ |
| RCL5<br>×<br>STOB | form and store $\omega_k$ |
| RCLE<br>- | form: $\omega_k - \Omega$ |
| X⇄Y<br>RCL6<br>×<br>STOA | form and store $\sigma_k$ |
| →P<br>X²<br>RCLA<br>X⇄Y<br>÷<br>ST+7 | form and sum: $\frac{\sigma_k}{\sigma_k^2 + (\omega_k - \Omega)^2}$ |
| RCLA<br>÷<br>ST×8 | form: $\frac{1}{\sigma_k^2 + (\omega_k - \Omega)^2}$ |
| X⇄Y<br>ST+9 | sum phase element |
| RCLA<br>X²<br>RCLB<br>X²<br>+<br>ST×8 | form in R8: $\prod_{k=1}^{n}{}_8 \left\{\frac{(\sigma_k^2 + \omega_k^2)}{\sigma_k^2 + (\omega_k - \Omega)^2}\right\}$ |
| DSZI<br>GTO0 | decrement k and test for loop exit |
| RCL7<br>Pi<br>ENT↑<br>+<br>÷ | calculate: $\frac{\Sigma_7}{2\pi}$ |
| RCL3<br>F0?<br>GTO8 | jump if highpass or bandstop |
| ÷<br>RCL2<br>RCL4<br>X²<br>÷<br>EEX<br>+<br>×<br>GTO9 | lowpass or bandpass $\frac{d\Omega}{d\omega}$<br>$\tau_g = \left\{1 + \frac{f_o^2}{f^2}\right\}\frac{\Sigma_7}{2\pi BW}$ |
| *LBL8<br>×<br>RCL4<br>X²<br>RCL2<br>+<br>×<br>RCL4<br>X²<br>RCL2<br>-<br>X²<br>÷ | highpass or bandstop $\frac{d\Omega}{d\omega}$<br>$\tau_g = \left\{\frac{f^2 + f_o^2}{(f^2 - f_o^2)^2}\right\}\frac{BW}{2\pi}\cdot\Sigma_7$ |
| *LBL9<br>RCL8<br>LOG<br>EEX<br>1<br>×<br>PRTX | calculate and print amplitude response in dB |
| R↓<br>RCL9<br>F0?<br>CHS<br>PRTX | calculate and print phase response in degrees |
| R↓<br>PRTX<br>SPC<br>RTN | print group delay |

| LABELS | | | | | FLAGS |
|---|---|---|---|---|---|
| A BUTTERWORTH n | B LP: $f_o$ | C BS: BW↑$f_o$ | D START SWEEP | E $f \rightarrow \tau_g$, etc | 0 CLR: LP or BP SET: HP or BS |
| a CHEBYSHEV n↑dB Ripple | b HP: $f_o$ | c BP: BW↑$f_o$ | d SELECT LOG/LIN SWP | e $f_{START}$↑Δf | 1 CLR: LINEAR SET: LOG |
| 0 SUMMATION LOOP START | 1 MULTIUSE LABEL | 2 | 3 | 4 | 2 |
| 5 | 6 | 7 SWEEP START | 8 BS, HP OUTPUT | 9 PRINT & SPACE SUBROUTINE | 3 |

| SET STATUS | | | |
|---|---|---|---|
| FLAGS | ON | OFF | TRIG | DISP |
| 0 | | ■ | DEG ■ | FIX |
| 1 | | ■ | GRAD | SCI |
| 2 | | | RAD | ENG ■ |
| 3 | | | | n 3 |

Suggested HP-67 program changes. The "print" command is used to output data in the program listing. These print commands are located at the following line numbers: 070, 191, 196, and 198. HP-67 users may prefer either a "pause" or "R/S" command replacing the "print" command at the above line numbers. If the R/S change is made, the program execution will stop at each data output point. To resume program execution, execute a "R/S" command from the keyboard.

## PROGRAM 2-3 BUTTERWORTH AND CHEBYSHEV LOWPASS NORMALIZED COEFFICIENTS.

Program Description and Equations Used

This program calculates the normalized (1 ohm, 1 radian/second cutoff) element values for either the Butterworth (maximally flat) or Chebyshev (equal ripple passband) all pole lowpass filter approximations. The filters can be either doubly terminated (resistors at both ends) or singly terminated (driven from a voltage or current source, i.e., $R_T$ approaches infinity). Because of duality, two filter topologies exist for the ladder filter as shown in Fig. 2-3.1. These topologies are bilateral and passive; therefore, the voltage source can be placed in series with the left-hand termination resistor as shown, or in series with the right-hand termination resistor. By proper selection of the filter topology and input port designation, the singly terminated filter can be driven from either a current or voltage source and resistively terminated, or driven from a Thevenin (or Norton) equivalent source and terminated in either a short or open circuit.

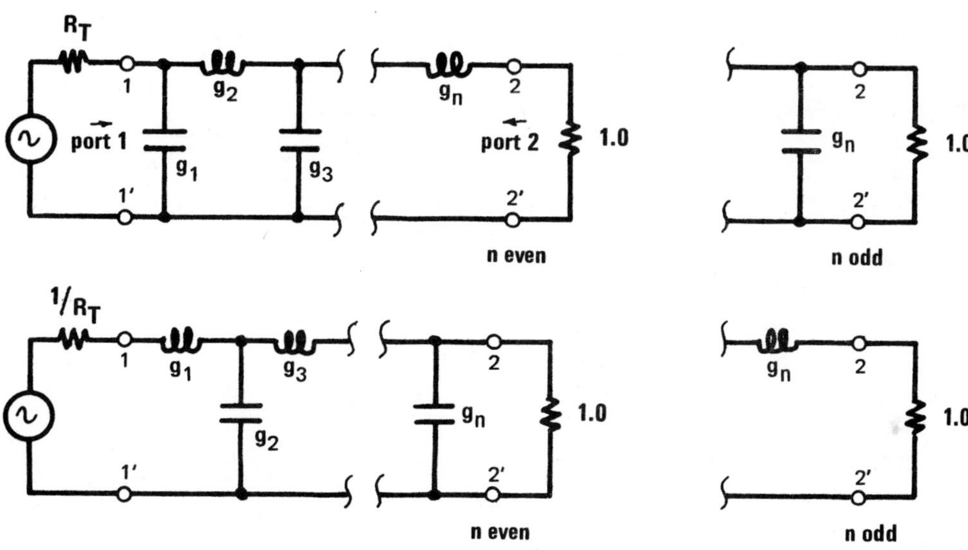


Figure 2-3.1 Lowpass ladder filter topologies.

The search for explicit formulas for ladder filter element values has extended over four decades. Bennett [ 7 ] provided the remarkedly simple formula for equally terminated Butterworth filters in 1932. Norton [39] provided the formulas for the open circuited Butterworth case in 1937. Belevitch [ 5 ] published formulas for the doubly terminated Chebyshev case in 1952. Orchard [40] gathered together this previous work and provided the missing fourth formula set for the open circuited Chebyshev case in 1953. Green [28] went on to generalize these formulas for any ratio of resistive terminations in 1954. These formulas had been numerically tested, but never formally proved. Doyle [22] provided a "hammer and tongs" brute force proof for the Butterworth case with arbitrary terminations. Meanwhile, in Japan, Takahasi [51], had made an ingenious proof of the formulas for the arbitrarily terminated Chebyshev case and extended it to the Butterworth case by a limiting process. Takahasi published his independent work in 1951 (in Japanese), but it was not discovered by the rest of the world until 1957. Weinberg and Slepian [54] discuss Takahasi's results. Takahasi's results can also be found in the back of Weinberg's book [53].

The recursion relations given by Eqs. (2-3.1) through (2-3.16) are adapted from Takahasi. If the filter order is odd, the filter can be terminated by 1 ohm at one port and by any resistance 1 ohm or larger at the other port. By using the dual topology, the termination resistance can be any resistance 1 ohm or smaller (including 0 ohms). If the filter is an even ordered Chebyshev design, then the first port termination resistance must be larger than 1 ohm. The minimum value of this termination resistance is given by Eq. (2-3.18).

Takahasi's recursion relationships:

$$g_{r+1} = \frac{A \cdot s_{r-\frac{1}{2}} \cdot s_{r+\frac{1}{2}}}{g_r \left(\xi^2 + \eta^2 - \xi \eta c_r + s_r^2\right)} \qquad (2\text{-}3.1)$$

where $r = 1, 2, \ldots, n-1$

$$g_1 = \frac{\sqrt{A} \cdot s_{\frac{1}{2}}}{R_T (\xi - \eta)} \qquad (2\text{-}3.2)$$

$$s_q = 2 \cdot \sin\left(\frac{\pi \cdot q}{n}\right) \qquad (2\text{-}3.3)$$

$$c_q = 2 \cdot \cos\left(\frac{\pi \cdot q}{n}\right) \qquad (2\text{-}3.4)$$

For normalized lowpass Butterworth coefficients:

$$A = 1 \tag{2-3.5}$$

$$\xi = 1 \tag{2-3.6}$$

$$\eta = \left(\frac{R_T - 1}{R_T + 1}\right)^{1/n} \tag{2-3.7}$$

$$s_r^{\,2} \equiv 0 \tag{2-3.8}$$

For normalized lowpass Chebyshev coefficients:

$$A = 4 \tag{2-3.9}$$

$$\xi = F(1) \tag{2-3.10}$$

$$\eta = F\left(1 - \frac{4 \cdot v\, R_T}{(1 + R_T)^2}\right) \tag{2-3.11}$$

$$v = \begin{Bmatrix} 1 + \xi^2, & n \text{ even} \\ 1, & n \text{ odd} \end{Bmatrix} \tag{2-3.12}$$

$$F(x) = u - \frac{1}{u} \tag{2-3.13}$$

$$u = \left(\sqrt{\frac{x}{\varepsilon^2}} + \sqrt{\frac{x}{\varepsilon^2} + 1}\right)^{1/n} \tag{2-3.14}$$

$$y = 10^{\varepsilon_{dB}/20} \tag{2-3.15}$$

$$\varepsilon^2 = y^2 - 1 \tag{2-3.16}$$

$$\omega_{-3dB} = \cosh\left(\frac{1}{n} \cosh^{-1} \frac{1}{\varepsilon}\right) \tag{2-3.17}$$

$$R_L \Big|_{\substack{\min \\ n \text{ even}}} = \left(\frac{\sqrt{\frac{y+1}{y-1}} - 1}{\sqrt{\frac{y+1}{y-1}} + 1}\right)^2 \tag{2-3.18}$$

When the termination ratio is neither 0, $\infty$ , or as close as possible to 1, there are more than one possible set of ladder element values for the same filtering function. These alternate sets are synthesized by realizing the reflection zeros in the RHP, or RHP-LHP alternating rather than in the LHP. The closed form formulas realize the LHP reflection zero case. This realization generally results in a ladder filter with minimum sensitivity to component value changes. For a more comprehensive discussion of reflection zeros and order of realization, see Weinberg [53], chapter 13.

The program is set up to calculate the minimum termination resistance, and if the value loaded by the user is less than the minimum, the minimum value replaces the user loaded value.

When the termination resistance is allowed to approach infinity (or 0 using the dual topology), the filter only has one termination resistor, and is called "singly terminated." These singly terminated filters are used where it is inconvenient, or wasteful of power, to use the doubly terminated filter. Because the loaded Q's of the resonant circuits become higher as the unloaded end of the filter is approached, the singly terminated design is more difficult to align.

Often, the LC filter is used as a basis for an active filter design such as Szentirmai's leapfrog topology [48], Bruton's frequency dependent negative resistor (FDNR) approach [10], or Orchard and Sheahans' type 11 active simulation [42]. Using the doubly terminated LC topologies for the active filter basis, will also mean that the active filters will be less critical toward alignment.

# User Instructions

| | | | | |
|---|---|---|---|---|
| BUTTERWORTH AND CHEBYSHEV LP NORMALIZED COEFFICIENTS | | | | |
| Load n | Load $R_T$ ($R_T \geqslant 1$) | calculate Butterworth values | calculate $-\epsilon_{dB}$ Cheb values | calculate $-3_{dB}$ Cheb values |

2

| STEP | INSTRUCTIONS | INPUT DATA/UNITS | KEYS | OUTPUT DATA/UNITS |
|---|---|---|---|---|
| 1 | Load both sides of magnetic card | | | |
| 2 | Load filter order (n = 12 maximum) | n | A | n |
| | If the normalized lowpass prototype is to be transformed to bandpass types 6, 7, 8, 9, 10, or 11, and Chebyshev response is desired, the filter order must be odd so the terminations will be equal resistance. | | | |
| 3 | Load the termination resistance desired | $R_T$ | B | |
| | The termination resistance must be 1 or larger. For terminations less than 1 ohm (normalized) load the reciprocal value and use the dual topology. See note after step 7. | | | |
| 4 | For Butterworth coeffieicnts | | C | $R_T$ |
| | | | | space |
| | | | | $g_1$ |
| | | | | $g_2$ |
| | | | | : |
| | | | | $g_n$ |
| | | | | space |
| | | | | $R_L = 1$ |
| 5 | For Chebyshev coefficients that define a filter that is $-\epsilon$ dB down at $\omega = 1$ | $\epsilon_{dB}$ | D | $\omega_{-3\ dB}$ |
| | If even ordered Chebyshev has been selected, the minimum source resistance is calculated and is used if the resistance loaded in step 3 is smaller. | | | space |
| | | | | $R_T$ |
| | | | | space |
| | | | | $g_1$ |
| | | | | $g_2$ |
| | | | | : |
| | | | | $g_n$ |
| | | | | space |
| | | | | $R_L = 1$ |

# 2-3 User Instructions

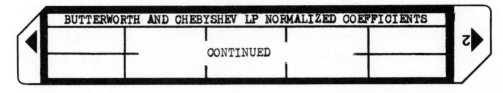

| BUTTERWORTH AND CHEBYSHEV LP NORMALIZED COEFFICIENTS |
|---|
| CONTINUED |

| STEP | INSTRUCTIONS | INPUT DATA/UNITS | KEYS | OUTPUT DATA/UNITS |
|---|---|---|---|---|
| 6 | For Chebyshev coefficients that define a filter that is 3 dB down at $\omega = 1$ | $\epsilon$dB | E | $\omega_{-\epsilon}$ dB |
| | | | | space |
| | The minimum source resistance comment for even ordered Chebyshev filters in step 5 also applies here. | | | $R_T$ |
| | | | | space |
| | | | | $g_1$ |
| | | | | $g_2$ |
| | | | | : |
| | | | | $g_n$ |
| | | | | space |
| | | | | $R_L$ 1 |
| 7 | Go back and repeat any step. | | | |
| | The last calculated coefficients will be in storage for use by other programs in this section. | | | |
| | Notes on termination resistance: | | | |
| | To enable the program to output coefficients for the singly terminated case, load $10^5$ ohms for $R_T$ if Chebyshev response is going to be selected, or load $10^9$ ohms if Butterworth response is going to be selected. Either one of these values is a reasonable approximation to infinity when compared to one ohm. The maximum termination resistance in the Chebyshev case is limited to $10^5$ ohms because of a small difference between big numbers problem. $10^5$ ohms is a compromise between an approximation to infinity and the number of significant digits in the coefficients. With $10^5$ ohms, the answers are significant to five places. | | | |

<u>Example 2-3.1</u>

Find the normalized lowpass coefficients for a 4th order, ½ dB ripple Chebyshev filter that is doubly terminated, and has the minimum termination resistance. The filter response should be 3 dB down at the passband edge ($\omega = 1$) relative to the response at dc.

HP-97 printout

| | | |
|---|---|---|
| 4. | GSBP | load filter order |
| 1. | GSBB | load termination resistance desired |
| .5 | GSBE | enter passband ripple in dB and calculate Chebyshev coefficients |
| 914.626-03 | *** | $\omega_{-\varepsilon dB}$ (output) |
| 1.98406+00 | *** | minimum termination resistance allowed at port 1 |
| 920.243-03 | *** | $g_1$ |
| 2.58640+00 | *** | $g_2$ |
| 1.30355+00 | *** | $g_3$ |
| 1.62581+00 | *** | $g_4$ |
| 1.00000-00 | *** | port 2 termination resistance |

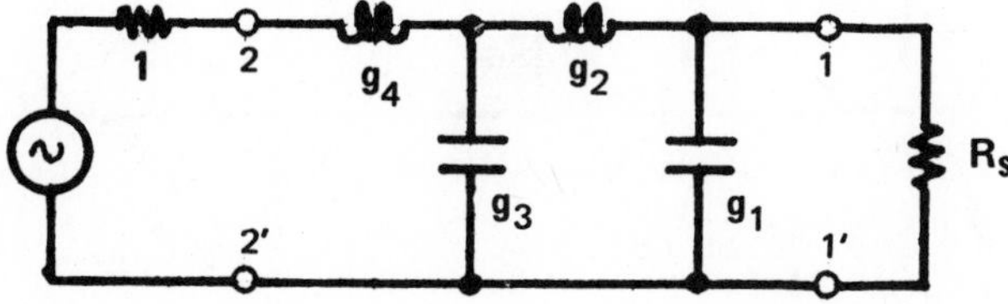


Figure 2-3.2 One topology for normalized lowpass filter (port ordering reversed).

Example 2-3.2

Find the normalized lowpass coefficients for a 10th order Butterworth filter that is singly terminated.

HP-97 printout

| | | |
|---|---|---|
| 10. | GSBA | load filter order |
| 1.+05 | GSBB | load termination resistance (use $10^5$ for Chebyshev) |
| | GSBC | calculate Butterworth coefficients |
| 1.00000+03 | *** | termination resistance at port 1 |
| 1.56434+00 | *** | $g_1$ |
| 1.85516+00 | *** | $g_2$ |
| 1.81211+00 | *** | $g_3$ |
| 1.55665+00 | *** | $g_4$ |
| 1.51062+00 | *** | $g_5$ |
| 1.39205+00 | *** | $g_6$ |
| 1.04062+00 | *** | $g_7$ |
| 762.527-03 | *** | $g_8$ |
| 465.379-03 | *** | $g_9$ |
| 156.434-03 | *** | $g_{10}$ |
| 1.00000+00 | *** | termination resistance at port 2 |

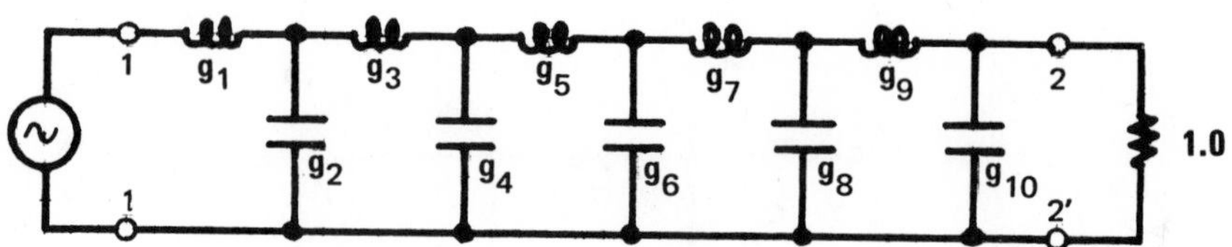


Figure 2-3.3 One form for normalized lowpass filter (dual topology used).

# Program Listing I

| | | |
|---|---|---|
| 001 | *LBLA | LOAD FILTER ORDER |
| 002 | STO6 | store filter order |
| 003 | Pi | |
| 004 | X≠Y | calculate and store $\pi/n$ |
| 005 | ÷ | |
| 006 | STO1 | |
| 007 | RCLE | |
| 008 | RTN | |
| 009 | *LBLE | LOAD DESIRED TERMINATION |
| 010 | STOD | RESISTANCE |
| 011 | RTN | |
| 012 | *LBLC | CALCULATE BUTTERWORTH COEFS |
| 013 | CF1 | |
| 014 | EEX | set $\omega_{-3dB} = 1$ |
| 015 | STO0 | |
| 016 | STO2 | set $\xi = 1$ |
| 017 | RCLD | calculate and store: |
| 018 | EEX | |
| 019 | - | |
| 020 | RCLD | |
| 021 | EEX | |
| 022 | + | |
| 023 | ÷ | $\eta = \left\{ \dfrac{R_T - 1}{R_T + 1} \right\}^{\frac{1}{n}} \to R_3$ |
| 024 | GSB4 | |
| 025 | STO3 | |
| 026 | GTO0 | jump around Cheb setup |
| 027 | *LBLE | CALCULATE −3dB CHEBYSHEV |
| 028 | SF0 | COEFFICIENTS |
| 029 | GTO2 | |
| 030 | *LBLD | CALCULATE − dB CHEBYSHEV |
| 031 | CF0 | COEFFICIENTS |
| 032 | *LBL2 | |
| 033 | SF1 | indicate Chebyshev |
| 034 | EEX | |
| 035 | 1 | calculate and store: |
| 036 | ÷ | |
| 037 | 10^x | |
| 038 | EEX | $\epsilon^2 = 10^{\epsilon dB/10} - 1 \to R_3$ |
| 039 | - | |
| 040 | STO3 | |
| 041 | EEX | calculate and store: |
| 042 | + | |
| 043 | √X | $y = 10^{\epsilon dB/20} \to R_E$ |
| 044 | STOE | |
| 045 | EEX | calculate: |
| 046 | + | |
| 047 | RCLE | |
| 048 | EEX | |
| 049 | - | $R_{T_{min}} = \left[ \dfrac{\sqrt{\frac{y+1}{y-1}} - 1}{\sqrt{\frac{y+1}{y-1}} + 1} \right]^2$ |
| 050 | ÷ | |
| 051 | √X | |
| 052 | STOE | |
| 053 | EEX | |
| 054 | + | |
| 055 | RCLE | |
| 056 | EEX | |

| | | |
|---|---|---|
| 057 | - | |
| 058 | ÷ | |
| 059 | X² | |
| 060 | RCLD | if filter order is even, |
| 061 | X≤Y? | and $R_T$ desired is less than |
| 062 | RJ | $R_{T_{min}}$, replace $R_T$ desired |
| 063 | GSB6 | by $R_{T_{min}}$ |
| 064 | F2? | |
| 065 | F2? | |
| 066 | STOD | |
| 067 | EEX | calculate and store: |
| 068 | GSB7 | $\xi = F(1) \to R_2$ |
| 069 | STO2 | |
| 070 | RCL3 | calculate and store: |
| 071 | 1/X | |
| 072 | √X | |
| 073 | LSTX | |
| 074 | EEX | |
| 075 | - | |
| 076 | √X | $\omega_{-3dB} = \cosh\left( \dfrac{1}{n} \cosh^{-1} \dfrac{1}{\epsilon} \right) \to R_0$ |
| 077 | + | |
| 078 | GSB4 | |
| 079 | 1/X | |
| 080 | ÷ | |
| 081 | 2 | |
| 082 | ÷ | |
| 083 | STO0 | |
| 084 | F0? | calculate $\omega_{\epsilon dB}$ if $\omega_{-3dB}$ |
| 085 | 1/X | coefficients requested |
| 086 | GSB3 | print $\omega_{-3dB}$, or $\omega_{-\epsilon dB}$ |
| 087 | GSB6 | calculate |
| 088 | RCL3 | |
| 089 | EEX | $v = \begin{cases} 1+\epsilon^2 & , \text{ n even} \\ 1 & , \text{ n odd} \end{cases}$ |
| 090 | ÷ | |
| 091 | F2? | |
| 092 | LSTX | |
| 093 | 4 | calculate and store: |
| 094 | X | |
| 095 | RCLD | |
| 096 | X | |
| 097 | RCLD | |
| 098 | EEX | |
| 099 | + | |
| 100 | X² | $\eta = F\left( 1 - \dfrac{4\,v\,R_T}{(1 + R_T)^2} \right) \to R_3$ |
| 101 | ÷ | |
| 102 | CHS | |
| 103 | EEX | |
| 104 | + | |
| 105 | X<0? | X<0 default |
| 106 | CLX | |
| 107 | GSB7 | |
| 108 | STO3 | |
| 109 | *LBL0 | |
| 110 | RCLD | |
| 111 | P≠S | |
| 112 | CLRG | clear coefficient registers |

**REGISTERS**

| 0 $\omega_{-3dB}$ | 1 $\dfrac{\pi}{n}$ | 2 $\xi$, 1 | 3 $\epsilon^2, \eta, \lambda$ | 4 $g_r$ | 5 | 6 $n$ | 7 $r$ | 8 $\dfrac{2r-1}{2}$ | 9 $S_{2r-1}$ |
|---|---|---|---|---|---|---|---|---|---|
| S0 $g_1$ | S1 $g_2$ | S2 $g_3$ | S3 $g_4$ | S4 $g_5$ | S5 $g_6$ | S6 $g_7$ | S7 $g_8$ | S8 $g_9$ | S9 $g_{10}$ |
| A $g_{11}$ | B $g_{12}$ | C $g_{13}$ | | D $R_T$ | | | E $y, \sqrt{\frac{y+1}{y-1}}, c_{2r}$ | I index | |

# Program Listing II

| # | Code | Note | # | Code | Note |
|---|------|------|---|------|------|
| 113 | P≷S | | 169 | GT01 | |
| 114 | STOD | | 170 | SPC | |
| 115 | GSB3 | print actual termination R | 171 | EEX | $R_L = 1$ |
| 116 | 1/X | | 172 | *LBL3 | print and space subroutine |
| 117 | STO4 | initialize registers | 173 | PRTX | |
| 118 | EEX | | 174 | SPC | |
| 119 | 1 | | 175 | RTN | |
| 120 | STOI | | 176 | *LBL5 | subroutine to finish $g_{r+1}$ |
| 121 | EEX | | 177 | - | |
| 122 | STO7 | | 178 | ST÷4 | calculation, store result, |
| 123 | . | | 179 | RCL0 | |
| 124 | 5 | | 180 | RCL4 | |
| 125 | STO8 | calculate and store: | 181 | ST÷4 | and setup $g_r$ for next |
| 126 | GSB8 | | 182 | ST÷4 | |
| 127 | STO9 | | 183 | F0? | iteration |
| 128 | ENT↑ | $g_1 = \dfrac{A^{1/2} \cdot s_{1/2}}{R_T(\xi - \eta)}$ | 184 | x | |
| 129 | F1? | | 185 | STOI | |
| 130 | + | | 186 | PRTX | |
| 131 | STx4 | if Chebyshev use A = 4, | 187 | RTN | |
| 132 | RCL2 | otherwise use A = 1 | 188 | *LBL6 | subroutine to set flag 2 |
| 133 | RCL3 | | 189 | RCL6 | if filter order is odd |
| 134 | GSB5 | | 190 | 2 | |
| 135 | *LBL1 | recursion loop start | 191 | ÷ | |
| 136 | ISZI | increment register index | 192 | FRC | |
| 137 | RCL9 | $s_{r+1/2}$  start $g_{r+1}$ calculation | 193 | X≠0? | |
| 138 | STx4 | | 194 | SF2 | |
| 139 | EEX | | 195 | R↓ | |
| 140 | ST+8 | | 196 | RTN | |
| 141 | RCL8 | | 197 | *LBL7 | subroutine to calculate: |
| 142 | GSB8 | $s_{r-1/2}$ | 198 | RCL3 | |
| 143 | STx4 | | 199 | ÷ | |
| 144 | STO3 | | 200 | √X | |
| 145 | 4 | | 201 | ENT↑ | $F(x) = u - \dfrac{1}{u}$ |
| 146 | F1? | if Chebyshev, use A = 4 | 202 | X² | |
| 147 | STx4 | | 203 | EEX | |
| 148 | RCL7 | finish $g_{r+1}$ calculation | 204 | + | |
| 149 | GSB8 | | 205 | √X | |
| 150 | X² | | 206 | ÷ | $u = \left\{\sqrt{\dfrac{x}{\epsilon^2}} + \sqrt{\dfrac{x}{\epsilon^2} + 1}\right\}^{1/n}$ |
| 151 | RCL2 | | 207 | GSB4 | |
| 152 | X² | | 208 | 1/X | |
| 153 | F1? | add $s_r^2$ if Chebyshev | 209 | - | |
| 154 | + | | 210 | RTN | |
| 155 | RCL3 | | 211 | *LBL4 | subroutine to calculate: |
| 156 | X² | | 212 | RCLE | |
| 157 | + | | 213 | 1/X | |
| 158 | RCLE | | 214 | Y^X | $( \ )^{1/n} \to R_x \to R_y$ |
| 159 | RCL2 | | 215 | ENT↑ | |
| 160 | x | | 216 | RTN | |
| 161 | RCL3 | | 217 | *LBL8 | subroutine to calculate: |
| 162 | x | | 218 | RCL1 | |
| 163 | GSB5 | | 219 | x | |
| 164 | EEX | increment r | 220 | 2 | $s_q = 2\sin\left(\dfrac{\pi q}{n}\right) \to R_x$ |
| 165 | ST+7 | | 221 | →R | |
| 166 | RCL7 | | 222 | STOE | |
| 167 | RCL6 | test for loop exit | 223 | R↓ | $c_q = 2\cos\left(\dfrac{\pi q}{n}\right) \to R_E$ |
| 168 | X>Y? | | 224 | RTN | NOTE TRIG MODE |

| LABELS | | | | | FLAGS | SET STATUS | | |
|--------|--------|--------|--------|--------|-------|---------|------|------|
| A filter order | B $R_T$ | C Butterworth coefficients | D -6dB Cheb coefficents | E -3dB Cheb coefficients | 0 -3dB Cheb | FLAGS | TRIG | DISP |
| a | b | c | d | e | 1 Chebyshev | ON OFF | | |
| 0 recursion loop setup | 1 recursion loop start | 2 Chebyshev -3dB jump | 3 print & space | 4 ( )^(1/n) | 2 odd number | 0 ■ / 1 ■ / 2 ■ | DEG / GRAD / RAD ■ | FIX / SCI / ENG ■ |
| 5 store $g_{r+1}$ | 6 SF2 if n odd | 7 F(x) | 8 $s_q$ & $c_q$ | 9 | 3 | 3 | | n __5__ |

## PROGRAM 2-4 NORMALIZED LOWPASS TO BANDSTOP, LOWPASS, OR HIGHPASS LC LADDER TRANSFORMATIONS.

Program Description and Equations Used

This program transforms the normalized lowpass coefficients (1 ohm, 1 radian/sec) into the frequency and impedance scaled lowpass, highpass, or bandstop topologies. The normalized lowpass coefficients are obtained from register storage and either must be loaded by the user (for other than Butterworth and Chebyshev filters), or are generated and stored by Program 2-3 for the Butterworth and Chebyshev approximations.

Every linear, passive, lumped, time-invariant, bilateral electrical network has a dual topology. LC filters are a member of this class of networks; hence, two electrically equivalent networks can be formed from the transformation or scaling of the normalized lowpass structure. These two forms are designated as form 1, and form 2 in the program. Having two forms available provides the designer some relief from awkward component values, or the opportunity to choose the minimum inductor topology.

The program is separated into three parts which share common subroutines. These sections are 1) de-normalization parameter input (bandwidth, termination resistance level, and center frequency), 2) bandstop denormalization and transformation, and 3) lowpass and highpass denormalization and transformation. In analytical form, these transformations are discussed next.

Lowpass filters: No transformation is necessary for converting the normalized lowpass to the un-normalized lowpass filters. The normalized lowpass values need only be scaled to the desired operating impedance level and cutoff frequency. The object of the scaling procedure is to end up with filter elements that have the same impedance ratios to the termination resistance at the cutoff frequency as the normalized filter has at 1 radian/second to 1 ohm. The mechanics of this scaling procedure are:

$$L,\ \text{scaled} = (L,\ \text{normalized}) \cdot (R/(2\pi \cdot BW)) \tag{2-4.1}$$

$$C,\ \text{scaled} = (C,\ \text{normalized}) \ / \ (2\pi \cdot BW \cdot R) \tag{2-4.2}$$

The normalized L's and C's are equal to the g's from Program 2-3, and BW and R represent the cutoff frequency in Hz and the load resistance in ohms respectively. Figure 2-4.1 shows the two forms of the lowpass filter; either port can be designated as input, i.e., the input voltage source can go in series with either termination resistor.

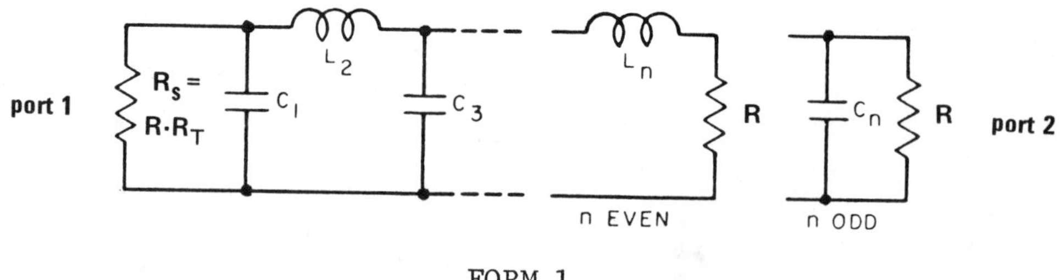


FORM 1

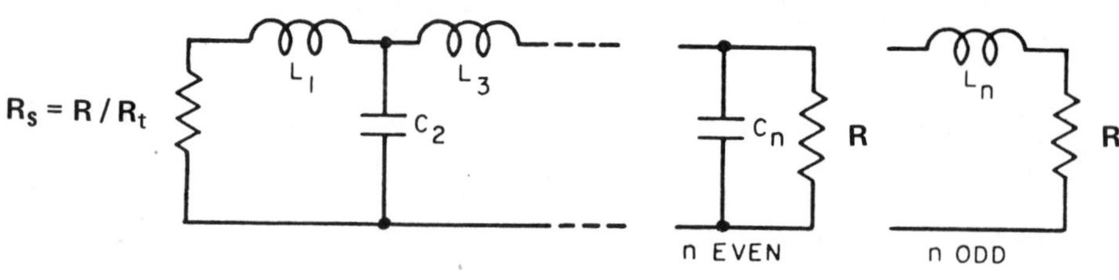


FORM 2

Figure 2-4.1 Two forms of lowpass filter.

Highpass filters: The highpass transformation is accomplished by replacing s by 1/s. Since sinusoidal frequencies are of primary interest, s may be replaced by $j\omega$, or 1/s by $-j/\omega$. Conceptually, this operation is equivalent to replacing each normalized lowpass capacitor with an inductor and vice-versa. The normalized values of the highpass elements are the reciprocals of the lowpass values, i.e., the g's calculated in Program 2-3 become 1/g's when converted to normalized highpass coefficients. Fig. 2-4.2 shows the two forms of the highpass filter, and the element values are calculated using Eqs. (2-4.1) and (2-4.2) with the normalized highpass coefficients. Either port can be designated as the input as in the lowpass case (or in any other passive LC case).

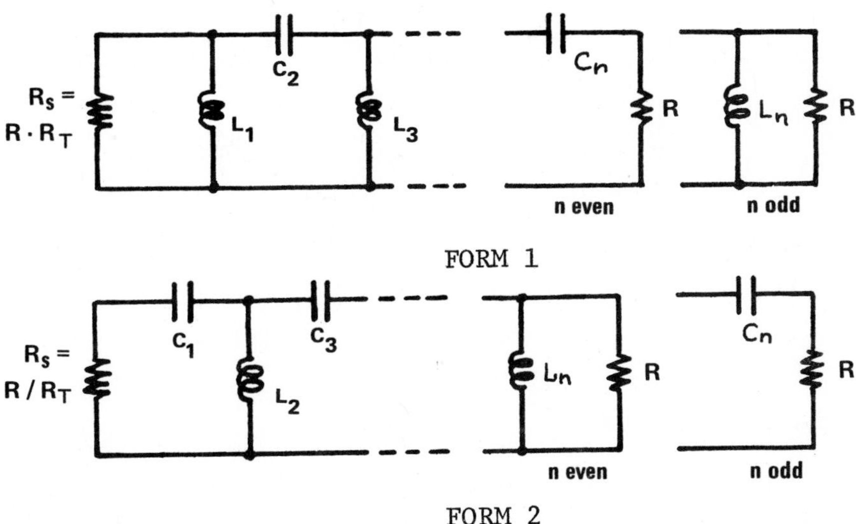


Figure 2-4.2 Two forms of highpass filter.

The highpass transformation may also be applied analytically; for example, the transformation is applied to the Butterworth normalized lowpass magnitude response equation (Eq. (2-4.3)) to convert it to the normalized highpass form (Eq. (2-4.4)).

$$|A(\omega)|_{LP} = \frac{1}{\sqrt{1 + \omega^{2n}}} \tag{2-4.3}$$

$$|A(\omega)|_{HP} = \frac{\omega^{n}}{\sqrt{1 + \omega^{2n}}} \tag{2-4.4}$$

For more information, see Weinberg [53]. Blinchikoff and Zverev [ 8 ] also has an excellent discussion of transformations both conventional as used herein, and unconventional to preserve LP transient characteristics.

Bandpass filters: The bandpass filter is a combination of a highpass and a lowpass filter. The loaded Q, $Q_L$, of the filter is a measure of the separation between the highpass and lowpass portions. To accomplish the transformation from normalized lowpass to un-normalized bandpass, s in the normalized lowpass expression is replaced by the function of s shown in Eq. (2-4.5).

$$s \Rightarrow Q_L \left\{ \frac{s}{\omega_o} + \frac{\omega_o}{s} \right\} \tag{2-4.5}$$

$$Q_L = \frac{f_o}{BW} \tag{2-4.6}$$

Where $f_o$ and BW are the center frequency and bandwidth in hertz.

Conceptually, the lowpass elements are replaced with new elements that exhibit the same impedance behavior at the bandpass filter center frequency as did the original elements at dc. Ideal inductors have zero reactance at dc, and are replaced with series resonant tank circuits which resonate at the bandpass filter center frequency, $f_o$. Ideal (lossless) series tank circuits have zero reactance at resonance. Likewise, each lowpass capacitor is replaced with a parallel resonant tank circuit which resonates at the bandpass filter center frequency. When the loaded Q is greater than 10 or so, the bandpass filter is called narrowband. In this case, other tank circuits can be synthesized to approximate the impedance behavior of the series and parallel resonant tank circuits for frequencies within the vicinity of the passband. Bandpass filters and narrowband transformations are discussed in Programs 2-5, 2-6, and 2-11.

Bandstop filters: The bandstop transformation is the reciprocal of the bandpass transformation, and is analogous to the lowpass-highpass transformation. Highpass filters are actually bandstop filters which have zero center frequency. To accomplish the bandstop transformation, s is replaced by:

$$s \Rightarrow \frac{1}{Q_L \left\{ \dfrac{s}{\omega_o} + \dfrac{\omega_o}{s} \right\}} \qquad (2\text{-}4.7)$$

Conceptually the bandstop transformation is accomplished by designing a highpass filter whose cutoff frequency equals the bandwidth of the desired bandstop filter. Each shunt inductor in the highpass filter is series resonated with a capacitor at the desired center frequency of the filter. Likewise, each series capacitor is parallel resonated with an inductor at the desired filter center frequency.

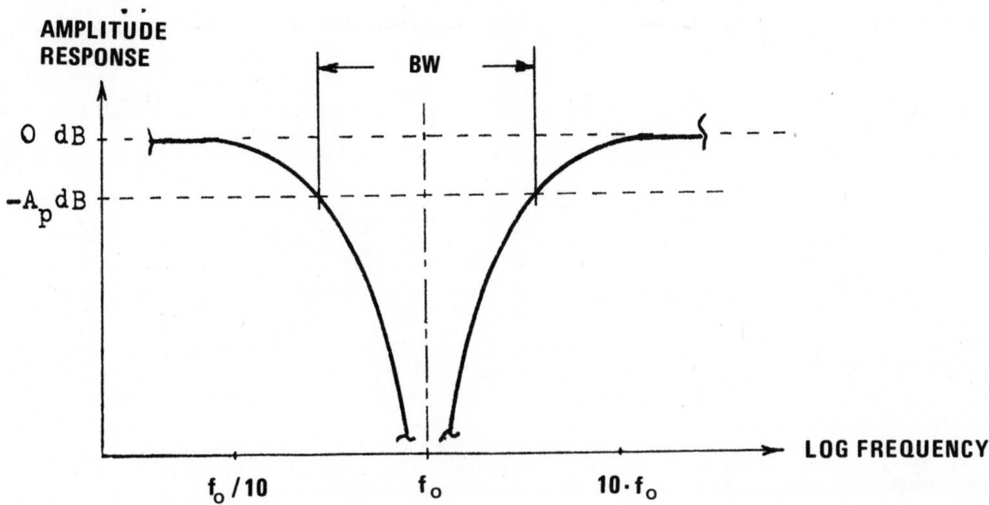


Figure 2-4.1 Bandstop filter parameters.

If $g_1$, $g_2$, .... , $g_n$ are the normalized lowpass coefficients and $R_T$ is the normalized termination resistance, then one form of the bandstop filter is shown by Fig. 2-4.2 .

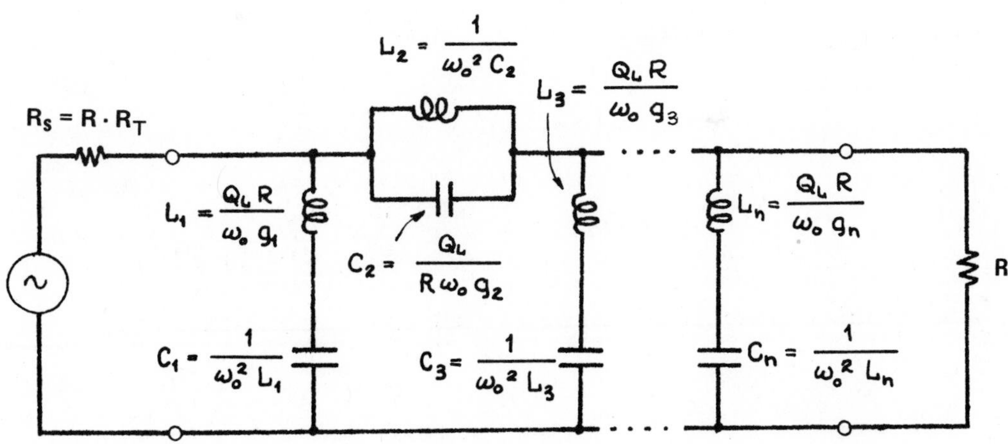


Figure 2-4.2 Bandstop filter form 1 (program output heading "21"), odd order filter shown; even order filter lacks last series tank circuit.

The other form of this filter is the dual of the first:

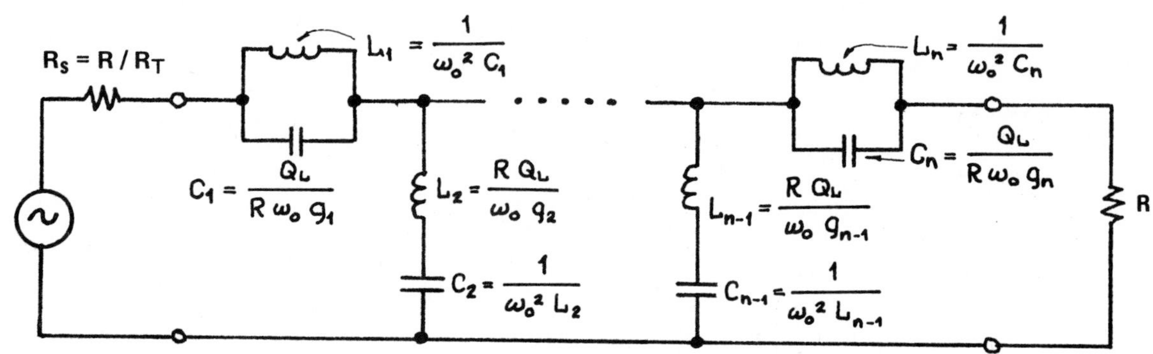


Figure 2-4.3 Bandstop form 2 (program output heading "22"), odd order filter shown; even order filter lacks last parallel tank circuit.

The program calculates both forms of these bandstop filters.

Filter physical realizability. The preceding transformations are used by this program and result in LC network schematics that will produce the desired response. Not all LC networks that can be drawn on paper as schematics are physically realizable. For example, a network branch consisting of a 1 μF capacitor in series with a 10 nh inductor would be nearly impossible to realize since the self inductance of the capacitor is much larger than the total required inductance. Table 2-4.1 is a reproduction of Table 7.1 from White [56], and shows the degree of physical realizability of lowpass and highpass filters. The physical realizability of a filter is assigned one of four possible scores. These scores are defined as follows:

Readily realizable (R): $1\ \mu h \le L \le 1\ h$
$5\ pF \le C \le 1\ \mu F$

Practical (P): $200\ nh \le L \le 10\ h$
$2\ pF \le C \le 10\ \mu F$

Marginally practical (M): $50\ nh \le L \le 100\ h$
$0.5\ pF \le C \le 500\ \mu F$

Impractical (I): All element values that lie outside the marginal range, i.e.,

$L < 50$ nh
$L > 100$ h
$C < 0.5$ pF
$C > 500$ μF

The table headings are meant to indicate ranges of filter cutoff frequency and termination impedance level. These ranges are defined as follows:

Frequency,

$f_o$ = 10 Hz implies: 3 Hz $\leq f_o <$ 30 Hz
$f_o$ = 100 Hz implies: 30 Hz $\leq f_o <$ 300 Hz
$f_o$ = 1 kHz implies: 300 Hz $\leq f_o <$ 3 kHz
$f_o$ = 10 kHz implies: 3 kHz $\leq f_o <$ 30 kHz
$f_o$ = 100 kHz implies: 30 kHz $\leq f_o <$ 300 kHz
$f_o$ = 1 MHz implies: 300 kHz $\leq f_o <$ 3 MHz
$f_o$ = 10 MHz implies: 3 MHz $\leq f_o <$ 30 MHz
$f_o$ = 100 MHz implies: 30 MHz $\leq f_o <$ 300 MHz

At frequencies above 300 MHz, lumped element filters are generally replaced with transmission line type filters.

Impedance Level (source and load resistances equal)

R = 3 ohms implies: $1 \leq R < 10$ (power filters)
R = 50 ohms implies: $10 \leq R < 150$
R = 500 ohms implies: $150 \leq R < 2.5k$
R = 10k ohms implies: $2.5k \leq R < 50k$

Table 2-4.1 Physical realizability of lowpass and highpass filters.

| R in ohms | Cutoff Frequency, $f_c$ | | | | | | | |
|---|---|---|---|---|---|---|---|---|
| | 10 Hz | 100 Hz | 1 kHz | 10 kHz | 100 kHz | 1 MHz | 10 MHz | 100 MHz |
| 3 | I | M | M | P | R | P | M | I |
| 50 | M | M | M | R | R | R | R | M |
| 500 | M | P | R | R | R | R | R | R |
| 10k | I | M | P | R | R | R | P | I |

Courtesy, Don White Consultants, Inc.

Bandstop filter physical realizability must include one additional parameter, the loaded Q of the filter, $Q_L$. As $Q_L$ becomes higher (filter becomes more narrow) the separation in element value between the series tank elements and the parallel tank elements increases as $Q_L$ . Table 2-4.2 is adapted from Table 7.2 in White and assigns realizability scores to bandstop (and bandpass) filters. The loaded Q ranges are defined as follows:

Loaded Q ($Q_L$), for bandpass and bandstop,

$$Q_L = 5 \text{ implies: } 3 \leq Q_L < 10$$
$$Q_L = 15 \text{ implies: } 10 \leq Q_L < 30$$
$$Q_L = 50 \text{ implies: } 30 \leq Q_L \leq 100$$

Table 2-4.2 Physical realizability of bandstop filters.

| Filter Prototype | $f_o$ = 1 kHz | | | | | | | | | $f_o$ = 10 kHz | | | | | | | | |
|---|---|---|---|---|---|---|---|---|---|---|---|---|---|---|---|---|---|---|
| | $Q_L = 5$ | | | $Q_L = 15$ | | | $Q_L = 50$ | | | $Q_L = 5$ | | | $Q_L = 15$ | | | $Q_L = 50$ | | |
| Type | 50 | 500 | 10K | 50 | 500 | 10K | 50 | 500 | 10K | 50 | 500 | 10K | 50 | 500 | 10K | 50 | 500 | 10K |
| 1st | I | P | P | I | I | I | I | I | I | M | R | P | I | M | P | I | M | P |
| 2nd | I | P | P | I | I | I | I | I | I | M | R | P | I | M | I | I | M | P |
| Filter Prototype | $f_o$ = 100 kHz | | | | | | | | | $f_o$ = 1 MHz | | | | | | | | |
| | $Q_L = 5$ | | | $Q_L = 15$ | | | $Q_L = 50$ | | | $Q_L = 5$ | | | $Q_L = 15$ | | | $Q_L = 50$ | | |
| Type | 50 | 500 | 10K | 50 | 500 | 10K | 50 | 500 | 10K | 50 | 500 | 10K | 50 | 500 | 10K | 50 | 500 | 10K |
| 1st | P | R | R | P | P | I | M | M | I | P | R | P | P | P | I | M | P | I |
| 2nd | P | R | R | P | P | I | M | M | I | P | R | P | P | P | I | M | M | I |
| Filter Prototype | $f_o$ = 10 MHz | | | | | | | | | $f_o$ = 100 MHz | | | | | | | | |
| | $Q_L = 5$ | | | $Q_L = 15$ | | | $Q_L = 50$ | | | $Q_L = 5$ | | | $Q_L = 15$ | | | $Q_L = 50$ | | |
| Type | 50 | 500 | 10K | 50 | 500 | 10K | 50 | 500 | 10K | 50 | 500 | 10K | 50 | 500 | 10K | 50 | 500 | 10K |
| 1st | M | P | M | I | P | I | I | I | I | I | I | I | I | I | I | I | I | I |
| 2nd | M | P | M | I | P | I | I | I | I | I | I | I | I | I | I | I | I | I |

Courtesy Don White Consultants Inc.

As the loaded Q increases, the element value spread can become unmanageable. This problem can be reduced by using narrowband transformations which are used in Programs 2-5 and 2-6 for the bandpass case. Narrowband transformation schematics for the bandstop case may be found on p. 217 of the ITT handbook [44]. The concept of coupling and narrowband transformations was introduced by Milton Dishal [21], and expanded by Seymour Cohn [16] for the bandpass case.

# User Instructions

| BANDSTOP, LOWPASS, OR HIGHPASS TRANSFORMATIONS | | | | |
|---|---|---|---|---|
| Lowpass Type 1 | Lowpass Type 2 | Highpass Type 1 | Highpass Type 2 | |
| Center Frequency | Bandwidth, Cutoff freq | Termination Resistance | Bandstop Type 1 | Bandstop Type 2 |

| STEP | INSTRUCTIONS | INPUT DATA/UNITS | KEYS | OUTPUT DATA/UNITS |
|---|---|---|---|---|
| 1 | Load both sides of magnetic card | | | |
| 2 | For lowpass filter component values: | | | |
| | a) load cutoff frequency in hertz | $f_{cutoff}$ | [B] | |
| | b) load termination resistance in ohms | R | [C] | |
| | c) for type 1 filter (capacitor first)* | | [f] [A] | $R_s$ |
| | | | | $C_1$ |
| | | | | $L_2$ |
| | | | | ⋮ |
| | | | | $C_n$ or $L_n$ |
| | | | | R |
| | d) for type 2 filter (inductor first)* | | [f] [B] | $R_s$ |
| | | | | $L_1$ |
| | | | | $C_2$ |
| | | | | ⋮ |
| | | | | $L_n$ or $C_n$ |
| | | | | R |
| 3 | For highpass filter component values: | | | |
| | a) load cutoff frequency in hertz | | [B] | |
| | b) load termination resistance in ohms | | [C] | |
| | c) for type 1 filter (inductor first)* | | [f] [C] | $R_s$ |
| | | | | $L_1$ |
| | | | | $C_2$ |
| | | | | ⋮ |
| | | | | $C_n$ or $L_n$ |
| | | | | R |

# User Instructions

BANDSTOP, LOWPASS, OR HIGHPASS TRANSFORMATIONS

CONTINUED

2

| STEP | INSTRUCTIONS | INPUT DATA/UNITS | KEYS | OUTPUT DATA/UNITS |
|---|---|---|---|---|
| 3 | Highpass component values continued | | | |
| | b) for type 2 filter (capacitor first)* | | [f] [D] | $R_s$ |
| | | | | $C_1$ |
| | | | | $L_2$ |
| | | | | : |
| | | | | $L_n$ or $C_n$ |
| | | | | R |
| 4 | For bandstop filter component values: | | | |
| | a) load filter center frequency in hertz | $f_o$ | [A] | |
| | b) load filter bandwidth in hertz | BW | [B] | |
| | c) load termination resistance in ohms | R | [C] | |
| | d) for type 1 filter (series tank first)* | | [D] | $R_s$ |
| | | | | $C_1$** |
| | | | | $L_1$ |
| | | | | $C_2$ |
| | | | | $L_2$ |
| | | | | : |
| | | | | $C_n$ |
| | | | | $L_n$ |
| | | | | R |
| | e) for type 2 filter (parallel tank first)* | | [E] | $R_s$ |
| | | | | $C_1$ |
| | | | | $L_1$ |
| | | | | : |
| | | | | $C_n$ |
| | | | | $L_n$ |
| | | | | R |

NOTES:

* All capacitor values are in farads, all inductor values are in henries and all resistor values are in ohms.

** In all section 2 programs where resonant tank components are printed, the capacitor is always printed first.

Example 2-4.1 Singly terminated lowpass filter

A maximally flat (Butterworth) lowpass filter must pass a 1 kHz signal with 1 dB or less attenuation relative to the filter response at dc, and must reject a 12 kHz signal by at least 75 dB. Program 2-1 is used to predict the required filter order, and -3 dB cutoff frequency (Butterworth cutoff frequency) with $Ap_{dB}$ = 1 dB, $As_{dB}$ = 75 dB, and $\lambda$ = 12. A filter order of 3.75 is calculated, which is rounded to the next largest integer, 4. Re-entering the program with $As_{dB}$ = 3 and n = 4, yields $\lambda$ = 1.183301, which means the 3 dB cutoff frequency is (1000)(1.183301) = 1183.301 Hz.

Next, Program 2-3 is loaded to obtain the normalized lowpass coefficients for a singly terminated 4th order Butterworth filter. The coefficients are automatically stored for use by this program.

Load this program, load the above cutoff frequency, and select an operating impedance level from Table 2-4.1 An impedance level of 500 ohms will result in a readily realizable filter. Both the type 1 and type 2 topologies can be calculated and the most attractive one selected. The HP-97 printout for the above operations is shown on the next page.

Programs 3-1 and 3-2 can be used to design the inductors needed for this design. If an active filter approach can be considered, see Program 2-9 for a lowpass active filter design.

**HP-97 printout for Example 2-4.1, lowpass filter design.**

**Load Program 2-1 to calculate required filter order:**

GSBa select Butterworth
1.00 GSBA load $Ap_{dB}$
75.00 GSBB load $As_{dB}$
12.00 GSBD load $\lambda$, and calculate n, the filter order
3.75 *** n (output)

3.00 GSBB load new $As_{dB}$
4.00 GSBC load integral filter order, n, and calculate $\lambda$
1.183301 *** $\lambda$ (output)

**Load Program 2-3 to generate and store the normalized lowpass coefs.**

4. GSBA load filter order
1.+09 GSBE load termination resistance desired
GSBC calculate Butterworth coefficients
1.00000+09 *** $R_T$ (normalized)

1.53073+00 *** $g_1$
1.57716+00 *** $g_2$
1.08239+00 *** $g_3$
382.683-03 *** $g_4$
} lowpass normalized coefficients

1.00000+00 *** R (normalized)

**Load this program (Program 2-4) to obtain un-normalized filter.**

1181.301 GSBE load un-normalized cutoff frequency
500. GSBC load termination resistance, R
GSBa calculate type 1 lowpass filter (capacitor first)

31. lowpass type 1 output code

500.0+03 *** $R_s$ (open circuit)

412.5-09 *** $C_1$
106.2-03 *** $L_2$
291.7-09 *** $C_3$
25.78-03 *** $L_4$

500.0+00 *** R

GSBb calculate type 2 lowpass filter (inductor first)

32. lowpass type 2 output code

500.0-09 *** $R_s$ (short circuit)

103.1-03 *** $L_1$
425.0-09 *** $C_2$
72.91-03 *** $L_3$
103.1-09 *** $C_4$

500.0+00 *** R

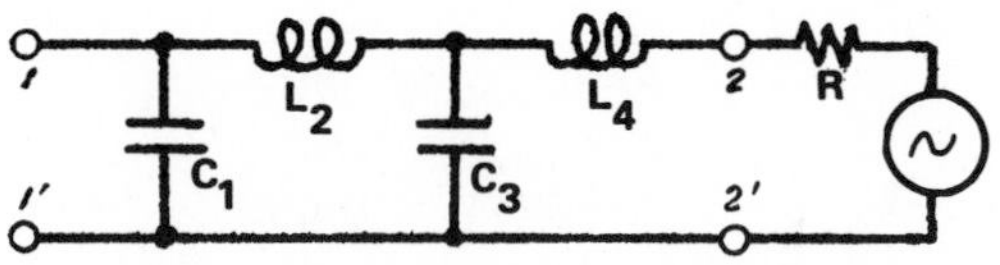

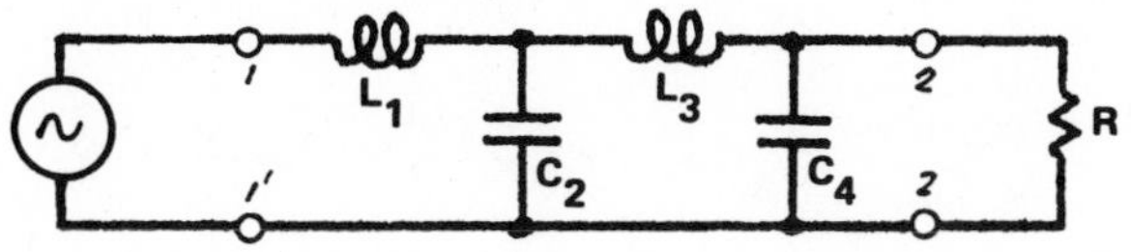

Example 2-4.2 Doubly terminated highpass filter

A highpass filter is required to keep the signal from a local CB transmitter from causing cross modulation interference in the tuner of a TV set. The filter will be placed in series with the 300 ohm balanced line from the antenna to the TV set, hence, the filter will be designed for a 300 ohm terminating impedance level. The filter must pass the TV spectrum which starts at 54 MHz, but must reject the CB radio band at 27 MHz. One dB of ripple is allowed across the TV spectrum, and at least 60 dB rejection is needed at the CB band frequencies. Because of the allowed ripple, a Chebyshev filter will be used. Program 2-1 calculates a minimum filter order of 7 as shown below along with the rest of the HP-97 printout for this design:

Load Program 2-1 to obtain minimum filter order required:

| | | |
|---|---|---|
| | GSBb | select Chebyshev |
| 1.00 | GSBA | load $Ap_{dB}$ |
| 60.00 | GSBB | load $As_{dB}$ |
| 2.00 | GSBD | load $\lambda$ and calculate filter order, n |
| 6.28 | *** | n (output) |
| 7.00 | GSBC | load integral filter order, n |
| 1.78 | *** | $\lambda$ where filter is 60 dB down (54/1.78 = 30.3) |
| 2.00 | GSBE | load $\lambda$ and calculate $As_{dB}$ |
| 68.16 | *** | $As_{dB}$ at 27 MHz |

Load Program 2-3 to generate and store the normalized lowpass coefficients:

| | | |
|---|---|---|
| 7. | GSBA | load filter order |
| 1. | GSBB | load termination resistance ratio |
| 1. | GSBD | load Chebyshev passband ripple in dB and start |
| 1.01721+00 | *** | normalized -3 dB frequency (output) |
| 1.00000+00 | *** | $R_T$ (normalized) |
| 2.16656+00 | *** | $g_1$ |
| 1.11151+00 | *** | $g_2$ |
| 3.09364+00 | *** | $g_3$ |
| 1.17352+00 | *** | $g_4$ — normalized lowpass coefficients ($g_1$ through $g_7$) |
| 3.09364+00 | *** | $g_5$ |
| 1.11151+00 | *** | $g_6$ |
| 2.16656+00 | *** | $g_7$ |
| 1.00000+00 | *** | R (normalized) |

This highpass example is for a balanced structure filter, and the program output is for an unbalanced structure (one side common). To convert the unbalanced structure to the balanced structure, capacitors are placed in each side of the filter, and their equivalent impedance is one-half the unbalanced value (twice the capacity).

Load this program, Program 2-4, to obtain the un-normalized filter:

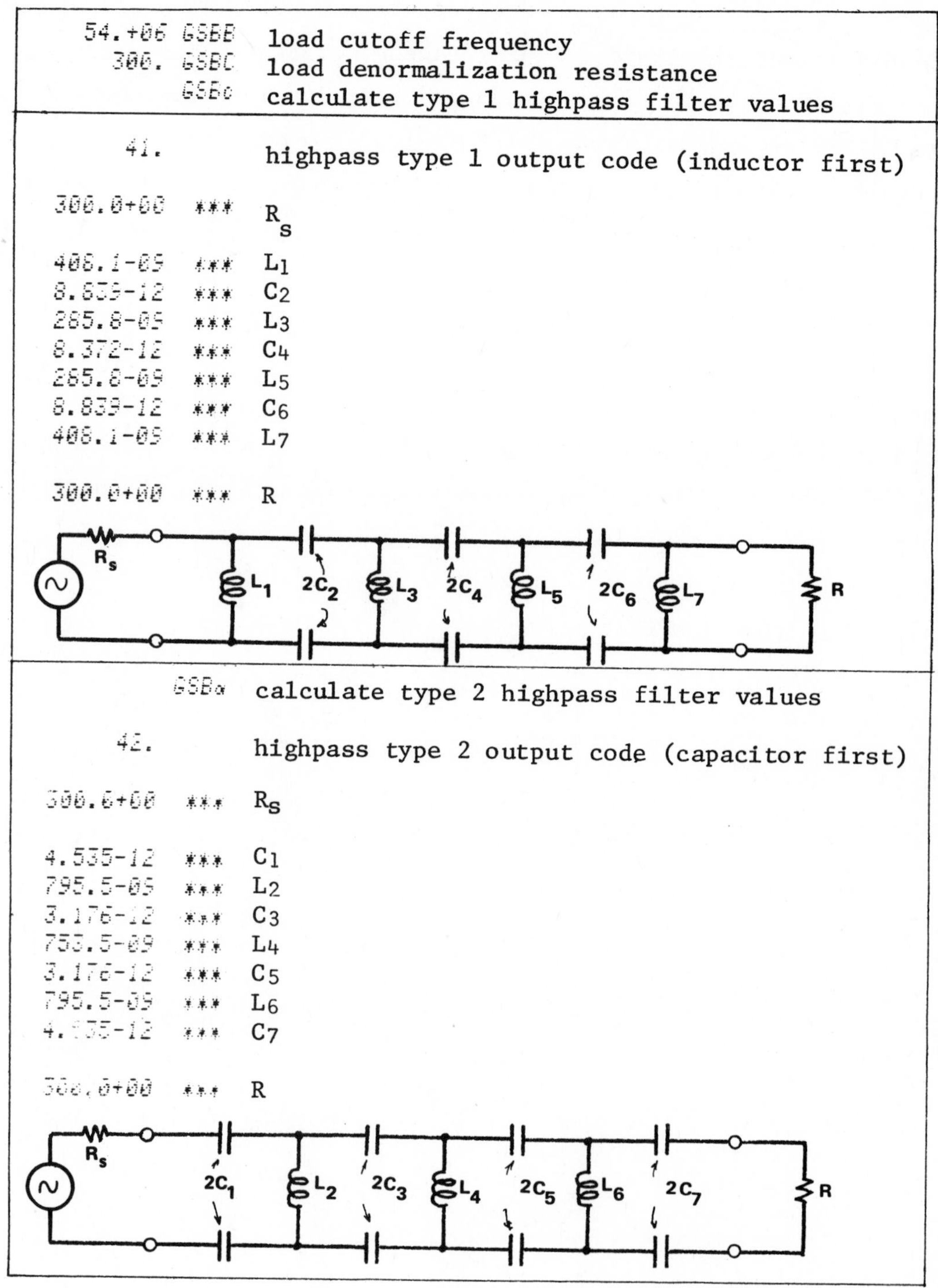

```
54.+06 GSBB     load cutoff frequency
  300. GSBC     load denormalization resistance
       GSBc     calculate type 1 highpass filter values

    41.         highpass type 1 output code (inductor first)

300.0+00  ***   Rs

408.1-09  ***   L1
8.839-12  ***   C2
265.8-09  ***   L3
8.372-12  ***   C4
265.8-09  ***   L5
8.839-12  ***   C6
408.1-09  ***   L7

300.0+00  ***   R
```



```
       GSBa     calculate type 2 highpass filter values

    42.         highpass type 2 output code (capacitor first)

300.0+00  ***   Rs

4.535-12  ***   C1
795.5-09  ***   L2
3.176-12  ***   C3
753.5-09  ***   L4
3.176-12  ***   C5
795.5-09  ***   L6
4.535-12  ***   C7

300.0+00  ***   R
```



Programs 3-5 and 3-6 can aid in the aircore inductor designs needed here.

Example 2-4.3 Bandstop filter

Consider implementing the filter cited in the previous example as a bandstop filter rather than as a highpass filter. The stopband required is from 26 MHz to 27 MHz. The center frequency of a bandstop (and bandpass) filter is the geometric mean of any two equal attenuation frequencies (this relationship does not hold for narrowband bandpass transformations for frequencies outside the passband). The center frequency of this bandstop filter is then 26.4953 MHz. If the upper -1 dB point is 54 MHz, then the lower -1 dB point is $(26.4953\ \text{MHz})^2/(54\ \text{MHz}) = 13$ MHz. The normalized frequency multiplier, $\lambda$ , is the ratio between the passband and the stopband, or $\lambda = (54 - 13)/(27 - 26) = 41$. From Program 2-1, the filter order that meets these requirements is 2. Even ordered Chebyshev filters do not have equal termination resistance levels, and this filter is to be placed in a 300 ohm system (equally terminated). To satisfy all requirements including equal termination, a third order bandstop filter will be designed. The HP-97 printout for this filter design follows.

Load Program 2-1 to calculate the minimum filter order required:

| | | |
|---|---|---|
| | GSBb | select Chebyshev |
| 1.00 | GSBa | load $Ap_{dB}$ |
| 60.00 | GSBE | load $As_{dB}$ |
| 41.00 | GSBD | load $\lambda$ and calculate filter order, n |
| 1.88 | *** | minimum n to meet requirements (use n = 2 min) |
| 3.00 | GSBC | load n desired and calculate $\lambda$ for $As_{dB}$ = 60 dB |
| 7.92 | *** | $\lambda$ |
| | 1/X | form $1/\lambda$ |
| 41.00 | X | |
| 5.18 | *** | stopband bandwidth (MHz) |
| 26.4953 | GSBd | enter center frequency (MHz) and calculate: |
| 29.21 | *** | upper stopband edge (MHz) |
| 24.03 | *** | lower stopband edge (MHz) |

| | | |
|---|---|---|
| 3. | GSBA | load filter order |
| 1. | GSBB | load termination resistance ratio desired |
| 1. | GSBD | load Chebyshev passband ripple in dB and start |
| 1.09487+00 | *** | $\lambda$ for 3 dB bandwidth (output) |
| 1.00000+00 | *** | $R_T$ (normalized) |
| 2.02359+00 | *** | normalized lowpass coefficients |
| 994.102-03 | *** | |
| 2.02359+00 | *** | |
| 1.00000+00 | *** | R (normalized) |

| | | |
|---|---|---|
| 26.4953+06 | GSBA | load filter center frequency |
| 41.+06 | GSBB | load filter bandwidth |
| 300. | GSBC | load de-normalization resistance level |
| | GSBD | calculate type 1 bandstop |
| 21. | | type 1 bandstop heading (series tank first) |
| 300.0+00 | *** | $R_s$ |
| 62.70-12 | *** | $C_1$ |
| 575.5-09 | *** | $L_1$ |
| 13.02-12 | *** | $C_2$ |
| 2.772-06 | *** | $L_2$ |
| 62.70-12 | *** | $C_3$ |
| 575.5-09 | *** | $L_3$ |
| 300.0+00 | *** | R |

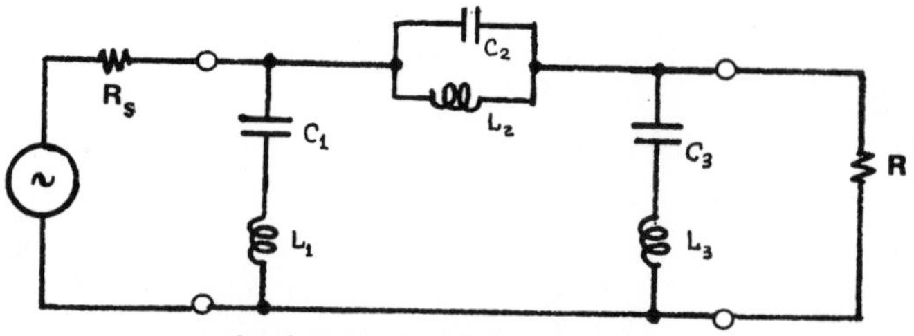

unbalanced structure

| | | |
|---|---|---|
| | GSBE | calculate type 2 bandstop |
| 22. | | type 2 bandstop heading (parallel tank first) |
| 300.0+00 | *** | $R_s$ |
| 6.394-12 | *** | $C_1$ |
| 5.643-06 | *** | $L_1$ |
| 30.80-12 | *** | $C_2$ |
| 1.171-06 | *** | $L_2$ |
| 6.394-12 | *** | $C_3$ |
| 5.643-06 | *** | $L_3$ |
| 300.0+00 | *** | R |

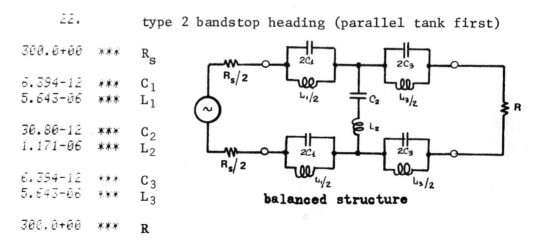

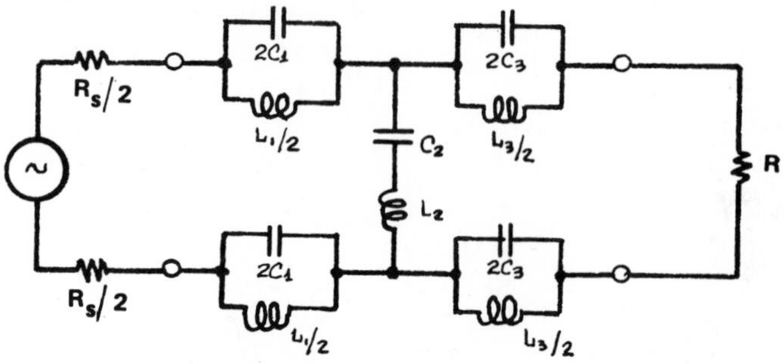

balanced structure

# Program Listing I

| | | |
|---|---|---|
| 001 | *LBLA | LOAD CENTER FREQUENCY |
| 002 | Pi | |
| 003 | ENT↑ | |
| 004 | + | $2\pi f_o \rightarrow R0$ |
| 005 | x | |
| 006 | ST00 | |
| 007 | RTN | |
| 008 | *LBLB | LOAD BANDWIDTH OR CUTOFF FREQ |
| 009 | Pi | |
| 010 | ENT↑ | |
| 011 | + | $2\pi BW \rightarrow R1$ |
| 012 | x | |
| 013 | ST01 | |
| 014 | RTN | |
| 015 | *LBLC | LOAD DENORMALIZATION RESIST |
| 016 | ST02 | $R \rightarrow R2$ |
| 017 | RTN | |
| 018 | *LBLD | BANDSTOP TYPE 1 ROUTINE |
| 019 | SPC | |
| 020 | 2 | |
| 021 | 1 | print heading "21" |
| 022 | PRTX | |
| 023 | CF1 | indicate type 1 topology |
| 024 | GT00 | |
| 025 | *LBLE | BANDSTOP TYPE 2 ROUTINE |
| 026 | SPC | |
| 027 | 2 | |
| 028 | 2 | print heading "22" |
| 029 | PRTX | |
| 030 | SF1 | indicate type 2 topology |
| 031 | *LBL0 | |
| 032 | SF2 | calculate and print $R_s$ |
| 033 | GSB2 | |
| 034 | RCL2 | |
| 035 | RCL1 | calculate and store: |
| 036 | x | |
| 037 | RCL0 | |
| 038 | X² | $\frac{R \cdot BW}{\omega_o^2} = \frac{R}{\omega_o \cdot Q_L} \rightarrow R4$ |
| 039 | ÷ | |
| 040 | ST04 | |
| 041 | RCL2 | |
| 042 | X² | $\frac{1}{R \cdot \omega_o \cdot Q_L} \rightarrow R5$ |
| 043 | ÷ | |
| 044 | ST05 | |
| 045 | CLX | |
| 046 | ST07 | initialize index registers |
| 047 | 9 | |
| 048 | STOI | |

| | | |
|---|---|---|
| 049 | *LBL1 | bandstop calculation loop |
| 050 | GSB9 | increment indices and |
| 051 | X>Y? | test for loop exit |
| 052 | GT04 | |
| 053 | SPC | |
| 054 | RCLi | recall $g_k$ |
| 055 | RCL4 | recall $R/(\omega_o \cdot Q_L)$ |
| 056 | CF0 | set print order for type 1 |
| 057 | F1? | test for type 1 filter |
| 058 | GT06 | |
| 059 | CLX | |
| 060 | RCL5 | substitute $1/(R \cdot \omega_o \cdot Q_L)$ in $R_x$ |
| 061 | SF0 | set print order for type 2 |
| 062 | *LBL6 | |
| 063 | GSB8 | gosub elt calculation & print |
| 064 | GSB9 | increment indices and |
| 065 | X>Y? | test for loop exit |
| 066 | GT04 | |
| 067 | SPC | |
| 068 | RCLi | recall $g_k$ |
| 069 | RCL5 | recall $1/(R \cdot \omega_o \cdot Q_L)$ |
| 070 | SF0 | set print order for type 1 |
| 071 | F1? | test for type 1 filter |
| 072 | GT06 | |
| 073 | CLX | |
| 074 | RCL4 | substitute $R/(\omega_o \cdot Q_L)$ in $R_x$ |
| 075 | CF0 | |
| 076 | *LBL6 | |
| 077 | GSB8 | gosub elt calculation & print |
| 078 | GT01 | goto loop start |
| 079 | *LBL8 | element calculation & print |
| 080 | x | form and store $g_k \cdot R_x \rightarrow R8$ |
| 081 | ST08 | |
| 082 | F0? | if flag 0 print R8 |
| 083 | PRTX | |
| 084 | RCL0 | calculate mating |
| 085 | X² | resonant element: |
| 086 | x | |
| 087 | 1/X | $C,L = \frac{1}{\omega_o^2 \cdot (L,C)}$ |
| 088 | PRTX | |
| 089 | F0? | if flag 0, return to |
| 090 | RTN | main program |
| 091 | RCL8 | recall and print R8 |
| 092 | PRTX | |
| 093 | RTN | return to main program |
| 094 | *LBLa | LOWPASS TYPE 1 ROUTINE |
| 095 | SPC | |
| 096 | 3 | |
| 097 | 1 | print heading "31" |
| 098 | PRTX | |
| 099 | CF0 | indicate lowpass filter |
| 100 | CF1 | indicate type 1 filter |
| 101 | GSB7 | calculate some constants |
| 102 | GT02 | goto output routine |

## REGISTERS

| 0 $2\pi f_c$ | 1 $2\pi BW$ | 2 $R$ | 3 | 4 scratch | 5 scratch | 6 $n$ | 7 $k$ | 8 | 9 |
|---|---|---|---|---|---|---|---|---|---|
| S0 $g_1$ | S1 $g_2$ | S2 $g_3$ | S3 $g_4$ | S4 $g_5$ | S5 $g_6$ | S6 $g_7$ | S7 $g_8$ | S8 $g_9$ | S9 $g_{10}$ |
| A $g_{11}$ | | B $g_{12}$ | | C $g_{13}$ | | D $R_T$ | | E | I index |

# Program Listing II

```
*LBLb   LOWPASS TYPE 2 ROUTINE
SPC
3       print heading "32"
2
PRTX
CF0     indicate lowpass filter
SF1     indicate type 2 filter
GSB7    compute LP type 1 constants
RCL2
X²      change to LP type 2 constants
ST÷4
ST×5
GTO2    goto output routine
*LBLd   HIGHPASS TYPE 2 ROUTINE
SPC
4       print heading "42"
2
PRTX
SF0     indicate highpass
SF1     indicate type 2
GSB7    compute LP type 1 constants
GTO2    goto output routine
*LBLc   HIGHPASS TYPE 1 ROUTINE
SPC
4       print heading "41"
1
PRTX
SF0     indicate highpass
CF1     indicate type 1
GSB7    calculate LP type 1 constants
RCL2
X²      change to HP type 1 constants
ST÷4
ST×5
*LBL2   LP & HP output routine
SPC     recall R_T
RCLD
F1?     if type 2 filter, form 1/R_T
1/X
RCL2
×       calculate and print R_s
PRTX
F2?     test for return to bandstop
RTN
SPC
*LBL3   LP and HP output loop start
GSB9    increment indices and
X>Y?    test for loop exit
GTO4
RCLi    recall g_k
F0?     if highpass, form 1/g_k
1/X
RCL5    calculate and print
×       first filter element
PRTX
GSB9    increment indices and
X>Y?    test for loop exit
GTO4
RCLi    recall g_k
F0?     if highpass, form 1/g_k
1/X
RCL4    calculate and print
×       other type of filter element
PRTX
GTO3    goto loop start
*LBL4   recall and print port 2
SPC     termination resistance
RCL2
PRTX
SPC
SPC
RTN     return control to keyboard
*LBL7   subroutine to calc LP - 1
RCL2    calculate and store
RCL1    inductor scaling:
÷       R/(2π.BW) → R4
STO4
RCL2    calculate and store
X²      capacitor scaling:
÷       1/(2π.BW.R) → R5
STO5
CLX
STO7    initialize indices
9
STOI
RTN
*LBL9   incr indices and loop exit
EEX
ST+7
ISZI
RCL6
RCL7
RTN
```

| LABELS | | | | | FLAGS |
|---|---|---|---|---|---|
| A load $f_o$ | B load BW | C load R | D $BS_1$ | E $BS_2$ | 0 Highpass |
| a $LP_1$ | b $LP_2$ | c $HP_1$ | d $HP_2$ | e | 1 Type 2 |
| 0 calculate BS coef | 1 BS loop rtn | 2 calc $R_T'$ | 3 LP/HP loop rtn | 4 print R | 2 lbl 2 return |
| 5 | 6 Local loop destination | 7 LP/HP coefs | 8 bandstop output | 9 index incr & loop exit test | 3 |

| SET STATUS | | | | |
|---|---|---|---|---|
| FLAGS | | | TRIG | DISP |
| | ON | OFF | USER'S CHOICE | |
| 0 | | ■ | DEG | FIX |
| 1 | | ■ | GRAD | SCI |
| 2 | | ■ | RAD | ENG |
| 3 | | | | n____ |

HP-67 suggested program changes. A print or R/S routine has not been provided, although register 9 and label "e" could have been used for this purpose. The reason for this omission is to preserve the heading format. Any program statements placed between a numeric entry and a print statement cause the printed format to be in the set status of the program; however, by placing the print statement directly after the numeric entry (see lines 20 through 22), "21" is printed without trailing zeros.

On the HP-67, the "print" statement causes the program halt for 5 seconds and a flashing decimal point. This situation slows program execution and may not be desirable. The HP-67 user may wish to have the program stop at the data output points. To cause the program to stop at these points, change the program as follows: Delete steps 019 - 022, 026 - 029, 095 - 098, 104 - 107, 117 - 120, and 126 - 129. Change the "print" statements to "R/S" statements at the following line numbers: 083, 088, 092, 144, 157, 166, and 171. To restart program execution after a program halt, execute a "R/S" from the keyboard.

Remember, when deleting steps from a program, always work from the back of the program forward. By observing this convention, the line numbers of steps not yet deleted will remain unaltered.

## PROGRAM 2-5 NORMALIZED LOWPASS TO BANDPASS FILTER TRANSFORMATIONS, TYPES 1, 2, 6, AND 7.

Program Description and Equations Used

This program converts normalized lowpass filter element values to a set of four bandpass topologies [16], [21], [56]. The four topologies are shown in Fig. 2-5.1, and the parameter $A_{ij}$ is defined by Eq. (2-5.1). Types 1 and 2 are exact transformations and will transform the lowpass response independent of the loaded filter Q (Eq. (2-4.7)). Types 6 and 7 of this program, and types 8, and 9 of Program 2-6 are narrowband approximations, and only provide accurate transformation results when the loaded Q is greater than 5, and preferably greater than 10.

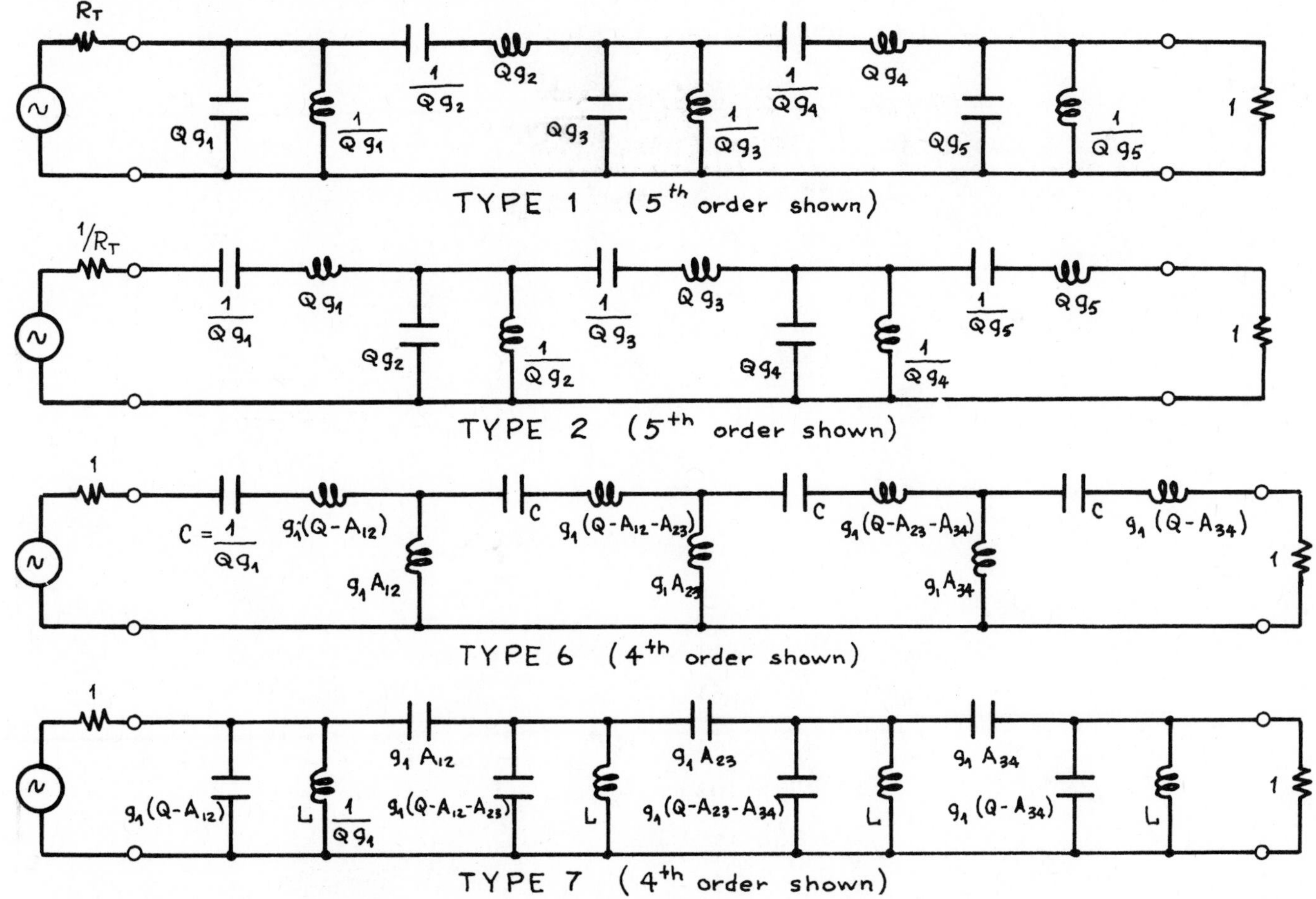


Figure 2-5.1 Bandpass filter topologies for types 1, 2, 6, & 7.

$$A_{ij} = (g_i \cdot g_j)^{-\frac{1}{2}} \qquad (2\text{-}5.1)$$

Figure 2-5.2 is a reproduction of Table 7.2 in White [56] and is intended as a guide to the best suited filter topology for a particular application. The physical realizability of a filter topology is assigned one of four possible scores based upon element values. These scores are defined as follows:

Readily realizable (R):

$1\ \mu h \leq L \leq 1\ h$

$5\ pF \leq C \leq 1\ \mu F$

Practical (P):

$0.2\ \mu h \leq L \leq 10\ h$

$2.\ \ pF \leq C \leq 10\ \mu F$

Marginally practical (M):

$50\ nh \leq L \leq 100\ h$

$0.5\ pF \leq C \leq 500\ \mu F$

Impractical (I):

All element values that lie outside the range of marginal i.e.,

$L < 50\ nh$

$L > 100\ h$

$C < .5\ pF$

$C > 500\ \mu F$

The table headings are meant to indicate ranges of loaded Q, filter center frequency, and termination resistance level. These ranges are:

Frequency;

$f_o$ = 10 Hz implies: $3\ Hz \leq f_o < 30\ Hz$

$f_o$ = 100 Hz implies: $30\ Hz \leq f_o < 300\ Hz$

$f_o$ = 1 kHz implies: $300\ Hz \leq f_o < 3\ kHz$

$f_o$ = 10 kHz implies $3\ kHz \leq f_o < 30\ kHz$

$f_o$ = 100 kHz implies: $30\ kHz \leq f_o < 300\ kHz$

$f_o$ = 1 MHz implies: $300\ kHz \leq f_o < 3\ MHz$

$f_o$ = 10 MHz implies: $3\ MHz \leq f_o < 30\ MHz$

$f_o$ = 100 MHz implies: $30\ MHz \leq f_o < 300\ MHz$

At frequencies above 300 MHz, lumped element filters are generally replaced with transmission line type filters.

Loaded Q ($Q_L$), for bandpass and bandstop,

$Q_L = 5$ implies: $3 \leq Q_L < 10$

$Q_L = 15$ implies: $10 \leq Q_L < 30$

$Q_L = 50$ implies: $30 \leq Q_L \leq 100$

Impedance Level (source and load resistances equal)

R = 3 ohms implies: $1 \leq R < 10$ (power filters)

R = 50 ohms implies: $10 \leq R < 150$

R = 500 ohms implies: $150 \leq R < 2.5k$

R = 10k ohms implies: $2.5k \leq R < 50k$

| Band-Pass Filter Prototype | $f_o = 1$ kHz | | | | | | | | | $f_o = 10$ kHz | | | | | | | | |
|---|---|---|---|---|---|---|---|---|---|---|---|---|---|---|---|---|---|---|
| | $Q_L = 5$ | | | $Q_L = 15$ | | | $Q_L = 50$ | | | $Q_L = 5$ | | | $Q_L = 15$ | | | $Q_L = 50$ | | |
| Type | 50 | 500 | 10K | 50 | 500 | 10K | 50 | 500 | 10K | 50 | 500 | 10K | 50 | 500 | 10K | 50 | 500 | 10K |
| 1st | I | P | P | I | I | I | I | I | I | M | R | P | I | M | P | I | M | P |
| 2nd | I | P | P | I | I | I | I | I | I | M | R | P | I | M | I | I | M | P |
| 3rd | I | M | I | I | I | I | I | I | I | M | P | M | I | P | P | I | M | I |
| 4th | I | M | P | I | I | P | I | I | M | M | P | P | I | P | P | I | M | P |
| 5th | P | P | P | P | I | P | P | P | I | R | R | P | R | P | P | R | P | M |
| 6th | P | P | I | P | P | I | P | P | I | R | R | P | R | P | P | R | P | M |
| 7th | I | M | P | I | I | P | I | I | M | M | P | R | I | P | R | I | M | P |
| 8th | M | P | I | M | P | I | M | P | I | P | R | P | P | P | P | P | P | M |
| 9th | I | M | P | I | I | P | I | I | M | M | P | P | I | P | P | I | M | P |
| 10th | M | P | M | P | R | P | R | R | P | P | R | P | R | R | R | R | R | R |
| 11th | M | P | P | M | P | P | M | M | P | P | R | R | P | R | R | M | P | R |

| Band-Pass Filter Prototype | $f_o = 100$ kHz | | | | | | | | | $f_o = 1$ MHz | | | | | | | | |
|---|---|---|---|---|---|---|---|---|---|---|---|---|---|---|---|---|---|---|
| | $Q_L = 5$ | | | $Q_L = 15$ | | | $Q_L = 50$ | | | $Q_L = 5$ | | | $Q_L = 15$ | | | $Q_L = 50$ | | |
| Type | 50 | 500 | 10K | 50 | 500 | 10K | 50 | 500 | 10K | 50 | 500 | 10K | 50 | 500 | 10K | 50 | 500 | 10K |
| 1st | P | R | R | P | P | I | M | M | I | P | R | P | P | P | I | M | P | I |
| 2nd | P | R | R | P | P | I | M | M | I | P | R | P | P | P | I | M | M | I |
| 3rd | P | R | P | P | R | P | M | P | P | R | R | P | R | R | R | M | P | I |
| 4th | P | R | R | P | R | R | M | P | R | R | R | R | P | R | R | M | P | R |
| 5th | R | R | P | R | R | P | R | R | P | R | R | P | R | R | M | R | P | I |
| 6th | R | R | P | R | R | P | R | P | P | R | R | P | R | R | M | R | P | I |
| 7th | P | R | R | P | R | R | M | P | R | R | R | R | P | R | R | M | P | R |
| 8th | R | R | P | R | R | P | R | R | P | R | R | P | R | R | M | R | P | I |
| 9th | P | R | R | P | R | R | M | P | R | R | R | R | P | R | R | M | P | R |
| 10th | R | R | R | R | R | P | R | R | P | R | R | P | R | R | M | R | R | M |
| 11th | R | R | R | R | R | R | P | R | R | R | R | R | R | R | R | R | R | R |

| Band-Pass Filter Prototype | $f_o = 10$ MHz | | | | | | | | | $f_o = 100$ MHz | | | | | | | | |
|---|---|---|---|---|---|---|---|---|---|---|---|---|---|---|---|---|---|---|
| | $Q_L = 5$ | | | $Q_L = 15$ | | | $Q_L = 50$ | | | $Q_L = 5$ | | | $Q_L = 15$ | | | $Q_L = 50$ | | |
| Type | 50 | 500 | 10K | 50 | 500 | 10K | 50 | 500 | 10K | 50 | 500 | 10K | 50 | 500 | 10K | 50 | 500 | 10K |
| 1st | M | P | M | I | P | I | I | I | I | I | I | I | I | I | I | I | I | I |
| 2nd | M | P | M | I | P | I | I | I | I | I | I | I | I | I | I | I | I | I |
| 3rd | P | R | M | R | P | I | I | M | I | I | M | I | I | I | I | I | I | I |
| 4th | M | R | R | I | P | R | I | M | R | I | M | R | I | I | P | I | I | M |
| 5th | P | R | M | M | P | I | P | M | I | M | M | I | I | I | I | M | I | I |
| 6th | R | R | M | P | P | I | P | M | I | P | M | I | M | I | I | M | I | I |
| 7th | M | R | P | I | P | P | I | P | P | I | P | M | I | I | I | I | M | I |
| 8th | R | R | M | R | P | I | P | M | I | P | M | I | P | I | I | M | I | I |
| 9th | M | R | R | I | P | R | I | M | R | I | M | R | I | I | P | I | I | M |
| 10th | P | R | I | P | M | I | P | M | I | P | M | I | M | I | I | M | I | I |
| 11th | M | R | M | M | P | M | I | P | M | I | M | I | I | M | I | I | I | I |

**Fig. 2-5.2 Physical realizability of bandpass filters.**

**Courtesy Don White Consultants Inc.**

To use the routines for types 6 through 9, the filter must have termination resistances as close to unity as possible. To achieve this result, a desired termination resistance level of 1.0 should be loaded into Program 2-3.

Of the filter types presented both in this program, and the accompanying program (types 1, 2, 6, 7, 8, 9, 10, and 11) only types 1, 2, 10, and 11 are exact transformations of the lowpass characteristic. All the remaining filter types are narrowband approximations, i.e., they will faithfully transform the lowpass characteristics within the passband and within a few octaves of the stopband. Types 6, 7, 8, and 9 do not have equal numbers of transmission zeros at both zero frequency and at infinite frequency. The result of this imbalance is to skew the filter response away from the frequency where the extra zeros exist. Figure 2-5.3 shows this occurrence.

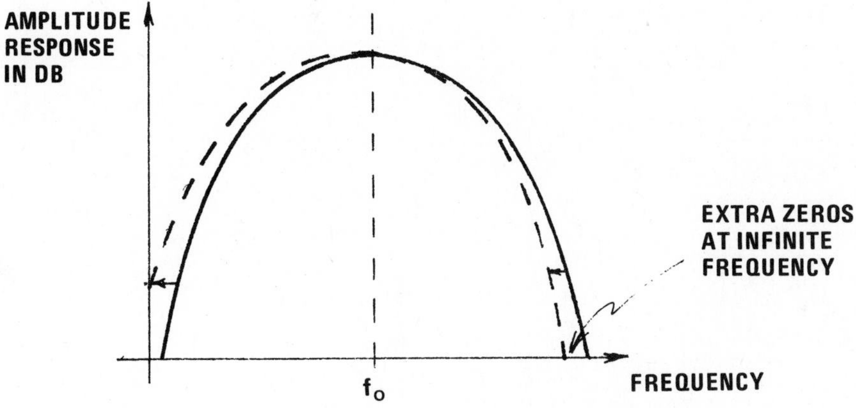


Figure 2-5.3 Bandpass filter response skewing due to extra transmission zeros at infinity.

One should not choose types 1, 2, 10, or 11 automatically. Types 1 and 2 may be difficult to realize in a narrowband application, and types 10 and 11 (also types 6 and 9) contain redundant inductors. Depending upon the frequency range and element values, these redundant inductors can be burdensome. As a guide, filters operating below 1 kHz may best be realized with an active filter (this subject is covered by other programs in this section); between 1 kHz and 100 kHz, the minimum inductor LC design should be considered and compared with active approaches; above 1 MHz the simplest LC topology should be sought to ease the tuning problem.

# User Instructions

| NORMALIZED LOWPASS TO BANDPASS TYPES 1, 2, 6, & 7 | | | | |
|---|---|---|---|---|
| load center frequency | load bandwidth | load termination resistance | | load filter # & start |

| STEP | INSTRUCTIONS | INPUT DATA/UNITS | KEYS | OUTPUT DATA/UNITS |
|---|---|---|---|---|
| 1 | Load both sides of program card | | | |
| 2 | Load center frequency in Hz | $f_o$ | [A] | $\omega_o$ |
| 3 | Load bandwidth in Hz | BW | [B] | Q |
| 4 | Load termination resistance in ohms | R | [C] | R |
| 5 | Load filter type number and start | type | [E] | R |
| | | | | tank C |
| | | | | tank L |
| | | | | cplg elt* |
| | | | | tank C |
| | | | | tank L |
| | | | | cplg elt* |
| | | | | tank C |
| | | | | tank L |
| | | | | ⋮ |
| | *The coupling element (L for type 6 or C for type 7) does not exist for types 1 or 2. | | | $R_T$ |
| 6 | For another case goto steps 2 through 5 as applicable | | | |

<u>Example 2-5.1 Type 6 filter</u>

A maximally flat passband (Butterworth) bandpass filter is to pass a 500 Hz band of frequencies centered around 10 kHz. In a bandpass (or bandstop) filter, the center frequency is the geometric mean of the upper and lower bandedge frequencies, i.e., $f_o = (9750 \cdot 10250)^{1/2}$, or $f_o = 9996.87$ Hz. The filter should reject by at least 30 dB those frequencies removed from the center frequency by more than 500 Hz. The required filter order is obtained from Program 2-1. Using this program, a minimum filter order of 5 is calculated given $As_{dB} = 3$, $Ap_{dB} = 30$, and $\lambda = 1000/500 = 2$. Program 2-3 is used to obtain the Butterworth normalized coefficients for use by this program.

The proper bandpass topology is selected from the table in Fig. 2-5.2 under the headings: $f_o = 10$ kHz, $Q_L = 10000/500 = 20$ (use $Q_L$ = 15 column), and R = 50 to find that a type 6 is readily realizable, therefore a type 6 filter will be designed. The HP-97 printout for the above operations is shown below.

Load Program 2-1 to calculate minimum filter order:

| Printout | | Operation |
|---|---|---|
| | GSBa | select Butterworth |
| 3.00 | GSBA | load $Ap_{dB}$ |
| 30.00 | GSBB | load $As_{dB}$ |
| 2.00 | GSBD | load $\lambda$ and calculate n |
| 4.99 | *** | filter. order, n (output) |
| 5.00 | GSBC | load integral n and calculate $\lambda$ |
| 2.00 | *** | $\lambda$ for given $Ap_{dB}$ and $As_{dB}$ |
| 2.00 | GSBE | load $\lambda$ and calculate $As_{dB}$ |
| 30.03 | *** | $As_{dB}$ |

Load Program 2-3 to calculate normalized LP Butterworth coefs:

| Printout | | Operation |
|---|---|---|
| 5. | GSBH | load filter order |
| 1. | GSBE | load desired termination resistance ratio |
| | GSBC | calculate Butterworth coefficients |
| 1.00000+00 | *** | $R_T$ (normalized port 1 termination resistor) |
| 618.034-03 | *** | $g_1$ normalized lowpass coefficients |
| 1.61803+00 | *** | $g_2$ normalized lowpass coefficients |
| 2.00000+00 | *** | $g_3$ normalized lowpass coefficients |
| 1.61803+00 | *** | $g_4$ normalized lowpass coefficients |
| 618.034-03 | *** | $g_5$ normalized lowpass coefficients |
| 1.00000+00 | *** | R (normalized port 2 termination resistor) |

Example 2-5.1, continued:

Load Program 2-5 (this program) and calculate type 6 elements.

| | |
|---|---|
| 9996.87 GSBA | load center frequency |
| 500. GSBB | load bandwidth |
| 50. GSBC | load termination resistance |
| 6. GSBE | load filter type desired and start |

```
50.000+00  ***   termination resistance

25.768-09  ***   C1
9.3443-03  ***   L1

491.97-06  ***   L12

25.768-09  ***   C2
9.0709-03  ***   L2

273.48-06  ***   L23

25.768-09  ***   C3
9.2894-03  ***   L3

273.48-06  ***   L34

25.768-09  ***   C4
9.0709-03  ***   L4

491.97-06  ***   L45

25.768-09  ***   C5
9.3443-03  ***   L5

50.000+00  ***   termination resistance
```

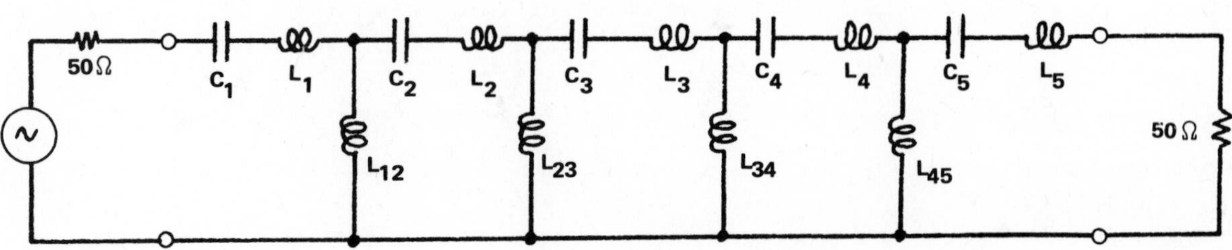


Figure 2-5.4 Type 6 bandpass filter schematic.

Type 6 tuning technique.* After the filter is designed, the inductors fabricated and adjusted, the capacitors obtained, and the filter constructed, the filter must be tuned. For series resonant tanks, such as in this filter and types 8 and 10, tuning is accomplished by decoupling individual tank circuits using open circuits.

Assume the inductors are wound on ferrite pot cores, and are the adjustable elements. Referring to Fig. 2-5.5, to tune $L_1$ temporarily open the circuit at "B" and tune L for series resonance of the $L_1$, $L_{12}$, C circuit at the center frequency of the filter, 9996.87 Hz in this case.

To tune $L_2$, $L_{12}$, $L_{23}$, and C, re-establish the connection at "B," and temporarily open the circuit at points "A" and "C." Tune $L_2$ for series resonance at the center frequency. Continue this procedure of opening adjacent tank circuits and tuning until all series resonant loops have been tuned to the filter center frequency.

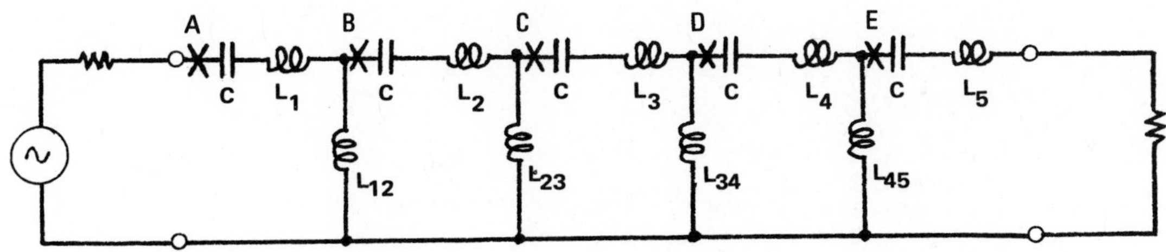


Figure 2-5.5 Type 6 filter showing circuit opens for tuning.

For information on ferrite pot core inductor design, see the Ferroxcube catalog "Linear Ferrite Materials and Components," and use Programs 3-1 and 3-2 to aid in the design of these inductors.

When designing the inductors, the designer must not allow the magnetic core excitation to drive the core near saturation. The voltage across an inductor is "Q" times the voltage across the series LC tank at

---

*For parallel tank filter tuning procedure, see the example in the type 8, 9, 10, and 11 transformations program.

resonance. With inductor Q's of 100 or better, inductor voltages can be large with respect to the voltage across the filter. The voltage across a filter element at center frequency is approximately $I_{in} \cdot X_{element}$ where $I_{in}$ is the filter input current and $X_{element}$ is the element reactance.

# Program Listing I

| | | |
|---|---|---|
| 001 | *LBLA | LOAD CENTER FREQUENCY |
| 002 | Pi | |
| 003 | ENT↑ | form and store: |
| 004 | + | |
| 005 | x | $2\pi f_o \rightarrow R0$ |
| 006 | STO0 | |
| 007 | RTN | |
| 008 | *LBLB | LOAD BANDWIDTH |
| 009 | Pi | |
| 010 | ENT↑ | |
| 011 | + | form and store: |
| 012 | x | |
| 013 | RCL0 | $Q = \dfrac{2\pi f_o}{2\pi BW} \rightarrow R_1$ |
| 014 | X≠Y | |
| 015 | ÷ | |
| 016 | STO1 | |
| 017 | RTN | |
| 018 | *LBLC | LOAD TERMINATION |
| 019 | STO2 | RESISTANCE |
| 020 | RTN | |
| 021 | *LBLE | LOAD FILTER TYPE (1,2,6,7) |
| 022 | STOI | |
| 023 | 8 | generate "ERROR" if other |
| 024 | X≠Y? | than filter types 1, 2, |
| 025 | GTOo | 6, or 7 loaded. |
| 026 | RCLI | |
| 027 | 3 | "ERROR" is generated by |
| 028 | X=Y? | calling unused label (a) |
| 029 | GTOo | |
| 030 | RCLI | |
| 031 | 4 | |
| 032 | X=Y? | |
| 033 | GTOo | |
| 034 | RCLI | |
| 035 | 5 | |
| 036 | X=Y? | |
| 037 | GTOo | |
| 038 | RCLI | calculate indirect label |
| 039 | 2 | corresponding to desired |
| 040 | ÷ | filter type |
| 041 | STOI | |
| 042 | INT | |
| 043 | X≠I | |
| 044 | FRC | |
| 045 | SF0 | set flag 0 if types 1 |
| 046 | X=0? | or 7 are entered otherwise |
| 047 | CF0 | clear flag 0 |
| 048 | GTOi | |

| | | |
|---|---|---|
| 049 | *LBL0 | type 1 calculation start |
| 050 | *LBL1 | type 2 calculation start |
| 051 | GSB9 | initialize flags & regs |
| 052 | *LBL2 | types 1 & 2 loop start |
| 053 | RCL7 | |
| 054 | 2 | set flag 2 if branch |
| 055 | ÷ | number is even where |
| 056 | FRC | k is the branch number |
| 057 | X=0? | |
| 058 | SF2 | |
| 059 | RCLi | |
| 060 | RCL1 | form $Q \cdot g_1$ |
| 061 | x | |
| 062 | F2? | if branch even, form $1/Q \cdot g_1$ |
| 063 | 1/X | |
| 064 | STOC | calculate and print |
| 065 | F0? | branch capacitor |
| 066 | GSB8 | |
| 067 | F1? | |
| 068 | GSB7 | |
| 069 | RCLC | |
| 070 | F0? | calculate and print |
| 071 | GSB7 | branch inductor |
| 072 | F1? | |
| 073 | GSB8 | |
| 074 | SPC | |
| 075 | DSZI | |
| 076 | EEX | increment indices |
| 077 | ST+7 | |
| 078 | RCL6 | |
| 079 | RCL7 | test for loop exit |
| 080 | X≠Y? | |
| 081 | GTO2 | |
| 082 | RCLD | |
| 083 | F0? | calculate and print |
| 084 | 1/X | termination resistance |
| 085 | RCL2 | |
| 086 | x | |
| 087 | GSB6 | |
| 088 | GTOb | |

## REGISTERS

| 0 $2\pi f_o$ | 1 Q | 2 R | 3 | 4 $\frac{1}{\omega_o R}$ or $\frac{R}{\omega_o}$ | 5 $\frac{R}{\omega_o}$ or $\frac{1}{\omega_o R}$ | 6 n | 7 k | 8 $g_n$ | 9 $A_{i, i+1}$ |
|---|---|---|---|---|---|---|---|---|---|
| S0 $g_1$ | S1 $g_2$ | S2 $g_3$ | S3 $g_4$ | S4 $g_5$ | S5 $g_6$ | S6 $g_7$ | S7 $g_8$ | S8 $g_9$ | S9 $g_{10}$ |

| A $g_{11}$ | B $g_{12}$ | C types 6&7 common element | D $R_T$ | E $g_{i+1}$ | I index |
|---|---|---|---|---|---|

# Program Listing II

| | | |
|---|---|---|
| 089 | *LBL3 | types 6 & 7 start |
| 090 | GSB9 | initialize flags & regs |
| 091 | RCLi | |
| 092 | STOE | recall and store $g_n$ |
| 093 | STO8 | |
| 094 | RCL1 | |
| 095 | x | calculate and store $Q \cdot g_n$ |
| 096 | STOC | |
| 097 | *LBL4 | types 6 & 7 loop start |
| 098 | F1? | if type 6 print common |
| 099 | GSB5 | tank capacitor value |
| 100 | DSZI | |
| 101 | EEX | increment indicies |
| 102 | ST+7 | |
| 103 | RCLi | recall $g_i$ |
| 104 | RCLE | |
| 105 | X⇌Y | interchange $g_i$ and $g_{i+1}$ |
| 106 | STOE | |
| 107 | x | |
| 108 | √X | calculate $A_{i, i+1}$ |
| 109 | 1/X | |
| 110 | RCL9 | interchange |
| 111 | X⇌Y | $A_{i, i+1}$ and $A_{i+1, i+2}$ |
| 112 | STO9 | |
| 113 | + | calculate type 6 tank L |
| 114 | GSB0 | or type 7 tank C |
| 115 | RCL9 | |
| 116 | RCL8 | |
| 117 | x | calculate coupling element |
| 118 | GSB8 | |
| 119 | SPC | |
| 120 | RCL7 | |
| 121 | RCL6 | |
| 122 | X>Y? | test for loop exit |
| 123 | GTO4 | |
| 124 | F1? | if type 6 print last tank |
| 125 | GSB5 | capacitor |
| 126 | RCL9 | calculate type 6 last tank |
| 127 | GSB0 | L, or type 7 last tank C |
| 128 | RCL2 | |
| 129 | GSB6 | print termination resistance |
| 130 | GTOb | |
| 131 | *LBL0 | types 6 & 7 common element |
| 132 | RCL8 | |
| 133 | x | calculate and print type 6 |
| 134 | CHS | tank inductor or type 7 |
| 135 | RCLC | tank capacitor |
| 136 | + | |
| 137 | GSB8 | |
| 138 | F0? | if type 7 print common tank |
| 139 | GSB5 | inductor value |
| 140 | GTOb | goto space and return |

| | | |
|---|---|---|
| 141 | *LBL5 | common element print subr |
| 142 | RCLC | |
| 143 | *LBL7 | type 6 C or type 7 L subr |
| 144 | 1/X | |
| 145 | RCL5 | |
| 146 | x | |
| 147 | PRTX | |
| 148 | RTN | |
| 149 | *LBL8 | type 6 L or type 7 C subr |
| 150 | RCL4 | |
| 151 | x | |
| 152 | PRTX | |
| 153 | RTN | |
| 154 | *LBL9 | initialization subroutine |
| 155 | SPC | |
| 156 | SF1 | if flag 0 is set, clear |
| 157 | F0? | flag 1 and vice-versa |
| 158 | CF1 | |
| 159 | RCL0 | if type 6: |
| 160 | 1/X | $\dfrac{R}{\omega_o} \rightarrow R_4$ ; $\dfrac{1}{R\omega_o} \rightarrow R_5$ |
| 161 | ST04 | |
| 162 | ST05 | |
| 163 | RCL2 | if type 7: |
| 164 | F1? | |
| 165 | 1/X | $\dfrac{1}{R\omega_o} \rightarrow R_4$ ; $\dfrac{R}{\omega_o} \rightarrow R_5$ |
| 166 | ST÷4 | |
| 167 | ST×5 | |
| 168 | EEX | initialize k |
| 169 | ST07 | |
| 170 | CLX | initialize $A_{n, n+1}$ |
| 171 | STO9 | |
| 172 | RCL6 | calculate register index |
| 173 | 9 | for $g_n$ |
| 174 | + | |
| 175 | STOI | |
| 176 | RCL2 | recall termination R |
| 177 | *LBL6 | print and space subroutine |
| 178 | PRTX | |
| 179 | *LBLb | space and return subroutine |
| 180 | SPC | |
| 181 | RTN | |

| LABELS | | | | |
|---|---|---|---|---|
| A load $f_o$ | B load BW | C load R | D | E load type |
| a | b space & rtn | c | d | e |
| 0 type 1 start | 1 type 2 start | 2 types 1&2 loop start | 3 types 6&7 start | 4 types 6&7 loop start |
| 5 print common element | 6 prt & space | 7 C or L output | 8 L or C output | 9 initialize |

| FLAGS | |
|---|---|
| 0 type 1 or 7 | |
| 1 type 2 or 6 | |
| 2 even branch | |
| 3 | |

| SET STATUS | | |
|---|---|---|
| FLAGS | TRIG | DISP |
| ON OFF | USERS | CHOICE |
| 0 ■ | DEG | FIX |
| 1 ■ | GRAD | SCI |
| 2 ■ | RAD | ENG |
| 3 | | n __ |

HP-67 suggested program changes. The "print" mode of output can be changed to the "R/S" mode by changing like statements at line numbers 147, 152, and 178. The program execution will halt at each data output point and await restart by the user via the "R/S" key.

## PROGRAM 2-6 NORMALIZED LOWPASS TO BANDPASS FILTER TRANSFORMATIONS, TYPES 8, 9, 10, AND 11.

Program Description and Equations Used

This program converts normalized lowpass filter element values to a set of four bandpass filter topologies [16], [56]. These four topologies are shown in Fig. 2-6.1 in normalized form (1 ohm, 1 radian/sec center frequency). The parameter $A_{ij}$ is defined by Eq. (2-5.1). Types 8 and 9 are narrowband transformations of types 2 and 1, while types 10 and 11 are exact transformations of types 2 and 1 obtained by applying Norton transformations to the shunt elements of type 2 to form type 10, or to the series elements of type 1 to form type 11. This transformation process is detailed in the equation derivation section following Example 2-6.2. The types 8 and 9 narrowband transformations will only provide accurate results when the loaded Q (ratio of center frequency to bandwidth) is greater than 5 or so. This restriction is not present with types 10 or 11. Because the type 8 or 9 coupling element causes extra zeros of transmission at either dc or infinite frequency, the frequency response will be skewed away from the extra transmission zero frequencies as implied by Fig. 2-5.3. Figure 2-5.2 should be consulted for picking the filter type best suited to the center frequency, loaded Q, and impedance level of the intended application.

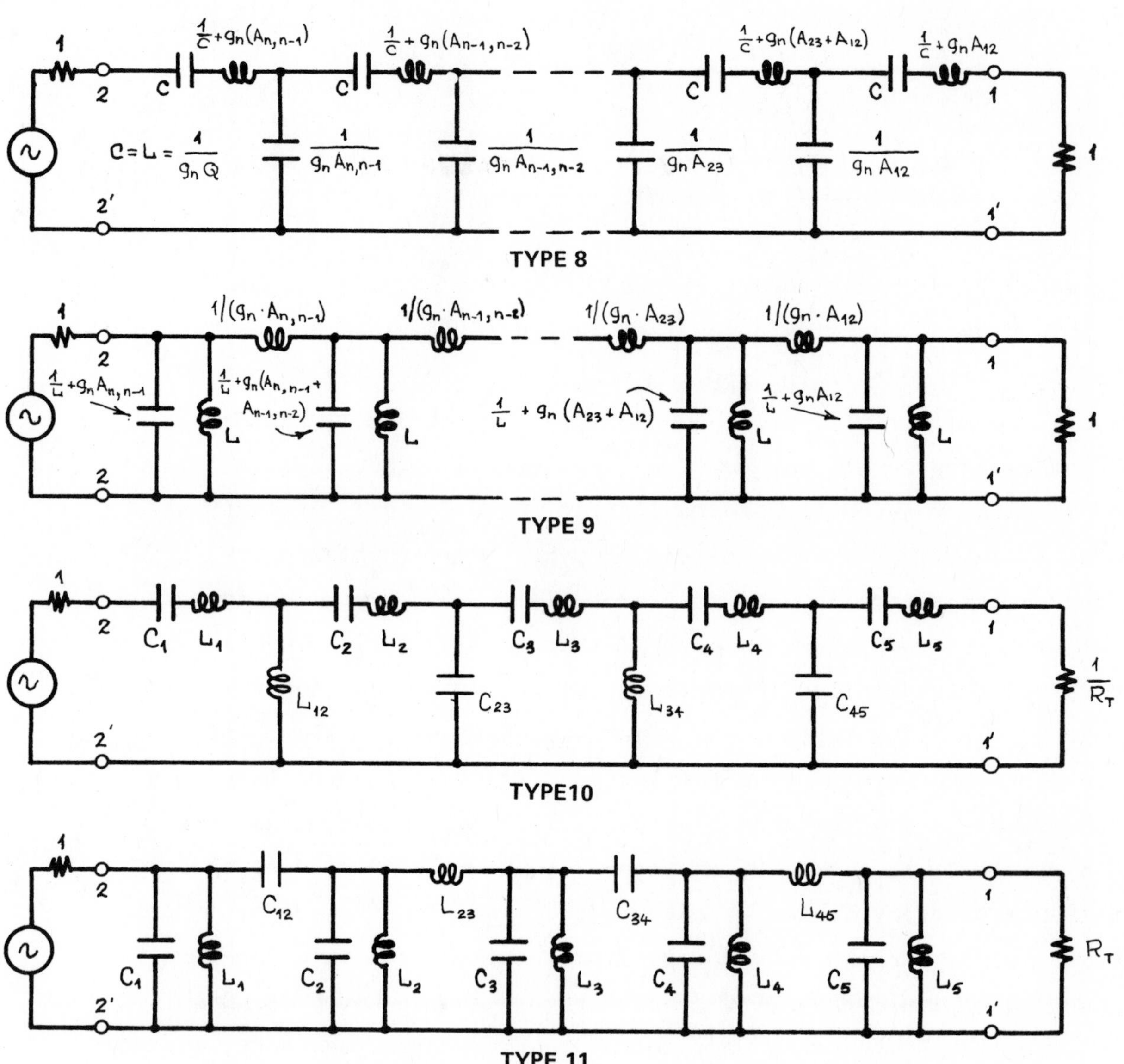


Figure 2-6.1 Normalized bandpass filter topologies for types 8, 9, 10, and 11.

Table 2-6.1 Types 10 and 11 normalized element values.

| Type 10 element | Type 11 element | normalized element value |
|---|---|---|
| $C_k$ | $L_k$ | $\left(Q \cdot g_i - \dfrac{N_{i+2} - 1}{Q \cdot g_{i+1}}\right)^{-1}$ |
| $L_k$ | $C_k$ | $Q \cdot g_i - \dfrac{N_i - 1}{Q \cdot g_{i-1}}$ |
| $L_{k,\ k+1}$ | $C_{k,\ k+1}$ | $\dfrac{N_i}{Q \cdot g_{i-1}}$ |
| $C_{k+1}$ | $L_{k+1}$ | $\dfrac{1}{Q \cdot g_n}$ |
| $L_{k+1}$ | $C_{k+1}$ | $Q \cdot g_n$ |
| $C_{k+1,\ k+1}$ | $L_{k+1,\ k+2}$ | $\dfrac{Q \cdot g_{i-1}}{N_i}$ |

$$N_i = \tfrac{1}{2}\left(1 + \sqrt{1 + 4Q^2 \cdot g_{i-1} \cdot g_n}\right) \quad ; \quad g_{n+1} \equiv 0$$

$k = 1, 3, 5, \ldots, n$ (n must be odd)

$i = n - k + 1$

The reverse ordering of the normalized lowpass coefficients from the element subscripts occurs because the dual form of the normalized lowpass filter is used. The dual is required to place the 1 ohm resistor next to the first shunt capacitor which is required for types 8 and 9 when transforming even ordered filters. Since the same register setup and recall routine is used for types 10 and 11, the dual form is carried over for convenience (it is not required).

Types 10 and 11 can be redrawn to show the ladder structure as T's or pi's of inductors and capacitors as shown in Fig. 2-6.2.

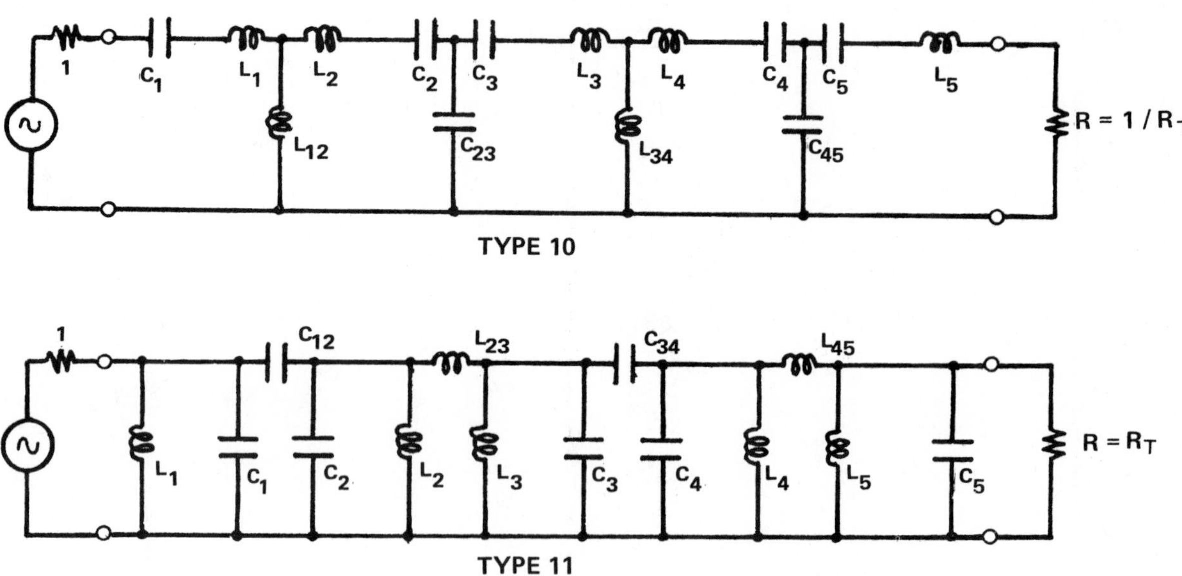


FIGURE 2-6.2 Types 10 and 11 showing T's and pi's of L's and C's.

These pi's and T's of inductors can be replaced with an active realization that contains only op-amps, resistors, and capacitors by using 2 back-to-back generalized impedance converter (GIC) circuits as detailed in Orchard and Sheahan's paper [42], and shown in Figs. 2-6.3 & 4.

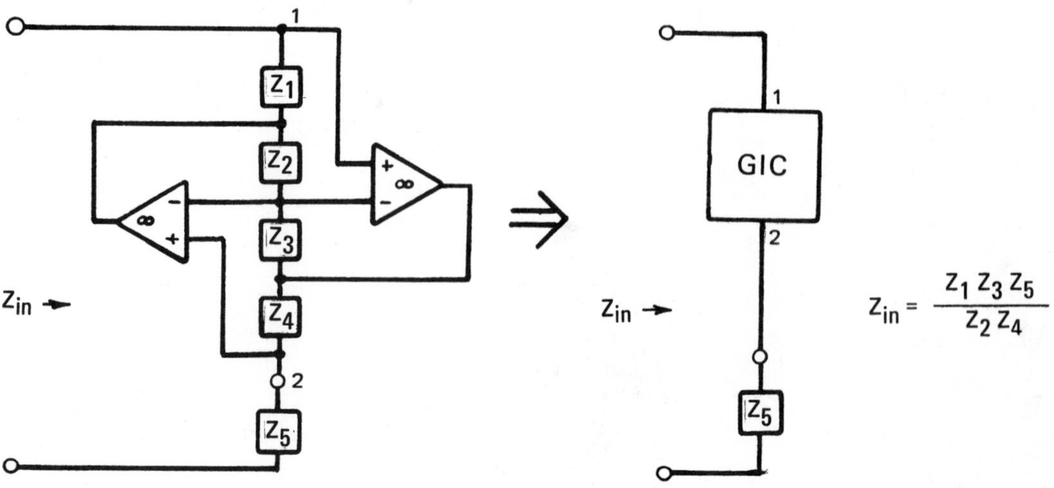


Figure 2-6.3 Antoniou GIC circuit [ 3 ].

If $Z_1$, $Z_2$, $Z_3$, and $Z_5$ are resistors and $Z_4$ is a capacitor, then,

$$Z_{in} = \frac{R_1 \ R_3 \ R_5}{R_2} \cdot sC_4 = sL \qquad (2\text{-}6.1)$$

Furthermore, if $R_2 = R_3$ (a Q enhancement condition), then,

$$L = R_1 C_4 R_5 \qquad (2\text{-}6.2)$$

Two GIC circuits with the component selection outlined above can be combined to produce a circuit that simulates a T or pi of inductances. These circuits are shown in Fig. 2-6.4.

Aside from the elimination of inductors, this particular mechanization is very easy to tune. Changing resistor $R_1$ in the GIC alters the apparent inductance seen at the terminals. The capacitor, $C_4$, needs to be stable (e.g., polystyrene or mica) but can have a large initial tolerance which is accommodated during the tuning procedure.

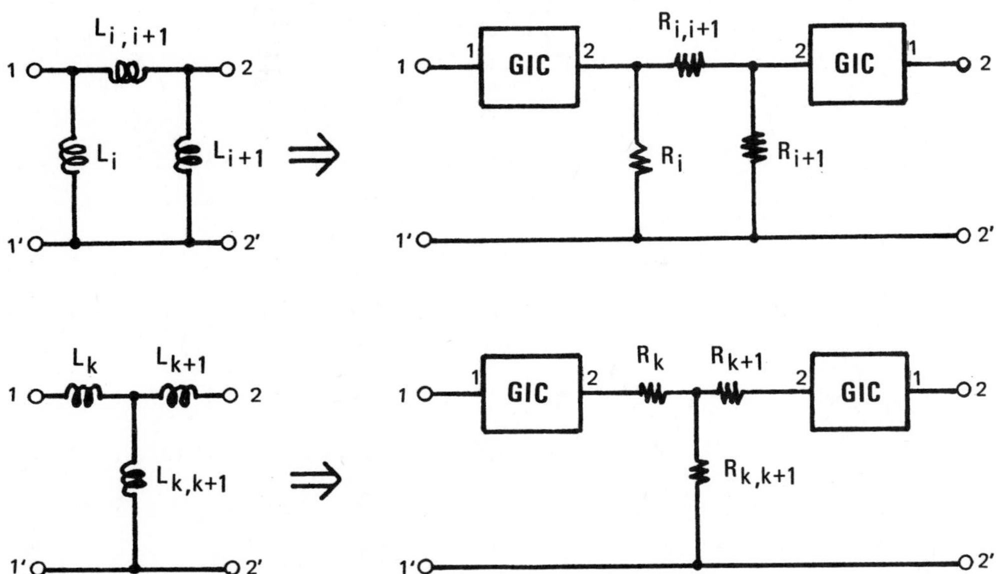


Figure 2-6.4 Pi or T inductance simulation circuits using GIC's.

The diagrams and discussion thus far have used the filters in normalized form, i.e., 1 ohm termination resistor, and 1 radian/second center frequency. The prototype filter is denormalized by multiplying each normalized inductor by $2\pi f_o/R$, and dividing each normalized capacitor by $2\pi f_o R$, where $f_o$ and R are the desired center frequency and termination resistance level respectively. The program accomplishes this denormalization by calling either subroutine 7 or 8. For types 8 and 10, subroutine 7 denormalizes capacitors and subroutine 8 denormalizes inductors, and the reverse is true for types 9 and 11.

Tuning procedure for types 7, 9, and 11*. After the component values have been calculated, the inductors designed,** fabricated and adjusted to value, and the capacitors selected and padded to the proper value, the filter may be assembled and tuned so it will exhibit the desired response.

Tuning is accomplished by adjusting each of the parallel tank elements. For low frequency filters, the inductor is usually chosen as the adjustable element. At higher frequencies the capacitor is usually chosen as the adjustable element. The resonance of the tank circuit must include the effects of the coupling elements. By temporarily shorting out adjacent tank circuits, the coupling element influence will be included. This tuning procedure is described next.

1) Temporarily place a short at location "B" and adjust $C_1$ (or $L_1$) to resonate the tank circuit at the center frequency of the filter, $f_o$. The connection (short) must be low inductance with respect to the other inductances in the circuit.

2) Remove the short at "B," and temporarily place shorts at locations "A" and "C." Adjust $C_2$ ( $L_2$) for tank circuit resonance at the filter center frequency.

3) Continue shorting out adjacent tanks with low inductance shorts at locations "B" & "D," "C" & "E," and "D," and adjusting each resulting tank circuit for resonance at the filter center frequency, $f_o$. These steps will complete the tuning of the filter.

---

** For more information on inductor design, see the ferromagnetic core and air core inductor design programs contained in another section of this book. Also see the Ferroxcube Inc. publication "Linear Ferrite Materials and Components" for information on ferrite pot core inductor design.

* See program 2-5 for the type 6, 8, and 10 tuning procedure.

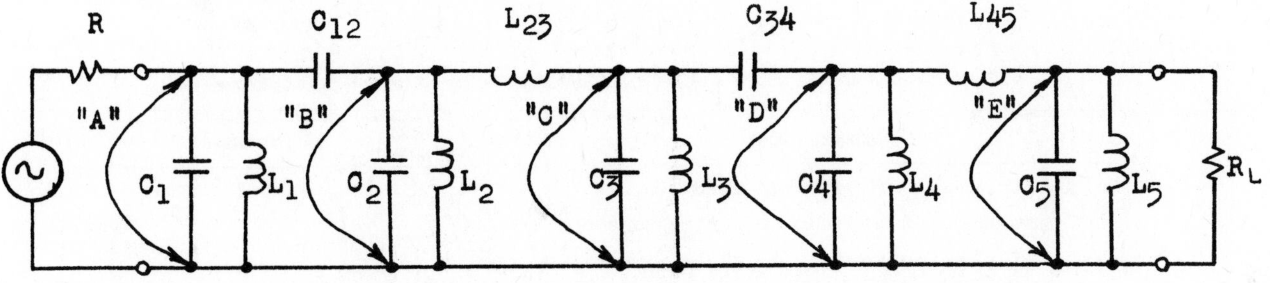


Figure 2-6.5 Circuit shorts for Types 7, 9, and 11 tuning.

# User Instructions

| NORMALIZED LOWPASS TO BANDPASS TYPES 8, 9, 10, & 11 | | | | |
|---|---|---|---|---|
| load center frequency | load bandwidth | load termination resistance | | load type # & start |

| STEP | INSTRUCTIONS | INPUT DATA/UNITS | KEYS | OUTPUT DATA/UNITS |
|---|---|---|---|---|
| 1 | Load both sides of program card (normalized lowpass coefficients and related parameters must be loaded into the registers either manually, or as output from Program 2-3) | | | |
| 2 | Load center frequency in Hz | $f_o$ | A | $\omega_o$ |
| 3 | Load bandwidth in Hz | BW | B | Q |
| 4 | Load termination resistance in ohms | R | C | |
| 5 | Load type number of filter desired | 8,9,10,11 | E | load R |
| | The tank capacitor is always printed first independent of filter type. | | | $C_{tank}$<br>$L_{tank}$ |
| | *The coupling element will be as follows:<br>Type 8, capacitor<br>Type 9, inductor<br>Type 10, alternating L's & C's<br>Type 11, alternating C's & L's<br>See Fig 2-6.1 for more details. | | | C,L cplg*<br><br>$C_{tank}$<br>$L_{tank}$<br><br>C,L cplg*<br><br>$C_{tank}$<br>⋮<br><br>load R |

## Example 2-6.1 Type 10 Filter Design

A Chebyshev response bandpass filter is required to pass a 20 Hz band of information geometrically centered about 1000 Hz with 0.5 dB ripple or less, and to operate in a 1000 ohm system. The filter stop-bandwidth is 60 Hz, and the filter should reject frequencies lying outside this band by at least 60 dB.

Referring to Fig. 2-5.2 under the headings f = 1 kHz, $Q_L$ = 1000/20 = 50, and R = 500, type 8 is practical, and type 10 is readily realizable. Since active inductor simulation is anticipated, type 10 will be selected.

Program 2-1 is used to calculate the filter order necessary to meet the requirements, and Program 2-3 is used to calculate and store the normalized lowpass coefficients for use by this program. The HP-97 printout for all these programs is shown below.

Load Program 2-1 and calculate required filter order

| | | |
|---|---|---|
| | GSBb | select Chebyshev response |
| .50 | GSBA | load $Ap_{dB}$ |
| 60.00 | GSBB | load $As_{dB}$ |
| 3.00 | GSBD | load λ and calculate minimum filter order |
| 4.31 | *** | n, the minimum filter order (output) |
| 5.00 | GSBC | load integral filter order and calculate λ |
| 2.31 | *** | λ to meet $Ap_{dB}$ and $As_{dB}$ given n = 5 |
| 3.00 | GSBE | load λ required and calculate actual $As_{dB}$ |
| 61.40 | *** | $As_{dB}$ for n = 5 and λ = 3 |

Load Program 2-3 and calculate Chebyshev LP normalized coefficients

| | | |
|---|---|---|
| 5. | GSBA | load required filter order |
| 1. | GSBB | load desired termination resistance ratio |
| .5 | GSBD | load Chebyshev passband ripple and start |
| 1.05926+00 | *** | normalized −3dB frequency (output) |
| 1.00000+00 | *** | $R_T$ (normalized port 1 termination resistance) |
| 1.70577+00 | *** | $g_1$ |
| 1.22963+00 | *** | $g_2$ |
| 2.54083+00 | *** | $g_3$ |
| 1.22963+00 | *** | $g_4$ |
| 1.70577+00 | *** | $g_5$ |
| 1.00000+00 | *** | R (normalized port 2 termination resistance) |

Example 2-6.1 (continued)

Load program 2-6 and calculate type 10 filter elements

```
        1000.  GSBA   load center frequency
          20.  GSBB   load bandwidth
        1000.  GSBC   load termination resistor
          10.  GSBE   select filter type and start

  1.00000+03   ***    R

  1.86608-09   ***    C1
  13.3879+00   ***    L1

  188.752-03   ***    L12

  1.86608-09   ***    C2
  13.5741+00   ***    L2

  134.199-09   ***    C23

  1.26442-09   ***    C3
  20.0331+00   ***    L3

  188.752-03   ***    L34

  1.86608-09   ***    C4
  13.5741+00   ***    L4

  134.199-09   ***    C45

  1.89263-09   ***    C5
  13.5741+00   ***    L5

  1.00000+03   ***    RT
```

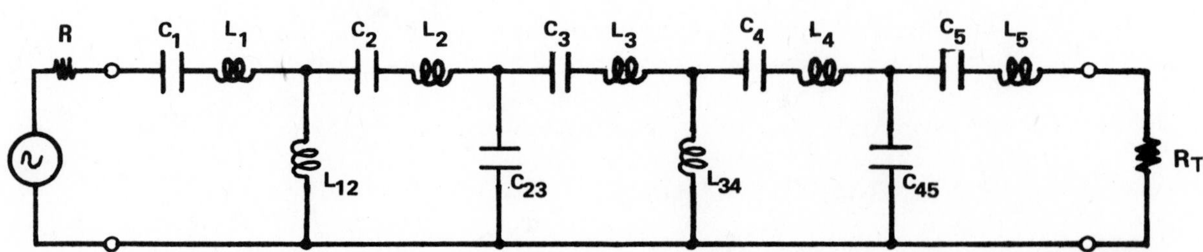


Figure 2-6.6 Type 10 bandpass filter schematic.

Example 2-6.2 Singly terminated type 10 filter design

Because the type 10 filter is an exact bandpass transformation of the lowpass prototype (as is the type 11), the terminating resistances need not be equal. This example will show the synthesis of a singly terminated type 10 filter, i.e., $R_T$ is allowed to approach infinite resistance. The equally terminated filter case is the least sensitive to component value changes. When the filter is singly terminated, the operating Q's of the tank circuits become higher as the open (or shorted) end of the filter is approached. This means that the changes in tank Q's will have a greater effect on the overall operating Q of the tank in the filter, and hence, the filter response. The HP-97 printout for the singly terminated type 10 filter follows. Refer to Fig. 2-6.6 for the filter schematic.

Load Program 2-3

| | | |
|---|---|---|
| 5. | GSBA | load n |
| 1.+05 | GSBB | load $R_T$ ratio |
| .5 | GSBD | load Chebyshev ripple |
| 1.05926+00 | *** | $\omega_{-3dB}$ (output) |
| 100.000+03 | *** | $R_T$ |
| 1.53866+00 | *** | $g_1$ |
| 1.64272+00 | *** | $g_2$ |
| 1.81407+00 | *** | $g_3$ |
| 1.42917+00 | *** | $g_4$ |
| 852.839-03 | *** | $g_5$ |
| 1.00000+00 | *** | R |

Load Program 2-6

| | | |
|---|---|---|
| 1000. GSBA | | load $f_o$ |
| 20. GSBB | | load bandwidth |
| 1000. GSBC | | load termination R |
| 10. GSBE | | select type & start |
| 1.00000+03 | *** | R |
| 3.73236-09 | *** | $C_1$ |
| 6.66484+00 | *** | $L_1$ |
| 124.064-03 | *** | $L_{12}$ |
| 3.73236-09 | *** | $C_2$ |
| 6.78668+00 | *** | $L_2$ |
| 204.171-09 | *** | $C_{23}$ |
| 1.76961-09 | *** | $C_3$ |
| 14.3222+00 | *** | $L_3$ |
| 115.649-03 | *** | $L_{34}$ |
| 3.73236-09 | *** | $C_4$ |
| 6.78668+00 | *** | $L_4$ |
| 219.026-09 | *** | $C_{45}$ |
| 2.08814-09 | *** | $C_5$ |
| 12.2443+00 | *** | $L_5$ |
| 10.0000-03 | *** | $R_T$ (short circuit) |

Derivation of types 10 and 11 transformations

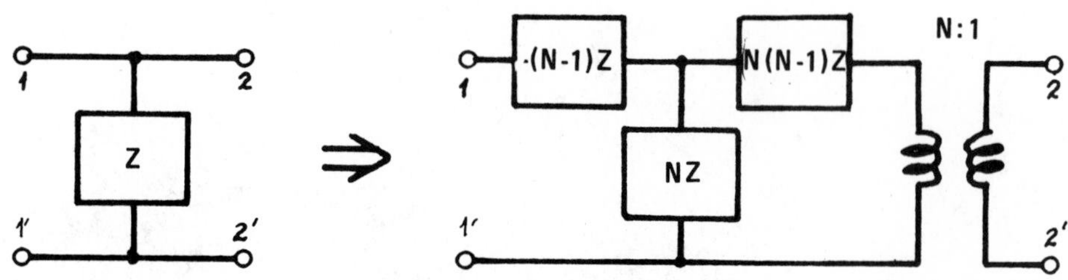


Figure 2-6.7 Norton's second transformation.

Figure 2-6.7 shows one form of Norton's second transformation [39]. This transformation changes a single shunt impedance into a T of impedances, one of which is negative, plus an ideal transformer with turns ratio N. Figure 2-6.8 shows how a parallel resonant tank circuit can be changed into a section of a type 10 bandpass filter structure.

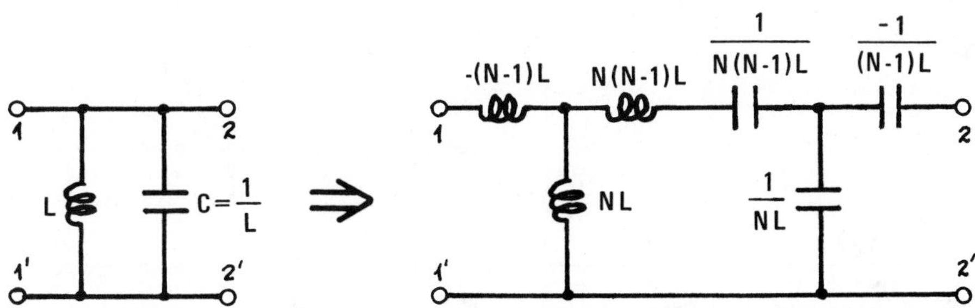


Figure 2-6.8 Norton's second transformation applied to a parallel LC tank circuit.

In Fig. 2-6.8, Norton's transformation has been applied back-to-back, i.e., the 2-2' terminals of the Norton transformation of the inductor have been connected to the 2-2' terminals of the Norton transformation of the capacitor. The same transformer ratio, N, is used for both transformations, therefore, the two ideal transformers are back-to-back providing an overall transformer ratio of unity and can be eliminated.

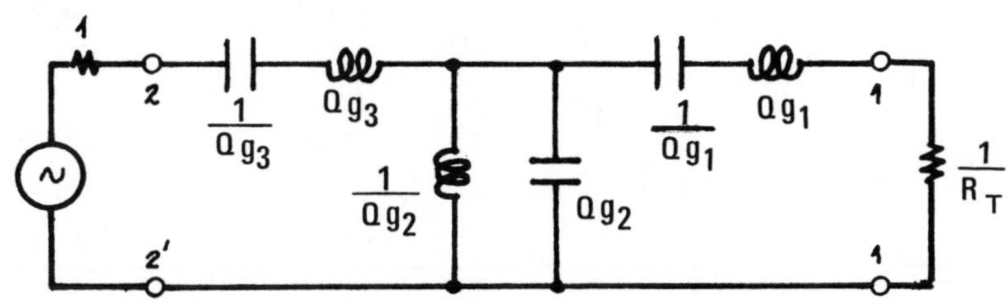


Figure 2-6.9 Type 2 normalized bandpass filter obtained from lowpass prototype (note port ordering).

Figure 2-6.9 shows a type 2 normalized bandpass filter obtained from the transformation of a lowpass prototype. The dual lowpass form is used (see Fig. 2-3.1 lower) and is scaled to a cutoff frequency of 1/Q (Q is the ratio of the filter center frequency to bandwidth); each frequency scaled series lowpass inductor is series resonated with a capacitor at $\omega = 1$, and each shunt scaled lowpass capacitor is parallel resonated with an inductor at $\omega = 1$. Next, the circuit of Fig. 2-6.8 is substituted for the parallel resonant tank, and the negative elements in the series arms combined with the positive series elements of Fig. 2-6.9. The results of this process yield the topology shown in Fig. 2-6.10. Higher ordered (odd order) filters are obtained by repeated application of this procedure.

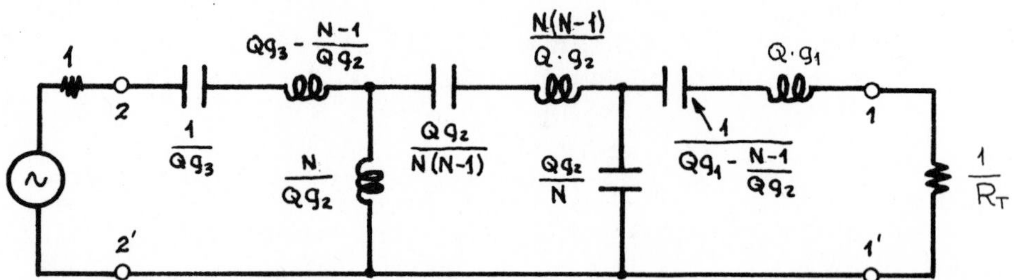


Figure 2-6.10 Type 10 normalized bandpass filter resulting from transformation.

The type 11 bandpass filter is shown in Fig. 2-6.1 and is the dual of the type 10 structure. Type 11 can be derived in a manner similar to the type 10 procedure by applying Norton's first transformation to a type 1 normalized bandpass filter. Norton's first transformation is shown in Fig. 2-8.1. Since type 11 is the dual of type 10 it can be more directly derived from the type 10 structure itself as shown by Fig. 2-6.1 and Table 2-6.1.

The value for $N_i$ given in Table 2-6.1 is derived by making the transformed tank capacitor (inductor) value the same as the first ladder tank capacitor (inductor) for type 10 (11), i.e.,

$$\frac{1}{Q \cdot g_n} = \frac{Q \cdot g_i - 1}{N_i \cdot (N_i - 1)} \tag{2-6.3}$$

Solving for $N_i$ yields:

$$N_i = \tfrac{1}{2}\left(1 + \sqrt{1 + 4Q^2 \cdot g_{i-1} \cdot g_n}\right) \tag{2-6.4}$$

# Program Listing I

| Step | Key | Comment |
|---|---|---|
| 001 | *LBLA | LOAD CENTER FREQUENCY |
| 002 | Pi | form and store $2\pi f_o \rightarrow$ R0 |
| 003 | ENT↑ | |
| 004 | + | |
| 005 | × | |
| 006 | STO0 | |
| 007 | RTN | |
| 008 | *LBLB | LOAD FILTER BANDWIDTH |
| 009 | Pi | form and store: $Q_L = \frac{2\pi f_o}{2\pi BW} \rightarrow R_1$ |
| 010 | ENT↑ | |
| 011 | + | |
| 012 | × | |
| 013 | RCL0 | |
| 014 | X⇄Y | |
| 015 | ÷ | |
| 016 | STO1 | |
| 017 | RTN | |
| 018 | *LBLC | LOAD TERMINATION RESISTANCE |
| 019 | STO2 | |
| 020 | RTN | |
| 021 | *LBLE | LOAD FILTER TYPE AND START |
| 022 | 2 | calculate starting label index |
| 023 | ÷ | |
| 024 | STOI | |
| 025 | INT | |
| 026 | 4 | |
| 027 | - | |
| 028 | X<0? | generate "ERROR" if filter type is less than 8 |
| 029 | GTOa | |
| 030 | X⇄I | store label index |
| 031 | SF0 | set flag 0 if order is odd |
| 032 | FRC | |
| 033 | X=0? | |
| 034 | CF0 | |
| 035 | GTOi | goto starting label |
| 036 | *LBL0 | type 8 and 9 routine |
| 037 | GSB9 | initialize registers |
| 038 | RCLi | recall and store $g_1$ for dual filter topology |
| 039 | STOE | |
| 040 | STO8 | |
| 041 | RCL1 | calculate and store common element value reciprocal |
| 042 | × | |
| 043 | STOC | |
| 044 | CLX | initialize $A_{01} = 0$ |
| 045 | STO9 | |
| 046 | *LBL2 | types 8 & 9 loop start |
| 047 | F1? | print type 9 tank capacitor |
| 048 | GSB5 | |
| 049 | DSZI | increment indices |
| 050 | EEX | |
| 051 | ST+7 | |
| 052 | RCLi | recall $g_{i+1}$ |
| 053 | RCLE | recall $g_i$ and store $g_{i+1}$ |
| 054 | X⇄Y | |
| 055 | STOE | |
| 056 | × | calculate $A_{i,\,i+1}$ |
| 057 | √X | |
| 058 | 1/X | |
| 059 | RCL9 | interchange $A_{i-1,i}$ & $A_{i,i+1}$ |
| 060 | X⇄Y | |
| 061 | STO9 | |
| 062 | + | form $A_{i-1,i} + A_{i,\,i+1}$, and output related element |
| 063 | GSB0 | |
| 064 | RCL9 | calculate and output coupling element |
| 065 | RCL8 | |
| 066 | × | |
| 067 | GSB7 | |
| 068 | SPC | test for loop exit |
| 069 | RCL7 | |
| 070 | RCL6 | |
| 071 | X>Y? | |
| 072 | GTO2 | |
| 073 | F1? | output type 9 tank capacitor |
| 074 | GSB5 | |
| 075 | RCL9 | output rest of last tank circuit |
| 076 | GSB0 | |
| 077 | RCL2 | recall and print terminating resistance value |
| 078 | GSB6 | |
| 079 | GTOb | |
| 080 | *LBL0 | types 8 & 9 output routine |
| 081 | RCL8 | output type 8 tank capacitor, or type 9 tank inductor |
| 082 | × | |
| 083 | RCLC | |
| 084 | + | |
| 085 | GSB8 | |
| 086 | F0? | output type 8 tank inductor |
| 087 | GSB5 | |
| 088 | GTOb | |
| 089 | *LBL1 | types 10 & 11 routine start |
| 090 | GSB9 | initialize registers |
| 091 | *LBL3 | types 10 & 11 loop start |
| 092 | RCL9 | $Q \cdot g_{i+1}$ |
| 093 | RCLi | $i = n, n-2, \cdots, 1$ |
| 094 | RCL1 | $Q \cdot g_i$ |
| 095 | × | |
| 096 | STO9 | |
| 097 | X⇄Y | |
| 098 | RCLE | $N_{i+2}$ $(N_{n+2} \equiv 1)$ |
| 099 | EEX | |
| 100 | - | |
| 101 | X⇄Y | |
| 102 | ÷ | |
| 103 | - | |
| 104 | STO3 | $Q \cdot g_i - \frac{N_{i+2}-1}{Q g_{i+1}}$ |
| 105 | F3? | if first time through loop, store value of first L or C |
| 106 | STOC | |
| 107 | F1? | output type 11 tank capacitor |
| 108 | GSB7 | |
| 109 | 2 | increment index, k |
| 110 | ST+7 | |

REGISTERS

| 0 | 1 | 2 | 3 | 4 | 5 | 6 | 7 | 8 | 9 |
|---|---|---|---|---|---|---|---|---|---|
| $2\pi f_o$ | $Q_L$ | R | scratch | $\frac{1}{\omega_o R}, \frac{R}{\omega_o}$ | $\frac{R}{\omega_o}, \frac{1}{\omega_o R}$ | n | k | scratch | scratch |

| S0 | S1 | S2 | S3 | S4 | S5 | S6 | S7 | S8 | S9 |
|---|---|---|---|---|---|---|---|---|---|
| $g_1$ | $g_2$ | $g_3$ | $g_4$ | $g_5$ | $g_6$ | $g_7$ | $g_8$ | $g_9$ | $g_{10}$ |

| A | B | C | D | E | I |
|---|---|---|---|---|---|
| $g_{11}$ | $g_{12}$ | common element | $R_T$ | N , $g_{i-1}$ | index |

# Program Listing II

| Step | Key | Comments |
|---|---|---|
| 111 | RCL6 | test for loop exit |
| 112 | RCL7 | |
| 113 | X>Y? | |
| 114 | GTO0 | |
| 115 | RCL9 | calculate and store transformer ratio for Norton transformation: $N_i = \frac{1}{2}\left(1+\sqrt{1+4Q^2 g_n \cdot g_{i-1}}\right)$ |
| 116 | DSZI | |
| 117 | RCLi | |
| 118 | RCL1 | |
| 119 | × | |
| 120 | STO9 | |
| 121 | 4 | |
| 122 | × | |
| 123 | RCLC | |
| 124 | × | |
| 125 | EEX | |
| 126 | + | |
| 127 | √X | |
| 128 | EEX | |
| 129 | + | |
| 130 | 2 | |
| 131 | ÷ | |
| 132 | STOE | |
| 133 | EEX | calculate and print tank inductor for type 10 or tank capacitor for type 11 |
| 134 | − | |
| 135 | RCL9 | |
| 136 | ÷ | |
| 137 | − | |
| 138 | GSB8 | |
| 139 | RCL3 | print type 11 tank inductor |
| 140 | F0? | |
| 141 | GSB7 | |
| 142 | SPC | calculate and print coupling element, L for type 10 or C for type 11 |
| 143 | RCLE | |
| 144 | RCL9 | |
| 145 | ÷ | |
| 146 | STO8 | |
| 147 | GSB8 | |
| 148 | SPC | print type 10 tank capacitor |
| 149 | RCLC | |
| 150 | F1? | |
| 151 | GSB7 | print type 10 tank inductor, or print type 11 tank capacitor |
| 152 | RCLC | |
| 153 | GSB8 | |
| 154 | RCLC | print type 11 tank inductor |
| 155 | F0? | |
| 156 | GSB7 | |
| 157 | SPC | |
| 158 | RCL8 | calculate and print coupling element, C for type 10 or L for type 11 |
| 159 | GSB7 | |
| 160 | SPC | |
| 161 | DSZI | decrement index and return to loop start |
| 162 | GTO3 | |
| 163 | *LBL0 | last tank output: C for type 10, or L for type 11 |
| 164 | RCL9 | |
| 165 | GSB8 | |
| 166 | RCL3 | output type 10 tank inductor |
| 167 | F0? | |
| 168 | GSB7 | |
| 169 | SPC | calculate and print termination resistance |
| 170 | RCL2 | |
| 171 | RCLD | |
| 172 | F1? | |
| 173 | 1/X | |
| 174 | × | |
| 175 | GSB6 | |
| 176 | GTOb | |
| 177 | *LBL5 | common element output subr |
| 178 | RCLC | recall common element |
| 179 | *LBL7 | L/C (odd/even) output subr |
| 180 | 1/X | |
| 181 | RCL5 | |
| 182 | × | |
| 183 | PRTX | |
| 184 | RTN | |
| 185 | *LBL8 | C/L (odd/even) output subr |
| 186 | RCL4 | |
| 187 | × | |
| 188 | PRTX | |
| 189 | RTN | |
| 190 | *LBL9 | initialization subroutine |
| 191 | SPC | |
| 192 | SF1 | |
| 193 | F0? | flag 1 $\overline{\text{flag 0}}$ |
| 194 | CF1 | |
| 195 | SF3 | setup denormalization constants for L's and C's (register order changed depending upon filter type being odd or even) |
| 196 | RCL0 | |
| 197 | 1/X | |
| 198 | STO4 | |
| 199 | STO5 | |
| 200 | RCL2 | |
| 201 | F1? | |
| 202 | 1/X | |
| 203 | ST÷4 | |
| 204 | ST×5 | |
| 205 | EEX | initialize registers |
| 206 | STO7 | |
| 207 | STO9 | |
| 208 | STOE | |
| 209 | RCL6 | initialize normalized LP coef recall index register |
| 210 | 9 | |
| 211 | + | |
| 212 | STOI | |
| 213 | RCL2 | recall termination R |
| 214 | *LBL6 | print and space subroutine |
| 215 | PRTX | |
| 216 | *LBLb | space and return subroutine |
| 217 | SPC | |
| 218 | RTN | |

| LABELS | | | | | FLAGS |
|---|---|---|---|---|---|
| A load $f_0$ | B load BW | C load R | D | E load type | 0 type 9 or 11 |
| a | b space & rtn | c | d | e | 1 type 8 or 10 |
| 0 types 8&9 start | 1 types 10&11 start | 2 types 8&9 loop start | 3 types 10&11 loop start | 4 | 2 |
| 5 print common elt. | 6 print, spc, return | 7 print C or L | 8 print L or C | 9 initialize | 3 first time thru loop |

| SET STATUS | | | |
|---|---|---|---|
| FLAGS | ON | OFF | TRIG | DISP |
| 0 | | ■ | DEG | FIX |
| 1 | | ■ | GRAD | SCI |
| 2 | ■ | | RAD | ENG ■ |
| 3 | | ■ | | n 5 |

HP-67 suggested program changes. To change from the "print" to "R/S" mode for program output, make the respective change at the following line numbers: 183, 188, and 217. The program will now stop at output points and await restart via the "R/S" command from the keyboard.

## PROGRAM 2-7 WYE-DELTA TRANSFORMATIONS FOR R, L, OR C.

Program Description and Equations Used

This program performs the Y-Δ transformation for groups of three resistors, capacitors, or inductors. These transformations find use whenever awkward or physically impractical element values result from electrical network design. The resistive transformation is often used with operational amplifier summing network design to keep the resistor values low. The inductive and capacitive transformations can be of assistance in filter design.

The Y-Δ transformations for one-of-a-kind elements are summarized below:

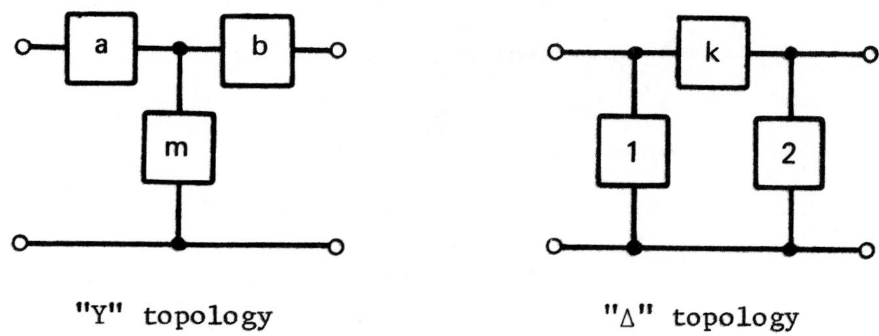


"Y" topology "Δ" topology

Figure 2-7.1 "Y" and "Δ" topology definitions.

For capacitors as network elements:

Y→Δ

$$C_1 = C_a \cdot C_m / \Sigma C$$
$$C_2 = C_b \cdot C_m / \Sigma C$$
$$C_k = C_a \cdot C_b / \Sigma C$$
$$\Sigma C = C_a + C_b + C_m$$

Δ→Y

$$C_a = \Sigma CC / C_2$$
$$C_b = \Sigma CC / C_1$$
$$C_m = \Sigma CC / C_k$$
$$\Sigma CC = C_1 C_2 + C_2 C_k + C_1 C_k$$

For inductors or resistors as network elements (read L's as R's):

$Y \to \Delta$

$$L_1 = \Sigma LL / L_b$$
$$L_2 = \Sigma LL / L_a$$
$$L_k = \Sigma LL / L_m$$
$$\Sigma LL = L_a L_b + L_a L_m + L_b L_m$$

$\Delta \to Y$

$$L_a = L_1 \cdot L_k / \Sigma L$$
$$L_b = L_2 \cdot L_k / \Sigma L$$
$$L_m = L_1 \cdot L_2 / \Sigma L$$
$$\Sigma L = L_1 + L_2 + L_k$$

# User Instructions

| Y→Δ ,Δ→Y TRANSFORMATION FOR L, R, OR C | | | | |
|---|---|---|---|---|
| set C | set L or R | | | print elements |
| load elt 1 or a | load elt k or m | load elt 2 or b | Y→Δ | Δ→Y |

2

| STEP | INSTRUCTIONS | INPUT DATA/UNITS | KEYS | OUTPUT DATA/UNITS |
|---|---|---|---|---|
| 1 | Load program card (one sided card) | | | |
| 2 | Select element type: | | | |
| | if capacitors | | f A | |
| | if inductors, or resistors | | f B | |
| 3 | Load element values | | | |
| | Load element 1 or a | | A | |
| | Load element k or m | | B | |
| | Load element 2 or b | | C | |
| 4 | Select transformation type: | | | |
| | Y→Δ transformation | | D | element a |
| | | | | element m |
| | | | | element b |
| | | | | Σ a,m,b |
| | | | | element 1 |
| | | | | element k |
| | | | | element 2 |
| | | | | Σ 1,k,2 |
| | Δ→Y transformation | | E | element 1 |
| | | | | element k |
| | | | | element 2 |
| | | | | Σ 1,k,2 |
| | | | | element a |
| | | | | element m |
| | | | | element b |
| | | | | Σ a,m,b |
| 5 | To print presently stored elements | | f E | elt 1,a |
| | | | | elt k,m |
| | | | | elt 2,b |
| | | | | Σ elts. |

Example 2-7.1

Convert the Y network of Fig. 2-7.2 into an equivalent Δ network. Compute the total capacitance both before and after the transformation.

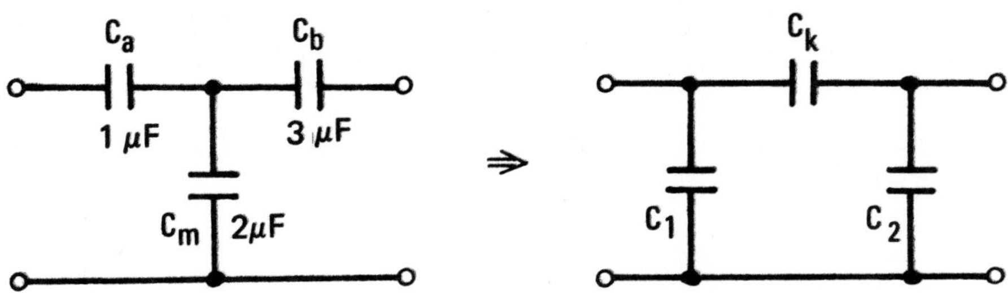


Figure 2-7.2 Capacitor networks for Example 2-7.1.

HP-97 printout

| | | | |
|---|---|---|---|
| 1.-06 | GSBA | $C_a$ | load capacitor values |
| 2.-06 | GSBB | $C_m$ | |
| 3.-06 | GSBC | $C_b$ | |
| | GSBa | select capacitors | |
| | GSBD | perform Y→Δ transformation | |
| 1.000-06 | *** | $C_a$ | before transformation |
| 2.000-06 | *** | $C_m$ | |
| 3.000-06 | *** | $C_b$ | |
| 6.000-06 | *** | ΣC's | |
| 333.3-09 | *** | $C_1$ | after transformation |
| 500.0-09 | *** | $C_k$ | |
| 1.000-06 | *** | $C_2$ | |
| 1.833-06 | *** | ΣC's | |

As a result of the transformation, the total capacity has been reduced by 69.4%.

Example 2-7.2

A top coupled parallel resonant bandpass filter of the type 7 topology has been designed with the element values shown in Fig. 2-7.3. The 1 picofarad coupling capacitor is a problem since it is the same relative value as the parasitic (stray) capacities of the printed circuit board. By converting from a Δ capacitor configuration to a Y configuration, the minimum filter capacity is 202 pF as seen in Fig. 2-7.4, and the parasitic capacities of the printed circuit board are easily managed.

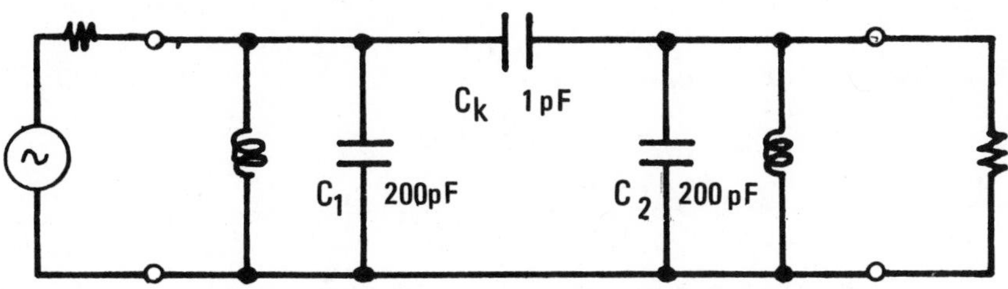


Figure 2-7.3 Type 7 filter design.

HP-97 printout for Δ→Y transformation:

```
200.-12 GSBA  C1 ⎫
        GSBC  C2 ⎬ load capacitor values
   1.-12 GSBB Ck ⎭
        GSBa  select capacitors
        GSBE  start Δ→Y transformation

200.0-12  ***  C1             ⎫
1.000-12  ***  Ck             ⎬ summary before
200.0-12  ***  C2             ⎪ transformation
401.0-12  ***  total capacity ⎭

202.0-12  ***  Ca             ⎫
40.40-09  ***  Cm             ⎬ summary after
202.0-12  ***  Cb             ⎪ transformation
40.80-09  ***  total capacity ⎭
```

Figure 2-7.4 Network after Δ→Y transformation.

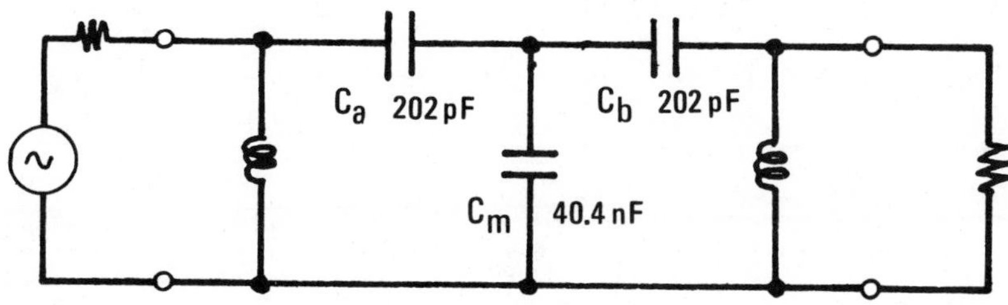

# Program Listing

| | | |
|---|---|---|
| 001 | *LBLA | LOAD element 1 or a |
| 002 | STOA | |
| 003 | RTN | |
| 004 | *LBLB | LOAD element k or m |
| 005 | STOB | |
| 006 | RTN | |
| 007 | *LBLC | LOAD element 2 or b |
| 008 | STOC | |
| 009 | RTN | |
| 010 | *LBLe | PRINT ELEMENTS |
| 011 | SPC | |
| 012 | RCLA | |
| 013 | PRTX | |
| 014 | RCLB | |
| 015 | PRTX | |
| 016 | + | |
| 017 | RCLC | |
| 018 | PRTX | |
| 019 | + | |
| 020 | PRTX | |
| 021 | SPC | |
| 022 | RTN | |
| 023 | *LBLD | START Y→Δ TRANSFORMATION |
| 024 | GSBe | print elements |
| 025 | F0? | jump if L or R |
| 026 | GTO0 | |
| 027 | *LBL1 | Δ→Y for L or R, Y→Δ for C |
| 028 | RCLA | form and store ΣX where |
| 029 | RCLB | X is L, R, or C |
| 030 | + | |
| 031 | RCLC | |
| 032 | + | |
| 033 | STOD | |
| 034 | RCLA | calculate element a or 1 |
| 035 | RCLB | and store in scratchpad |
| 036 | × | |
| 037 | RCLD | |
| 038 | ÷ | |
| 039 | STOE | |
| 040 | RCLA | calculate element m or k |
| 041 | RCLC | |
| 042 | × | |
| 043 | RCLD | |
| 044 | ÷ | |
| 045 | RCLE | store element a or 1 |
| 046 | STOA | |
| 047 | R↓ | |
| 048 | STOE | temporarily store element m or k in scratchpad |
| 049 | RCLB | calculate element b or 2 |
| 050 | RCLC | |
| 051 | × | |
| 052 | RCLD | |
| 053 | ÷ | |
| 054 | STOC | |
| 055 | RCLE | store element m or k |
| 056 | STOB | |
| 057 | GTOe | print element values |
| 058 | *LBLE | START Δ→Y TRANSFORMATION |
| 059 | GSBe | print elements |
| 060 | F0? | jump if L or R |
| 061 | GTO1 | |
| 062 | *LBL0 | Y→Δ for L or R, Δ→Y for C |
| 063 | RCLA | form and store ΣXX where |
| 064 | RCLB | X is L, R, or C |
| 065 | × | |
| 066 | RCLB | |
| 067 | RCLC | |
| 068 | × | |
| 069 | + | |
| 070 | RCLA | |
| 071 | RCLC | |
| 072 | × | |
| 073 | + | |
| 074 | STOD | |
| 075 | RCLC | calculate element 2 or c |
| 076 | ÷ | and store in scratchpad |
| 077 | STOE | |
| 078 | RCLD | calculate element k or m |
| 079 | RCLB | |
| 080 | ÷ | |
| 081 | STOB | |
| 082 | RCLD | calculate element 1 or a |
| 083 | RCLA | |
| 084 | ÷ | |
| 085 | STOC | |
| 086 | RCLE | store element 2 or c |
| 087 | STOA | |
| 088 | GTOe | print element values |
| 089 | *LBLa | SET CAPACITORS AS ELEMENTS |
| 090 | CF0 | |
| 091 | RTN | |
| 092 | *LBLb | SET INDUCTORS OR RESISTORS AS ELEMENTS |
| 093 | SF0 | |
| 094 | RTN | |

## REGISTERS

| 0 | 1 | 2 | 3 | 4 | 5 | 6 | 7 | 8 | 9 |
|---|---|---|---|---|---|---|---|---|---|
| | | | | | | | | | |
| S0 | S1 | S2 | S3 | S4 | S5 | S6 | S7 | S8 | S9 |
| | | | | | | | | | |

| A element 1 or a | B element k or m | C element 2 or b | D ΣX or ΣXX X is L, R, or C | E scratchpad | I |
|---|---|---|---|---|---|

## LABELS

| | | | | | | FLAGS | SET STATUS | | |
|---|---|---|---|---|---|---|---|---|---|
| A load 1 or a | B load k or m | C load 2 or b | D Y→Δ | E Δ→Y | 0 L or R | | | | |
| a set C | b set L, R | c | d | e print elements | 1 | FLAGS | TRIG | DISP | |
| 0 L or R dest. | 1 L or R dest. | 2 | 3 | 4 | 2 | ON OFF | USER'S CHOICE | | |
| 5 | 6 | 7 | 8 | 9 | 3 | 0 ■ | DEG | FIX | |
| | | | | | | 1 | GRAD | SCI | |
| | | | | | | 2 | RAD | ENG | |
| | | | | | | 3 | | n___ | |

## PROGRAM 2-8 NORTON TRANSFORMATIONS.

Program Description and Equations Used

Two network equivalence transformations developed by Edward L. Norton are shown below. They can be extremely useful for modifying network element values or topology.

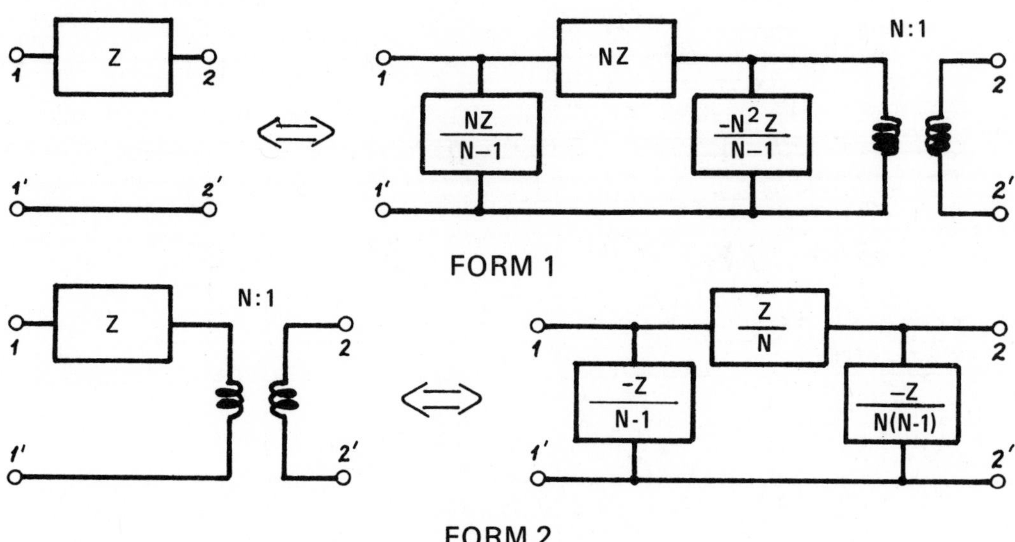


Figure 2-8.1 Two forms of Norton's first transformation.

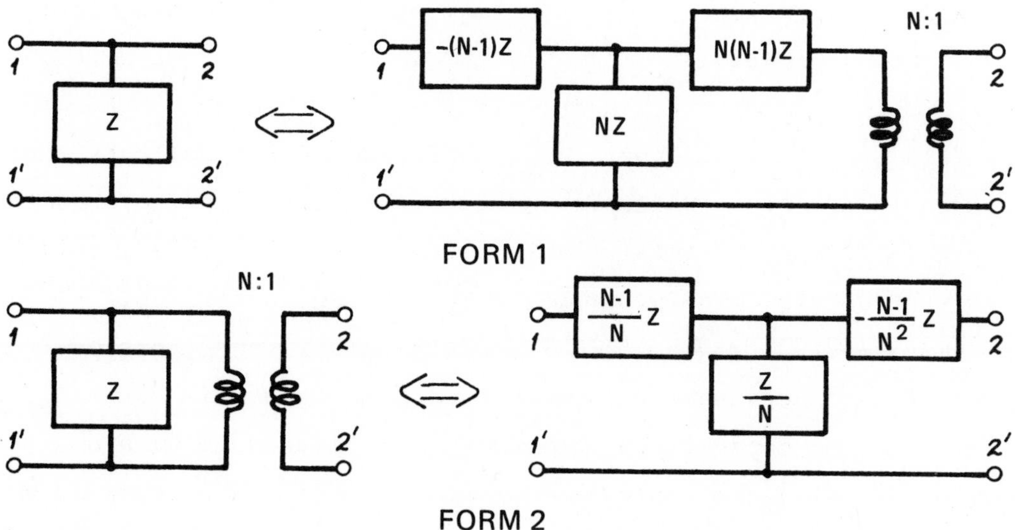


Figure 2-8.2 Two forms of Norton's second transformation.

Figure 2-8.1 shows two forms of Norton's first transformation, and Fig. 2-8.2 shows two forms of Norton's second transformation. The transformed network always contains a negative element, which is combined with a positive element not involved in the transformation. N must be chosen so this combination results in a zero or positive element value if the element is to be realized passively (there are active circuits which can simulate negative elements). When N is chosen so the negative and positive elements annihilate one-another, the overall network topology changes. This technique can be used to reverse an "L" network as shown in Fig. 2-8.3

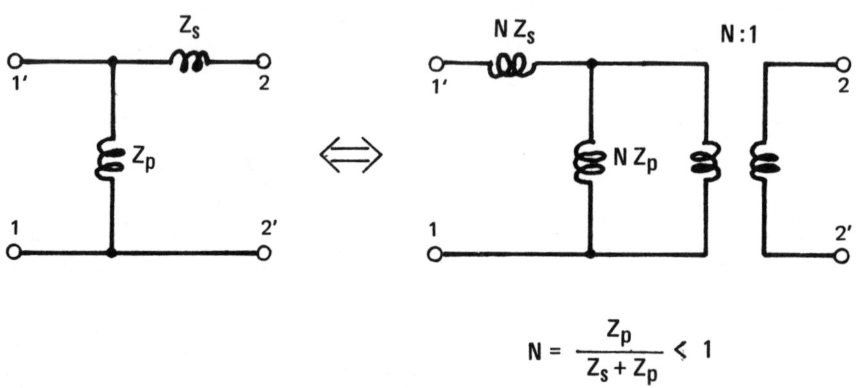


Figure 2-8.3 Norton transformation applied to an "L" network.

Chapter 10 of Zverev [58] has many example of the application of Norton's transformations. Some insight into the power of Norton's transformations is related in the article "Reminiscences" by W.R. Bennett in CAS-24 no. 12 (Dec. 1977). Dr. Bennett recollects that Ed Norton could efficiently furnish a network to give a prescribed loss characteristic with the minimum number of elements by using only a very ordinary sliderule, his intuition, and his transformations.

This HP-67/97 program will transform either capacitors or inductors and resistors. Because the impedance of a capacitor is inversely proportional to the capacitance, multiplying an impedance by N has the effect of dividing the capacitance by N. Figure 2-8.4 shows form 1 of Norton's first transformation when the element being transformed is a capacitor.

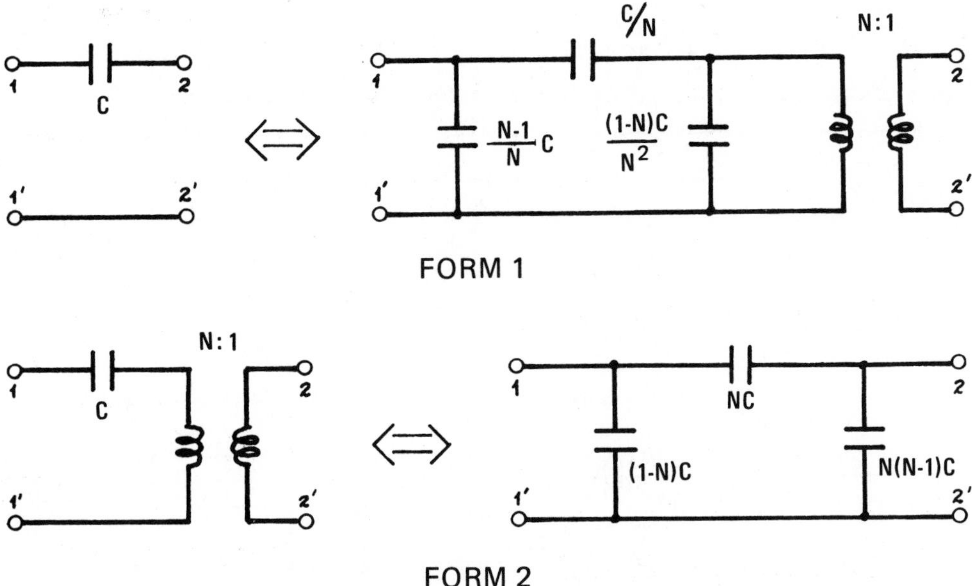

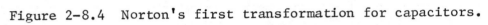

Figure 2-8.4 Norton's first transformation for capacitors.

The same reciprocal relations hold for Norton's second transformation as applied to capacitor networks.

# User Instructions

| NORTON TRANSFORMATIONS | | | | |
|---|---|---|---|---|
| load C | OR load L or R | load N | calculate 1st xfm forms | calculate 2nd xfm forms |

| STEP | INSTRUCTIONS | INPUT DATA/UNITS | KEYS | OUTPUT DATA/UNITS |
|---|---|---|---|---|
| 1 | Load program card | | | |
| 2 | If a capacitor network is being transformed, load capacitor value | C | A | |
| | OR | | | |
| | If an inductor or resistor network is being transformed, load L or R value | L, R | B | |
| 3 | Load ideal transformer ratio desired | N | C | |
| 4 | To calculate both forms of Norton's first transformation | | D | |
| | | | form one | shunt elt |
| | | | | series elt |
| | | | | shunt elt |
| | | | | space |
| | | | | xfmr ratio |
| | | | | space |
| | | | | space |
| | | | form two | shunt elt |
| | | | | series elt |
| | | | | shunt elt |
| 5 | To calculate both forms of Norton's second transformation | | E | |
| | | | form one | series elt |
| | | | | shunt elt |
| | | | | series elt |
| | | | | space |
| | | | | xfmr ratio |
| | | | | space |
| | | | | space |
| | | | form two | series elt |
| | | | | shunt elt |
| | | | | series elt |

Example 2-8.1

An impedance stepdown of 3:1 is required at the output of the band-pass filter shown in Fig. 2-8.5. A transformer could be used to provide this function. Instead, use Norton's first transformation to provide the impedance stepdown without a transformer.

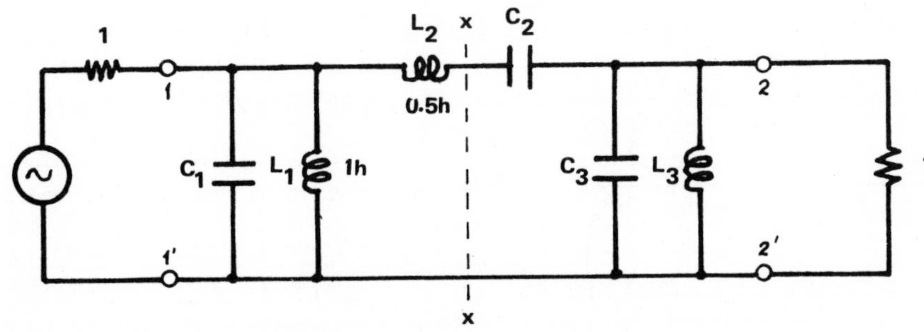


Figure 2-8.5 Bandpass filter network for Ex. 2-8.1.

A hypothetical $\sqrt{3}$:1 turns ratio transformer is inserted at x-x, and all network elements to the right scaled down in impedance by a factor of 3 as shown in Fig. 2-8.6.

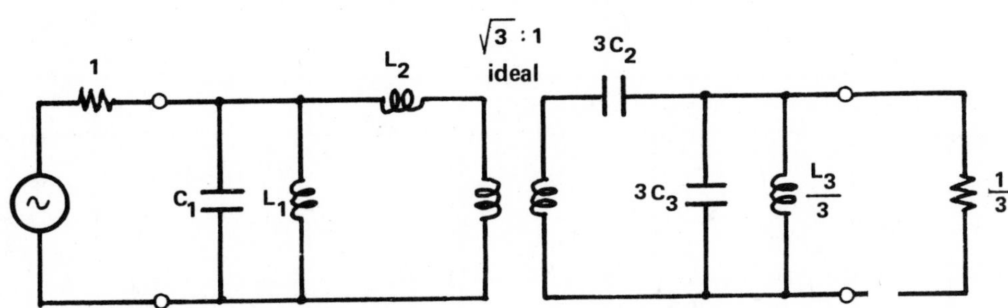


Figure 2-8.6 Network of Fig. 2-8.5 after insertion of hypothetical transformer.

Form 2 of Norton's first transformation is applied to $L_2$ and the transformer as shown in Fig. 2-8.7. The resulting negative shunt inductor is combined with $L_1$ as shown in Fig. 2-8.8.

HP-97 printout for Norton's first transformation

```
        .5 GSBB   L2

        3.   √X
           GSBC   } N

           GSBD   calculate Norton's first transformation

  1.183+00  ***   La   )
  866.0-03  ***   Lb   )
 -2.049+00  ***   Lc   )  form 1
                       )
  1.732+00  ***   transformer ratio

 -683.0-03  ***   La   )
  288.7-03  ***   Lb   )  form 2
  394.3-03  ***   Lc   )
```

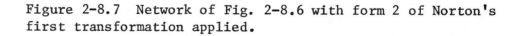

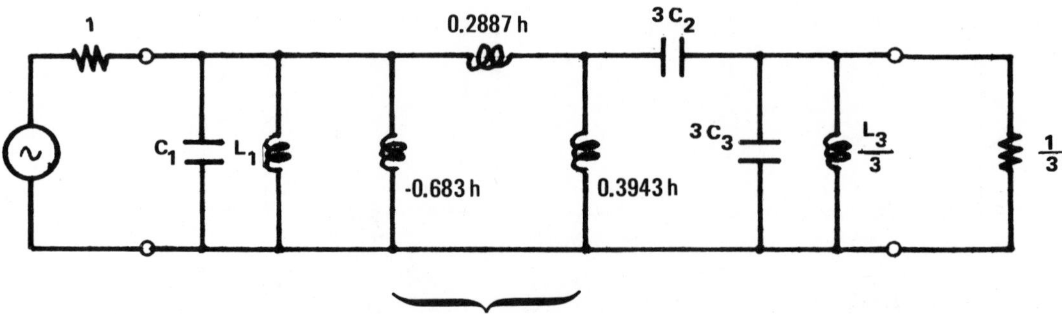


Figure 2-8.7 Network of Fig. 2-8.6 with form 2 of Norton's first transformation applied.

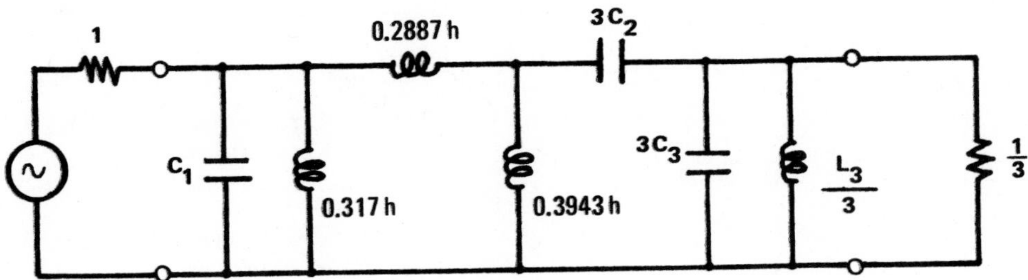


Figure 2-8.8 Final network with all negative elements absorbed.

# Program Listing I

| | | |
|---|---|---|
| 001 | *LBLA | LOAD C |
| 002 | SF0 | indicate capacitor entry |
| 003 | 1/X | form and store reciprocal |
| 004 | STO0 | of entry |
| 005 | 1/X | restore entry |
| 006 | RTN | |
| 007 | *LBLB | LOAD L OR R |
| 008 | CF0 | indicate L or R entry |
| 009 | STO0 | store entry |
| 010 | RTN | |
| 011 | *LBLC | LOAD N |
| 012 | STO1 | |
| 013 | RTN | |
| 014 | *LBLD | CALCULATE FIRST TRANSFORM |
| 015 | SPC | |
| 016 | RCL1 | |
| 017 | RCL1 | form 1 shunt element |
| 018 | EEX | calculation |
| 019 | - | |
| 020 | ÷ | |
| 021 | RCL0 | |
| 022 | × | |
| 023 | STO2 | |
| 024 | GSB0 | |
| 025 | RCL0 | |
| 026 | RCL1 | form 1 series element |
| 027 | × | calculation |
| 028 | GSB0 | |
| 029 | RCL2 | |
| 030 | RCL1 | form 1 shunt element |
| 031 | × | calculation |
| 032 | CHS | |
| 033 | GSB0 | |
| 034 | SPC | |
| 035 | RCL1 | recall and print transformer |
| 036 | PRTX | turns ratio |
| 037 | SPC | |
| 038 | SPC | |
| 039 | RCL0 | |
| 040 | RCL1 | form 2 shunt element |
| 041 | EEX | calculation |
| 042 | - | |
| 043 | ÷ | |
| 044 | STO2 | |
| 045 | CHS | |
| 046 | GSB0 | |
| 047 | RCL0 | |
| 048 | RCL1 | form 2 series element |
| 049 | ÷ | calculation |
| 050 | GSB0 | |
| 051 | RCL2 | form 2 shunt element |
| 052 | GTO1 | calculation |

| | | |
|---|---|---|
| 053 | *LBLE | CALCULATE SECOND TRANSFORM |
| 054 | SPC | |
| 055 | RCL0 | |
| 056 | RCL1 | form 1 series element |
| 057 | EEX | calculation |
| 058 | | |
| 059 | × | |
| 060 | STO2 | |
| 061 | CHS | |
| 062 | GSB0 | |
| 063 | RCL0 | |
| 064 | RCL1 | form 1 shunt element |
| 065 | × | calculation |
| 066 | GSB0 | |
| 067 | RCL2 | |
| 068 | RCL1 | form 1 series element |
| 069 | × | calculation |
| 070 | GSB0 | |
| 071 | SPC | |
| 072 | RCL1 | recall and print ideal |
| 073 | PRTX | transformer turns ratio |
| 074 | SPC | |
| 075 | SPC | |
| 076 | RCL1 | |
| 077 | EEX | form 2 series element |
| 078 | - | calculation |
| 079 | RCL1 | |
| 080 | ÷ | |
| 081 | RCL0 | |
| 082 | × | |
| 083 | STO2 | |
| 084 | GSB0 | |
| 085 | RCL0 | |
| 086 | RCL1 | form 2 shunt element |
| 087 | ÷ | calculation |
| 088 | GSB0 | |
| 089 | RCL2 | |
| 090 | CHS | |
| 091 | *LBL1 | |
| 092 | RCL1 | form 2 series element |
| 093 | ÷ | calculation |
| 094 | GSB0 | |
| 095 | SPC | |
| 096 | SPC | |
| 097 | RTN | |
| 098 | *LBL0 | output subroutine |
| 099 | F0? | |
| 100 | 1/X | |
| 101 | PRTX | |
| 102 | RTN | |

| REGISTERS | | | | | | | | | |
|---|---|---|---|---|---|---|---|---|---|
| 0 $\frac{1}{C}$ or L | 1 N | 2 scratch | 3 | 4 | 5 | 6 | 7 | 8 | 9 |
| S0 | S1 | S2 | S3 | S4 | S5 | S6 | S7 | S8 | S9 |
| A | B | C | D | E | | I | | | |

# Program Listing II

| LABELS | | | | | FLAGS |
|---|---|---|---|---|---|
| A load C | B load L | C load N | D calc type 1 | E calc type 2 | 0 capacitor |
| a | b | c | d | e | 1 |
| 0 output subr. | 1 | 2 | 3 | 4 | 2 |
| 5 | 6 | 7 | 8 | 9 | 3 |

| SET STATUS | | |
|---|---|---|
| FLAGS | TRIG | DISP |
| ON OFF | USER'S CHOICE | |
| 0 ■ | DEG | FIX |
| 1 | GRAD | SCI |
| 2 | RAD | ENG |
| 3 | | n ____ |

## PROGRAM 2-9 BUTTERWORTH AND CHEBYSHEV ACTIVE LOWPASS FILTER DESIGN AND POLE LOCATIONS.

Program Description and Equations Used

This program calculates the pole locations and Sallen and Key topology element values for un-normalized Butterworth or Chebyshev all pole lowpass filter approximations.

The program is designed to allow the use of capacitors with specified values as might result from the actual capacity measurement of a selected capacitor. The design process starts by assuming that all resistors are equal to the design resistance level, and the capacitor values are calculated to meet the filter requirements. The user may select new capacitor values near the original values, and the program will calculate new resistor values to meet the filter requirements. These resistor values can generally be selected from the nearest standard 0.1% resistor values.

The normalized pole locations of a Butterworth lowpass filter lie on a circle of unit radius as shown by Fig. 2-2.1 with the generalized pole locations given by Eqs. (2-2.12) and (2-2.13). The normalized pole locations for a Chebyshev lowpass filter lie on an ellipse as shown by Fig. 2-2.3 with the generalized pole locations given by Eqs. (2-2.15), (2-2.16), (2-2.17), and (2-2.18).

Each complex conjugate pole pair can be expressed in either the cartesian (real and imaginary parts) or the polar (magnitude and angle) co-ordinate systems. A variation on the polar system allows the pole pair to be defined in terms of the natural frequency (polar radius), $\omega_n$, and "Q," or quality factor. The relationship between these co-ordinate systems is shown in Fig. 2-9.1, and described by Eqs. (2-9.1) through (2-9.3).

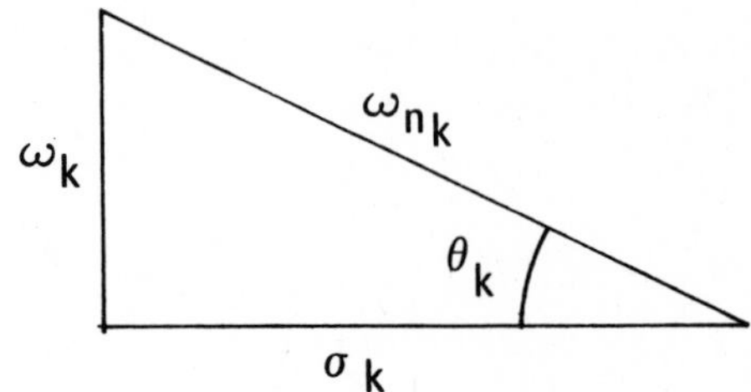


Figure 2-9.1 Co-ordinate system relationships.

$$\omega_{n_k} = \sigma_k^{\,2} + \omega_k^{\,2} \tag{2-9.1}$$

$$\theta_k = \tan^{-1}\left(\frac{\omega_k}{\alpha_k}\right) \tag{2-9.2}$$

$$Q_k = \frac{1}{2 \cos \theta_k} = \frac{\omega_{n_k}}{2\alpha_k} \tag{2-9.3}$$

The element values for the Sallen and Key type active resonator are easily expressed in terms of $\omega_n$ and Q as follows:

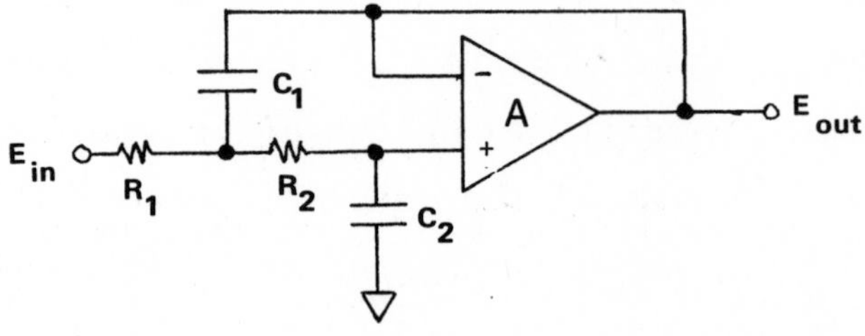

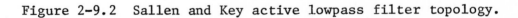

Figure 2-9.2 Sallen and Key active lowpass filter topology.

$$C_1 = \frac{Q(R_1 + R_2)}{\omega_n R_1 R_2} = \frac{2Q}{\omega_n R} \tag{2-9.4}$$

$$C_2 = \frac{1}{\omega_n Q (R_1 + R_2)} = \frac{C_1}{4Q^2} \tag{2-9.5}$$

$$R_1 = R_2 = R$$

The Sallen and Key resonator topology is chosen over other types because of the low parameter sensitivities to element changes. This type of filter synthesis is called the cascade method. Each pole pair is synthesized by an isolated op-amp resonator circuit. The entire filter is formed from a cascade of these resonator circuits. With each pole pair being independent, the overall filter sensitivities to component value changes are higher than an equivalent LC filter. See reference [49] (page 314) for more details.

If higher order filters are required (n greater than 9 or so), either the leapfrog (Szentirmai) topology using Deliyannis resonators [48], [20] or Cauer-Chebyshev filters using biquadratic sections [35] should be considered.

If the two capacitors in the Sallen and Key circuit are specified, then the following equations express the resistor values.

$$R_1 = \frac{1 + \sqrt{1 - 4Q^2 C_2/C_1}}{2Q\omega_n C_2} \tag{2-9.6}$$

$$R_2 = \frac{1}{\omega_n^2 C_1 C_2 R_1} \tag{2-9.7}$$

To ensure the quantity under the radical is positive in the equation for $R_1$, $C_2$ should be selected to be a lower value, and $C_1$ a higher value than given by Eqs. (2-9.4) and (2-9.5).

If the filter order is odd, then a real pole exists. A third order op-amp resonator circuit may be used to produce both the real pole and a complex conjugate pair. The lowest Q pole pair is selected for realization by this circuit to minimize sensitivities, and to keep the element value spread within bounds. The third order section topology is shown in Fig. 2-9.3.

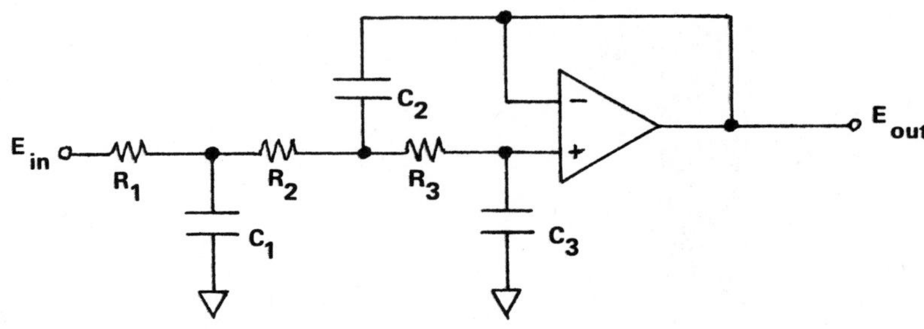


Figure 2-9.3 Third order op-amp resonator circuit.

$$\frac{E_{out}}{E_{in}} = \frac{1}{D(s)} \tag{2-9.8}$$

where

$$D(s) = s^3 C_1 C_2 C_3 R_1 R_2 R_3 + s^2 C_3 \{C_1 R_1 (R_2 + R_3) + C_2 R_3 (R_1 + R_2)\} + s\{C_1 R_1 + C_3 (R_1 + R_2 + R_3)\} + 1$$

$$\frac{E_{out}}{E_{in}} = \frac{1}{Cs^3 + Bs^2 + As + 1} = \frac{1}{\frac{s^2}{\omega_n^2} + \frac{s}{\omega_n Q} + 1} \cdot \frac{1}{\tau s + 1} \tag{2-9.9}$$

$$\text{for } R_1 = R_2 = R_3 = 1 \tag{2-9.10}$$

$$A = C_1 + 3C_3 = \tau + \frac{1}{\omega_n Q} \tag{2-9.11}$$

$$B = 2C_3(C_1 + C_2) = \frac{\tau}{\omega_n Q} + \frac{1}{\omega_n^2} \tag{2-9.12}$$

$$C_1 = C_1 C_2 C_3 = \frac{\tau}{\omega_n^2} \tag{2-9.13}$$

The equations for A, B, and C represent three equations in three unknowns, $C_1$, $C_2$, and $C_3$. By algebraic manipulation, a cubic equation in $C_1$ alone may be obtained.

$$C_1{}^3 - C_1{}^2\,(A) + C_1(\tfrac{3}{2}\,B) - 3C = 0 \tag{2-9.14}$$

A Newton-Raphson iterative solution is used to find the real root of this equation (there will be at least one). Once $C_1$ is found, the remaining two capacitors are found as follows:

$$C_3 = \frac{A - C_1}{3} \tag{2-9.15}$$

$$C_2 = \frac{C}{C_1 C_3} \tag{2-9.16}$$

If the three capacitors are specified, then the transmission function (Eq. (2-9.9)) may be used to obtain three equations in terms of the three unknown resistors. Equating like powers of s, as before, these equations result:

$$A = C_1R_1 + C_3(R_1 + R_2 + R_3) = \tau + \frac{1}{\omega_n Q} \tag{2-9.17}$$

$$B = C_3\{C_1R_1(R_2 + R_3) + C_2R_3\,(R_1 + R_2)\} = \frac{\tau}{\omega_n Q} + \frac{1}{\omega_n{}^2} \tag{2-9.18}$$

$$C = C_1C_2C_3R_1R_2R_3 = \frac{\tau}{\omega_n{}^2} \tag{2-9.19}$$

By algebraic manipulation, $R_2$ may be eliminated leaving two equations in two unknowns, $R_3$ as a cubic function of $R_1$ alone, and a quadratic equation in $R_1$ with $R_3$ as a parameter. The quadratic formula is used to reduce the second equation to R as a function of $R_1$ alone. These two non-linear equations in two unknowns are solved using an iterative method given in an unpublished paper by Robert Esperti of Delco Electronics.

$$R_3 = \frac{1}{R_1{}^2C_2C_3}\left\{R_1{}^2(C_1(C_1 + C_3)) + R_1{}^2(AC_1) + R_1\,(B) + \frac{C}{C_1}\right\} \tag{2-9.20}$$

$$R_1 = \frac{-b}{2a} + \sqrt{\left(\frac{b}{2a}\right)^2 - \frac{c}{a}} \tag{2-9.21}$$

$$\frac{-b}{2a} = \frac{A - C_3R_3}{2(C_1 + C_3)}\;;\quad \frac{c}{a} = \frac{C}{(C_1 + C_3)\cdot C_1C_2R_3} \tag{2-9-22}$$

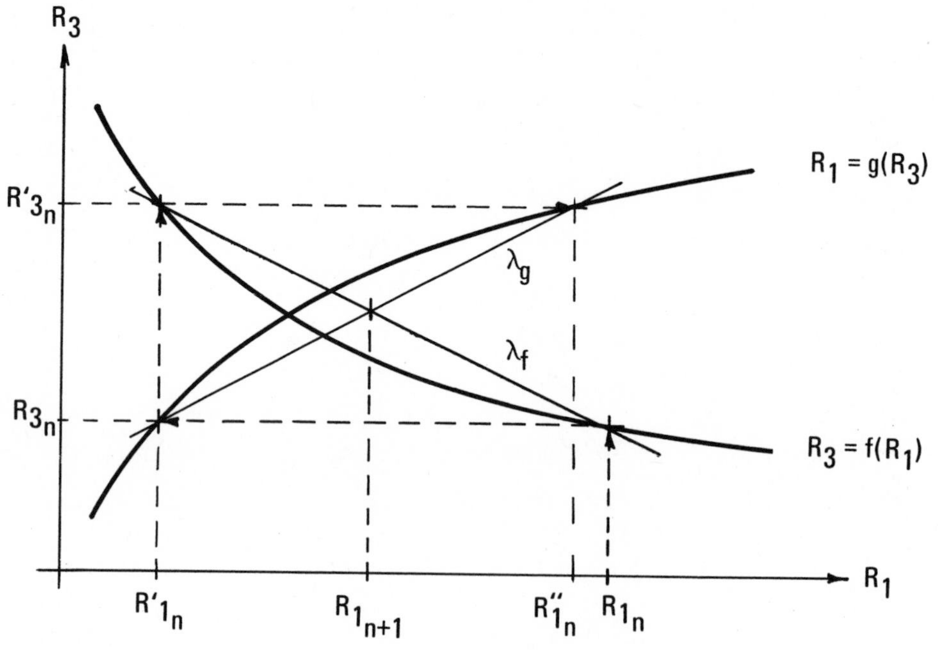


Figure 2-9.4 Esperti's iterative method.

Referring to Fig. 2-9.4, an initial guess for $R_1$ is made. The corresponding value for $R_3$ is calculated using $R_3 = f(R_1)$. The corresponding value for $R_1$ (say $R'_1$) is calculated using the above value for $R_3$ in $R'_1 = g(R_3)$. Using $R_3 = f(R'_1)$, a second value of $R_3$ is calculated; this value of $R_3$ is designated $R'_3$. Finally, a second value of $R_1$ is calculated using $R_1 = g(R'_3)$; this value of $R_1$ is designated $R''_1$. Straight lines designated $\lambda_f$ and $\lambda_g$ are drawn as shown. The intersection of these two lines defines the next guess for $R_1$. The iteration is halted when the new and old values for $R_1$ agree within $10^{-6}$%. The convergence of this method is quite fast with four iterations generally providing the above accuracy. Furthermore, the method will converge when direct substitution type iteration proves to be divergent.

The above procedure may be done algebraically to yield a recursion relationship as shown below:

$$R_{1_{n+1}} = R_{1_n} + \cfrac{g(f(R_{1_n})) - R_{1_n}}{1 - \cfrac{g(f(g(f(R_{1_n})))) - g(f(R_{1_n}))}{g(f(R_{1_n})) - R_{1_n}}} \tag{2-9.23}$$

The recursion relationship may be further reduced to an algorithm that can be used to program the HP-97. This algorithm is shown below:

$$R'_{1_n} = g(f(R_{1_n})) \tag{2-9.24}$$

$$R''_{1_n} = g(f(R'_{1_n})) \tag{2-9.25}$$

$$\delta = R'_{1_n} - R_{1_n} \tag{2-9.26}$$

$$\delta' = R''_{1_n} - R'_{1_n} \tag{2-9.27}$$

$$\varepsilon = \frac{\delta}{1 - \delta'/\delta} \tag{2-9.28}$$

$$R_{1_{n+1}} = R_{1_n} + \varepsilon \tag{2-9.29}$$

$$\text{Terminate if } \left| \frac{\varepsilon}{R_{1_{n+1}}} \right| \leq 10^{-8} \tag{2-9.30}$$

Each time through the $R''_1 = g(f(R_1))$ calculation, the value of $R_3$ is stored in a scratchpad register. After the iteration loop termination, values for $R_1$ and $R_3$ will be at hand. The following formula relates $R_2$ to these resistors and the other known quantities:

$$R_2 = \frac{C}{C_1 C_2 C_3 R_1 R_3} \tag{2-8.31}$$

To simplify the initial guess for $R_1$ and to keep the range of numbers within bounds, the selected values for the capacitors are normalized to 1 ohm, 1 radian/second values for use by the program. After the corresponding normalized resistors are calculated, the resistance values are de-normalized before output.

# User Instructions

| BUTTERWORTH & CHEBYSHEV ACTIVE LP FILTER DESIGN & POLES | | | | |
|---|---|---|---|---|
| C: n↑ $\epsilon_{dB}$ | | | enter $f_{-\epsilon dB}$ & start | |
| B: n | B: $-\epsilon_{dB}$ | R | enter $f_{-3dB}$ & start | enter $C_1' \uparrow C_2'$ |

| STEP | INSTRUCTIONS | INPUT DATA/UNITS | KEYS | OUTPUT DATA/UNITS |
|---|---|---|---|---|
| 1 | Load both sides of program card # 1 | | | |
| 2 | If Chebyshev: | | | |
| | enter filter order | n | ENT↑ | |
| | enter passband ripple | $\epsilon_{dB}$ | f A | |
| | go to step 4 | | | |
| 3 | If Butterworth: | | | |
| | enter filter order | n | A | |
| | if bandedge is defined by other than the -3dB point, enter the dB down defining the bandedge | $-\epsilon_{dB}$ | B | |
| 4 | Enter the design resistance level | R, Ω | C | |
| 5 | If bandedge is -3dB point, enter f-3dB & start | $f_{-3dB}$, Hz | D | if Cheb $f_{-\epsilon dB}$ see below for rest |
| 6 | If bandedge is -εdB point, enter $f_{-\epsilon dB}$ & start | $f_{-\epsilon dB}$, Hz | f D | if Buttw $f_{-3dB}$ |
| | | | | space |
| | | | | $\omega_n$ |
| | The data is for the second order filter section, and alternate capacitor values entered in next step are also for the second order section. The third order section (for odd filter order) is output last and is described on the next page. | | 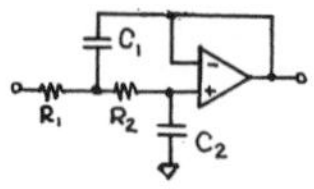 | Q |
| | | | | $C_1$, F |
| | | | | $C_2$, F |
| | | | | stop |
| | | | third order section output | $\omega_n$ |
| | | | | Q |
| | | | | σ |
| | | | | flashing display |
| 7 | If alternate capacitor values are desired, | | | |
| | enter $C_1'$ } to skip this step, press | $C_1'$, F | ENT↑ | |
| | enter $C_2'$ } "E" without numeric entry | $C_2'$, F | E | $R_1$, Ω |
| | | | | $R_2$, Ω |
| | After the second resistor value output, the program execution will automatically return to step six until all second order sections have been outputted. If the filter is odd order, the display will flash to indicate the reading of the second card is required. | | | |

# User Instructions

BUTTERWORTH & CHEBYSHEV ACTIVE LP FILTERS - ODD ORDER

THIS SECOND CARD IS USED WITH ODD ORDER BUTTERWORTH AND CHEBYSHEV ACTIVE LP FILTER DESIGN.

enter capacitor changes $C_1' \uparrow C_2' \uparrow C_3'$

| STEP | INSTRUCTIONS | INPUT DATA/UNITS | KEYS | OUTPUT DATA/UNITS |
|---|---|---|---|---|
| 9 | Read both sides of second card when display flashes with first program. Program operation will automatically resume after the second side of this card is read. | | | |
| 10 | The three capacitor values for the equal resistor topology will be printed. | | | $C_1$, F<br>$C_2$, F<br>$C_3$, F |
| 11 | If alternate capacitor values are desired, key those values via key "E". If the third order section requirements cannot be met with those resistors, the program execution will halt displaying "ERROR". Press any key to clear the display, and enter another set of capacitors using key "E". By staying close to the capacitor values printed in step 2, the error situation will generally be avoided. | $C_1'$, F<br>$C_2'$, F<br>$C_3'$, F | ENT↑<br>ENT↑<br>E | $R_1$, Ω<br>$R_2$, Ω<br>$R_3$, Ω |
| 12 | To run another case, reload both sides of card 1, and return to step 3 | | | |

Example 2-9.1

A 1 dB ripple Chebyshev lowpass active filter must pass all frequencies between dc and 1000 Hz within 3 dB, and must reject all frequencies higher than 2000 Hz by more than 60 dB. Program 2-1 may be used to determine the necessary filter order. This program calculates a minimum filter order of 6.19, which is rounded to the next highest integer, 7. A 7th order, 1 dB ripple Chebyshev lowpass filter that is 3 dB down at 1000 Hz, will be 1 dB down at 983.1 Hz and 69.4 dB down at 2000 Hz ( $\lambda$ = 2000/983.1 = 2.035).

This program (Program 2-9) is used to calculate the element values for a 7th order, 1 dB ripple, 1000 Hz -3 dB cutoff frequency Chebyshev filter. A design resistance level of 10000 ohms is chosen which will make the capacitor values around $1/(2\pi fR)$ = 0.016 μF.

## PROGRAM INPUT

| | | |
|---|---|---|
| 7. | ENT↑ | n |
| 1. | GSBa | $\varepsilon_{dB}$ |
| 10000. | GSBC | design resistance level |
| 1000. | GSBD | -3dB frequency |
| 983.1+00 | *** | -1dB frequence (output) |

## PROGRAM OUTPUT

section one

| | | | |
|---|---|---|---|
| 6.154+03 | *** | $\omega_{n_a}$ | |
| 10.90+00 | *** | $Q_a$ | |
| 354.2-09 | *** | $C_{1_a}$ | |
| 745.5-12 | *** | $C_{2_a}$ | |
| .47-06 | ENT↑ | $C_{1_a}$ | alternate values |
| 750.-12 | GSBE | $C_{2_a}$ | alternate values |
| 14.83+03 | *** | $R_{1_a}$ | |
| 5.052+03 | *** | $R_{2_a}$ | |

section two

| | | | |
|---|---|---|---|
| 4.993+03 | *** | $\omega_{n_b}$ | |
| 3.156+00 | *** | $Q_b$ | |
| 126.4-09 | *** | $C_{1_b}$ | |
| 3.173-09 | *** | $C_{2_b}$ | |
| .22-06 | ENT↑ | $C_{1_b}$ | alternate values |
| 3.-09 | GSBE | $C_{2_b}$ | alternate values |
| 17.72+03 | *** | $R_{1_b}$ | |
| 3.429+03 | *** | $R_{2_b}$ | |

section three

| | | | |
|---|---|---|---|
| 2.965+03 | *** | $\omega_n$ | of second order pair |
| 1.297+00 | *** | $Q$ | of second order pair |
| 1.269+03 | *** | σ, real pole location | |
| 85.66-09 | *** | $C_{1_c}$ | |
| 163.9-09 | *** | $C_{2_c}$ | |
| 6.385-09 | *** | $C_{3_c}$ | |
| .1-06 | ENT↑ | $C_{1_c}$ | alternate values |
| .22-06 | ENT↑ | $C_{2_c}$ | alternate values |
| 6.2-09 | GSBE | $C_{3_c}$ | alternate values |
| 8.800+03 | *** | $R_{1_c}$ | |
| 6.113+03 | *** | $R_{2_c}$ | |
| 12.22+03 | *** | $R_{3_c}$ | |

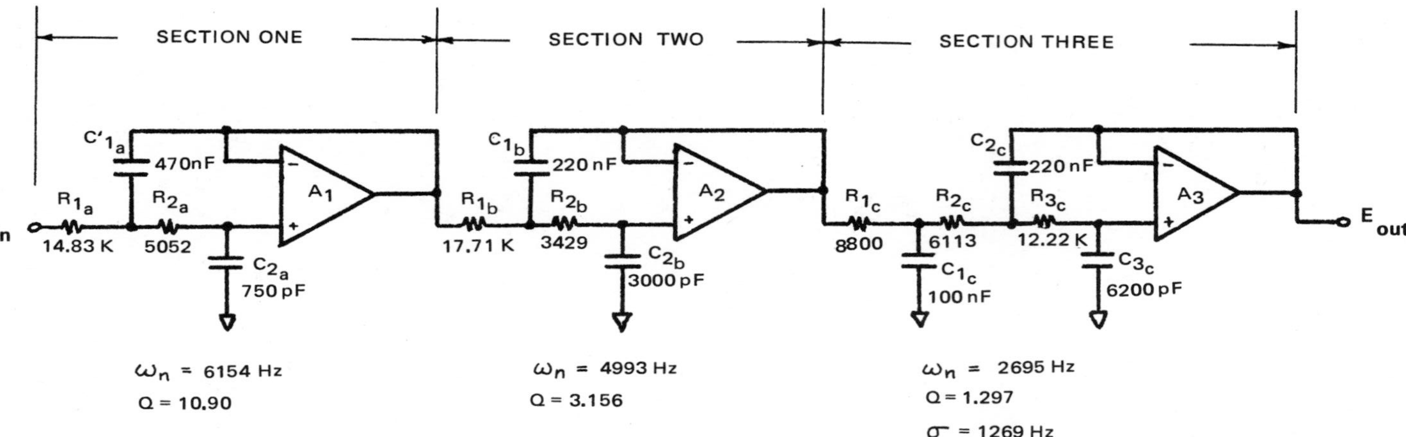

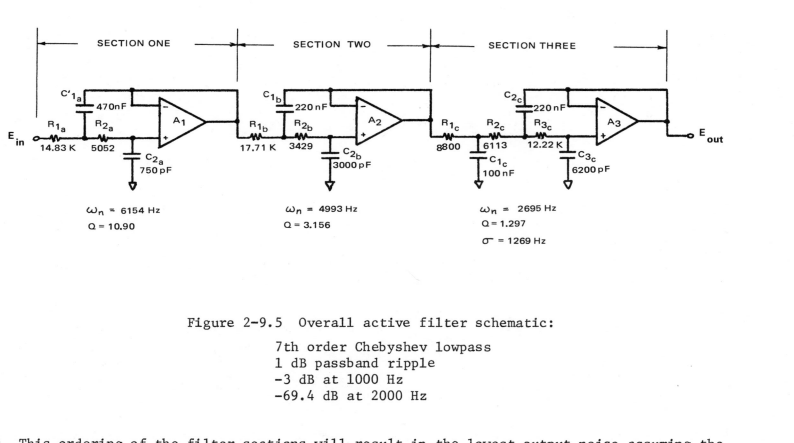

Figure 2-9.5 Overall active filter schematic:

7th order Chebyshev lowpass
1 dB passband ripple
-3 dB at 1000 Hz
-69.4 dB at 2000 Hz

Note: This ordering of the filter sections will result in the lowest output noise assuming the resistance levels in the resonator sections are low enough so the op-amp voltage noise dominates (see Program 1-6). Because the highest Q resonator is first, it will be prone to overload at frequencies near the resonant peak. For filters operating at higher signal levels where self noise is not a concern, the ordering of the sections should be reversed with the lowest Q section placed first.

Example 2-9.2

An active Butterworth lowpass filter must pass all frequencies between dc and 1000 Hz within 1 dB, and must reject all frequencies higher than 3000 Hz by at least 60 dB. Program 2-1 may be used to determine the minimum filter order. This program calculates a minimum filter order of 6.90, which is rounded to 7, the next highest integer. This filter will be 60.9 dB down at 3000 Hz ($\lambda$ = 3000/1000 = 3).

This program (Program 2-9) is used to find the element values for a 7th order, 1000 Hz -1 dB cutoff, Butterworth lowpass active filter. A design resistance level of 10000 ohms will keep the capacitor values centered around $1/(2\pi fR)$ = 0.016 $\mu$F.

**PROGRAM INPUT**

```
      7.  GSBA    n
      1.  GSBB    ε dB
  10000.  GSBC    R, design resist level
   1000.  GSBa    f-εdB
1.101+03   ***    f-3dB (output)
```

**PROGRAM OUTPUT**

section one

```
6.920+03   ***    ωn
2.247+00   ***    Q
64.94-09   ***    C1
3.216-09   ***    C2
  68.-03  ENT↑    C'1  }
3000.-12  GSBE    C'2  }  alternate values
14.26+03   ***    R1
7.180+03   ***    R2
```

section two

```
6.920+03   ***    ωn
801.9-03   ***    Q
23.18-09   ***    C1
9.010-09   ***    C2
  24.-09  ENT↑    C'1  }
8200.-12  GSBE    C'2  }  alternate values
14.81+03   ***    R1
7.164+03   ***    R2
```

section three

```
6.920+03   ***    ωn  }
555.6-03   ***    Q   }  of second order pair
6.920+03   ***    σ
19.32-09   ***    C1
22.14-09   ***    C2
7.058-09   ***    C3
  22.-09  ENT↑    C'1  }
  22.-09  ENT↑    C'2  }  alternate values
6800.-12  GSBE    C'3  }
9.172+03   ***    R1
7.675+03   ***    R2
13.03+03   ***    R3
```

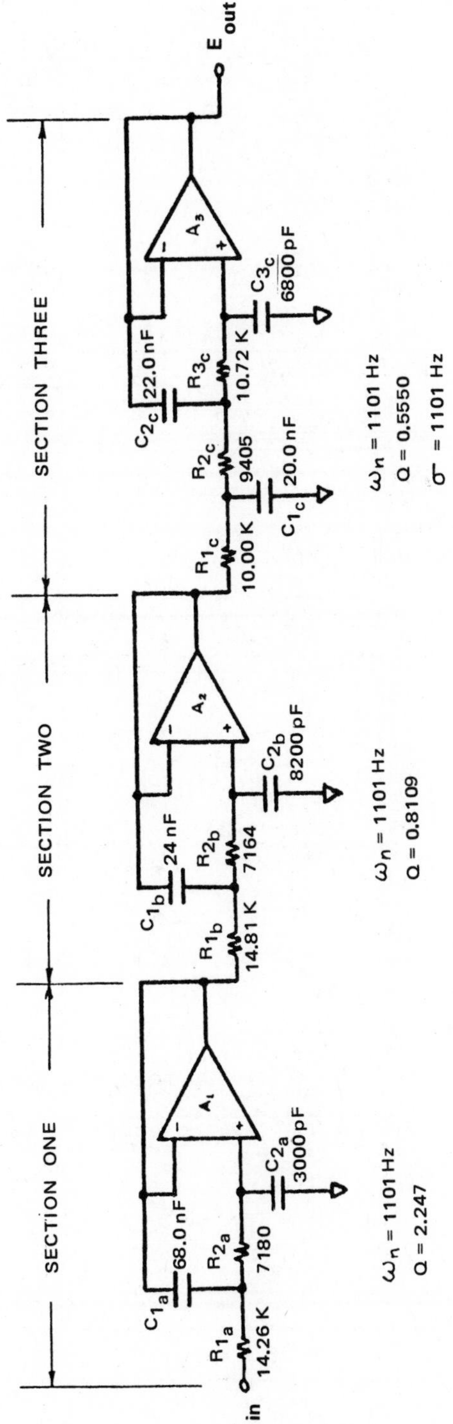


Figure 2-8.6 Overall active filter schematic:
7th order Butterworth lowpass filter
-1 dB @ 1000 Hz
-3 dB @ 1101 Hz
-60.9 dB @ 2000 Hz

# Program Listing I

| | | |
|---|---|---|
| 001 | *LBLA | BUTTERWORTH; LOAD n |
| 002 | SF1 | indicate Butterworth |
| 003 | EEX | setup registers: |
| 004 | STOB | $f_{-3dB}/f_{-\varepsilon dB} = 1$ |
| 005 | STOD | $\cosh a = 1$ |
| 006 | STOE | $\sinh \alpha = 1$ |
| 007 | R↓ | recover n |
| 008 | GTO8 | goto filter order entry subr. |
| 009 | *LBLa | CHEBYSHEV; LOAD n↑εdB |
| 010 | STOB | store $\varepsilon dB$ |
| 011 | R↓ | recover filter order, n |
| 012 | CF1 | indicate Chebyshev |
| 013 | GSB8 | gosub filter order entry subr |
| 014 | RCLB | |
| 015 | EEX | |
| 016 | 1 | calculate: |
| 017 | ÷ | |
| 018 | 10ˣ | $\varepsilon = \sqrt{10^{0.1\varepsilon_{dB}} - 1}$ |
| 019 | EEX | |
| 020 | - | |
| 021 | √X | |
| 022 | 1/X | $1/\varepsilon \rightarrow R5$ |
| 023 | STO5 | |
| 024 | ENT↑ | |
| 025 | X² | |
| 026 | EEX | calculate and store: |
| 027 | + | |
| 028 | √X | $a = \dfrac{1}{n} \sinh^{-1}\left(\dfrac{1}{\varepsilon}\right) \rightarrow R2$ |
| 029 | + | |
| 030 | RCLA | |
| 031 | 1/X | |
| 032 | Yˣ | |
| 033 | STO2 | |
| 034 | ENT↑ | |
| 035 | 1/X | calculate and store: |
| 036 | - | |
| 037 | 2 | $\sinh a \rightarrow R_E$ |
| 038 | ÷ | |
| 039 | STOE | |
| 040 | RCL2 | |
| 041 | ENT↑ | calculate and store: |
| 042 | 1/X | |
| 043 | + | $\cosh a \rightarrow R_D$ |
| 044 | 2 | |
| 045 | ÷ | |
| 046 | STOD | |
| 047 | GTO5 | go to data entry flag clear |
| 048 | *LBLB | LOAD $-\varepsilon_{dB}$ FOR BUTTERWORTH |
| 049 | EEX | if bandedge is not defined |
| 050 | 1 | by -3dB point |
| 051 | ÷ | calculate and store: |
| 052 | 10ˣ | |
| 053 | EEX | $\dfrac{f_{-3dB}}{f_{-\varepsilon_{dB}}} = \left[10^{0.1\varepsilon_{dB}} - 1\right]^{\frac{1}{2n}} \rightarrow R_B$ |
| 054 | - | |
| 055 | RCLA | |
| 056 | ENT↑ | |
| 057 | + | |
| 058 | 1/X | |
| 059 | CHS | |
| 060 | Yˣ | |
| 061 | STOB | |
| 062 | GTO5 | goto data entry flag clear |
| 063 | *LBLC | LOAD OPERATING RESISTANCE |
| 064 | STO6 | LEVEL |
| 065 | GTO5 | goto data entry flag clear |
| 066 | *LBLD | LOAD $f_{-3dB}$ & START |
| 067 | F1? | jump, if Butterworth |
| 068 | GTO7 | |
| 069 | STO9 | |
| 070 | RCL5 | |
| 071 | ENT↑ | |
| 072 | X² | |
| 073 | EEX | |
| 074 | - | |
| 075 | √X | for Chebyshev, calculate |
| 076 | + | $f_{-\varepsilon dB} = \dfrac{f_{-3\,dB}}{\cosh\left[\dfrac{1}{n}\cosh^{-1}\left(\dfrac{1}{\varepsilon}\right)\right]}$ |
| 077 | RCLA | |
| 078 | 1/X | |
| 079 | Yˣ | |
| 080 | ENT↑ | |
| 081 | 1/X | |
| 082 | + | |
| 083 | ÷ | |
| 084 | ENT↑ | |
| 085 | + | |
| 086 | SF3 | set data entry flag |
| 087 | PRTX | print $f_{-\varepsilon dB}$ |
| 088 | *LBLd | LOAD $f_{-\varepsilon dB}$ AND START |
| 089 | F1? | if Butterworth, calculate |
| 090 | RCLB | and print $f_{-3dB}$ |
| 091 | F1? | |
| 092 | x | |
| 093 | F1? | |
| 094 | PRTX | |
| 095 | *LBL7 | |
| 096 | Pi | |
| 097 | ENT↑ | |
| 098 | + | |
| 099 | x | if flag 3, $2\pi f \rightarrow R3$ |
| 100 | F3? | |
| 101 | STO3 | |
| 102 | EEX | |
| 103 | STO0 | setup for next loop |
| 104 | SPC | |
| 105 | *LBL1 | second order filter loop |
| 106 | SPC | |
| 107 | RCL0 | |
| 108 | RCLI | |
| 109 | x | |
| 110 | EEX | |

**REGISTERS**

| 0 | 1 | 2 | 3 | 4 | 5 | 6 | 7 | 8 | 9 |
|---|---|---|---|---|---|---|---|---|---|
| $2k - 1$ | $2Q$ | $a$ or $\omega_n$ | $\omega_{-3dB}$ | $C_1$ | $1/\varepsilon$ | $R$ | $\omega_k$ | $\sigma_k$ | scratch |
| S0 | S1 | S2 | S3 | S4 | S5 | S6 | S7 | S8 | S9 |
| | | | | | | | | | |

| A | B | C | D | E | I |
|---|---|---|---|---|---|
| filter order, n | $\varepsilon_{dB}$, 1, or $\dfrac{f_{-3dB}}{f_{-\varepsilon dB}}$ | $C_2$ | $\cosh a$ or 1 | $\sinh a$ or 1 | $\pi/(2n)$ |

# Program Listing II

| Step | Key | Comments |
|---|---|---|
| 111 | →R | |
| 112 | RCLD | calculate pole positions: |
| 113 | x | |
| 114 | STO7 | $\sigma_k = (\sinh a)(\sin \frac{2k-1}{2n}\pi)$ |
| 115 | X⇄Y | |
| 116 | RCLE | $\omega_k = (\cosh a)(\cos \frac{2k-1}{2n}\pi)$ |
| 117 | x | |
| 118 | STO8 | |
| 119 | →P | |
| 120 | RCL3 | |
| 121 | x | calculate $\omega_{n_k}$ and $Q_k$ |
| 122 | PRTX | |
| 123 | STO2 | $\omega_{n_k}^2 = \sigma_k^2 + \omega_k^2$ |
| 124 | X⇄Y | |
| 125 | COS | $Q_k = 1/(2 \cos( \tan^{-1} \frac{\omega_k}{\sigma_k} ))$ |
| 126 | 1/X | |
| 127 | STO1 | |
| 128 | 2 | |
| 129 | ÷ | |
| 130 | PRTX | |
| 131 | LSTX | increment k by 2 |
| 132 | ST+0 | |
| 133 | F0? | jump if n is even |
| 134 | GTO3 | |
| 135 | RCL0 | |
| 136 | EEX | odd order filter: |
| 137 | + | test for last section |
| 138 | RCLA | (3rd order section) |
| 139 | X≤Y? | |
| 140 | GTO2 | |
| 141 | *LBL3 | calculate $C_1$ for 2nd order |
| 142 | RCL1 | |
| 143 | RCL2 | |
| 144 | ÷ | $C_1 = \frac{2Q}{\omega_n \cdot R}$ |
| 145 | RCL6 | |
| 146 | ÷ | |
| 147 | PRTX | |
| 148 | ENT↑ | save $C_1$ in stack |
| 149 | ENT↑ | |
| 150 | RCL1 | calculate $C_2$ for 2nd order |
| 151 | X² | |
| 152 | ÷ | $C_2 = \frac{C_1}{4 \cdot Q^2}$ |
| 153 | PRTX | |
| 154 | RTN | |
| 155 | *LBLE | LOAD ALT CAPACITOR VALUES |
| 156 | F3? | |
| 157 | F3? | if numeric entry, store, |
| 158 | GTO4 | otherwise jump |
| 159 | STO9 | |
| 160 | X⇄Y | calculate $R_1$: |
| 161 | STO4 | |
| 162 | ÷ | |
| 163 | RCL1 | $R_1 = \frac{1 + \sqrt{1 - 4Q^2 \cdot C_2'/C_1'}}{2 \cdot Q \cdot \omega_n \cdot C_2'}$ |
| 164 | X² | |
| 165 | x | |
| 166 | CHS | |
| 167 | EEX | $R_1$ calculation (continued) |
| 168 | + | |
| 169 | √X | |
| 170 | EEX | |
| 171 | + | |
| 172 | RCL1 | |
| 173 | ÷ | |
| 174 | RCL2 | |
| 175 | ÷ | |
| 176 | RCL9 | |
| 177 | ÷ | |
| 178 | PRTX | |
| 179 | RCL4 | |
| 180 | x | $R_2$ calculation: |
| 181 | RCL9 | |
| 182 | x | |
| 183 | RCL2 | $R_2 = 1/(\omega_n^2 \cdot C_1' \cdot C_2' \cdot R_1)$ |
| 184 | X² | |
| 185 | x | |
| 186 | 1/X | |
| 187 | PRTX | |
| 188 | *LBL4 | |
| 189 | RCL0 | test for loop exit |
| 190 | RCLA | |
| 191 | X>Y? | |
| 192 | GTO1 | |
| 193 | SPC | space paper upon loop exit |
| 194 | SPC | |
| 195 | RTN | |
| 196 | *LBL2 | calculate real 3rd order pole |
| 197 | RCLE | |
| 198 | RCL3 | |
| 199 | x | |
| 200 | PRTX | |
| 201 | *LBL0 | wait loop for 2nd card read |
| 202 | PSE | |
| 203 | GTO0 | |
| 204 | *LBL8 | filter order entry subr |
| 205 | STOA | |
| 206 | 2 | |
| 207 | ÷ | |
| 208 | ENT↑ | set flag 0 if n is even |
| 209 | INT | |
| 210 | CF0 | |
| 211 | X=Y? | |
| 212 | SF0 | |
| 213 | Pi | |
| 214 | RCLA | calculate and store: |
| 215 | ENT↑ | |
| 216 | + | $\pi/(2n) \rightarrow R_I$ |
| 217 | ÷ | |
| 218 | STOI | |
| 219 | *LBL5 | data entry flag clear subr |
| 220 | CF3 | |
| 221 | RTN | |

**LABELS**

| | | | | |
|---|---|---|---|---|
| A load n ↑ dB | B load R | C $f_{-3dB}$ & go | D $f_{-\epsilon dB}$ & go | E load $C_1$↑$C_2$ |
| a capacitor entry tog | b | c | d | e |
| 0 2nd card read loop | 1 n & Q calculation | 2 odd order output | 3 even ord output | 4 loop exit test |
| 5 clr data entry flag | 6 | 7 | 8 | 9 |

**FLAGS**

| | |
|---|---|
| 0 | n even |
| 1 | set for Buttr |
| 2 | |
| 3 | data entry |

**SET STATUS**

| FLAGS | ON | OFF |
|---|---|---|
| 0 | | ■ |
| 1 | ■ | |
| 2 | | ■ |
| 3 | | ■ |

| TRIG | |
|---|---|
| DEG | |
| GRAD | |
| RAD | ■ |

| DISP | |
|---|---|
| FIX | |
| SCI | |
| ENG | ■ |
| n | 3 |

# Program Listing I

| | | | |
|---|---|---|---|
| 001 | RCL7 | $\omega_k$ | for 3rd order section |
| 002 | RCL8 | $\sigma_k$ | |
| 003 | RCL6 | R | |
| 004 | P⇄S | | |
| 005 | SF2 | | |
| 006 | ST06 | | store denormalization R |
| 007 | R↓ | | |
| 008 | ST00 | | calculate and store: |
| 009 | →P | | |
| 010 | X² | | $\omega_{n_k}{}^2 = \omega_k{}^2 + \sigma_k{}^2$ |
| 011 | ST01 | | |
| 012 | 2 | | $2\sigma_k = \dfrac{\omega_n}{Q}$ |
| 013 | ST×0 | | |
| 014 | RCLE | | calculate and store: |
| 015 | RCL1 | | |
| 016 | × | | $C = \dfrac{\tau}{\omega_n{}^2}$ |
| 017 | 1/X | | |
| 018 | STOC | | |
| 019 | ST05 | | |
| 020 | RCLE | | calculate and store: |
| 021 | RCL0 | | |
| 022 | + | | $B = \dfrac{\tau}{\omega_n \cdot Q} + \dfrac{1}{\omega_n{}^2}$ as |
| 023 | × | | |
| 024 | STOB | | $\left(\dfrac{\tau}{\omega_n{}^2}\right)\left(\dfrac{1}{\tau} + \dfrac{\omega_n}{Q}\right)$ |
| 025 | ST04 | | |
| 026 | RCLE | | calculate and store: |
| 027 | RCL0 | | |
| 028 | × | | $A = \tau + \dfrac{1}{\omega_n Q}$ as |
| 029 | RCL1 | | |
| 030 | + | | |
| 031 | RCLC | | $\left(\dfrac{\tau}{\omega_n{}^2}\right)\left(\omega_n{}^2 + \dfrac{\omega_n}{Q}\right)$ |
| 032 | × | | |
| 033 | STOA | | |
| 034 | 3 | | use register arithmetic |
| 035 | ST×4 | | to form and store: |
| 036 | ST×5 | | 3B/2, and 3C |
| 037 | 2 | | |
| 038 | ST÷4 | | |
| 039 | ST03 | | initialize registers for |
| 040 | EEX | | Newton–Raphson iteration |
| 041 | CHS | | |
| 042 | 8 | | |
| 043 | ST09 | | |
| 044 | *LBL0 | | Newton–Raphson routine to |
| 045 | RCL3 | | find the real 3rd order |
| 046 | RCL3 | | root of $f(C_1) = 0$ |
| 047 | RCL3 | | |
| 048 | RCLA | | |
| 049 | – | | calculate $f(C_1)$ as: |
| 050 | × | | |
| 051 | RCL4 | | $f(C_1) = C_1{}^3 - AC_1{}^2 + \dfrac{3B}{2}C_1 - 3C$ |
| 052 | + | | |
| 053 | × | | |
| 054 | RCL5 | | |
| 055 | – | | |

| | | | |
|---|---|---|---|
| 056 | ST00 | | |
| 057 | CLX | | calculate $f'(C_1)$ as |
| 058 | 3 | | |
| 059 | × | | $f'(C_1) = 3C_1{}^2 - 2AC_1 + \dfrac{3B}{2}$ |
| 060 | RCLA | | |
| 061 | 2 | | |
| 062 | × | | |
| 063 | – | | |
| 064 | × | | |
| 065 | RCL4 | | |
| 066 | + | | |
| 067 | ST÷0 | | form and store: |
| 068 | RCL0 | | |
| 069 | ST–3 | | $C_{1_{n+1}} = C_{1_n} - \dfrac{f(C_{1_n})}{f'(C_{1_n})}$ |
| 070 | RCL3 | | iterate again if |
| 071 | ÷ | | |
| 072 | ABS | | $\left| \dfrac{\frac{f(C_{1_n})}{f'(C_{1_n})}}{C_{1_n}} \right| \geqslant 10^{-8}$ |
| 073 | RCL9 | | |
| 074 | X≤Y? | | |
| 075 | GT00 | | |
| 076 | RCLA | | calculate and store: |
| 077 | RCL3 | | |
| 078 | – | | |
| 079 | 3 | | $C_3 = \dfrac{A - C_1}{3}$ |
| 080 | ÷ | | |
| 081 | ST04 | | |
| 082 | RCL3 | | calculate: |
| 083 | × | | |
| 084 | RCLC | | $C_2 = \dfrac{C}{C_1 \cdot C_3}$ |
| 085 | X⇄Y | | |
| 086 | ÷ | | |
| 087 | RCL4 | | order $C_1$, $C_2$, and $C_3$ in |
| 088 | X⇄Y | | the stack |
| 089 | RCL3 | | |
| 090 | GSB9 | | restore P S order |
| 091 | GSB1 | | denormalize and print |
| 092 | GSB1 | | capacitors |
| 093 | *LBL1 | | capacitor denormalization |
| 094 | RCL3 | | |
| 095 | ÷ | | |
| 096 | RCL6 | | $C_{den} = C_{nor}/(\omega_{\varepsilon dB} \cdot R)$ |
| 097 | ÷ | | |
| 098 | PRTX | | |
| 099 | R↓ | | |
| 100 | RTN | | |
| 101 | *LBLE | | LOAD ALTERNATE CAPACITOR |
| 102 | GSB9 | | VALUES FOR $C_1$, $C_2$, & $C_3$ |
| 103 | RCL3 | | |
| 104 | P⇄S | | |
| 105 | SF2 | | |
| 106 | R↓ | | initialize registers |
| 107 | ST02 | | store $C_1$, $C_2$, & $C_3$ |
| 108 | R↓ | | |
| 109 | ST01 | | |
| 110 | R↓ | | |

### REGISTERS

| 0 $2k-1$ | 1 | 2 | 3 $\omega_{-3dB}$ | 4 | 5 $1/\varepsilon$ | 6 R | 7 $\omega_k$ | 8 $\sigma_k$ | 9 |
|---|---|---|---|---|---|---|---|---|---|
| S0 $C_1'$, $\dfrac{\omega_n}{Q}$ | S1 $C_2'$, $\omega_n{}^2$ | S2 $C_3'$ | S3 $R_1$ | S4 $R_1'$, $\dfrac{3B}{2}$ | S5 $R_1''$, $3C$ | S6 R | S7 scratch | S8 scratch | S9 $10^{-8}$ |
| A $A = \tau + \dfrac{1}{\omega_n Q}$ | | B $B = \dfrac{\tau}{\omega_n Q} + \dfrac{1}{\omega_n{}^2}$ | | C $C = \dfrac{\tau}{\omega_n{}^2}$ | | D cosh a | E sinh a | | I $C/(C_1 \cdot C_2)$ |

2–9, CARD 2

# Program Listing II

```
STO0
R↓
RCL6        form ω₋εdB * R
x
STx0
STx1        normalize C1', C2', C3'
STx2
EEX         store initial guess for R1
STO3
RCLC
RCL0        form and store:  C / (C1'·C2')
÷
RCL1
÷
STOI
*LBL7       Esperti iteration loop start
RCL3        calculate and store:
GSB8        R1' = f(g(R1))
STO4
GSB8        calculate and store
STO5        R1'' = f(g(R1'))
RCL4        calculate: δ = R1' - R1
ST-5
RCL3        calculate: δ' = R1'' - R1'
ST-4
RCL4
X=0?        δ = 0 escape
GTO6
EEX
RCL5
RCL4        form: ΔR1 = δ / (1 - δ'/δ)
÷
-
÷
ST+3        form R1(n+1) = R1(n) + ΔR1
RCL3
÷           iterate again if
ABS
RCL9        |ΔR1 / R1| ≥ 10^-8
X≤Y?
GTO7
*LBL6
RCLI
RCL2
÷           calculate R2 = C / (C1C2C3R1R3)
RCL3
÷
RCL8
÷
RCL6
STx3        denormalize resistors
STx8
x
RCL3        print R1, R2, and R3
PRTX
X⇄Y
PRTX
RCL8
PRTX
*LBL9
F2?         if flag 2, restore
P⇄S         P⇄S register order
RTN
*LBL8       subroutine for R1 = f(g(R1))
RCL0
RCL0  C1    R3 = g(R1)
RCL2  C3    as defined by:
+
STO7        R3 = [R1³C1(C1+C3) - R1²AC1 + R1B - C/C1] / (R1²C2C3)
x
x
RCLA  A
RCL0  C1
x
-
x
RCLB  B
+
RCLC  C
RCL0  C1
÷
-
RCL1  C2
RCL2  C3
x
÷
X⇄Y
X²
÷
STO8        store R3
RCL2  C3;   R1 = f(R3) as defined by:
x
RCLA  A
-           R1 = -b/2a + √[(b/2a)² - c/a]
CHS
RCL7
ENT↑        a = C1 + C3
+
÷  -b/2a    -b = A - C3R3
ENT↑
X²          c = C/(C1C2R3)
RCLI
RCL8
÷
RCL7
÷  c/a
-
√X
+  R1
RTN
```

| LABELS | | | | | FLAGS | SET STATUS | | |
|---|---|---|---|---|---|---|---|---|
| A | B | C | D | E load $C_1, C_2, C_3$ | 0 | FLAGS | TRIG | DISP |
| a | b | c | d | e | 1 | ON OFF 0 | DEG | FIX |
| 0 Newton-Raphson | 1 denormalize routine | 2 | 3 | 4 | 2 P⇄S used odd # time | 1 | GRAD | SCI |
| 5 | 6 escape | 7 Esperti routine go | 8 R1=f(g(R1)) | 9 P⇄S routine | 3 | 2 ■ (OFF) | RAD ■ | ENG ■ |
| | | | | | | 3 | | n 3 |

HP-67 suggested program changes. Program space does not allow the addition of a print, R/S toggle and associated output routine. If the HP-67 user would like the program to stop instead of halting for 5 seconds (print command) change the "print" statements to "R/S" at the following line numbers: (program 1); 122, 130, 147, 153, 178, 187, and 200; (program 2); 098, 165, 167, and 169. To resume program execution with the above changes, execute a "R/S" command from the keyboard after each data output point.

## PROGRAM 2-10 BUTTERWORTH AND CHEBYSHEV ACTIVE HIGHPASS FILTER DESIGN AND POLE LOCATIONS.

### Program Description and Equations Used

This program calculates the normalized pole locations and provides element values for the un-normalized, unity gain Sallen and Key type second and third order highpass active resonator circuit. Higher order filters are formed by cascading second order sections, and one third order section if the filter order is odd. The program uses either the Butterworth (maximally flat) or Chebyshev (equiripple passband) all pole filter descriptions.

The program is designed to allow the use of specified capacitor values such as would result from the actual measurement of a standard value capacitor. The corresponding resistor values are calculated for each section. The nearest 1% standard value precision resistor will generally suffice for the calculated value.

The design process starts by finding the normalized lowpass pole locations for the desired filter type. If the passband cutoff frequency is different from the conventional definition of the bandedge, a scaling of the normalized cutoff frequency is done. The Butterworth amplitude response is 3 dB down at the passband edge, while the Chebyshev amplitude response is $\varepsilon$ dB down at the passband edge, where $\varepsilon$ dB is the passband ripple in dB. The scaling factor is K, and the normalized filter cutoff frequency is denoted by $\omega_n$.

The normalized and scaled lowpass pole locations are sequentially found as complex conjugate pairs, and, if the filter order is odd, the real pole location. The lowpass, unity-gain, Sallen and Key, normalized active filter circuit element values may be found in terms of these pole locations. The element values of the highpass normalized active resonator may be found from the normalized lowpass structure. The normalized lowpass structure is transformed to the normalized highpass structure by replacing each lowpass resistor with a capacitor and vice versa.

The normalized highpass element values are the reciprocals of the corresponding converted lowpass element, i.e., a 2 farad capacitor becomes a ½ ohm resistor. This conversion is equivalent to replacing s by 1/s in the lowpass transfer function equation. The un-normalized highpass equation is found by replacing s by $\omega_c/s$, where $\omega_c = 2\pi f_c$, and $f_c$ is the highpass cutoff frequency in hertz.

Each complex conjugate pole pair can be expressed in either the cartesian (real and imaginary parts) or the polar (magnitude and angle) co-ordinate system. A variation on the polar system allows the pole pair to be defined in terms of the natural frequency, $\omega_n$, and "Q" or quality factor. The relationships between these co-ordinate systems is shown in Fig. 2-9.1 The Butterworth and Chebyshev pole locations are given in Program 2-2. By putting all the foregoing concepts together, the denormalized highpass element values can be expressed in terms of $\omega_n$ and Q with the second order circuit topology as shown in Fig. 2-10.1.

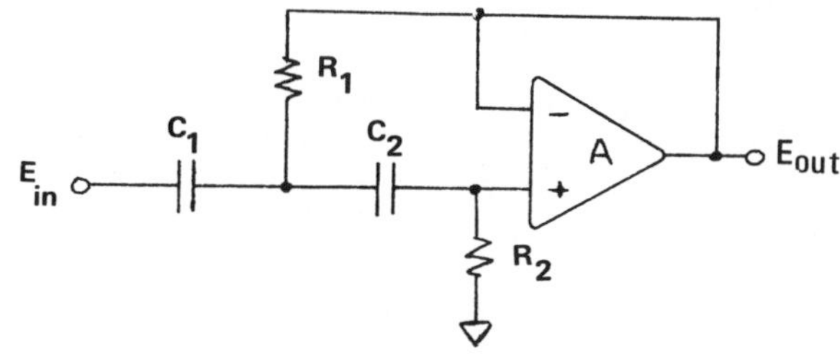


Figure 2-10.1 Highpass Sallen and Key circuit.

$$R_1 = \frac{\omega_n/\omega_c}{Q(C_1 + C_2)} \tag{2-10.1}$$

$$R_2 = \frac{(\omega_n/\omega_c)^2}{R_1 \cdot C_1 \cdot C_2} \tag{2-10.2}$$

The Sallen and Key unity-gain op-amp resonator is chosen over other types because of its low component count and low parameter sensitivities to element value changes (see [19]). High Q realizations are difficult with this resonator type since the resistor value spread is $4Q^2$ when the capacitor values are equal, however, this constraint is not a problem here since the pole Q's are rarely greater than 10.

High pole Q's occur with higher order filters (n greater than 9 or so). In these cases, the Szentirmai leapfrog topology [48], should be given consideration, or else an elliptic response lower order filter might meet the amplitude response requirements (the phase response will be less linear however).

All operational amplifiers have bandwidth limitations, i.e., the μA-741 has unity open loop gain at 500 kHz typically. When the operating frequency range of the active filter contains frequencies that approach 1% of the op-amp unity gain crossover frequency (500 kHz for the μA-741), then the contribution of the operational amplifier compensation pole and lower open loop gain must be considered. Program 1-3 can be used to calculate the pole location shifts. Positive and negative feedback resonators of the Deliyannis type can accommodate the op-amp compensation pole and open loop gain characteristic (see [19]).

If the filter order is odd, then a real pole exists. A third order op-amp active resonator circuit may be used to produce both the real pole and a complex conjugate pair. The lowest Q pole pair is chosen for realization by this circuit to keep the element value spread within bounds, and also to minimize sensitivities. The third order active highpass topology is shown in Fig. 2-10.2.

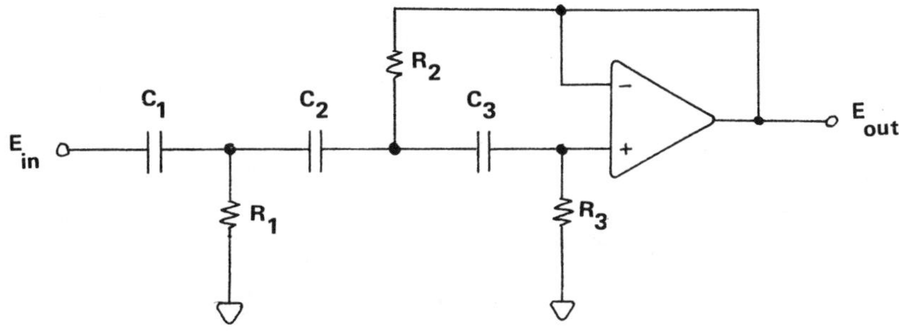


Figure 2-10.2 Third order highpass active filter section.

The transfer function in terms of the R's and C's assuming an ideal operational amplifier is:

$$\frac{E_{out}}{E_{in}} = \frac{s^3 R_1 R_2 R_3 C_1 C_2 C_3}{D(s)} \tag{2-10.3}$$

where

$$D(s) = s^3 R_1 R_2 R_3 C_1 C_2 C_3 + s^2 R_2 \{R_3 C_2 C_3 + R_1 \ \Sigma CC\}$$

$$+ s\{R_1(C_1 + C_2) + R_2(C_2 + C_3)\} + 1$$

and

$$\Sigma CC = C_1 C_2 + C_2 C_3 + C_1 C_3 \tag{2-10.4}$$

The resistor values may be obtained from the capacitor values and the pole locations by the simultaneous solution of three equations in three unknowns. These three equations are generated by equating like powers of s between the desired transfer function as expressed with the pole locations and the above transfer function. The desired transfer function in terms of the complex conjugate pole pair as expressed through $\omega_n$ and Q, and the real pole location, $1/\tau$, is:

$$\frac{E_{out}}{E_{in}} = \frac{s^3 \left(\frac{1}{\omega_c \tau}\right) \cdot \left(\frac{\omega_n}{\omega_c}\right)^2}{\left\{\frac{s}{\omega_c \tau} + 1\right\}\left\{s^2\left(\frac{\omega_n}{\omega_c}\right)^2 + s\left(\frac{1}{Q}\right)\left(\frac{\omega_n}{\omega_c}\right) + 1\right\}} \tag{2-10.5}$$

or, in descending powers of s:

$$\frac{E_{out}}{E_{in}} = \frac{s^3 \left(\frac{\omega_n}{\omega_c}\right)^2 \cdot \left(\frac{1}{\omega_c \tau}\right)}{s^3 \left(\frac{\omega_n}{\omega_c}\right)^2 \left(\frac{1}{\omega_c \tau}\right) + s^2 \left(\frac{\omega_n}{\omega_c}\right)^2 \left(1 + \frac{1}{\omega_n Q \tau}\right) + s\left(\frac{\omega_n}{\omega_c}\right)\left(\frac{1}{Q} + \frac{1}{\omega_n \tau}\right) + 1} \tag{2-10.6}$$

The resulting three equations in three unknowns are:

$$R_1R_2R_3C_1C_2C_3 = \left(\frac{\omega_n}{\omega_c}\right)^2 \left(\frac{1}{\omega_c\tau}\right) \quad (2\text{-}10.7)$$

$$R_2\ (R_3C_2C_3 + R_1\Sigma CC) = \left(\frac{\omega_n}{\omega_c}\right)^2 \left(1 + \frac{1}{\omega_n Q\tau}\right) \quad (2\text{-}10.8)$$

$$R_1\ (C_1 + C_2) + R_2(C_2 + C_3) = \left(\frac{\omega_n}{\omega_c}\right) \left(\frac{1}{Q} + \frac{1}{\omega_n\tau}\right) \quad (2\text{-}10.9)$$

After algebraic manipulation, a cubic equation in $R_1$ alone is obtained:

$$R_1{}^3K_3 + R_1{}^2\ K_2 - R_1K_1 + K_0 = 0 \quad (2\text{-}10.10)$$

where the constants $K_3$, $K_2$, $K_1$, and $K_0$ are defined by:

$$K_3 = -\ (C_1 + C_2)(C_1\ \Sigma\, CC) \quad (2\text{-}10.11)$$

$$K_2 = \left(\frac{1}{Q} + \frac{1}{\omega_n\tau}\right)\left(C_1\Sigma CC\right) \left(\frac{\omega_n}{\omega_c}\right) \quad (2\text{-}10.12)$$

$$K_1 = \left(1 + \frac{1}{\omega_n Q\tau}\right)\left(C_1(C_2 + C_3)\right) \left(\frac{\omega_n}{\omega_c}\right)^2 \quad (2\text{-}10.13)$$

$$K_0 = (C_2 + C_3) \left(\frac{1}{\omega_c\tau}\right) \left(\frac{\omega_n}{\omega_c}\right)^2 \quad (2\text{-}10.14)$$

The program uses a Newton-Raphson iterative solution to find the real root of Eq. (2-10.10) for $R_1$ (there will be at least one real root). The details of the Newton-Raphson technique are shown in Program 1-5.

Once $R_1$ has been obtained, the values for $R_2$ and $R_3$ are obtained using the following equations:

$$R_2 = \left(\frac{1}{C_2 + C_3}\right)\left\{\frac{\omega_n}{\omega_c}\left(\frac{1}{Q} + \frac{1}{\omega_n\tau}\right) - R_1(C_1 + C_2)\right\} \quad (2\text{-}10.15)$$

$$R_3 = \left(\frac{\omega_n}{\omega_c}\right)^2 \left(\frac{1}{\omega_c\tau}\right) \left(\frac{1}{R_1R_2C_1C_2C_3}\right) \quad (2\text{-}10.16)$$

# User Instructions

| BUTTERWORTH AND CHEBYSHEV ACTIVE HIGHPASS FILTERS | | | | |
|---|---|---|---|---|
| C: n↑ε dB | | | load f-ε dB & start | |
| B: n | B: ε dB | R | load f-3dB & start | load $C_1$ ↑ $C_2$ |

| STEP | INSTRUCTIONS | INPUT DATA/UNITS | KEYS | OUTPUT DATA/UNITS |
|---|---|---|---|---|
| 1 | Read both sides of program card one | | | |
| 2 | If Chebyshev response is desired: | | | |
| | a) Load filter order | n | [ENT↑] | |
| | b) Load passband ripple in dB | ε dB | [f] [A] | |
| | c) go to step 4 | | | |
| 3 | If Butterworth response is desired: | | | |
| | Load filter order | n | [A] | |
| | If the passband edge is defined at other than the -3dB point, enter the bandedge attenuation in dB (attenuation is expressed as a positive number) | ε dB | [B] | |
| 4 | Load operating resistance level *** | R | [C] | |
| | The calculated resistor values will usually be within a decade of this value. | | | |
| 5 | If the passband edge is defined by the -3dB amplitude response point, enter f-3dB *** | f-3dB | [D] | f-εdB* |
| | *The Chebyshev bandedge is usually defined by the -εdB point since the passband response oscillates within a band εdB wide. If a Chebyshev response has been selected, the frequency where the amplitude response exits the εdB ripple band will be printed. | | | See step6 continuation on next page for rest of output. |
| | go to step 7 (read step 6 commentary) | | | |
| 6 | If the passband edge is defined by the -εdB point, enter f-εdB *** | f-εdB | [f] [D] | f-3dB** |
| | **If Butterworth response has been selected, the frequency where the response is 3dB down will be printed. | | | |

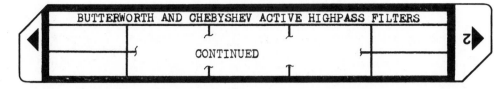

BUTTERWORTH AND CHEBYSHEV ACTIVE HIGHPASS FILTERS

CONTINUED

| STEP | INSTRUCTIONS | INPUT DATA/UNITS | KEYS | OUTPUT DATA/UNITS |
|---|---|---|---|---|
| 6 | | | | $C_{design}$ |
| | The design capacitance value is outputted.*** If this value is unacceptable from a circuit or practicality point of view, alter the design resistance level accordingly using key "C", then recalculate the design capacitance level using key "D". The design cutoff frequency need not be re-entered even though the original frequency entry was via keys "f", "D". | new R | C | |
| | | | D | new $C_{des}$ |
| | When an acceptable design capacitance level has been found, continue program output by using "R/S". | | R/S | $\omega_{n1}$ |
| | | | | $Q_1$ |
| | | | | stop |
| 7 | Enter capacitor values to be used in this second order filter section*** | $C_1$ | ENT↑ | |
| | | $C_2$ | E | $R_1$ |
| | | | | $R_2$ |
| | | | | space |
| | | | | n2 |
| | | | | $Q_2$ |
| | | | | stop |
| | Keep entering capacitor values for succeeding sections until all second order sections have been defined. | $C1_2$ | | $R1_2$ |
| | | $C2_2$ | | ⋮ |
| | | ⋮ | | ⋮ |
| | If an odd order filter is being designed, the last printout will be a set of three numbers, and the display will flash to indicate that the loading of the second card is required. It is not necessary to stop the program, just insert the second card into the card reader and read both sides. | $C1_n$ | | |
| | | $C2_n$ | | $R2_n$ |
| | | | | odd order filter: last sect |
| | After the second card reading is complete, load the three capacitor values to be used with this third order filter section using key "E". | | | $\omega_n$ |
| | | | | Q |
| | | | | $1/\tau$ |
| | | | | flashing display |
| | | $C_1$ | ENT↑ | |
| | *** The unit of resistance is ohms, capacitance is farads, and frequency is hertz. | $C_2$ | ENT↑ | |
| | | $C_3$ | E | $R_1$ |
| | | | | $R_2$ |
| | | | | $R_3$ |

Example 2-10.1

A fifth order, ½ dB passband ripple Chebyshev active highpass filter is to have 3 dB or less attenuation at 10 Hz. A National Semiconductor type LF-156 bi-fet operational amplifier is chosen as the active element in the filter.

Design an active filter to meet these specifications and choose the operating resistance level to achieve the lowest capacitance values in the filter without affecting the dc drift characteristics of the operational amplifier by more than 10%. The operating temperature range is -25°C to +85°C.

From the LF-156 data sheet, the maximum input bias current occurs at the highest operating temperature, +85°C, and is approximately 1 nA. The typical input offset voltage is 3 millivolts. The resistance level that will generate 0.3 millivolts with 1 nA flowing is:

$$R = (3 \times 10^{-4}\ \text{V})/(1 \times 10^{-9}\ \text{A}) = 300\ \text{k}\Omega$$

The filter is then designed with this value in mind as the largest resistance value which has an effect on the dc output of the last filter stage. Being a highpass filter, each stage of the filter blocks the dc voltage present from the preceding stage.

The filter design will be done twice, once with 300 kΩ as the design resistance level to determine the value of $R_2$ in the last (third order) section. The operating resistance level is then scaled to cause the highest resistance value ($R_2$) to be 300 kΩ. The HP-97 printout for these operations is shown on the next page.

In the second run of the program, the design capacitance level is 0.1749 μF. The nearest larger standard capacitor value is 0.22 μF. The filter will require five capacitors, therefore, five 0.22 μF mylar capacitors were drawn from stock, and their capacities measured. The measured values were: .2236 μF, .2014 μF, .1965 μF, .2173 μF, and 0.2542 μF. The filter resistances are designed around these capacitor values.

**Example 2-10.1 printout**

FIRST PROGRAM RUN

LOAD FIRST PROGRAM CARD

| | | |
|---|---|---|
| 5. | ENT↑ | load filter order |
| .5 | GSBa | load passband ripple |
| 300000. | GSBC | load design resist |
| 10. | GSBD | load −3dB frequency |
| 10.59+00 | *** | $-\frac{1}{2}$dB frequency (o/p) |
| 53.05-09 | *** | design capacitance level (output) |
| | R/S | continue execution |
| 960.8-03 | *** | $\omega_n$ first section |
| 4.545+00 | *** | Q |
| 53.05-09 | ENT↑ | enter first section |
| | GSBE | design capacitance |
| 31.71+03 | *** | $R_1$ first section |
| 2.620+06 | *** | $R_2$ resistor values |
| 651.9-03 | *** | $\omega_n$ second section |
| 1.178+00 | *** | Q |
| 342.1-03 | *** | $1/\tau$ |
| | | LOAD SECOND CARD |
| 53.05-09 | ENT↑ | |
| | ENT↑ | enter design cap |
| | GSBE | |
| 90.47+03 | *** | $R_1$ second section resistor values |
| 43.86+03 | *** | $R_2$ |
| 989.1+03 | *** | $R_3$ |
| 989.1+03 | ENT↑ | |
| 300.+03 | ÷ | scale design resistance level to make $R_3$ become 300 k Ω |
| | 1/X | |
| 303.3-03 | *** | |
| 300000. | × | |
| 90.99+03 | *** | |

SECOND PROGRAM RUN

LOAD FIRST PROGRAM CARD

| | | |
|---|---|---|
| 5. | ENT↑ | |
| .5 | GSBa | |
| 90.99+03 | GSBC | load new design resistance level |
| 10. | GSBD | |
| 10.59+00 | *** | |
| 174.9-09 | *** | new design capacitor value (output) |
| | R/S | |
| 960.8-03 | *** | $\omega_n$ |
| 4.545+00 | *** | Q |
| .2236-06 | ENT↑ | $C_1$ first section |
| .2014-06 | GSBE | $C_2$ selected caps |
| 7.916+03 | *** | $R_1$ first section |
| 655.9+03 | *** | $R_2$ resistor values |
| 651.9-03 | *** | $\omega_n$ second section |
| 1.178+00 | *** | Q |
| 342.1-03 | *** | $1/\tau$ |
| | | LOAD SECOND CARD |
| .1965-06 | ENT↑ | $C_1$ second section input (third order filter) |
| .2173-06 | ENT↑ | $C_2$ |
| .2542-06 | GSBE | $C_3$ |
| 24.17+03 | *** | $R_1$ second section resistor values |
| 9.014+03 | *** | $R_2$ |
| 247.8+03 | *** | $R_3$ |

FINAL SCHEMATIC

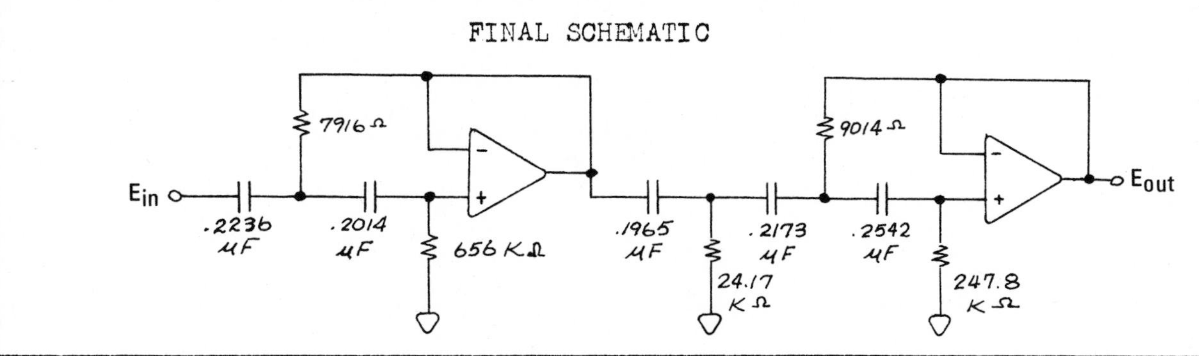

# Program Listing I

| Step | Key | Comment |
|---|---|---|
| 001 | *LBLA | BUTTERWORTH: LOAD n |
| 002 | SF1 | indicate Butterworth |
| 003 | EEX | setup registers: |
| 004 | STOB | f-3dB/f-εdB = 1 |
| 005 | STOD | cosh a = 1 |
| 006 | STOE | sinh a = 1 |
| 007 | GSB5 | |
| 008 | GTO6 | |
| 009 | *LBLa | CHEBYSHEV: LOAD n ↑ εdB |
| 010 | CF1 | indicate Chebyshev |
| 011 | STOB | store εdB |
| 012 | GSB5 | gosub input routine |
| 013 | RCLB | calculate: |
| 014 | EEX | |
| 015 | 1 | $\epsilon = (10^{0.1\epsilon dB} - 1)^{\frac{1}{2}}$ |
| 016 | ÷ | |
| 017 | 10ˣ | |
| 018 | EEX | |
| 019 | - | |
| 020 | √X | |
| 021 | 1/X | store $1/\epsilon$ → R5 |
| 022 | ST05 | |
| 023 | ENT↑ | calculate and store: |
| 024 | X² | |
| 025 | EEX | |
| 026 | + | |
| 027 | √X | $a = \frac{1}{n} \sinh^{-1}(\frac{1}{\epsilon})$ → R2 |
| 028 | + | |
| 029 | RCLA | |
| 030 | 1/X | |
| 031 | Yˣ | |
| 032 | ST02 | |
| 033 | ENT↑ | calculate and store: |
| 034 | 1/X | |
| 035 | - | sinh a → RE |
| 036 | 2 | |
| 037 | ÷ | |
| 038 | STOE | |
| 039 | RCL2 | calculate and store: |
| 040 | ENT↑ | |
| 041 | 1/X | |
| 042 | + | cosh a → RD |
| 043 | 2 | |
| 044 | ÷ | |
| 045 | STOD | |
| 046 | LSTX | calculate and store: |
| 047 | RCL5 | |
| 048 | ENT↑ | |
| 049 | X² | |
| 050 | EEX | $\frac{f\text{-}\epsilon dB}{f\text{-}3dB} = \cosh(\frac{1}{n}\cosh^{-1}(\frac{1}{\epsilon}))$ |
| 051 | - | |
| 052 | √X | |
| 053 | + | |
| 054 | RCLA | |
| 055 | 1/X | |
| 056 | Yˣ | |
| 057 | ENT↑ | |
| 058 | 1/X | |
| 059 | + | |
| 060 | ÷ | |
| 061 | STOB | |
| 062 | GTO6 | |
| 063 | *LBLB | LOAD εdB for Butterworth |
| 064 | EEX | calculate and store: |
| 065 | 1 | |
| 066 | ÷ | |
| 067 | 10ˣ | |
| 068 | EEX | |
| 069 | - | $\frac{f\text{-}3dB}{f\text{-}\epsilon dB} = \left[10^{0.1\epsilon dB} - 1\right]^{\frac{1}{2n}}$ |
| 070 | RCLA | |
| 071 | 1/X | |
| 072 | Yˣ | |
| 073 | √X | |
| 074 | 1/X | |
| 075 | STOB | |
| 076 | GTO6 | |
| 077 | *LBLC | LOAD OPERATING RESISTANCE LEVEL |
| 078 | ST06 | |
| 079 | GTO6 | |
| 080 | *LBLD | LOAD f-3dB and START |
| 081 | STOC | temporarily store f-3dB |
| 082 | F1? | jump if Butterworth |
| 083 | GTO0 | |
| 084 | RCLB | recall Cheb denorm ratio |
| 085 | ST03 | |
| 086 | ÷ | form -εdB frequency |
| 087 | F3? | print f-εdB if data entered |
| 088 | GSB4 | |
| 089 | RCLC | recall f-3dB |
| 090 | *LBLd | LOAD f-εdB and START |
| 091 | STOC | temporarily store frequency |
| 092 | RCLB | recall Buttr denorm ratio |
| 093 | F1? | if Buttr, store ratio |
| 094 | ST03 | |
| 095 | ÷ | if Butterworth, calculate and print f-3dB |
| 096 | F1? | |
| 097 | PRTX | |
| 098 | *LBL0 | |
| 099 | SPC | |
| 100 | CF2 | |
| 101 | RCLC | if flag 3, $2\pi f_c$ → R5 |
| 102 | ENT↑ | |
| 103 | + | |
| 104 | Pi | |
| 105 | x | |
| 106 | F3? | |
| 107 | ST05 | |
| 108 | RCL5 | calculate and print nominal capacitor value |
| 109 | RCL6 | |
| 110 | x | |

(An arrow runs from step 083 GTO0 to step 098 *LBL0.)

REGISTERS

| 0 | 1 | 2 | 3 | 4 | 5 | 6 | 7 | 8 | 9 |
|---|---|---|---|---|---|---|---|---|---|
| 2k-1 | Q | a or $\omega_n$ | K | $C_1$ | $\omega_c$, $1/\epsilon$ | R | $\omega_n/\omega_c$ | | $C_2$ |
| S0 | S1 | S2 | S3 | S4 | S5 | S6 | S7 | S8 | S9 |
| | | | | | | | | | |

| A | B | C | D | E | I |
|---|---|---|---|---|---|
| filter order, n | εdB, 1, $\frac{f\text{-}3dB}{f\text{-}\epsilon dB}$ | cutoff frequency | cosh a or 1 | sinh a or 1 | $\frac{\pi}{2n}$ |

# Program Listing II

| Key | Comment |
|---|---|
| 1/X | print design capacitance |
| PRTX | |
| SPC | stop program execution and |
| R/S | await operator decision |
| EEX | setup for next loop |
| STO0 | |
| *LBL1 | second order filter loop |
| SPC | |
| RCL0 | calculate normalized |
| RCLI | pole locations: |
| × | |
| EEX | |
| →R | $\sigma_k = (\sinh a)(\sin((2k-1)\frac{\pi}{2n}))$ |
| RCLD | |
| × | $\omega_k = (\cosh a)(\cos((2k-1)\frac{\pi}{2n}))$ |
| X⇄Y | |
| RCLE | |
| × | |
| →P | calculate $\omega_{n_k}$ and $Q_k$, scale |
| RCL3 | $\omega_{n_k}$ for proper normalized |
| × | bandedge |
| PRTX | |
| STO2 | $\omega_{n_k} = \left[\omega_k^2 + \sigma_k^2\right]^{\frac{1}{2}} \cdot (K)$ |
| X⇄Y | |
| COS | |
| ENT↑ | $Q_k = \dfrac{1}{2\cos(\tan^{-1}\frac{\omega_k}{\sigma_k})}$ |
| + | |
| 1/X | |
| STO1 | |
| PRTX | |
| 2 | |
| ST+0 | increment 2k by 2 |
| F0? | if even order filter, rtn |
| RTN | and await capacitor values |
| RCL0 | odd order filter: |
| RCLA | jump if last section |
| X≤Y? | |
| GTO2 | |
| RTN | await capacitor values |
| *LBLE | LOAD CAPACITOR VALUES |
| F2? | reject input if 3rd order |
| GTO3 | section has been outputted |
| STO9 | store $C_2$ |
| X⇄Y | store $C_1$ |
| STO4 | |
| + | calculate and print $R_1$ |
| RCL1 | |
| × | $R_1 = \dfrac{\omega_n/\omega_c}{Q(C_1 + C_2)}$ |
| RCL2 | |
| RCL5 | |
| ÷ | |
| STO7 | |
| X⇄Y | |
| ÷ | |
| PRTX | |
| RCL4 | calculate and print $R_2$ |
| × | |
| RCL9 | |
| × | $R_2 = \dfrac{(\omega_n/\omega_c)^2}{R_1 \cdot C_1 \cdot C_2}$ |
| RCL7 | |
| X² | |
| X⇄Y | |
| ÷ | |
| PRTX | |
| RCL0 | test for loop exit |
| RCLA | |
| X>Y? | |
| GTO1 | |
| SPC | loop exit |
| SPC | |
| RTN | |
| *LBL2 | 3rd order filter section |
| RCLE | calculate and print |
| RCL3 | real 3rd order pole location |
| × | |
| PRTX | |
| SPC | |
| *LBL3 | wait loop for second |
| SF2 | card read |
| PSE | |
| GTO3 | |
| *LBL4 | print and set flag 3 |
| PRTX | |
| SF3 | |
| RTN | |
| *LBL5 | entry subroutine |
| R↓ | recover and store n |
| STOA | |
| 2 | |
| ÷ | set flag 0 if n is even |
| FRC | |
| CF0 | |
| X=0? | |
| SF0 | |
| Pi | calculate and store: |
| RCLA | |
| ENT↑ | $\frac{\pi}{2n} \rightarrow$ RI |
| + | |
| ÷ | |
| STOI | |
| EEX | |
| STO3 | $\omega_n$ initialization |
| RTN | |
| *LBL6 | exit routine, |
| SPC | clear flag 3 and space |
| CF3 | |
| RTN | |

NOTE TRIG MODE

**LABELS**

| | | | | |
|---|---|---|---|---|
| A Buttr load n | B Buttr load ε dB | C LOAD R | D LOADf−3dB & START | E LOAD CAPACITORS |
| a Cheb load n↑dB | b | c | d LOADf−εdB & START | e |
| 0 2πf calc | 1 2nd order filter loop | 2 3rd order filter lp | 3 | 4 print & set flag 3 |
| 5 entry subroutine | 6 exit subroutine | 7 | 8 | 9 |

**FLAGS**

| | |
|---|---|
| 0 | n even |
| 1 | Buttr |
| 2 | go to wait loop |
| 3 | data in |

**SET STATUS**

| FLAGS | ON | OFF | TRIG | | DISP | |
|---|---|---|---|---|---|---|
| 0 | | ■ | DEG | | FIX | |
| 1 | | ■ | GRAD | | SCI | |
| 2 | | ■ | RAD | ■ | ENG | ■ |
| 3 | | ■ | | | n | 3 |

# Program Listing I

| | | |
|---|---|---|
| 001 | R/S | cancel pause after card read |
| 002 | *LBLE | LOAD C1↑C2↑C3 and START |
| 003 | SPC | |
| 004 | GSB9 | test for P⇄S |
| 005 | P⇄S | execute and signal P⇄S |
| 006 | SF2 | |
| 007 | ST03 | store C3 |
| 008 | R↓ | store C2 |
| 009 | ST02 | |
| 010 | R↓ | store C1 |
| 011 | ST01 | |
| 012 | RCL2 | calculate and store: |
| 013 | x | |
| 014 | RCL2 | $C_1 \cdot \Sigma CC \rightarrow R7$ |
| 015 | RCL3 | |
| 016 | x | |
| 017 | + | |
| 018 | RCL3 | |
| 019 | RCL1 | |
| 020 | x | |
| 021 | + | |
| 022 | RCL1 | |
| 023 | x | |
| 024 | ST07 | |
| 025 | GSB9 | P⇄S and reset flag 2 |
| 026 | RCL5 | obtain and store $\omega_o$ |
| 027 | ST0I | |
| 028 | RCLE | calculate $1/\tau$ |
| 029 | RCL3 | |
| 030 | x | |
| 031 | RCL1 | recall: Q |
| 032 | RCL2 | $\omega_n$ |
| 033 | RCL6 | R |
| 034 | P⇄S | execute and signal P⇄S |
| 035 | SF2 | |
| 036 | ST00 | store R |
| 037 | R↓ | store $\omega_n$ |
| 038 | ST04 | |
| 039 | R↓ | form and store $1/Q$ |
| 040 | 1/X | |
| 041 | ST06 | |
| 042 | X⇄Y | store $1/\tau$ |
| 043 | ST05 | |

| | | |
|---|---|---|
| 044 | x | |
| 045 | RCL4 | form $C_1(\frac{1}{\tau Q} + \omega_n)$ |
| 046 | + | |
| 047 | RCL1 | |
| 048 | x | |
| 049 | RCL2 | |
| 050 | RCL3 | form and store C2 + C3 |
| 051 | + | |
| 052 | STOA | |
| 053 | x | form and store: |
| 054 | RCL4 | |
| 055 | x | $K_1 = \frac{\omega_n}{\omega_c^2}(\frac{1}{\tau Q} + \omega_n)C_1(C_2+C_3)$ |
| 056 | RCLI | |
| 057 | X² | |
| 058 | ÷ | |
| 059 | STOB | |
| 060 | RCL4 | |
| 061 | RCLI | |
| 062 | ÷ | form and store: |
| 063 | X² | |
| 064 | RCLI | |
| 065 | ÷ | $K_0 = (\frac{\omega_n^2}{\tau})(C2 + C3)(\frac{1}{\omega_c^3})$ |
| 066 | RCL5 | |
| 067 | x | |
| 068 | RCLA | |
| 069 | x | |
| 070 | STOA | |
| 071 | RCL5 | |
| 072 | RCL4 | |
| 073 | RCL6 | |
| 074 | x | form and store: |
| 075 | + | |
| 076 | RCL7 | |
| 077 | x | $K_2 = (\frac{1}{\tau} + \frac{\omega_n}{Q})(C_1 \Sigma CC)\frac{1}{\omega_c}$ |
| 078 | RCLI | |
| 079 | ÷ | |
| 080 | STOC | |
| 081 | RCL1 | |
| 082 | RCL2 | form and store: |
| 083 | + | |
| 084 | RCL7 | |
| 085 | x | $K_3 = -(C_1 + C_2)(C_1 \Sigma CC)$ |
| 086 | CHS | |
| 087 | STOD | |
| 088 | RCL0 | |
| 089 | EEX | form and store $10^{-8} \cdot R$ |
| 090 | 8 | for iteration loop |
| 091 | ÷ | exit test |
| 092 | ST09 | |

**REGISTERS**

| 0 | 1 | 2 | 3 | 4 | 5 | 6 | 7 | 8 | 9 |
|---|---|---|---|---|---|---|---|---|---|
| S0 R1 | S1 C1 | S2 C2 | S3 C3 | S4 $\omega_n$ | S5 $1/\tau$ | S6 $1/Q$ | S7 $C_1 \cdot \Sigma CC$ | S8 f/f' | S9 $10^{-8} \cdot R$ |
| A $K_0$ | B $-K_1$ | C $K_2$ | D $K_3$ | | E sinh a or 1 | | I $\omega_c$ | | |

# Program Listing II

| Step | Key | Comments |
|---|---|---|
| 093 | *LBL0 | Newton-Raphson loop for $R_1$ |
| 094 | RCL0 | form and store: |
| 095 | RCL0 | $f(R_1) = K_3R_1^3 + K_2R_1^2 + K_1R_1 + K_0$ |
| 096 | RCL0 | |
| 097 | RCLD | |
| 098 | x | |
| 099 | RCLC | |
| 100 | + | |
| 101 | x | |
| 102 | RCLB | |
| 103 | − | |
| 104 | x | |
| 105 | RCLA | |
| 106 | + | |
| 107 | STO8 | |
| 108 | CLX | form: |
| 109 | + | $f'(R_1) = 3K_3R_1^2 + 2K_2R_1 + K_1$ |
| 110 | + | |
| 111 | + | |
| 112 | RCLD | |
| 113 | x | |
| 114 | RCLC | |
| 115 | ENT↑ | |
| 116 | + | |
| 117 | + | |
| 118 | x | |
| 119 | RCLB | |
| 120 | − | |
| 121 | ST÷8 | form $-\Delta R_1 = f(R_1)/f'(R_1)$ |
| 122 | RCL8 | form $R_{1_{n+1}} = R_{1_n} + \Delta R_1$ |
| 123 | ST−0 | |
| 124 | ABS | iterate again if |
| 125 | RCL9 | $\lvert\Delta R_1\rvert \geq 10^{-6}\cdot R_1$ |
| 126 | X≤Y? | |
| 127 | GTO0 | |

| Step | Key | Comments |
|---|---|---|
| 128 | RCL0 | recall and print $R_1$ |
| 129 | PRTX | |
| 130 | RCL5 | calculate and print $R_2$ |
| 131 | RCL4 | $R_2 = \dfrac{\frac{1}{\omega_c}\left(\frac{1}{\tau} + \frac{\omega_n}{Q}\right) - R_1(C_1 + C_2)}{C_2 + C_3}$ |
| 132 | RCL6 | |
| 133 | x | |
| 134 | + | |
| 135 | RCLI | |
| 136 | ÷ | |
| 137 | RCL1 | |
| 138 | RCL2 | |
| 139 | + | |
| 140 | RCL0 | |
| 141 | x | |
| 142 | − | |
| 143 | RCL2 | |
| 144 | RCL3 | |
| 145 | + | |
| 146 | ÷ | |
| 147 | PRTX | |
| 148 | RCL0 | calculate and print $R_3$ |
| 149 | x | $R_3 = \left(\frac{1}{\omega_c^3}\right)\dfrac{\omega_n^2/\tau}{R_1R_2C_1C_2C_3}$ |
| 150 | RCL1 | |
| 151 | x | |
| 152 | RCL2 | |
| 153 | x | |
| 154 | RCL3 | |
| 155 | x | |
| 156 | 1/X | |
| 157 | RCL4 | |
| 158 | RCLI | |
| 159 | ÷ | |
| 160 | X² | |
| 161 | x | |
| 162 | RCLI | |
| 163 | ÷ | |
| 164 | RCL5 | |
| 165 | x | |
| 166 | PRTX | |
| 167 | SPC | |
| 168 | *LBL9 | if flag 2, execute P⇄S |
| 169 | F2? | |
| 170 | P⇄S | |
| 171 | RTN | |

**LABELS**

| A | B | C | D | E load capacitors |
|---|---|---|---|---|
| a | b | c | d | e |
| 0 Newton-Raphson | 1 | 2 | 3 | 4 |
| 5 | 6 | 7 | 8 | 9 P⇄S |

**FLAGS**

| | |
|---|---|
| 0 | |
| 1 | |
| 2 | P⇄S |
| 3 | |

**SET STATUS**

| FLAGS | ON | OFF | TRIG | DISP |
|---|---|---|---|---|
| 0 | | | DEG | FIX |
| 1 | | | GRAD | SCI |
| 2 | | ■ | RAD | ENG ■ |
| 3 | | | | n 3 |

## PROGRAM 2-11 DELIYANNIS POSITIVE AND NEGATIVE FEEDBACK ACTIVE RESONATOR DESIGN ( USED FOR ACTIVE BANDPASS FILTERS ).

### Program Description and Equations Used

Active filter resonators are constrained by component value ranges (10 ohms to 10 megohms, 100 pF to 10 μF), operational amplifier gain-bandwidth limitations, and overall circuit sensitivities. The Deliyannis resonator circuit allows high Q realizations and also compensates for the finite gain and bandwidth of the operational amplifier [20].

This resonator synthesizes a second order pole pair of given $\omega_n$ and Q. The natural frequency, $\omega_n$, and the quality factor, Q, are provided as outputs from the active Butterworth and Chebyshev filter programs contained in this section.

This resonator type has the ability to synthesize a resonator with infinite Q. The infinite Q resonator is used in the interior stages of the Szentirmai leapfrog filter topology [48]. The leapfrog active filter is a direct simulation of a passive LC filter, and generally has the same low sensitivity characteristics of the LC topology. When narrow-band active filters are required, the leapfrog topology will be one of the viable candidates for filter realization (also see the GIC realization in Program 2-6).

The circuit for the Deliyannis second order bandpass circuit is shown in Fig. 2-11.1.

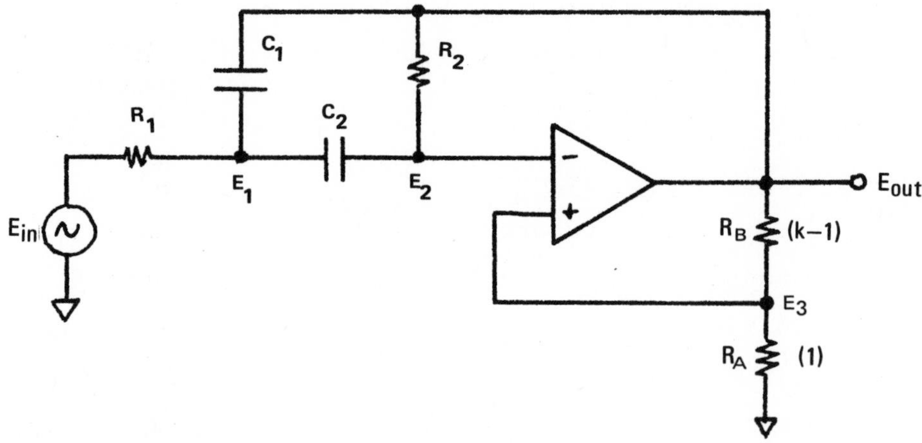


Figure 2-11.1 Deliyannis bandpass resonator circuit.

The transmission function is obtained using nodal analysis. In matrix form, the nodal equations are:

$$E_{out} = A(s)[E_3 - E_2], \text{ (op-amp transmission fcn)} \tag{2-11.1}$$

$$\begin{bmatrix} \{\frac{1}{R_1} + s(C_1 + C_2)\} & \{-sC_2\} \\ \{-sC_2\} & \{\frac{1}{R_2} + sC_2\} \end{bmatrix} \cdot \begin{bmatrix} E_1 \\ E_2 \end{bmatrix} = \begin{bmatrix} \frac{1}{R_1} & sC_1 \\ 0 & \frac{1}{R_2} \end{bmatrix} \cdot \begin{bmatrix} E_{in} \\ E_{out} \end{bmatrix} \tag{2-11.2}$$

where

$$E_3 = E_{out}/k \tag{2-11.3}$$

Solving for $E_2$ from Eqs. (2-11.1) and (2-11.3):

$$E_2 = E_{out}\left[\frac{1}{k} - \frac{1}{A(s)}\right] \tag{2-11.4}$$

The transmission function is first obtained for the general case using $A(s)$, then more specifically using $A(s) = A_o/(\tau s)$. The passive sensitivities may be obtained from the general solution, and the active sensitivities obtained from the specific solution, $A(s)=A_o/(\tau s)$.

The matrix equation is rewritten to bring $1/k - 1/A(s)$ inside the coefficient matrix, and to bring all dependent variables to the right hand side of the equation:

$$\begin{bmatrix} \left\{\frac{1}{R_1} + s(C_1 + C_2)\right\} & \left\{-s\left[C_1 - C_2\left(\frac{1}{k} - \frac{1}{A(s)}\right)\right]\right\} \\ \left\{-sC\right\} & \left\{\left(\frac{1}{R_2}\right)\left(\frac{1}{k} - \frac{1}{A(s)} - 1\right) + sC_2\left(\frac{1}{k} - \frac{1}{A(s)}\right)\right\} \end{bmatrix} \cdot \begin{bmatrix} E_1 \\ E_{out} \end{bmatrix} = \begin{bmatrix} \frac{1}{R_1} \\ 0 \end{bmatrix} \cdot E_{in} \tag{2-11.5}$$

Cramer's rule is used to find the expression for $E_{out}/E_{in}$, the filter transmission function.

$$\frac{E_{out}}{E_{in}} = \frac{-\dfrac{s}{R_1C_1\left(1 + {}^1/A(s) - {}^1/k\right)}}{s^2 + s\left\{\dfrac{1}{R_2C_1} + \dfrac{1}{R_2C_2} + \dfrac{1}{R_1C_1} \cdot \dfrac{{}^1/A(s) - {}^1/k}{1 + {}^1/A(s) - {}^1/k}\right\} + \dfrac{1}{R_1R_2C_1C_2}} \tag{2-11.6}$$

The passive sensitivities may be evaluated assuming the op-amp to be ideal, i.e., the open loop gain is allowed to approach infinity. In this situation, the transmission function becomes:

$$\frac{E_{out}}{E_{in}} = \frac{-\dfrac{ks}{R_1C_1(k-1)}}{s^2 + s\left\{\dfrac{1}{R_2C_1} + \dfrac{1}{R_2C_2} - \dfrac{1}{(k-1)\ R_1C_1}\right\} + \dfrac{1}{R_1R_2C_1C_2}} \tag{2-11.7}$$

The coefficients of the denominator of this equation may be compared with the like coefficients in the standard second order form to derive expressions for $\omega_n$ and Q. The standard second order form of the transmission function is:

$$\frac{E_{out}}{E_{in}} = \frac{ks}{s^2 + \frac{\omega_n}{Q}s + \omega_n^2} \tag{2-11.8}$$

The following expressions for $\omega_n$, Q, and K are obtained:

$$K = -\frac{k}{R_1 C_1 (k-1)} \qquad (2\text{-}11.9)$$

$$\omega_n = (R_1 R_2 C_1 C_2)^{-\frac{1}{2}} \qquad (2\text{-}11.10)$$

$$Q = \frac{\sqrt{\dfrac{R_2}{R_1}}}{\sqrt{\dfrac{C_2}{C_1}} + \sqrt{\dfrac{C_1}{C_2}} - \dfrac{1}{k-1} \cdot \dfrac{R_2}{R_1} \cdot \sqrt{\dfrac{C_2}{C_1}}} \qquad (2\text{-}11.11)$$

Let $\mu = R_2/R_1$ , and $\delta = C_2/C_1$, then:

$$Q = \frac{\sqrt{\mu\delta}}{\delta + 1 - \mu\delta/(k-1)} \qquad (2\text{-}11.12)$$

The denominator of Eq. (2-11.12) can be made arbitrarily small by proper choice of $\mu$. The denominator can be made to vanish completely causing Q to become infinite, thus generating the infinite Q resonator required for the interior stages of the leapfrog filter topology.

Sensitivities are a way of expressing how much a given parameter, say Q, is affected by a change in one of the circuit elements. The general convention is to express sensitivities as a demensionless number formed from the ratio of individual percentage changes:

$$S_R^Q = \lim_{\Delta R \to 0} \frac{\Delta Q/Q}{\Delta R/R} = \frac{R}{Q} \cdot \frac{\partial Q}{\partial R} \qquad (2\text{-}11.13)$$

Applying this definition to the expressions for $\mu_n$, Q, and K, the following passive sensitivities result:

$$S^{\omega_n}_{R_1,\, R_2,\, C_1,\, C_2} = -\tfrac{1}{2} \qquad (2\text{-}11.14)$$

$$S^Q_{R_1} = -S^Q_{R_2} = -\tfrac{1}{2} - Q\,\frac{\sqrt{\mu\delta}}{k-1} \qquad (2\text{-}11.15)$$

$$S^Q_{C_1} = -S^Q_{C_2} = -\tfrac{1}{2} + Q\sqrt{\mu\delta}\left(\frac{1}{\mu} - \frac{1}{k-1}\right) \qquad (2\text{-}11.16)$$

$$S^Q_{R_B} = -S^Q_{R_A} = Q\,\frac{\sqrt{\mu\delta}}{k-1} \qquad (2\text{-}11.17)$$

$$S^{K}_{R_1,\ C_2} = -1 \tag{2-11.18}$$

$$S^{K}_{R_A} = -S^{K}_{R_B} = {}^{1}/k \tag{2-11.19}$$

The break frequency of the open loop transmission function of most operational amplifiers is around 10 Hz, and the gain-bandwidth product (GBP) is about $10^6$ Hz thus, the finite gain characteristics of the op-amp begin to affect the active filter response when kilohertz frequencies are involved. In this frequency range, the operational amplifier transmission function, $A(s) = A_o/(1 + \tau s)$, may be approximated by $A(s) = A_o/\tau s$. With this approximation, the active filter transmission function becomes:

$$\frac{E_{out}}{E_{in}} = \frac{-\dfrac{s}{(R_1C_1)(1 + \tau s/A_o - 1/k)}}{s^2 + s\left\{\dfrac{1}{R_2C_1} + \dfrac{1}{R_2C_2} + \dfrac{1}{R_1C_1}\cdot\dfrac{\tau s/A_o - 1/k}{1 + \tau s/A_o - 1/k}\right\} + \dfrac{1}{R_1R_2C_1C_2}} \tag{2-11.20}$$

This expression is expanded, and like powers of s collected to form the final expression for the active filter transmission function:

$$\frac{E_{out}}{E_{in}} = \frac{s\,\dfrac{-k}{R_1C_1}}{D(s)} \tag{2-11.21}$$

where

$$D(s) = s^3\frac{k\tau}{A_o} + s^2\left\{k - 1 + \frac{k\tau}{A_o}\left(\frac{1}{R_2C_1} + \frac{1}{R_2C_2} + \frac{1}{R_1C_1}\right)\right\}$$

$$+ s\left\{(k-1)\left(\frac{1}{R_2C_1} + \frac{1}{R_2C_2}\right) - \frac{1}{R_1C_1} + \frac{\tau k}{A_oR_1R_2C_1C_2}\right\} + \frac{k-1}{R_1R_2C_1C_2}$$

The denominator is factored into a single pole and a complex conjugate pair:

$$\frac{E_{out}}{E_{in}} = \frac{H\cdot\dfrac{s}{\omega_nQ}}{\left(\dfrac{s}{\sigma} + 1\right)\left(\dfrac{s^2}{\omega_n^2} + \dfrac{s}{\omega_nQ} + 1\right)} \tag{2-11.22}$$

The natural frequency, $\omega_n$, and the quality factor, Q, are derived by equating like powers of s between Eqs. (2-11.21) and (2-11.22):

$$\omega_n = \frac{1}{R_1 R_2 C_1 C_2} \cdot \sqrt{1 - \frac{\tau\, k^2}{A_o (k-1)\, R_1 C_1}} \qquad (2\text{-}11.23)$$

$$BW = \frac{\omega_n}{Q} = \left\{\frac{1}{R_2 C_1} + \frac{1}{R_2 C_2} + \frac{1}{R_1 C_1 (k-1)}\right\}\left\{1 - \frac{\tau k^2}{A_o (k-1) R_1 R_2}\right\} \qquad (2\text{-}11.24)$$

From these equations, the active sensitivities are derived:

$$S^{\omega_n}_{A/\tau} = S^{Q}_{A/\tau} = \tfrac{1}{2} \cdot \frac{\omega_n \tau}{A_o} \cdot \left(\frac{k}{k-1}\right)^2 \cdot \sqrt{\mu\delta} \qquad (2\text{-}11.25)$$

where $\mu = R_2/R_1$ (2-11.26)

and $\delta = C_2/C_1$ (2-11.27)

as defined previously. The objective is to choose $\mu$ or $\delta$ to strike a happy medium between the active and the passive sensitivities (see [19], p . 319).

The Designers Guide to Active Filters [26], has the set of equations that generate the element values for this positive and negative feedback biquad. The point is made that by choosing $\delta < 1$ some of the active sensitivities may be reduced at the expense of resistor value spread ( $\mu$ increases).

Equations (2-11.28) through (2-11.42) are used by the HP-67/97 program. The equation solution starts with a choice for the capacitor ratio, $\delta$ , and positive feedback ratio, k, and the operational amplifier dc gain, $A_o$, and gain bandwidth product, GBP. The resonant frequency is $f_o$ and $p = 1/k$ ($f_a = 1/(2\pi\tau)$).

$$\Omega = f_a/f_o = GBP/(f_o A_o) \qquad (2\text{-}11.28)$$

$$\gamma = A_o\, \Omega = GBP/f_o \qquad (2\text{-}11.29)$$

$$d = 1/Q \qquad (2\text{-}11.30)$$

$$\beta = \Omega - p\gamma = (1 - \frac{A_o}{k}) \qquad (2\text{-}11.31)$$

$$m = \gamma + \beta = \Omega\left\{1 + A_o\left(1 - \frac{1}{k}\right)\right\} \tag{2-11.32}$$

$$a_2 = (\delta + 1)\{m(m-d) + 1\} \tag{2-11.33}$$

$$a_1 = \delta m - (\delta + 1)\beta - (m-d)(md-1) \tag{2-11.34}$$

$$a_0 = m(\beta - d) + 1 \tag{2-11.35}$$

$$\left.\begin{array}{l} C_1 = 1 \\ \\ C_2 = \delta \end{array}\right\} \text{normalized values} \tag{2-11.36}$$

The quadratic equation is used to find the positive real root ($R_1$) of:

$$a_2 R_1^2 + a_1 R_1 + a_0 = 0 \tag{2-11.38}$$

i.e.,

$$R_1 = \frac{-a_1}{2a_2} + \sqrt{\left(\frac{a_1}{2a_2}\right)^2 - \frac{a_0}{a_2}} \tag{2-11.39}$$

then

$$R_2 = \frac{m(\delta + 1)R_1 - (dm-1)}{(R_1 - \beta)\delta} \tag{2-11.40}$$

H is the gain of the filter at resonance:

$$H = \frac{-R_2 \cdot \delta \cdot Q}{1 - \frac{1}{k} + \frac{1}{A_o}} \tag{2-11.41}$$

A parasitic pole also exists. The location of this pole is at $-\sigma$, where:

$$\sigma = \frac{m}{\delta R_1 R_2} \tag{2-11.42}$$

The normalized transmission function with the above element values becomes:

$$G(s) = \frac{E_{out}}{E_{in}} = \frac{\frac{H}{Q}s}{\left(s^2 + \frac{s}{Q} + 1\right)\left(\frac{s}{\sigma} + 1\right)} \tag{2-11.43}$$

The design of this filter type is somewhat cut and try if low sensitivities are to be achieved. The program is written to take the desired resonant frequency, the operational amplifier parameters, the capacitor ratio, one capacitor value, and the positive feedback ratio, and provides the remaining element values.

Because the resonator design exhibits a gain, H, at resonance, the input resistor, $R_1$, may be split into two resistors to provide a Thevenin equivalent circuit with gain $H_{desired}/H = 1/H'$ and impedance $R_1$. This equivalent circuit is shown in Fig. 2-11.2.

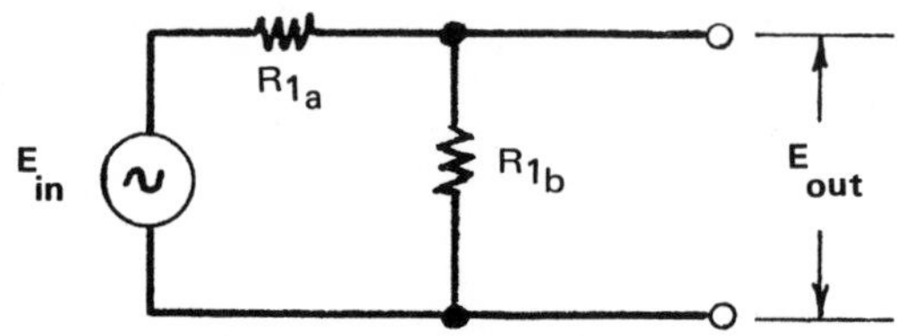


Figure 2-11.2 Equivalent input resistor network.

$$Eout/Ein = 1/H' = R_{1b}/(R_{1a} + R_{1b}) \tag{2-11.44}$$

$$R_{equiv} = (R_{1a} \cdot R_{1b})/(R_{1a} + R_{1b}) = R_1 \tag{2-11.45}$$

Equation (2-11.44) is solved for $R_{1a} + R_{1b}$, and substituted into Eq. (2-11.45) to yield an expression for $R_{1a}$:

$$R_{1a} = H' \cdot R_1 \tag{2-11.46}$$

Substituting Eq. (2-11.46) into Eq. (2-11.44) yields an expression for $R_{1b}$:

$$R_{1b} = R_{1a}/(H'-1) \tag{2-11.47}$$

Equations (2-11.46) and (2-11.47) are used by the program to split the input resistor and provide the desired resonator gain at the resonant frequency.

# 2-11 User Instructions

| DELIYANNIS POSITIVE AND NEGATIVE FEEDBACK RESONATOR | | | | |
|---|---|---|---|---|
| resistance level | $\delta$ | $H_{desired}$ | | |
| Q | p | op-amp gain-BW | op-amp dc gain | load $f_o$ & start |

| STEP | INSTRUCTIONS | INPUT DATA/UNITS | KEYS | OUTPUT DATA/UNITS |
|---|---|---|---|---|
| 1 | Load both sides of program card | | | |
| 2 | Load Q, the quality factor | Q | [A] | |
| 3 | Load p, the positive feedback ratio (p = 1/k) | p | [B] | |
| 4 | Load R, the operating resistance level | R, Ω | [f] [A] | |
| 5 | Load $\delta$, the ratio of $C_2$ to $C_1$ (Eq. (2-10.27)) | $\delta$ | [f] [B] | |
| 6 | Load desired gain at resonance | $H_{desired}$ | [f] [C] | |
| 7 | Load op-amp gain-bandwidth product | GBP, Hz | [C] | |
| 8 | Load op-amp dc gain | $A_o$ | [D] | |
| 9 | Load resonant frequency desired and start<br><br>note:<br>Flag 3 is tested on all input routines to determine whether input or output of the respective parameter is desired. If an input key ("A" - "D" and "a" - "c") is keyed without numeric entry, or following the clear key (e), the presently stored parameter will be displayed. | $f_o$, Hz | | $R_1$<br>$R_2$<br>H<br>$\sigma$<br>$R_B$ } normalized<br><br>$R_1$<br>$R_2$<br>$C_1$<br>$C_2$<br>$R_{1a}$<br>$R_{1b}$ } denormalized<br><br>$S^{\omega_n}_{R_1,R_2,C_1,C_2}$<br>$S^Q_{R_B}, -S^Q_{R_A}$<br>$S^Q_{R_1}, -S^Q_{R_2}$<br>$S^Q_{C_1}, -S^Q_{C_2}$<br>$S^Q_{A/\tau}, -S^Q_{A/\tau}$ |
| 10 | Go back and change any parameters in any order, and rerun program. The center frequency need not be reloaded unless it is being changed. | | | |

Example 2-11.1

A second order Deliyannis resonator is to be designed using a type 741 operational amplifier. The operational amplifier characteristics and resonator specifications are:

| | |
|---|---|
| Center frequency: | 1000 Hz |
| Q: | 100 |
| gain at resonance: | 1.0 |
| capacitor ratio: | 1.0 |
| p, positive fdbk ratio: | 0.04 |
| resistance level: | 10000 Ω |
| | |
| op-amp gain-bandwidth: | 500000 Hz |
| op-amp dc gain: | 100000 |

Find the element values and calculate the sensitivities for this design. Investigate the effect of different values of positive feedback on the component value spread and sensitivities. The HP-97 printout for this problem is shown on the next page, and the schematic is shown in Fig. 2-11.3.

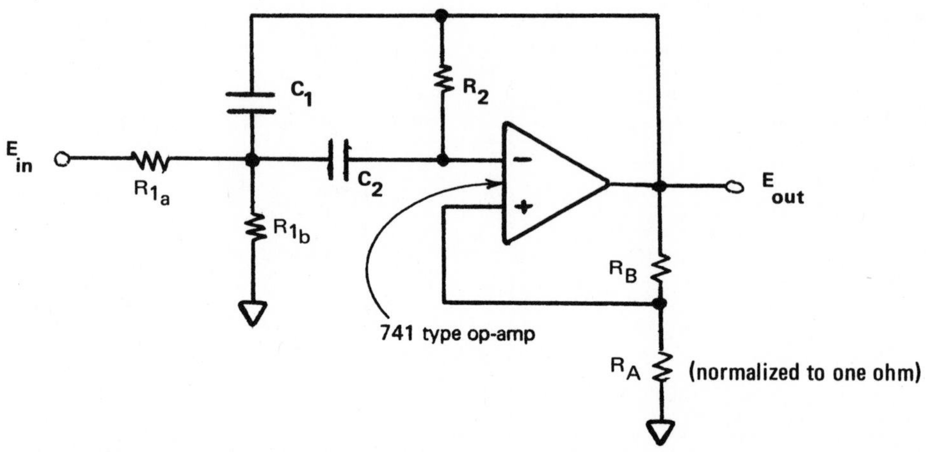


Figure 2-11.3 Deliyannis resonator schematic.

HP-97 printout for Example 2-11.1

```
       100. GSBA  load Q
     10000. GSBa  load denormalization resistance level, R
       .04 GSBB  load positive feedback ratio, p
         1. GSBb  load capacitor ratio, δ
         1. GSBc  load gain desired at resonance, H_desired
    500000. GSBC  load op-amp GBP
    100000. GSBD  load op-amp dc gain, A_o
      1000. GSBE  load f_o and start

 145.770-03  ***  R1                 }
 6.75947+00  ***  R2                 }  normalized values
-704.104+00  ***  H                  }  (C1 = 1)
 487.151+00  ***  σ                  }
 24.0000+00  ***  RB (RA = 1)        }

 10.0000+03  ***  R1                 }
 463.707+03  ***  R2                 }  denormalized values
 2.32001-09  ***  C1                 }
 2.32001-09  ***  C2                 }

 7.04104+06  ***  R1A     Thevenin equivalent input resistor pair
 10.0142+03  ***  R1B
```

| | | |
|---|---|---|
| -500.000-03 | *** | $S^{\omega_n}_{R_1, R_2, C_1, C_2}$ |
| 28.3733+00 | *** | $S^Q_{R_B}$, $-S^Q_{R_A}$ |
| -28.8733+00 | *** | $S^Q_{R_1}$, $-S^Q_{R_2}$ |
| -14.1882+00 | *** | $S^Q_{C_1}$, $-S^Q_{C_2}$ |
| 7.38889-03 | *** | $S^Q_{A/\tau}$, $-S^{\omega_n}_{A/\tau}$ |

The following printouts have all parameters the same except the positive feedback ratio, p. Notice passive sensitivities increase and active decrease.

| 1.-09 GSBB p<br>GSBE | | .004 GSBB p<br>GSBE | | .4 GSBB p<br>GSBE | |
|---|---|---|---|---|---|
| 3.79141-03 | *** | 46.3615-03 | *** | 577.077-03 | *** |
| 172.670+00 | *** | 20.6707+00 | *** | 1.71635+00 | *** |
| -17.2668+03 | *** | -2.07535+03 | *** | -286.053+00 | *** |
| 763.761+00 | *** | 519.661+00 | *** | 302.893+00 | *** |
| 1.00000+09 | *** | 249.000+00 | *** | 1.50000+00 | *** |
| | | | | | |
| 10.0000+03 | *** | 10.0000+03 | *** | 10.0000+03 | *** |
| 455.423+06 | *** | 4.45860+06 | *** | 29.7421+03 | *** |
| 60.3422-12 | *** | 737.866-12 | *** | 9.18446-09 | *** |
| 60.3422-12 | *** | 737.866-12 | *** | 9.18446-09 | *** |
| | | | | | |
| 172.668+06 | *** | 20.7535+06 | *** | 2.86053+06 | *** |
| 10.0006+03 | *** | 10.0048+03 | *** | 10.0351+03 | *** |
| | | | | | |
| -500.000-03 | *** | -500.000-03 | *** | -500.000-03 | *** |
| 21.3406-06 | *** | 8.48008+00 | *** | 114.973+00 | *** |
| -500.021-03 | *** | -8.98008+00 | *** | -115.473+00 | *** |
| -31.4320-03 | *** | -4.24420+00 | *** | -57.4880+00 | *** |
| 213.406-03 | *** | 21.2853-03 | *** | 4.79053-03 | *** |

# Program Listing I

| Step | Key | Comment |
|---|---|---|
| 001 | *LBLA | **LOAD Q** |
| 002 | 1/X | |
| 003 | STO0 | **store d = 1/Q** |
| 004 | GTO0 | |
| 005 | *LBLa | **LOAD DENORMALIZATION RESISTANCE LEVEL** |
| 006 | STO8 | |
| 007 | GTO0 | |
| 008 | *LBLB | **LOAD p** |
| 009 | STO1 | |
| 010 | GTO0 | |
| 011 | *LBLb | **LOAD $C_1/C_2$ RATIO** |
| 012 | STO2 | |
| 013 | GTO0 | |
| 014 | *LBLC | **LOAD OP-AMP GBP** |
| 015 | STO3 | |
| 016 | GTO0 | |
| 017 | *LBLc | **LOAD $H_{desired}$** |
| 018 | P⇄S | |
| 019 | STO0 | |
| 020 | P⇄S | |
| 021 | GTO0 | |
| 022 | *LBLD | **LOAD OP-AMP $A_o$** |
| 023 | STO4 | |
| 024 | *LBL0 | **clear flag 3 subroutine** |
| 025 | CF3 | |
| 026 | RTN | |
| 027 | *LBLE | **LOAD $f_o$ AND START ANALYSIS** |
| 028 | F3? | **store $f_o$ if entered** |
| 029 | STO5 | **from keyboard** |
| 030 | SPC | |
| 031 | RCL3 | $\gamma = \frac{A_o}{f_o} \rightarrow R_A$ |
| 032 | RCL5 | |
| 033 | ÷ | |
| 034 | STOA | |
| 035 | RCL4 | $\beta = \frac{\gamma}{A_o} - \frac{\gamma}{k} \rightarrow R_B$ |
| 036 | ÷ | |
| 037 | RCLA | |
| 038 | RCL1 | |
| 039 | x | |
| 040 | - | |
| 041 | STOB | |
| 042 | RCLA | $m = \gamma + \beta$ |
| 043 | + | |
| 044 | STOC | |
| 045 | RCL2 | $\delta + 1 \rightarrow R9$ |
| 046 | EEX | |
| 047 | + | |
| 048 | STO9 | |
| 049 | x | $m(\delta+1)$ |
| 050 | RCLC | $m - d \rightarrow R_E$ |
| 051 | RCL0 | |
| 052 | - | |
| 053 | STOE | |
| 054 | x | $a_2 = (\delta+1)\{m(m-d)+1\} \rightarrow R_D$ |
| 055 | RCL9 | |
| 056 | + | |
| 057 | STOD | |
| 058 | RCL2 | $a_1 = \delta m - (\delta+1)\beta - (m-d)(dm-1)$ |
| 059 | RCLC | |
| 060 | x | |
| 061 | RCL9 | |
| 062 | RCLB | |
| 063 | x | |
| 064 | - | |
| 065 | RCLC | $dm - 1 \rightarrow R_I$ |
| 066 | RCL0 | |
| 067 | x | |
| 068 | EEX | |
| 069 | - | |
| 070 | STOI | |
| 071 | RCLE | $\frac{a_1}{2} \rightarrow R6$ |
| 072 | x | |
| 073 | - | |
| 074 | 2 | |
| 075 | ÷ | |
| 076 | STO6 | |
| 077 | RCL0 | $a_o = m(\beta - d) + 1$ |
| 078 | RCLB | |
| 079 | - | |
| 080 | RCLC | |
| 081 | x | |
| 082 | EEX | |
| 083 | - | |
| 084 | RCLD | $R_1 = \sqrt{\left(\frac{a_1}{2a_2}\right)^2 - \frac{a_o}{a_2}} - \frac{a_1}{2a_2}$ |
| 085 | ST÷6 | |
| 086 | ÷ | |
| 087 | RCL6 | |
| 088 | X² | |
| 089 | + | |
| 090 | √X | |
| 091 | RCL6 | |
| 092 | - | |
| 093 | STOD | |
| 094 | PRTX | |
| 095 | RCLC | $R_2 = \frac{m(\delta+1)R_1 - (dm-1)}{(R_1 - \beta)\delta}$ |
| 096 | RCL9 | |
| 097 | x | |
| 098 | x | |
| 099 | RCLI | |
| 100 | - | |
| 101 | RCLD | |
| 102 | RCLB | |
| 103 | - | |
| 104 | ÷ | |
| 105 | RCL2 | |
| 106 | ÷ | |
| 107 | STOE | |
| 108 | PRTX | |
| 109 | RCL2 | |
| 110 | x | |

**REGISTERS**

| 0 | 1 | 2 | 3 | 4 | 5 | 6 | 7 | 8 | 9 |
|---|---|---|---|---|---|---|---|---|---|
| $d = \frac{1}{Q}$ | $p = \frac{1}{k}$ | $\delta = \frac{C_2}{C_1}$ | op-amp GBP | op-amp dc gain, $A_o$ | $f_o$ | H, or $a_1/a_2$ | $R_2\delta$, or $\mu$ | resistance level | $\delta+1$, or $Q\sqrt{\mu\delta}$ |

| S0 | S1 | S2 | S3 | S4 | S5 | S6 | S7 | S8 | S9 |
|---|---|---|---|---|---|---|---|---|---|
| $H_{desired}$ | | | | | | | | | |

| A | B | C | D | E | I |
|---|---|---|---|---|---|
| $\gamma$ | $\beta$ | $m$ or $\epsilon = \frac{1}{k-1}$ | $a_2$, or $R_1$ | $m-d$, or $R_2$ | $dm-1$, or $-0.5$ |

# Program Listing II

| Step | Key | Description |
|---|---|---|
| 111 | STO7 | $H_{actual} = \dfrac{-R_2 \cdot \delta \cdot Q}{1 - \frac{1}{k} + \frac{1}{A_o}}$ |
| 112 | EEX | |
| 113 | RCL1 | |
| 114 | - | |
| 115 | RCL4 | |
| 116 | 1/X | |
| 117 | + | |
| 118 | ÷ | |
| 119 | RCL0 | |
| 120 | ÷ | |
| 121 | STO6 | |
| 122 | CHS | |
| 123 | PRTX | |
| 124 | RCLC | $\sigma = \dfrac{m}{\delta \cdot R_1 \cdot R_2}$ |
| 125 | RCLD | |
| 126 | ÷ | |
| 127 | RCL7 | |
| 128 | ÷ | |
| 129 | PRTX | |
| 130 | RCL1 | $R_B = k - 1$ |
| 131 | 1/X | |
| 132 | EEX | |
| 133 | - | |
| 134 | GSB9 | |
| 135 | 1/X | $\epsilon = \dfrac{1}{k-1}$ |
| 136 | STOC | |
| 137 | RCL8 | recall and print denormalized $R_1$ |
| 138 | PRTX | |
| 139 | RCLE | calculate and print denormalized $R_2$ |
| 140 | x | |
| 141 | RCLD | |
| 142 | ÷ | |
| 143 | PRTX | |
| 144 | RCL5 | calculate and print denormalized $C_1$: |
| 145 | Pi | |
| 146 | x | |
| 147 | ENT↑ | |
| 148 | + | $C_1 = \dfrac{R_1}{2\pi \cdot f_o \cdot R}$ |
| 149 | RCL8 | |
| 150 | x | |
| 151 | RCLD | |
| 152 | ÷ | |
| 153 | 1/X | |
| 154 | PRTX | |
| 155 | RCL2 | calculate and print denormalized $C_2$ |
| 156 | x | |
| 157 | GSB9 | |
| 158 | P⇄S | calculate Thevenin equivalent for $R_1$ to provide desired gain at resonance: |
| 159 | RCL0 | |
| 160 | P⇄S | |
| 161 | ST÷6 | |
| 162 | RCL6 | |
| 163 | RCL8 | |
| 164 | x | $R_{1a} = \dfrac{H_{actual}}{H_{desired}} \cdot R_1$ |
| 165 | PRTX | |
| 166 | RCL6 | $R_{1b} = \dfrac{R_{1a}}{\frac{H_{actual}}{H_{desired}} - 1}$ |
| 167 | EEX | |
| 168 | - | |
| 169 | ÷ | |
| 170 | GSB9 | |
| 171 | . | $-0.5 \rightarrow R_I$ |
| 172 | 5 | |
| 173 | CHS | |
| 174 | STOI | |
| 175 | PRTX | print: $S^{\omega_n}_{C_1, C_2, R_1, R_2}$ |
| 176 | RCLE | $\mu = \dfrac{R_2}{R_1} \rightarrow R_7$ |
| 177 | RCLD | |
| 178 | ÷ | |
| 179 | STO7 | |
| 180 | RCL2 | $S^Q_{R_B} = -S^Q_{R_A} = Q\dfrac{\sqrt{\mu\delta}}{k-1}$ |
| 181 | x | |
| 182 | √X | |
| 183 | RCL0 | |
| 184 | ÷ | |
| 185 | STO9 | |
| 186 | RCLC | |
| 187 | x | |
| 188 | PRTX | |
| 189 | CHS | $S^Q_{R_1} = -S^Q_{R_2} = -\frac{1}{2} - Q\dfrac{\sqrt{\mu\delta}}{k-1}$ |
| 190 | RCLI | |
| 191 | + | |
| 192 | PRTX | |
| 193 | RCL7 | $S^Q_{C_1} = -S^Q_{C_2} = -\frac{1}{2} + Q\sqrt{\mu\delta}\left(\frac{1}{\mu} - \frac{1}{k-1}\right)$ |
| 194 | 1/X | |
| 195 | RCLC | |
| 196 | - | |
| 197 | RCL9 | |
| 198 | x | |
| 199 | RCLI | |
| 200 | + | |
| 201 | PRTX | |
| 202 | RCL9 | $S^{\omega}_{A/2} = -S^Q_{A/\tau} = \dfrac{\sqrt{\mu\delta}}{2} \cdot \dfrac{\omega_n \tau}{A_o} \cdot \left(\dfrac{k}{k-1}\right)^2$ |
| 203 | RCL0 | |
| 204 | x | |
| 205 | RCLA | |
| 206 | ENT↑ | |
| 207 | + | |
| 208 | ÷ | |
| 209 | RCLC | |
| 210 | RCL1 | |
| 211 | ÷ | |
| 212 | X² | |
| 213 | x | |
| 214 | *LBL9 | print and space subroutine |
| 215 | PRTX | |
| 216 | SPC | |
| 217 | RTN | |

| LABELS | | | | | FLAGS |
|---|---|---|---|---|---|
| A Load Q | B Load p | C Load GBP | D Load $A_o$ | E Load $f_o$ & Start | 0 |
| a Load R | b Load δ | c Load $H_{desired}$ | d | e | 1 |
| 0 | 1 | 2 | 3 | 4 | 2 |
| 5 | 6 | 7 | 8 | 9 Print & Space | 3 Data entry |

**SET STATUS**

| FLAGS | ON | OFF | TRIG | DISP |
|---|---|---|---|---|
| 0 | | ■ | USER'S CHOICE DEG | FIX |
| 1 | | | GRAD | SCI |
| 2 | | | RAD | ENG |
| 3 | | ■ | | n____ |

## PROGRAM 2-12 ELLIPTIC FILTER ORDER AND LOSS POLE LOCATIONS.

Program Description and Equations Used

This program finds the lowest elliptic (also called Cauer-Chebyshev) lowpass filter order that will meet the requirements for Amax, Amin, fmax, and fmin. These parameters are defined with the aid of Fig. 2-12.1.

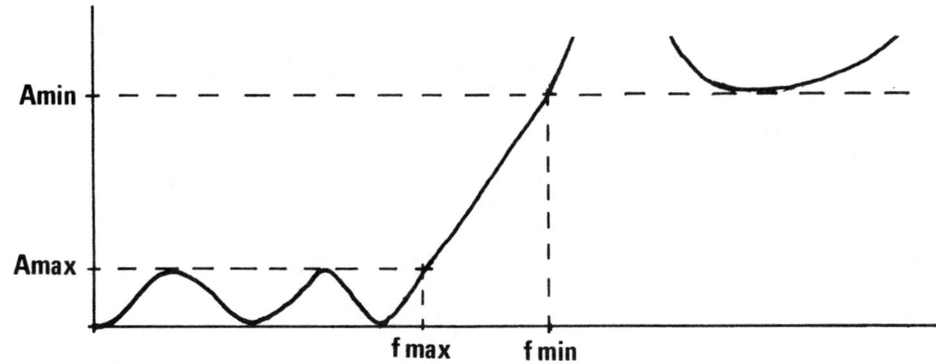


Figure 2-12.1 Elliptic filter loss function, where:

Amax : maximum passband ripple in dB
Amin : minimum stopband attenuation in dB
fmax : maximum passband frequency (passband edge)
fmin : minimum frequency where Amin is achieved.

The program also calculates the attenuation pole frequencies. From these frequencies the filter response at any frequency outside the passband may be determined by using the Z transformation. This transformation technique is described in the next program, and also in chapter 8 of Daniels' book [17]. The analog Z transformation should not be confused with the digital z transformation.

The elliptic filter response is not monotonic in the stopband as can be seen in Fig. 2-12.1. This stopband response is the characteristic difference between the Chebyshev and elliptic filter responses. Both filter types have equiripple behavior in the passband, but Chebyshev (and Butterworth) filters have all attenuation poles located at infinite frequency, while elliptic filters have finite attenuation poles. Because of these finite attenuation poles, the elliptic filter has a sharper transition from passband to stopband for a given filter order.

The elliptic response also has its drawbacks. As the transition band becomes sharper (the filter more selective) the transfer function phase angle changes more rapidly with frequency, and so the group delay becomes peaked near the passband edge frequency. Uniform group delay is required for filters that must process pulses without exhibiting ringing amplitude responses; thus, the transmission function of the elliptic filter tends toward the optimum only from the point of view of the attenuation requirement.

If the LC filter is being designed as a basis for an active filter design such as the leapfrog topology, or an elliptic response is being contemplated for active simulation by cascaded active resonators, the elliptic filter transmission zero (attenuation pole) simulation will require a biquadratic resonator circuit. The designer should always compare the sensitivities of the elliptic active filter circuit versus the sensitivities of a higher order all-pole active design which meets the overall same specifications. In general, as the active resonator circuit becomes more complicated, or the operating gain-bandwidth requirements approach the op-amp gain-bandwidth, the circuit sensitivities become worse, and the final filter design may not meet the specification requirements when component drift due to temperature and aging is considered.

The following formulas are discussed in detail in the equation derivation section and the results brought forward. The loss function, L, is defined by Eq. (2-12.1) (refer to Fig. 2-12.1).

$$L^2 = \frac{10^{0.1\ Amin} - 1}{10^{0.1\ Amax} - 1} \qquad (2\text{-}12.1)$$

Furthermore, $x_L$ is the ratio of the lowpass stopband edge frequency to the lowpass passband edge frequency (refer to Fig. 2-12.1):

$$x_L^{-1} = \frac{f_{max}}{f_{min}} \qquad (2\text{-}12.2)$$

The minimum elliptic filter order that will meet the requirements for Amax, Amin, fmax, and fmin is calculated from Eq. (2-12.28).

$$n = \frac{K\left(x_L^{-1}\right) \cdot K'\left(L^{-1}\right)}{K'\left(x_L^{-1}\right) \cdot K\left(L^{-1}\right)} \qquad (2\text{-}12.30)$$

where K( ) is the complete elliptic integral of the first kind, and K'( ) is the complementary complete elliptic integral of the first kind. These functions are defined by Eqs. (2-12.11) through (2-12.14) and are calculated by a truncated infinite series as given by Eqs. (2-12.18) through (2-12.21).

The loss poles of the elliptic filter transfer function are given by Eqs. (2-12.31) and (2-12.32).

$$x_\nu = \frac{x_L}{x_{z\nu}} \qquad (2\text{-}12.31)$$

where

$$x_{z\nu} = \begin{cases} \operatorname{sn}\left\{\frac{2\nu}{n} K\left(x_L^{-1}\right), x_L^{-1}\right\} & n \text{ odd} \\ \operatorname{sn}\left\{\frac{2\nu-1}{n} K\left(x_L^{-1}\right), x_L^{-1}\right\} & n \text{ even} \end{cases} \qquad (2\text{-}12.32)$$

The elliptic sine is evaluated by means of a Fourier series given by Eqs. (2-12.24) and (2-12.25).

The even ordered elliptic filters have a stopband loss that approaches a constant, finite value as the frequency approaches infinity, i.e., the even ordered elliptic filter does not have a loss pole at infinite frequency. The lossless LC synthesis of such a filter cannot be done without the use of mutual inductive coupling between the filter sections. On the other hand, active filter realizations can be done without the loss pole locations being a constraint.

A special form of the Möbius transformation (a bilinear change of variables) may be applied to the even ordered elliptic loss pole frequencies to move the highest frequency loss pole to infinity and thereby allow LC synthesis without mutual inductance. The even ordered elliptic filter element value tables in Zverev [58], already have this transformation applied, hence $x_L^{-1} = \sin\theta$ only for odd order filters ($\theta$ is the tabulated modular angle).

The general form of the Möbius transformation is:

$$s^2 = \left\{\frac{\Omega_C^2 - \Omega_B^2}{\Omega_B^2 - \Omega_0^2}\,\Omega_B^2\right\} \cdot \left\{\frac{S^2 + \Omega_0^2}{S^2 + \Omega_C^2}\right\} \tag{2-12.3}$$

This transformation converts frequencies as follows:

1) $S = j\Omega_0$ to $s = 0$
2) $S = j\Omega_B$ to $s = j\Omega_B$ (no change in passband edge)
3) $S = j\Omega_C$ to $s = \infty$

It is not desired to transform the dc, or zero frequency, location in the lowpass filter, hence, $\Omega_0 = 0$; furthermore, the loss poles lie directly on the $j\omega$ axis so the transformation need only apply to $s = j\omega$, thus Eq. (2-12.3) becomes:

$$\omega^2 = \left(\Omega_C^2 - \Omega_B^2\right) \frac{\Omega^2}{\Omega_C^2 - \Omega^2} \tag{2-12.4}$$

The program calculates and prints (displays) the original even-ordered pole locations as calculated from Eq. (2-12.32) applies Eq. (2-12.4), and prints and stores the transformed pole locations. For odd-ordered filters, the program calculates, prints, and stores the finite loss pole locations from Eq. (2-12.32) without transformation. In both the even and odd cases, the loss pole frequencies are stored in normalized form ($\Omega = 1$), but are denormalized for printout or display.

The normalized loss pole frequencies are used by the next program in this section to calculate the filter attenuation at any frequency within the passband or the stopband by using the Z transform.

# User Instructions

| ELLIPTIC FILTER ORDER AND LOSS POLE LOCATIONS | | | | |
|---|---|---|---|---|
| Amin | fmin | change n | | |
| Amax | fmax | compute n | compute loss poles | |

| STEP | INSTRUCTIONS | INPUT DATA/UNITS | KEYS | OUTPUT DATA/UNITS |
|---|---|---|---|---|
| 1 | Load both sides of magnetic card | | | |
| 2 | Load maximum passband ripple in dB | Amax | [A] | |
| 3 | Load minimum stopband loss in dB | Amin | [f] [A] | |
| 4 | Load passband cutoff frequency | fmax | [B] | |
| 5 | Load minimum stopband loss frequency | fmin | [f] [B] | |
| 6 | Calculate filter order to meet requirements | | [C] | n<br>n* |
| | *The first n will be the result of the calculations and will generally not be an integer. The second n is the next highest integer, and is the stored value. Both values are given so the designer can get a feeling for the design margin. If the two values are close, the next higher filter order might be considered.<br><br>If the program stops displaying "Error", the input data for Amax and Amin are too far apart (.005dB and 100dB for example) and calculations for $K(L^{-1})$ exceed the precision capability of the HP-97. The filter order may be obtained from the Kawakami CC nomograph [34], [58], and the program restarted with step 7. Step 8 will still run correctly. | | | |
| 7 | To change filter order (integers only) | n | [f] [C] | |
| 8 | To calculate loss poles (frequencies of maximum attenuation) | | [D] | $f_1$<br>$f_2$<br>⋮<br>$f_{n/2}$** <br>space<br>$f_1'$ ***<br>$f_2'$<br>⋮<br>$f'_{(n-1)/2}$ |
| | **The number of loss poles will be the integral part of n/2, i.e., a fifth order filter will have two loss poles.<br><br>***If n is even, the Möbius transformation is done to ensure a loss pole at infinity. The primed frequencies (f') are the Möbius transformed frequencies. The highest original loss frequency has been transformed to infinite frequency, and is not printed out, i.e., a sixth order filter only has two transformed loss frequencies printed out. The original frequency, $f_{n/2}$, is the transformed fmin frequency. | | | |

Example 2-12.1

Compute the filter order and loss pole locations for an elliptic filter to meet the following specifications.

Amax = .28 dB ($\rho$= 25%, Amax = $-10 \log(1-\rho^2)$)

Amin = 63 dB

fmax = 1000 Hz

fmin = 2000 Hz

HP-97 input/output

```
        .28 GSBe  load Amax
      63.00 GSBa  load Amin
    1000.00 GSBB  load fmax
    2000.00 GSBb  load fmin
            GSBC  calculate minimum filter order

       4.97  ***  actual calculated filter order, n
       5.00  ***  nearest integral value for n to meet specs

            GSBD  calculate loss pole locations
3250.804880  ***
2089.246565  ***
```

These results may be checked by comparing them to the 30° modular angle filter design shown in the "Catalog of Normalized Lowpass Models" on page 220 of Zverev [58].

Example 2-12.2

Compute the minimum filter order and loss pole locations for an elliptic filter which meets the following specifications:

$A_{max}$ = .1773 dB ($\rho$ = 20%, $A_{max} = -10 \log(1-\rho^2)$)

$A_{min}$ = 78 dB

$f_{max}$ = 1000 Hz

$f_{min}$ = 2000 Hz

```
      .1773 GSBA   load Amax
      78.00 GSBa   load Amin
    1000.00 GSBB   load fmax
    2000.00 GSBb   load fmin
            GSBC   calculate minimum filter order

       5.90  ***   actual calculated filter order, n
       6.00  ***   nearest integral n to meet specs

            GSBD   calculate loss pole locations:
7235.802719  ***  }
2732.053611  ***  }    untransformed loss poles
2061.165330  ***  }
     <------------ also represents transformed fmin
2922.132266  ***  }
2129.548771  ***  }    transformed loss pole locations
```

Derivation of Equations Used

The elliptic response is governed by the Chebyshev rational function, which is a ratio of polynomials. The development of the Chebyshev rational function in terms of elliptic functions is beyond the scope of this discussion. This development is discussed in Chapter 5 of Daniels' book [17]. A few highlights of the Chebyshev rational function and elliptic functions will be used to show the development of the equations used by this program.

The Chebyshev response becomes the elliptic response when the Chebyshev polynomial, $T_n(x)$, is replaced by the Chebyshev rational function, $R_n(x,L)$, in the filter transfer function (Feldtkeller equation).

$$|H(j\omega)|^2 = 1 + |K(j\omega)|^2 \qquad (2\text{-}12.5)$$

for Chebyshev response, $|K(j\omega)|^2 = \varepsilon^2 \cdot T_n\ (x)$ (2-12.6)

for elliptic response, $|K(j\omega)|^2 = \varepsilon^2 \cdot R_n\ (x,L)$ (2-12.7)

Hence, the elliptic attenuation function is:

$$A(\omega)_{dB} = 20 \cdot \log|H(j\omega)| \tag{2-12.8}$$

$$= 10 \cdot \log\left\{1 + \varepsilon^2 \cdot R_n^{\ 2}(x,L)\right\} ;$$

$$\text{where } x = \omega/\omega max = f/fmax \tag{2-12.9}$$

The Chebyshev rational function, $R_n(x,L)$, has the following properties (also see Fig. 2-11.2).

1) $R_n$ is odd when n is odd and vice versa.

2) All the zeros of $R_n$ lie within the interval $-1 < x < 1$, while all the poles lie outside this interval.

3) $R_n(x,L)$, like $T_n(x)$, oscillates between $\pm 1$ for $-1 < x < 1$. This interval defines the passband.

4) $R_n(1,L) = +1$ (passband edge).

5) $|R_n| > L$ (oscillates outside of L) for $|x| > x_L$, where $x_L$ is defined as the first value of x where $R_n(x,L) = L$, and hence, Amin is achieved (defines stopband).

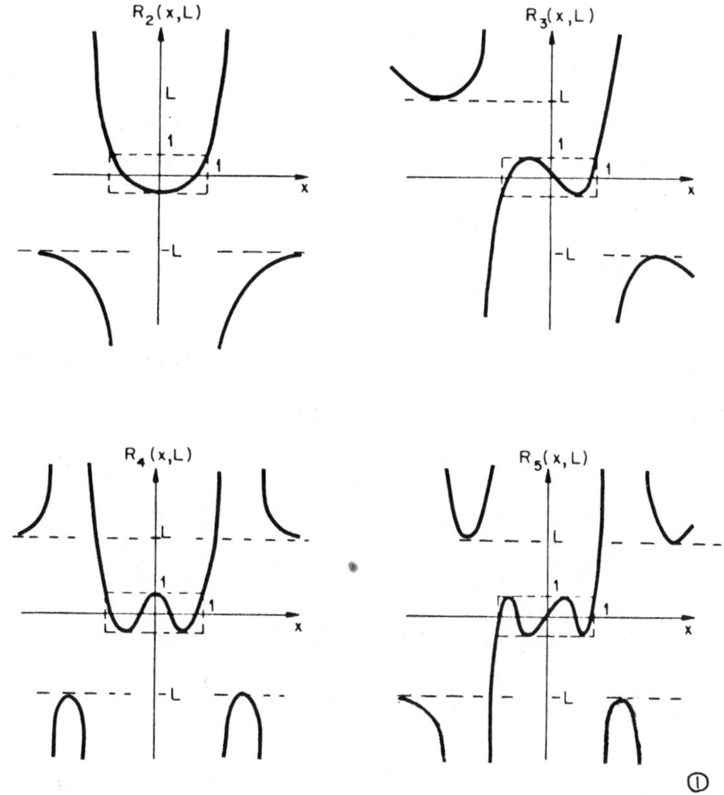


Figure 2-11.2 Chebyshev rational functions for n = 2 to 5.

By using Eq. (2-12.8) and condition 5, an expression for L can be found in terms of the filter parameters Amin and $\varepsilon$.

$$L^2 = \frac{10^{0.1Amin} - 1}{\varepsilon^2} \qquad (2\text{-}12.10)$$

Since $A(\omega)$ = Amax at the passband edge, fmax, condition 4 and Eq. (2-12.8) can be used to find an expression for $\varepsilon$.

$$\varepsilon^2 = 10^{0.1Amax} - 1 \qquad (2\text{-}12.11)$$

Not surprisingly, this is the same expression as is used in the Chebyshev case, and for the same reasons (condition 3).

By putting Eqs. (2-12.10) and (2-12.11) together, the expression for L is obtained:

$$L^2 = \frac{10^{0.1Amin} - 1}{10^{0.1Amax} - 1} \qquad (2\text{-}12.12)$$

## ELLIPTIC FUNCTIONS

There are three kinds of elliptic integrals (see Abramowitz and Stegun, [1]). Only the elliptic integral of the first kind is needed for elliptic filters. The elliptic integral of the first kind is defined by the following equation:

$$u(\phi,k) = \int_{0}^{\phi} \frac{dx}{(1 - k^2 \cdot \sin^2 x)^{1/2}} \tag{2-12.13}$$

The two variables, $\phi$ and k, are called the amplitude and modulus respectively. Some elliptic function tables [1], and some elliptic filter tables [58], are parametric in terms of the modular angle, $\theta$, instead of the modulus, k. The modular angle is defined by:

$$k = \sin \theta \tag{2-12.14}$$

The complete elliptic integral of the first kind results when $\phi$, the limit of integration, is taken as $\pi/2$ radians. This value, $u(\pi/2,k)$ is defined as K(k).

Figure 2-12.3 shows $u(\phi,k)$ parametric with the modular angle, $\theta$. $u(\phi,k)$ has been normalized with respect to K(k). Figure 2-12.4 shows the complete elliptic integral, K(k) by itself.

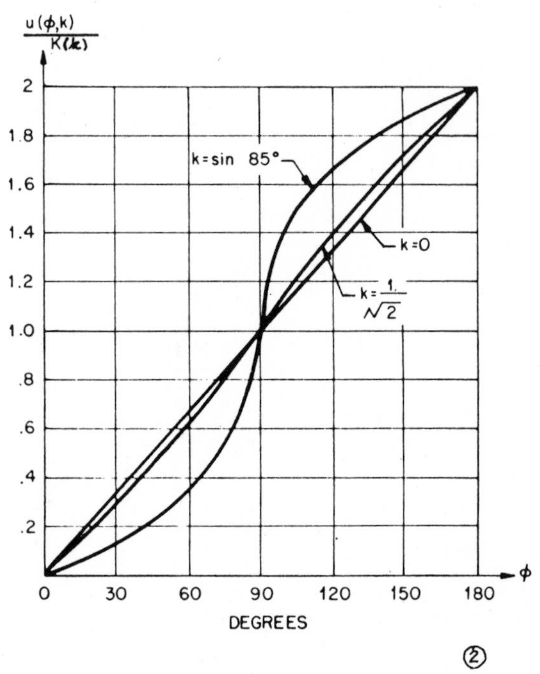


Figure 2-12.3 Elliptic integral.

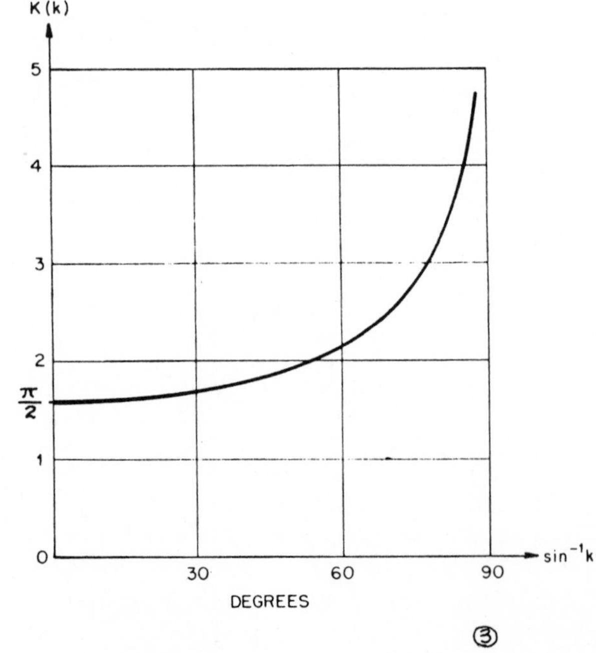


Figure 2-12.4 Complete elliptic integral.

The complementary modulus is defined in terms of the modulus, k, or the modular angle, θ, as:

$$k' = (1 - k^2)^{\frac{1}{2}} = \cos\theta \qquad (2\text{-}12.13)$$

The complementary complete elliptic integral is defined in terms of the complementary modulus:

$$K'(k) = K(k') = u(\pi/2,\ k') \qquad (2\text{-}12.16)$$

The elliptic sine is an elliptic function, and is defined in a somewhat reverse manner from the elliptic integral:

$$u(\phi,k) = \int_0^{\phi} (1 - k^2 \cdot \sin^2(x))^{-\frac{1}{2}}\, dx \qquad (2\text{-}12.17)$$

$$sn(u,k) = \sin\phi \qquad \text{(elliptic sine)} \qquad (2\text{-}12.18)$$

$$cn(u,k) = \phi \qquad \text{(elliptic cosine)} \qquad (2\text{-}12.19)$$

The definition is "reverse" since the limit of integration, $\phi$, must be found to yield the "input," $u(\phi,k)$ and k. Figure 2-12.5 shows the elliptic sine and elliptic cosine functions.

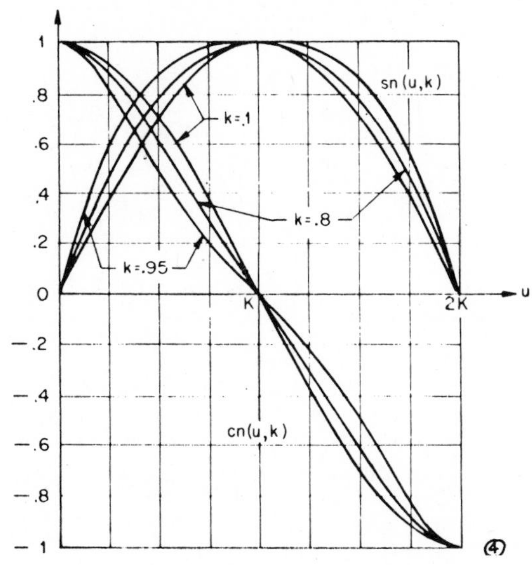


Figure 2-12.5 Elliptic sine and cosine functions.

Luckily, there are rapidly converging series expansions for both K(k) and sn(u,k), [12], and the programmable calculator can be used to perform the iterative calculations. These series expansions are:

Complete elliptic integral

$$K(k) = \frac{\pi}{2} \prod_{m=o}^{\infty} (1 + k_{m+1}) \; ; \qquad (2\text{-}12.20)$$

where

$$k_{m+1} = (1 = k_m')/(1 + k_m') \qquad (2\text{-}12.21)$$

$$k_m' = (1 = k_m{}^2)^{\frac{1}{2}} \text{ , (complementary modulus)} \qquad (2\text{-}12.22)$$

$$k_o \equiv k \qquad (2\text{-}12.23)$$

The terms of the infinite product expansion rapidly converge toward unity. The series is terminated when $k_m < 10^{-9}$. This accuracy is generally achieved in four iterations or less.

Elliptic sine

The elliptic sine is calculated from the following Fourier series:

$$s_n(u,k) = \frac{2\pi}{K(k) \cdot k} \sum_{m=o}^{\infty} \left\{ \frac{q^{m+\frac{1}{2}}}{1 - q^{2m+1}} \right\} \cdot \sin\left( (2m+1) \frac{\pi u}{2K(k)} \right) \qquad (2\text{-}12.24)$$

where q is Jacobi's nome (also called modular elliptic function):

$$q = e^{-\frac{\pi K'(k)}{K(k)}} \qquad (2\text{-}12.25)$$

The series is terminated when $(q^{m+\frac{1}{2}})/(1 - q^{2m+1}) < 10^{-9} q$

This particular algorithm for the elliptic sine is only one of many which can be used to calculate the function. For sharp cutoff filters, the convergence is slow; however, of all the algorithms researched by the author, the Fourier series method could be coded to fit into the HP-97 program memory and still leave enough room for the coding needed for the rest of the program.

If more registers were available, the descending Landen transformation method could have been combined with the calculation of K(k) to simultaneously yield K(k) and sn (u,k) as outlined in Skwirzynski and Zdunek's article [46]. If more program space were available, the elliptic sine could be calculated from the ratios of sums of hyperbolic sines and cosines as recommended by Orchard [41]. Also, if more program space were available, the calculation of the transmission zeros could be done directly from adaptations of the elliptic sine as represented by infinite products of hyperbolic tangents given by Amstutz [ 2 ] or as interpreted by Geffe [27]. Darlington's algorithm [18] is used in Program 2-15, and is a concise method for calculating the transmission zeros and poles when the filter order is odd.

Filter order calculation: Just as the trigonometric sine is periodic, so is the elliptic sine, although the elliptic sine is doubly periodic with a real period of $4 \cdot K(k)$, and an imaginary period of $2 \cdot K'(k)$. The Chebyshev rational function, $R(x,L)$ may be expressed in terms of the complete elliptic integral and the elliptic sine. By relating the real and imaginary periods of the elliptic sine function to the real and imaginary periods of the Chebyshev rational function, two equations in two unknowns, C and n, may be formulated. These equations are:

Chebyshev rational function and elliptic functions

$$R_n(x,L) = \begin{cases} \operatorname{sn}\left(uL/C,\ L^{-1}\right) & n \text{ odd} \\ \operatorname{sn}\left(uL/C + (-1)^{\frac{n}{2}} \cdot K(L^{-1}),\ L^{-1}\right) & n \text{ even} \end{cases} \tag{2-12.26}$$

where C is a constant, and u is the solution to:

$$x = \operatorname{sn}(x_L \cdot u,\ x_L^{-1}) \tag{2-12.27}$$

Simultaneous equations in C and n:

$$x_L^{-1} \cdot K(x_L^{-1}) = n \cdot C \cdot L^{-1} \cdot K(L^{-1}) \quad \text{(real periods)} \tag{2-12.28}$$

$$x_L^{-1} \cdot K'(x_L^{-1}) = C \cdot L^{-1} \cdot K'(L^{-1}) \quad \text{(imaginary periods)} \tag{2-12.29}$$

Eliminating C by simultaneous solution of Eqs. (2-12.28) and (2-12.29) results in the following expression for the filter order, n:

$$n = \frac{K(x_L^{-1}) \cdot K'(L^{-1})}{K'(x_L^{-1}) \cdot K(L^{-1})} \tag{2-12.30}$$

where $x_L^{-1}$ is defined by Eq. (2-12.2) and $L^{-1}$ by Eq. (2-12.18):

$$x_L^{-1} = (fmax)/(fmin)$$

$$L^{-1} = \left\{ \frac{10^{0.1Amax} - 1}{10^{0.1Amin} - 1} \right\}^{\frac{1}{2}}$$

The loss poles of the elliptic filter transfer function, Eq. (2-12.5), are given by:

$$x_\nu = \frac{x_L}{x_{z\nu}} \tag{2-12.31}$$

where:

$$x_{z\nu} = \left\{ \begin{array}{ll} sn\left(\frac{2\nu}{n} K(x_L^{-1}), x_L^{-1}\right) & n \text{ odd} \\ sn\left(\frac{(2\nu-1)}{n} K(x_1^{-1}), x_L^{-1}\right) & n \text{ even} \end{array} \right\} \nu = 1, 2, \ldots, n \tag{2-12.32}$$

In Eq. (2-12.22) k becomes $x_1^{-1}$ for the above elliptic sine computation, hence:

$$x_\nu = \frac{K(x_L^{-1})}{2\pi\Sigma} \tag{2-12.33}$$

where $\Sigma$ is the term summation in Eq. (2-12.24).

# Program Listing I

| | | | |
|---|---|---|---|
| 001 | *LBLA | LOAD | Amax (passband ripple) |
| 002 | ST00 | | |
| 003 | RTN | | |
| 004 | *LBLc | LOAD | Amin (min stopband loss) |
| 005 | STO1 | | |
| 006 | RTN | | |
| 007 | *LBLB | LOAD | fmax |
| 008 | STO2 | | |
| 009 | RTN | | |
| 010 | *LBLb | LOAD | fmin |
| 011 | STO3 | | |
| 012 | RTN | | |
| 013 | *LBLC | calculate filter order, n | |
| 014 | RCL2 | compute and store: | |
| 015 | RCL3 | $x_L^{-1} = \dfrac{f_{max}}{f_{min}} \rightarrow R9$ | |
| 016 | ÷ | | |
| 017 | STO9 | | |
| 018 | GSB5 | compute and store: | |
| 019 | STO4 | $K(x_L^{-1}) \rightarrow R4 \rightarrow R7$ | |
| 020 | STO7 | | |
| 021 | RCL9 | compute and store: | |
| 022 | GSB4 | $K'(x_L^{-1}) \rightarrow R8$ | |
| 023 | STO8 | | |
| 024 | ST÷4 | continue n calculation | |
| 025 | RCL0 | compute and store: | |
| 026 | GSB7 | | |
| 027 | RCL1 | $L^{-1} = \sqrt{\dfrac{10^{0.1\,Amax} - 1}{10^{0.1\,Amin} - 1}} \rightarrow R_E$ | |
| 028 | GSB7 | | |
| 029 | ÷ | | |
| 030 | √X | | |
| 031 | STOE | | |
| 032 | X² | generate error message if | |
| 033 | RCLC | $L^{-1}$ is smaller than $10^{-5}$ | |
| 034 | X>Y? | | |
| 035 | GTO9 | call to unused label: "ERROR" | |
| 036 | RCLE | compute: $K'(L^{-1})$ | |
| 037 | GSB4 | | |
| 038 | ST×4 | continue n calculation | |
| 039 | RCLE | compute: $K(L^{-1})$ | |
| 040 | GSB5 | | |
| 041 | ST÷4 | finish n computation | |
| 042 | RCL4 | recall n | |
| 043 | SPC | | |
| 044 | PRTX | print non-integral n | |
| 045 | EEX | convert n to next highest | |
| 046 | STOD | integer, print and store | |
| 047 | + | | |
| 048 | INT | | |
| 049 | PRTX | | |
| 050 | *LBLc | LOAD ALTERNATE n VALUE | |
| 051 | STO4 | | |
| 052 | GTO3 | | |
| 053 | *LBLD | CALCULATE LOSS POLES | |
| 054 | DSP9 | set display format | |
| 055 | 1 | initialize index register | |
| 056 | 3 | | |
| 057 | STOI | | |
| 058 | . | calculate starting $\nu$ : | |
| 059 | 5 | | |
| 060 | STO6 | n even, $\nu = \frac{1}{2}$ | |
| 061 | RCL4 | n odd, $\nu = 1$ | |
| 062 | X | | |
| 063 | FRC | | |
| 064 | ST+6 | | |
| 065 | SF0 | set flag 0 if n is odd | |
| 066 | X=0? | | |
| 067 | CF0 | | |
| 068 | Pi | compute and store q: | |
| 069 | RCL8 | | |
| 070 | X | $q = e^{-\pi\frac{K'}{K}}$ | |
| 071 | RCL7 | | |
| 072 | ÷ | | |
| 073 | CHS | | |
| 074 | e^x | | |
| 075 | STOE | | |
| 076 | RCLC | calculate error limit for | |
| 077 | X | loop exit | |
| 078 | STOC | | |
| 079 | *LBL0 | loop to calculate elliptic | |
| 080 | Pi | sine ($sn(x, x_L^{-1})$) | |
| 081 | RCL6 | | |
| 082 | X | compute and store: $(\pi\nu)/n \rightarrow x$ | |
| 083 | RCL4 | | |
| 084 | ÷ | | |
| 085 | P≷S | | |
| 086 | STO0 | | |
| 087 | EEX | initialize 2m + 1 | |
| 088 | STO1 | | |
| 089 | CLX | initialize summation ($\Sigma$) | |
| 090 | STO3 | | |
| 091 | *LBL1 | elliptic sine loop | |
| 092 | RCLE | compute and store: | |
| 093 | RCL1 | | |
| 094 | Y^x | | |
| 095 | √X | $\dfrac{q^{m+\frac{1}{2}}}{1 - q^{2m+1}} \rightarrow S2$ | |
| 096 | LSTX | | |
| 097 | CHS | | |
| 098 | EEX | | |
| 099 | + | | |
| 100 | ÷ | | |
| 101 | STO2 | | |
| 102 | RCL1 | compute and add to sum ($\Sigma$): | |
| 103 | RCL0 | | |
| 104 | X | | |
| 105 | SIN | (S2)sin(($2m+1$) $\pi\nu$ /n) | |
| 106 | X | | |
| 107 | ST+3 | | |
| 108 | 2 | increment 2m | |
| 109 | ST+1 | | |
| 110 | RCLC | test for loop exit: | |
| 111 | RCL2 | | |
| 112 | X>Y? | | |

REGISTERS

| 0 Amax | 1 Amin | 2 fmax | 3 fmin | 4 n | 5 scratch | 6 index, $\nu$ | 7 $K(x_L^{-1})$ | 8 $K'(x_L^{-1})$ | 9 $x_L^{-1}$ |
|---|---|---|---|---|---|---|---|---|---|
| S0 $(\pi\nu)/n$ | S1 $2m+1$ | S2 $\dfrac{q^{m+\frac{1}{2}}}{1-q^{2m+1}}$ | S3 $\Sigma$ | S4 | S5 | S6 | S7 | S8 | S9 |
| | | | | ←————————— loss pole storage registers | | | | | |
| A | B | C $10^{-10}$ | | D NINF (used by next program) | | E scratchpad | | I storage reg. index | |
| ←————— loss pole storage —————→ | | | | | | | | | |

# Program Listing II

| Step | Key | Comments |
|---|---|---|
| 113 | GT01 | |
| 114 | RCL3 | recall summation & compute sn: |
| 115 | P⇄S | |
| 116 | ENT↑ | $\frac{sn(x,x_L^{-1})}{x_L} = \frac{2\pi\sum}{K(x_L^{-1})}$ |
| 117 | + | |
| 118 | Pi | |
| 119 | x | |
| 120 | RCL7 | |
| 121 | ÷ | |
| 122 | 1/X | compute and store normalized loss pole locations |
| 123 | ISZI | |
| 124 | STOi | |
| 125 | RCL2 | denormalize and print loss pole locations |
| 126 | x | |
| 127 | PRTX | |
| 128 | EEX | increment register index |
| 129 | ST+6 | |
| 130 | RCL6 | test for loop exit: |
| 131 | ENT↑ | loop if $n > 2\nu$ |
| 132 | + | |
| 133 | RCL4 | |
| 134 | X>Y? | |
| 135 | GT00 | |
| 136 | SPC | |
| 137 | F0? | jump if n is odd |
| 138 | GT03 | |
| 139 | 1 | initialize index register and store highest register number for later exit test |
| 140 | 4 | |
| 141 | X⇄I | |
| 142 | STOE | |
| 143 | RCLi | recall $\Omega_c$ |
| 144 | X² | store $\Omega_c^2$ |
| 145 | STO5 | |
| 146 | *LBL2 | Möbius transformation loop |
| 147 | ISZI | calculate Möbius transform for even ordered lowpass: |
| 148 | RCLi | |
| 149 | X² | |
| 150 | RCL5 | |
| 151 | LSTX | |
| 152 | X² | |
| 153 | - | $\omega^2 = (\Omega_c^2 - 1)\frac{\Omega^2}{\Omega_c^2 - \Omega^2}$ |
| 154 | ÷ | |
| 155 | RCL5 | |
| 156 | EEX | |
| 157 | - | |
| 158 | x | |
| 159 | ABS | |
| 160 | √X | |
| 161 | DSZI | |
| 162 | STOi | store normalized & xfmed loss pole location |
| 163 | ISZI | |
| 164 | RCL2 | denormalize and print loss pole location |
| 165 | x | |
| 166 | PRTX | |
| 167 | RCLI | |
| 168 | RCLE | |
| 169 | X≠Y? | test for loop exit |
| 170 | GT02 | |
| 171 | DSZI | restore highest reg. index |
| 172 | 2 | NINF = 2 for transformed even ordered filters |
| 173 | STOD | |
| 174 | *LBL3 | |
| 175 | DSP2 | set original display format |
| 176 | SPC | |
| 177 | RTN | return control to keyboard |
| 178 | *LBL4 | compute K (k) |
| 179 | X² | |
| 180 | CHS | form complementary modulus: |
| 181 | EEX | |
| 182 | + | $k' = \sqrt{1 - k^2}$ |
| 183 | √X | |
| 184 | *LBL5 | compute K'(k) |
| 185 | STO5 | store argument, k |
| 186 | Pi | initialize product register |
| 187 | 2 | |
| 188 | ÷ | |
| 189 | STO6 | |
| 190 | *LBL6 | complete elliptic integral |
| 191 | EEX | |
| 192 | RCL5 | |
| 193 | X² | |
| 194 | - | $K(x) = \frac{\pi}{2}\prod_{m=0}^{\infty}(1 + k_m)$ |
| 195 | √X | |
| 196 | EEX | |
| 197 | X⇄Y | $k_{m-1} = \frac{1 - k_m'}{1 + k_m'}$ |
| 198 | - | |
| 199 | LSTX | |
| 200 | EEX | $k_i' = \sqrt{1 - k_i^2}$ |
| 201 | + | |
| 202 | ÷ | |
| 203 | STO5 | |
| 204 | EEX | |
| 205 | + | |
| 206 | ST×6 | |
| 207 | RCL5 | |
| 208 | EEX | |
| 209 | CHS | test for loop exit: |
| 210 | 1 | loop if $k_m > 10^{-10}$ |
| 211 | 0 | |
| 212 | STOC | |
| 213 | X≤Y? | |
| 214 | GT06 | |
| 215 | RCL6 | recall K(k) |
| 216 | RTN | return to main program |
| 217 | *LBL7 | subroutine to compute: |
| 218 | EEX | |
| 219 | 1 | $10^{0.1A} - 1$ |
| 220 | ÷ | |
| 221 | 10ˣ | |
| 222 | EEX | |
| 223 | - | |
| 224 | RTN | |

**LABELS**

| A load Amax | B load fmax | C calc n | D calc loss poles | E |
|---|---|---|---|---|
| a load Amin | b load fmin | c enter n | d | e |
| 0 sn(u,k) | 1 sn loop start | 2 Mobius transform | 3 jump dest | 4 K(k) |
| 5 K'(k) | 6 K'(k) loop | 7 conversion subroutine | 8 | 9 |

**FLAGS**

| | |
|---|---|
| 0 | n odd |
| 1 | |
| 2 | |
| 3 | |

**SET STATUS**

| FLAGS | ON | OFF | TRIG | | DISP | |
|---|---|---|---|---|---|---|
| 0 | | ■ | DEG | | FIX | ■ |
| 1 | | | GRAD | | SCI | |
| 2 | | | RAD | ■ | ENG | |
| 3 | | | | | n | 2 |

## PROGRAM 2-13 RESPONSE OF A FILTER WITH CHEBYSHEV PASSBAND AND ARBITRARY STOPBAND LOSS POLES.

Program Description and Equations Used

This program will calculate the passband and stopband attenuation of lowpass, highpass, bandpass, and bandstop filters having Chebyshev (equi-ripple) passbands and arbitrary stopband losspole locations. The elliptic filter is a special case of this filter class in that the loss pole locations are chosen to provide equi-ripple stopband behavior.

Bandpass and bandstop filters are assumed to be the classic transformations of the lowpass structure, i.e., equal numbers of attenuation poles on either side of the passband, and geometrical symmetry of those poles about the center frequency. The program is designed to take either stored normalized lowpass loss pole frequencies provided by Program 2-12, or to accept normalized lowpass loss pole frequencies, number of poles at infinite frequency, and passband ripple as provided by the user.

This program is adapted from an unpublished HP-67/97 elliptic stopband attenuation program written by Philip R. Geffe. The basis of the program is the Z transformation, and the associated loss function, L(Z). This function allows the calculation of the stopband attenuation of equi-ripple passband elliptic filters from a knowledge of the loss pole frequencies only [17]. The transformed variable, Z, is defined by:

$$Z^2 = (s^2 + \omega_B^2)/(s^2 + \omega_A^2) \qquad (2\text{-}13.1)$$

This function spreads the passband ($s = j\omega_A$ to $j\omega_B$) over the entire imaginary Z axis, and spreads the stopbands along the real Z axis. Although use of the Z transform allows greater numerical accuracy due to the spreading out of the passband poles, the prime reason for its use in this program is the mathematical expressions for elliptic filters are simpler in the Z domain than in the s domain.

Given a filter with equiripple passband extending from $\omega_A$ to $\omega_B$, having NZ attenuation poles at the origin, N finite loss poles, and NINF attenuation poles at infinite frequency, the loss function in terms of Z is:

$$L(Z) = \left\{\frac{Z + \omega_B/\omega_A}{Z - \omega_B/\omega_A}\right\}^{\frac{NZ}{2}} \left\{\frac{Z + 1}{Z - 1}\right\}^{\frac{NINF}{2}} \prod_{i=1}^{N} \frac{Z + Z_i}{Z - Z_i} \qquad (2\text{-}13.2)$$

If L(Z) represents a normalized lowpass filter, then $\omega_A = 0$, $\omega_B = 1$, and NZ = 0. Letting $s = j\Omega$, Z and L(Z) become:

$$Z = (1 - 1/\Omega^2)^{\frac{1}{2}} \qquad (2\text{-}13.3)$$

$$L(Z) = \left\{\frac{Z + 1}{Z - 1}\right\}^{\frac{NINF}{2}} \prod_{i=1}^{N} \frac{Z + Z_i}{Z - Z_i} \qquad (2\text{-}13.4)$$

The attenuation function, A(Ω), is defined in terms of the loss function, L(Z), as follows:

$$A(\Omega) = 10 \cdot \log\left\{1 + \frac{\varepsilon^2}{4}\left(L(Z) + \frac{(-1)^{NINF}}{L(Z)}\right)^2\right\} \qquad (2\text{-}13.5)$$

$$\varepsilon^2 = 10^{0.1Amax} - 1 \qquad (2\text{-}13.6)$$

In the stopband, the attenuation function may be simplified:

$$A(\Omega) = 10 \log\left[1 + \frac{\varepsilon^2}{4}\left\{|L(Z)| + 1/|L(Z)|\right\}^2\right] \qquad (2\text{-}13.7)$$

The filter passband ripple (Amax) may sometimes be expressed in terms of a reflection coefficient, ρ. The relationship between these quantities is:

$$Amax = -10 \log(1 - \rho^2) \qquad (2\text{-}13.8)$$

Within the normalized lowpass passband (Ω<1), Z becomes purely imaginary. Equation (2-13.4) may be rewritten in exponential form to eliminate the need for complex arithmetic:

$$L(Z) = e^{jB} \qquad (2\text{-}13.9)$$

where

$$B = \frac{NINF}{2} \tan^{-1}\left\{\frac{-2|Z|}{|Z|^2 - 1}\right\} + \sum_{i=1}^{N} \tan^{-1}\left\{\frac{-2|Z|Z_i}{|Z|^2 - Z_i^2}\right\} \qquad (2\text{-}13.10)$$

substituting Eq. (2-13.9) into (2-13.5) yields:

$$A(\Omega) = 10 \log (1 + \varepsilon^2 \cos^2 B) \text{ for NINF even,} \qquad (2\text{-}13.11)$$

and

$$A(\Omega) = 10 \log (1 + \varepsilon^2 \sin^2 B) \text{ for NINF odd.} \qquad (2\text{-}13.12)$$

The program uses Eqs. (2-13.3) through (2-13.12) to find the filter loss at any frequency. Two ancillary relations are used to convert unnormalized bandpass or bandstop frequencies to the normalized lowpass frequency, $\Omega$. Lowpass and highpass filters are only special cases of bandpass and bandstop filters respectively, in that the center frequency is zero. These two ancillary equations are:

<u>Bandpass to normalized lowpass</u>

$$\Omega_{BP} = \frac{1}{BW} \left\{ f - \frac{f_o^2}{f} \right\} \qquad (2\text{-}13.13)$$

where

BW = bandwidth

$f_o$ = center frequency

<u>Bandstop to normalized lowpass</u>

$$\Omega_{BS} = 1/\Omega_{BP} \qquad (2\text{-}13.14)$$

Equation (2-13.4) will predict the stopband attenuation for even ordered elliptic filters of Cauer types A and B (the Möbius transformation - see previous program for description). The type A, even-ordered filter has no attenuation poles at infinite frequency, and can only be realized with mutual inductive coupling between filter sections, while the Möbius transformed pole locations (type B) can be realized with a ladder structure containing only L's and C's. The even ordered type B ladder structure possesses a double pole of attenuation at infinite frequency.

Equation (2-13.4) will not work with the pole locations resulting from a transformation to Cauer type C filters (equal resistive termination for even-ordered elliptic filters), i.e., one must use types A and B only. See Saal and Ulbrich [45] for details.

# User Instructions

| CHEBYSHEV PASSBAND - ARBITRARY STOPBAND RESPONSE | | | | |
|---|---|---|---|---|
| load $p_i$ | load NINF | load $+\rho$ or $-$Amax | | |
| bandpass: $f_o \uparrow$ BW | bandstop: $f_o \uparrow$ BW | load $f_{st} \uparrow f_{sp} \uparrow \Delta f$ | start sweep | calculate $f \rightarrow A(f)$ |

| STEP | INSTRUCTIONS | INPUT DATA/UNITS | KEYS | OUTPUT DATA/UNITS |
|---|---|---|---|---|
| 1 | Load both sides of magnetic card | | | |
| 2 | If this program is being used concurrently with Program 2-11, the loss poles, Amax, and NINF are already stored by that program. Go to step 6 and continue. | | | |
| 3 | Load normalized loss pole frequencies | setup | [f] [A] | |
| | | $p_1$ | [R/S] | |
| | | $p_2$ | [R/S] | |
| | | ⋮ | ⋮ | |
| | | $p_n$ | [R/S] | |
| 4 | Load number of loss poles at infinite frequency | NINF | [f] [B] | |
| 5 | Load either the reflection coefficient or the passband ripple in dB (related quantities). The program differentiates the quantities by sign. Both quantities are normally positive | | | |
| | Reflection coefficient | $\rho$ | [f] [C] | Amax |
| | or | | | |
| | Passband ripple in dB (note sign) | $-$Amax | [f] [C] | Amax |
| 6 | Select filter type: | | | |
| | Bandpass or Lowpass: | $f_o$ | [ENT↑] | |
| | The lowpass filter is a special case of the bandpass filter in that the center frequency is zero. The bandwidth is the lowpass cutoff frequency. | BW | [A] | |
| | Bandstop or Highpass: | $f_o$ | [ENT↑] | |
| | The highpass filter is a special case of the bandstop filter in that the center frequency is zero. The bandwidth is the highpass cutoff frequency. | BW | [B] | |

# User Instructions

CHEBYSHEV PASSBAND - ARBITRARY STOPBAND RESPONSE

CONTINUED

| STEP | INSTRUCTIONS | INPUT DATA/UNITS | KEYS | OUTPUT DATA/UNITS |
|---|---|---|---|---|
| 7 | Load denormalized stopband frequency and calculate stopband attenuation | f | E | A(f) |
| 8 | If a sweep of frequencies is desired: | | | |
| | a) Load sweep parameters | $f_{start}$ | ENT↑ | |
| | The frequency increment is either an additive delta, or a multiplicative delta depending upon lin/log sweep. If linear sweep is desired, then the increment should be entered as a negative quantity, i.e., for 100 Hz linear steps, the increment should be entered as -100. Whether the increment is linear or logrithmic, the sweep will be always in the direction of increasing frequency. | $f_{stop}$<br>$f_{incr}$ | ENT↑<br>C | |
| | b) Start sweep | | D | f<br>A(f)<br>space<br>f<br>A(f)<br>⋮ |
| 9 | Go back to any step desired, modify, and rerun program | | | |

Example 2-13.1

An elliptic bandpass filter is required to pass frequencies between 5 kHz and 15 kHz with 0.0436 dB ripple or less (10% reflection coefficient), and reject frequencies lying outside a 4.1 kHz to 19 kHz band by at least 60 dB. Find the minimum filter order that will satisfy these requirements, and predict the stopband response.

The center frequency is the geometric mean of the upper and lower passband edge frequencies. Likewise, the stopband edge frequencies must be geometrically symmetrical about the center frequency. In this example, the above frequencies do not satisfy this requirement, hence, the narrowest stopband with geometric symmetry must be defined. The filter center frequency is calculated from the passband edge frequencies:

$$f_o = (5000 \cdot 15000)^{\frac{1}{2}} = 8660.25 \text{ Hz}$$

The narrowest stopband may be found by calculating the geometrical mating frequencies to the given stopband frequencies, and taking the narrowest set:

$$f_u = f_o^2/4100 = 18292.68 \text{ Hz}$$

$$f_L = f_o^2/19000 = 3947.37 \text{ Hz}$$

The narrowest stopband is 4100 Hz to 18292.68 Hz for a stopband width of 14192.68 Hz.

The stopband and passband data are loaded into Program 2-12 to find the minimum filter order and loss pole locations. Because bandpass data was loaded, the loss pole frequencies that are output represent loss pole bandwidths, or the separation of loss pole frequencies in the upper and lower stopbands that are geometrically related to the filter center frequency. To convert these bandwidths into loss pole frequencies, the subprogram contained in Program 2-1 can be used. These equivalent bandpass loss pole frequencies are not necessary for proper operation of this program, but are calculated for information only. They can also be useful when tuning the final filter. All normalized loss pole information is automatically stored by Program 2-12 for use by this program.

**Example 2-13.1 continued**

Load Program 2-12 and calculate filter order and loss poles.

```
      .0436 GSBA  load Amax
      60.00 GSBa  load Amin
   10000.00 GSBE  load fmax (passband bandwidth)
   14192.68 GSBb  load fmin (stopband minimum bandwidth)

            GSBC  calculate minimum filter order

       6.72  ***
       7.00  ***  minimum integral filter order, n

            GSBD  calculate loss pole bandwidths

28.69564+03  ***  loss pole bandwidth #1
17.08919+03  ***  loss pole bandwidth #2
14.44925+03  ***  loss pole bandwidth #3
```

Load Program 2-1 to calculate loss pole locations from loss pole bandwidths.

```
   28695.64 ENT↑  load loss pole bandwidth #1
    8660.25 GSBd  load fo
   31106.69  ***  upper BP loss pole frequency #1
    2411.05  ***  lower BP loss pole frequency #1

   17089.19 ENT↑  load loss pole bandwidth #2
    8660.25 GSBd  load fo
   20710.53  ***  upper BP loss pole frequency #2
    3621.34  ***  lower BP loss pole frequency #2

   14449.25 ENT↑  load loss pole bandwidth #3
    8660.25 GSBd  load fo
   18502.71  ***  upper BP loss pole frequency #3
    4053.46  ***  lower BP loss pole frequency #3
```

Load this program (Program 2-13) and calculate filter response.

```
    8660.25 ENT↑  load fo
   10000.00 GSBA  load passband width and select bandpass

    2000.00 ENT↑  load f-start
    5000.00 ENT↑  load f-stop
    -200.00 GSBC  load f-increment (a negative value
                        means linear sweep increments)
            GSBD  start sweep:
                        the output is on the next page.
```

(sweep step size changes were made between output segments)

**PROGRAM OUTPUT FOR EXAMPLE 2-13.1**

| LOWER STOPBAND | | PASSBAND | | | | UPPER STOPBAND | | | |
|---|---|---|---|---|---|---|---|---|---|
| f | A(f) dB | f | A(f) | f | A(f) | f | A(f) | f | A(f) |
| 2000.00 | 68.02 | 5000.0000 | 0.0436 | 10000.0000 | 0.0434 | 15000.00 | 0.04 | 30000.00 | 79.85 |
| 2200.00 | 73.03 | 5500.0000 | 0.0020 | 10500.0000 | 0.0342 | 16000.00 | 12.98 | 31000.00 | 100.57 |
| 2400.00 | 98.12 | 6000.0000 | 0.0389 | 11000.0000 | 0.0115 | 17000.00 | 31.72 | 32000.00 | 82.55 |
| 2600.00 | 73.25 | 6500.0000 | 0.0002 | 11500.0000 | 0.0000 | 18000.00 | 52.97 | 33000.00 | 76.47 |
| 2800.00 | 67.19 | 7000.0000 | 0.0248 | 12000.0000 | 0.0144 | 19000.00 | 64.35 | 34000.00 | 73.25 |
| 3000.00 | 64.45 | 7500.0000 | 0.0434 | 12500.0000 | 0.0389 | 20000.00 | 68.65 | 35000.00 | 71.15 |
| 3200.00 | 63.90 | 8000.0000 | 0.0234 | 13000.0000 | 0.0385 | 21000.00 | 77.55 | 36000.00 | 69.63 |
| 3400.00 | 66.45 | 8500.0000 | 0.0016 | 13500.0000 | 0.0082 | 22000.00 | 66.70 | 37000.00 | 68.49 |
| 3600.00 | 84.71 | 9000.0000 | 0.0065 | 14000.0000 | 0.0090 | 23000.00 | 64.24 | 38000.00 | 67.60 |
| 3800.00 | 66.03 | 9500.0000 | 0.0293 | 14500.0000 | 0.0430 | 24000.00 | 63.83 | 39000.00 | 66.89 |
| 4000.00 | 67.53 | | | 15000.0000 | 0.0436 | 25000.00 | 64.45 | 40000.00 | 66.31 |
| 4200.00 | 49.19 | | | | | 26000.00 | 65.75 | 41000.00 | 65.84 |
| 4400.00 | 32.55 | | | | | 27000.00 | 67.65 | 42000.00 | 65.45 |
| 4600.00 | 18.89 | | | | | 28000.00 | 70.25 | 43000.00 | 65.13 |
| 4800.00 | 5.63 | | | | | 29000.00 | 73.91 | 44000.00 | 64.66 |
| 5000.00 | 0.04 | | | | | | | 45000.00 | 64.64 |

NOTE:
The display was changed manually to DSP4 for the passband printout, then changed back to DSP2 for the upper stopband output.

Example 2-13.2

Compute the minimum stopband attenuation of an eleventh order, 20% reflection coefficient, 75 degree modular angle elliptic filter (see p. 326 of Saal and Ulbrich [45]).

Load Program 2-12 and calculate filter order and loss pole locations.

```
      1.00 ENT↑  }
       .20   X²  }
              -  }  calculate Amax = 10 log (1- ρ²)
            LOG  }
     10.00    X  }
            CHS  }
  0.1772877 ***  }

           GSBA  load Amax
    100.00 GSBa  load dummy Amin large enough to cause "error" halt
      1.00 GSBB  load normalized passband edge
     75.00  D→R  }
            SIN  }  calculate stopband edge from modular angle
            1/X  }
   1.035276 ***  }
           GSBb  load normalized stopband edge

           GSBC  start filter order calculation (computes K(k))
          ERROR  program halt since L⁻¹ is too small

       11. GSBc  load desired filter order

           GSBD  output loss pole locations and store for next program
2.222241138  ***
1.344326902  ***
1.128566299  ***
1.05[illegible]17641  ***
1.0375195[illegible]4  ***
```

Load this program (Program 2-13) and calculate filter response.

```
     0.000 ENT↑  load filter center frequency (lowpass)
     1.000 GSBA  load bandwidth (normalized for this example)

     1.000 GSBb  load number of poles at infinity

    75.000  SIN  }  calculate normalized stopband edge frequency
            1/X  }
           GSBE  calculate stopband loss at this frequency
    60.606  ***  minimum stopband loss in dB (Amin defined at fmin)
```

# Program Listing I

| Step | Key | Comment |
|---|---|---|
| 001 | *LBLa | SETUP LOSS POLE ENTRY |
| 002 | 1 | initialize index register |
| 003 | 3 | |
| 004 | STOI | |
| 005 | SF2 | indicate initialization reqd |
| 006 | *LBL0 | enter normalized loss pole |
| 007 | R/S | |
| 008 | ISZI | |
| 009 | STOi | |
| 010 | GTO0 | |
| 011 | *LBLb | LOAD NINF, the number of lowpass loss poles at infinite freqeuncy |
| 012 | STOD | |
| 013 | GTO6 | |
| 014 | *LBLc | LOAD ρ or -Amax |
| 015 | X<0? | if negative entry, jump |
| 016 | GTO1 | |
| 017 | X² | calculate: Amax $= \lvert 10\log(1-\rho^2)\rvert$ |
| 018 | CHS | |
| 019 | GSB7 | |
| 020 | *LBL1 | store $\lvert$Amax$\rvert$ |
| 021 | ABS | |
| 022 | STO0 | |
| 023 | GTO6 | goto space and return |
| 024 | *LBLA | LOAD $f_o$ & BW for bandpass |
| 025 | CF0 | indicate bandpass |
| 026 | GTO1 | |
| 027 | *LBLB | LOAD $f_o$ & BW for bandstop |
| 028 | SF0 | indicate bandstop |
| 029 | *LBL1 | store BW (bandwidth) |
| 030 | STO9 | |
| 031 | R↓ | form and store $f_o^2$ |
| 032 | X² | |
| 033 | STO8 | |
| 034 | GTO6 | goto space and return |
| 035 | *LBLC | LOAD f-start, f-stop, Δf |
| 036 | P⇄S | store f-increment (Δf) |
| 037 | STO1 | |
| 038 | R↓ | store f-stop |
| 039 | STO2 | |
| 040 | R↓ | store f-start |
| 041 | STO0 | |
| 042 | P⇄S | restore register order |
| 043 | GTO6 | goto space and return |
| 044 | *LBLD | START SWEEP |
| 045 | P⇄S | |
| 046 | RCL0 | recall and print present frequency |
| 047 | P⇄S | |
| 048 | PRTX | |
| 049 | GSBE | calculate and print A(f) |
| 050 | P⇄S | recall frequency increment |
| 051 | RCL1 | |
| 052 | X<0? | if increment negative, use additive delta |
| 053 | ST-0 | |
| 054 | X<0? | |
| 055 | GTO1 | |
| 056 | STx0 | if plus, use product delta |
| 057 | *LBL1 | test for loop exit |
| 058 | RCL2 | |
| 059 | RCL0 | |
| 060 | P⇄S | |
| 061 | X≤Y? | |
| 062 | GTOD | |
| 063 | RTN | |
| 064 | *LBLE | LOAD f, calculate A(f) |
| 065 | STO6 | temporarily store f |
| 066 | F2? | if first time through here, goto initialization routine |
| 067 | GSB8 | |
| 068 | RCL6 | calculate: $\Omega = \frac{1}{BW}\left[f - \frac{f_o^2}{f}\right]$ |
| 069 | RCL8 | |
| 070 | RCL6 | |
| 071 | ÷ | |
| 072 | - | |
| 073 | ABS | |
| 074 | RCL9 | |
| 075 | ÷ | |
| 076 | X=0? | $\Omega = 0$ escape |
| 077 | RTN | |
| 078 | F0? | if bandstop, form inverse |
| 079 | 1/X | |
| 080 | EEX | test for passband $(\Omega < 1)$ |
| 081 | CF3 | set flag 3 if passband |
| 082 | X>Y? | |
| 083 | SF3 | |
| 084 | X⇄Y | form and store: $\lvert Z\rvert = \left(\left\lvert 1 - \frac{1}{\Omega}\right\rvert\right)^{\frac{1}{2}}$ |
| 085 | X² | |
| 086 | 1/X | |
| 087 | - | |
| 088 | ABS | |
| 089 | √X | |
| 090 | STO6 | |
| 091 | F3? | jump if in passband |
| 092 | GTO3 | |
| 093 | EEX | stopband attenuation, form and store: $\left[\frac{Z+1}{Z-1}\right]^{NINF/2}$ |
| 094 | + | |
| 095 | RCL6 | |
| 096 | EEX | |
| 097 | - | |
| 098 | ÷ | |
| 099 | ABS | |
| 100 | RCLD | |
| 101 | Yˣ | beginning of L(Z) calc |
| 102 | √X | |
| 103 | STO5 | |
| 104 | RCL7 | initialize index register |
| 105 | STOI | |
| 106 | *LBL2 | L(Z) calculation loop |
| 107 | ISZI | |
| 108 | RCL6 | calculate $\frac{Z+Z_i}{Z-Z_i}$ |
| 109 | RCLi | |
| 110 | + | |
| 111 | RCL6 | |
| 112 | RCLi | |

**REGISTERS**

| 0 | 1 | 2 | 3 | 4 | 5 | 6 | 7 | 8 | 9 |
|---|---|---|---|---|---|---|---|---|---|
| Amax | $\epsilon^2/4$ | | | | L | scratch | "13" | $f_o^2$ | BW |
| S0 present freq | S1 freq incr | S2 stop freq | S3 | S4 ← loss pole storage registers | S5 | S6 | S7 | S8 | S9 → |

| A | B | C | D | E | I |
|---|---|---|---|---|---|
| ← loss pole storage | → | $10^{-9}$ | NINF | $I_{max}$ | storage register index |

# Program Listing II

NOTE FLAG SET STATUS

|  |  |
|---|---|
| - | |
| ÷ | |
| STx5 | form running product of L(Z) |
| RCLI | |
| RCLE | test for loop exit |
| X≠Y? | |
| GTO2 | |
| RCL5 | |
| 1/X | form (L + 1/L) |
| LSTX | |
| GTO5 | goto output routine |
| *LBL3 | passband attenuation calc |
| ENT↑ | |
| + | |
| CHS | |
| RCL6 | form and store: |
| X² | |
| EEX | $\frac{NINF}{2}\beta_{INF}$ ; |
| - | |
| →P | |
| X⇄Y | $\beta_{INF} = \tan^{-1}\left[\frac{-2\|Z\|}{\|Z\|^2 - 1}\right]$ |
| 2 | |
| ÷ | |
| RCLD | |
| x | |
| STO5 | |
| RCL7 | initialize index register |
| STOI | |
| SF1 | |
| RCLD | |
| 2 | set flag 1 if NINF is odd |
| ÷ | |
| FRC | |
| X=0? | |
| CF1 | |
| *LBL4 | L(Z) calculation loop |
| ISZI | increment index register |
| RCL6 | |
| RCLi | |
| x | form $\beta_i$: |
| ENT↑ | |
| + | $\beta_i = \tan^{-1}\frac{-2\|Z\|Z_i}{\|Z\|^2 - Z_i^2}$ |
| CHS | |
| RCL6 | |
| X² | |
| RCLi | |
| X² | |
| - | |
| →P | |
| X⇄Y | |
| ST+5 | add $\beta_i$ to running sum |
| RCLI | |
| RCLE | test for loop exit |
| X≠Y? | |
| GTO4 | |
| RCL5 | recall β |
| EEX | |
| →R | form sin β, and cos β |
| F1? | recall sin β→$R_x$ if NINF odd |
| X⇄Y | |
| ENT↑ | prepare to double $R_x$ |
| *LBL5 | Output routine; form |
| + | $\epsilon^2/4\ (L+1/L)^2$ if stopband |
| X² | |
| RCL1 | $\epsilon^2 \frac{\sin^2\beta}{\cos^2\beta}$ if passband |
| x | |
| GSB7 | calculate and print |
| RND | 10 log(1 + $R_x$) |
| PRTX | |
| *LBL6 | space and return subroutine |
| SPC | |
| RTN | |
| *LBL7 | subroutine to calculate: |
| EEX | |
| + | 10 log(1 + (·)) |
| LOG | |
| EEX | |
| 1 | |
| x | |
| RTN | |
| *LBL8 | initialization routine |
| RCLI | store highest loss pole |
| STOE | register number |
| RCL0 | |
| EEX | calculate and store: |
| 1 | |
| ÷ | |
| 10ˣ | $\frac{\epsilon^2}{4} = \frac{10^{0.1Amax} - 1}{4}$ |
| EEX | |
| - | |
| 4 | |
| ÷ | |
| STO1 | |
| 1 | store index register |
| 3 | initialization, and |
| STO7 | initialize index register |
| STOI | |
| *LBL9 | loss pole Z transform loop |
| ISZI | increment index register |
| EEX | calculate and store: |
| RCLi | |
| X² | $Z_i = (1 - 1/(p_i)^2)^{\frac{1}{2}}$ |
| 1/X | where $p_i$ are the normalized |
| - | loss pole frequencies |
| √X | |
| STOi | |
| RCLI | test for loop exit |
| RCLE | |
| X≠Y? | |
| GTO9 | |
| RTN | return to main program |

**LABELS**

| | | | | |
|---|---|---|---|---|
| A BANDPASS f0↑BW | B BANDSTOP f0↑BW | C fst↑fsp↑f | D START SWEEP | E f→A(f) |
| a losspole entry | b load NINF | c load ρor-Amax | d | e |
| 0 losspole ent loop | 1 local lbl | 2 L(Z) stop band | 3 passband atten | 4 L(Z) pass band |
| 5 output routine | 6 space & return | 7 A(f) | 8 init | 9 losspole Z xfms |

**FLAGS**

| | |
|---|---|
| 0 | bandstop |
| 1 | NINF odd |
| 2 | init |
| 3 | passband |

**SET STATUS**

| FLAGS | ON | OFF | TRIG | | DISP | |
|---|---|---|---|---|---|---|
| 0 | | ■ | DEG | ■ | FIX | ■ |
| 1 | | ■ | GRAD | | SCI | |
| 2 | ■ | | RAD | | ENG | |
| 3 | | | | | n 2 | |

## PROGRAM 2-14 POLE AND ZERO LOCATIONS OF A FILTER WITH CHEBYSHEV PASSBAND AND ARBITRARY STOPBAND LOSS POLE LOCATIONS.

### Program Description and Equations Used

This program calculates the complex zero locations of the filter transfer function, $H(s) = E_{in}/E_{out}$, from the loss pole frequencies (frequencies of infinite attenuation). The zero locations are also called the natural modes of H(s). The pole locations of H(s), are the loss pole frequencies and lie on the $j\omega$ axis. The transmission function, T(s), is the reciprocal of the filter transfer function, and may be more familiar to some readers. When active elliptic filters are being designed [35], one approach is to divide the transmission function into bi-quadratic factors with each factor (second order pole pair, and second order zero pair) being synthesized with a separate active network [38].

The loss pole frequencies can be supplied by the user in the case of arbitrary stopband, equiripple passband filters, or can be generated by Program 2-12 for elliptic filters (equiripple stopband and passband).

This program works in the Z-domain to spread out the pole and zero frequencies, and enhance the numerical accuracy of the final output. The s-domain frequencies are Z transformed using Eq. (2-14.1), which is the normalized lowpass form of the more generalized Z transform.

$$Z^2 = 1 + \frac{1}{s^2}\bigg|_{s=j\omega} = 1 - \frac{1}{\omega^2} \qquad (2\text{-}14.1)$$

The filter transfer function is a rational function, i.e., it is a ratio of polynomials:

$$H(s) = \frac{e(s)}{q(s)} \qquad (2\text{-}14.2)$$

This transfer function is related to the filter characteristic function, K(s), by the Feldtkeller equation:

$$H(s)H(-s) = 1 + K(s)K(-s) \qquad (2\text{-}14.3)$$

where the characteristic function has been defined in terms of the Chebyshev rational function, R(x,L), by Eq. (2-12.3), and also is a ratio of polynomials:

$$K(s) = \frac{f(s)}{q(s)} \tag{2-14.4}$$

Expanding the Feldtkeller equation to remove the denominator polynomial, q(s), yields:

$$e(s)e(-s) = q(s)q(-s) + f(s)f(-s) \tag{2-14.5}$$

If the normalized lowpass Z transformation of these s-domain polynomials are defined by:

$$F(Z) \Leftrightarrow f(s)/s^m \tag{2-14.6}$$

$$Q(Z) \Leftrightarrow q(s)/s^m \tag{2-14.7}$$

$$Z_i^2 = 1 + \left(\frac{\omega i}{s}\right)^2$$

where

$$m = NINF + N \tag{2-14.8}$$

$$NINF = \text{number of attenuation poles at } \infty \tag{2-14.9}$$

$$N = \text{number of finite loss pole freqs} \tag{2-14.10}$$

then the Z transform equivalent of Eq. (2-14.5) becomes:

$$E(Z)E^*(Z) = Q^2(Z) + F^2(Z) \tag{2-14.11}$$

where

$$E(Z) \Leftrightarrow e(s)/s^m \tag{2-14.11a}$$

$$E^*(Z) \Leftrightarrow e(-s)/s^m \tag{2-14.11b}$$

The derivation of $Q^2(Z)$ and $F^2(Z)$ in terms of the Z transformed loss pole frequencies, $Z_i$, is done later and the results brought forward:

$$Q^2(Z) = (1-Z^2)^{NINF} \prod_{i=1}^{N} (Z^2 - Z_i^2)^2 \tag{2-14.12}$$

$$F^2(Z) = \varepsilon^2 (Ev\ A(Z))^2 \tag{2-14.13}$$

$$A(Z) = (Z + 1)^{NINF} \prod_{i=1}^{N} (Z + Z_i)^2 \tag{2-14.14}$$

The program Z transforms the loss pole frequencies using Eq. (2-14.1) then forms E(Z)E*(Z) using Eqs. (2-14.11), (2-14.12), (2-14.13), and (2-14.14). The roots of E(Z)E*(Z) are found using the secant iteration method (described later), and exist as quads, i.e.:

$$(Z+\sigma+j\omega)(Z+\sigma-j\omega)(Z-\sigma+j\omega)(Z-\sigma-j\omega) = Z^4 + pZ^2 + q \qquad (2\text{-}14.15)$$

Equation (2-14.1) may be used in reverse to convert Eq. (2-14.15) to the s-domain equivalent. The right half s plane (RHP) poles are assigned to e(-s), and the LHP poles assigned to e(s). These LHP poles represent the natural modes of the filter, and may be defined by a natural frequency, $\omega_n$, and a quality factor, Q:

$$\omega_n = (1 + p + q)^{\frac{1}{2}} \qquad (2\text{-}14.16)$$

$$Q = \left[2\left\{1 - (1 + \frac{p}{2})(1 + p + q)\right\}\right]^{\frac{1}{2}} \qquad (2\text{-}14.17)$$

The natural frequency and Q represent the program output.

# User Instructions

CARD # 1, CARD # 2

| TRANSFER FUNCTION ZEROS FROM LOSS POLE LOCATIONS | | | | |
|---|---|---|---|---|
| | | | | |
| | | | | START |

| STEP | INSTRUCTIONS | INPUT DATA/UNITS | KEYS | OUTPUT DATA/UNITS |
|---|---|---|---|---|
| | NOTE: This program takes loss pole frequencies stored in registers S4 through S8. Program 2-11 automatically stores the loss pole frequencies in these registers. If the loss pole frequencies are provided by the user, they should be loaded before proceeding. | | | |
| 1 | Load both sides of program card one | | | |
| 2 | Start program execution | | E | flashing display |
| 3 | Insert second card into card reader, this card will be read by the program at the appropriate time. If the card is not inserted, the display will flash when the second card is to be read. | | | |
| 4 | Read both sides of second program card The program execution will automatically resume. If the first program is halted ("R/S" key) when the display flashes, the second program execution may be resumed by depressing key "E" after the second card loading. | | | $\omega_{n_N}$<br>$Q_N$<br>space<br>$\omega_{n_{N-1}}$<br>$Q_{N-1}$<br>⋮<br>⋮<br>$\omega_{n_1}$<br>$Q_1$<br>space<br>$\sigma_0$ (if odd) |

Example 2-14.1

Find the natural modes for the elliptic filter given in Example 2-12.2.

Load Program 2-11 and calculate loss pole frequencies.

```
1.00 ENT↑
 .20   X²     convert 20% reflection coefficient into
       -      passband ripple in dB using:
       LOG        Ap_dB = -10log(1-ρ²)
10.00  x
       CHS
       DSP6
0.177288 ***  Ap_dB, passband ripple in dB
       DSP2
       GSBA
78.00 GSBa    load stopband attenuation reqd, As_dB
 1.00 GSBB    load normalized cutoff frequency
 2.00 GSBb    load normalized minimum stopband frequency
      GSBC    calculate minimum filter order

 5.90  ***    calculated filter order
 6.00  ***    nearest integral filter order

      GSBD    calculate loss pole frequencies
7.235803+00 ***   untransformed even order
2.732051+00 ***   loss pole frequencies
2.061105+00 ***

2.922132+00 ***   Möbius transformed loss pole frequencies
2.129549+00 ***
```

Load this program (Program 2-14) and calculate the natural modes.

```
      GSBE    start E(Z)E*(Z) calculation

0.83278696 ***  ωn1
1.57099957 ***  Q1

1.03809259 ***  ωn2     complex zero locations describing
5.89989189 ***  Q2      natural modes

0.50079327 ***  ωn3
0.62665941 ***  Q3
```

The complex zero locations may be converted from the $\omega_n$ and Q description to real and imaginary parts to enable checking results against elliptic filter tables (see p. 248 of Zverev [58]). Equations (2-9.1), (2-9.2), and (2-9.3) are used for the conversion.

| | | |
|---:|---:|---|
| 1.57099957 | ENT↑ | load $Q_1$ and calculate $\theta_1$ |
| | + | |
| | 1/X | |
| | COS⁻¹ | |
| 71.44174416 | *** | $\theta_1$ (degrees) |
| .83278696 | →R | load $\omega_{n1}$ and calculate real and imag parts |
| 0.26505003 | *** | $\sigma_1$ |
| | X⇄Y | |
| 0.78948249 | *** | $\omega_1$ |
| 5.89989189 | ENT↑ | load $Q_2$ and calculate $\theta_2$ |
| | + | |
| | 1/X | |
| | COS⁻¹ | |
| 85.13850531 | *** | $\theta_2$ (degrees) |
| 1.03805259 | →R | load $\omega_{n_2}$ and calculate real and imag parts |
| 0.08797556 | *** | $\sigma_2$ |
| | X⇄Y | |
| 1.03435603 | *** | $\omega_2$ |
| .62665941 | ENT↑ | load $Q_3$ and calculate $\theta_3$ |
| | + | |
| | 1/X | |
| | COS⁻¹ | |
| 37.07171837 | *** | $\theta_3$ (degrees) |
| .50079327 | →R | load $\omega_{n3}$ and calculate real and imag parts |
| 0.39957373 | *** | $\sigma_3$ |
| | X⇄Y | |
| 0.30188530 | *** | $\omega_3$ |

## Derivation of Equations Used

The characteristic function, K(s), is a ratio of polynomials as indicated by Eqs. (2-14.4) and (2-12.3). The denominator of this function is already known in terms of the loss pole frequencies. In low-pass form, this polynomial is:

$$q(s) = \prod_{i=1}^{N} (s^2 + \omega_i^2) \tag{2-14.18}$$

H(s), the filter transfer function, is described in terms of the polynomials of the characteristic function by Eqs. (2-14.2) and (2-14.5). Since H(s) describes a realizable transfer function, the zeros of H(s) must lie in the LHP. With this condition in mind, the LHP zeros of e(s) e(-s) are assigned to e(s) and the RHP zeros assigned to e(-s). This root splitting brings us to the concept of a quad. Assume that e(s) is represented by complex conjugate root pairs and a real root if e(s) is odd, i.e.,

$$e(s) = (s + \sigma_o) \prod_{i=1}^{N} \left\{ s^2 + s(2\sigma_i) + \sigma_i^2 + \omega_i^2 \right\} \tag{2-14.19}$$

Then the right half s-plane roots are represented by e(-s):

$$e(-s) = (-s + \sigma_o) \prod_{i=1}^{N} \left\{ s^2 - s(2\sigma_i) + \sigma_i^2 + \omega_i^2 \right\} \tag{2-14.20}$$

hence:

$$e(s)\ e(-s) = (-s^2 + \sigma_o^2) \prod_{i=1}^{N} \left\{ s^4 + s^2\ 2(\omega_i^2 - \sigma_i^2) + (\omega_i^2 + \sigma_i^2)^2 \right\} \tag{2-14.21}$$

This concept is illustrated in Fig. 2-14.1.

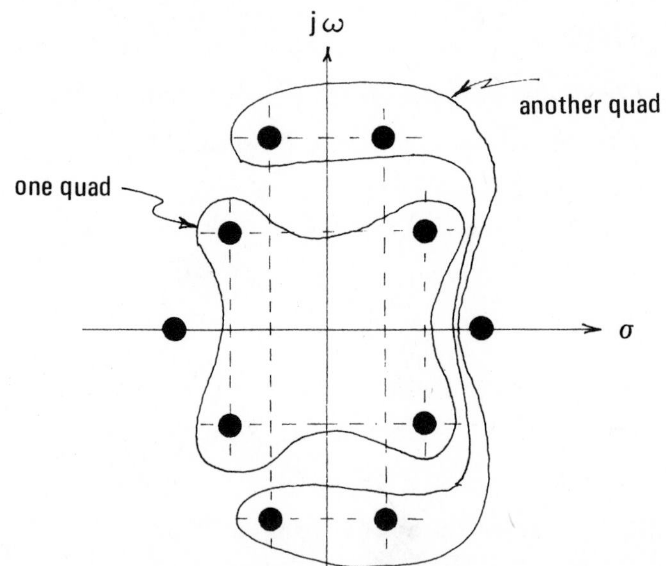


Figure 2-14.1 Concept of a quad.

The importance of this concept is once one root of e(s) e(-s) is found, three other roots of the quad are also defined, and may be removed to reduce the order of e(s) e(-s) by four.

The Characteristic Function in Terms of the Transformed Variable

The actual finding of the polynomials of H(s) is done in the Z-plane rather than the s-plane for two reasons: 1) The solution is numerically more accurate because the roots are spread out and the small difference between big numbers problem is much reduced. 2) The expressions for $F^2(Z)$ and $Q^2(Z)$ are much simpler in terms of the transformed loss pole frequencies than are $f^2(s)$ and $q^2(s)$ in terms of the actual loss pole frequencies, $\omega_i$. These transformations are defined as follows:

$$F(Z) \Leftrightarrow \frac{f(s)}{(s^2 + \omega_a^2)^{m/2}} \tag{2-14.22}$$

$$Q(Z) \Leftrightarrow \frac{q(s)}{(s^2 + \omega_a^2)^{m/2}} \tag{2-14.23}$$

where

$$Z^2 = \frac{s^2 + \omega_b^2}{s^2 + \omega_a^2} \tag{2-14.24}$$

and

$$m = NZERO + NINF + N \tag{2-14.25}$$

$$NZERO = \text{number of attenuation poles at dc (equals zero for lowpass filters)} \tag{2-14.26}$$

$$NINF = \text{number of attenuation poles at infinity} \tag{2-14.9}$$

$$N = \text{number of finite loss pole frequencies} \tag{2-14.10}$$

In the normalized lowpass case, the lower bandedge transformation frequency, $\omega_a$ is dc ($\omega_a = 0$), and the upper bandedge transformation frequency, $\omega_b$, is unity. Under these conditions the Z transformation becomes:

$$F(Z) \Leftrightarrow \frac{f(s)}{s^m} \tag{2-14.6}$$

$$Q(Z) \Leftrightarrow \frac{q(s)}{s^m} \tag{2-14.7}$$

with

$$Z^2 = 1 + 1/s^2, \text{ or for } s = j\omega,\ Z^2 = 1 - 1/\omega^2$$

The lowpass form of q(s) is given by Eq. (2-14.18):

$$q(s) = \prod_{i=1}^{N} (s^2 + \omega_i^2)$$

The Z transformed equivalent is:

$$Q(Z) \Leftrightarrow \frac{1}{s^m} \prod_{i=1}^{N} (s^2 + \omega_i^2) \tag{2-14.27}$$

$$= \frac{1}{s^{NINF}} \prod_{i=1}^{N} \left(\frac{s^2 + \omega_i^2}{s^2}\right) \tag{2-14.28}$$

The filter poles can be found from the zeros of the attenuation function, Eq. (2-13.5), i.e.,

$$1 + \frac{\varepsilon^2}{4}\left\{ L(Z) + \frac{(-1)^{NINF}}{L(Z)} \right\}^2 = 0 \qquad (2\text{-}14.29)$$

where L(Z) is defined by Eq. (2-13.4):

$$L(Z) = \left\{ \frac{Z+1}{Z-1} \right\}^{\frac{NINF}{2}} \cdot \prod_{i=1}^{N} \frac{Z + Z_i}{Z - Z_i} \qquad (2\text{-}13.4)$$

then Q(Z), as defined by Eq. (2-14.28), is the common denominator for Eq. (2-14.29). The quantity inside the brackets of Eq. (2-14.29) can be written in terms of Q(Z) and A(Z) (Eq. (2-14.14)) as follows:

$$L(Z) + \frac{(-1)^{NINF}}{L(Z)} = \frac{A(Z) + (-1)^{NINF} \cdot A(-Z)}{Q(Z)} \qquad (2\text{-}14.30)$$

Fortunately, the sign of $(-1)^{NINF}$ causes the numerator to be an even polynomial in Z as is required for the resulting polynomials of the Chebyshev rational function to be Hurwitz.

Thus, the equation whose zeros are to be found is:

$$1 + \frac{\varepsilon^2}{4}\left\{ \frac{A(Z) + (-1)^{NINF} \cdot A(-Z)}{Q(Z)} \right\}^2 = 0 \qquad (2\text{-}14.31)$$

Because of the even numerator polynomial, Eq. (2-14.31) becomes:

$$1 + \frac{\varepsilon^2}{4}\left\{ \frac{2 \cdot Ev\,(A(Z))}{Q(Z)} \right\}^2 = 0 \qquad (2\text{-}14.32)$$

Cancelling out constants and placing the entire expression over a common denominator yields:

$$Q^2(Z) + \varepsilon^2 \left\{ Ev\ A(Z) \right\}^2 = 0 \qquad (2\text{-}14.33)$$

Substituting F(Z) from Eq. (2-14.13) results the desired expression for the transfer function zeros:

$$Q^2(Z) + F^2(Z) = 0 \qquad (2\text{-}14.34)$$

<u>Secant iteration method</u>

The secant iterative method finds the values for the variable, x, where the function f(x) = 0 (zeros of x). It is similar to the

Newton-Raphson method except the derivative of the function is numerically approximated from the present and past values of f(x):

$$x_{i+1} = x_i - f(x_i)\left\{\frac{x_i - x_{i-1}}{f(x_i) - f(x_{i-1})}\right\} \qquad (2\text{-}14.35)$$

where $x_i$ is the present estimate for the variable.

The iteration is continued until the correction term magnitude becomes smaller than a given error radius. For this program, that error radius is chosen to be $10^{-9}$.

Two values for x are needed to start the secant iteration, a past value and a present value. In this program, the past value is chosen as 0 and the present value as 1460°. As the iteration starts, the method may not converge, but may get sent far away from the desired solution. This can happen if the present and past estimates lie on opposite sides of a saddle (see Fig. 2-14.3). To help force convergence, the magnitude of the correction radius is limited to 0.1. When the iteration starts, the estimates have a random nature, but can't get far away from the origin. As a zero is approached, the method rapidly converges.

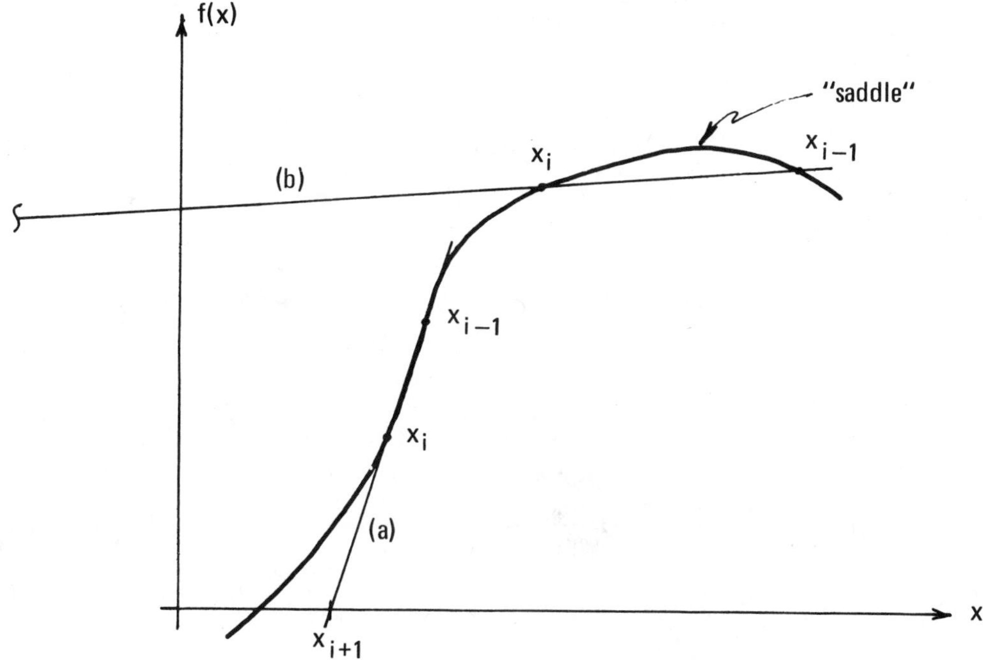


Figure 2-14.3 Secant method, two cases a) normal convergence, and b) divergence caused by the presence of a "saddle" in the function.

Figure 2-14.3 shows a two dimensional representation of the method, but in the present instance, the application is three dimensional because of the complex nature of the variable. As each complex zero is found, three others are defined automatically because of the quadrangle symmetry (quads) in the zeros of the filter transfer function (see Fig. 2-14.1), thus the order of the equation may be reduced by four through polynomial division. If the filter order is odd, a real zero exists in the transfer function. After all quads have been removed from the transfer function, the remainder will be the real zero. This technique is used herein, zeros are removed from $E(Z)E^*(Z)$ until a second order polynomial or less remains. If the filter order is even, no remainder exists, but if the filter order is odd, the second order remainder represents the LHP and RHP parts of the real zero. The RHP zero is discarded since it belongs to $H(-s)$, and the LHP zero location is transformed back to the s-domain for output.

2–14, CARD 1

# Program Listing I

ALGORITHM TO FORM $E(Z)E^*(Z)$ FROM $F^2(Z) + Q^2(Z)$

| Step | Key | Comments |
|---|---|---|
| 001 | *LBLE | START |
| 002 | RCLI | store index number of |
| 003 | STOB | highest register w/ coefs |
| 004 | RCL0 | |
| 005 | EEX | |
| 006 | 1 | calculate $\epsilon^2$: |
| 007 | ÷ | |
| 008 | $10^x$ | $\epsilon^2 = 10^{0.1\epsilon dB} - 1$ |
| 009 | EEX | |
| 010 | − | |
| 011 | RCLD | |
| 012 | + | store NINF + $\epsilon^2$ |
| 013 | STOD | |
| 014 | 1 | |
| 015 | 3 | initialize index register |
| 016 | STOI | |
| 017 | *LBL0 | Z transform loss pole freqs |
| 018 | ISZI | |
| 019 | EEX | |
| 020 | RCLi | $Z_i^2 = 1 - 1/\omega_i^2$ |
| 021 | $X^2$ | |
| 022 | 1/X | |
| 023 | − | |
| 024 | STOi | |
| 025 | RCLI | |
| 026 | RCLB | test for loop exit |
| 027 | X≠Y? | |
| 028 | GTO0 | |
| 029 | RCLD | set flag 2 if NINF = 2 |
| 030 | INT | |
| 031 | 2 | |
| 032 | CF0 | |
| 033 | X=Y? | |
| 034 | SF0 | |
| 035 | EEX | start $Q^2(Z)$ calculation: |
| 036 | STOA | |
| 037 | CHS | |
| 038 | STOC | form and store $(1 - Z^2)^{NINF}$ |
| 039 | F0? | |
| 040 | CHS | for NINF = 1 or 2 |
| 041 | STO1 | |
| 042 | CHS | |
| 043 | STO0 | |
| 044 | F0? | |
| 045 | GSB9 | |
| 046 | 1 | |
| 047 | 3 | initialize index register |
| 048 | STOI | |
| 049 | *LBL1 | $Q^2(Z)$ calculation loop |
| 050 | ISZI | |
| 051 | RCLi | |
| 052 | CHS | $Q^2(Z) = (1-Z^2)^{NINF} \prod_{i=1}^{N} (Z^2 - Z_i^2)^2$ |
| 053 | STOC | |
| 054 | GSB9 | |
| 055 | GSB9 | $-Z_i^2 \rightarrow R_C$ |
| 056 | RCLI | |
| 057 | RCLB | |
| 058 | X≠Y? | test for loop exit |
| 059 | GTO1 | |
| 060 | CLX | start A(Z) calculation |
| 061 | STOA | |
| 062 | 3 | initialize index register |
| 063 | STOI | |
| 064 | P⇄S | place $Q^2(Z)$ in secondary regs |
| 065 | EEX | initialize polynomial |
| 066 | STO0 | product registers |
| 067 | RCLB | |
| 068 | EEX | reduce highest loss pole |
| 069 | 1 | register number by 10 to |
| 070 | − | reflect P⇄S of registers |
| 071 | STOB | |
| 072 | *LBL2 | A(Z) calculation loop start |
| 073 | ISZI | |
| 074 | RCLi | $A(Z) = (Z+1)^{NINF} \prod_{i=1}^{N} (Z+Z_i)^2$ |
| 075 | √X | |
| 076 | STOC | $Z_i \rightarrow R_C$ |
| 077 | GSB9 | multiply existing polynomial |
| 078 | GSB9 | product by $(Z + Z_i)^2$ |
| 079 | RCLI | |
| 080 | RCLB | test for loop exit |
| 081 | X≠Y? | |
| 082 | GTO2 | |
| 083 | EEX | setup to form $(Z + 1)^{NINF}$ |
| 084 | STOC | |
| 085 | GSB9 | multiply existing polynomial |
| 086 | F0? | by $(Z + 1)^{NINF}$, (NINF = 1 or 2) |
| 087 | GSB9 | |
| 088 | EEX | calculate highest register |
| 089 | RCLB | number containing polynomial |
| 090 | RCLB | coefficients: |
| 091 | + | |
| 092 | 5 | 2B + 10 + F0 → RB |
| 093 | + | |
| 094 | F0? | |
| 095 | + | |
| 096 | STOB | |
| 097 | STOI | initialize index register |
| 098 | *LBL3 | |
| 099 | ISZI | clear registers not contain- |
| 100 | CLX | ing polynomial coefficients |
| 101 | STOi | |
| 102 | P⇄S | |
| 103 | STOi | |
| 104 | P⇄S | |
| 105 | RCLI | |
| 106 | 1 | |
| 107 | 9 | test for loop exit |
| 108 | X≠Y? | |
| 109 | GTO3 | |
| 110 | RCL0 | form (Ev A(Z))$^2$: |
| 111 | RCL2 | |
| 112 | × | |

REGISTERS

| 0 | 1 | 2 | 3 | 4 | 5 | 6 | 7 | 8 | 9 |
|---|---|---|---|---|---|---|---|---|---|
| $Q_0, A_0, A_0$ | $Q_1, A_1, A_2$ | $Q_2, A_2, A_4$ | $Q_3, A_3, A_6$ | $Q_4, A_4, A_8$ | $Q_5, A_5, A_{10}$ | $Q_6, A_6, A_{12}$ | $Q_7, A_7, A_{14}$ | $Q_8, A_8, A_{16}$ | $Q_9, A_9, A_{18}$ |

| S0 | S1 | S2 | S3 | S4 | S5 | S6 | S7 | S8 | S9 |
|---|---|---|---|---|---|---|---|---|---|
| $Q_0, F_0$ | $Q_1, F_1$ | $Q_2, F_2$ | $Q_3, F_3$ | $Q_4, F_4, Z_1$ | $Q_5, F_5, Z_2$ | $Q_6, F_6, Z_3$ | $Q_7, F_7, Z_4$ | $Q_8, F_8$ | $Q_9, F_9$ |

| A | B | C | D | E | I |
|---|---|---|---|---|---|
| Q & F index | highest reg. number used | $Z_i^2$ | $\epsilon^2$ + NINF | Z index | index |

# Program Listing II

```
STOI    
ST+1     A2' = 2A0A2
-----------------------------------------------
RCL0     (NOTE: the primed coefs
RCL6      represent the coefs of
x         A^2(Z). After this part
RCL2      of the program is done
RCL4      the coefficients of
x         A^2(Z) have replaced the
+         coeffients of A(Z).)
STO3
ST+3     A6' = 2(A0A6 + A2A4)
-----------------------------------------------
RCL2
RCL8
x
RCL4     A10' = 2(A2A8 + A4A6)
RCL6
x
+
STO5
ST+5
-----------------------------------------------
RCL6
RCL8
x        A14' = 2A6A8
STO7
ST+7
-----------------------------------------------
6
STOI     initialize index register
-----------------------------------------------
RCL8
STx8     A16' = A8^2
-----------------------------------------------
RCL4
x        A12' = A6^2 + 2A4A8
GSB7
-----------------------------------------------
RCL2
x
RCL8
√X       A8' = A4^2 + 2(A2A6 + A0A8)
RCL0
x
+
GSB7
-----------------------------------------------
RCL0
x        A4' = A2^2 + 2A0A4
GSB7
-----------------------------------------------
RCL0     A0' = A0^2
STx0
-----------------------------------------------
RCLD     recall ε^2
FRC
-----------------------------------------------
STx0
STx1     form F^2(Z) = ε^2(Ev(A(Z)))^2
STx2
STx3
STx4
STx5
STx6
STx7
STx8
```

```
9        initialize index register
STOI
-----------------------------------------------
*LBL4
DSZI     form E(Z)E*(Z)
SF2
RCLi     E(Z)E*(Z) = Q^2(Z) + F^2(Z)
P⇄S
ST+i
P⇄S
F2?
GTO4     test for loop exit
-----------------------------------------------
*LBL5
PSE      wait loop for 2nd card read
GTO5
-----------------------------------------------
*LBL7    A^2(Z) calculation subr
RCLi     forms:
STxi
R↓       R(i)^2 + 2(Rx), and returns
ST+i
ST+i     R(i) → Rx
R↑
DSZI
DSZI
RTN
RTN
-----------------------------------------------
*LBL9    polynomial multiplication
SF2      flag 2 indicates 1st time
-----------------------------------------------
RCLA     initialize index register
X⇄I      with Q or F index
-----------------------------------------------
STOE     save existing index
-----------------------------------------------
*LBL8    polynomial mult loop
RCLi
ISZI
RCLC     a_(k+1) = C·a_(k+1) + a_k
F2?
CLX          C = 0 for k = n
STxi
R↓
ST+i
-----------------------------------------------
CF1      decrement I register, and
DSZI     set flag 1 if I = 0
SF1
-----------------------------------------------
DSZI     decrement I register
-----------------------------------------------
F1?      test for loop exit
GTO8
-----------------------------------------------
RCLC     finish poly multiplication
STx0     ao = C·ao
-----------------------------------------------
RCLE     restore pre-existing index
STOI
-----------------------------------------------
RCLA     increment F or Q index
EEX
+
STOA
-----------------------------------------------
RTN      return to main program
```

| LABELS | | | | | FLAGS |
|---|---|---|---|---|---|
| A | B | C | D | E START | 0 NINF = 2 |
| a | b | c | d | e | 1 |
| 0 $Z_i$ calc | 1 $Q^2(Z)$ | 2 A(Z) | 3 clear unused reg | 4 E(Z)E*(Z) | 2 I = ∅ |
| 5 wait loop | 6 | 7 $F^2(Z)$ subr | 8 poly multiply | 9 poly multiply | 3 |

| SET STATUS | | | | |
|---|---|---|---|---|
| FLAGS | ON | OFF | TRIG | DISP |
| 0 | | ■ | DEG | FIX ■ |
| 1 | | | GRAD | |
| 2 | | ■ | RAD | |
| 3 | | | | n 2 |

# Program Listing I

SECANT ITERATION TO FIND ROOTS OF E(Z)E*(Z)

```
001  *LBLE   START SECANT ITERATION
002    EEX
003    CHS   set correction radius for
004      9   loop exit
005   STOE
006  *LBLe   secant outer loop start
007    CLX
008   STO0   set Z0 = 0 + j0
009   STO1
010   STO5
011    P⇄S
012   RCL0   set F(Z0) = E0 + j0
013    P⇄S
014   STO4
015      6   set Z1 = 1∠60°
016      0
017   ENT↑
018    EEX
019     →R
020   STO2
021    X⇄Y
022   STO3
023  *LBL0   prepare for polynomial
024   RCL2   evaluation:
025   RCL3
026      ×   form Z^2 = (σ - jω)^2;
027   ENT↑
028      +
029   STOD   Im(Z^2) = 2σω → RD → R7
030   STO7
031   RCL2
032     X²
033   RCL3   Re(Z^2) = σ^2 - ω^2 → RC → R6
034     X²
035      -
036   STOC
037   STO6
038   RCLB   set index to highest register
039   STOI   number that has coefficients
040   RCLi   start polynomial evaluation
041   ST×6   by forming E2n·Z^2
042   ST×7
043  *LBL1   polynomial eval loop start,
044   DSZI   decrement register index
045   RCLi   recall E2k
046   ST+6   add to calculation real part
047   RCLI
048    EEX   test for loop exit
049      1
050   X=Y?
051   GTO2
052   RCL6   perform complex multiply
053   RCLC   by Z^2 on the ongoing
054      ×   calculation
055   RCL7
056   RCLD   continue complex multiply
057      ×   (a + jb)(Re(Z^2) + jIm(Z^2)) =
058      -   a·Re(Z^2) - b·Im(Z^2) +
059   RCL6   j(a·Im(Z^2) + b·Re(Z^2))
060   RCLD
061      ×
062   RCL7
063   RCLC
064      ×
065      +
066   STO7
067     R↓
068   STO6
069   GTO1
070  *LBL2   form Z estimate correction:
071   RCL7
072   RCL6   ΔZk = F(Zk)[(Zk - Zk-1)/(F(Zk) - F(Zk-1))]
073     →P
074   STO8
075    X⇄Y
076   STO9
077   RCL3
078   RCL1
079      -
080   RCL2
081   RCL0
082      -
083     →P
084   ST×8
085    X⇄Y
086   ST+9
087   RCL7
088   RCL5
089      -
090   RCL6
091   RCL4
092      -
093     →P
094   X=0?   escape if F(Zk)-F(Zk-1) = 0
095   GTO3
096   ST÷8   finish ΔZk calculation
097    X⇄Y
098   ST-9
099   RCL7   shift register contents,
100   STO5   Zk becomes Zk-1, and
101   RCL6   F(Zk) becomes F(Zk-1) for
102   STO4   the next iteration
103   RCL3
104   STO1
105   RCL2
106   STO0
107   RCL8   recall |ΔZk|
108      .   limit |ΔZk| to 0.1 to help
109      1   ensure convergence
110   X>Y?
```

Branch annotations: GTO e, GTO 0, GTO 1, GTO 2, GTO 3

**REGISTERS**

| 0 | 1 | 2 | 3 | 4 | 5 | 6 | 7 | 8 | 9 |
|---|---|---|---|---|---|---|---|---|---|
| Re $Z_{k-1}$ | Im $Z_{k-1}$ | Re $Z_k$ | Im $Z_k$ | ReF($Z_{k-1}$) | ImF($Z_{k-1}$) | ReF($Z_k$) | ImF($Z_k$) | scratch | scratch |
| S0 $E_0$ | S1 $E_2$ | S2 $E_4$ | S3 $E_6$ | S4 $E_8$ | S5 $E_{10}$ | S6 $E_{12}$ | S7 $E_{14}$ | S8 $E_{16}$ | S9 $E_{18}$ |

| A | B | C | D | E | I |
|---|---|---|---|---|---|
| | highest register # | Re($Z_k^2$) | Im($Z_k^2$) | error radius for loop exit | index |

# Program Listing II

| Step | Key | Comment |
|---|---|---|
| 111 | R↓ | |
| 112 | RCL9 | apply Z correction: |
| 113 | X⇄Y | |
| 114 | →R | $Z_{k+1} = Z_k - \Delta Z$ |
| 115 | ST−2 | |
| 116 | X⇄Y | |
| 117 | ST−3 | |
| 118 | RCL8 | |
| 119 | RCLE | |
| 120 | X≤Y? | test for loop exit |
| 121 | GTO0 | |
| 122 | *LBL3 | Z factor output and |
| 123 | RCL3 | polynomial deflation by |
| 124 | X² | degree 4, i.e., the quad is: |
| 125 | RCL2 | |
| 126 | X² | $z^4 + pz^2 + q$ |
| 127 | − | |
| 128 | ENT↑ | $p = 2\left((\text{Im } Z_i)^2 - (\text{Re } Z_i)^2\right)$ |
| 129 | + | |
| 130 | STOC | p → RC |
| 131 | RCL3 | |
| 132 | X² | |
| 133 | RCL2 | |
| 134 | X² | $q = \left((\text{Im } Z_i)^2 + (\text{Re } Z_i)^2\right)^2$ |
| 135 | + | |
| 136 | X² | |
| 137 | STOD | q → RD |
| 138 | + | calculate and output the |
| 139 | EEX | s-plane LHP complex-conjugate |
| 140 | + | pole pair natural frequency: |
| 141 | √X | |
| 142 | 1/X | $\omega_n = (1 + p + q)^{-\frac{1}{4}}$ |
| 143 | √X | |
| 144 | PRTX | |
| 145 | EEX | calculate and output pole |
| 146 | LSTX | pair "Q": |
| 147 | RCLC | |
| 148 | 2 | |
| 149 | ÷ | |
| 150 | EEX | |
| 151 | + | $Q^2 = \left(2\left(1-(1+p/2)(1+p+q)\right)\right)^{-1}$ |
| 152 | × | |
| 153 | − | |
| 154 | ENT↑ | |
| 155 | + | |
| 156 | 1/X | |
| 157 | √X | |
| 158 | PRTX | print Q |
| 159 | SPC | |
| 160 | RCLB | set index to highest register |
| 161 | STOI | number that has coefficients |
| 162 | *LBL5 | polynomial deflation loop |
| 163 | RCLi | |
| 164 | RCLC | |
| 165 | × | |
| 166 | ISZI | let the primed values |
| 167 | RCLi | represent the coeffic- |
| 168 | RCLD | ients of the deflated |
| 169 | × | polynomial: |
| 170 | + | |
| 171 | DSZI | $E'_k = E_k - pE'_{k+2} - qE'_{k+4}$ |
| 172 | DSZI | |
| 173 | ST−i | |
| 174 | RCLI | |
| 175 | 1 | |
| 176 | 3 | test for loop exit |
| 177 | X≤Y? | |
| 178 | GTO5 | |
| 179 | *LBL6 | move coefficients down two |
| 180 | RCLi | register numbers in storage |
| 181 | DSZI | so $E_0$ resides in register $S_0$ |
| 182 | DSZI | |
| 183 | STOi | |
| 184 | ISZI | |
| 185 | ISZI | |
| 186 | ISZI | |
| 187 | RCLB | |
| 188 | RCLI | test for loop exit |
| 189 | X≤Y? | |
| 190 | GTO6 | |
| 191 | DSZI | |
| 192 | CLX | |
| 193 | STOi | clear top two registers. |
| 194 | DSZI | |
| 195 | STOi | |
| 196 | DSZI | |
| 197 | RCLI | store index number of highest |
| 198 | STOB | register containing coefs |
| 199 | 1 | |
| 200 | 2 | |
| 201 | X≤Y? | test for outer loop exit |
| 202 | GTOe | |
| 203 | EEX | |
| 204 | 1 | if filter order is even, |
| 205 | RCLI | exit loop here |
| 206 | X≤Y? | |
| 207 | RTN | |
| 208 | RCLi | calculate real pole location |
| 209 | DSZI | in s-plane for odd ordered |
| 210 | RCLi | filter |
| 211 | X⇄Y | |
| 212 | ÷ | |
| 213 | ABS | $\lvert\sigma_0\rvert = (E_2/E_0 - 1)^{-\frac{1}{2}}$ |
| 214 | EEX | |
| 215 | − | |
| 216 | √X | |
| 217 | 1/X | |
| 218 | PRTX | |
| 219 | SPC | |
| 220 | RTN | |

Branch annotations (left margins): GTO e, GTO 0, GTO 3, GTO 6, GTO e, GTO 5.

| LABELS | | | | | FLAGS |
|---|---|---|---|---|---|
| A | B | C | D | E START | 0 |
| a | b | c | d | e main loop start | 1 |
| 0 poly eval | 1 poly eval | 2 ΔZ calc | 3 factor output | 4 | 2 |
| 5 poly deflate | 6 coef reorder | 7 | 8 | 9 | 3 |

| SET STATUS | | |
|---|---|---|
| FLAGS (ON OFF) | TRIG | DISP |
| 0 | DEG | FIX ■ |
| 1 | GRAD | SCI |
| 2 | RAD | ENG |
| 3 | | n 8 |

## PROGRAM 2-15 DARLINGTON'S ELLIPTIC FILTER ALGORITHMS.

Program Description and Equations Used

This program calculates the normalized transmission function pole and zero locations, and minimum stopband rejection for odd order elliptic filters. The program is based on Professor Sidney Darlington's paper which describes simple elliptic filter algorithms using transformations on elliptic sines and their moduli [18], and his unpublished HP-65 program on the same subject.

The output data is normalized to the passband cutoff frequency ($f_p$), however, the algorithm is normalized to the geometric mean of the passband and stopband edge frequencies as shown by Fig. 2-15.1.

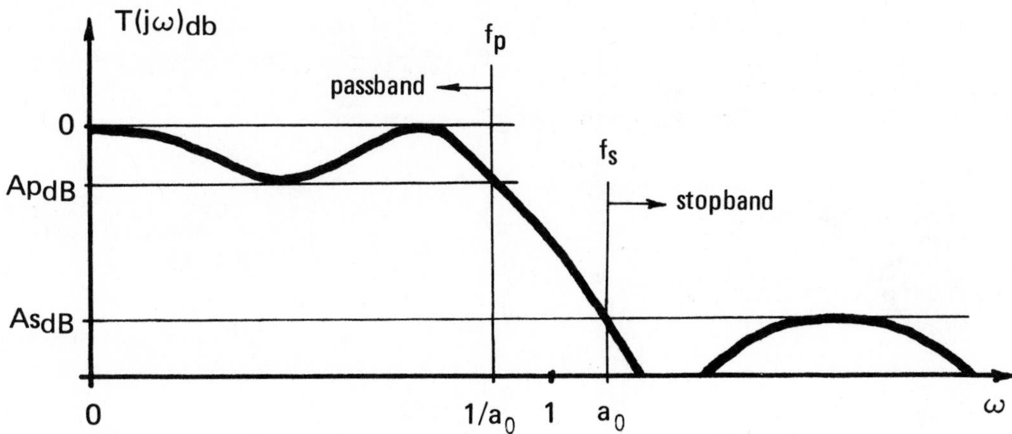


Figure 2-15.1 Definition of elliptic filter terms.

Thus, the transition ratio, $\lambda$ , becomes:

$$\lambda = \frac{f_s}{f_p} = \frac{a_0}{1/a_0} = a_0^{\;2} \tag{2-15.1}$$

or

$$a_0 = \sqrt{\lambda} \tag{2-15.2}$$

The filter transmission function, T(s), is the reciprocal of the filter transfer function, H(s), which is related to the filter characteristic function, K(s), through the Feldtkeller equation:

$$|T(j\omega)|^2 = \frac{\text{power out}}{\text{power in}} = \left|\frac{1}{H(j\omega)}\right|^2 = \frac{1}{1+\varepsilon^2|K(j\omega)|^2} \tag{2-15.3}$$

where the characteristic function is the Chebyshev rational function described in Program 2-12. Darlington's algorithms are a very elegant way of approximating the Chebyshev rational function using simple recursive relationships. These relationships can also be used to find the LHP poles and zeros of:

$$T(s)T(-s) = \frac{1}{1+\varepsilon^2 K(s)K(-s)} \tag{2-15.4}$$

<u>Normalized transmission zero frequencies.</u> If Yo represents geometrically normalized frequency (Fig. 2-15.1) and $Y_{0k}$ $(k = 1, 2, \ldots, \frac{n-1}{2})$ represents the normalized transmission zero frequencies where n is the filter order, then the characteristic function for odd order, equiripple passband, lowpass filters is given by:

$$|K(Y_0)|^2 = |J_0 \cdot F_o(Y_0)|^2 \tag{2-15.5}$$

where Jo is a constant and

$$F_o(Y_0) = Y_0 \prod_{k=1}^{(n-1)/2} \frac{1 - Y_{0k}^2 Y_0^2}{Y_0^2 - Y_{0k}^2} \tag{2-15.6}$$

For the elliptic filter case (equal ripple passband and stopband):

$$\varepsilon^2 = 10^{0.1Ap_{dB}} - 1 \tag{2-15.7}$$

$$J_0 = F_o(a_0) \tag{2-15.8}$$

$$F_o\left(\frac{1}{Y_0}\right) = \frac{1}{F_o(Y_0)} \tag{2-15.9}$$

These quantities and $Y_{0k}$ may be found through recursive use of a variable transformation which spreads out the transition interval.

Let

$$a_{k+1} = a_k^{\,2} + \sqrt{a_k^{\,4} - 1} \qquad (2\text{-}15.10)$$

then, given $a_0$ as defined by Eq. (2-15.2), find and store $a_1$, $a_2$, $a_3$, and $a_4$. Four applications of the recursion formula will provide precision which will be calculator limited rather than algorithm limited (see p. 37 of [18]).

Let h represent the index for the transmission zero frequencies; h = 1, 2, ... , (n-1)/2, then let

$$Y_{4h} = \frac{a_4}{\cos\{\,(2h-1)(90/n)\,\}} \qquad (2\text{-}15.11)$$

and recursively calculate:

$$Y_{(k-1)h} = \frac{1}{2a_k}\,(Y_{kh} - 1/Y_{kh}) \qquad (2\text{-}15.12)$$

$$k = 4,\ 3,\ 2,\ 1$$

The transmission zero frequencies normalized with respect to the passband edge are:

$$a_o \cdot Y_{0h} \qquad (2\text{-}15.13)$$

<u>Minimum stopband rejection.</u> The minimum stopband rejection for elliptic filters first occurs at the stopband frequency edge (geometrically normalized frequency $a_o$) and may be found from Jo and Eqs. (2-15.4), (2-15.5), and (2-15.8 ), i.e.:

$$As_{dB} = 10 \log\,(1 + \varepsilon^2 J_0^{\,2} J_0^{\,2}) \qquad (2\text{-}15.14)$$

Jo is found from another recursion relationship; let

$$J_4 \cong 2^{n-1} \cdot\ a_4^{\,n} = \frac{(2 \cdot a_4)^n}{2} \qquad (2\text{-}15.15)$$

then recursively calculate and store $J_k$'s using:

$$J_{k-1} = \tfrac{1}{2}\sqrt{(J_k - 1/J_k)} \qquad (2\text{-}15.16)$$

$$k = 4,\ 3,\ 2,\ 1$$

Transmission function pole locations. Let $s_{oh}$ represent the complex pole location, and let

$$J_o \cdot s_{oo} = 1/\varepsilon \tag{2-15.17}$$

Then recursively calculate:

$$s_{(k+1)o} = J_k \cdot s_{ko} + \sqrt{(J_k \cdot s_{ko})^2 + 1} \tag{2-15.18}$$

$$k = 0,\ 1,\ 2$$

As the index increases, the terms $J_k \cdot s_{ko}$ become numerically very large since the $J_k$'s increase nearly geometrically for $J_k$ large. To avoid numeric overflow ($10^{99}$) use:

$$s_{40} \cong 2 \cdot J_3 \cdot s_{30} \tag{2-15.19}$$

Calculate and store:

$$s_{50} = \left\{ \frac{J_4}{s_{40}} + \sqrt{\left(\frac{J_4}{s_{40}}\right)^2 + 1} \right\}^{\frac{1}{n}} \tag{2-15.20}$$

To calculate the pole locations, let:

$$s_{5h} = s_{50} \cdot e^{jh(\pi/n)} \tag{2-15.21}$$

$$h = 0,\ 1,\ 2,\ \ldots,\ (n-1)/2$$

Using complex arithmetic, recursively calculate:

$$s_{(k-1)h} = \frac{1}{2.a_{k-1}}(s_{kh} - 1/s_{kh}) \tag{2-15.22}$$

$$k = 5,\ 4,\ 3,\ 2,\ 1$$

The pole locations normalized to the passband edge are given by:

$$s_{oh} \cdot a_o \tag{2-15.23}$$

The subroutine that calculates Eq. (2-15.22) may seem obscure to some readers. The particular coding that is used minimizes the amount of data that must undergo polar-to-rectangular and rectangular-to-polar conversions, and hence, maximizes the numerical accuracy of the routine. The normal format for the pole locations is polar as given by Eq. (2-15.21). In general, let:

$$s_{kh} = \rho_{kh} \cdot e^{j\beta_{kh}} \tag{2-15.24}$$

In rectangular format, Eq. (2-15.24) becomes:

$$s_{kh} = \rho_{kh} \cos \beta_{kh} + j\, \rho_{kh} \sin \beta_{kh} \qquad (2\text{-}15.25)$$

For the reciprocal case, let:

$$\frac{1}{s_{kh}} = \frac{1}{\rho_{kh}}\, e^{-j\beta_{kh}} \qquad (2\text{-}15.26)$$

which using rectangular format becomes:

$$\frac{1}{s_{kh}} = \frac{1}{\rho_{kh}} \cos \beta_{kh} - j\,\frac{1}{\rho_{kh}} \sin \beta_{kh} \qquad (2\text{-}15.27)$$

hence,

$$s_{kh} - \frac{1}{s_{kh}} = \left(\rho_{kh} + \frac{1}{\rho_{kh}}\right) \cos \beta_{kh} + j\left(\rho_{kh} - \frac{1}{\rho_{kh}}\right) \sin \beta_{kh} \qquad (2\text{-}15.28)$$

or,

$$s_{kh} - \frac{1}{s_{kh}} = \left(1 + \frac{1}{\rho_{kh}^2}\right) \rho_{kh} \cos \beta_{kh} + j\left(1 - \frac{1}{\rho_{kh}^2}\right) \rho_{kh} \cdot \sin \beta_{kh} \qquad (2\text{-}15.29)$$

In Eq. (2-15.29), the terms $\rho_{kh} \cos \beta_{kh}$ and $\rho_{kh} \sin \beta_{kh}$ are the output components of a polar-to-rectangular conversion, and $\rho_{kh}$ is saved in the last x register, and has not undergone any conversion. The stack is used to hold the intermediate parts of Eq. (2-15.29). A rectangular-to-polar conversion then completes the subroutine.

# User Instructions

| DARLINGTON'S ELLIPTIC FILTER ALGORITHMS | | | | |
|---|---|---|---|---|
| load +$Ap_{dB}$, or $-\rho$ | load $\lambda = f_s/f_p$ | load filter order (odd only) | calculate xmsn zero freqs & min loss | print ? / calculate pole locations |

| STEP | INSTRUCTIONS | INPUT DATA/UNITS | KEYS | OUTPUT DATA/UNITS |
|---|---|---|---|---|
| 1 | Load both sides of program card | | | |
| 2 | Select print or R/S option (toggle) | | f E | 0 (R/S) |
| | | | f E | 1 (print) |
| | | | f E | 0 (R/S) |
| | | | | ⋮ |
| 3 | Load passband ripple in dB or | $Ap_{dB}$ | A | $\epsilon^2$ |
| | reflection coefficient | $\rho$ | chs A | $\epsilon^2$ |
| 4 | Load stopband to passband frequency ratio | $\lambda$ | B | |
| 5 | Load filter order (must be odd) | n | C | |
| 6 | Calculate normalized transmission zero | | | |
| | frequencies and minimum stopband loss | | D | $\Omega_1$ |
| | | | | $\Omega_2$ |
| | | | | ⋮ |
| | | | | $\Omega_{\frac{n-1}{2}}$ |
| | | | | $As_{dB}$ |
| 7 | Calculate real and imaginary parts of | | | |
| | normalized transmission function poles | | E | Re $s_{o1}$ |
| | | | | Im $s_{o1}$ |
| | | | | Re $s_{o2}$ |
| | | | | Im $s_{o2}$ |
| | | | | ⋮ |
| | | | | Re $s_{on}$ |
| | | | | Im $s_{on}$ |

<u>Example 2-15.1</u>

Find the transmission function poles and zeros for a 9th order, elliptic filter having a 85° modular angle, and 50% reflection coefficient. Also calculate the minimum stopband attenuation in dB. Compare the results to the output of Program 2-11.

| PROGRAM 2–15 INPUT | | |
|---|---|---|
| -.5 | GSBA | load – $\rho$ |
| 85. | SIN | calculate |
| | 1/X | and load $\lambda$ |
| 1.003819836+00 | *** | |
| | GSBE | |
| 9. | GSBC | load n, the filter order |

| PROGRAM 2–15 OUTPUT | | |
|---|---|---|
| | GSBD | calc xmsn 0's |
| 1.004553794+00 | *** | $z_1$ |
| 1.014264420+00 | *** | $z_2$ |
| 1.071140576+00 | *** | $z_3$ |
| 1.449931830+00 | *** | $z_4$ |
| 33.62429965+00 | *** | $As_{dB}$ min |
| | GSBE | calc xmsn fcn poles |
| 372.8205714-03 | *** | Re $p_o$ |
| 0.000000000+00 | *** | Im $p_o$ |
| 182.7207935-03 | *** | Re $p_1$ |
| 739.3062101-03 | *** | Im $p_1$ |
| 41.53031846-03 | *** | Re $p_2$ |
| 951.6294634-03 | *** | Im $p_2$ |
| 7.869871966-03 | *** | Re $p_3$ |
| 992.6118076-03 | *** | Im $p_3$ |
| 1.191142481-03 | *** | Re $p_4$ |
| 995.5098960-03 | *** | Im $p_4$ |

Load Program 2-12 and calculate transmission zeros (loss poles) for the same conditions.

| PROGRAM 2–12 INPUT | PROGRAM 2–12 OUTPUT |
|---|---|
| 1. ENT↑<br>.5 X²<br>- calculate<br>LOG and load<br>10. × $Ap_{dB}$ for<br>CHS 50% refl<br>1.249387366+00 *** coef<br>GSBA<br><br>30. GSBa load $As_{dB}$<br><br>1. GSBB load $f_p$<br><br>85. SIN calculate and<br>1/X load $f_s$ for<br>1.003819838+00 *** 85° modular<br>GSBb angle | GSBC calculate filter order<br><br>8.352734615+00 *** calc order<br>9.000000000+00 *** integral order to meet specs<br><br>GSBD calculate xmsn zero freq's<br><br>1.449931802+00 *** $z_4$<br>1.071140568+00 *** $z_3$<br>1.014284416+00 *** $z_2$<br>1.004553794+00 *** $z_1$ |

Comparing these results to those obtained from Program 2-15, differences exist in the 9th and 10th places sometimes. It is the author's opinion that the output from Program 2-12 is accurate to 2 parts in $10^{10}$, since the elliptic sine algorithm and complete elliptic integral algorithm have been checked against the elliptic function tables in Abramowitz and Stegun [ 1 ] and disagree by at most one in the least significant digit of the HP-97 output (see Program 5-1 for details).

# Program Listing I

| Step | Key | Comment |
|---|---|---|
| 001 | *LBLA | LOAD $A_{PdB}$ or $-\rho$ |
| 002 | X<0? | test for $-\rho$ |
| 003 | GTOa | |
| 004 | EEX | calculate and store: |
| 005 | 1 | $\epsilon^2 = 10^{0.1 A_{PdB}} - 1$ |
| 006 | ÷ | |
| 007 | 10ˣ | |
| 008 | EEX | |
| 009 | - | |
| 010 | STOA | |
| 011 | GTO9 | |
| 012 | *LBLa | |
| 013 | X² | calculate and store: |
| 014 | CHS | |
| 015 | EEX | |
| 016 | + | |
| 017 | 1/X | $\epsilon^2 = \frac{1}{1-\rho^2} - 1$ |
| 018 | EEX | |
| 019 | - | |
| 020 | STOA | |
| 021 | GTO9 | |
| 022 | *LBLB | LOAD λ, the stopband to |
| 023 | STOB | passband frequency ratio |
| 024 | GTO9 | |
| 025 | *LBLC | LOAD n, the filter order |
| 026 | STOC | (must be odd) |
| 027 | GTO9 | |
| 028 | *LBLD | CALC. xmsn zeros & $A_{sdB}$ |
| 029 | 9 | calculate and store: |
| 030 | 0 | |
| 031 | RCLC | $\frac{90}{n} \rightarrow R_E$ |
| 032 | ÷ | |
| 033 | STOE | |
| 034 | EEX | |
| 035 | STOI | initialize k+1, 2h-1 |
| 036 | STO9 | |
| 037 | RCLB | $a_o = \sqrt{f_s / f_p}$ |
| 038 | √X | |
| 039 | GSB7 | |
| 040 | GSB7 | $a_{k+1} = a_k^2 + \sqrt{a_k^4 - 1}$ |
| 041 | GSB7 | $k = 0, 1, 2, 3$ |
| 042 | GSB7 | |
| 043 | *LBL0 | |
| 044 | 3 | initialize k-1 |
| 045 | STOI | |
| 046 | RCL4 | calculate: |
| 047 | RCL9 | |
| 048 | RCLE | $Y_{4h} = \frac{a_4}{\cos\{(2h-1)\frac{90}{n}\}}$ |
| 049 | × | |
| 050 | COS | |
| 051 | ÷ | $h = 1, 2, \ldots, \frac{n-1}{2}$ |
| 052 | SF0 | indicate early subr exit |
| 053 | *LBL1 | |
| 054 | GSB8 | $Y_{(k-1)h} = \frac{1}{2a_k}\left(Y_{kh} - \frac{1}{Y_{kh}}\right)$ |
| 055 | RCLi | |
| 056 | ÷ | $k = 4, 3, 2$ |
| 057 | DSZI | test for loop exit |
| 058 | GTO1 | |
| 059 | GSB8 | $Y_o$ $a_o$ = xmsn zero freq |
| 060 | GSBd | print xmsn zero freq |
| 061 | 2 | increment 2h-1 |
| 062 | ST+9 | |
| 063 | RCL9 | |
| 064 | RCLC | |
| 065 | X>Y? | test for loop exit |
| 066 | GTO0 | |
| 067 | GSB9 | space if flag 1 is set |
| 068 | EEX | initialize k-1 |
| 069 | STOI | |
| 070 | RCL4 | calculate and store: |
| 071 | ENT↑ | |
| 072 | + | $J_4 \cong \frac{(2a_4)^n}{2}$ |
| 073 | RCLC | |
| 074 | Yˣ | |
| 075 | 2 | |
| 076 | ÷ | |
| 077 | P⇄S | |
| 078 | STO0 | |
| 079 | CF0 | indicate full subr |
| 080 | GSB8 | |
| 081 | GSB8 | $J_{k-1} = \sqrt{\frac{1}{2}\left(J_k - \frac{1}{J_k}\right)}$ |
| 082 | GSB8 | |
| 083 | GSB8 | $k = 4, 3, 2, 1$ |
| 084 | P⇄S | calculate and print: |
| 085 | X² | |
| 086 | X² | |
| 087 | RCLA | |
| 088 | × | |
| 089 | EEX | $A_{sdB} = 10 \log(1 + \epsilon^2 J_o^4)$ |
| 090 | + | |
| 091 | LOG | |
| 092 | 1 | |
| 093 | 0 | |
| 094 | × | |
| 095 | PRTX | |
| 096 | GTO9 | goto space and return subr |
| 097 | *LBL7 | subroutine to calculate: |
| 098 | X² | |
| 099 | ENT↑ | |
| 100 | X² | |
| 101 | EEX | |
| 102 | - | |
| 103 | √X | $a_{k+1} = a_k^2 + \sqrt{a_k^4 - 1}$ |
| 104 | + | |
| 105 | STOi | |
| 106 | ISZI | |
| 107 | RTN | |

**REGISTERS**

| 0 | 1 | 2 | 3 | 4 | 5 | 6 | 7 | 8 | 9 |
|---|---|---|---|---|---|---|---|---|---|
| $a_o$ | $a_1$ | $a_2$ | $a_3$ | $a_4$ | | | | | index |

| S0 | S1 | S2 | S3 | S4 | S5 | S6 | S7 | S8 | S9 |
|---|---|---|---|---|---|---|---|---|---|
| $J_4$ | $J_3$ | $J_2$ | $J_1$ | $J_o$ | | | | | |

| A | B | C | D | E | I |
|---|---|---|---|---|---|
| $\epsilon^2$ | λ | n | s | 90/n | register index |

# Program Listing II

|  |  |
|---|---|
| *LBL8 | subroutine to calculate: |
| ENT↑ | |
| 1/X | $u_{k-1} \cdot c_{k-1} = \frac{1}{2}\left(u_k + \frac{1}{u_k}\right)$ |
| + | |
| 2 | |
| ÷ | |
| F0? | test for early exit |
| RTN | |
| √X | $J_{k-1} = \sqrt{\frac{1}{2}\left(J_k - \frac{1}{J_k}\right)}$ |
| STOi | |
| ISZI | |
| RTN | |
| *LBLE | CALCULATE POLE LOCATIONS |
| 3 | initialize 3-k |
| STOI | |
| RCLA | $J_0 \, s_\infty = \frac{1}{\epsilon}$ |
| √X | |
| 1/X | |
| P⇄S | |
| *LBL2 | calculate: $s_{(k+1)o} = J_k s_{ko} + \sqrt{J_k^2 s_{ko}^2 + 1}$, $k = 0, 1, 2,$ |
| GSB6 | |
| RCLi | |
| x | |
| DSZI | test for loop exit |
| GTO2 | |
| ENT↑ | to avoid overflow, use: $s_{4o} \cong 2\, J_3\, s_{3o}$ |
| + | |
| RCLi | calculate and store: $s_{5o} = \left\{\frac{J_4}{s_{4o}} + \sqrt{\left(\frac{J_4}{s_{4o}}\right)^2 + 1}\right\}^{\frac{1}{n}}$ |
| P⇄S | |
| X⇄Y | |
| ÷ | |
| GSB6 | |
| RCLC | |
| 1/X | |
| Yˣ | |
| STOD | |
| CLX | initialize 2h |
| STO9 | |
| *LBL4 | pole location calc loop |
| 4 | initialize k-1 |
| STOI | |
| RCL9 | calc $s_{5h} = s_{5o}\, e^{jh\frac{\pi}{n}}$, $h = 0, 1, 2, \cdots, \frac{n-1}{2}$ |
| RCLE | |
| x | |
| RCLD | |
| *LBL3 | $s_{(k-1)h} = \frac{1}{2a_{k-1}}\left(s_{kh} - \frac{1}{s_{kh}}\right)$, $k = 5, 4, 3, 2$ |
| GSB5 | |
| RCLi | |
| ÷ | |
| DSZI | test for loop exit |
| GTO3 | |
| GSB5 | finish pole location calculation and print pole locations |
| →R | |
| GSBd | |
| X⇄Y | |
| GSBd | |
| GSB9 | |
| 2 | increment 2h |
| ST+9 | |
| RCL9 | test for loop exit |
| RCLC | |
| X>Y? | |
| GTO4 | |
| *LBL9 | space and return subr |
| F1? | space if flag 1 is set |
| SPC | |
| RTN | |
| GTO9 | R/S lockup |
| *LBL5 | subroutine to calculate using complex arithmetic: $s_{k-1} \cdot a_{k-1} = \frac{1}{2}\left(s_k - \frac{1}{s_k}\right)$ |
| →R | |
| LSTX | |
| 1/X | |
| X² | |
| EEX | |
| - | |
| x | |
| LSTX | |
| 2 | |
| + | |
| R↑ | |
| x | |
| X⇄Y | |
| →P | |
| 2 | |
| ÷ | |
| RTN | |
| *LBL6 | subroutine to calculate: $s_{(k+1)o} = J_k s_{ko} + \sqrt{(J_k s_{ko})^2 + 1}$ |
| ENT↑ | |
| X² | |
| EEX | |
| + | |
| √X | |
| + | |
| RTN | |
| *LBLd | print or R/S subroutine |
| F1? | |
| PRTX | print and return if flag 1 is set, otherwise |
| F1? | |
| RTN | |
| R/S | stop program execution |
| RTN | |
| *LBLe | PRINT-R/S TOGGLE |
| CF1 | clear flag 1 and place a zero in the display |
| CLX | |
| RTN | |
| *LBLe | set flag 1 and place a one in the display |
| SF1 | |
| EEX | |
| RTN | |

| LABELS | | | | | FLAGS |
|---|---|---|---|---|---|
| A LOAD $A_{PdB}$ or $-\rho$ | B LOAD λ | C LOAD n | D CALC zeros | E CALC poles | 0 subr exit |
| a calc $\epsilon^2$ | b | c | d prt-R/S | e print? | 1 print |
| 0 h loop | 1 k loop | 2 k loop | 3 k loop | 4 h loop | 2 |
| 5 subr | 6 subr | 7 subr | 8 subr | 9 subr | 3 |

| SET STATUS | | |
|---|---|---|
| FLAGS (ON OFF) | TRIG | DISP |
| 0 | DEG ■ | FIX |
| 1 | GRAD | SCI |
| 2 | RAD | ENG |
| 3 | | n |

# Part 3

# ELECTROMAGNETIC COMPONENT DESIGN

## PROGRAM 3-1 FERROMAGNETIC CORE INDUCTOR DESIGN – MAGNETICS.

Program Description and Equations Used

This program calculates the various parameters relating to inductor or transformer design on closed magnetic cores. Given the core relative permeability ($\mu$), the core length ($\ell_c$), the core area (A), the air gap ($\ell_{air}$), the required inductance (L), the dc current ($I_{dc}$), the applied ac voltage (E), and the excitation frequency (f), the program will calculate the number of turns required (N), the core H (oersteds) and B (gauss) resulting from the dc excitation, the ac excitation, and the total from both excitations. The dimensions of the core and air-gap can be entered in either centimeter or inch units. Program 3-2 will calculate the wire size and winding resistance given the window area and mean turn length. The program will also calculate the coil inductance if the number of turns, the core permeability and dimensions, and the air gap dimensions are given.

If the inductance in millihenries per 1000 turns is given (the $A_L$ value) along with the core dimensions and permeability, the effective air gap will be calculated and stored in place of the given air gap. The inductance or turns, and core excitation will then be calculated on the basis of the calculated air gap.

The magnetic equations used are:

$$H = \frac{0.4\ \mu N I}{\ell_c + \mu_c \cdot \ell_{air}} \qquad (3.1.1)$$

$$E = 10^{-8} \cdot N \frac{d\phi}{dt} = 10^{-8} N A \frac{dB}{dt} \qquad (3\text{-}1.2)$$

where I is the current in the coil. Equation (3-1.2) can be rearranged to yield B, the core flux density:

$$B = \frac{10^8}{N A} \int E \cdot dt \qquad (3\text{-}1.3)$$

If $E = \sqrt{2} \cdot E_{rms} \cdot \sin(2\pi ft)$ is the sinewave excitation, then:

$$B_{peak} = \frac{10^8 \cdot E_{rms}}{\sqrt{2}\pi\ ANf} \tag{3-1.4}$$

If E is a symmetrical squarewave with voltage $E_{pk}$ as shown by Fig. 3-1.1, then:

$$B_{peak} = \frac{10^8\ Epk}{4\,ANf} \tag{3-1.5}$$

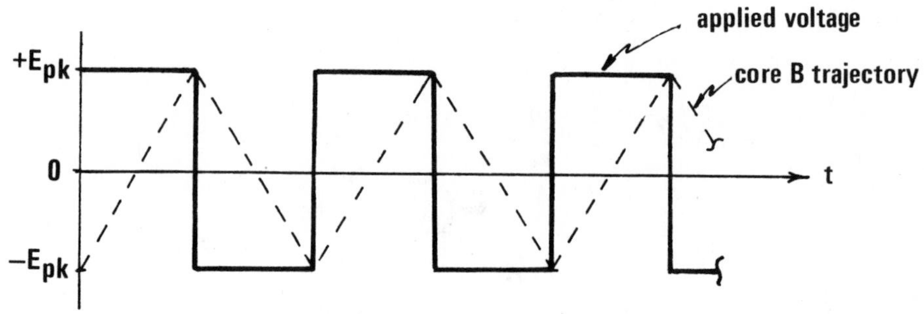


Figure 3-1.1 Square wave coil excitation and magnetic flux density trajectory.

Remembering the differential relationship between current and voltage in an inductor, $E = L(dI/dt)$, an expression can be derived relating the inductance, L, to the magnetic circuit quantities:

$$B = \mu H \tag{3-1.6}$$

From Eqs. (3-1.2) and (3-1.6):

$$E = 10^{-8} N \cdot A \mu \frac{dH}{dt} \tag{3-1.7}$$

From Eq. (3-1.1):

$$\frac{dH}{dt} = \frac{0.4\mu\ N}{\ell_c + \mu\ell_{air}} \cdot \frac{dI}{dt} \tag{3-1.8}$$

Combining Eqs. (3-1.7) and(3-1.8) yields the inductance expression:

$$E = \frac{0.4\pi\ N^2\ A \cdot 10^{-8}}{\ell_c + \mu\ell_{air}} \cdot \frac{dI}{dt} \tag{3-1.9}$$

hence

$$L = \frac{0.4\pi\ N^2 \mu A \cdot 10^{-8}}{\ell_c + \mu\ell_{air}} \tag{3-1.10}$$

This equation may be rearranged to yield the equivalent air gap if the inductance per turn squared and core dimensions are known:

$$\ell_{air} = \frac{0.4\pi\ N^2 A \cdot 10^{-8}}{L} - \frac{\ell_c}{\mu}\text{, cm} \qquad (3\text{-}1.11)$$

Generally the inductance index in millihenries per 1000 turns is provided by the core manufacturer:

$$L^* = \text{millihenries per 1000 turns} \qquad (3\text{-}1.12)$$

hence,

$$\ell_{air} = \frac{4\pi A}{L^*} - \frac{\ell_c}{\mu} \quad \text{cm} \qquad (3\text{-}1.13)$$

Equation (3-1.10) can be rearranged to yield an expression for N, the number of turns, required to achieve a given inductance, L:

$$N = \left\{ L \frac{(\ell_c + \mu\,\ell_{air}) \cdot 10^8}{0.4\ \pi\ \mu\,A} \right\}^{1/2} \qquad (3\text{-}1.14)$$

The program uses these equations as follows: Labels "A," "a," "B," and "b" are used to load and store the core parameters. The actual stored parameters are in centimeters, and entries with inch units (Labels "A" and "B") are converted before storage. Label "C" uses Eq. (3-1.14) to calculate N given L. Label "c" uses Eq. (3-1.10) to calculate L given N. Label "d" uses Eq. (3-1.13) to calculate the equivalent air gap given the inductance index, L*. The new air gap dimension replaces the presently stored air gap dimension. Label "D" uses Eq. (3-1.1) to calculate the dc magnetizing force, H, given the dc current through the core. Since the number of turns are required for this calculation, the use of "C" or "c" must precede the use of "D." The dc flux density, $B_{dc}$, is calculated using Eq. (3-1.6). Label "E" uses Eq. (3-1.4) to calculate the peak core flux density given the ac coil excitation. The flux in the core will vary sinusoidally with sinusoidal excitation. The peak ac magnetizing force is calculated using Eq. (3-1.6). The peak ac and dc core magnetic parameters are added together and printed to provide the peak excitation in the core. The peak excitation should be kept below the magnetic saturation level of the core material for linear operation. Label "e" uses Eq. (3-1.5) to calculate peak core flux density from squarewave coil excitation, and provides a summary as above.

# User Instructions

| INDUCTOR DESIGN - MAGNETICS | | | | |
|---|---|---|---|---|
| $\mu\uparrow\ell_c\uparrow A_c$ cm | $\ell_{air}$ cm | N → L | L*, $\frac{mh}{1000T}$ | $E_{pk}\uparrow f_{Hz}$ H, $B_{ac}$, pk |
| $\mu\uparrow\ell_c\uparrow A_c$ inches | $\ell_{air}$ inches | L → N | $I_{dc}$→H, $B_{dc}$ | $E_{rms}\uparrow f_{Hz}$ H, $B_{ac}$, pk |

| STEP | INSTRUCTIONS | INPUT DATA/UNITS | KEYS | OUTPUT DATA/UNITS |
|---|---|---|---|---|
| 1 | Load both sides of magnetic card | | | |
| 2 | Load magnetic core parameters | | | |
| | a) for dimensions in inches | | | |
| | i) relative permeability of core | μ | [ENT↑] | |
| | ii) effective core length | $\ell_c$ | [ENT↑] | |
| | iii) effective core cross-sectional area | $A_c$ | [A] | μ |
| | b) for dimensions in centimeters | | | |
| | i) relative permeability of core | μ | [ENT↑] | |
| | ii) effective core length | $\ell_c$ | [ENT↑] | |
| | iii) effective core cross-sectional area | $A_c$ | [f] [A] | μ |
| 3 | Load air gap length (if L* is to be used, skip this step) | | | |
| | a) for dimensions in inches | $\ell_{air}$ | [B] | $\ell_{air}$, cm |
| | b) for dimensions in centimeters | $\ell_{air}$ | [f] [B] | $\ell_{air}$, cm |
| 4 | Load L* (mh/1000T) if air gap is unknown | L* | [f] [D] | $\ell_{air}$, cm |
| 5 | To calculate the number of turns to achieve a given inductance | L, h | [C] | N |
| 6 | To calculate the inductance given the number of turns | N | [f] [C] | L, h |
| 7 | Load dc coil current | $I_{dc}$ | [D] | $H_{dc}$, Oe |
| | | | | $B_{dc}$, G |
| 8 | If sinewave ac coil excitation is present | | | |
| | a) load the rms voltage | $E_{rms}$, V | [ENT↑] | |
| | b) load the frequency | f, Hz | [E] | $H_{ac}$ pk, Oe |
| | | | | $H_{dc}$, Oe |
| | | | | $H_{total}$, Oe |
| | | | | $B_{ac}$ pk, G |
| | | | | $B_{dc}$, G |
| | | | | $B_{total}$, G |

# User Instructions

INDUCTOR DESIGN - MAGNETICS

CONTINUED

2

| STEP | INSTRUCTIONS | INPUT DATA/UNITS | KEYS | OUTPUT DATA/UNITS |
|---|---|---|---|---|
| 9 | If square-wave coil excitation is present | | | |
| | a) load the peak voltage (see Fig. 3-1.1) | $E_{pk}$ | [ENT↑] | |
| | b) load the frequency | f, Hz | [f] [E] | $H_{ac\ pk}$, Oe |
| | | | | $H_{dc}$, Oe |
| | | | | $H_{total}$, Oe |
| | | | | $B_{ac\ pk}$, G |
| | | | | $B_{dc}$, G |
| | | | | $B_{total}$, G |
| 10 | To obtain the wire size and winding resistance for the above winding, load Program 3-2. | | | |

Example 3-1.1

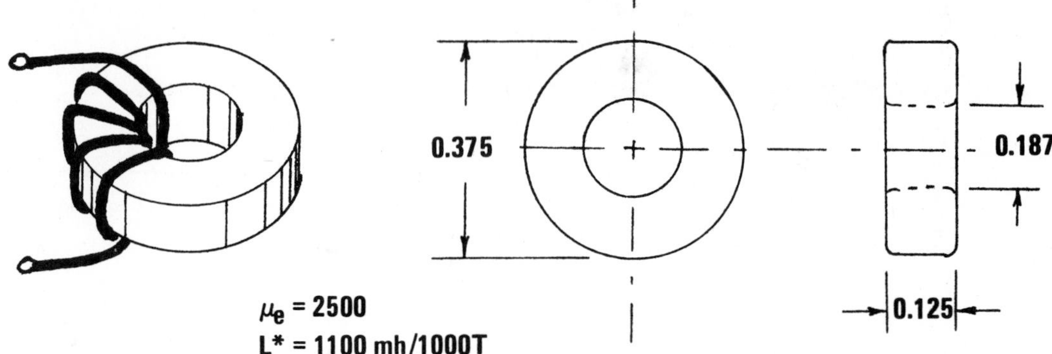


Design an inductor to have an inductance of 20 millihenries using the above core (a Ferroxcube 266CT1253B7). The operating frequency is 10 kHz, and the applied ac voltage is 1 Vrms sinewave. There will be 1 mA of dc flowing in the winding.

The core physical constants are needed first:

$A = (.125)(.375 - .187)/2 = 11.8 \times 10^{-3}$ inches$^2$
$\ell_c = \pi(.375 + .187)/2 = .883$ inches (mfgr says .852 in)
$\ell_{air} = 0$ (no air gap)

These dimensions along with $\mu_e$ = 2500 are loaded using the A & B keys.

| | | |
|---|---|---|
| 2500. | ENT↑ | $\mu_e$ |
| .852 | ENT↑ | $\ell_c$, inches |
| 11.8-03 | GSBA | A , inches$^2$ |
| 0. | GSBB | $\ell_{air}$ |
| 1100. | GSBd | L* (mh/1000T) |
| 4.062-06 | *** | $\ell_{air}$ calculated, cm |
| .020 | GSBC | L required, h |
| 134.8+00 | *** | N calculated (use 135T) |
| 1.-03 | GSBD | Idc, amps |
| 77.93-03 | *** | Hdc, oersteds |
| 194.8+00 | *** | Bdc, gauss |
| 1. | ENT↑ | Vrms |
| 10000. | GSBE | freq, Hz, sinewave |
| 87.71-03 | *** | Hac peak, oersteds |
| 77.93-03 | *** | Hdc " |
| 165.6-03 | *** | H total " |
| 219.3+00 | *** | Bac peak, gauss |
| 194.8+00 | *** | Bdc " |
| 414.1+00 | *** | B total " |

Since the core saturates at around 2500 gauss, and this design only excites the core to 414 gauss peak, the design appears adequate from a magnetics standpoint.

Example 3-1.2

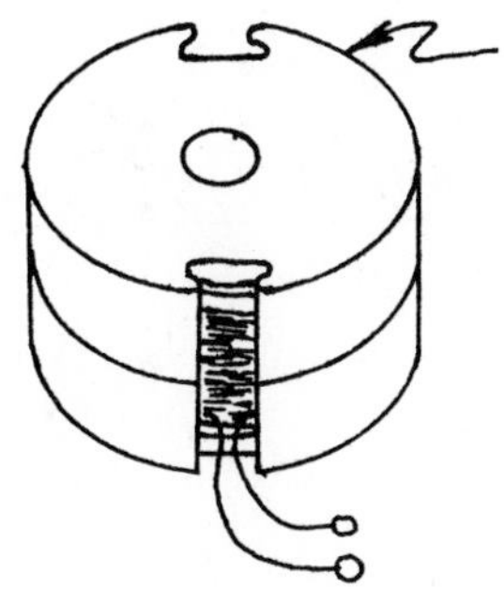

Ferrite pot core: Ferroxcube 2213C A400 3B7

$\ell_c$ = 3.15 cm
$A_c$ = 0.635 $cm^2$
$\mu_e$ = 1845
L* = 400 mh/1000T
$B_{max}$ < 2000 gauss for stable inductance

This pot core is to be used in a tank circuit of a class A tuned amplifier operating at 50 kHz. The dc current is 30 mA, and the applied ac voltage is 10 Vrms. The required inductance is 40 mh (the resonating capacitor is 253 pF). Calculate the effective air gap, the number of turns required, the dc and ac core excitation, and the peak flux density. The following HP-97 printout shows the data entry and calculated parameter output.

```
   1845. ENT↑    μe
   3.15 ENT↑     ℓc, centimeters
   .635 GSBa     Ac, cm²

   400. GSBd     L* (mh/1000T)
18.24-03  ***    ℓair calculated

   .040 GSBC     L required, h
316.2+00  ***    N calculated (use 316)

   .030 GSBD     Idc, amps
323.9-03  ***    Hdc, oersteds
597.6+00  ***    Bdc, gauss

    10. ENT↑     Vrms
 50000. GSBE     Freq, Hz, sinewave
12.15-03  ***    Hac peak, oersteds
323.9-03  ***    Hdc,           "
336.1-03  ***    H total,       "

22.42+00  ***    Bac peak, gauss
597.6+00  ***    Bdc,           "
620.0+00  ***    B total,       "
```

A printout of the registers reveals this stored information:

```
          PREG

1.845+03   0
3.150+00   1    ℓc cm
635.0-03   2    Ac, cm²
18.24-03   3    ℓair, cm
316.2+00   4    N, turns
50.00+03   5    freq, Hz
323.9-03   6    Hdc, Oe
597.6+00   7    Bdc, gauss
0.000+00   8
22.42+00   9    Bac pk, gauss
10.00+00   A    Vac, volts
30.00-03   B    Idc, amps
4.000+06   C    L x 10^8
400.0+00   D    L*, mh/1000T
0.000+00   E
0.000+00   I
```

Example 3-1.3

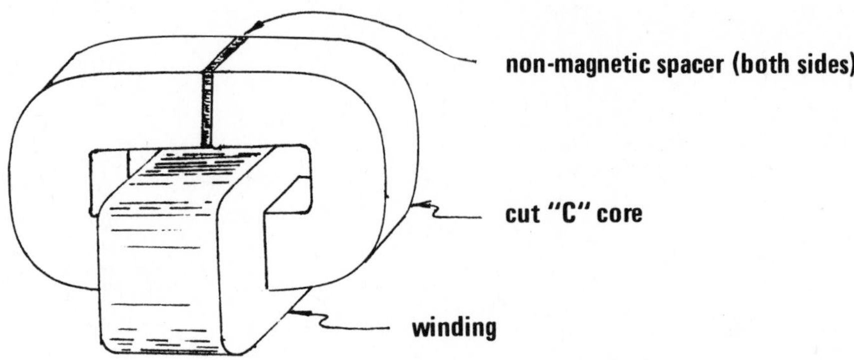


Figure 3-1.2 Inductor on cut C-core.

An inductor to carry dc is needed for the power separation assembly at the end of a coax cable. One ampere dc must flow through the inductor without forcing the B-H loop into a nonlinear region. The inductance needed is 1 henry. Ac signals of 10 Vrms across a frequency band covering 10 Hz to 1000 Hz will be applied in addition to the dc current. A tentative selection is a cut "C" core (see Fig. 3-1.2) with dimensions $A_c = 1.0\ in^2$, $\ell_c = 6$ inches, and $\mu = 1000$ (silectron transformer steel). To ensure linear inductance, the peak flux level in the core should not exceed 10000 gauss.

| | | | | | |
|---|---|---|---|---|---|
| 1000. | ENT↑ | $\mu$ | | | |
| 6. | ENT↑ | $\ell_c$, inches | | | |
| 1. | GSBA | $A_c$, inches$^2$ | | | |
| .062 | GSBB | $\ell_{air}$, inches (.031 each side) | .125 | GSBB | new air gap, inches (0.625" each side) |
| 1. | GSBC | L, h, required | | GSBC | recalculate N |
| 1.460+03 | *** | N, # turns calc | 2.026+03 | *** | N, # turns |
| 1. | GSBD | Idc, amps | | GSBD | recalc, H, Bdc |
| 10.62+00 | *** | Hdc, oersteds | 7.651+00 | *** | Hdc, oersteds |
| 10.62+03 | *** | Bdc, gauss | 7.651+03 | *** | Bdc, gauss |
| 10. | ENT↑ | Vrms | | | |
| 10. | GSBE | freq, Hz, sinewave | | GSBE | recalc H, Bac, etc. |
| 2.390+00 | *** | Hac peak, oersteds | 1.722+00 | *** | Hac peak, oersteds |
| 10.62+00 | *** | Hdc, " | 7.651+00 | *** | Hdc, " |
| 13.01+00 | *** | H total, " | 9.373+00 | *** | H total, " |
| 2.390+03 | *** | Bac peak, gauss | 1.722+03 | *** | Bac peak, guass |
| 10.62+03 | *** | Bdc " | 7.651+03 | *** | Bdc, " |
| 13.01+03 | *** | B total, " | 9.373+03 | *** | B total, " |
| B total exceeds 10000 gauss, use a thicker spacer (larger air gap). | | | B total is less than 10000 gauss, magnetic design is complete. | | |

# Program Listing I

| | | |
|---|---|---|
| 001 | *LBLa | LOAD CORE PARAMS, CM UNITS |
| 002 | ST02 | store core area |
| 003 | R↓ | |
| 004 | ST01 | store core length |
| 005 | R↓ | |
| 006 | ST00 | store core permeability |
| 007 | F2? | test for initialization |
| 008 | GSB5 | |
| 009 | GT04 | goto spc, CF3 and rtn |
| 010 | *LBLA | LOAD CORE PARAMS, IN. UNITS |
| 011 | F2? | test for initialization |
| 012 | GSB5 | |
| 013 | RCLI | convert area in $in^2$ to $cm^2$ |
| 014 | X² | and store |
| 015 | x | |
| 016 | ST02 | |
| 017 | R↓ | |
| 018 | RCLI | convert core length in in. |
| 019 | x | to cm and store |
| 020 | ST01 | |
| 021 | R↓ | |
| 022 | ST00 | store core permeability |
| 023 | GT04 | goto spc, CF3 and rtn |
| 024 | *LBLB | LOAD AIR GAP LENGTH, INCHES |
| 025 | F2? | test for initialization |
| 026 | GSB5 | |
| 027 | RCLI | convert air gap length |
| 028 | x | to cm |
| 029 | *LBLb | LOAD AIR GAP LENGTH, CM |
| 030 | F2? | test for initialization |
| 031 | GSB5 | |
| 032 | ST03 | store air gap length in cm |
| 033 | GT04 | goto spc, CF3, and rtn |
| 034 | *LBLC | LOAD INDUCTANCE REQUIRED |
| 035 | F3? | if no numeric input, jump |
| 036 | F.? | |
| 037 | GT00 | |
| 038 | RCLE | |
| 039 | x | calculate and store $L·10^8$ |
| 040 | STOC | |
| 041 | *LBL0 | |
| 042 | RCLC | calculate and store the |
| 043 | GSB6 | number of turns required |
| 044 | x | by using Eq. (3-1.14) |
| 045 | RCL2 | |
| 046 | ÷ | |
| 047 | RCL0 | |
| 048 | ÷ | |
| 049 | √x | |
| 050 | ST04 | |
| 051 | GT03 | print number of turns |

$$N = \left\{ \frac{L(l_c + \mu\, l_{air}) \cdot 10^8}{0.4\pi \, \mu \, A_c} \right\}^{1/2}$$

| | | |
|---|---|---|
| 052 | *LBLc | LOAD NUMBER OF TURNS |
| 053 | F3? | if numeric input, |
| 054 | ST04 | store value |
| 055 | RCL4 | calculate and store $L·10^8$: |
| 056 | X² | |
| 057 | GSB6 | |
| 058 | | |
| 059 | RCL2 | $L·10^8 = \dfrac{0.4\pi N^2 \mu A}{l_c + \mu\, l_{air}}$ |
| 060 | x | |
| 061 | RCL0 | |
| 062 | x | |
| 063 | STOC | |
| 064 | RCLE | divide by $10^8$ |
| 065 | ÷ | |
| 066 | GT03 | goto print subroutine |
| 067 | *LBLD | LOAD $I_{dc}$ |
| 068 | F3? | if numeric input, |
| 069 | STOB | store value |
| 070 | RCLB | |
| 071 | GSB6 | calculate and print $H_{dc}$: |
| 072 | ÷ | |
| 073 | RCL4 | |
| 074 | x | $H_{dc} = \dfrac{0.4\pi NI}{l_c + \mu\, l_{air}}$ |
| 075 | PRTX | |
| 076 | ST06 | |
| 077 | RCL0 | |
| 078 | x | calculate and store $B_{dc}$ |
| 079 | ST07 | $B_{dc} \quad \mu·H_{dc}$ |
| 080 | GT03 | goto print subroutine |
| 081 | *LBLd | LOAD L*, MH PER 1000 TURNS |
| 082 | STOD | |
| 083 | 1/X | |
| 084 | 4 | calculate and store |
| 085 | x | equivalent air gap: |
| 086 | Pi | |
| 087 | x | |
| 088 | RCL2 | $l_{air} = \dfrac{4\pi A}{L^*} - \dfrac{l_c}{\mu}$ |
| 089 | x | |
| 090 | RCL1 | |
| 091 | RCL0 | |
| 092 | ÷ | |
| 093 | − | |
| 094 | ST03 | |
| 095 | GT03 | goto print subroutine |

| REGISTERS | | | | | | | | | |
|---|---|---|---|---|---|---|---|---|---|
| 0 $\mu$ | 1 $l_c$ | 2 $A_c$ | 3 $l_{air}$ | 4 $N$ | 5 $f$ | 6 $H_{dc}$ | 7 $B_{dc}$ | 8 | 9 $B_{ac,pk}$ |
| S0 | S1 | S2 | S3 | S4 | S5 | S6 | S7 | S8 | S9 |
| A $V_{ac}$ | B $I_{dc}$ | C $L \times 10^8$ | D $L^*$ | E $10^8$ | I 2.54 | | | | |

# Program Listing II

NOTE FLAG SET STATUS

```
096 *LBLE   LOAD E_rms, f_Hz; CALC H,B
097   F3?
098   F3?   jump if no numeric entry
099  GTO1
100  STO5   store frequency
101   X⇄Y
102  STOA   store rms voltage
103 *LBL1   setup for B_peak calculation
104  RCLA
105     2
106    √X   k = √2 π
107    Pi
108     x
109  GTO2   goto B calculation
110 *LBLe   LOAD E_pk, f_Hz; calc H, B
111   F3?
112   F3?   jump if no numeric entry
113  GTO1
114  STO5   store frequency
115   X⇄Y
116  STOA   store peak voltage
117 *LBL1   setup for B calculation
118  RCLA
119     4   k = 4
120 *LBL2   common B calculation routine
121     ÷
122  RCL5
123     ÷
124  RCL2
125     ÷   B_peak = 10^8 · E / kANf
126  RCL4
127     ÷
128  RCLE
129     x
130  STO9   store B_ac, pk
131  RCL0   calculate and print H_ac, pk
132     ÷   H = B/μ
133  PRTX
134  RCL6   recall and print H_dc
135  PRTX
136     +
137  PRTX   calc and print H_total
138   SPC
139  RCL9   recall and print B_ac, pk
140  PRTX
141  RCL7   recall and print B_dc
142  PRTX
143     +   calculate B_total
144 *LBL3   print and space subroutine
145  PRTX
146 *LBL4   space and CF3 subroutine
147   SPC
148   CF3
149   RTN
150 *LBL5   initialization subroutine
151   EEX
152     8   generate and store 10^8
153  STOE
154    R↓   recover x register
155     2
156     .
157     5   generate and store 2.54
158     4
159  STOI
160    R↓   recover x register
161   RTN   return to main program
162 *LBL6   common magnetics subroutine
163  RCL3
164  RCL0
165     x   calculate:
166  RCL1
167     +       (l_c + μ l_air) / (0.4 π)
168    Pi
169     ÷
170     .
171     4
172     ÷
173   RTN   return to main program
```

**NOTE:**

To change from the "print" mode to the "R/S" mode for output, change the "print" statements to "R/S" statements at the following line numbers: 075, 133, 135, 137, 140, 142, and 145.

NOTE FLAG SET STATUS

| LABELS | | | | | FLAGS |
|---|---|---|---|---|---|
| A $\mu \uparrow l_c \uparrow A_c$ [in] | B $l_{air}$ [in] | C L → N | D $I_{dc} \rightarrow H_{dc}, B_{dc}$ | E $V_{rms} \uparrow f_{Hz} \rightarrow H_{pk}, B_{pk}$ | 0 |
| a $\mu \uparrow l_c \uparrow A_c$ [cm] | b $l_{air}$ [cm] | c N → L | d Load $L^*$ | e $V_{pk} \uparrow f_{Hz} \rightarrow H_{pk}, B_{pk}$ | 1 |
| 0 loop c destination | 1 ac flux output routine | 2 ac flux output routine | 3 print, space, CF3, rtn | 4 space CF3, rtn | 2 store constants |
| 5 initialize constants | 6 $\frac{l_c + \mu_c l_{air}}{0.4\pi}$ | 7 | 8 | 9 | 3 data entry |

| SET STATUS | | | |
|---|---|---|---|
| FLAGS | | TRIG | DISP |
| | ON OFF | | |
| 0 | | DEG | FIX |
| 1 | | GRAD | SCI |
| 2 | ■ | RAD | ENG ■ |
| 3 | ■ | | n 3 |

## PROGRAM 3-2 FERROMAGNETIC CORE INDUCTOR DESIGN — WIRE SIZE.

Program Description and Equations Used

This program is a companion program to Program 3-1. Given the window area and the number of turns (stored by companion program), this program will calculate the wire size with heavy insulation (class 2) that will fill the window area. If the length of the mean turn is known, the program will also calculate the winding resistance.

The program is also designed to provide information on the wire diamter over class 2 insulation and wire resistance in ohms/inch given the wire size in AWG. The program will also calculate the AWG given the wire diameter over class 2 insulation.

The operation of the program centers around the logarithmic relationship between AWG and the wire cross-sectional area. This logarithmic relationship is:

$$AWG = \frac{1}{b} \ln \frac{\text{diameter in inches}}{a} \qquad (3\text{-}2.1)$$

where $a' = 0.3245574964$, $b' = -.1159489227$ } bare wire

$a = 0.3137250775$, $b = -.1097881513$ } wire with class 2 insulation

If the total area for a winding of N turns is known, then the area for one turn may be calculated. If the wire is assumed to just fit inside a square with the wire diameter tangent to the sides of the square, then the waste space due to wire stacking can be accommodated (see Fig. 3-6.2). The wire diameter becomes the square root of the square's area. The program uses this algorithm. Once the wire diameter is found, the AWG can be calculated using the logarithmic relationships. The constants for heavy insulation are used. The AWG that is used and is output is the upward rounded value of (1.5 + calculated AWG).

The wire resistance per unit length is inversely proportional to the copper cross-section, hence, the wire size in AWG also bears a logarithmic relationship to the wire resistance. When the wire resistance is desired as a function of the wire AWG, the relationship becomes exponential:

$$R/\ell \text{ (ohms/inch)} = c \cdot e^{(d \cdot AWG)} \qquad (3\text{-}2.2)$$

where $c = 8.371747114 \times 10^{-6}$, $d = -.2317635483$ (annealed copper wire)

This exponential relationship is used in conjunction with the mean turn length and the number of turns to calculate the total resistance of the winding. The window area and mean turn length may be entered in either units of inches or centimeters. Centimeter dimensions are converted to inch dimensions before storage within the program.

If the AWG is known and the overall wire diameter including the heavy insulation is desired, Eq. (3-2.1) can be rearranged to yield:

$$\text{diameter in inches} = a \cdot e^{(b \cdot AWG)} \qquad (3\text{-}2.3)$$

This equation is evaluated under label e.

# User Instructions

| INDUCTOR DESIGN - WIRE SIZE AND RESISTANCE | | | | |
|---|---|---|---|---|
| window area, $cm^2$ | mean turn length, cm | change # of turns | AWG → ohms/inch | wire diam. → AWG |
| window area, $in^2$ | mean turn length, in | calculate AWG | calculate winding R | AWG→wire diameter |

| STEP | INSTRUCTIONS | INPUT DATA/UNITS | KEYS | OUTPUT DATA/UNITS |
|---|---|---|---|---|
| 1 | Load both sides of magnetic card | | | |
| 2 | Enter window area available for winding | | | |
| | a) for dimensions in square inches | $A_w$, $in^2$ | [A] | |
| | b) for dimensions in square centimeters | $A_w$, $cm^2$ | [f] [A] | |
| 3 | Enter the length of a mean turn (a turn through the middle of the winding) | | | |
| | a) for dimensions in inches | $\ell_t$, in | [B] | |
| | b) for dimensions in centimeters | $\ell_t$, cm | [f] [B] | |
| 4 | To change the number of turns, or to enter the number of turns if the previous program was not run | N | [f] [C] | |
| 5 | Calculate the wire AWG that will fill the window area. Heavy insulation (class 2) is assumed. | | [C] | AWG |
| 6 | Calculate the winding resistance in ohms | | [D] | R, ohms |
| 7 | To find the AWG given the wire diameter over heavy insulation in inches | $D_W$ | [f] [E] | AWG |
| 8 | To find the wire diameter over heavy insulation given AWG | AWG | [E] | $D_W$, in |
| 9 | To find the wire resistance per inch of annealed copper wire given AWG | AWG | [f] [D] | ohms/in |

Example 3-2.1

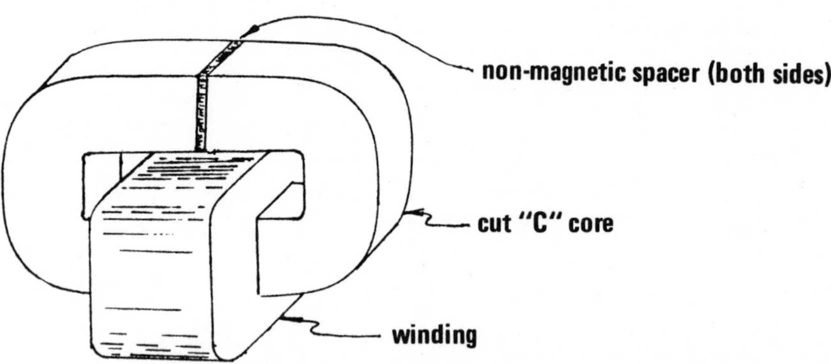


Figure 3-2.1 Inductor on cut C-core.

The inductor in Fig. 3-2.1 was designed to carry dc in Example 3-1.3. If the winding window area is 2 square inches, and the mean turn length is 6 inches, what wire size will fill the winding window, and what will be the total winding resistance?

```
         2.  GSBA   window area in square inches
         6.  GSBB   mean turn length in inches
             GSBC   start wire size calculation
        22.   ***   wire size in AWG

             GSBD   start winding resistance calculation
  16.67+00    ***   winding resistance in ohms
```

# Program Listing I

```
001  *LBLa   LOAD WINDOW AREA IN cm^2
002  F0?     test for initialization
003  GSB2
004  RCLI
005  X^2     convert area to inches^2
006  ÷
007  *LBLA   LOAD WINDOW AREA IN in^2
008  STOA    store window area
009  F0?     test for initialization
010  GSB2
011  RTN     return control to keyboard
012  *LBLb   LOAD MEAN TURN LENGTH IN cm
013  F0?     test for initialization
014  GSB2
015  RCLI
016  ÷       convert length to inches
017  *LBLB   LOAD MEAN TURN LENGTH IN in
018  STOC    store mean turn length
019  F0?     test for initialization
020  GSB2
021  RTN     return control to keyboard
022  *LBLc   LOAD NUMBER OF TURNS CHANGE
023  STO4    store new number of turns
024  RTN
025  *LBLC   CALCULATE WIRE AWG
026  RCLA    calculate wire diameter:
027  RCL4        d = sqrt(A_window / n)
028  ÷
029  √X
030  GSB6    calculate AWG from wire diam
031  EEX     using Eq. (3-2.1)
032  +
033  STOB
034  GTO4    goto print, space & dsp subr
035  *LBLD   CALCULATE WINDING RESISTANCE
036  RCLB    use Eq. (3-2.2) to calc
037  GSB5    ohms/inch
038  RCLC
039  x       multiply by total winding
040  RCL4    length to get total
041  x       resistance
042  GTO4    print resistance
043  *LBLd   CONVERT AWG TO OHMS/INCH
044  GSB5    perform conversion
045  GTO4    print result
046  *LBLe   CONVERT WIRE DIAMETER TO AWG
047  GSB6    perform conversion
048  GTO4    print result
049  *LBLE   CONVERT AWG TO WIRE DIAMETER
050  GSB0    interchange registers
051  RCL1
052  x       use Eq. (3-2.3) for
053  e^x     conversion
054  RCL0
055  x
056  GSB1    interchange registers
057  *LBL4   print, spc, & eng3 subr
058  PRTX
059  SPC
060  ENG
061  DSP3
062  RTN
063  *LBL5   AWG to ohms/inch subroutine
064  GSB0    interchange registers
065  RCL3
066  x       use Eq. (3-2.2) for
067  e^x     conversion
068  RCL2
069  x
070  GTO1    test for register interchg
071  *LBL6   wire diameter to AWG subr
072  GSB0    interchange registers
073  RCL0
074  ÷       use Eq. (3-2.1) for
075  LN      conversion
076  RCL1
077  ÷
078  .
079  5
080  +
081  FIX
082  DSP0
083  RND
084  GTO1    interchange registers
085  *LBL0   register interchange subr
086  F0?     test for initialization
087  GSB2
088  P⇄S
089  SF2
090  RTN
```

**NOTE:**
**To change from the "print" to "R/S" mode for output, change the "print" statement at line 058 to a "R/S" statemdnt.**

REGISTERS

| 0 | 1 | 2 | 3 | 4 | 5 | 6 | 7 | 8 | 9 |
|---|---|---|---|---|---|---|---|---|---|
| | | | | N | | | | | |

| S0 | S1 | S2 | S3 | S4 | S5 | S6 | S7 | S8 | S9 |
|---|---|---|---|---|---|---|---|---|---|
| .3137250775 | -.1097881513 | $\times 10^{-6}$ 8.371747114 | .231765483 | | | | | | |

| A | B | C | D | E | I |
|---|---|---|---|---|---|
| Window Area, in² | AWG | Mean Turn, in | | | 2.54 |

# Program Listing II

NOTE FLAG SET STATUS

| Step | Key | Comment |
|---|---|---|
| 091 | *LBL2 | initialization subroutine |
| 092 | ENG | set engr 3 format |
| 093 | DSP3 | |
| 094 | F2? | test if P⇄S needed |
| 095 | P⇄S | |
| 096 | P⇄S | execute and note P⇄S |
| 097 | SF2 | |
| 098 | CF0 | indicate initialization done |
| 099 | . | |
| 100 | 3 | |
| 101 | 1 | |
| 102 | 3 | |
| 103 | 7 | |
| 104 | 2 | .3137250775 → S0 |
| 105 | 5 | |
| 106 | 0 | |
| 107 | 7 | |
| 108 | 7 | |
| 109 | 5 | |
| 110 | STO0 | |
| 111 | CLX | |
| 112 | . | |
| 113 | 1 | |
| 114 | 0 | |
| 115 | 9 | |
| 116 | 7 | |
| 117 | 8 | −.1097881513 → S1 |
| 118 | 8 | |
| 119 | 1 | |
| 120 | 5 | |
| 121 | 1 | |
| 122 | 3 | |
| 123 | CHS | |
| 124 | STO1 | |
| 125 | CLX | |
| 126 | 8 | |
| 127 | . | |
| 128 | 3 | |
| 129 | 7 | |
| 130 | 1 | |
| 131 | 7 | |
| 132 | 4 | $8.371747114 \times 10^{-6}$ → S2 |
| 133 | 7 | |
| 134 | 1 | |
| 135 | 1 | |
| 136 | 4 | |
| 137 | EEX | |
| 138 | CHS | |
| 139 | 6 | |
| 140 | STO2 | |
| 141 | CLX | |
| 142 | . | |
| 143 | 2 | |
| 144 | 3 | |
| 145 | 1 | |
| 146 | 7 | |
| 147 | 6 | .231765483 → S3 |
| 148 | 5 | |
| 149 | 5 | |
| 150 | 4 | |
| 151 | 8 | |
| 152 | 3 | |
| 153 | STO3 | |
| 154 | CLX | |
| 155 | 2 | |
| 156 | . | 2.54 → RI |
| 157 | 5 | |
| 158 | 4 | |
| 159 | STOI | |
| 160 | R↓ | restore x register |
| 161 | *LBL1 | subroutine to interchange |
| 162 | F2? | registers if flag 2 is set |
| 163 | P⇄S | |
| 164 | RTN | |

NOTE FLAG SET STATUS

| LABELS | | | | | FLAGS |
|---|---|---|---|---|---|
| A load window area in in² | B load mean turn in inches | C calculate AWG | D calculate winding R | E AWG → wire diam | 0 store constants |
| a load window area in cm² | b load mean turn in cm | c | d | e wire diam → AWG | 1 |
| 0 P⇄S SF2 | 1 P⇄S if F2 | 2 Constant storage | 3 | 4 Print & space | 2 P⇄S used |
| 5 AWG → Ω/in | 6 wire diam → AWG | 7 | 8 | 9 | 3 |

| SET STATUS | | | | |
|---|---|---|---|---|
| FLAGS | ON | OFF | TRIG | DISP |
| 0 | ■ | | DEG | FIX ■ |
| 1 | | | GRAD | SCI |
| 2 | | ■ | RAD | ENG |
| 3 | | | | n 0 |

## PROGRAM 3-3 TRANSFORMER LEAKAGE INDUCTANCE AND WINDING CAPACITANCES.

Program Description and Equations Used

This program will calculate the leakage inductance and winding capacitances of a two winding transformer. Both the interwinding capacitance and winding self-capacitances are calculated. The output for both the leakage inductance and winding capacitances are reflected to the primary winding.

Leakage inductance. The total magnetic flux in a transformer is composed of the mutual flux and the leakage flux. The mutual flux follows the core path and links both primary and secondary windings, and results in the mutual, or open-circuit inductance of the transformer. The leakage flux is the relatively small flux which originates in the primary winding and does not link the secondary winding, or vice-versa, and results in the leakage inductance. The leakage flux will be less as the primary and secondary windings are interleaved up to the limit imposed by the space occupied by the insulation between windings. To a degree, the interleaving process is self-defeating, as too much interleaving generates much nonconductive space, and most of the leakage flux flows therein.

Of the many formulas that have been derived for the calculation of leakage inductance, the one by Fortescue [25] is generally accurate and errs, if at all, on the conservative side:

$$L_{leak} = 10 \cdot 6 \times 10^{-9} \frac{N^2 \cdot MT(2nc + a)}{n^2 b} \tag{3-3.1}$$

where

$L_{leak}$ = leakage inductance in henries, referred to the winding having N turns (the primary in this program)

MT = mean-turn length in inches for the whole coil (both windings)

n = number of dielectrics between windings

a = winding buildup in inches

b = winding traverse in inches

c = dielectric thickness between windings in inches

Interleaving provides the greatest reduction in leakage inductance when the dielectric height, c, is small compared to the window height. When *nc* is comparable to the window height, the leakage inductance does not decrease substantially as the number of interleaves, n, is increased. The lowest leakage inductance will be obtained with a transformer having a small number of turns, a short mean turn length, and a low, wide winding window.

The term "a" in Eq. (3-3.1) refers to the total winding buildup composed of the primary buildup, the secondary buildup, and the insulation layers buildup. If $a_p$ represents the buildup of all the primary interleaves, and $a_s$ represents the buildup of all the secondary interleaves, then:

$$2nc + a = 3nc + a_p + a_s \qquad (3\text{-}3.2)$$

The basis for Eq. (3-3.2) may be seen from Fig. 3-3.1.

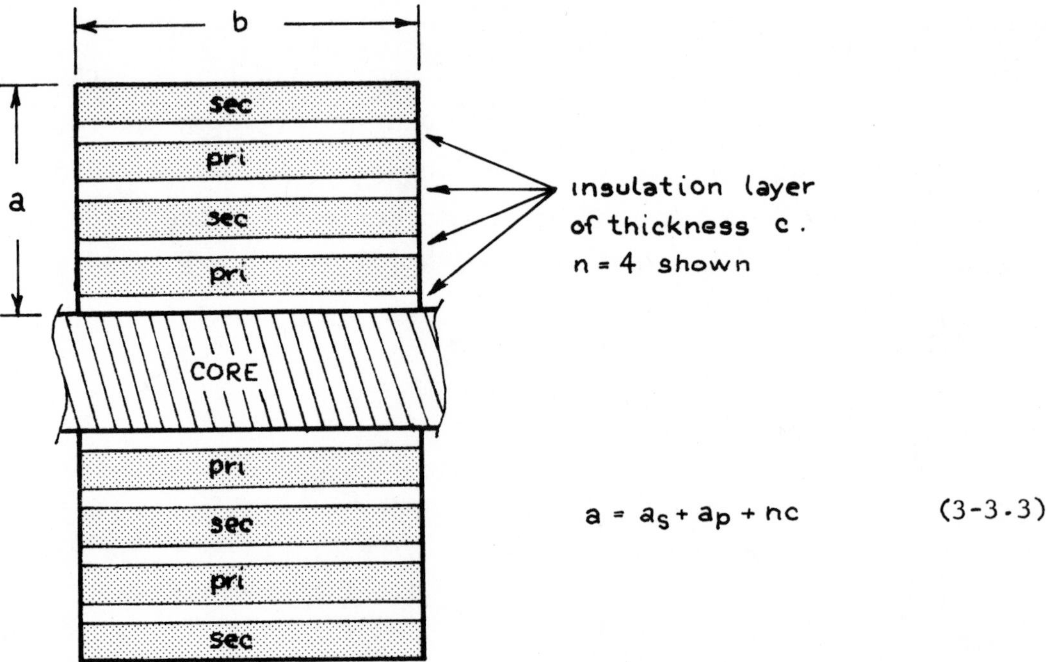


Figure 3-3.1 Cross-section of transformer winding on a core leg.

Interwinding capacitance. The interwinding capacitance is the primary-secondary capacitance. This capacitance is calculated by considering the primary and secondary windings as single conducting sheets separated by the dielectric formed by the insulating layer and wire insulation. The capacitance of two flat plates separated by a dielectric is:

$$C = .225 \times 10^{-12}\ \varepsilon \frac{A}{t} \tag{3-3.4}$$

where

$\varepsilon$ is the relative dielectric constant of the dielectric

A is the area of one plate in inches$^2$

t is the dielectric thickness in inches

For the transformer

$$A = n \cdot MT \cdot b \tag{3-3.5}$$

and

$$t = c + t_{\text{primary wire insulation}} + t_{\text{secondary wire insulation}} \tag{3-3.6}$$

The wire insulation thickness for heavy insulation (heavy formvar, etc.) can be obtained from the wire AWG. The AWG is obtained from the wire diameter over class 2 insulation by using Eq. (3-2.1), where the wire diameter is calculated by assuming the wire plus insulation just fits in a box as shown by Fig. 3-6.2. The wire diameter over the insulation then becomes:

$$t_{\text{wire, primary}} = \sqrt{\frac{a_p \cdot b}{N_p}} \tag{3-3.7}$$

and

$$t_{\text{wire, secondary}} = \sqrt{\frac{a_s \cdot b}{N_s}} \tag{3-3.8}$$

The diameter of the bare wire is obtained from AWG by using Eq. (3-2.3). Hence, the thickness of the wire insulation is:

$$t_{\text{wire insulation}} = \tfrac{1}{2}\left(t_{\text{wire + insulation}} - t_{\text{wire}}\right) \tag{3-3.9}$$

The wire insulation thickness calculations are performed in the subroutine under label 6 in the HP-67/97 program.

Winding self-capacitance. In a multilayer winding, the voltage between layers is zero at one end of the layer, and $2E/N_L$ at the other where

E is the total winding voltage, and $N_L$ is the number of layers. This voltage gradient model serves as the basis for the total winding capacity as given by Reuben Lee [36].

$$C_i = 1.333 \frac{C_{L_i}}{N_{L_i}} \left\{ 1 - \frac{1}{N_{L_i}} \right\} \qquad (3\text{-}3.10)$$

$$i = \text{pri or sec}$$

$C_{L_i}$ is the layer-to-layer capacitance, and is found from Eq. (3-3.4) where

$$A = MT \cdot b \qquad (3\text{-}3.11)$$

and

$$t = t_d + 2t_{\text{wire insulation}} \qquad (3\text{-}3.12)$$

The basis of Eqs. (3-3.11) and (3-3.12) are shown by Fig. 3-3.2.

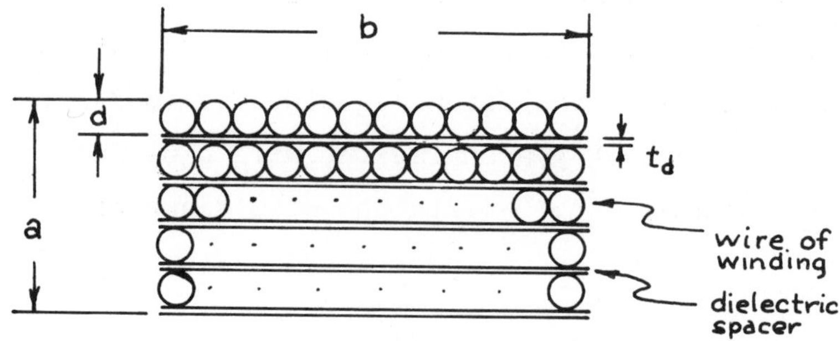


Figure 3-3.2 Cross-section of a winding showing dimensioning.

The number of layers is needed for Eq. (3-3.10) and is found from the number of turns, the interwinding dielectric thickness, and the winding dimensions. The wire cross-sectional area (per Fig. 3-6.2) and the dielectric cross-sectional area must equal the total area available for that winding, i.e.,

$$N_L(d + t_d) = a \qquad (3\text{-}3.13)$$

$$\text{volume} = a \cdot b = \underbrace{N_L \cdot t_d \cdot b}_{\text{spacer volume}} + \underbrace{N \cdot d^2}_{\text{wire volume}} \qquad (3\text{-}3.14)$$

Substituting Eq. (3-3.13) into (3-3.14) and solving for $N_L$ yields:

$$N_{L_i} = \frac{N_i \, d_i}{b_i} \tag{3-3.15}$$

where d is the quadratic solution to:

$$N_i d_i^{\,2} + \left(N_i t_{d_i}\right) d_i - a_i b_i = 0 \tag{3-3.16}$$

$$i = \text{pri or sec}$$

The program calculates the secondary winding capacity and reflects it to the primary winding:

$$C_{sec}\text{@ primary} = C_{sec} \cdot \left(\frac{N_s}{N_p}\right)^2 \tag{3-3.17}$$

The total winding capacity seen at the primary is the sum of the reflected secondary winding capacitance, and the primary winding capacitance.

# User Instructions

| TRANSFORMER LEAKAGE L AND WINDING C | | | | |
|---|---|---|---|---|
| winding traverse | $N_p \uparrow N_s$ | # of dielectrics | print? | Calculate L leakage C winding C interwinding |
| pri buildup ↑ sec buildup | average mean turn length | $t_{d_p} \uparrow t_{d_s} \uparrow t_d$ | $\varepsilon_{pri} \uparrow \varepsilon_{sec} \uparrow \varepsilon_{sp}$ | |

| STEP | INSTRUCTIONS | INPUT DATA/UNITS | KEYS | OUTPUT DATA/UNITS |
|---|---|---|---|---|
| 1 | Load both sides of program card | | | |
| | (note flag status) | | | |
| 2 | Load both sides of data card | | | |
| 3 | Select print or R/S option using toggle | | [f] [D] | 0, R/S |
| | | | [f] [D] | 1, print |
| | | | [f] [D] | 0, R/S |
| | | | | ⋮ |
| 4 | Load winding traverse in inches | b, in | [f] [A] | |
| 5 | Load winding buildup in inches: | | | |
| | a) primary buildup | $a_p$, in | [ENT↑] | |
| | b) secondary buildup | $a_s$, in | [A] | |
| 6 | Load number of turns: | | | |
| | a) primary turns | $N_p$ | [ENT↑] | |
| | | | [f] [B] | |
| 7 | load average mean-turn length for the whole | | | |
| | transformer winding in inches | MT, in | [B] | |
| 8 | load the number of dielectrics | n | [f] [C] | |
| 9 | load dielectric thickness in inches: | | | |
| | a) primary interwinding dielectric | $t_{d_p}$, in | [ENT↑] | |
| | b) secondary interwinding dielectric | $t_{d_s}$, in | [ENT↑] | |
| | c) primary-secondary dielectric | $t_d$, in | [C] | |
| 10 | Load relative dielectric constants: | | | |
| | a) average for primary interwinding | $\varepsilon_{pri}$ | [ENT↑] | |
| | dielectric and wire insulation | | | |
| | b) average for secondary interwinding | $\varepsilon_{sec}$ | [ENT↑] | |
| | dielectric and wire insulation | | | |
| | c) primary-secondary spacer | $\varepsilon_{sp}$ | [D] | |

# User Instructions

TRANSFORMER LEAKAGE L AND WINDING C

CONTINUED

2

| STEP | INSTRUCTIONS | INPUT DATA/UNITS | KEYS | OUTPUT DATA/UNITS |
|---|---|---|---|---|
| 11 | Calculate L's and C's | | E | |
| | Primary leakage inductance | | | $L_{leak}$, h |
| | | | | space |
| | Secondary wire AWG | | | AWG, sec |
| | Number of secondary winding layers | | | # layers |
| | Secondary winding C reflected to primary, F | | | $C_{sec@pri}$ |
| | | | | space |
| | Primary wire AWG | | | AWG, pri |
| | Number of primary layers | | | # layers |
| | Primary winding capacity in farads | | | $C_{primary}$ |
| | Total winding capacity reflected to primary | | | $C_{total}$ |
| | | | | space |
| | primary-secondary interwinding capacitance, F | | | $C_{pri-sec}$ |
| 12 | Data review: Go back and key any entry key without keying in any numeric entry to view the presently stored variable. See Example 3-3.1. | | | |

Example 3-3.1

Find the primary leakage inductance and winding capacitances of a transformer having the following specifications:

traverse: 2"

number of pri-sec dielectrics: 4 (3 interleaves)

dielectric thickness: 0.050"

pri-sec insulator dielectric constant: 10

mean turn length for whole transformer: 5"

Primary

number of turns: 100

buildup: 0.25"

interwinding dielectric thickness: 0.002"

average interwinding dielectric and wire insulation dielectric constant: 10

Secondary

number of turns: 1000

buildup: 0.3"

interwinding dielectric thickness: 0

average interwinding dielectric and wire insulation dielectric constant: 5

HP printout for Example 3-3.1

```
      2. GSBa   winding traverse

    .25 ENT↑   primary winding buildup
     .3 GSBA   secondary winding buildup

   100. ENT↑   primary winding turns
  1000. GSBb   secondary winding turns

     5. GSBB   mean turn length for whole transformer

     4. GSBc   number of pri-sec dielectrics

   .002 ENT↑   primary interwinding dielectric thickness
     0. ENT↑   secondary interwinding dielectric thickness
    .05 GSBC   pri-sec dielectric thickness

    10. ENT↑   average primary dielectric constant
     5. ENT↑   average secondary dielectric constant
    10. GSBD   pri-sec dielectric, dielectric constant


           GSBE   calculate L's and C's
19.05-06    ***   primary leakage inductance, henrys

24.00+00    ***   secondary wire AWG
24.49+00    ***   number of secondary layers
23.19-09    ***   secondary interwinding C seen @ primary, F

14.00+00    ***   primary wire AWG
6.972+00    ***   number of primary layers
678.6-12    ***   primary interwinding capacity, F
23.87-09    ***   total interwinding capacity @ primary, F

1.699-09    ***   pri-sec winding capacity, F
```

Data Review printout for Example 3-3.1

```
             GSBa
 2.000+00    ***   traverse

             GSBA
 300.0-03    ***   secondary winding buildup
 250.0-03    ***   primary winding buildup

             GSBb
 1.000+03    ***   secondary turns
 100.0+00    ***   primary turns

             GSBB
 5.000+00    ***   mean turn length

             GSBc
 4.000+00    ***   number of dielectrics

             GSBC
 50.00-03    ***   primary-sec dielectric thickness
 0.000+00    ***   secondary interwinding dielectric thickness
 2.000-03    ***   primary interwinding dielectric thickness

             GSBD
 10.00+00    ***   pri-sec dielectric, dielectric constant
 5.000+00    ***   secondary average dielectric constant
 10.00+00    ***   primary average dielectric constant
```

# Program Listing I

| Step | Key | Comment |
|---|---|---|
| 001 | *LBLA | I/O PRIMARY & SEC BUILDUP |
| 002 | EEX | |
| 003 | GSB0 | |
| 004 | 0 | |
| 005 | GTO1 | |
| 006 | *LBLa | I/O WINDING TRAVERSE (b) |
| 007 | 2 | |
| 008 | GTO1 | |
| 009 | *LBLB | I/O AVERAGE MEAN TURN (MT) |
| 010 | 3 | |
| 011 | GTO1 | |
| 012 | *LBLb | I/O PRIMARY AND SEC TURNS |
| 013 | 5 | |
| 014 | GSB0 | |
| 015 | 4 | |
| 016 | GTO1 | |
| 017 | *LBLC | I/O DIELECTRIC THICKNESSES |
| 018 | 8 | I/O pri-sec spacer thickness |
| 019 | GSB0 | |
| 020 | 7 | I/O secondary intrawinding dielectric thickness |
| 021 | GSB0 | |
| 022 | 6 | I/O primary intrawinding dielectric thickness |
| 023 | GTO1 | |
| 024 | *LBLc | I/O NUMBER OF DIELECTRICS |
| 025 | 9 | |
| 026 | GTO1 | |
| 027 | *LBLD | I/O DIELECTRIC CONSTANTS |
| 028 | 1 | I/O dielectric constant of pri-sec spacer |
| 029 | 2 | |
| 030 | GSB0 | |
| 031 | 1 | I/O secondary insulation dielectric constant |
| 032 | 1 | |
| 033 | GSB0 | |
| 034 | EEX | I/O primary insulation dielectric constant |
| 035 | 1 | |
| 036 | *LBL1 | subroutine to I/O last item |
| 037 | GSB0 | |
| 038 | GTO8 | |
| 039 | *LBL0 | main I/O subroutine |
| 040 | STOI | store index |
| 041 | R↓ | recover entry |
| 042 | F3? | if flag 3, set flag 1 |
| 043 | SF1 | |
| 044 | F1? | if flag 1, store entry |
| 045 | STOi | |
| 046 | F1? | if flag 1, recover previous entry |
| 047 | R↓ | |
| 048 | F1? | if flag 1, return |
| 049 | RTN | |
| 050 | RCLi | recall and print item |
| 051 | GTO7 | |
| 052 | *LBLd | PRINT-R/S TOGGLE |
| 053 | F0? | |
| 054 | GTO2 | (→ 058) |
| 055 | SF0 | |
| 056 | EEX | |
| 057 | GTO8 | |
| 058 | *LBL2 | |
| 059 | CF0 | |
| 060 | CLX | |
| 061 | GTO8 | |
| 062 | *LBLE | CALCULATE L's & C's |
| 063 | P⇄S | calculate leakage inductance |
| 064 | RCL4 | |
| 065 | P⇄S | |
| 066 | RCL4 | |
| 067 | RCL9 | |
| 068 | ÷ | |
| 069 | X² | |
| 070 | × | |
| 071 | RCL3 | |
| 072 | × | |
| 073 | RCL9 | $L_{leak} = \dfrac{10.6\, N_p^2 \cdot MT \cdot (3nc + a_p + a_s)}{10^{+9}\, n^2\, b}$ |
| 074 | RCL8 | |
| 075 | × | |
| 076 | 3 | |
| 077 | × | |
| 078 | RCL0 | |
| 079 | + | |
| 080 | RCL1 | |
| 081 | + | |
| 082 | × | |
| 083 | RCL2 | |
| 084 | ÷ | |
| 085 | GSB3 | |
| 086 | RCL1 | calculate and store $2 \cdot t_{wire}$, secondary |
| 087 | RCL2 | |
| 088 | × | |
| 089 | RCL5 | |
| 090 | ÷ | |
| 091 | RCL7 | |
| 092 | GSB6 | |
| 093 | STOB | |
| 094 | R↓ | recover d/b |
| 095 | RCL5 | recall $N_s$ |
| 096 | GSB5 | calc secondary capacitance: |
| 097 | P⇄S | |
| 098 | RCL1 | |
| 099 | P⇄S | |
| 100 | RCLB | |
| 101 | RCL7 | |
| 102 | + | |
| 103 | GSB4 | |
| 104 | × | |
| 105 | RCL5 | reflect secondary capacitance to primary: |
| 106 | RCL4 | |
| 107 | ÷ | |
| 108 | X² | |
| 109 | × | |
| 110 | STOC | |
| 111 | GSB3 | |
| 112 | RCL0 | |

**REGISTERS**

| 0 | 1 | 2 | 3 | 4 | 5 | 6 | 7 | 8 | 9 |
|---|---|---|---|---|---|---|---|---|---|
| $a_p$, pri buildup | secondary buildup | b, winding traverse | MT, mean turn length | $N_p$ | $N_s$ | $t_{D\,pri}$ | $t_{D\,sec}$ | $C, t_{D\,spacer}$ | n, the # of dielectrics |

| S0 | S1 | S2 | S3 | S4 | S5 | S6 | S7 | S8 | S9 |
|---|---|---|---|---|---|---|---|---|---|
| $\epsilon_{pri}$ | $\epsilon_{sec}$ | $\epsilon_{spacer}$ | $225 \times 10^{-15}$ | $10.6 \times 10^{-9}$ | $k_1$ = .3137250775 | $k_1'$ = .3245574964 | $k_2$ = -.1097881513 | $k_2'$ = -0.1159489227 | |

| A | B | C | D | E | I |
|---|---|---|---|---|---|
| 2x primary wire insulation thickness | 2x secondary wire insulation thickness | Csec, or dsec | | 1.33333··· | index or scratchpad |

# Program Listing II

NOTE FLAG SET STATUS

| Step | Key | Comment |
|---|---|---|
| 113 | RCL2 | calculate and store $2 \cdot t_{wire}$, primary |
| 114 | × | |
| 115 | RCL4 | |
| 116 | ÷ | |
| 117 | RCL6 | |
| 118 | GSB6 | |
| 119 | STOA | |
| 120 | R↓ | calc primary capacitance |
| 121 | RCL4 | |
| 122 | GSB5 | |
| 123 | P⇄S | |
| 124 | RCL0 | |
| 125 | P⇄S | |
| 126 | RCLA | |
| 127 | RCL6 | |
| 128 | + | |
| 129 | GSB4 | |
| 130 | × | |
| 131 | GSB7 | |
| 132 | RCLC | calculate and print: |
| 133 | + | $C_{pri} - N^2 \cdot C_{sec}$ |
| 134 | GSB3 | |
| 135 | RCL9 | calculate interwinding cap.: |
| 136 | P⇄S | |
| 137 | RCL2 | |
| 138 | P⇄S | |
| 139 | × | |
| 140 | RCLA | |
| 141 | RCLB | |
| 142 | + | |
| 143 | 2 | |
| 144 | ÷ | |
| 145 | RCL8 | |
| 146 | + | |
| 147 | GSB4 | |
| 148 | *LBL3 | print or R/S subroutine |
| 149 | GSB7 | |
| 150 | GTO8 | |
| 151 | *LBL4 | capacity subroutine |
| 152 | ÷ | |
| 153 | RCL3 | MT |
| 154 | × | |
| 155 | RCL2 | b |
| 156 | × | |
| 157 | P⇄S | |
| 158 | RCL3 | $.225 \times 10^{-12}$ |
| 159 | P⇄S | |
| 160 | × | |
| 161 | RTN | |
| 162 | *LBL5 | intrawinding capacity subr |
| 163 | × | calc and print # of layers |
| 164 | GSB7 | |
| 165 | 1/X | calculate winding capacity term: |
| 166 | ENT↑ | |
| 167 | ENT↑ | |
| 168 | EEX | |
| 169 | X⇄Y | |
| 170 | − | |
| 171 | × | |
| 172 | RCLE | |
| 173 | × | |
| 174 | RTN | |
| 175 | *LBL6 | wire AWG and insulation thk. |
| 176 | 2 | calculate wire diameter: |
| 177 | ÷ | |
| 178 | STOI | |
| 179 | X² | |
| 180 | + | |
| 181 | √X | |
| 182 | RCLI | |
| 183 | − | |
| 184 | STOI | |
| 185 | RCL2 | calculate d/b |
| 186 | ÷ | |
| 187 | RCLI | calculate insulation thick. |
| 188 | RCLI | calculate wire AWG |
| 189 | P⇄S | |
| 190 | RCL5 | $k_1$ |
| 191 | ÷ | |
| 192 | LN | |
| 193 | RCL7 | $k_2$ |
| 194 | ÷ | |
| 195 | ENT↑ | |
| 196 | ENT↑ | |
| 197 | EEX | calculate and print integral wire size |
| 198 | + | |
| 199 | INT | |
| 200 | GSB7 | |
| 201 | R↓ | calculate bare wire diameter from AWG |
| 202 | RCL8 | |
| 203 | $y^x$ | |
| 204 | $e^x$ | |
| 205 | RCL6 | |
| 206 | P⇄S | |
| 207 | × | |
| 208 | − | calculate $2 \cdot t_{insulation}$ |
| 209 | RTN | |
| 210 | *LBL7 | print or R/S subroutine |
| 211 | F0? | |
| 212 | PRTX | |
| 213 | F0? | |
| 214 | RTN | |
| 215 | R/S | |
| 216 | RTN | |
| 217 | *LBL8 | space and clear flag 3 subr |
| 218 | F0? | |
| 219 | SPC | |
| 220 | CF1 | |
| 221 | CF3 | |
| 222 | RTN | |
| 223 | GTO8 | |

NOTE FLAG SET STATUS

| LABELS | | | | | FLAGS |
|---|---|---|---|---|---|
| A I/O of pri & sec buildup | B I/O of mean turn length | C I/O of dielectric thick | D I/O of relative dielectric const. | E calculate L & C's | 0 print |
| a I/O winding traverse | b I/O turns Np, Ns | c I/O of # of dielectrics | d print or R/S toggle | e | 1 input |
| 0 I/O subroutine | 1 I/O subroutine | 2 print or R/S toggle | 3 print or R/S and space | 4 capacitance subroutine | 2 |
| 5 winding C subroutine | 6 wire diameter subroutine | 7 print or R/S subroutine | 8 space & CF1,3 subr | 9 | 3 input |

| SET STATUS | | | | |
|---|---|---|---|---|
| FLAGS | ON | OFF | TRIG | DISP |
| 0 | ■ | | DEG | FIX |
| 1 | | ■ | GRAD | SCI |
| 2 | | | RAD | ENG ■ |
| 3 | | ■ | | n 3 |

## PROGRAM 3-4 STRAIGHT WIRE AND LOOP WIRE INDUCTANCE.

### Program Description and Equations Used

This program calculates the inductance of straight wire lengths and single square wire loops. The permeability of the wire is taken into account only for the inductance calculation, but not for skin depth; therefore, the inductance calculated is the low frequency inductance.

The calculation of wire inductance can be an important design parameter in some instances. For example, the bonding wire inductance of high speed, wideband hybrid integrated circuits affects circuit performance. Wire self-inductance is also important in the design of high frequency (1000 Hz), high power (megawatt) power conversion equipment such as SCR inverters, choppers, cycloconverters, and phase delay rectifiers.

The inductance of a straight wire increases with permeability and length, and decreases with increasing diameter. The combined effect of permeability, length, and diameter is not described simply, but can be easily solved with a scientific calculator. For example, the inductance of copper wire is strongly influenced by diameter while the inductance of a high permeability wire such as permalloy is relatively unaffected by diameter.

The formulas used herein come from Grover [30], and can also be found in Terman [52]. Two basic formulas are used, one for straight wire, and another for wire loops. These formulas are algebraically manipulated to obtain expressions for each of the four variables; wire diameter (d), wire length ($\ell$), relative permeability ($\mu$), and inductance in $\mu$h (L). The program works in the units of centimeters, but the user may input data in either inch or centimeter units.

Figure 3-4.1 shows the definitions of the wire terms.

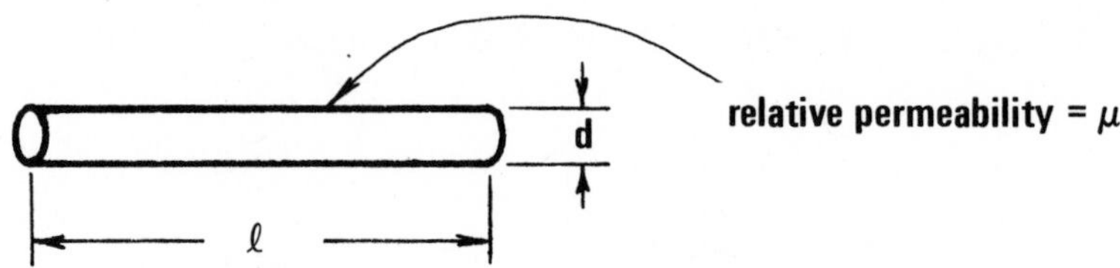


Figure 3-4.1 Straight wire terms.

The formulas for the straight wire case are:

$$L = (2 \times 10^{-3})\, \ell \left\{ \ell n\left(\frac{4\ell}{d}\right) + \frac{\mu}{4} - 1 \right\},\ \mu h \tag{3-4.1}$$

$$d = \frac{4\ell}{e^{(L/(2\ell \times 10^{-3}) - \mu/4 + 1)}} \tag{3-4.2}$$

$$\mu = 4\left\{ \frac{L}{2\ell \times 10^{-3}} + 1 - \ell n\left(\frac{4\ell}{d}\right) \right\} \tag{3-4.3}$$

To obtain the wire length, a Newton-Raphson iterative solution is employed (see Program 1-3 for details), because the equation for $\ell$ has a logarithm containing $\ell$.

$$\ell = \frac{L}{(2 \times 10^{-3})\left\{ \ell n\left(\frac{4\ell}{d}\right) + \frac{\mu}{4} - 1 \right\}} \tag{3-4.4}$$

The Newton-Raphson solution finds where a function is zero, therefore, let:

$$f(\ell) = \ell - \frac{L}{(2 \times 10^{-3})\left\{ \ell n\left(\frac{4\ell}{d}\right) + \frac{\mu}{4} - 1 \right\}} = 0 \tag{3-4.5}$$

and

$$f'(\ell) = \frac{df(\ell)}{d\ell} = 1 + \frac{L}{(2 \times 10^{-3}\ell)\left\{ \ell n\left(\frac{4\ell}{d}\right) + \frac{\mu}{4} - 1 \right\}} \tag{3-4.6}$$

The initial guess for $\ell$ is 1, and the $\ell$ value for each succeeding iteration is given by:

$$\ell_{i+1} = \ell_i - \frac{f(\ell_i)}{f'(\ell_i)} \tag{3-4.7}$$

The iteration is terminated when:

$$\left| \ell_{i+1} - \ell_i \right| < 10^{-6} \qquad (3\text{-}4.8)$$

Figure 3-4.2 shows the definitions of the loop wire terms.

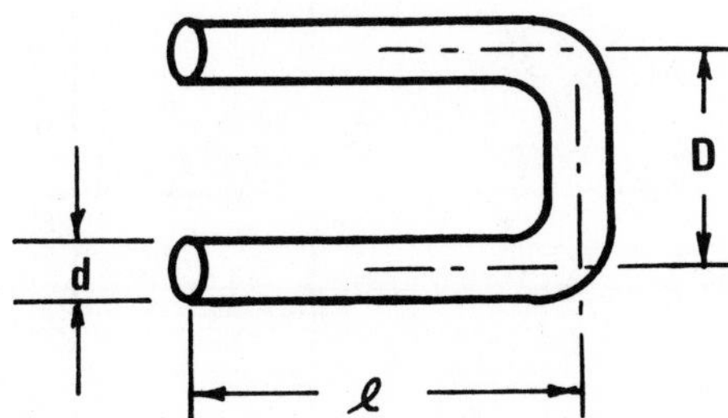


Figure 3-4.2 Loop wire terms.

The formulas for the loop wire case are:

$$L = (4 \times 10^{-3}\, \ell) \left\{ \ell n\left(\frac{2D}{d}\right) + \frac{\mu}{4} - \frac{D}{\ell} \right\}, \ \mu h \qquad (3\text{-}4.9)$$

$$d = \frac{2D}{e^{(L/(4 \times 10^{-3}\ell) - \mu/4 + D/\ell)}} \qquad (3\text{-}4.10)$$

$$\ell = \frac{\dfrac{L}{4 \times 10^{-3}} + D}{\ell n\left(\dfrac{2D}{d}\right) + \dfrac{\mu}{4}} \qquad (3\text{-}4.11)$$

$$\mu = 4\left\{ \frac{L}{4 \times 10^{-3}\ell} + \frac{D}{\ell} - \ell n\left(\frac{2D}{d}\right) \right\} \qquad (3\text{-}4.12)$$

Keys "a" through "d" set up the dimension units to be used for input or output (inches or centimeters), and the configuration (straight wire or loop wire). When the loop wire configuration is selected (key "c"), the loop separation, D, must also be entered via key "c."

Keys "A" through "D" provide the program input/output functions. Use of these keys following numeric input signals an input to the program. Use of these keys without numeric entry, or following the clear key (E) signals an output is required from the program. Flag 3 is used to indicate input or output within the program.

# User Instructions

| STRAIGHT WIRE AND LOOP WIRE INDUCTANCE | | | | |
|---|---|---|---|---|
| centimeter units | inch units | wire loop, enter D | straight wire | |
| wire diam d | wire length ℓ | permeablty μ | inductance L | clear input mode |

| STEP | INSTRUCTIONS | INPUT DATA/UNITS | KEYS | OUTPUT DATA/UNITS |
|---|---|---|---|---|
| 1 | Load both sides of data card | | | |
| 2 | Select dimension units | | | |
| | a) centimeter units | | f A | 1.000 |
| | b) inch units | | f B | 2.540 |
| 3 | Select configuration | | | |
| | a) wire loop, load loop separation | D | f C | |
| | b) straight wire | | f D | |
| 4 | To calculate wire diameter, d | | | |
| | a) load wire length | ℓ | B | |
| | b) load wire permeability | μ | C | |
| | c) load required inductance | L, μh | D | |
| | d) start solution | | A | d |
| 5 | To calculate wire length, ℓ | | | |
| | a) load wire diameter | d | A | |
| | b) load wire permeability | μ | C | |
| | c) load required inductance | L, μh | D | |
| | d) start solution execution | | B | ℓ |
| 6 | To calculate permeability, μ | | | |
| | a) load wire diameter | d | A | |
| | b) load wire length | ℓ | B | |
| | c) load required inductance | L, μh | D | |
| | d) start solution execution | | C | μ |
| 7 | To calculate inductance, L | | | |
| | a) load wire diameter | d | A | |
| | b) load wire length | ℓ | B | |
| | c) load permeability | μ | C | |
| | d) start solution execution | | D | L, μh |
| 8 | To clear input mode (reset flag 3) | | E | |

<u>Example 3-4.1</u>

Find the inductance of a straight gold wire 0.001 inch in diameter and 0.3 inch long (a hybrid integrated circuit interconnect wire).

```
        GSBb  set inches
        GSBa  set straight wire mode
   .001 GSBA  load wire diameter in inches
   .300 GSBB  load wire length in inches
  1.000 GSBC  load wire relative permeability
        GSBD  calculate inductance
  0.010  ***  inductance in microhenries
```

<u>Example 3-4.2</u>

Find the length of a 4/0 copper cable (.528 in diam) having an inductance of 6 microhenries

```
          GSBb  set inches
          GSBd  set straight wire mode
     .528 GSBA  load wire diameter
    1.000 GSBC  load relative permeability of wire
    6.000 GSBD  load required inductance
          GSBB  calculate wire length*
  182.258  ***  length, inches

   12.000   ÷
   15.188  ***  length, feet
```

*Computation time takes about 1 minute.

Example. 3-4.3

A pair of 4/0 wires run 20 feet between a capacitor module and an inverter module in an ac traction motor controller. The wire separation is twice the wire diameter. What parasitic inductance does the wire add in series with the capacitors? 4/0 wire is .528 inches in diameter.

```
         GSBb   set inch mode
    .528 ENT↑   }
            +   }  calculate and enter the wire separation,
   1.056  ***   }  and select wire loop configuration
         GSBc   }
    .528 GSBA   load wire diameter in inches
  20.000 ENT↑   }
  12.000    ×   }  calculate and load wire length in inches
 240.000  ***   }
         GSBB   }
   1.000 GSBC   load permeability of wire
         GSBD   calculate inductance of wire loop
   3.979  ***   inductance, microhenries
```

If the maximum parasitic inductance that can be tolerated is 2 microhenries, how long can the feeder wires be if the other parameters don't change?

```
   2.000 GSBD   load required inductance in μh
         GSBE   calculate loop length
 120.948  ***   loop length, inches

  12.000    ÷
  10.079  ***   loop length, feet
```

# Program Listing I

| Step | Key | Comment |
|---|---|---|
| 001 | *LBLa | SET CM UNIT MODE |
| 002 | EEX | |
| 003 | STO9 | store cm → cm conversion |
| 004 | RTN | |
| 005 | *LBLb | SET INCH UNIT MODE |
| 006 | 2 | |
| 007 | . | |
| 008 | 5 | store in → cm conversion |
| 009 | 4 | |
| 010 | STO9 | |
| 011 | RTN | |
| 012 | *LBLc | LOAD WIRE LOOP SEPARATION |
| 013 | SF0 | indicate wire loop mode |
| 014 | CF3 | |
| 015 | 4 | goto data entry subroutine |
| 016 | GTO0 | |
| 017 | *LBLd | SET STRAIGHT WIRE MODE |
| 018 | CF0 | indicate straight wire mode |
| 019 | RTN | |
| 020 | *LBLA | I/O OF WIRE DIAMETER, d |
| 021 | 2 | |
| 022 | EEX | |
| 023 | CHS | store 0.002 |
| 024 | 3 | |
| 025 | STO8 | |
| 026 | R↓ | recover input |
| 027 | 0 | |
| 028 | F3? | if numeric input, |
| 029 | GTO0 | goto data input subroutine |
| 030 | F0? | |
| 031 | GTO1 | jump if wire loop mode |
| 032 | RCL1 | |
| 033 | 4 | calculate and store d for |
| 034 | x | straight wire case: |
| 035 | GSB6 | |
| 036 | + | $d = \dfrac{4\ell}{e^{\left(\frac{L}{2\ell\times10^{-3}} - \frac{\mu}{4} + 1\right)}}$ |
| 037 | RCL2 | |
| 038 | - | |
| 039 | $e^x$ | |
| 040 | ÷ | |
| 041 | STO0 | |
| 042 | GTO7 | goto unit conversion & print |
| 043 | *LBL1 | calculate and store d for |
| 044 | GSB8 | loop wire case |
| 045 | GSB6 | |
| 046 | x | |
| 047 | 2 | |
| 048 | ÷ | |
| 049 | - | |
| 050 | $e^x$ | $d = \dfrac{2D}{e^{\left(\frac{L}{4\ell\times10^{-3}} - \frac{\mu}{4} + \frac{D}{\ell}\right)}}$ |
| 051 | RCL4 | |
| 052 | x | |
| 053 | ENT↑ | |
| 054 | + | |
| 055 | STO0 | |
| 056 | GTO7 | goto unit conv and print |
| 057 | *LBLB | I/O OF WIRE LENGTH, $\ell$ |
| 058 | EEX | |
| 059 | F3? | if numeric input, |
| 060 | GTO0 | goto input subroutine |
| 061 | F0? | |
| 062 | GTO1 | jump if loop wire mode |
| 063 | STO1 | store "1" for initial guess |
| 064 | *LBL4 | Newton-Raphson loop start |
| 065 | RCL1 | |
| 066 | 4 | |
| 067 | x | calculate and store $f(\ell)$: |
| 068 | RCL0 | |
| 069 | ÷ | |
| 070 | LN | |
| 071 | EEX | |
| 072 | - | $\ln\left\{\frac{4\ell}{d}\right\} + \frac{\mu}{4} - 1$ |
| 073 | RCL2 | |
| 074 | + | |
| 075 | F2? | test for subroutine exit |
| 076 | RTN | |
| 077 | STOE | finish $f(\ell)$ calculation |
| 078 | RCL8 | |
| 079 | x | |
| 080 | 1/X | |
| 081 | RCL5 | $f(\ell) = \ell - \dfrac{L}{2\times10^{-3}\left\{\ln\left(\frac{4\ell}{d}\right) + \frac{\mu}{4} - 1\right\}}$ |
| 082 | x | |
| 083 | CHS | |
| 084 | RCL1 | |
| 085 | + | |
| 086 | STO7 | |
| 087 | RCL5 | |
| 088 | RCL8 | calculate and apply $f'(\ell)$: |
| 089 | RCL1 | |
| 090 | x | |
| 091 | RCLE | $f'(\ell) = 1 + \dfrac{L}{(2\times10^{-3}\ell)\left\{\ln\left(\frac{4\ell}{d}\right) + \frac{\mu}{4} - 1\right\}^2}$ |
| 092 | $X^2$ | |
| 093 | x | |
| 094 | ÷ | |
| 095 | EEX | |
| 096 | + | |
| 097 | ST÷7 | calculate correction |
| 098 | RCL7 | apply correction |
| 099 | ST-1 | |
| 100 | ABS | |
| 101 | EEX | |
| 102 | CHS | test for loop exit |
| 103 | 6 | |
| 104 | X≤Y? | |
| 105 | GTO4 | |
| 106 | RCL1 | recall and print |
| 107 | GTO7 | |
| 108 | *LBL1 | calculate $\ell$ for loop wire |
| 109 | RCL5 | case |
| 110 | RCL8 | |

**REGISTERS**

| 0 | 1 | 2 | 3 | 4 | 5 | 6 | 7 | 8 | 9 |
|---|---|---|---|---|---|---|---|---|---|
| diameter cm | length cm | $\mu/4$ | | wire separation, cm | inductance L | | scratch | $2\times10^{-3}$ | 1 or 2.54 |
| S0 | S1 | S2 | S3 | S4 | S5 | S6 | S7 | S8 | S9 |
| | | | | | | | | | |

| A | B | C | D | E | I |
|---|---|---|---|---|---|
| | | | | scratch | index |

# Program Listing II

| Step | Key | Comment |
|---|---|---|
| 111 | ENT↑ | |
| 112 | + | |
| 113 | ÷ | |
| 114 | RCL4 | |
| 115 | + | |
| 116 | RCL4 | $\ell = \dfrac{\dfrac{L}{4\times10^{-3}} + D}{\ln\left(\dfrac{2D}{d}\right) + \dfrac{\mu}{4}}$ |
| 117 | ENT↑ | |
| 118 | + | |
| 119 | RCL0 | |
| 120 | ÷ | |
| 121 | LN | |
| 122 | RCL2 | |
| 123 | + | |
| 124 | ÷ | |
| 125 | STO1 | store $\ell$ |
| 126 | *LBL7 | unit conversion & prt subr |
| 127 | RCL9 | recall unit conversion |
| 128 | ÷ | |
| 129 | *LBL2 | print and space subroutine |
| 130 | PRTX | -- can be R/S statement |
| 131 | SPC | |
| 132 | RTN | |
| 133 | *LBLC | I/O OF PERMEABILITY, $\mu$ |
| 134 | 4 | |
| 135 | ÷ | |
| 136 | RCL9 | undo unit conversion |
| 137 | ÷ | |
| 138 | 2 | if numeric input, goto data input subroutine |
| 139 | F3? | |
| 140 | GTO0 | |
| 141 | F0? | jump if wire loop mode |
| 142 | GTO3 | |
| 143 | GSB6 | start calculation for straight wire |
| 144 | + | |
| 145 | RCL1 | |
| 146 | 4 | |
| 147 | GTO1 | |
| 148 | *LBL3 | loop wire calculation |
| 149 | GSB6 | $\dfrac{L}{4\ell\times10^{-3}}$ |
| 150 | 2 | |
| 151 | ÷ | |
| 152 | RCL4 | $\dfrac{D}{\ell}$ |
| 153 | RCL1 | |
| 154 | ÷ | |
| 155 | + | |
| 156 | RCL4 | D |
| 157 | 2 | |
| 158 | *LBL1 | common calculation routine |
| 159 | × | |
| 160 | RCL0 | |
| 161 | ÷ | |
| 162 | LN | |
| 163 | - | |
| 164 | STO2 | store $\mu/4$ |
| 165 | 4 | |
| 166 | × | calculate $\mu$ |
| 167 | GTO2 | goto print and space subr |
| 168 | *LBLD | I/O OF INDUCTANCE, L |
| 169 | RCL9 | undo unit conversion |
| 170 | ÷ | |
| 171 | 5 | if numeric input, goto data input subroutine |
| 172 | F3? | |
| 173 | GTO0 | |
| 174 | F0? | jump if loop wire mode |
| 175 | GTO3 | |
| 176 | SF2 | calc: $\ln\left(\dfrac{4\ell}{d}\right) + \dfrac{\mu}{4} - 1$ |
| 177 | GSB4 | |
| 178 | GTO1 | jump |
| 179 | *LBL3 | calculate: $2\left\{\ln\left(\dfrac{2D}{d}\right) + \dfrac{\mu}{4} - \dfrac{D}{\ell}\right\}$ |
| 180 | RCL4 | |
| 181 | ENT↑ | |
| 182 | + | |
| 183 | RCL0 | |
| 184 | ÷ | |
| 185 | LN | |
| 186 | GSB8 | |
| 187 | + | |
| 188 | ENT↑ | |
| 189 | + | |
| 190 | *LBL1 | common inductance calculation $\times(2\ell\times10^{-3})$ |
| 191 | RCL8 | |
| 192 | × | |
| 193 | RCL1 | |
| 194 | × | |
| 195 | STO5 | store inductance |
| 196 | GTO2 | goto print and space subr |
| 197 | *LBL0 | data input subroutine |
| 198 | STOI | store register index |
| 199 | R↓ | recover input |
| 200 | RCL9 | apply unit conversion and store entry |
| 201 | × | |
| 202 | STOi | |
| 203 | RTN | return to main program |
| 204 | *LBL6 | subroutine to calculate: $\dfrac{L}{2\ell\times10^{-3}}$ |
| 205 | EEX | |
| 206 | RCL5 | |
| 207 | RCL8 | |
| 208 | ÷ | |
| 209 | RCL1 | |
| 210 | ÷ | |
| 211 | RTN | |
| 212 | *LBL8 | subroutine to calculate: $\dfrac{\mu}{4} - \dfrac{D}{d}$ |
| 213 | RCL2 | |
| 214 | RCL4 | |
| 215 | RCL1 | |
| 216 | ÷ | |
| 217 | - | |
| 218 | RTN | |
| 219 | *LBLE | CLEAR INPUT MODE |
| 220 | CF3 | |
| 221 | RTN | |

**LABELS**

| | | | | |
|---|---|---|---|---|
| A d | B $\ell$ | C $\mu$ | D L | E clear input |
| a cm units | b inch units | c wire loop | d straight wire | e |
| 0 data entry | 1 used | 2 output routine w/o unit conv | 3 partial calc of loop wire $\mu$ | 4 Newton-Raphson Loop |
| 5 | 6 calc $L/(.002\ell)$ | 7 output routine w/ unit conv | 8 calc of $\mu/4 - D/\ell$ | 9 calc of $\ln(4\ell/d)+\mu/4-1$ |

**FLAGS**

| | |
|---|---|
| 0 | wire loop |
| 1 | |
| 2 | subr 4 exit |
| 3 | data entry |

**SET STATUS**

| FLAGS | ON | OFF | TRIG | DISP |
|---|---|---|---|---|
| 0 | | ■ | DEG | FIX ■ |
| 1 | | | GRAD | SCI |
| 2 | | ■ | RAD | ENG |
| 3 | | ■ | | n 3 |

## PROGRAM 3-5 AIR-CORE SINGLE-LAYER INDUCTOR DESIGN.

Program Description and Equations Used

This program uses Wheeler's equation [55] to solve for the various parameters relating to single-layer, air-core inductor design. The basic form of Wheeler's equation is:

$$L(\mu h) = \frac{a^2n^2}{9a + 10\ell} \quad \text{(use inch dimensions)} \qquad (3\text{-}5.1)$$

This equation provides answers within 1% accuracy for all values of $2a/\ell$ less than 3, and the results will be about 4% low when $2a/\ell = 5$ (short coils).

There are five parameters that can be used to describe an air-core inductor: the coil radius in inches (a), the coil length in inches ($\ell$), the number of turns (n), the winding pitch ($p = \ell/n$), and the inductance in microhenries (L). Of this set of five parameters, only four are independent since $\ell$, n, and p are interrelated; hence, given any three independent parameters, the fourth independent parameter, and the remaining dependent parameter can be found. For example, L can be calculated given a, $\ell$, and n, or a, n, and p.

Wheeler's equation may be algebraically manipulated to yield the other independent variables.

Solving for $\ell$ given a, n, and L:

$$\ell = \frac{a^2n^2 - 9a\,L}{10\,L} \qquad (3\text{-}5.2)$$

Solving for $\ell$ given n and p:

$$\ell = n \cdot p \qquad (3\text{-}5.3)$$

Solving for n given a, $\ell$, and L:

$$n = \frac{1}{a}\sqrt{L(9a + 10\ell)} \qquad (3\text{-}5.4)$$

Solving for n given a, p, and L: find quadratic solution of

$$a^2n^2 - 10Lpn - 9aL = 0 \qquad (3\text{-}5.5)$$

Solving for p given $\ell$ and n:

$$p = \ell/n \qquad (3\text{-}5.6)$$

Solving for p given a, n, and L:

$$p = \frac{1}{10n}\left\{\frac{a^2n^2}{L} - 9a\right\} \qquad (3\text{-}5.7)$$

Solving for L given a, n, and p:

$$L = \frac{a^2n^2}{9a + 10np} \qquad (3\text{-}5.8)$$

Solving for a given $\ell$, n, and L: find quadratic solution of

$$n^2a^2 - 9La = 10\ell L = 0 \qquad (3\text{-}5.9)$$

The program uses these equations as follows. The appropriate input keys are assumed to have been executed prior to an output request. Label "A" inputs or outputs the coil radius in inches, a. The input is stored in R0, and Eq. (3-5.9) is used for output.

Label "B" inputs or outputs the number of turns, n. The input is stored in R1, and if p was previously entered, $\ell$ is calculated using Eq. (3-5.3). For output, Eq. (3-5.5) is used if p, $\ell$, and a are specified, otherwise, Eq. (3-5.4) is used.

Label "C" inputs or outputs the coil length, $\ell$. For input, the coil length is stored in R2, flag 0 is cleared, and a new p is calculated and stored using Eq. (3-5.6). For output, if p has been previously entered, use Eq. (3-5.3), otherwise use Eq. (3-5.2).

Label "D" inputs or outputs the winding pitch, p. For input, the new pitch is stored in R3, flag 0 is set, and new $\ell$ is calculated with Eq. (3-5.3). For output, Eq. (3-5.6) is used.

Label "E" inputs or outputs the coil inductance, L, in microhenries. For input, the value is stored in R4. For output, Eq. (3-5.1) is used, and the new inductance value stored.

Label "c" calculates the wire diameter given the wire AWG with heavy insulation. The wire diameter over heavy insulation bears an exponential relationship to the wire gauge:

$$\text{Diameter (inches)} = k_1 \cdot e^{k_2 \cdot \text{AWG}} \qquad (3\text{-}5.10)$$

where $k_1 = 0.31373$
and $k_2 = -.109788$

On the first execution of this routine, the constants $k_1$ and $k_2$ are stored into R8 and R9 respectively. Flag 2 is initially set after magnetic card reading to indicate constant storage required, and is reset upon test.

Label "d" calculates the AWG of the wire given the diameter over the insulation in inches:

$$\text{AWG} = \frac{1}{k_2} \cdot \ln \left\{ \frac{\text{Diameter}}{k_1} \right\} \qquad (3\text{-}5.11)$$

Label "e" is used to clear flag 3 to indicate data output desired.

Keys "A" through "E" leave flag 3 cleared after the associated routine finishes, i.e., data output mode is set unless further numeric entry is made.

The routines under keys "d" and "e" do not alter the state of flag 3. For example, one may load the wire AWG, use key "c" to convert to wire diameter, and then use key "D" to load this value as the winding pitch (close wound coils).

Highest coil Q's are generally obtained when the space between the wires equals the wire diameter (pitch equals twice the wire diameter). Callendar's equation [13] can be used to estimate the Q of a coil with this pitch:

$$Q = \frac{\sqrt{\text{freq in Hz}}}{\frac{2.71}{a} + \frac{2.13}{\ell}} \quad \text{(use inch dimensions)} \qquad (3\text{-}5.12)$$

For RF coils where the skin depth is less than the wire diameter, Callendar's equation is accurate to within a few percent. For close wound coils, the calculated Q will be high by a factor of 1.9.

HP-67 users may want to make the following program changes to make the final number in the display unambiguous. For example, label "C" causes both the number of turns and the coil length to be printed with the coil length being displayed last. To change the program so only the number of turns is displayed and printed, change lines 122 through 126 of the program as follows:

```
122   RCL3
123     x
124   STO2
125   RCL1
126   GTO8
```

# User Instructions

| AIR-CORE, SINGLE-LAYER, SOLENOIDAL INDUCTOR DESIGN | | | | |
|---|---|---|---|---|
| | | AWG → diam | diam → AWG | clear input mode |
| coil radius a, in | # of turns n | coil length ℓ, in | pitch p = ℓ/n | inductance L, μh |

| STEP | INSTRUCTIONS | INPUT DATA/UNITS | KEYS | OUTPUT DATA/UNITS |
|---|---|---|---|---|
| 1 | Load both sides of program card | | | |
| 2 | Select problem type: | | | |
| | a) to find L & p given a, n, & ℓ | | | |
| | i) load the coil radius | a, in | [A] | |
| | ii) load the number of turns | n | [B] | |
| | iii) load the coil length | ℓ, in | [C] | |
| | iv) calculate the coil inductance | | [E] | L, μh |
| | v) calculate the winding pitch | | [D] | p, in/T |
| | b) to find L & ℓ given a, n, & p | | | |
| | i) load the coil radius | a, in | [A] | |
| | ii) load the number of turns | n | [B] | |
| | iii) load the winding pitch | p, in/T | [D] | |
| | iv) calculate the coil inductance | | [E] | L, μh |
| | v) calculate the coil length | | [C] | ℓ, in |
| | c) to find n & p given a, ℓ, & L | | | |
| | i) load the coil radius | a, in | [A] | |
| | ii) load a dummy value for n* | 1 | [B] | |
| | iii) load the winding length | ℓ, in | [C] | |
| | iv) load desired inductance | L, μh | [E] | |
| | v) calculate the # of turns and | | [B] | n, turns |
| | the winding pitch | | | p, in/T |
| | d) to find n & ℓ given a, n, & L | | | |
| | i) load the coil radius | a, in | [A] | |
| | ii) load the winding pitch | p, in/T | [D] | |
| | iii) load desired inductance | L, μh | [E] | |
| | iv) calculate the number of turns | | [B] | n, turns |
| | and the winding length | | | ℓ, in |
| | e) to find ℓ & p given a, n, & L | | | |
| | i) load the coil radius | a, in | [A] | |
| | ii) load the desired number of turns | n | [B] | |
| | iii) load the desired inductance | L, μh | [E] | |
| | iv) calculate the inductor length ** | | [C] | ℓ, in |
| | v) calculate the winding pitch | | [D] | p, in/T |

# User Instructions

AIR-CORE, SINGLE-LAYER, SOLENOIDAL INDUCTOR DESIGN

CONTINUED

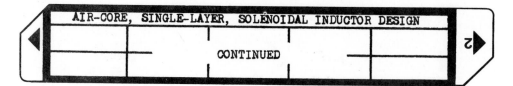

| STEP | INSTRUCTIONS | INPUT DATA/UNITS | KEYS | OUTPUT DATA/UNITS |
|---|---|---|---|---|
| 2 | f) to find a & $\ell$ given n, p, & L | | | |
| | i) load the desired number of turns | n | B | |
| | ii) load the desired winding pitch | p, in/T | D | |
| | iii) load the desired inductance | L, µh | E | |
| | iv) calculate the coil radius | | A | a, in |
| | v) calculate the coil length | | C | $\ell$, in |
| | g) to find a & p given n, $\ell$, & L | | | |
| | i) load the desired number of turns | n | B | |
| | ii) load the desired coil length | $\ell$, in | C | |
| | iii) load the desired inductance | L, µh | E | |
| | iv) calculate the coil radius | | A | a, in |
| | v) calculate the winding pitch | | D | p, in/T |
| 3 | Go back to any part of step 2, or stop | | | |
| 4 | To convert wire AWG to diameter over heavy (class 2) insulation | AWG | f C | diam, in |
| 5 | To convert wire diameter over heavy insulation to AWG | diam, in | f D | AWG |
| 6 | To clear input mode, i.e., to request output after numeric operations have been performed from the keyboard | | f E | |

Notes:

* $p = \ell/n$, a non-zero n is required for proper program operation. The dummy n is replaced with the calculated n under label B.

** A negative value for the inductor length means the required inductance cannot be realized with the chosen radius and number of turns. Either increase n or a.

<u>Example 3-5.1</u>

An air-core coil is to be wound in a ½ inch form using #18 AWG HF wire at a pitch of twice the wire diameter. What number of turns are required for an inductance of 500 nanohenry (0.5 μh), and what will the winding length be?

```
  .250 GSBA  load coil radius in inches
18.000 GSBc  load wire AWG
 0.043  ***  wire diameter over HF insulation

 2.000    ×  calculate winding pitch (2 x diam)
       GSBD  load winding pitch
  .500 GSBE  load required inductance in microhenry
       GSBB  calculate turns and coil length
 8.958  ***  number of turns (use 9 turns)
 0.778  ***  coil length in inches
```

<u>Example 3-5.2</u>

A 6 turn coil on a 6 inch form is closewound with #4/0 wire. The wire is 0.750 inches over the insulation. What is the coil inductance and length?

```
3.000 GSBA  load the coil radius in inches
6.000 GSBE  load the number of turns
 .750 GSBD  load winding pitch
      GSBE  calculate inductance
4.500  ***  inductance in microhenries

      GSBC  calculate coil length
4.500  ***  coil length in inches
```

# Program Listing I

| | | | | | | |
|---|---|---|---|---|---|---|
| 001 | *LBLA | I/O OF COIL RADIUS, a | 053 | *LBL1 | calculate and store | |
| 002 | F3? | jump if numeric entry | 054 | RCL1 | | |
| 003 | GT00 | | 055 | RCL3 | $\ell = n(\ell/n)$ | |
| 004 | RCL1 | use quadratic equation to find a in: | 056 | x | | |
| 005 | X² | | 057 | ST02 | | |
| 006 | ST05 | | 058 | GT08 | goto print and space subr | |
| 007 | 9 | $a^2 n^2 - 9aL - 10\ell L = 0$ | 059 | *LBLD | I/O OF COIL PITCH, p | |
| 008 | RCL4 | | 060 | F3? | jump if numeric entry | |
| 009 | x | | 061 | GT00 | | |
| 010 | CHS | | 062 | RCL2 | calculate and store | |
| 011 | ST06 | | 063 | RCL1 | | |
| 012 | RCL2 | | 064 | ÷ | $p = \ell/n$ | |
| 013 | RCL4 | | 065 | ST03 | | |
| 014 | x | | 066 | GT08 | goto print and space subr | |
| 015 | EEX | | 067 | *LBL0 | | |
| 016 | 1 | | 068 | ST03 | store p | |
| 017 | x | | 069 | RCL1 | calculate and store | |
| 018 | CHS | | 070 | x | $\ell = p \cdot n$ | |
| 019 | ST07 | | 071 | ST02 | | |
| 020 | GSB9 | gosub quadratic solution | 072 | SF0 | indicate p entered last | |
| 021 | ST00 | store a | 073 | RTN | | |
| 022 | GT08 | goto print & space subr | 074 | *LBLB | I/O OF COIL TURNS, n | |
| 023 | *LBL0 | coil radius data input | 075 | F3? | jump if numeric entry | |
| 024 | ST00 | store coil radius | 076 | GT00 | | |
| 025 | RTN | return control to keyboard | 077 | F0? | jump if p entered last | |
| 026 | *LBLC | I/O OF COIL LENGTH, | 078 | GT01 | | |
| 027 | F3? | jump if numeric entry | 079 | GSB3 | calculate and store n: | |
| 028 | GT00 | | 080 | RCL4 | | |
| 029 | F0? | jump if p entered last | 081 | x | | |
| 030 | GT01 | | 082 | √X | | |
| 031 | RCL0 | calculate and store: | 083 | RCL0 | $n = \frac{1}{a} \sqrt{L(9a - 10\ell)}$ | |
| 032 | RCL1 | | 084 | ÷ | | |
| 033 | x | | 085 | ST01 | | |
| 034 | X² | | 086 | PRTX | | |
| 035 | RCL4 | | 087 | 1/X | | |
| 036 | ÷ | $\ell = \frac{1}{10}\left(\frac{a^2 n^2}{L} - 9a\right)$ | 088 | RCL2 | | |
| 037 | RCL0 | | 089 | x | | |
| 038 | 9 | | 090 | ST03 | | |
| 039 | x | | 091 | GT08 | | |
| 040 | - | | 092 | *LBL1 | calculate and store n from quadratic solution to: | |
| 041 | EEX | | 093 | RCL0 | | |
| 042 | 1 | | 094 | X² | | |
| 043 | ÷ | | 095 | ST05 | | |
| 044 | ST02 | | 096 | RCL3 | | |
| 045 | GT08 | goto print and space subr | 097 | RCL4 | | |
| 046 | *LBL0 | | 098 | x | $a^2 n^2 - 10Lpn - 9aL = 0$ | |
| 047 | CF0 | indicate ℓ entered last | 099 | EEX | | |
| 048 | ST02 | store ℓ | 100 | 1 | | |
| 049 | RCL1 | | 101 | x | | |
| 050 | ÷ | calculate and store $p = \ell/n$ | 102 | CHS | | |
| 051 | ST03 | | 103 | ST06 | | |
| 052 | RTN | | 104 | RCL0 | | |
| | | | 105 | RCL4 | | |
| | | | 106 | x | | |

## REGISTERS

| 0 a | 1 n | 2 ℓ | 3 p | 4 L | quadratic equation terms | | wire AWG | constants |
|---|---|---|---|---|---|---|---|---|
| | | | | | 5 a | 6 b | 7 c | 8 $k_1$ | 9 $k_2$ |
| S0 | S1 | S2 | S3 | S4 | S5 | S6 | S7 | S8 | S9 |
| A | B | C | D | E | I |

# Program Listing II

NOTE FLAG SET STATUS

```
107       9
108       x
109     CHS
110     STO7
111     GSB9
112     STO1
113     PRTX
114     RCL3
115       x
116     STO2
117     GTO8
118   *LBL0
119     STO1    store number of turns
120     F0?     jump if p entered last
121     GTO0
122     RTN
123   *LBL0     calculate and store new
124     RCL3    coil length
125       x
126     STO2
127     RTN
128   *LBLE     I/O OF INDUCTANCE, L (μh)
129     F3?     jump if numeric entry
130     GTO0
131     RCL0    use Wheeler's equation
132     RCL1    to calculate inductance
133       x     (Eq. (3-5.1)):
134      X²
135     GSB3    L = a²n² / (9a + 10ℓ)
136       ÷
137     STO4
138   *LBL8     print and space subroutine
139     PRTX
140     SPC
141     RTN
142   *LBL0
143     STO4    store inductance input
144     RTN
145   *LBL9     quadratic equation solution
146     RCL5    subroutine.
147     ST÷6
148     ST÷7    If ax² + bx + c = 0
149       2
150     ST÷6    then the positive root is:
151     RCL6
152     CHS     x = -b/2a + √((b/2a)² + c/a)
153     ENT↑
154      X²
155     RCL7
156       -
157      √X
158       +
159     RTN
160   *LBL3     9a + 10ℓ calculation subr
161     RCL0
162       9
163       x
164     RCL2
165     EEX
166       1
167       x
168       +
169     RTN
170   *LBLc     AWG → WIRE DIAMETER
171     F2?     constant initialization
172     GSB2    needed?
173     RCL9
174       x
175      eˣ     diameter = k1·e^(k2·AWG)
176     RCL8
177       x
178     GTO8
179   *LBLd     WIRE DIAMETER → AWG
180     F2?     constant initialization
181     GSB2    needed?
182     RCL8
183       ÷
184      LN
185     RCL9    AWG = (1/k2) ln{diameter/k1}
186       ÷
187     INT
188     GTO8
189   *LBL2     constant initialization
190       .
191       3
192       1
193       3
194       0
195       4
196     STO8    store k1
197      R↓     recover x register
198       .
199       1
200       0
201       9
202       7
203       3
204       3
205     CHS
206     STO9    store k2
207      R↓     recover x register
208     RTN
209   *LBLe     CLEAR INPUT MODE
210     CF3
211     RTN
```

Equations in the listing comments:

$$L = \frac{a^2n^2}{9a + 10\ell}$$

If $ax^2 + bx + c = 0$, then the positive root is:

$$x = -\frac{b}{2a} + \sqrt{\left(\frac{b}{2a}\right)^2 + \frac{c}{a}}$$

$$\text{diameter} = k_1 \cdot e^{k_2 \cdot \text{AWG}}$$

$$\text{AWG} = \frac{1}{k_2} \ln\left\{\frac{\text{diameter}}{k_1}\right\}$$

**NOTE:**

Print statements are located at steps 086 and 139 and may be changed to R/S if desired.

NOTE FLAG SET STATUS

| LABELS | | | | | FLAGS |
|---|---|---|---|---|---|
| A I/O coil radius | B I/O coil length | C I/O # of turns | D I/O pitch | E I/O inductance | 0 p entered last |
| a | b | c | d | e | 1 |
| 0 local label | 1 local label | 2 constant storage | 3 9a + 10ℓ | 4 | 2 store coefficients |
| 5 | 6 | 7 | 8 print & space | 9 quadratic solution | 3 data entry |

| SET STATUS | | | | |
|---|---|---|---|---|
| FLAGS | ON | OFF | TRIG | DISP |
| 0 | | ■ | DEG | FIX ■ |
| 1 | | | GRAD | SCI |
| 2 | ■ | | RAD | ENG |
| 3 | | ■ | | n 3 |

## PROGRAM 3-6 AIR-CORE MULTILAYER INDUCTOR DESIGN.

Program Description and Equations Used

This program uses a modification of Bunet's formula [11], Eq. (3-6.1), to design air-core, multilayer solenoidal inductors (inch dimensions).

$$L\ (\mu h) = \frac{a^2 n^2}{9a + 10\ell + 8.4c + 3.2\, c\ell/a} \qquad (3\text{-}6.1)$$

The coil dimensions are shown in Fig. 3-6.1, and the range of usefulness of the program can be ascertained from Table 3-6.1.

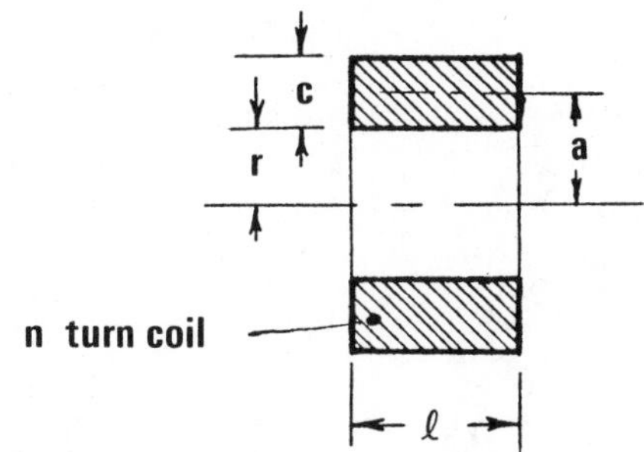


Figure 3-6.1 Multilayer coil dimensions.

Table 3-6.1 Accuracy estimates for Bunet's equation.

| c/a ratio | 2a/ℓ ratio for 1% accuracy | other accuracies 2a/ℓ | % |
|---|---|---|---|
| 1/20 | ≤ 3 | 5 | 4 |
| 1/5 | ≤ 5 | 10 | 2 |
| 1/2 | ≤ 2 | 5 | 3 |
| 1/1 | ≤ 1.5 | 5 | 5 |

The modification to Eq. (3-6.1) consists of replacing the mid-coil radius, a, by the inner radius, r:

$$a = r + \frac{c}{2} \tag{3-6.2}$$

The coil is generally wound on a coil form, hence, r and $\ell$ are known from the coil form dimensions. The coil mid-radius, a, is dependent upon the coil buildup, and is generally not known at the inception of the design.

If the wire and insulation occupy a box as shown in Fig. 3-6.2,

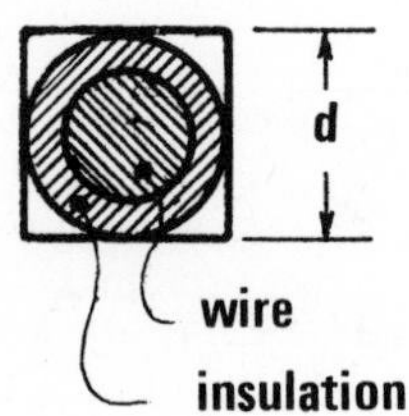


Figure 3-6.2 Wire cross-section.

then the total area occupied by n turns of this wire would be:

$$A_{total} = n \cdot d^2 \tag{3-6.3}$$

This area is also expressible in terms of the coil dimensions:

$$A_{total} = c \cdot \ell \tag{3-6.4}$$

Hence,

$$n \cdot d^2 = c \cdot \ell \tag{3-6.5}$$

or

$$c = \frac{n \cdot d^2}{\ell} \tag{3-6.6}$$

A fifth order polynomial in n may be derived to yield the number of turns of wire with diameter d, given the required inductance, L, the coil inner radius, r, and the coil width, $\ell$. Taking Eq. (3-6.1), multiplying both sides by the denominator term, and clearing fractions yields:

$$a^3n^2 - L\{9a^2 + (10\ell + 8.4c)\,a + 3.2c\,\ell\} = 0 \tag{3-6.7}$$

Substituting Eq. (3-6.2) for a, and Eq. (3-6.6) for c, and collecting terms in like powers of n results in the following 5th order polynomial equation:

$$f(n) = An^5 + Bn^4 + Cn^3 + Dn^2 - En - F = 0 \tag{3-6.8}$$

$$A = \left(\frac{d^2}{2\ell}\right)^3 \tag{3-6.9}$$

$$B = 3r\left(\frac{d^2}{2\ell}\right)^2 \tag{3-6.10}$$

$$C = 3r^2\left(\frac{d^2}{2\ell}\right) \tag{3-6.11}$$

$$D = r^3 - \left(\frac{d^2}{2\ell}\right)^2 (25.8\ L) \tag{3-6.12}$$

$$E = L\left\{\frac{d^2}{2\ell}(34.8r + 10\ell) + 3.2d^2\right\} \tag{3-6.13}$$

$$F = rL\,(10\ell + 9r) \tag{3-6.14}$$

The Newton-Raphson iterative procedure described in Program 1-3 is used to find the largest positive real root for n in Eq. (3-6.8). If the initial guess for n is larger than the largest root, the method will converge to the largest root when the function is a polynomial as in the present case. An initial guess of 10000 turns is used. If a larger number of turns is expected, the user may want to increase the initial guess which is located at step 084 of the program.

If r, c, $\ell$, and L are specified, then the solution for n becomes somewhat simpler. Since r and c are both known, a can be calculated from Eq. (3-6.2). With this calculation, all parameters except n are known in Eq. (3-6.1), and n becomes:

$$n = \frac{1}{a}\left\{L(9a + 10 + c(8.4) + 3.2\ell/a\ )\right\}^{\frac{1}{2}} \tag{3-6.15}$$

Once n has been calculated, the wire diameter, d, can be calculated from Eq. (3-6.6) as given below:

$$d = \sqrt{\frac{c\ell}{n}} \tag{3-6.16}$$

So far, the two cases for the number of turns have been derived. Likewise, there are two cases for the calculation of L. Given r, $\ell$, c, and n, Eqs. (3-6.2) and (3-6.1) may be used to calculate L. If the wire diameter, d, had been specified instead of the coil thickness, c, then

Eqs. (3-6.6) and (3-6.1) are used to calculate L.

Program constants

Since all program steps were used to code the program equations, no room remains for the program constants. These constants are recorded on another magnetic card, and are loaded after the program magnetic card loading. Load the following registers, and record the data on both sides of the data card (2 WDATA commands):

8.4 → R7

3.2 → R8

10. → R9

# User Instructions

| AIR-CORE MULTILAYER INDUCTOR DESIGN | | | | |
|---|---|---|---|---|
| coil inner radius, r (I) | wire diam, d (I) / winding thickness, c (I) | winding length, ℓ (I) | number of turns, n (I/O) | inductance in µh, L (I/O) |

| STEP | INSTRUCTIONS | INPUT DATA/UNITS | KEYS | OUTPUT DATA/UNITS |
|---|---|---|---|---|
| 1 | Load both sides of program card and either side of data card | | | |
| 2 | Load inner coil radius | r, in | [A] | |
| 3 | Load wire diameter | d, in | [f] [B] | |
| | or | or | | |
| | Load winding thickness | c, in | [B] | |
| 4 | Load winding width | ℓ, in | [C] | |
| 5 | To calculate inductance in microhenries | | | |
| | a) load the number of coil turns | n | [D] | |
| | b) calculate inductance | | [E] | L, µh |
| 6 | To calculate the number of turns | | | |
| | a) load the desired inductance | L, µh | [E] | |
| | b) calculate the number of turns | | [D] | n |

Example 3-6.1

Find the number of turns of #24 HF wire (0.0224 inches over insulation) to be wound on a bobbin that has a 0.3 inch inner radius and is 0.5 inch wide to obtain an inductance of 200 microhenries. Also find the coil thickness.

```
     .30 GSBA   load bobbin inner radius (in)

   .0224 GSBb   load wire diameter over insulation (in)

     .50 GSBC   load bobbin width (in)

  200.00 GSBE   load inductance required (μh)

         GSBD   calculate # of turns & coil thickness*
  122.66  ***   number of turns (use 123)
  0.1231  ***   coil thickness, inches
```

Example 3-6.2

Calculate the inductance of an 18 turn coil of 4/0 wire with 6 turns per layer wound on a 6 inch diameter form. 4/0 wire is 0.75 inch over the insulation.

```
    3.00 GSBA   load coil inner radius (in)

     .75 GSBb   load wire diameter over insulation (in)

    6.00    X   calculate coil width:
    4.50  ***   coil turns per layer x thickness per turn
         GSBC   load coil width

   18.00 GSBD   load number of turns

         GSBE   calculate inductance
 50.6345  ***   inductance in microhenries
```

* Requires about a minute to compute.

# Program Listing I

```
001  *LBLA   LOAD COIL INNER RADIUS
002  STO1
003  GTO9
004  *LBLB   LOAD COIL THICKNESS
005  SF0     indicate thickness loaded
006  STO2    store thickness
007  GTO9    goto CF3, space & return
008  *LBLb   LOAD WIRE DIAMETER
009  CF0     indicate wire diam. loaded
010  STO6    store wire diameter
011  GTO9    goto CF3, space & return
012  *LBLC   LOAD WINDING LENGTH
013  STO3    store
014  GTO9    goto CF3, space, & return
015  *LBLD   I/O OF COIL TURNS
016  F3?     if input, jump
017  GTO0
018  F0?     if coil thickness loaded,
019  GTO1    use other routine
020  RCL6    calculate n given r, ℓ,
021  X²      d, and L
022  RCL3
023  ENT↑    calculate and temporarily
024  +       store d²/(2ℓ)
025  ÷
026  STOI
027  3       calculate and store n⁵ coef
028  Yˣ      A = {d²/(2ℓ)}³
029  STOA
030  RCLI
031  X²      calculate and store n⁴ coef
032  RCL1
033  3       B = 3r(d²/2ℓ)²
034  GSB5
035  STOB
036  RCLI
037  RCL1    calculate and store n³ coef
038  X²
039  3
040  GSB5    C = 3r²(d²/2ℓ)
041  STOC
042  RCL1
043  3
044  Yˣ
045  2       calculate and store n² coef
046  5
047  .
048  8       D = r³ - (d²/2ℓ)² (25.8·L)
049  RCLI
050  X²
051  RCL4
052  GSB5
053  -
054  STOD
055  3
056  4
057
058  8
059  RCL1    calculate and store n¹ coef
060  x
061  RCL9
062  RCL3
063  GSB4    E = L{ d²/2ℓ (34.8r + 10ℓ) + 3.2d² }
064  RCLI
065  x
066  RCL8
067  RCL6
068  X²
069  GSB4
070  RCL4
071  x
072  STOE
073  RCL9
074  RCL3
075  x       calculate and store n⁰ coef
076  9
077  RCL1
078  GSB4
079  RCL4    F = rL(9r + 10ℓ)
080  RCL1
081  GSB5
082  STOI
083  EEX     setup initial guess for n
084  4       in Newton-Raphson soln
085  STO5
086  *LBL8   Newton-Raphson start
087  RCL5
088  ENT↑
089  ENT↑
090  ENT↑
091  RCLA    calculate and store
092  x
093  RCLB    f(nᵢ) = Anᵢ⁵ + Bnᵢ⁴ + Cnᵢ³ + Dnᵢ² - Enᵢ - F
094  +
095  x
096  RCLC
097  +
098  x
099  RCLD
100  +
101  x
102  RCLE
103  -
104  x
105  RCLI
106  -
107  STO2
108  CLX     calculate
109  RCL5
110  RCLA    f'(nᵢ) = 5Anᵢ⁴ + 4Bnᵢ³ + 3Cnᵢ² + 2Dnᵢ - E
111  5
112  GSB5
```

REGISTERS

| 0 a | 1 r | 2 c | 3 ℓ | 4 L | 5 n | 6 d | 7 8.4 | 8 3.2 | 9 10 |
|---|---|---|---|---|---|---|---|---|---|
| S0 | S1 | S2 | S3 | S4 | S5 | S6 | S7 | S8 | S9 |

| A A | B B | C C | D D | E E | I F |
|---|---|---|---|---|---|

# Program Listing II

| Step | Key | Comment |
|---|---|---|
| 113 | RCLB | |
| 114 | 4 | |
| 115 | x | |
| 116 | + | |
| 117 | x | |
| 118 | RCLC | |
| 119 | 3 | |
| 120 | x | |
| 121 | + | |
| 122 | x | |
| 123 | RCLD | |
| 124 | ENT↑ | |
| 125 | + | |
| 126 | + | |
| 127 | x | |
| 128 | RCLE | |
| 129 | − | |
| 130 | ST÷2 | calc & store $f(n_i)/f'(n_i)$ |
| 131 | RCL2 | apply correction: |
| 132 | ST−5 | $n_{i+1} = n_i - f(n_i)/f'(n_i)$ |
| 133 | ABS | |
| 134 | . | test for loop exit |
| 135 | 1 | |
| 136 | X≤Y? | |
| 137 | GTO8 | |
| 138 | RCL6 | |
| 139 | X² | |
| 140 | RCL5 | can be R/S statement |
| 141 | PRTX | print n |
| 142 | x | |
| 143 | RCL3 | calculate, print and store |
| 144 | ÷ | coil thickness, c: |
| 145 | STO2 | $c = nd^2/\ell$ |
| 146 | GTO2 | |
| 147 | *LBL0 | input storage routine for |
| 148 | STO5 | number of turns input |
| 149 | GTO9 | goto CF3, space and return |
| 150 | *LBL1 | calculate the number of turns |
| 151 | GSB3 | given r, $\ell$, c, and L |
| 152 | RCL4 | |
| 153 | x | |
| 154 | √X | $n = \frac{1}{a}\left\{L\left(9a + 10\ell + 8.4c + 3.2\frac{c\ell}{a}\right)\right\}^{1/2}$ |
| 155 | RCL0 | |
| 156 | ÷ | |
| 157 | STO5 | |
| 158 | PRTX | ← can be R/S statement |
| 159 | 1/X | |
| 160 | RCL2 | |
| 161 | RCL3 | |
| 162 | GSB5 | |
| 163 | √X | |
| 164 | STO6 | |
| 165 | GTO2 | |
| 166 | *LBLE | I/O OF INDUCTANCE |
| 167 | STO4 | store inductance entry |
| 168 | F3? | |
| 169 | GTO9 | jump if input |
| 170 | F0? | if winding thickness loaded, |
| 171 | GTO1 | skip thickness calculation |
| 172 | RCL6 | |
| 173 | X² | |
| 174 | RCL3 | calculate and store thickness: |
| 175 | ÷ | |
| 176 | RCL5 | $c = nd^2/\ell$ |
| 177 | x | |
| 178 | STO2 | |
| 179 | *LBL1 | |
| 180 | GSB3 | |
| 181 | 1/X | calculate and store inductance: |
| 182 | RCL0 | |
| 183 | RCL5 | $L = \frac{a^2n^2}{9a + 10\ell + 8.4c + 3.2\,c\ell/a}$ |
| 184 | x | |
| 185 | X² | |
| 186 | x | |
| 187 | STO4 | |
| 188 | *LBL2 | print and space subroutine |
| 189 | DSP4 | |
| 190 | PRTX | ← can be R/S statement |
| 191 | DSP2 | |
| 192 | *LBL9 | CF3 and space subroutine |
| 193 | CF3 | |
| 194 | SPC | |
| 195 | RTN | |
| 196 | *LBL3 | inductance factor calculation subroutine |
| 197 | RCL1 | |
| 198 | RCL2 | |
| 199 | 2 | calculate and store: |
| 200 | ÷ | |
| 201 | + | $a = r + c/2$ |
| 202 | STO0 | |
| 203 | 9 | |
| 204 | x | |
| 205 | RCL3 | calculate: |
| 206 | RCL9 | $9a + 10\ell + 8.4c + 3.2\frac{c\ell}{a}$ |
| 207 | GSB4 | |
| 208 | RCL7 | |
| 209 | RCL8 | |
| 210 | RCL0 | |
| 211 | ÷ | |
| 212 | RCL3 | |
| 213 | GSB4 | |
| 214 | RCL2 | |
| 215 | *LBL4 | x, + subroutine |
| 216 | x | |
| 217 | + | |
| 218 | RTN | |
| 219 | *LBL5 | x, x subroutine |
| 220 | x | |
| 221 | x | |
| 222 | RTN | |

**LABELS**

| A load inner radius | B load winding thickness | C load winding length | D I/O number of turns | E I/O inductance |
|---|---|---|---|---|
| a | b | c | d | e |
| 0 local loop destination | 1 local label | 2 print & space subroutine | 3 inductance subroutine | 4 x, + subroutine |
| 5 x, x subroutine | 6 | 7 | 8 turns subroutine | 9 space & rtn subroutine |

**FLAGS**

| | |
|---|---|
| 0 | set for winding thickness |
| 1 | |
| 2 | |
| 3 | data entry |

**SET STATUS**

| FLAGS | ON | OFF | TRIG | DISP |
|---|---|---|---|---|
| 0 | ■ | | DEG | FIX ■ |
| 1 | | | GRAD | SCI |
| 2 | | | RAD | ENG |
| 3 | ■ | | | n 2 |

## PROGRAM 3-7 CYLINDRICAL SOLENOID DESIGN.

Program Description and Equations Used

This program provides the coil winding particulars and the coil electrical characteristics given the specifications for a cylindrical solenoid. These specifications are:

1) Minimum plunger attractive force in pounds (F),
2) Initial air gap length in inches ($\ell_{air}$),
3) Maximum flux density in the air gap ($B_{max}$) in gauss,
4) Maximum coil current density in amperes/in$^2$ ($\Delta$),
5) Maximum coil buildup, or thickness, (w) in inches,
6) Coil excitation voltage (E) in volts, or current (I) in amperes,
7) Optionally, the magnetic path area ($A_{iron}$) in inches$^2$, the magnetic path length ($\ell_{iron}$) in inches, and the magnetic permeability ($\mu$).

The length of the magnetic path is assumed to be zero unless step 7 is exercised.

The characteristics that the program calculates are:

1) Plunger diameter in inches ($D_p$),
2) Number of turns in the coil (N),
3) Coil wire AWG using class 2 or heavy insulation,
4) Coil length in inches ($\ell_{coil}$),
5) Coil inductance in henries (L),
6) Coil resistance in ohms (R),
7) Coil power dissipation in watts (P),
8) Actual B in the core and in the air-gap, and
9) Actual F.

With the maximum flux density in the air gap and plunger attractive force specified, the area of the air gap can be calculated from:

$$A_{air} = F \cdot k_1 / (B_{air}{}^2) \qquad (3\text{-}7.1)$$

where $k_1$ is the constant of proportionality relating flux density in the air gap to pressure in pounds/in$^2$

$$k_1 = 1.73 \times 10^6 \tag{3-7.2}$$

If the plunger area is assumed equal to the air gap area, the plunger diameter can be calculated using:

$$D_p = 2 \cdot \left(A_{air}/\pi\right)^{\frac{1}{2}} \tag{3-7.3}$$

Once the plunger diameter is known, then a value for the winding thickness may be loaded into the program. The smallest dimension of the winding should not exceed 3 inches to allow adequate thermal conduction for the heat generated with the coil, thus avoiding high internal coil temperatures. If the program calculates a short coil length, then the thickness is not restrained. A long coil restrains the coil thickness to 3 inches or less. Several iterations of the program solution may be required until satisfactory values for coil length and width (thickness) are found.

Given the excitation voltage, inverse current density in the coil (M) in circular mils per ampere, and the coil dimensions as defined by Fig. 3-7.1, the number of turns required is given by Eq. (3-7.4). The derivation of this equation is given later.

$$N = E \cdot M/(\pi(D_p + w)) \tag{3-7.4}$$

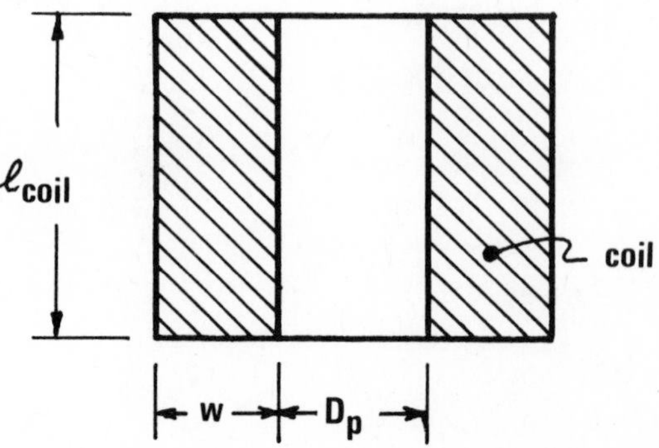


Figure 3-7.1 Solenoid coil dimensions.

If the coil is excited with a current, then the number of turns is:

$$N = (NI)/I \tag{3-7.5}$$

where NI is the coil ampere-turns which is calculated from $B_{max}$ later.

The cross-sectional area of the coil ($w \cdot \ell_{coil}$) consists of current carrying wire and noncurrent carrying insulation and space. The shape factor (sf) is the ratio of the current carrying area to the total area of the coil. If the wire plus insulation is assumed to occupy a square with side d as shown in Fig. 3-6.2, and the winding cross-section is occupied by N of these squares, then the shape factor is:

$$sf = \frac{\pi}{4}\left\{\frac{\text{diameter of bare wire}}{d}\right\}^2 \tag{3-7.6}$$

The diameters of both the bare wire and the wire with insulation bear exponential relationships to the wire AWG as given by Eq. (3-2.1). Substituting these relationships into Eq. (3-7.6) yields:

$$sf = \frac{\pi}{4}\left\{\frac{a'}{a} e^{AWG(b' - b)}\right\}^2 \tag{3-7.7}$$

where

$$\frac{\pi}{4}\left\{\frac{a'}{a}\right\}^2 = .8418900745 \tag{3-7.8a}$$

$$2(b' - b) = -1.21690938 \times 10^{-2} \tag{3-7.8b}$$

The coil has N wires each carrying in current, I; thus the current density in the coil is:

$$\Delta = (NI)/(sf \cdot l_{coil} \cdot w) \tag{3-7.9}$$

where $\Delta$ is specified by the user through M:

$$k_2 = M \cdot \Delta = (\text{cir-mils/A})(\text{A/in}^2) = (4 \times 10^6)/\pi \tag{3-7.10}$$

Solving for the coil length between Eqs. (3-7.9) and (3-7.10) yields:

$$l_{coil} = (NI \cdot M)/(sf \cdot k_2 \cdot w) \tag{3-7.11}$$

The coil ampere-turns, NI, is calculated from $B_{max}$ using the "Ohm's law" of magnetics:

$$MMF = \phi \cdot \mathcal{R} \tag{3-7.12}$$

where $\phi$ is the flux and is continuous throughout the magnetic and air paths and is analogous to electric current. The reluctance, $\mathcal{R}$, is the magnetic resistance, and the magnetomotive force, MMF, is the magnetic "voltage" source. The total reluctance is the sum of the individual reluctances making up the magnetic circuit and the MMF is proportional to the current in the coil:

$$MMF = 0.4\mu NI \tag{3-7.13a}$$

$$\mathcal{R} = \sum_i \frac{\ell_i}{\mu_i \cdot A_i} \tag{3-7.13b}$$

The electromagnet model used by this program has two sections, the magnetic path, and the air gap. Usually the air gap reluctance is the dominant term. Noting that the relative permeability for air is unity, and

$$\phi = B_{iron} \cdot A_{iron} = B_{max} \cdot A_{air} \tag{3-7.14}$$

then solving Eq. (3-7.12) for NI yields:

$$NI = \frac{B_{max} A_{air}}{A_{iron}} \left\{ \frac{\ell_{iron}}{\mu_{iron}} + \ell_{air} \frac{A_{iron}}{A_{air}} \right\} \frac{k_3}{0.4\pi} \tag{3-7.15}$$

where $k_3 = 2.54$, the inch to centimeter conversion ratio. The iron area, $A_{iron}$, refers to the smallest iron area, which may not be next to the air gap.

An iterative method is required to find the wire AWG and coil length. An initial shape factor of 0.5 is assumed, the coil length is obtained using Eq. (3-7.11). The wire diameter over insulation is obtained using

$$d = (w \cdot \ell_{coil}/N)^{\frac{1}{2}} \tag{3-7.16}$$

The wire AWG is obtained from the wire diameter over insulation from Eq. (3-2.1), and a new shape factor calculated from the AWG using Eq. (3-7.7). The new shape factor replaces the old shape factor and the calculations run again. The iteration is terminated when the new and old shape factors agree within .001.

The coil physical dimensions and number of turns have now been determined, and other electrical characteristics can be calculated.

$$L = \frac{0.4\pi \cdot N^2 \cdot A_{iron} \cdot k_3 \times 10^{-8}}{\frac{\ell_{iron}}{\mu_{iron}} + \ell_{air} \frac{A_{iron}}{A_{air}}} \qquad (3\text{-}7.17)$$

$$R = (R/\ell)(\text{mean turn})(N) \qquad (3\text{-}7.18)$$

where $R/\ell$ is obtained from:

$$R/\ell, (\text{ohms/inch}) = k_4 \cdot e^{k_5 \cdot AWG} \qquad (3\text{-}7.19)$$

hence,

$$R = N \cdot \pi \cdot (D_p + w) \cdot k_4 \cdot e^{k_5 \cdot AWG} \qquad (3\text{-}7.20)$$

For the coil temperature at 60°C, the constants are:

$$\pi \cdot k_4 = 2.9185212367 \times 10^{-5}$$

$$k_5 = 0.2317635483$$

If the coil excitation is a constant voltage, then the coil current will have to be recalculated due to the downward rounding of the wire size to the nearest integral value:

$$I = \frac{E}{R} \qquad (3\text{-}7.21)$$

The power dissipated in the coil is:

$$P = I^2 R \qquad (3\text{-}7.22)$$

If constant voltage excitation is used, the peak flux density ($B_{max}$) and initial plunger attractive force will be slightly larger than the initial values again due to the downward rounding of the wire AWG. The larger wire will have lower resistance causing higher coil current and a higher NI product. Equations (3-7.15) and (3-7.1) are rearranged and used to find $B_{iron}$ and F.

$$B_{iron} = \frac{0.4\pi\, NI}{\left\{\frac{\ell_{iron}}{\mu_{iron}} + \ell_{air} \frac{A_{iron}}{A_{air}}\right\} k_3} \qquad (3\text{-}7.23)$$

$$F = \frac{B_{max}^{2} \cdot A_{air}}{k_1} = \frac{(B_{iron} \cdot A_{iron})^2}{k_1 \cdot A_{air}} \tag{3-7.24}$$

In addition to the program card, a data card is necessary to load the registers with these constants:

| | | |
|---|---|---|
| $\mu_o$ default: | 500 | $\rightarrow R_5$ |
| $B_{max}$ default: | 15000 | $\rightarrow R_8$ |
| Initial shape factor: | 0.5 | $\rightarrow R_E$ |
| $(\pi/4)(a'/a)$: | 0.8418900745 | $\rightarrow S_o$ |
| $2(b' - b)$: | $-1.216909380 \times 10^{-2}$ | $\rightarrow S_1$ |
| a: | $3.130387015 \times 10^{-1}$ | $\rightarrow S_2$ |
| b: | $-1.097333787 \times 10^{-1}$ | $\rightarrow S_3$ |
| $\pi \cdot k_4$: | $2.985212367 \times 10^{-5}$ | $\rightarrow S_4$ |
| $k_5$: | $2.317635483 \times 10^{-1}$ | $\rightarrow S_5$ |
| $k_3$: | 2.54 | $\rightarrow S_6$ |
| $k_2 = \frac{4}{\pi} \times 10^6$: | $1.273239545 \times 10^6$ | $\rightarrow S_7$ |
| $k_1$: | $1.73 \times 10^6$ | $\rightarrow S_8$ |
| M default: | 1000 | $\rightarrow S_9$ |

If the user wants to work in centimeter units instead of inch units, then a different set of constants can be loaded. All constants are the same except for the following:

| | | |
|---|---|---|
| a: | $7.951183018 \times 10^{-1}$ | $\rightarrow S_2$ |
| $\pi \cdot k_4$: | $1.175280459 \times 10^{-5}$ | $\rightarrow S_4$ |
| $k_3$: | 1.0 | $\rightarrow S_6$ |
| $k_2$: | $5.012754114 \times 10^5$ | $\rightarrow S_7$ |
| $k_1$: | $1.11613 \times 10^7$ | $\rightarrow S_8$ |

The inverse current density, M, is now in hybrid units. The circular-mils/A must be multiplied by 2.54 before entry, and the current density, $\Delta$, is in $A/cm^2$. The plunger attractive force is still in pounds. If this force is desired in kilograms, change $k_1$ as follows:

| | | |
|---|---|---|
| $k_1$: | $2.46064 \times 10^7$ | $\rightarrow S_8$ |

The HP-67 user may wish the program to stop at data output points rather than executing a 5 second "print" halt. To cause the program to stop at the data output points, change the "print" statements to "R/S" statements at the following line numbers: 047, 084, 131, 144, 160, 176, 180, 185, and 194.

# User Instructions

| CYLINDRICAL SOLENOID DESIGN | | | | |
|---|---|---|---|---|
| $B_{max}$ in air gap ↑ air gap (I) | $\ell_{iron}$ ↑ $A_{iron}$ ↑ $\mu$ (I) | + Volts or − Amps (I) | load M, cir mils / A (I/O) | calculate coil design and electrical parameters (O) |
| Force, lbs (I) | calculate pole diameter (O) | winding width (I) | | |

| STEP | INSTRUCTIONS | INPUT DATA/UNITS | KEYS | OUTPUT DATA/UNITS |
|---|---|---|---|---|
| 1 | Load both sides of program card and both sides of data card | | | |
| 2 | Load force required (in pounds) at maximum air gap (plunger all the way out) | F | A | |
| 3 | Load maximum flux in the iron (gauss) and | $B_{max}$ | ENT | |
| | the air gap in inches | $\ell_{air}$ | f A | |
| 4 | Optional, load magnetic circuit parameters: | | | |
| | a) load magnetic path length | $\ell_{iron}$, in | ENT | |
| | b) load magnetic path minimum area | $A_{iron}$, $in^2$ | ENT | |
| | c) load relative permeability | $\mu$ | f B | |
| | If this step is not executed, the program will use $A_{iron} = A_{air}$ and $\ell_{iron} = 0$ | | | |
| 5 | Calculate pole diameter<br>To, change the pole diameter, change $B_{max}$, a larger $B_{max}$ will result in a smaller pole. $B_{max}$ is material dependent, and generally should not exceed 15000 gauss. | | B | pole diameter in inches |
| 6 | Load winding thickness | w, in | C | |
| 7 | Load excitation voltage or current | | | |
| | a) excitation voltage | E, V | f C | |
| | b) excitation current (note neg value) | −I, A | f C | |
| 8 | Load a value for M, the inverse coil current density in circular-mils per ampere. If no value is loaded, a default value of 1000 will be used. Execution of this step without numeric entry causes currently stored value to be printed and displayed. | M | f D | M<br>Δ |
| | | | | |

# User Instructions

CYLINDRICAL SOLENOID DESIGN

CONTINUED

2

| STEP | INSTRUCTIONS | INPUT DATA/UNITS | KEYS | OUTPUT DATA/UNITS |
|---|---|---|---|---|
| 9 | Calculate coil design and electrical | | E | N |
| | parameters | | | AWG |
| | | | | $\ell_{coil}$ |
| | | | | L, h |
| | | | | R, Ω |
| | | | | P, watts |
| | | | | $B_{iron}$, G |
| | | | | $B_{max}$, G |
| | | | | F, pounds |

<u>Example 3-7.1</u>

Figure 3-7.2 shows a plunger-type, iron-clad cylindrical solenoid. Design the solenoid to have a 1 inch travel and exert an initial pull of 500 pounds when connected to a 55 volt dc source. The initial flux density in the iron shall be 7000 gauss, and the coil inverse current density shall be 700 circular-mils/A. Assume all the reluctance to be in the air gap.

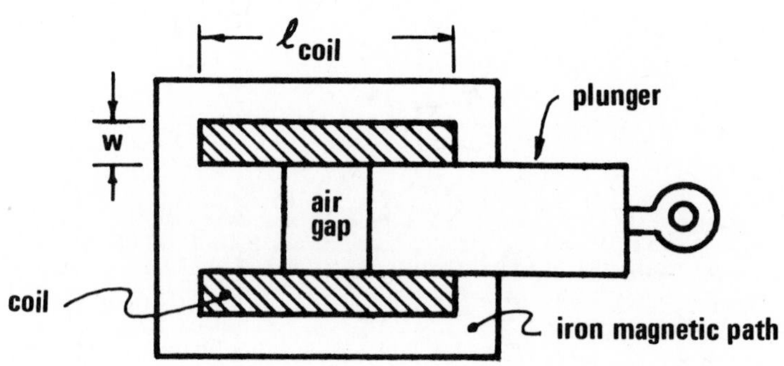


Figure 3-7.2 Plunger-type, iron-clad cylindrical solenoid.

| | | |
|---|---|---|
| 500.00 | GSB A | load initial force required in pounds (F) |
| 7000.00 | ENT↑ | load maximum B field in gauss $(B_{max})$ |
| 1.00 | GSB a | load $\ell_{air}$ |
| | GSB B | calculate plunger diameter required $(D_p)$ |
| 4.74 | *** | plunger diameter in inches |
| 3.00 | GSB C | load winding width in inches (w) |
| 55.00 | GSB c | load excitation voltage in volts (E) |
| 700.00 | GSB D | load inverse current density, M, in cir-mils/A |
| 700.00 | *** | M |
| 1818.91 | *** | $\Delta$, A/in$^2$ |
| | GSB E | calculate coil design and electrical parameters |
| 1563.00 | *** | N, the number of turns |
| 12.00 | *** | AWG of wire with heavy or class 2 insulation |
| 3.57 | *** | coil length in inches $(\ell_{coil})$ |
| 1.41 | *** | coil inductance in henries (L) |
| 5.90 | *** | coil resistance in ohms (R) |
| 512.43 | *** | coil power dissipation in watts (P) |
| 7296.69 | *** | actual maximum flux density in the iron |
| 7296.69 | *** | $B_{max}$, the flux density in the air gap |
| 543.28 | *** | F, the plunger attractive force actually achieved |

Example 3-7.2

A small solenoid is needed which has 0.050 inch travel, exerts an initial pull of 5 pounds, and is used intermittently with a 0.10 duty cycle. The coil excitation current is 3 A, and an initial flux density of 6000 gauss is to be used. Because of the intermittent duty cycle, an M of 100 cir-mils/A is used. The magnetic path is 1.5 inches long, has a cross-sectional area of 0.4 inch$^2$, and has a relative permeability of 500. Investigate the solenoid design with and without consideration for the magnetic path reluctance. A much more thorough analysis can be done with Program 3-8.

| | | |
|---|---|---|
| 5.000 | GSBA | load initial force required in pounds (F) |
| 6000.000 | ENT↑ | load maximum flux density in gauss ($B_{max}$) |
| .050 | GSBa | load initial air gap in inches ($\ell_{air}$) |
| | GSBE | calculate plunger diameter in inches ($D_p$) |
| 0.553 | *** | $D_p$ |
| .250 | GSBC | load winding width in inches (w) |
| -3.000 | GSBc | load excitation current in A (-I) |
| 100.000 | GSBD | load inverse current density in cir-mils/A (M) |
| 100.000 | *** | M |
| 12732.395 | *** | $\Delta$, A/inch$^2$ |
| | GSBE | calculate coil design etc. without considering iron path |
| 202.000 | *** | the number of turns (N) |
| 25.000 | *** | AWG of coil wire with heavy insulation |
| 0.308 | *** | coil length in inches ($\ell_{coil}$) |
| 0.006 | *** | coil inductance in henries (L) |
| 1.590 | *** | coil resistance in ohms (R) |
| 14.311 | *** | coil power dissipation in watts (P) |
| 5996.237 | *** | maximum flux density in the iron, gauss |
| 5996.237 | *** | $B_{max}$, maximum flux density in the air gap, gauss |
| 4.994 | *** | actual initial force, F, in pounds |

Rerun program with magnetic (iron) path considered

| | | |
|---|---|---|
| 1.500 | ENT↑ | load magnetic path length in inches |
| .400 | ENT↑ | load magnetic path area in inches$^2$ |
| 500.000 | GSBE | load relative magnetic permeability |
| | GSBE | calculate coil design and electrical parameters |
| 209.000 | *** | N |
| 25.000 | *** | AWG |
| 0.319 | *** | $\ell_{coil}$ |
| 0.006 | *** | L |
| 1.645 | *** | R |
| 14.807 | *** | P |
| 3597.060 | *** | B in iron area defined |
| 5988.202 | *** | B in air gap and in iron pole pieces |
| 4.980 | *** | F |

Derivation of Equations Used. The number of coil turns can be calculated from the applied voltage, the desired inverse current density, and the coil inner diameter and thickness. Conveniently, copper has a resistance of 1 ohm per circular mil per inch of length at 60°C; therefore, with a uniform coil temperature of 60°C, the wire resistance is:

$$R = \frac{\ell_w}{M} \tag{3-7.24}$$

where $\ell_w$ is the winding wire length in the coil in inches, and m is the wire cross-sectional area in circular mils. If M is defined as the inverse current density in circular-mils/A, then the cross-section of a wire carrying a current I is:

$$m = M \cdot I \tag{3-7.25}$$

Since

$$R = \frac{E}{I}, \text{(Ohm's law)} \tag{3-7.26}$$

then

$$\frac{E}{I} = \frac{\ell_w}{M \cdot I} \tag{3-7.27}$$

Rearranging Eq. (3-7.27) and cancelling I yields:

$$E = \frac{\ell_w}{M} \tag{3-7.28}$$

The winding wire length can be found by multiplying the mean turn length by the number of turns:

$$\ell_w = N \cdot \pi \cdot (D_p + w) \tag{3-7.29}$$

where Fig. 3-7.1 defines the coil dimensions $D_p$ and w. Substituting Eq. (3-7.29) into Eq. (3-7.28) and solving for N yields:

$$N = \frac{E \cdot M}{\pi (D_p + w)} \tag{3-7.30}$$

The best reference on the subject known to the author is rather old [47] since it was first published in 1924.

# Program Listing I

| | | |
|---|---|---|
| 001 | *LBLA | LOAD FORCE REQUIRED |
| 002 | ST07 | |
| 003 | RTN | |
| 004 | *LBLα | LOAD $B_{max}$ & $\ell_{air}$ |
| 005 | ST05 | |
| 006 | R↓ | |
| 007 | ST08 | |
| 008 | GT05 | goto CF3 and return subr |
| 009 | *LBLB | CALCULATE POLE DIAMETER, $D_p$ |
| 010 | RCL7 | |
| 011 | RCL8 | |
| 012 | X² | |
| 013 | ÷ | $A_{air} = \dfrac{F \cdot k_1}{B_{air}^2}$ |
| 014 | P≠S | |
| 015 | RCL8 | |
| 016 | P≠S | |
| 017 | X | |
| 018 | ST06 | store air gap area |
| 019 | F1? | minimum magnetic area equals |
| 020 | ST03 | airgap area if flag 1 is set |
| 021 | 4 | |
| 022 | X | |
| 023 | Pi | $D_p = \sqrt{\dfrac{4 \cdot A_{air}}{\pi}}$ |
| 024 | ÷ | |
| 025 | √X | |
| 026 | STOD | store pole diameter |
| 027 | GT04 | goto prt, spc, & CF3 subr |
| 028 | *LBLb | LOAD $\ell_{iron}$ & $A_{iron}$ & $\mu$ |
| 029 | CF1 | indicate magnetic path used |
| 030 | ST04 | |
| 031 | R↓ | |
| 032 | ST03 | store data |
| 033 | R↓ | |
| 034 | ST02 | |
| 035 | RTN | |
| 036 | *LBLC | LOAD WINDING WIDTH, w |
| 037 | ST00 | |
| 038 | RTN | |
| 039 | *LBLc | LOAD COIL EXCITATION, |
| 040 | ST09 | +E, or –I |
| 041 | GT05 | goto CF3 and return subr |
| 042 | *LBLD | I/O OF CIRCULAR-MILS/AMP, M |
| 043 | P≠S | interchange registers |
| 044 | F3? | store input if present |
| 045 | ST09 | |
| 046 | RCL9 | recall and print M |
| 047 | PRTX | |
| 048 | RCL7 | calculate and print Δ : |
| 049 | X≠Y | |
| 050 | ÷ | $\Delta = \dfrac{M}{k_2}$ |
| 051 | P≠S | |
| 052 | GT04 | goto prt, spc, & CF3 subr |
| 053 | *LBLE | CALCULATE MAIN OUTPUT |
| 054 | RCL8 | |
| 055 | RCL6 | |

| | | |
|---|---|---|
| 056 | X | |
| 057 | RCL3 | calculate and store NI |
| 058 | ÷ | using Eq. (3-7.15) |
| 059 | GSB9 | |
| 060 | ÷ | |
| 061 | STOA | |
| 062 | RCL9 | test for current excitation |
| 063 | X<0? | |
| 064 | GT00 | |
| 065 | P≠S | voltage excitation: |
| 066 | RCL9 | calculate the number of |
| 067 | P≠S | turns using Eq. (3-7.4): |
| 068 | X | |
| 069 | RCLD | |
| 070 | RCL0 | |
| 071 | + | $N = \dfrac{E \cdot M}{\pi(D_p + w)}$ |
| 072 | Pi | |
| 073 | X | |
| 074 | ÷ | |
| 075 | GT01 | |
| 076 | *LBL0 | current excitation, calculate |
| 077 | RCLA | the number of turns using |
| 078 | X≠Y | Eq. (3-7.5): |
| 079 | ÷ | $N = (NI)/I$ |
| 080 | CHS | |
| 081 | *LBL1 | calculate, store and print |
| 082 | INT | the integral number of turns |
| 083 | STOI | |
| 084 | PRTX | |
| 085 | *LBL7 | iteration loop start |
| 086 | RCLA | calculate and store coil |
| 087 | RCLE | length using Eq. (3-7.11): |
| 088 | ÷ | |
| 089 | RCL0 | |
| 090 | ÷ | |
| 091 | P≠S | |
| 092 | RCL9 | $\ell_{coil} = \dfrac{NI \cdot M}{sf \cdot k_2 \cdot w}$ |
| 093 | X | |
| 094 | RCL7 | |
| 095 | P≠S | |
| 096 | ÷ | |
| 097 | ST01 | |
| 098 | RCLI | calculate wire diameter over |
| 099 | 1/X | insulation using Eq. (3-7.16) |
| 100 | RCL0 | |
| 101 | X | |
| 102 | RCL1 | $d = \sqrt{\dfrac{w \cdot \ell_{coil}}{N}}$ |
| 103 | X | |
| 104 | √X | |
| 105 | P≠S | |
| 106 | RCL2 | calculate and store wire AWG |
| 107 | ÷ | using Eq. (3-2.1) |
| 108 | LN | |
| 109 | RCL3 | $AWG = \dfrac{1}{b} \ell n \left\{ \dfrac{\text{wire diameter}}{a} \right\}$ |
| 110 | ÷ | |

## REGISTERS

| 0 | 1 | 2 | 3 | 4 | 5 | 6 | 7 | 8 | 9 |
|---|---|---|---|---|---|---|---|---|---|
| w | $\ell_{coil}$ | $\ell_{iron}$ | $A_{iron}$ | $\mu$ | $\ell_{air}$ | $A_{air}$ | F | $B_{max}$ | +volts or –amps |
| S0 $\frac{\pi}{4}\left(\frac{a'}{a}\right)^2$ | S1 $2(b'-b)$ | S2 $a$ | S3 $b$ | S4 $\pi \cdot k_4$ | S5 $k_5$ | S6 $k_3 = 2.54$ | S7 $k_2 = \frac{4 \times 10^6}{\pi}$ | S8 $k_1 = 1.73 \times 10^6$ | S9 $M$ |
| A $NI , I$ | B $AWG$ | C $R$ | D $D_p$ | E $sf$ | I $N$ | | | | |

# Program Listing II

NOTE FLAG SET STATUS

```
STOE
RCL1
x
e^x
RCL0
P⇄S
x
```

calculate shape factor using Eq. (3-7.7):

$$sf = \frac{\pi}{4}\left(\frac{a'}{a}\right)^2 e^{AWG \cdot 2(b'-b)}$$

```
RCLE
X⇄Y
STOE
```

recall old sf and store new sf

```
-
ABS
EEX
CHS
3
X≤Y?
GTO7
```

test for loop exit

```
RCLB
INT
STOB
PRTX
```

print & store integral AWG

```
RCL1
PRTX
```

recall and print the number of turns

```
SF2
```

indicate $k_3$ on top

```
GSB9
RCLI
X²
x
RCL3
x
EEX
8
÷
PRTX
```

calculate and print inductance using Eq. (3-7.17)

$$L = \frac{0.4\pi \cdot N^2 \cdot A_{iron} \cdot k_3 \cdot 10^{-8}}{\frac{\ell_{iron}}{\mu_{iron}} + \frac{\ell_{air} \cdot A_{iron}}{A_{air}}}$$

```
RCLB
P⇄S
RCL5
x
e^x
RCL4
P⇄S
x
RCLD
RCL0
+
x
RCL1
x
STOC
PRTX
```

calculate and print resistance using Eq. (3-7.20)

$$R = N\pi\,(D_p + w)\,k_4\,e^{k_5 \cdot AWG}$$

```
RCL9
X<0?
GTO0
```

test for current excitation

```
RCLC
÷
```

calculate current using Ohm's law

```
*LBL0
ABS
STOA
X²
RCLC
x
PRTX
```

calculate and print coil power dissapation using Eq. (3-7.21):

$$P = I^2R$$

```
GSB9
RCLA
x
RCLI
x
PRTX
```

calculate and print new $B_{iron}$ using Eq. (3-7.22):

$$B_{iron} = \frac{0.4\pi\, NI/k_3}{\frac{\ell_{iron}}{\mu_{iron}} + \frac{\ell_{air} \cdot A_{iron}}{A_{air}}}$$

```
RCL3
x
RCL6
÷
PRTX
```

calculate and print:

$$B_{max} = \frac{B_{iron} \cdot A_{iron}}{A_{air}}$$

```
X²
RCL6
x
P⇄S
RCL8
P⇄S
÷
```

calculate and print new F using Eq. (3-7.23):

$$F = \frac{B_{max}^{2} \cdot A_{air}}{k_1}$$

```
*LBL4
PRTX
SPC
```

print, spc, CF3 subroutine

```
*LBL5
CF3
RTN
```

CF3 and return subroutine

```
*LBL9
RCL2
RCL4
÷
RCL5
RCL3
x
RCL6
÷
+
1/X
7
2
D→R
x
P⇄S
RCL6
P⇄S
F2?
1/X
÷
RTN
```

magnetics subroutine to calculate:

$$\frac{0.4\pi}{\frac{\ell_{iron}}{\mu_{iron}} + \frac{\ell_{air} \cdot A_{iron}}{A_{air}}} \cdot \frac{k_3(F2=1)}{k_3(F2=0)}$$

7, 2, D→R: generates $0.4\pi$ in 3 steps

NOTE FLAG SET STATUS

| LABELS | | | | | FLAGS |
|---|---|---|---|---|---|
| A load F | B calc Dp | C load w | D load M | E calc coil & elect params | 0 |
| a $B_{max}$↑ air gap | b $\ell_{iron}$↑$A_{iron}$↑$\mu$ | c load +E, −I | d | e | 1 magnetic path data not loaded |
| 0 Local label | 1 Local label | 2 | 3 | 4 output routine | 2 conversion order |
| 5 CF3, RTN | 6 | 7 sf iteration routine | 8 | 9 subroutine | 3 data entry |

| SET STATUS | | | | |
|---|---|---|---|---|
| FLAGS | ON | OFF | TRIG | DISP |
| 0 | | | DEG ■ | FIX ■ |
| 1 | ■ | | GRAD | SCI |
| 2 | | ■ | RAD | ENG |
| 3 | | ■ | | n 2 |

## PROGRAM 3-8 CYLINDRICAL SOLENOID ANALYSIS.

Program Description and Equations Used

This program analyzes a cylindrical coil solenoid, or other magnetic circuits having many parts of varying reluctance. The information required to run the program is as follows:

1) The air gap in inches ($\ell_{air}$),

2) The number of turns in the coil (N),

3) The AWG of the coil wire,

4) The length of the coil in inches ($\ell_{coil}$),

5) The coil inner diameter in inches ($ID_{coil}$),

6) The plunger outer diameter in inches ($OD_p$),

7) The plunger inner diameter in inches if the plunger is hollow ($ID_p$),

8) The length, area, and permeability of each different magnetic section ($\ell_{iron}$, $A_{iron}$, $\mu$),

8a) If the magnetic section is a cylindrical shell with axial flux flow, the height (h), the ID which may be zero, the OD, and the permeability ($\mu$), can be entered, and the reluctance and cross-sectional area will be returned and automatically loaded into the program,

8b) If the magnetic section consists of a disc (or washer) with radial flux flow, the thickness (t), the ID, the OD, and the permeability can be entered, and the reluctance and minimum cross-sectional area will be returned and automatically loaded into the program, and

9) The coil excitation in either volts or amperes (E or -I).

The program will then calculate the following parameters:

1) Reluctance and area of each different magnetic section ($\mathcal{R}$ & $A_{iron}$),

2) Coil inductance and resistance (R and L),

3) Coil circular-mils/A, A/in$^2$, and power dissipation M, Δ, & P),

4) The flux density in the air gap, and in the magnetic section with the smallest cross-sectional area ($B_{air}$, $B_{iron}$), and

5) The plunger attractive force in pounds (F).

This program uses the Ohm's law of magnetics as given by Eqs. (3-7.12) and (3-7.13), which combined yield:

$$0.4\pi NI = \phi \cdot \sum_i \frac{\ell_i}{\mu_i A_i} \tag{3-8.1}$$

As magnetic path data is entered, the program keeps a running sum of the reluctances, $\frac{\ell_i}{\mu_i A_i}$, and also stores the smallest magnetic area. The iron part will saturate first where the area is the smallest, and the flux density (B) the highest. The total flux can be found from Eq. (3-8.1):

$$\phi = \frac{0.4\mu NI k_3}{\sum\limits_{\substack{\text{iron}\\ \text{parts}}} \frac{\ell_i}{\mu_i A_i} + \frac{\ell_{air}}{A_{air}}} \tag{3-8.2}$$

where

$$A_{air} = \frac{\pi}{4}\left(OD_p^{\ 2} - ID_p^{\ 2}\right) \tag{3-8.3}$$

$$k_3 = 2.54$$

The plunger attractive force is found in terms of the flux:

$$F = \frac{\phi^2}{k_1 \cdot k_3^4 \cdot A_{air}} \tag{3-8.4}$$

where the air gap area is in inches$^2$ and the constant $k_1$ is:

$$k_1 = 1.73 \times 10^6$$

The inductance of the N turn coil wound on the magnetic circuit is:

$$L = \frac{N^2 k_3}{10^8} \left\{ \frac{0.4\pi}{\sum\limits_{\substack{\text{iron}\\\text{parts}}} \frac{\ell}{\mu A} + \frac{\ell_{air}}{A_{air}}} \right\} \tag{3-8.5}$$

This expression is basically derived in Eqs. (3-1.1) through (3-1.10).

The coil width (w) can be expressed in terms of the coil length ($\ell_{coil}$), the number of turns (N), and the wire AWG. The wire is assumed to occupy a box as shown in Fig. 3-6.2.

$$\text{coil area} = w \cdot \ell_{coil} = N \cdot (\text{wire diameter})^2 \tag{3-8.6}$$

Substituting the exponential relationship between AWG and wire diameter given by Eq. (3-5.10) yields:

$$w = \frac{N}{\ell_{coil}} \left( a \cdot e^{b \cdot AWG} \right)^2 \tag{3-8.7}$$

The coil resistance can now be calculated using Eq. (3-7.20):

$$R = N \cdot \pi \left( ID_{coil} + w \right) \left( k_4 \, e^{k_5 \cdot AWG} \right)$$

The coil power dissipation is:

$$P = I^2 R \tag{3-8.8}$$

If voltage excitation is used, the coil current is calculated using Ohm's law, then the power dissipation is calculated.

The coil circular mils per A is given by:

$$M = \underbrace{10^6 \cdot \left( a' \cdot e^{b' \cdot AWG} \right)^2}_{\substack{\text{wire area in}\\\text{circular mils}}} \Big/ I \tag{3-8.9}$$

The coil current density in $A/in^2$ is given by Eq. (3-8.10), i.e.:

$$\Delta = \frac{k_2}{M} \tag{3-8.10}$$

Two commonly encountered part shapes in the magnetic path are the cylindrical shell as shown in Fig. 3-8.1 and the disc or washer as shown in Fig. 3-8.2. Two subroutines are provided to calculate the reluctance and minimum cross-sectional area of these two shapes.

<u>Subroutine 1, thin cylindrical shell with permeability μ.</u>

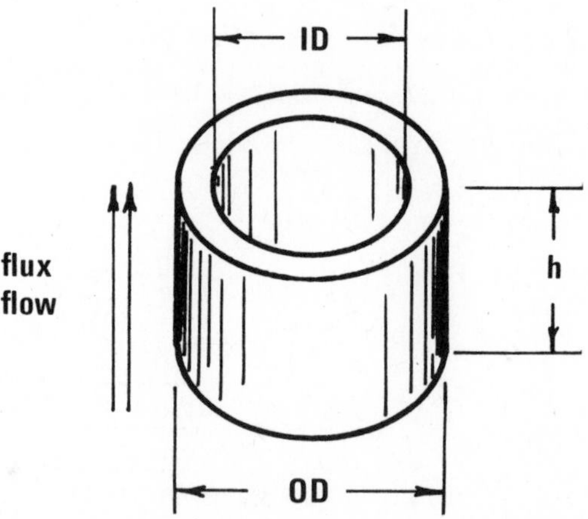


Figure 3-8.1 Thin cylindrical shell.

The cross-sectional area is given by Eq. (3-8.3) and the reluctance is:

$$\mathcal{R} = \frac{h}{\mu A}$$

This subroutine output becomes the input for the program coding under label B, and the reluctance is calculated under label B. The subroutine output is stored in the stack in the same format as data entered from the keyboard for arbitrary magnetic section, i.e.:

| stack register | contents |
|---|---|
| t | not used |
| z | h |
| y | cross-sectional area |
| x | permeability |

<u>Subroutine 2, disc or washer with radial flux flow.</u>

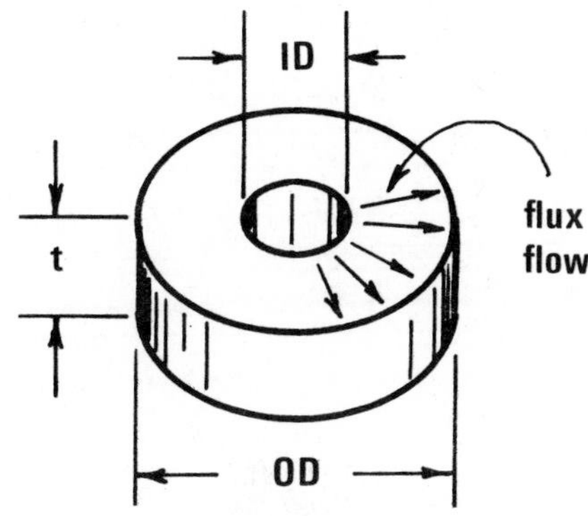


Figure 3-8.2 Disc or washer with radial flux flow.

The disc is composed of an infinite number of annular shells each with infinitesimal thickness dr. The cross-sectional area of each annulus is $2\pi rt$. In this instance, the summation of Eq. (3-8.1) is expressed as an integral:

$$\mathcal{R} = \sum \frac{\ell}{\mu A} = \frac{1}{\mu t} \int_{r_1 = \frac{ID}{2}}^{r_2 = \frac{OD}{2}} \frac{dr}{2\pi r} = \frac{\ell n(OD/ID)}{2\pi t \mu} \qquad (3\text{-}8.11)$$

The disc has the smallest cross-sectional area at the inner diamater, hence:

$$A = A' = \pi \cdot ID \cdot t \qquad (3\text{-}8.12)$$

This subroutine output becomes the input for the program coding under label B. The data format used with label B is the equivalent length of a constant cross-section magnetic path, the path area, and the path permeability. The equivalent length having the above reluctance and cross-sectional area A' is:

$$\ell = \mu A' \cdot \mathcal{R} = \left(\frac{\pi \cdot ID \cdot t \cdot \mu}{2\pi \cdot t \cdot \mu}\right) \cdot \ell n \frac{OD}{ID} = \frac{ID}{2} \ell n \frac{OD}{ID} \tag{3-8.13}$$

Subroutine 2 output is transferred to the program coding under label B using the stack in the same way that subroutine 1 operates.

In addition to the program card, a data card is required to load the registers with the program constants. All registers contain zero except for the following:

| | |
|---|---|
| a' for AWG | $3.241013109 \times 10^{-1} \rightarrow S_o$ |
| b' for AWG | $-1.158179256 \times 10^{-1} \rightarrow S_1$ |
| a for AWG | $3.130387015 \times 10^{-1} \rightarrow S_2$ |
| b for AWG | $-1.097333787 \times 10^{-1} \rightarrow S_3$ |
| $\pi \cdot k_4$ for resistance | $2.985212367 \times 10^{-5} \rightarrow S_4$ |
| $k_5$ for resistance | $2.317635483 \times 10^{-1} \rightarrow S_5$ |
| $k_3$, cm $\rightarrow$ inch | $2.54 \rightarrow S_6$ |
| $k_2$, $4/\pi \times 10^6$ | $1.273239545 \times 10^6 \rightarrow S_7$ |
| $k_1$ | $1.73 \times 10^6 \rightarrow S_8$ |

If metric units are preferred, i.e., linear dimensions in cm, force in kg, current density in A/cm$^2$ and inverse current density in hybrid units (circular mil-milli-centimeter/A), change the following constants.

| | |
|---|---|
| a' for AWG | $8.232173297 \times 10^{-1} \rightarrow S_o$ |
| a for AWG | $7.951183108 \times 10^{-1} \rightarrow S_2$ |
| $\pi \cdot k_4$ for resistance | $1.175280459 \times 10^{-5} \rightarrow S_4$ |
| $k_3$ cm $\rightarrow$ cm | $1.0 \rightarrow S_6$ |
| $k_2$, $4/(2.54\pi) \times 10^6$ | $5.012754114 \times 10^5 \rightarrow S_7$ |
| $k_1$ | $2.4606 \times 10^7 \rightarrow S_8$ |

HP-67 users may want the program to stop instead of executing a "print" statement. This can be accomplished by changing the "print" statements to "R/S" statements at the following line numbers: 102, 105, 124, and 130. To continue program execution after a stop, key a "R/S" command from the keyboard.

# User Instructions

| CYLINDRICAL SOLENOID ANALYSIS | | | | |
|---|---|---|---|---|
| $N \uparrow AWG \uparrow ID_{coil} \uparrow \ell_{coil}$ | $ID_p \uparrow OD_p$ | +E or -I | calculate inductance & resistance | calculate M, Δ, & P |
| $\ell_{air}$ | $\ell_{iron} \uparrow A_{iron} \uparrow \mu$ | calculate $B_{air}$, $B_{iron, max}$ | calculate initial plunger attractive force | calculate complete summary |

| STEP | INSTRUCTIONS | INPUT DATA/UNITS | KEYS | OUTPUT DATA/UNITS |
|---|---|---|---|---|
| 1 | Load both sides of program card and both sides of data card | | | |
| 2 | Load air gap length in inches | $\ell_{air}$ | [A] | |
| 3 | Load plunger ID and OD in inches. The ID can be zero if the plunger is solid | $ID_p$ | [ENT↑] | |
| | | $OD_p$ | [f] [B] | |
| 4 | Load coil parameters: | | | |
| | number of wire turns in coil | N | [ENT↑] | |
| | wire AWG | AWG | [ENT↑] | |
| | coil ID in inches | $ID_{coil}$ | [ENT↑] | |
| | coil length in inches | $\ell_{coil}$ | [f] [A] | |
| 5 | Load coil excitation | | | |
| | voltage excitation in volts | E | [f] [C] | |
| | current excitation in A (note minus) | -I | [f] [C] | |
| 6 | Optional step, the main source of reluctance in the magnetic path is the air gap. For added accuracy, the length, area, and permeability of each magnetic section may be entered: | | | |
| | effective magnetic path length in inches | $\ell_{iron}$ | [ENT↑] | |
| | effective magnetic path area in inches² | $A_{iron}$ | [ENT↑] | |
| | magnetic permeability of path | $\mu$ | [B] | $\mathcal{R}$ |
| | | | | A |
| | If the magnetic section is either a cylindrical shell or a disc, then a subroutine can be used to calculate and enter the above parameters from the section dimensions. | | | |
| | For cylindrical shells with axial flux flow: | | | |
| | load shell height in inches | h | [ENT↑] | |
| | load shell ID in inches (may be zero) | ID | [ENT↑] | |
| | load shell OD in inches | OD | [ENT↑] | |
| | load shell permeability | $\mu$ | [GSB] [1] | $\mathcal{R}$ |
| | | | | A |

# User Instructions

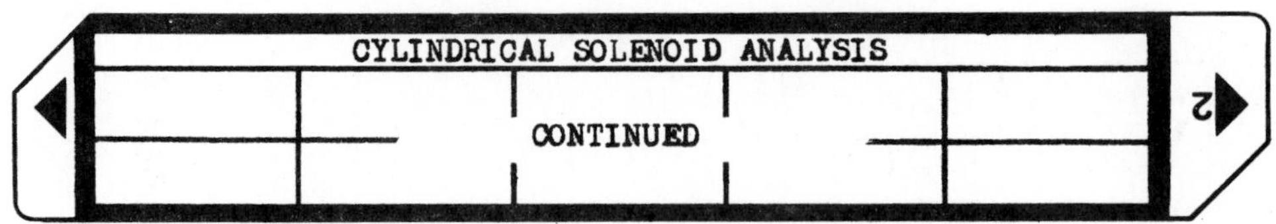


| STEP | INSTRUCTIONS | INPUT DATA/UNITS | KEYS | OUTPUT DATA/UNITS |
|---|---|---|---|---|
| 6 | continued | | | |
| | For discs with radial flux flow: | | | |
| | load disc thickness in inches | t | ENT ↑ | |
| | load disc ID in inches | ID | ENT ↑ | |
| | load disc OD in inches | OD | ENT ↑ | |
| | load permeability of material | $\mu$ | GSB 2 | $\mathcal{R}$ |
| | | | | A |
| | Repeat step 6 for each separate magnetic section in the magnetic circuit. | | | |
| 7 | To calculate the flux density in the air gap and in the smallest iron cross-sectional area (the smallest area has the highest flux dens) | | C | $B_{air}$, G |
| | | | | $B_{iron}$, G |
| | If step 6 is omitted, $\mathcal{R}_{iron} = 0$, $A_{iron} = A_{air}$ is assumed, hence, $B_{iron} = B_{air}$ | | | |
| 8 | To calculate the initial plunger attractive force in pounds | | D | F |
| 9 | To calculate the electrical inductance and resistance at 60°C of the coil | | f D | L, h |
| | | | | R, ohms |
| 10 | To calculate the coil M, Δ, and power dissipation | | f E | M, $\frac{\text{cir-mils}}{A}$ |
| | | | | Δ, $A/in^2$ |
| | | | | P, watts |
| 11 | To calculate all the information contained in steps 8, 9, 10, and 11 | | E | L, h |
| | | | | R, ohms |
| | | | | M, $\frac{\text{cir-mils}}{A}$ |
| | | | | Δ, $A/in^2$ |
| | | | | P, watts |
| | | | | $B_{air}$, G |
| | | | | $B_{iron}$, G |
| | | | | F, lbs |
| 12 | To run a new case, goto step 1 and start over | | | |

Example 3-8.1

The cylindrical solenoid shown in cross-section by Fig. 3-8.3 has the following characteristics:

1) The coil is 150 turns of #24 AWG HF wire,
2) 0.5 A excitation current flows through the coil, and
3) The magnetic materials are 1010 mild carbon steel.

For the analysis, neglect the force required to compress the return spring.

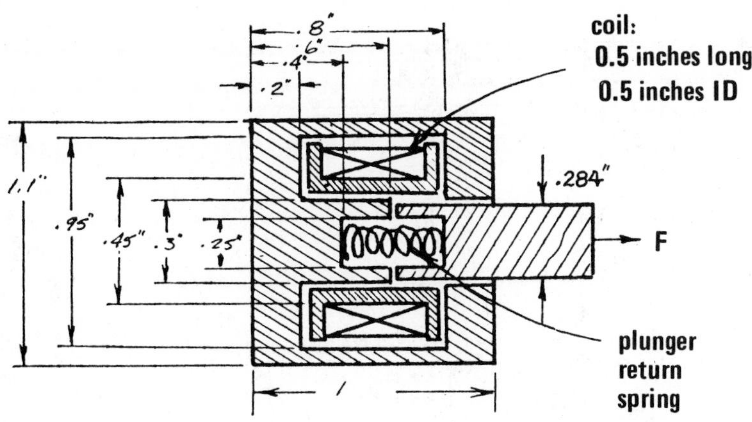


Figure 3-8.3 Cylindrical solenoid construction.

Analyze the solenoid and determine its electrical and magnetic characteristics. Also analyze the solenoid for the same characteristics if the coil is excited by 0.6 Vdc.

The analysis is begun by breaking down the solenoid into its component geometric shapes as shown by Fig. 3-8.4.

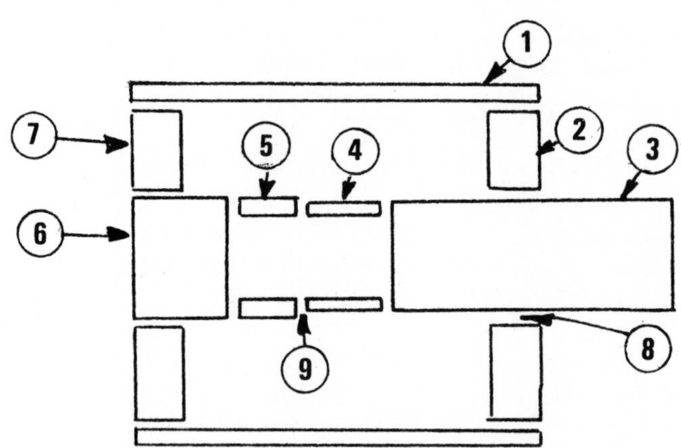


Figure 3-8.4 Component geometric shapes of solenoid.

The component geometric shapes of the solenoid are as follows:

1) Cylindrical shell, 1.0" long, 0.95" ID, 1.1" OD, and $\mu$= 1000,

2) Disc, 0.2" thick, 0.3" ID, 0.95" OD, and $\mu$ = 1000,

3) Solid cylinder, 0.2" long (active magnetic part), 0.0" ID, 0.284" OD, and $\mu$ = 1000,

4) Cylindrical shell, 0.2" long, 0.25" ID, 0.284" OD, and $\mu$ = 1000,

5) Cylindrical shell, 0.2" long, 0.25" ID, 0.3" OD, and $\mu$ = 1000,

6) Solid cylinder, 0.4" long, 0.0" ID, 0.3" OD, and $\mu$ = 1000,

7) Disc, 0.2" thick, 0.3" ID, 0.95" OD, and $\mu$ = 1000,

8) Disc (air gap), 0.2" thick, 0.284" ID, 0.3" OD, and $\mu$ = 1,

9) Operating air gap, 0.005" thick, 0.25" ID, 0.284" OD, & $\mu$ = 1.

The air gap data is loaded, and the complete summary calculated, then the magnetic path component parts are loaded and the summary run again to show the difference that the magnetic circuit reluctance makes on the electrical and magnetic characteristics. This sequence is repeated with the coil excitation at 0.6 Vdc.

**HP-97 PRINTOUT FOR EXAMPLE 3-8.1**

.005 GSBA load $\ell_{air}$

150. ENT↑ load N
24. ENT↑ load AWG
.5 ENT↑ load ID
.5 GSBa load $\ell_{coil}$

.25 ENT↑ load $ID_p$
.284 GSBb load $OD_p$

-.5 GSBc load -I

calc all *
GSBE parameters
2.048-03 *** L, h
759.9-03 *** R, ohms

809.2+00 *** M, cir-mils/A
1.574+03 *** Δ, A/in$^2$
190.0-03 *** P, watts

7.421+03 *** max $B_{iron}$
7.421+03 *** $B_{air}$, G

453.9-03 *** F, pounds

* Magnetic reluctance is assumed zero since flag 0 is set. Flag 0 is cleared under label B.

load magnetic path data

cylindrical shell
1. ENT↑ length
.95 ENT↑ ID
1.1 ENT↑ OD
1000. GSB1 μ

4.141-03 *** ℛ
241.5-03 *** area

disc
.2 ENT↑ thickness
.3 ENT↑ ID
.95 ENT↑ OD
1000. GSB2 μ

917.3-06 *** ℛ
188.5-03 *** area

solid cylinder .2 ENT↑ length
0. ENT↑ ID
.284 ENT↑ OD
1000. GSB1 u

3.157-03 *** ℛ
63.35-03 *** area

cylindrical shell
.2 ENT↑ length
.25 ENT↑ ID
.284 ENT↑ OD
1000. GSB1 μ

14.03-03 *** ℛ
14.26-03 *** area

cylindrical shell
.2 ENT↑ length
.25 ENT↑ ID
.3 ENT↑ OD
1000. GSB1 μ

9.260-03 *** ℛ
21.60-03 *** area

solid cylinder
.4 ENT↑ length
0. ENT↑ ID
.3 ENT↑ OD
1000. GSB1 μ

5.659-03 *** ℛ
70.69-03 *** area

disc
.2 ENT↑ thickness
.3 ENT↑ ID
.95 ENT↑ OD
1000. GSB2 μ

917.3-06 *** ℛ
188.5-03 *** min area

disc
.2 ENT↑ thickness
.284 ENT↑ ID
.3 ENT↑ OD
1. GSB2 μ

43.62-03 *** ℛ
178.4-03 *** min area

GSBE calc all params
1.661-03 *** L, h
759.9-03 *** R, ohms

809.2+00 *** M, cir-mils/A
1.574+03 *** Δ, A/in$^2$
190.0-03 *** P, watts

6.019+03 *** max $B_{iron}$
6.019+03 *** $B_{air}$, G

298.6-03 *** F, pounds

Look at voltage excitation. Set flag 0 so magnetic reluctance is ignored and calculate electrical & magnetic parameters.

SF0
.6 GSBc load E

GSBE calc params
2.048-03 *** L, h
759.9-03 *** R, ohms

512.4+00 *** M, cir-mils/A
2.485+03 *** Δ, A/in$^2$
473.7-03 *** P, watts

11.72+03 *** max $B_{iron}$
11.72+03 *** $B_{air}$, G

1.132+00 *** F, pounds

Clear flag 0 to use magnetic reluctance.

CF0
GSBE calc params
1.661-03 *** L, h
759.9-03 *** R, ohms

512.4+00 *** M, cir-mils/A
2.485+03 *** Δ, A/in$^2$
473.7-03 *** P, watts

9.505+03 *** max $B_{iron}$
9.505+03 *** $B_{air}$, G

744.6-03 *** F, pounds

# Program Listing I

| Step | Key | Comment |
|---|---|---|
| 001 | *LBLA | LOAD AIR GAP IN INCHES |
| 002 | STO2 | store entry |
| 003 | GTO0 | goto space and return |
| 004 | *LBLa | LOAD N ↑ AWG ↑ $ID_{coil}$ ↑ $\ell_{coil}$ |
| 005 | STO1 | store coil length |
| 006 | R↓ | recover and store $ID_{coil}$ |
| 007 | STOD | |
| 008 | R↓ | recover and store AWG |
| 009 | STOB | |
| 010 | R↓ | recover and store N |
| 011 | STOE | |
| 012 | GTO0 | goto space and return |
| 013 | *LBL2 | SUBROUTINE FOR DISC |
| 014 | R↓ | |
| 015 | X⇄Y | |
| 016 | STOI | |
| 017 | ÷ | $\ell_{effective} = \frac{ID}{2} \ln \frac{OD}{ID}$ |
| 018 | LN | |
| 019 | RCLI | |
| 020 | × | |
| 021 | 2 | |
| 022 | ÷ | |
| 023 | X⇄Y | |
| 024 | RCLI | |
| 025 | × | $A_{min} = \pi \cdot ID \cdot t$ |
| 026 | Pi | |
| 027 | × | |
| 028 | R↑ | recover $\mu$ |
| 029 | *LBLB | LOAD $\ell_{iron}$ ↑ $A_{iron}$ ↑ $\mu$ |
| 030 | X⇄Y | store $\mu$ |
| 031 | STOI | |
| 032 | F0? | store $A_{iron}$ on first |
| 033 | STO4 | execution of this routine |
| 034 | × | |
| 035 | ÷ | $\mathcal{R}_i = \frac{\ell_{iron_i}}{\mu_i \cdot A_{iron_i}}$ |
| 036 | SPC | |
| 037 | PRTX | |
| 038 | ST+5 | add $\mathcal{R}_i$ to $\Sigma$ |
| 039 | RCL4 | test to see if present area |
| 040 | RCLI | is smaller than minimum |
| 041 | X≤Y? | stored area, if so, store |
| 042 | STO4 | present area |
| 043 | CF0 | indicate magnetic params |
| 044 | GSB8 | print area and space |
| 045 | GTO0 | goto space and return |
| 046 | *LBLb | LOAD $ID_p$ ↑ $OD_p$ |
| 047 | GSB4 | calculate and store |
| 048 | STO3 | annular area |
| 049 | GTO0 | goto space and return |

NOTE:

The "print" statements at line numbers 037, 102, 105, 124, and 130 may be changed to "R/S" statements if desired.

| Step | Key | Comment |
|---|---|---|
| 050 | *LBLC | CALCULATE $B_{air}$ and $B_{iron}$ |
| 051 | GSB6 | calculate R, I, and NI |
| 052 | GSB9 | calc $(0.4\pi/k_3)/(\Sigma\mathcal{R}_i + \ell_{air}/A_{air})$ |
| 053 | RCL4 | use $A_{air}$ if magnetic params |
| 054 | F0? | not entered, otherwise use |
| 055 | RCL3 | min $A_{iron}$ |
| 056 | 1/X | take reciprocal area |
| 057 | RCLI | calculate and print $\phi$ |
| 058 | RCLA | using Eq. (3-7.2) |
| 059 | × | |
| 060 | STO6 | |
| 061 | × | calculate and print: |
| 062 | P⇄S | |
| 063 | RCL6 | |
| 064 | P⇄S | $B_{iron,\,max} = \frac{\phi}{\min A_{iron} \cdot k_3^2}$ |
| 065 | X² | |
| 066 | STOI | |
| 067 | ÷ | |
| 068 | PRTX | |
| 069 | RCL6 | calculate and print: |
| 070 | RCL3 | |
| 071 | ÷ | $B_{max} = \frac{\phi}{A_{air} \cdot k_3^2}$ |
| 072 | RCLI | |
| 073 | ÷ | |
| 074 | GTO8 | |
| 075 | *LBLE | PRINT COMPLETE SUMMARY |
| 076 | GSBd | |
| 077 | GSBe | |
| 078 | GSBC | |
| 079 | *LBLD | CALCULATE AND PRINT F |
| 080 | GSB6 | |
| 081 | SF2 | |
| 082 | GSB9 | |
| 083 | RCLA | |
| 084 | × | |
| 085 | X² | |
| 086 | RCL3 | $F = \frac{\phi^2}{k_1 \cdot k_3^4 \cdot A_{air}}$ |
| 087 | ÷ | |
| 088 | P⇄S | |
| 089 | RCL8 | |
| 090 | P⇄S | |
| 091 | ÷ | |
| 092 | GTO8 | |
| 093 | *LBLd | CALCULATE AND PRINT L & R |
| 094 | GSB6 | |
| 095 | GSB9 | |
| 096 | RCLE | |
| 097 | X² | |
| 098 | × | |
| 099 | EEX | $L = \frac{N^2 k_3}{10^8} \cdot \frac{0.4\pi}{\sum_{iron} \mathcal{R} + \frac{\ell_{air}}{A_{air}}}$ |
| 100 | 8 | |
| 101 | ÷ | |
| 102 | PRTX | |
| 103 | RCLC | recall and print resistance |

**REGISTERS**

| 0 | 1 | 2 | 3 | 4 | 5 | 6 | 7 | 8 | 9 |
|---|---|---|---|---|---|---|---|---|---|
| $w$ | $\ell_{coil}$ | $\ell_{air}$ | $A_{air}$ | min $A_{iron}$ | $\sum \frac{\ell}{\mu A}$ | $\phi$ | scratch | $I$ | $E$ |

| S0 | S1 | S2 | S3 | S4 | S5 | S6 | S7 | S8 | S9 |
|---|---|---|---|---|---|---|---|---|---|
| $a'$ | $b'$ | $a$ | $b$ | $\pi k_4$ | $k_5$ | $k_3$ | $k_2$ | $k_1$ | |

| A | B | C | D | E | I |
|---|---|---|---|---|---|
| NI | AWG | R | coil OD | N | scratchpad |

# Program Listing II

NOTE FLAG SET STATUS

```
104  *LBL8    print and space subroutine
105   PRTX
106   GTO0
107  *LBLc    LOAD COIL EXCITATION
108   STO9
109  *LBL0    space and return subroutine
110    SPC
111    RTN
112  *LBLe    CALCULATE AND PRINT M, ,P
113   GSB6
114    P⇄S
115   RCL0
116   RCL1
117   GSB3
118     X²
119   RCL8
120      ÷
121    EEX
122      6
123      x
124   PRTX
125    1/X
126    P⇄S
127   RCL7
128    P⇄S
129      x
130   PRTX
131   RCL8
132     X²
133   RCLC
134      x
135   GTO8
136  *LBL1    CYLINDRICAL SHELL SUBR
137   STOI
138     R↓
139   GSB4
140   RCLI
141   GTOB
142  *LBL3    subroutine to calculate:
143    P⇄S
144   RCLB
145      x
146     eˣ
147      x
148    RTN
149  *LBL4    subroutine to calculate:
150     X²
151    X⇄Y
152     X²
153      -
154     Pi
155      x
156      4
157      ÷
158    RTN
```

Steps 113–124: $M = 10^6\left(a' e^{b' \cdot AWG}\right)^2$

Steps 125–130: $\Delta = \frac{k_2}{M}$

Steps 131–135: $P = I^2 R$

Steps 142–148: $R_y \cdot e^{R_x \cdot AWG}$

Steps 149–158: $\text{Area} = \frac{\pi}{4}\left(OD^2 - ID^2\right)$

```
159  *LBL6    subr to calc R, I, and NI
160    P⇄S
161   RCL2
162   RCL3
163   GSB3
164     X²
165   RCLE
166      x
167   RCL1
168      ÷
169   STO0
170   RCLD
171      +
172   RCLE
173      x
174    P⇄S
175   RCL4
176   RCL5
177   GSB3
178      x
179   STOC
180   RCL9
181   X<0?    test for current excitation
182   GTO0
183      ÷
184    1/X
185  *LBL0    jump destination
186    ABS    store |I|
187   STO8
188   RCLE    calculate and store NI
189      x
190   STOA
191    RTN
192  *LBL9    magnetics subroutine
193      7
194      2
195    D→R
196   RCL2
197   RCL3
198      ÷
199   RCL5
200    F0?
201    CLX
202      +
203      ÷
204    P⇄S
205   RCL6
206    P⇄S
207    F2?
208    1/X
209      x
210   STOI
211    RTN    return to main program
```

Steps 160–169: $W = \frac{N}{\ell_{coil}}\left(a \cdot e^{b \cdot AWG}\right)^2$

Steps 170–179: $R = N\pi\left(ID_{coil} + W\right)k_4 e^{k_5 \cdot AWG}$

Steps 183–184: $I = E/R$

Steps 193–195: $0.4\pi$

Steps 196–210: $\dfrac{0.4\pi}{\sum_{iron} \mathcal{R}_i + \dfrac{\ell_{air}}{A_{air}}} \cdot \dfrac{k_3 \ (F2=0)}{k_3 \ (F2=1)}$

NOTE FLAG SET STATUS

| LABELS | | | | | FLAGS |
|---|---|---|---|---|---|
| A $\ell_{air}$ | B $\ell_{iron} \uparrow A_{iron} \uparrow \mu$ | C calculate $B_{air}$, max $B_{iron}$ | D calc F | E complete summary | 0 magnetic parameters entered |
| a $N \uparrow AWG \uparrow ID_{coil} \uparrow \ell_{coil}$ | b $ID_p \uparrow OD_p$ | c +E or −I | d calc L, R | e calc M, Δ, & P | 1 |
| 0 local label | 1 cylindrical section entry | 2 disc section entry | 3 wire size subroutine | 4 circular section area | 2 subroutine 9 control |
| 5 | 6 R, I & NI subroutine | 7 | 8 print & space subroutine | 9 magnetics calc subr | 3 |

| SET STATUS | | | | |
|---|---|---|---|---|
| FLAGS | ON | OFF | TRIG | DISP |
| 0 | ■ | | users choice | |
| 1 | | | DEG | FIX |
| 2 | | ■ | GRAD | SCI |
| 3 | | | RAD | ENG ■ |
| | | | | n 3 |

## PROGRAM 3-9 MAGNETIC RELUCTANCE OF TAPERED CYLINDRICAL SECTIONS.

Program Description and Equations Used

This program calculates the magnetic reluctance of tapered cylindrical sections with axial flux flow as shown by Fig. 3-9.1. The magnetic reluctance is analogous to electrical resistance, and is used in the Ohm's law of magnetics as given by Eq. (3-8.1).

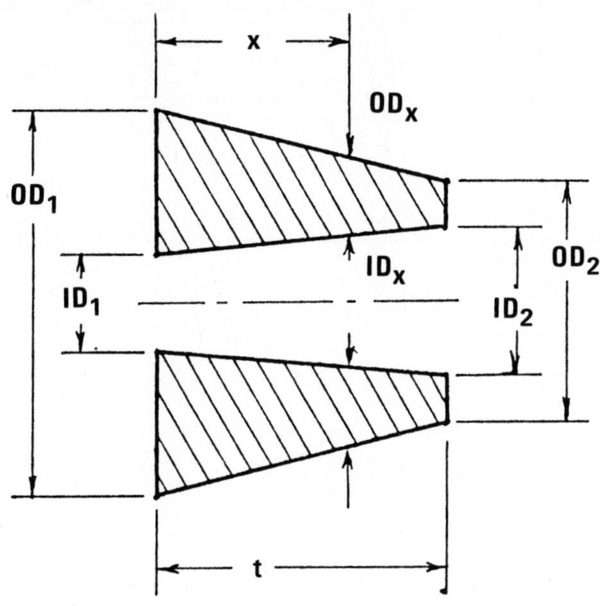


Figure 3-9.1 Tapered cylindrical section and dimensions.

Consider the section to be composed of an infinite number of washers each of infinitesimal thickness dx, then the reluctance of a washer is:

$$d\mathcal{R} = dx/(\mu \cdot A_x) \tag{3-9.1}$$

where

$$A_x = (\pi/4)(OD_x^2 - ID_x^2) \tag{3-9.2}$$

The inner and outer diameters at location x can be found by linearly interpolating between the known end diameters:

$$ID_x = ID_1 + (1/t)(ID_2 - ID_1)\cdot x \qquad (3\text{-}9.3)$$

$$OD_x = OD_1 + (1/t)(OD_2 - OD_1)\cdot x \qquad (3\text{-}9.4)$$

Substituting Eqs. (3-9.3) and (3-9.4) into Eq. (3-9.2) and collecting like powers of x results in a quadratic:

$$A_x = (\pi/4)(a + bx + cx^2) \qquad (3\text{-}9.5)$$

where

$$a = OD_1{}^2 - ID_1{}^2$$

$$b = (2/t)\{OD_1(OD_2 - OD_1) - ID_1(ID_2 - ID_1)\}$$

$$c = (1/t^2)\{(OD_2 - OD_1)^2 - (ID_2 - ID_1)^2\}$$

hence,

$$\mathcal{R} = \frac{4}{\mu\pi}\int_0^t \frac{dx}{a + bx + cx^2} \qquad (3\text{-}9.6)$$

The result of this integration can have any one of three forms; let

$$q = b^2 - 4ac \qquad (3\text{-}9.7)$$

and

$$r = (2cx + b)\Big/\sqrt{|q|} \qquad (3\text{-}9.8)$$

then if $q>0$ and $|r|<1$, the solution is:

$$\mathcal{R} = -\frac{8}{\mu\pi\sqrt{|q|}}\tanh^{-1} r \qquad (3\text{-}9.9)$$

if $q>0$ and $|r| \geq 1$, the solution is:

$$\mathcal{R} = \frac{4}{\mu\pi\sqrt{|q|}}\ \ell n\left(\frac{r-1}{r+1}\right) \qquad (3\text{-}9.10)$$

if $q < 0$, the solution for all r is:

$$\mathcal{R} = \frac{8}{\mu\pi\sqrt{|q|}}\tan^{-1} r \qquad (3\text{-}9.11)$$

# User Instructions

| MAGNETIC RELUCTANCE OF TAPERED CYLINDRICAL SECTIONS | | | | |
|---|---|---|---|---|
| load $ID_1 \uparrow ID_2$ | load $OD_1 \uparrow OD_2$ | load section length, t | load permea-bility, $\mu$ | print ? / calculate $\mathcal{R}$ |

| STEP | INSTRUCTIONS | INPUT DATA/UNITS | KEYS | OUTPUT DATA/UNITS |
|---|---|---|---|---|
| 1 | Load both sides of the magnetic card | | | |
| 2 | select print/ no-print option | | f E | 0 (no prt) |
| | | | f E | 1 (print) |
| | | | f E | 0 (no prt) |
| | | | | ⋮ |
| 3 | Load inner diameters | $ID_1$* | ENT↑ | |
| | | $ID_2$* | A | |
| 4 | Load outer diameters | $OD_1$* | ENT↑ | |
| | | $OD_2$* | B | |
| 5 | Load section length | t* | C | |
| 6 | Load magnetic permeability of material | | D | |
| 7 | Calculate reluctance | | E | $\mathcal{R}$** |

Notes

* Any units of the users choosing may be used as long as the same unit is used throughout. If the reluctance is going to be loaded into Program 3-7, then inch units should be used.

** The units of reluctance are in inverse dimension units, i.e., $inches^{-1}$, $cm^{-1}$, $ft^{-1}$, etc.

## Example 3-9.1

Given the conical section shown in Fig. 3-9.2, calculate the reluctance in inch units.

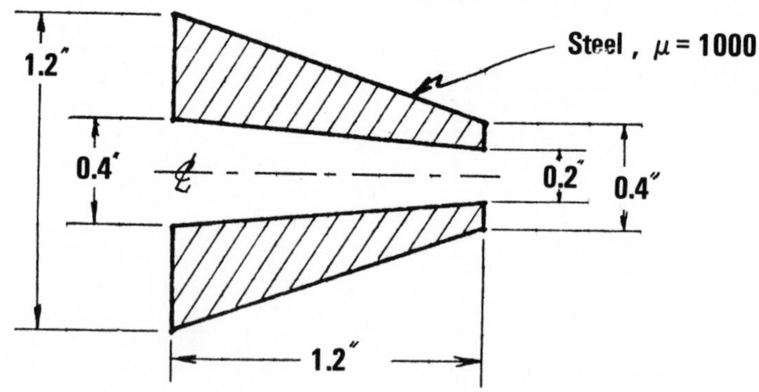


Figure 3-9.2 Tapered conical section.

.2 ENT↑    $ID_1$
.4 GSBA    $ID_2$

.4 ENT↑    $OD_1$
1.2 GSBB    $OD_2$

1.2 GSBC    t

1000. GSBD    μ

GSBE    calculate reluctance
3.872-03 ***    $\mathcal{R}$, $in^{-1}$

# Program Listing I

|  |  |
|---|---|
| *LBLA | LOAD $ID_1 \uparrow ID_2$ |
| STO1 | |
| R↓ | store entries |
| STO0 | |
| GTO0 | goto space and return subr |
| *LBLB | LOAD $OD_1 \uparrow OD_2$ |
| STO3 | |
| R↓ | store entries |
| STO2 | |
| GTO0 | goto space and return subr |
| *LBLC | LOAD SECTION LENGTH |
| STO4 | |
| GTO0 | |
| *LBLD | LOAD PERMEABILITY |
| STO5 | |
| *LBL0 | space and return subroutine |
| SPC | |
| RTN | |

|  |  |
|---|---|
| *LBLE | CALCULATE RELUCTANCE |
| RCL3 | calculate and store: |
| RCL2 | |
| - | $(OD_2 - OD_1)^2$ |
| X² | |
| STO8 | |
| LSTX | calculate and retain in stk: |
| RCL2 | $OD_1(OD_2 - OD_1)$ |
| × | |
| RCL1 | calculate w/ register arith: |
| RCL0 | |
| - | $(OD_2 - OD_1)^2 - (ID_2 - ID_1)^2$ |
| ENT↑ | |
| X² | |
| ST-8 | |
| R↓ | calculate and store b: |
| RCL0 | |
| × | |
| - | |
| ENT↑ | $\frac{2}{t}\left\{OD_1(OD_2 - OD_1) - ID_1(ID_2 - ID_1)\right\}$ |
| + | |
| RCL4 | |
| ÷ | |
| STO7 | |
| RCL4 | finish c calculation |
| X² | |
| ST÷8 | |
| RCL7 | calculate and store q: |
| X² | |
| RCL2 | |
| X² | |
| RCL0 | |
| X² | |
| - | $q = b^2 - 4ac$ |
| RCL8 | |
| × | |
| 4 | |
| × | |
| - | |
| STOB | |
| ABS | calculate and store: |
| √X | $\sqrt{\lvert q \rvert}$ |
| STOA | |
| RCL4 | calculate and store: |
| GSB0 | |
| STO9 | $\int_0^t \frac{dx}{a + bx + cx^2}$ |
| CLX | |
| GSB0 | |
| ST-9 | |

**REGISTERS**

| 0 | 1 | 2 | 3 | 4 | 5 | 6 | 7 | 8 | 9 |
|---|---|---|---|---|---|---|---|---|---|
| $ID_1$ | $ID_2$ | $OD_1$ | $OD_2$ | t | $\mu$ | scratch | b | c | $\int_0^t$ |
| S0 | S1 | S2 | S3 | S4 | S5 | S6 | S7 | S8 | S9 |
| | | | | | | | | | |

| A | B | C | D | E | I |
|---|---|---|---|---|---|
| $\sqrt{\lvert q \rvert}$ | q | 2cx + b | | $\mathcal{R}$ | |

# Program Listing II

```
068 RCL9   calculate and store
069 4      reluctance
070 x
071 RCL5
072 Pi
073 x
074 ÷
075 STOE
```

$$\mathcal{R} = \frac{4}{\mu\pi}\int_0^t \frac{dx}{a + bx + cx^2}$$

```
076 F1?    print reluctance and space
077 PRTX   if flag 1 is set
078 F1?
079 SPC
080 RTN
081 *LBL0  integral evaluation
082 ENT↑   subroutine
083 +
084 RCL8   calculate and store r:
085 x
086 RCL7
087 +
088 STOC
089 RCLA
090 ÷
091 STO6
```

$$r = \frac{2cx + b}{\sqrt{|q|}}$$

```
092 ABS    set flag 0 if the magnitude
093 EEX    of r is greater than 1
094 SF0
095 X>Y?
096 CF0
097 RCLB
098 X<0?   jump if q is less than 0
099 GTO0
100 F0?    jump if flag 0 is set
101 GTO2
102 EEX    calculate tanh⁻¹ r
103 RCL6
104 +
105 EEX
106 RCL6
107 -
108 ÷
109 √X
110 LN
111 CHS    change sign per Eq. (3-8.9)
112 GTO1   jump
```

$$\tanh^{-1} r = \frac{1}{2}\ln\frac{1+r}{1-r}$$

```
113 *LBL2  logarithmic solution
114 RCLC
115 RCLA
116 -
117 RCLC
118 RCLA
119 +
120 ÷
121 LN
122 RCLA
123 ÷
124 RTN    return to main program
125 *LBL0  trigonometric solution
126 RCL6   calculate tan⁻¹ r
127 TAN⁻¹
128 *LBL1  common portion of
129 ENT↑   hyperbolic and trigonometric
130 +      solutions
131 RCLA
132 ÷
133 RTN    return to main program
134 *LBLe  PRINT OR R/S TOGGLE
135 F1?    jump if flag 1 is set
136 GTO3
137 SF1    set flag 1
138 EEX    place 1 in display
139 RTN    return control to keyboard
140 *LBL3  clear flag 1 and place a
141 CF1    zero in the display
142 CLX
143 RTN    return control to keyboard
```

Flag 1 should be set (cleared) before magnetic card recording depending upon the user's desire for the program to normally be in the print (R/S) mode after the card read.

**LABELS**

| A load $ID_1 \uparrow ID_2$ | B load $OD_1 \uparrow OD_2$ | C load t | D load permeability | E calculate reluctance |
|---|---|---|---|---|
| a | b | c | d | e print / R/S toggle |
| 0 local label | 1 subroutine destination | 2 subroutine destination | 3 print / R/S destination | 4 |
| 5 | 6 | 7 | 8 | 9 |

**FLAGS**

| | |
|---|---|
| 0 | r > 1 |
| 1 | print |
| 2 | |
| 3 | |

**SET STATUS**

| FLAGS | ON | OFF | TRIG | | DISP | |
|---|---|---|---|---|---|---|
| 0 | | ■ | DEG | | FIX | |
| 1 | | | GRAD | | SCI | |
| 2 | | | RAD | ■ | ENG | ■ |
| 3 | | | | | n 3 | |

# Part 4

# HIGH FREQUENCY CIRCUIT DESIGN

## PROGRAM 4-1 BILATERAL TRANSISTOR AMPLIFIER DESIGN USING S PARAMETERS.

Program Description and Equations Used

When $s_{12}$, the reverse transmission coefficient, cannot be reduced to near zero using unilateral design methods,* or the unilateral figure of merit is not sufficiently near zero, the bilateral design method must be used. Since $s_{12}$ is related to the capacitive reactance of the transistor base-collector capacity, and this reactance becomes smaller as frequency increases, the bilateral design requirement generally occurs when the amplifier is to be used at UHF frequencies and above.

The bilateral stability factor, K, is computed using Eq. (4-1.1). For the amplifier to be unconditionally stable, K must be greater than one, and the magnitudes of $s_{11}$ and $s_{22}$ must be smaller than one. Since $s_{11}$ and $s_{22}$ are reflection coefficients, this last requirement implies that the input and output impedances are positive. Unconditional stability means the amplifier will not oscillate for any choice of input and output terminations.

$$K = \frac{1 + |\Delta|^2 - |s_{11}| - |s_{22}|}{2\,|s_{21} \cdot s_{12}|} \qquad (4\text{-}1.1)$$

$$\Delta = s_{11} \cdot s_{22} - s_{21} \cdot s_{12} \qquad (4\text{-}1.2)$$

When K is less than one, the amplifier will oscillate with certain source and load impedances, hence, these impedances must be carefully selected. The HP EE pac Program 18 will calculate the stability circles to aid in the termination impedance selection.

The scattering parameters are:

$s_{11}$ is the input reflection coefficient,
$s_{12}$ is the reverse transmission coefficient,
$s_{21}$ is the forward transmission coefficient, and
$s_{22}$ is the output reflection coefficient.

---

* See the HP EE pac Program 16 for unilateral design methods.

Scattering parameters are obtained from reflection coefficient measurements applied to a two port network with both ports loaded with a reference impedance, $Z_o$, which is typically 50 ohms resistive. The reflection coefficient is defined by Eq. (1-1.2). For a more comprehensive discussion of s parameters, see Froehner [24], HP application note 95 [32], or Carson [15].

If the proposed amplifier is unconditionally stable, then the maximum gain can be calculated using Eq. (4-1.3)

$$G_{max} = \left|\frac{s_{21}}{s_{12}}\right| \cdot (K \pm \sqrt{K^2 - 1}) \tag{4-1.3}$$

The negative sign is used when $B_1$ is positive and vice-versa:

$$B_1 = 1 + |s_{11}|^2 - |s_{22}|^2 - |\Delta|^2 \tag{4-1.4}$$

The source and load reflection coefficients necessary to provide $G_{max}$ are given by Eqs. (4-1.5) and (4-1.6). These loads present a conjugate match to the transistor.

$$\rho_{MS} = C_1^* \cdot \frac{B_1 \pm \sqrt{B_1^2 - 4|C_1|^2}}{2|C_1|^2} \tag{4-1.5}$$

$$\rho_{ML} = C_2^* \cdot \frac{B_2 \pm \sqrt{B_2^2 - 4|C_2|^2}}{2|C_1|^2} \tag{4-1.6}$$

$$B_2 = 1 + |s_{22}|^2 - |s_{11}|^2 - |\Delta|^2 \tag{4-1.7}$$

$$C_1 = s_{11} - \Delta \cdot s_{22}^* \tag{4-1.8}$$

$$C_2 = s_{22} - \Delta \cdot s_{11}^* \tag{4-1.9}$$

The minus sign in Eqs. (4-1.5) and (4-1.6) is used when $B_1$ is positive and vice-versa. The asterisk (*) means the complex conjugate, i.e., the sign of the imaginary part is reversed, or the sign of the angle is reversed for rectangular or polar formats respectively.

Equations (4-1.5) and (4-1.6) are used to calculate reflection coefficients. The corresponding impedances can be obtained if Eq. (1-1.2) is rearranged to provide $Z_L$ in terms of $Z_s$:

$$Z_L = Z_o \frac{1 + \rho}{1 - \rho} \tag{4-1.10}$$

This routine is contained under label E of the program.

# User Instructions

| BILATERAL TRANSISTOR AMPLIFIER DESIGN USING S PARAMETERS | | | | |
|---|---|---|---|---|
| | | calculate $\rho_{Source, max}$ | | print, R/S toggle |
| load $\Theta_{ij} \uparrow s_{ij} \uparrow ij$ | calculate K, $G_{max}$ | calculate $\rho_{Load, max}$ | | $\measuredangle\rho \uparrow \|\rho\| \uparrow Z_o \rightarrow Im, Re Z$ |

| STEP | INSTRUCTIONS | INPUT DATA/UNITS | KEYS | OUTPUT DATA/UNITS |
|---|---|---|---|---|
| 1 | Load both sides of magnetic card | | | |
| 2 | Select print or R/S option | | f E | 0 (R/S) |
| | | | f E | 1 (print) |
| | | | f E | 0 (R/S) |
| | | | | ⋮ |
| 3 | Load elements of s parameter matrix for ij = 11, 12, 21, 22 (any order) | | | |
| | a) load angle of $s_{ij}$ in degrees | $\Theta_{ij}^{o}$ | ENT↑ | |
| | b) load magnitude of $s_{ij}$ | $\|s_{ij}\|$ | ENT↑ | |
| | c) load subscript | ij | A | |
| 4 | Calculate stability factor and maximum gain | | B | K |
| | | | | $G_{max}$, dB |
| 5 | Calculate angle and magnitude of load reflection coefficient to obtain $G_{max}$ | | C | $\measuredangle \rho_{mL}$ |
| | | | | $\|\rho_{mL}\|$ |
| | Calculate real and imaginary parts of load impedance | $Z_o$ | E | Re $Z_L$ |
| | | | | Im $Z_L$ |
| 6 | Calculate angle and magnitude of source reflection coefficient to obtain $G_{max}$ | | f C | $\measuredangle \rho_{ms}$ |
| | | | | $\|\rho_{ms}\|$ |
| | Calculate real and imaginary parts of source impedance | $Z_o$ | E | Re $Z_s$ |
| | | | | Im $Z_s$ |
| 7 | Calculate real and imaginary parts of impedances corresponding to a reflection coefficient and $Z_o$ | $\measuredangle \rho$ | ENT↑ | |
| | | $\|\rho\|$ | ENT↑ | |
| | | $Z_o$ | E | Re Z |
| | | | | Im Z |

Example 4-1.1

Given a 2N3570 transistor operating at $I_c$ = 4 mA and $V_{ce}$ = 10 V and having the following s parameters at 750 MHz,

$$\begin{bmatrix} s_{11} & s_{12} \\ s_{21} & s_{22} \end{bmatrix} = \begin{bmatrix} 0.277 \measuredangle -59° & 0.078 \measuredangle 93° \\ 1.920 \measuredangle 60° & 0.848 \measuredangle -31° \end{bmatrix}$$

calculate the stability factor, the maximum power gain in dB, the source reflection coefficient and impedance to obtain $G_{max}$, and the load reflection coefficient and impedance to obtain $G_{max}$.

| PROGRAM INPUT | | PROGRAM OUTPUT | |
|---|---|---|---|
| -59.000 ENT↑ | $\theta_{11}$, angle in degrees | GSBB | calculate K & $G_{max}$ |
| .277 ENT↑ | $s_{11}$, magnitude | 1.033+00 *** | K > 1, uncond stable |
| 11. GSBA | ij | 12.81+00 *** | $G_{max}$, dB |
| 93.000 ENT↑ | $\theta_{12}$ | GSBc | calculate $\rho_{MS}$ |
| .078 ENT↑ | $s_{12}$ | 135.4+00 *** | $\measuredangle\rho_{MS}$, degrees |
| 12. GSBA | ij | 729.6-03 *** | $\lvert\rho_{MS}\rvert$ |
| 64.000 ENT↑ | $\theta_{21}$ | 50. GSBE | calculate $Z_S$ |
| 1.920 ENT↑ | $s_{21}$ | 9.063+00 *** | Re $Z_S$, ohms |
| 21. GSBA | ij | 19.90+00 *** | Im $Z_s$, ohms |
| -31.000 ENT↑ | $\theta_{22}$ | GSBC | calculate $\rho_{ML}$ |
| .848 ENT↑ | $s_{22}$ | 33.85+00 *** | $\measuredangle\rho_{ML}$, degrees |
| 22. GSBA | ij | 951.1-03 *** | $\lvert\rho_{ML}\rvert$ |
| | | 50. GSBE | calculate $Z_L$ |
| | | 14.69+00 *** | Re $Z_L$, ohms |
| | | 163.1+00 *** | Im $Z_L$, ohms |

# Program Listing I

| Step | Key | Comment |
|---|---|---|
| 001 | *LBLA | **LOAD** $\theta_{ij} \uparrow s_{ij} \uparrow ij$ |
| 002 | ENT↑ | |
| 003 | + | calculate storage register index |
| 004 | 2 | |
| 005 | 1 | |
| 006 | - | |
| 007 | STOI | |
| 008 | R↓ | recover and store $s_{ij}$ |
| 009 | STOi | |
| 010 | ISZI | increment register index |
| 011 | R↓ | recover and store $\theta_{ij}$ |
| 012 | STOi | |
| 013 | GTO3 | goto space and return |
| 014 | *LBLB | **CALCULATE K, $G_{max}$** |
| 015 | RCL2 | calculate and store $s_{11} \cdot s_{22}$ |
| 016 | RCL1 | |
| 017 | RCLD | |
| 018 | RCLE | |
| 019 | GSB9 | |
| 020 | STO6 | $\lvert s_{11} \cdot s_{22} \rvert$ |
| 021 | R↓ | |
| 022 | STO7 | $\measuredangle\, s_{11}\, s_{22}$ |
| 023 | RCL4 | calculate and store: |
| 024 | RCL3 | |
| 025 | RCLB | |
| 026 | RCLC | |
| 027 | GSB9 | $\Delta = s_{11} \cdot s_{22} - s_{12} \cdot s_{21}$ |
| 028 | CHS | |
| 029 | RCL7 | |
| 030 | RCL6 | |
| 031 | GSB8 | |
| 032 | STO6 | $\lvert\Delta\rvert$ |
| 033 | R↓ | |
| 034 | STO7 | $\measuredangle \Delta$ |
| 035 | RCLD | finish K calculation |
| 036 | RCL1 | |
| 037 | GSB7 | $B_1 = \lvert s_{11}\rvert^2 - \lvert s_{22}\rvert^2 - \lvert\Delta\rvert^2 + 1$ |
| 038 | RCL6 | |
| 039 | X² | |
| 040 | EEX | |
| 041 | + | |
| 042 | RCL1 | |
| 043 | X² | |
| 044 | - | |
| 045 | RCLD | |
| 046 | X² | |
| 047 | - | $1 + \lvert\Delta\rvert^2 - \lvert s_{11}\rvert^2 - \lvert s_{22}\rvert^2$ |
| 048 | RCL3 | |
| 049 | RCLB | |
| 050 | × | |
| 051 | ABS | |
| 052 | ENT↑ | |
| 053 | + | |
| 054 | ÷ | |
| 055 | STO9 | $K = \dfrac{1 + \lvert\Delta\rvert^2 - \lvert s_{11}\rvert^2 - \lvert s_{22}\rvert^2}{2\lvert s_{21} \cdot s_{12}\rvert}$ |
| 056 | GSB5 | goto print routine |
| 057 | X² | calculate $G_{max}$: |
| 058 | LSTX | |
| 059 | X⇄Y | |
| 060 | EEX | |
| 061 | - | |
| 062 | √X | |
| 063 | RCL5 | $G_{max} = \left\lvert \dfrac{s_{21}}{s_{12}} \right\rvert \cdot \left(K \pm \sqrt{K^2 - 1}\right)$ |
| 064 | × | |
| 065 | - | |
| 066 | RCLB | – used when $B_1$ is + |
| 067 | × | |
| 068 | RCL3 | |
| 069 | ÷ | |
| 070 | ABS | convert $G_{max}$ to dB power gain |
| 071 | LOG | |
| 072 | EEX | |
| 073 | 1 | |
| 074 | × | |
| 075 | GTO0 | goto print and space subr |
| 076 | *LBLc | **CALCULATE $\rho_{source,\,max}$** |
| 077 | RCL7 | calculate $-\Delta \cdot s_{22}$ |
| 078 | RCL6 | |
| 079 | RCLD | |
| 080 | RCLE | |
| 081 | CHS | |
| 082 | GSB9 | |
| 083 | CHS | |
| 084 | RCL2 | recall $s_{11}$ |
| 085 | RCL1 | |
| 086 | GSB2 | calc and print $\measuredangle\, \rho_{source,\,max}$ |
| 087 | RCLD | $\lvert s_{22}\rvert$ |
| 088 | RCL1 | $\lvert s_{11}\rvert$ |
| 089 | GSB7 | calc $\lvert s_{11}\rvert^2 - \lvert s_{22}\rvert^2 - \lvert\Delta\rvert^2 + 1 = B_1$ |
| 090 | GTO1 | jump |
| 091 | *LBLC | **CALCULATE $\rho_{load,\,max}$** |
| 092 | RCL7 | calculate $-\Delta \cdot s_{11}$ |
| 093 | RCL6 | |
| 094 | RCL1 | |
| 095 | RCL2 | |
| 096 | CHS | |
| 097 | GSB9 | |
| 098 | CHS | |
| 099 | RCLE | recall $s_{22}$ |
| 100 | RCLD | |
| 101 | GSB2 | calc and print $\measuredangle\, \rho_{load,\,max}$ |
| 102 | RCL1 | $\lvert s_{11}\rvert$ |
| 103 | RCLD | $\lvert s_{22}\rvert$ |
| 104 | GSB7 | calc $\lvert s_{22}\rvert^2 - \lvert s_{11}\rvert^2 - \lvert\Delta\rvert^2 - 1 = B_2$ |
| 105 | *LBL1 | calculate refl coef mag |
| 106 | RCLA | $-\measuredangle B$ |
| 107 | RCL8 | $\lvert B\rvert$ |
| 108 | RCL0 | $\lvert C\rvert$ |
| 109 | ENT↑ | |
| 110 | + | |

**REGISTERS**

| 0 | 1 | 2 | 3 | 4 | 5 | 6 | 7 | 8 | 9 |
|---|---|---|---|---|---|---|---|---|---|
| $\lvert C\rvert$ | $\lvert s_{11}\rvert$ | $\measuredangle\, s_{11}$ | $\lvert s_{12}\rvert$ | $\measuredangle\, s_{12}$ | sign($B_1$) | scratch, $\lvert\Delta\rvert$ | scratch, $\measuredangle\, \Delta$ | scratch, $B_2$ or $B_1$ | K |

| S0 | S1 | S2 | S3 | S4 | S5 | S6 | S7 | S8 | S9 |
|---|---|---|---|---|---|---|---|---|---|
| Re $\rho$ | Im $\rho$ | $Z_o$ , $Z_s$ | $\measuredangle\, Z_s$ | | | | | | |

| A | B | C | D | E | I |
|---|---|---|---|---|---|
| $\measuredangle\, C^*, -\measuredangle B$ | $\lvert s_{21}\rvert$ | $\measuredangle\, s_{21}$ | $\lvert s_{22}\rvert$ | $\measuredangle\, s_{22}$ | index |

# Program Listing II

```
÷
ENT↑        |ρ| = B/2C - (sign B)√((B/2C)² - 1)
X²
EEX
-
√X
RCL5
×
-
*LBL0       print and space subroutine
GSB5
*LBL3       space subroutine
F0?         space if flag 0 is set
SPC
GTO6        goto R/S lock
*LBLE       CONVERT ∡ρ↑|ρ|↑Z₀ → Im, Re Z
P⇄S
STO2
R↓
→R
STO0        Re ρ
EEX
+
X⇄Y
STO1        Im ρ
X⇄Y
→P          1+ρ
ST×2        Z₀·(1+ρ)
X⇄Y
STO3        ∡(1+ρ)
RCL1
CHS         -Im ρ
EEX
RCL0        Re ρ
-
→P          1-ρ
ST÷2        |Z₀|·|(1+ρ)/(1-ρ)| = |Z|
X⇄Y
ST-3        ∡(1+ρ) - ∡(1-ρ) = ∡Z
RCL3        ∡Z
RCL2        |Z|
P⇄S
→R          convert to rectangular fmt
GSB5        print Re Z
X⇄Y         recover Im Z
GTO0        print Im Z and space
*LBL7       subroutine to calculate:
X²
X⇄Y         X² - Y² - |Δ|² + 1 = B
X²
-           sign(B) → R5
EEX
+
RCL6
X²
-
STO8
X=0?
EEX
ABS
LSTX
÷
STO5
RTN
*LBL8       complex add subroutine
→R
R↓
R↓
→R
X⇄Y
R↓
+
R↓
+
R↑
→P
RTN
*LBL9       complex multiply subroutine
R↓
×
R↓
+
R↑
RTN
*LBL2       subroutine to finish C
GSB8        calculation, store results
STO0        and print angle of
X⇄Y         reflection coefficient
CHS
STOA
*LBL5       print subroutine
F0?
PRTX        print and return if flag 0
F0?         is set, otherwise stop
RTN
R/S
RTN
*LBL6       R/S lock
R/S         prevents inadvertent use
GTO6        of program fcns w/ R/S
*LBLe       PRINT, R/S TOGGLE
CF0         clear flag 0 to indicate
CLX         R/S mode and place a zero
RTN         in the display
*LBLe
SF0         set flag 0 to indicate
EEX         print and continue mode
RTN         and place a one in display
```

NOTE FLAG SET STATUS

| LABELS | | | | | FLAGS |
|---|---|---|---|---|---|
| A $\theta_{ij}\uparrow s_{ij}\uparrow ij$ | B → K, $G_{max}$ | C → $\rho_{mL}$ | D | E $\rho\uparrow Z_o \rightarrow Z$ | 0 print |
| a | b | c → $\rho_{ms}$ | d | e | 1 |
| 0 prt, spc, rtn | 1 local label w/ C, fC | 2 subroutine w/ C, fC | 3 space, rtn | 4 | 2 |
| 5 print, R/S subroutine | 6 R/S lock | 7 subroutine | 8 complex add | 9 complex multiply | 3 |

| SET STATUS | | |
|---|---|---|
| FLAGS (ON OFF) | TRIG | DISP |
| 0 ■ | DEG ■ | FIX |
| 1 | GRAD | SCI |
| 2 | RAD | ENG ■ |
| 3 | | n 3 |

## PROGRAM 4-2 UHF OSCILLATOR DESIGN USING S PARAMETERS.

Program Description and Equations Used

At UHF frequencies, the interelement capacities of a UHF transistor can function as the feedback elements to allow the device to oscillate when connected to an external tuned circuit (usually a ¼-wave transmission line section). The emitter circuit is generally left unbypassed while the base circuit is bypassed with a capacitor to provide an ac ground. The collector-emitter capacity provides the necessary feedback to allow the collector to exhibit negative output impedance and oscillate with the external tuned circuit.

The program starts with the common base s parameters, reverses the port ordering so the collector is the input, and calculates the reflection coefficient of the "input." If the magnitude of the reflection coefficient is greater than one, the real part of the input impedance will be negative. The routine under label E provides the conversion from reflection coefficient to impedance, while the routine under label e provides the reverse conversion.

Equation (4-2.1) calculates the input reflection coefficient when the output port is loaded with $R_L$ as shown by Fig. 4-2.1. Equation (4-2.1) holds for any transistor configuration.

$$s_{11}' = s_{11} + \frac{s_{12} \cdot s_{21} \cdot \rho_L}{1 - s_{22} \cdot \rho_L} \qquad (4\text{-}2.1)$$

where $\rho_L$ is defined by Eq. (1-1.2) with $Z_r = R_L$.

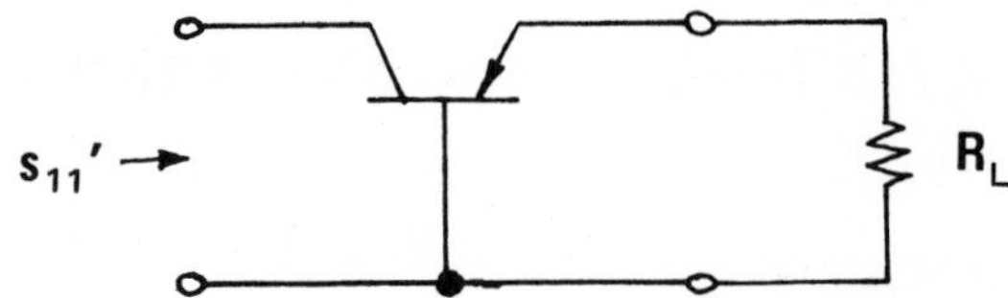


Figure 4-2.1 Common base transistor with collector as input port.

If the tuned source is connected to the collector, and the reflection coefficient of the source is denoted $\rho_S$, the circuit will oscillate if:

$$\rho_S \cdot s_{11}' \geq 1 \tag{4-2.2}$$

This equation is used in reverse to calculate the source reflection coefficient necessary for oscillation, i.e.:

$$\rho_S = \frac{1}{s_{11}'} \tag{4-2.3}$$

This reflection coefficient can be converted to its equivalent impedance using Eq. (4-1.10). The "Q," or quality factor, of this impedance is the ratio of the imaginary part to the real part, i.e.:

$$Q = \frac{\text{Im } Z_S}{\text{Re } Z_S} \tag{4-2.4}$$

The transistor negative input impedance can also be used to make a reflection amplifier if a circulator is used to separate the input from the output. The noise figure will be poor because of the large unbypassed emitter resistance.

For more information see the HP Journal [33], or HP application note number 95 [32].

Notes for User Instructions. Most UHF transistors are four lead devices (emitter, base, collector, and case). The case is electrically isolated from the transistor, in fact, the transistor chip is so small that it is mounted on the end of the collector lead inside the case. Because of the fourth element, the case, the parasitic capacities from it to the other leads will introduce errors into the common-emitter to common-base s parameter conversion. See G. Bodway's article [ 9 ] on characterization of transistors by means of three port scattering parameters as one way of dealing with this problem.

If the common base s parameters are available, or can be measured, they are the highly preferred form of data input for the program. Common-base parameters notwithstanding, the common-emitter conversion can be used with the knowledge that $s_{11}'$ will not be very accurate.

# User Instructions

| UHF OSCILLATOR DESIGN USING S PARAMETERS | | | | |
|---|---|---|---|---|
| interchange ports 1&2 | fA, C, fD, E | print s matrix | calculate $1/S_{11}' = \rho_s$ | Im Z ↑ Re Z ↑ $Z_o$ → ∡ρ, \|ρ\| |
| load data $\theta_{ij}$ ↑ \|$s_{ij}$\| ↑ ij | load ∡ $\rho_L$ ↑ \|$\rho_L$\| | calculate $s_{11}'$ | load ∡ $\rho_s$ ↑ \|$\rho_s$\| calc $s_{11}' \cdot \rho_s$ | ∡ρ ↑ \|ρ\| ↑ $Z_o$ → Im Z, Re Z |

| STEP | INSTRUCTIONS | INPUT DATA/UNITS | KEYS | OUTPUT DATA/UNITS |
|---|---|---|---|---|
| 1 | Load both sides of program card or load Program 4-3 if parameter conversion reqd | | | |
| 2 | Load s parameters. If already in common base form, goto step 10 after executing this step. | | | |
| | a) load angle of scattering parameter | $\theta_{ij}$ | ENT↑ | |
| | b) load magnitude of scattering parameter | \|$s_{ij}$\| | ENT↑ | |
| | c) load subscript of scattering parameter | ij | A | |
| | Repeat this step for ij = 11, 12, 21, 22 in any order | | | |
| 3 | To convert common emitter s parameters to common base, load EE1-06A, parameter conversions: s ⇄ Y, G, Z, H. (see notes in step 16) | | | |
| 4 | Convert s parameters to Y parameters | $Z_o$ | B | |
| 5 | Load Program 4-3 to convert common emitter Y parameters to common base Y parameters | | | |
| 6 | Perform CE to CB conversion | | B | |
| 7 | Reload EE1-06A to convert Y parameters back to s parameters | | | |
| 8 | Convert Y parameters to s parameters | $Z_o$ | f B | |
| 9 | Reload both sides of this program card (4-2) | | | |
| 10 | Calculate load reflection coefficient | | | |
| | a) load imaginary part of $Z_{emitter}$ | Im $Z_L$ | ENT↑ | |
| | b) load real part of $Z_{emitter}$ | Re $Z_L$ | ENT↑ | |
| | c) load reference impedance | $Z_o$ | f E | ∡ $\rho_L$<br>\|$\rho_L$\| |

# User Instructions

UHF OSCILLATOR DESIGN USING S PARAMETERS

CONTINUED

| STEP | INSTRUCTIONS | INPUT DATA/UNITS | KEYS | OUTPUT DATA/UNITS |
|---|---|---|---|---|
| 11 | Enter load reflection coefficient (if step 10 is used, the reflection coefficient magnitude and angle are already in the stack--- use key "B" alone) | $\angle \rho_L$<br>$\lvert\rho_L\rvert$ | ENT↑<br>B | |
| 12 | Interchange port ordering 1⇄2 | | f A | |
| 13 | Calculate $s_{11}'$ | | C | $\angle s_{11}'$<br>$\lvert s_{11}'\rvert$ |
| 14 | Calculate $\rho_s = 1/s_{11}'$ | | f D | $\angle 1/s_{11}'$<br>$\lvert 1/s_{11}'\rvert$ |
| 15 | Convert $\rho_s$ to $Z_s$: enter reference impedance | $Z_o$ | E | Im $Z_s$<br>Re $Z_s$ |
| | To find the minimum resonator Q | | ÷ | $Q_{min}$ |
| 16 | The load reflection coefficient is not erased when Program 4-3 or EE1-06A* is used, hence, for another case, the keystrokes in steps 12, 13, 14, and 15 are contained in user definable key fB, therefore, for another case, do steps 1 through 9, then execute fB | | f B | $\angle s_{11}$<br>$\lvert s_{11}\rvert$<br>$\angle 1/s_{11}'$<br>$\lvert 1/s_{11}'\rvert$<br>Im $Z_s$<br>Re $Z_s$<br>$Q_{min}$ |
| | * In HP EE pac (supplied by HP) | | | |

Example 4-2.1

A UHF oscillator using a RCA 2N5179 transistor is to operate between 300 MHz and 400 MHz. The transistor is to be operated at 1.5 mA collector current and 4 volts $V_{ce}$ per the manufacturer's recommendations. At 300 MHz the common-emitter y parameters are:

$$\begin{bmatrix} \{(6.5 + j9.0) \times 10^{-3}\} & \{-j1.35 \times 10^{-3}\} \\ \{(32 - j32) \times 10^{-3}\} & \{(0.25 + j2.6) \times 10^{-3}\} \end{bmatrix}$$

and at 400 MHz the common-emitter y parameters are:

$$\begin{bmatrix} \{(9.2 + j10.7) \times 10^{-3}\} & \{-j1.8 \times 10^{-3}\} \\ \{(25 - j34) \times 10^{-3}\} & \{(0.3 + j4.0) \times 10^{-3}\} \end{bmatrix}$$

The proposed oscillator schematic is shown in Fig. 4-2.2, and biasing networks have been added to achieve the manufacturer's recommended bias. The 100 ohm resistor in series with the RFC lowers the Q of the resonant circuit formed by the RFC and the coax capacity so the circuit will not preferentially oscillate at that lower frequency.

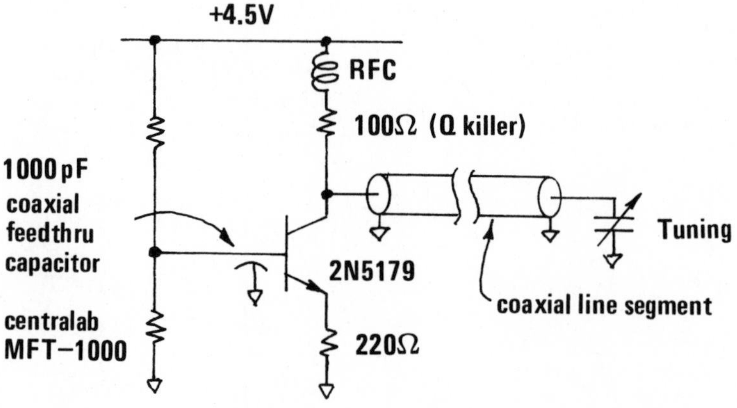


Figure 4-2.2 Oscillator schematic for Example 4-2.1.

**HP-97 PRINTOUT FOR EXAMPLE 4-2.1 , 300MHz CASE**

Load Program 4–3 & load y params

| | | | |
|---|---|---|---|
| 1. | GSBe | | select y parameters |
| 9. | ENT↑ | Im | load $y_{ie}$ and |
| 6.5 | →P | Re | convert to |
| 1.-03 | × | | polar format |
| 11. | GSBA | ij | |
| -90. | ENT↑ | Θ | load $y_{re}$ in |
| 1.35-03 | | mag | polar format |
| 12. | GSBA | ij | |
| -32. | ENT↑ | Im | load $y_{fe}$ and |
| | CHS | Re | convert to |
| | →P | | polar format |
| 1.-03 | × | | |
| 21. | GSBA | ij | |
| 2.6 | ENT↑ | Im | load $y_{oe}$ and |
| .25 | →P | Re | convert to |
| 1.-03 | × | | polar format |
| 22. | GSBA | ij | |

| | | |
|---|---|---|
| | GSBE | print stored params |
| 54.16+00 | *** | $\measuredangle y_{11}$ or $\measuredangle y_{ie}$ |
| 11.10-03 | *** | $\|y_{11}\|$ or $\|y_{ie}\|$ |
| -90.00+00 | *** | $\measuredangle y_{12}$ or $\measuredangle y_{re}$ |
| 1.350-03 | *** | $\|y_{12}\|$ or $\|y_{re}\|$ |
| -45.00+00 | *** | $\measuredangle y_{21}$ or $\measuredangle y_{fe}$ |
| 45.25-03 | *** | $\|y_{21}\|$ or $\|y_{fe}\|$ |
| 84.51+00 | *** | $\measuredangle y_{22}$ or $\measuredangle y_{oe}$ |
| 2.612-03 | *** | $\|y_{22}\|$ or $\|y_{oe}\|$ |

| | | |
|---|---|---|
| | GSBB | CE → CB conversion |
| | GSBE | print stored params |
| -29.31+00 | *** | $\measuredangle y_{ib}$ |
| 44.44-03 | *** | $\|y_{ib}\|$ |
| 78.69+00 | *** | $\measuredangle y_{rb}$ |
| -1.275-03 | *** | $\|y_{rb}\|$ |
| -42.35+00 | *** | $\measuredangle y_{fb}$ |
| -43.64-03 | *** | $\|y_{fb}\|$ |
| 84.51+00 | *** | $\measuredangle y_{ob}$ |
| 2.612-03 | *** | $\|y_{ob}\|$ |

Load Program EE1-06A (EE pac)

| | | |
|---|---|---|
| 50. | GSBb | load reference Z & convert y params to s parameters |

load this program (Program 4–2)

| | | |
|---|---|---|
| | GSBc | print s parameters |
| 147.6+00 | *** | $\measuredangle s_{11}$ |
| 464.4-03 | *** | $\|s_{11}\|$ |
| 93.63+00 | *** | $\measuredangle s_{12}$ |
| 41.01-03 | *** | $\|s_{12}\|$ |
| -27.41+00 | *** | $\measuredangle s_{21}$ |
| 1.404+00 | *** | $\|s_{21}\|$ |
| -10.62+00 | *** | $\measuredangle s_{22}$ |
| 1.024+00 | *** | $\|s_{22}\|$ |

load $R_L$ and calculate $\rho_L$ using 50 ohm $Z_o$

| | | |
|---|---|---|
| 0. | ENT↑ | Im $R_L$ |
| 220. | ENT↑ | Re $R_L$ |
| 50. | GSBe | $Z_o$ |
| 0.000+00 | *** | $\measuredangle \rho_L$ |
| 629.6-03 | *** | $\|\rho_L\|$ |
| | GSBB | load $\rho_L$ into program |
| | GSBb | execute design |
| -9.018+00 | *** | $\measuredangle s_{11}'$ |
| 1.027+00 | *** | $\|s_{11}'\|$ |
| 9.018+00 | *** | $\measuredangle 1/s_{11}'$ |
| 973.4-03 | *** | $\|1/s_{11}'\|$ |
| 616.0+00 | *** | Im $Z_L$ for $Z_o = 50\ \Omega$ |
| 105.9+00 | *** | Re $Z_L$ |
| 5.817+00 | *** | $Q_{min}$ = Im $Z_L$ / Re $Z_L$ |

A transmission line segment is designed to provide the load reactance of j616 ohms to resonate at 300 MHz. The real part of the load reactance is ignored since the Q of the resonant line will be much larger than the minimum Q required. The amplitude of the oscillation will increase until the amplifier becomes non-linear and its power gain is reduced to the point that Eq. (4-2.2) is satisfied with the equals sign.

Because of the high load reactance required, a high $Z_o$ in the resonant line is desired. For the transmission line, use a #12 AWG wire spaced 0.25" off a ground plane as shown by Fig. 4-2.3.

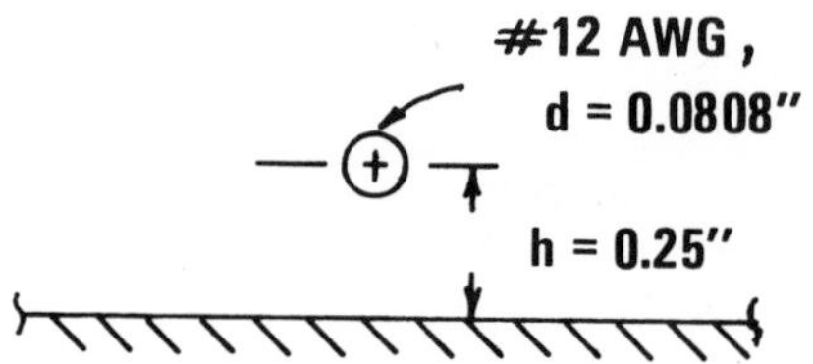


Figure 4-2.3 Air dielectric transmission line.

The characteristic impedance, $Z_o$, of this line is:

$$Z_o = \frac{138}{\sqrt{\varepsilon_r}} \log \frac{4h}{d} \qquad (4\text{-}2.5)$$

where $\varepsilon_r$ is the relative dielectric constant of the dielectric, and is unity for air. Using this $\varepsilon_r$, and the d and h shown in Fig. 4-2.3, the characteristic impedance of the line is 150.6 ohms.

If the trimmer capacitor at the far end of the line is a 1 - 10 pF piston trimmer, its reactance with 10 pF at 300 MHz is:

$$X_c = -j/(2\pi fC) = -\ j53.05 \text{ ohms} \qquad (4\text{-}2.6)$$

The length of transmission line that transforms -j53.05 ohms to j616 ohms is needed. Equation (1-1.1) can be manipulated to provide the solution for line length i.e.:

$$e^{2\gamma\ell} = \frac{\rho}{\rho_t} \qquad (4\text{-}2.7)$$

where $\rho_t$ is defined by Eq. (1-2.7). Since the transmission line load impedance is purely imaginary, as is the required input impedance, and the line is essentially lossless, the expressions for the reflection coefficients are the ratios of complex conjugates, and Eq. (4-2.7) can be reduced to the following forms:

$$\ell = \frac{\lambda}{2\pi}\left\{\tan^{-1}\left(\frac{j\cdot Z_r}{Z_o}\right) - \tan^{-1}\left(\frac{j\cdot Z_s}{Z_o}\right)\right\} \qquad (4\text{-}2.8)$$

where

$$\gamma = j\beta = j\,\frac{2\pi}{\lambda}$$

Using Eq. (4-2.8) with $Z_r$ = -j53.05 ohms, $Z_s$ = 616 ohms, $Z_o$ = 150.6 ohms, and $\lambda = 3 \times 10^8$/freq = 1 meter = 39.27 inches yields $\ell$ = 10.46 inches. This length is too long to be practical. If capacity is added to the transistor collector circuit, less inductance will be required from the transmission line stub, and a shorter stub can be used. If 10 pF is added from the collector to ground, the susceptance of this capacitor will be:

$$B = 2\pi fC = (2\pi)(300 \times 10^6)(10^{-11}) = 18.85 \text{ mmho}$$

This susceptance is subtracted from the susceptance required from the transmission line stub to obtain the new transmission line susceptance and hence, input reactance:

$$B_{line} = \frac{-1}{616} - 0.01885 = -\ 0.02047 \text{ mho}$$

or

$$X_{line} = \frac{-1}{B_{line}} = 48.84 \text{ ohms}$$

Using Eq. (4-2.8) with $Z_s$ = j48.84 and the other parameters unchanged yields $\ell$ = 4.09 inches, which is much more practical. With this line length, the trimmer capacitor value for oscillation at 400 MHz is calculated as shown by the HP-97 printout in Fig. (4-2.5). Again, neglecting the real part of $Z_L$, and accommodating the susceptance of the additional 10 pF at the transistor collector, the line must present a reactance of 36.22 ohms to the collector. Using Eq. (4-2.8) and solving for $Z_r$ given $\ell$ = 4.09 inches, $\lambda$ = 29.53 inches, $Z_s$ = j36.22 ohms and $Z_o$ = 150.6 ohms yields $Z_r$ = -j110.8 ohms. At 400 MHz, -j110.8 ohms is the reactance of a 3.6 pF capacitor, which is within the tuning range of the piston trimmer capacitor. The complete schematic of the oscillator is shown in Fig. 4-2.4, which was breadboarded and does oscillate over the 300 to 400 MHz range. This type of oscillator is often used as the local oscillator in UHF tv tuners.

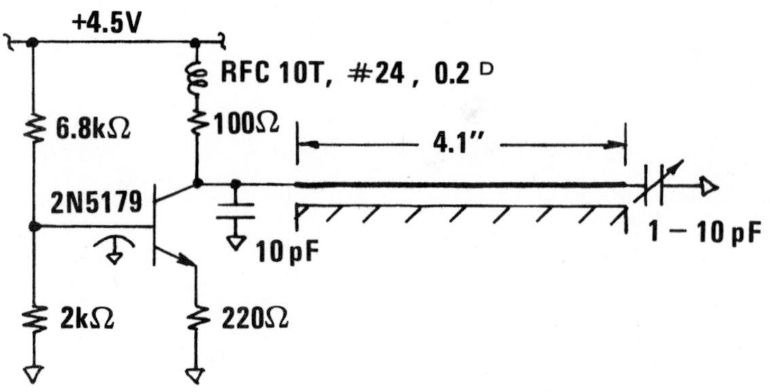


Figure 4-2.4 UHF oscillator schematic.

Load Program 4-3 and load y params

| | | |
|---|---|---|
| 1. | GSBe | select y parameters |
| 10.7 | ENT↑ | Im $y_{ie}$ |
| 9.2 | →P | Re $y_{ie}$ |
| 1.-03 | × | |
| 11. | GSBA | ij |
| -90. | ENT↑ | ∡ $y_{re}$ |
| 1.8-03 | ENT↑ | $\lvert y_{re}\rvert$ |
| 12. | GSBA | ij |
| -34. | ENT↑ | Im $y_{fe}$ |
| 25. | →P | Re $y_{fe}$ |
| 1.-03 | × | |
| 21. | GSBA | ij |
| 4. | ENT↑ | Im $y_{oe}$ |
| .3 | →P | Re $y_{oe}$ |
| 1.-03 | × | |
| 22. | GSBA | ij |
| | GSBE | print stored values |
| 49.31+00 | *** | ∡ $y_{ie}$ |
| 14.11-03 | *** | $\lvert y_{ie}\rvert$ |
| -90.00+00 | *** | ∡ $y_{re}$ |
| 1.800-03 | *** | $\lvert y_{re}\rvert$ |
| -53.67+00 | *** | ∡ $y_{fe}$ |
| 42.20-03 | *** | $\lvert y_{fe}\rvert$ |
| 85.71+00 | *** | ∡ $y_{oe}$ |
| 4.011-03 | *** | $\lvert y_{oe}\rvert$ |
| | GSBB | convert CE → CB |
| | GSBE | print CB values |
| -31.45+00 | *** | ∡ $y_{ib}$ |
| 40.44-03 | *** | $\lvert y_{ib}\rvert$ |
| 82.23+00 | *** | ∡ $y_{rb}$ |
| -2.220-03 | *** | $\lvert y_{rb}\rvert$ |
| -49.86+00 | *** | ∡ $y_{fb}$ |
| -39.24-03 | *** | $\lvert y_{fb}\rvert$ |
| 85.71+00 | *** | ∡ $y_{ob}$ |
| 4.011-03 | *** | $\lvert y_{ob}\rvert$ |

Load Program EE1-06A (EE pac)

| | | |
|---|---|---|
| 50. | GSBb | load reference Z & convert y parameters to s parameters |

Load this program (Program 4-2)

| | | |
|---|---|---|
| | GSBc | print s parameters |
| 139.2+00 | *** | ∡ $s_{11}$ |
| 450.8-03 | *** | $\lvert s_{11}\rvert$ |
| 95.19+00 | *** | ∡ $s_{12}$ |
| 77.48-03 | *** | $\lvert s_{12}\rvert$ |
| -36.90+00 | *** | ∡ $s_{21}$ |
| 1.369+00 | *** | $\lvert s_{21}\rvert$ |
| -15.96+00 | *** | ∡ $s_{22}$ |
| 1.059+00 | *** | $\lvert s_{22}\rvert$ |
| | | load $R_L$ and calc $\rho_L$ using 50 ohm $Z_o$ |
| 0. | ENT↑ | Im $R_L$ |
| 220. | ENT↑ | Re $R_L$ |
| 50. | GSBe | $Z_o$ |
| 0.000+00 | *** | ∡ $\rho_L$ |
| 629.6-03 | *** | $\lvert\rho_L\rvert$ |
| | GSBB | load $\rho_L$ into program |
| | GSBb | execute design |
| -13.06+00 | *** | ∡ $s_{11}'$ |
| 1.067+00 | *** | $\lvert s_{11}'\rvert$ |
| 13.06+00 | *** | ∡ $1/s_{11}'$ |
| 937.0-03 | *** | $\lvert 1/s_{11}'\rvert$ |
| 403.8+00 | *** | Im $Z_L$ for $Z_o = 50$ |
| 116.3+00 | *** | Re $Z_L$ |
| 3.471+00 | *** | $Q_{min} = \text{Im } Z_L / \text{Re } Z_L$ |

Fig. 4-2.5 HP-97 printout for 400 MHz case.

# Program Listing I

| Step | Key | Comment |
|---|---|---|
| 001 | *LBLA | **LOAD S PARAMETERS:** |
| 002 | ENT↑ | |
| 003 | + | |
| 004 | 2 | calculate storage index |
| 005 | 1 | |
| 006 | - | |
| 007 | STOI | |
| 008 | R↓ | recover and store $\theta_{ij}$ |
| 009 | STOi | |
| 010 | ISZI | increment index |
| 011 | R↓ | recover and store $s_{ij}$ |
| 012 | STOi | |
| 013 | GTO9 | goto space and return |
| 014 | *LBLB | **ENTER LOAD REFLECTION COEF** |
| 015 | STO6 | store magnitude |
| 016 | X⇄Y | |
| 017 | STO7 | store angle |
| 018 | GTO9 | goto space and return |
| 019 | *LBLC | **CALCULATE $s_{11}'$** |
| 020 | RCL3 | $\|s_{12}\|$ |
| 021 | STO8 | |
| 022 | RCL4 | $\measuredangle s_{12}$ |
| 023 | STO9 | |
| 024 | RCLB | $\|s_{21}\|$ $\quad s_{11}' = s_{11} + \dfrac{s_{12}\, s_{21}\, \rho_L}{1 - s_{22}\, \rho_L}$ |
| 025 | ST×8 | |
| 026 | RCLC | $\measuredangle s_{21}$ |
| 027 | ST+9 | |
| 028 | RCL6 | $\|\rho_L\|$ |
| 029 | ST×8 | |
| 030 | RCL7 | $\measuredangle \rho_L$ |
| 031 | ST+9 | |
| 032 | RCLE | $\measuredangle s_{22}$ |
| 033 | RCL7 | $\measuredangle \rho$ |
| 034 | + | |
| 035 | RCLD | $\|s_{22}\|$ |
| 036 | RCL6 | $\|\rho\|$ |
| 037 | × | |
| 038 | CHS | |
| 039 | →R | |
| 040 | EEX | |
| 041 | + | |
| 042 | →P | $1 - s_{22}\cdot \rho_L$ |
| 043 | ST÷8 | |
| 044 | X⇄Y | |
| 045 | ST-9 | |
| 046 | RCL9 | $\dfrac{s_{12}\cdot s_{21}\cdot \rho_L}{1 - s_{22}\cdot \rho_L}$ in polar coordinates (steps 046–047) |
| 047 | RCL8 | |
| 048 | →R | |
| 049 | STO8 | $\dfrac{s_{12}\cdot s_{21}\cdot \rho_L}{1 - s_{22}\cdot \rho_L}$ in rect coordinates (steps 049–051) |
| 050 | X⇄Y | |
| 051 | STO9 | |
| 052 | RCL2 | $s_{11}$ |
| 053 | RCL1 | |
| 054 | →R | |
| 055 | ST+8 | |
| 056 | X⇄Y | |
| 057 | ST+9 | |
| 058 | RCL9 | $s_{11} - \dfrac{s_{12}\cdot s_{21}\cdot \rho_L}{1 - s_{22}\cdot \rho_L}$ rect (steps 058–059) |
| 059 | RCL8 | |
| 060 | →P | |
| 061 | STO8 | $s_{11} - \dfrac{s_{12}\cdot s_{21}\cdot \rho_L}{1 - s_{22}\cdot \rho_L}$ polar (steps 061–063) |
| 062 | X⇄Y | |
| 063 | STO9 | |
| 064 | GTO8 | goto print subroutine |
| 065 | *LBLD | **CALCULATE $\rho\cdot s_{11}'$ GIVEN $\rho$** |
| 066 | P⇄S | |
| 067 | STO0 | $\|\rho\|$ |
| 068 | X⇄Y | |
| 069 | STO1 | $\measuredangle \rho$ |
| 070 | P⇄S | |
| 071 | RCL9 | $\measuredangle s_{11}'$ |
| 072 | RCL8 | $\|s_{11}'\|$ |
| 073 | P⇄S | |
| 074 | ST×0 | $\|\rho\|\cdot\|s_{11}'\|$ |
| 075 | X⇄Y | |
| 076 | ST+1 | $\measuredangle\rho + \measuredangle s_{11}'$ |
| 077 | RCL0 | |
| 078 | RCL1 | |
| 079 | P⇄S | |
| 080 | GTO8 | goto print subroutine |
| 081 | *LBLd | **CALCULATE $1/s_{11}'$** |
| 082 | 1/X | reciprocate magnitude |
| 083 | X⇄Y | |
| 084 | CHS | change sign of angle |
| 085 | GTO8 | goto print subroutine |
| 086 | *LBLE | **CALC** Re, Im $Z$ **GIVEN** $\measuredangle\rho\uparrow\|\rho\|\uparrow Z_o$ |
| 087 | P⇄S | |
| 088 | STO4 | $Z_o$ |
| 089 | R↓ | |
| 090 | →R | |
| 091 | STO2 | Re $\rho$ $\quad Z = Z_o\,\dfrac{1+\rho}{1-\rho}$ |
| 092 | EEX | |
| 093 | + | 1 + Re $\rho$ |
| 094 | X⇄Y | |
| 095 | STO3 | Im $\rho$ |
| 096 | X⇄Y | |
| 097 | →P | $\|1+\rho\|$ |
| 098 | ST×4 | $Z_o\cdot(1+\rho)$ (steps 098–100) |
| 099 | X⇄Y | |
| 100 | STO5 | |
| 101 | RCL3 | |
| 102 | CHS | |
| 103 | EEX | |
| 104 | RCL2 | |
| 105 | - | |
| 106 | →P | $1-\rho$ |
| 107 | ST÷4 | calc $Z$ (steps 107–109) |
| 108 | X⇄Y | |
| 109 | ST-5 | |
| 110 | RCL5 | |

**REGISTERS**

| 0 | 1 | 2 | 3 | 4 | 5 | 6 | 7 | 8 | 9 |
|---|---|---|---|---|---|---|---|---|---|
| | $\|s_{11}\|$ | $\measuredangle s_{11}$ | $\|s_{12}\|$ | $\measuredangle s_{12}$ | | $\|\rho_L\|$ | $\measuredangle \rho_L$ | scratch | scratch |

| S0 | S1 | S2 | S3 | S4 | S5 | S6 | S7 | S8 | S9 |
|---|---|---|---|---|---|---|---|---|---|
| scratch | scratch | Im $\rho_L$ | Re $\rho_L$ | $Z_o$, $\|Z_L\|$ | scratch, $\measuredangle Z_L$ | scratch | | | |

| A | B | C | D | E | I |
|---|---|---|---|---|---|
| | $\|s_{21}\|$ | $\measuredangle s_{21}$ | $\|s_{22}\|$ | $\measuredangle s_{22}$ | index |

# Program Listing II

| | | | |
|---|---|---|---|
| 111 | RCL4 | | |
| 112 | P⇄S | | |
| 113 | →R | | |
| 114 | X⇄Y | | |
| 115 | GTO8 | goto print subroutine | |
| 116 | *LBLe | CALC ∡ρ, \|ρ\| GIVEN Im Z↑Re Z↑Z₀ | |
| 117 | P⇄S | | |
| 118 | STO4 | Z₀ | |
| 119 | R↓ | | |
| 120 | STO3 | Re Z | |
| 121 | R↓ | | |
| 122 | STO2 | Im Z | |
| 123 | R↑ | | |
| 124 | R↑ | | |
| 125 | − | Z₀ − Re Z | |
| 126 | →P | | |
| 127 | STO5 | \|Z₀ − Z\| | |
| 128 | X⇄Y | | |
| 129 | STO6 | ∡(Z₀ − Z) | |
| 130 | RCL2 | | |
| 131 | RCL3 | | |
| 132 | RCL4 | | |
| 133 | + | | |
| 134 | →P | \|Z₀ + Z\| | |
| 135 | ST÷5 | | |
| 136 | X⇄Y | | |
| 137 | ST−6 | | |
| 138 | RCL5 | \|ρ\| | |
| 139 | RCL6 | ∡ρ | |
| 140 | P⇄S | | |
| 141 | GTO8 | goto print subroutine | |
| 142 | *LBLα | INTERCHANGE PORTS 1 AND 2 | |
| 143 | RCLE | | |
| 144 | RCL2 | | |
| 145 | STOE | ∡ S₁₁ ⇄ ∡ S₂₂ | |
| 146 | X⇄Y | | |
| 147 | STO2 | | |
| 148 | RCLD | | |
| 149 | RCL1 | | |
| 150 | STOD | \|S₁₁\| ⇄ \|S₂₂\| | |
| 151 | X⇄Y | | |
| 152 | STO1 | | |
| 153 | RCLC | | |
| 154 | RCL4 | | |
| 155 | STOC | ∡ S₁₂ ⇄ ∡ S₂₁ | |
| 156 | X⇄Y | | |
| 157 | STO4 | | |
| 158 | RCLB | | |
| 159 | RCL3 | | |
| 160 | STOB | \|S₁₂\| ⇄ \|S₂₁\| | |
| 161 | X⇄Y | | |
| 162 | STO3 | | |
| 163 | GTO7 | goto R/S lockup | |
| 164 | *LBLb | EXECUTE fA, C, fD, 50 E | |
| 165 | GSBα | | |

$$\rho = \frac{Z - Z_0}{Z + Z_0}$$

| | | | |
|---|---|---|---|
| 166 | GSBC | | |
| 167 | GSBd | | |
| 168 | 5 | } use 50 ohm Z₀ | |
| 169 | 0 | | |
| 170 | GSBE | | |
| 171 | ÷ | | |
| 172 | GSB5 | | |
| 173 | GTO9 | goto space and return subr | |
| 174 | *LBLc | PRINT S PARAMETER MATRIX | |
| 175 | RCL1 | | |
| 176 | RCL2 | S₁₁ | |
| 177 | GSB8 | | |
| 178 | RCL3 | | |
| 179 | RCL4 | S₁₂ | |
| 180 | GSB8 | | |
| 181 | RCLB | | |
| 182 | RCLC | S₂₁ | |
| 183 | GSB8 | | |
| 184 | RCLD | | |
| 185 | RCLE | S₂₂ | |
| 186 | *LBL8 | print subroutine | |
| 187 | GSB5 | | |
| 188 | X⇄Y | | |
| 189 | GSB5 | | |
| 190 | *LBL9 | space and return subroutine | |
| 191 | F0? | space if flag 0 is set | |
| 192 | SPC | | |
| 193 | RTN | | |
| 194 | *LBL7 | R/S lockup subroutine | |
| 195 | R/S | | |
| 196 | GTO7 | | |
| 197 | *LBL5 | print or R/S subroutine | |
| 198 | F0? | if flag 0 is set, print | |
| 199 | PRTX | and return | |
| 200 | F0? | | |
| 201 | RTN | | |
| 202 | R/S | otherwise stop | |
| 203 | RTN | | |

## Notes

Flag 0 controls the print or R/S decision. It should be set or reset to reflect the users choice of printed output, or program halts for output respectively at the time the magnetic card is recorded.

| LABELS | | | | |
|---|---|---|---|---|
| A load S parameters | B enter load reflection coef | C calculate S₁₁ | D calculate S₁₁·ρ | E ρ, Z₀ → Z |
| a interchange ports 1 & 2 | b fA, C, fD, E | c print s matrix | d calculate 1/S₁₁' | e Z, Z₀ → ρ |
| 0 | 1 | 2 | 3 | 4 |
| 5 print or R/S subroutine | 6 | 7 R/S lockup | 8 print & space subroutine | 9 space subroutine |

| FLAGS | |
|---|---|
| 0 | print |
| 1 | |
| 2 | |
| 3 | |

| SET STATUS | | |
|---|---|---|
| FLAGS | TRIG | DISP |
| ON OFF<br>0 ☐ ☐<br>1<br>2<br>3 | DEG ■<br>GRAD<br>RAD | FIX<br>SCI<br>ENG ■<br>n 3 |

## PROGRAM 4-3 TRANSISTOR CONFIGURATION CONVERSION.

Program Description and Equations Used

This program allows conversion between common emitter, common base, and common collector configurations of transistor h parameters or y parameters, as well as conversions between the h and the y parameters.

The configuration conversions is done by operating on the y parameters and converting to and from the h parameters for data input and output. To make the program operate in either h or y parameters, the conversion process is skipped for the y parameter case. Label 7 of the program contains the coding that accomplishes the h to y, or y to h conversion. Label 7 is called at the beginning and end of the configuration conversion, and flag 0 is used to indicate whether or not the subroutine under label 7 should be skipped or not.

Figure 4-3.1 Two-port network conventions.

Given a two-port network with port voltages and currents as defined by Fig. 4-3.1, the y and h parameters are defined as follows:

h parameters

$$\begin{bmatrix} E_1 \\ I_2 \end{bmatrix} = \begin{bmatrix} h_{11} & h_{12} \\ h_{21} & h_{11} \end{bmatrix} \cdot \begin{bmatrix} I_1 \\ E_2 \end{bmatrix} \qquad (4\text{-}3.1)$$

y parameters

$$\begin{bmatrix} I_1 \\ I_2 \end{bmatrix} = \begin{bmatrix} y_{11} & y_{12} \\ y_{21} & y_{22} \end{bmatrix} \cdot \begin{bmatrix} E_1 \\ E_2 \end{bmatrix} \quad (4\text{-}3.2)$$

The network ports correspondence to the transitor elements is shown in Table 4-3.1.

Table 4-3.1 Transistor 2-port correspondences

| Configuration | 1 | 1' or 2' | 2 |
|---|---|---|---|
| CE | B | E | C |
| CB | E | B | C |
| CC | B | C | E |

The h parameters are converted to y parameters with the following transformation [15]:

$$\begin{bmatrix} y_{11} & y_{12} \\ y_{21} & y_{22} \end{bmatrix} = \frac{1}{h_{11}} \begin{bmatrix} 1\,, & -h_{12} \\ h_{21}, & h_{11}h_{22} - h_{12}h_{21} \end{bmatrix} \quad (4\text{-}3.3)$$

Likewise, the y parameters are converted to h parameters in similar fashion:

$$\begin{bmatrix} h_{11} & h_{12} \\ h_{21} & h_{22} \end{bmatrix} = \frac{1}{y_{11}} \cdot \begin{bmatrix} 1\,, & -y_{12} \\ y_{21}\,, & y_{11}y_{22} - y_{21}y_{12} \end{bmatrix} \quad (4\text{-}3.4)$$

Since the form of both conversions is identical, the same subroutine is used for both conversions (subroutine 7).

The y matrix representing the present transistor configuration is transformed into another y matrix representing the new transistor configuration. This new matrix is designated y' for clarity. These transformations are:

For CE → CB or CB → CE,

$$\begin{bmatrix} y_{11}' & y_{12}' \\ y_{21}' & y_{22}' \end{bmatrix} = \begin{bmatrix} \{y_{11} + y_{22} + y_{12} + y_{21}\} & \{-(y_{12} + y_{22})\} \\ \{-(y_{21} + y_{22})\} & \{ y_{11} \} \end{bmatrix} \tag{4-3.5}$$

For CC → CE or CE → CC,

$$\begin{bmatrix} y_{11}' & y_{12}' \\ y_{21}' & y_{22}' \end{bmatrix} = \begin{bmatrix} \{ y_{11} \} & \{ -(y_{11} + y_{12}) \} \\ \{-(y_{11} + y_{21})\} & \{ y_{11} + y_{22} + y_{21} + y_{12}\} \end{bmatrix} \tag{4-3.6}$$

For CC → CB,

$$\begin{bmatrix} y_{11}' & y_{12}' \\ y_{21}' & y_{22}' \end{bmatrix} = \begin{bmatrix} \{ y_{22} \} & \{ -(y_{21} + y_{22}) \} \\ \{-(y_{12} + y_{22})\} & \{y_{11} + y_{12} + y_{21} + y_{22}\} \end{bmatrix} \tag{4-3.7}$$

For CB → CC,

$$\begin{bmatrix} y_{11}' & y_{12}' \\ y_{21}' & y_{22}' \end{bmatrix} = \begin{bmatrix} \{y_{11} + y_{22} + y_{21} + y_{12}\} & \{-(y_{11} + y_{21}) \} \\ \{-(y_{11} + y_{12})\} & \{ y_{11} \} \end{bmatrix} \tag{4-3.8}$$

After the respective conversion is complete, the y' matrix has replaced the y matrix in storage.

In looking over the various conversions, one will notice similarities in the operations used. There are four basic operations used to perform all the conversions:

1) no change;
2) ($y_{11}$ or $y_{22}$) + $y_{12}$;
3) ($y_{11}$ or $y_{22}$) + $y_{21}$; and
4) $y_{11} + y_{22} + y_{12} + y_{21}$.

The choice between $y_{11}$ and $y_{22}$ or $y_{12}$ and $y_{22}$ can be taken care of by interchanging the appropriate y matrix elements prior to these calculations. This matrix reordering is accomplished under label 3. The matrix conversion calculation is done under label 6 (two places); thus, these subroutines are selectively used to achieve all conversions.

# User Instructions

| TRANSISTOR CONFIGURATION CONVERSION | | | | |
|---|---|---|---|---|
| | CB → CE | CB → CC | CE → CC | h or y ? 0 or 1 |
| load $\theta_{ij}\uparrow \lvert\ \rvert_{ij}\uparrow ij$ | CE → CB | CC → CB | CC → CE | print matrix |

| STEP | INSTRUCTIONS | INPUT DATA/UNITS | KEYS | OUTPUT DATA/UNITS |
|---|---|---|---|---|
| 1 | Load both sides of program card | | | |
| 2 | Select h or y matrix mode | | | |
| | a) h parameters | 0 | f E | 0 |
| | b) y parameters | 1 | f E | 1 |
| 3 | Load matrix to be converted | | | |
| | a) angle of $h_{ij}$ or $y_{ij}$ | $\theta_{ij}$ | ENT↑ | |
| | b) magnitude of $h_{ij}$ or $y_{ij}$ | $\lvert\ \rvert_{ij}$ | ENT↑ | |
| | c) subscript | ij | A | |
| | repeat this step for ij = 11, 12, 21, 22 in any order | | | |
| 4 | Select conversion desired | | | |
| | a) common emitter to common base | | B | |
| | b) common base to common emitter | | f B | |
| | c) common collector to common base | | C | |
| | d) common base to common collector | | f C | |
| | e) common collector to common emitter | | D | |
| | f) common emitter to common collector | | f D | |
| 5 | Print converted matrix | | E | $\theta_{11}$ |
| | | | | $\lvert\ \rvert_{11}$ |
| | | | | $\theta_{12}$ |
| | | | | $\lvert\ \rvert_{12}$ |
| | | | | $\theta_{21}$ |
| | | | | $\lvert\ \rvert_{21}$ |
| | | | | $\theta_{22}$ |
| | | | | $\lvert\ \rvert_{22}$ |

Example 4-3.1

Convert the following common collector h parameter matrix to a common base h parameter matrix:

$$\begin{bmatrix} h_{ic} & h_{rc} \\ h_{fc} & h_{oc} \end{bmatrix} = \begin{bmatrix} 1000 \angle 40^\circ & 10^{-4} \angle -50^\circ \\ 100 \angle 40^\circ & 50 \times 10^{-6} \angle 0 \end{bmatrix}$$

| PROGRAM INPUT | | PROGRAM OUTPUT | |
|---|---|---|---|
| 40. ENT↑ | $\angle h_{ic}$ | 0. GSBe | select h parameters |
| 1000. ENT↑ | $\|h_{ic}\|$ | | |
| 11. GSBA | ij | GSBC | execute CC → CB conv |
| -50. ENT↑ | $\angle h_{rc}$ | GSBE | print stored matrix |
| 1.-04 ENT↑ | $\|h_{rc}\|$ | -9.971+00 *** | $\angle h_{ib}$ |
| 12. GSBA | ij | 22.60+03 *** | $\|h_{ib}\|$ |
| 40. ENT↑ | $\angle h_{fc}$ | -9.967+00 *** | $\angle h_{rb}$ |
| 100. ENT↑ | $\|h_{fc}\|$ | 2.261+03 *** | $\|h_{rb}\|$ |
| 21. GSBA | ij | | |
| | | -179.9+00 *** | $\angle h_{fb}$ |
| 0. ENT↑ | $\angle h_{oc}$ | 1.000+00 *** | $\|h_{fb}\|$ |
| 50.-06 ENT↑ | $\|h_{oc}\|$ | | |
| 22. GSBA | ij | -49.97+00 *** | $\angle h_{oc}$ |
| | | 1.130-03 *** | $\|h_{oc}\|$ |

Common base h parameter matrix from HP-97 output:

$$\begin{bmatrix} h_{ib} & h_{rb} \\ h_{fb} & h_{ob} \end{bmatrix} = \begin{bmatrix} 22600 \angle -9.971^\circ & 2261 \angle -9.967^\circ \\ 1.000 \angle -179.9^\circ & 1.130 \times 10^{-3} \angle -49.97^\circ \end{bmatrix}$$

# Program Listing I

| | | |
|---|---|---|
| 001 | *LBLA | LOAD MATRIX ELEMENTS, |
| 002 | ENT↑ | |
| 003 | + | calculate storage index |
| 004 | 2 | from subscript |
| 005 | 1 | |
| 006 | - | |
| 007 | STOI | |
| 008 | R↓ | recover and store $\mid\ \mid_{ij}$ |
| 009 | STOi | |
| 010 | ISZI | increment storage index |
| 011 | R↓ | recover and store $\theta_{ij}$ |
| 012 | STOi | |
| 013 | GTO4 | return control to keyboard |
| 014 | *LBLC | CONVERT CC → CB PARAMETERS |
| 015 | GSB6 | take [h]→[y]→[y'] |
| 016 | *LBL3 | reorder matrix elements |
| 017 | RCL1 | |
| 018 | RCLD | |
| 019 | STO1 | $\mid\ \mid_{11} \rightleftharpoons \mid\ \mid_{22}$ |
| 020 | R↓ | |
| 021 | STOD | |
| 022 | RCL3 | |
| 023 | RCLB | |
| 024 | STO3 | $\mid\ \mid_{12} \rightleftharpoons \mid\ \mid_{21}$ |
| 025 | R↓ | |
| 026 | STOB | |
| 027 | RCL2 | |
| 028 | RCLE | |
| 029 | STO2 | $\theta_{11} \rightleftharpoons \theta_{22}$ |
| 030 | R↓ | |
| 031 | STOE | |
| 032 | RCL4 | |
| 033 | RCLC | |
| 034 | STO4 | $\theta_{12} \rightleftharpoons \theta_{21}$ |
| 035 | R↓ | |
| 036 | STOC | |
| 037 | GTO7 | convert y' → h |
| 038 | *LBLb | CONVERT CB → CE PARAMETERS |
| 039 | *LBLB | CONVERT CE → CB PARAMETERS |
| 040 | GSB6 | take [h]→[y]→[y'] |
| 041 | GTO7 | convert [y']→[h] |
| 042 | *LBL6 | |
| 043 | GSB7 | convert h params to y params |
| 044 | RCLC | |
| 045 | RCLB | calculate and store: |
| 046 | RCLE | |
| 047 | RCLD | |
| 048 | GSB8 | |
| 049 | CHS | $y_{21}' = -(y_{21} + y_{22})$ |
| 050 | STOB | |
| 051 | R↓ | |
| 052 | STOC | |
| 053 | RCL4 | |
| 054 | RCL3 | |
| 055 | RCLE | |
| 056 | RCLD | |
| 057 | GSB8 | calculate and store: |
| 058 | CHS | |
| 059 | STO3 | $y_{12}' = -(y_{12} + y_{22})$ |
| 060 | X⇄Y | |
| 061 | STO4 | |
| 062 | X⇄Y | |
| 063 | RCLC | |
| 064 | RCLB | calculate and store: |
| 065 | GSB8 | |
| 066 | RCLE | |
| 067 | RCLD | |
| 068 | GSB8 | |
| 069 | CHS | $y_{11}' = -y_{22} + (y_{21}' + y_{12}') + y_{11}$ |
| 070 | RCL2 | |
| 071 | RCL1 | $= y_{11} + y_{12} + y_{21} + y_{22}$ |
| 072 | GSB8 | |
| 073 | STO1 | |
| 074 | R↓ | |
| 075 | STO2 | |
| 076 | RTN | |
| 077 | *LBLd | CONVERT CE → CC PARAMETERS |
| 078 | *LBLD | CONVERT CC → CE PARAMETERS |
| 079 | GSB6 | take [h]→[y]→[y'] |
| 080 | GTO7 | convert [y']→[h] |
| 081 | *LBLc | CONVERT CB → CC PARAMETERS |
| 082 | GSB6 | take [h]→[y]→[y'] |
| 083 | GTO3 | reorder matrix elements |
| 084 | *LBL6 | |
| 085 | GSB7 | transform [h]→[y] |
| 086 | RCL2 | |
| 087 | RCL1 | calculate and store: |
| 088 | RCL4 | |
| 089 | RCL3 | |
| 090 | GSB8 | |
| 091 | CHS | $y_{12}' = -(y_{11} + y_{12})$ |
| 092 | STO3 | |
| 093 | R↓ | |
| 094 | STO4 | |
| 095 | RCL2 | |
| 096 | RCL1 | calculate and store: |
| 097 | RCLC | |
| 098 | RCLB | |
| 099 | GSB8 | |
| 100 | CHS | $y_{21}' = -(y_{11} + y_{21})$ |
| 101 | STOB | |
| 102 | X⇄Y | |
| 103 | STOC | |
| 104 | X⇄Y | |
| 105 | RCL4 | |
| 106 | RCL3 | calculate and store: |
| 107 | GSB8 | |
| 108 | RCL2 | |
| 109 | RCL1 | $y_{22}' = y_{11} + y_{12} + y_{21} + y_{22}$ |
| 110 | GSB8 | |

### REGISTERS

| 0 | 1 $\mid\ \mid_{11}$ | 2 $\theta_{11}$ | 3 $\mid\ \mid_{12}$ | 4 $\theta_{12}$ | 5 | 6 $\mid\Delta\mid$ | 7 $\measuredangle\Delta$ | 8 | 9 |
|---|---|---|---|---|---|---|---|---|---|
| S0 | S1 | S2 | S3 | S4 | S5 | S6 | S7 | S8 | S9 |
| A | B $\mid\ \mid_{21}$ | C $\theta_{21}$ | D $\mid\ \mid_{22}$ | E $\theta_{22}$ | | I index | | | |

# Program Listing II

| | | |
|---|---|---|
| 111 | CHS | |
| 112 | RCLE | |
| 113 | RCLD | |
| 114 | GSB8 | |
| 115 | STOD | |
| 116 | R↓ | |
| 117 | STOE | |
| 118 | RTN | return to main program |
| 119 | *LBL7 | subroutine to convert [y]⇄[h] |
| 120 | F0? | if flag 0 is set |
| 121 | RTN | |
| 122 | RCL2 | |
| 123 | RCL1 | |
| 124 | RCLD | given: |
| 125 | RCLE | |
| 126 | GSB9 | $$\begin{bmatrix} a_{11} & a_{12} \\ a_{21} & a_{22} \end{bmatrix} = A$$ |
| 127 | STO6 | |
| 128 | R↓ | |
| 129 | STO7 | |
| 130 | RCL4 | |
| 131 | RCL3 | calculate and store the determinant of A: |
| 132 | RCLB | |
| 133 | RCLC | $$\Delta A = a_{11} \cdot a_{22} - a_{21} \cdot a_{12}$$ |
| 134 | GSB9 | |
| 135 | CHS | |
| 136 | RCL7 | |
| 137 | RCL6 | |
| 138 | GSB8 | |
| 139 | STO6 | |
| 140 | R↓ | |
| 141 | STO7 | |
| 142 | RCL2 | calculate and store: |
| 143 | CHS | |
| 144 | STO2 | |
| 145 | RCL1 | $$a_{11}' = \frac{1}{a_{11}}$$ |
| 146 | 1/X | |
| 147 | STO1 | |
| 148 | RCL3 | |
| 149 | CHS | calculate and store: |
| 150 | RCL4 | |
| 151 | GSB9 | $$a_{12}' = -\frac{a_{12}}{a_{11}}$$ |
| 152 | STO3 | |
| 153 | R↓ | |
| 154 | STO4 | |
| 155 | RCL2 | |
| 156 | RCL1 | calculate and store: |
| 157 | RCLB | |
| 158 | RCLC | |
| 159 | GSB9 | $$a_{21}' = -\frac{a_{21}}{a_{11}}$$ |
| 160 | STOB | |
| 161 | R↓ | |
| 162 | STOC | |
| 163 | RCL2 | |
| 164 | RCL1 | |
| 165 | RCL6 | |

| | | |
|---|---|---|
| 166 | RCL7 | calculate and store: |
| 167 | GSB9 | |
| 168 | STOD | |
| 169 | R↓ | |
| 170 | STOE | $$a_{22}' = \frac{\Delta A}{a_{11}}$$ |
| 171 | RTN | return to subroutine call |
| 172 | GTO2 | goto R/S lockup |
| 173 | *LBL8 | complex addition subroutine |
| 174 | →R | |
| 175 | R↓ | input and output are in |
| 176 | R↓ | polar co-ordinates |
| 177 | →R | |
| 178 | X⇄Y | |
| 179 | R↓ | |
| 180 | + | |
| 181 | R↓ | |
| 182 | + | |
| 183 | R↑ | |
| 184 | →P | |
| 185 | RTN | |
| 186 | *LBL9 | complex multiply subroutine |
| 187 | R↓ | |
| 188 | × | input and output are in |
| 189 | R↓ | polar co-ordinates |
| 190 | + | |
| 191 | R↑ | |
| 192 | →R | |
| 193 | →P | |
| 194 | RTN | |
| 195 | *LBLE | PRINT STORED MATRIX |
| 196 | RCL1 | |
| 197 | RCL2 | |
| 198 | GSB5 | |
| 199 | RCL3 | |
| 200 | RCL4 | |
| 201 | GSB5 | |
| 202 | RCLB | |
| 203 | RCLC | |
| 204 | GSB5 | |
| 205 | RCLD | |
| 206 | RCLE | |
| 207 | *LBL5 | print subroutine |
| 208 | PRTX-- | or R/S |
| 209 | X⇄Y | |
| 210 | PRTX-- | or R/S |
| 211 | *LBL4 | space and return subroutine |
| 212 | SPC | |
| 213 | RTN | |
| 214 | *LBL2 | R/S lockup subroutine |
| 215 | R/S | |
| 216 | GTO2 | |
| 217 | *LBLe | SELECT y OR h PARAMETERS |
| 218 | CF0 | |
| 219 | X>0? | set flag 0 if "1" entered |
| 220 | SF0 | |
| 221 | RTN | return to keyboard control |

| LABELS | | | | | FLAGS | SET STATUS | | |
|---|---|---|---|---|---|---|---|---|
| A load data | B CE→CB | C CC→CB | D CC→CE | E print matrix | 0 set for y | FLAGS | TRIG | DISP |
| a | b CB→CE | c CB→CC | d CE→CC | e select y or h | 1 | ON OFF | DEG ■ | FIX |
| 0 | 1 | 2 | 3 rearrange matrix | 4 space & rtn subroutine | 2 | 0 ■ / 1 | GRAD | SCI |
| 5 print subroutine | 6 [h]→[h'] | 7 [h]⇄[y] | 8 complex add | 9 complex multiply | 3 | 2 / 3 | RAD | ENG ■ / n 3 |

## PROGRAM 4-4 COMPLEX 2x2 MATRIX OPERATIONS – PART 1.

### Program Description and Equations Used

This program is one of two programs to manipulate complex 2x2 matrices. When dealing with high frequency amplifiers employing feedback, and input and output networks, one way of obtaining the overall amplifier response is to operate on the matrices that describe these 2-port networks. Shunt feedback may be included within the transistor transfer matrix through Y matrix addition. Y matrices can be converted to Z matrices using the complex matrix inverse routine. Series feedback is included by adding Z matrices. The input and output networks are included by multiplying ABCD (transmission) matrices.

This program will perform matrix addition ($A + B \rightarrow A$), subtraction ($A - B \rightarrow A$), multiplication ($AB \rightarrow A$), and interchange ($A \rightleftarrows B$) with 2x2 matrices having complex coefficients. Data entry and output may be in either rectangular or polar format. All data stored and used by the program is in rectangular format. If flag 1 is set, polar format is indicated and the data is converted to and from rectangular format upon data input or output respectively.

The program operation is very straightforward, and matrix operations are done in the conventional manner. Two subroutines are used, one for complex addition and the other for complex multiplication. See [ 6 ], [14] for matrix algebra details.

Both this program and the companion program (Program 4-5) share common register storage allocations; thus, matrix manipulations requiring functions contained in different programs are easily accommodated.

Matrix addition and subtraction:

$$\begin{bmatrix} a_{11} & a_{12} \\ a_{21} & a_{22} \end{bmatrix} \pm \begin{bmatrix} b_{11} & b_{12} \\ b_{21} & b_{22} \end{bmatrix} = \begin{bmatrix} r_{11} & r_{12} \\ r_{21} & r_{22} \end{bmatrix}$$

$$r_{11} = a_{11} \pm b_{11}$$
$$r_{22} = a_{22} \pm b_{22}$$
$$r_{21} = a_{21} \pm b_{21}$$
$$r_{22} = a_{22} \pm b_{22}$$

The R matrix replaces the A matrix at the completion of the routine.

Matrix multiplication:

$$\begin{bmatrix} a_{11} & a_{12} \\ a_{21} & a_{22} \end{bmatrix} \times \begin{bmatrix} b_{11} & b_{12} \\ b_{21} & b_{22} \end{bmatrix} = \begin{bmatrix} r_{11} & r_{12} \\ r_{21} & r_{22} \end{bmatrix}$$

$$r_{11} = a_{11}\, b_{11} + a_{12}\, b_{21}$$
$$r_{12} = a_{11}\, b_{12} + a_{12}\, b_{22}$$
$$r_{21} = a_{21}\, b_{11} + a_{22}\, b_{21}$$
$$r_{22} = a_{21}\, b_{12} + a_{22}\, b_{22}$$

Again, the R matrix replaces the A matrix at the completion of the routine.

Matrix interchange:

$$\begin{bmatrix} a_{11} & a_{12} \\ a_{21} & a_{22} \end{bmatrix} \rightleftarrows \begin{bmatrix} b_{11} & b_{12} \\ b_{21} & b_{22} \end{bmatrix}$$

$$a_{11} \rightleftarrows b_{11}$$
$$a_{12} \rightleftarrows b_{12}$$
$$a_{21} \rightleftarrows b_{21}$$
$$a_{22} \rightleftarrows b_{22}$$

# User Instructions

| COMPLEX 2x2 MATRIX OPERATIONS – PART 1 | | | | |
|---|---|---|---|---|
| print A | print B | rect/polar 0 / 1 | A ⇄ B | |
| load A | load B | A + B → A | A – B → A | A x B → A |

| STEP | INSTRUCTIONS | INPUT DATA/UNITS | KEYS | OUTPUT DATA/UNITS |
|---|---|---|---|---|
| 1 | Load both sides of the program card | | | |
| 2 | select polar or rectangular format | | f C | 0 (rect) |
| | | | f C | 1 (polar) |
| | | | f C | 0 (rect) |
| | | | | ⋮ |
| 3 | Load A matrix in selected format (step 2) | | | |
| | rectangular format shown here | | | |
| | a) imaginary part of matrix element | Im $a_{ij}$ | ENT↑ | |
| | b) real part of matrix element | Re $a_{ij}$ | ENT↑ | |
| | c) load element subscript | ij | A | |
| | Do this step for subscripts 11, 12, 21, 22 in any order. | | | |
| 4 | Load B matrix in selected format (step 2) | | | |
| | polar format shown here | | | |
| | a) load angle of matrix element | $\measuredangle b_{ij}$ | ENT↑ | |
| | b) load magnitude of matrix element | $\|b_{ij}\|$ | ENT↑ | |
| | c) load element subscript | ij | B | |
| | Do this step for subscripts 11, 12, 21, 22 in any order | | | |
| 5 | To print matrices in chosen format (say polar) | | | |
| | a) A matrix -- use f A | | f * | $\measuredangle_{11}$ |
| | b) B matrix -- use f B | | | $\|\ \|_{11}$ |
| | | | | $\measuredangle_{12}$ |
| | | | | $\|\ \|_{12}$ |
| | | | | $\measuredangle_{21}$ |
| | | | | $\|\ \|_{21}$ |
| | | | | $\measuredangle_{22}$ |
| | | | | $\|\ \|_{22}$ |

# User Instructions

COMPLEX 2x2 MATRIX OPERATIONS – PART 1

CONTINUED

2

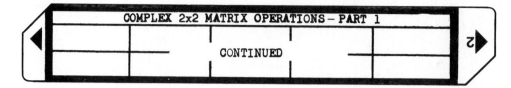

| STEP | INSTRUCTIONS | INPUT DATA/UNITS | KEYS | OUTPUT DATA/UNITS |
|---|---|---|---|---|
| 6 | To add matrices A and B with result replacing A (use step 5 to print result) | | [C] | |
| 7 | To subtract matrices A and B with result replacing A (use step 5 to print results) | | [D] | |
| 8 | To multiply matrices A and B with result replacing A (use step 5 to print results) | | [E] | |
| 9 | To interchange matrices A and B (A⇄B) (use step 5 to print results) | | [f] [D] | |
| | General notes<br>1) Matrix data and operations are stored and manipulated in rectangular format and converted to and from polar for data input and output if flag 1 is set.<br><br>2) After any operation or input, the presently stored matrices can be recorded on a magnetic card using the WDATA command, and later re-entered into storage. | | | |

Example 4-4.1

Given

$$A = \begin{bmatrix} (3 + j4) & (4 + j5) \\ (5 + j6) & (2 + j4) \end{bmatrix}, \quad B = \begin{bmatrix} (4 + j5) & (5 + j6) \\ (6 + j7) & (7 + j8) \end{bmatrix}$$

Load the above matrices, store them on a data card, then perform A + B, A - B, and A x B. The HP-97 printout for the matrix loading is shown below, and the program output is shown on the next page. The B matrix is loaded in scrambled order to demonstrate the free form loading feature of the program.

**HP-97 PRINTOUT FOR EXAMPLE 4-4.1 INPUT**

| A MATRIX LOADING | | B MATRIX LOADING | |
|---|---|---|---|
| 4.00 ENT↑ | Im $a_{11}$ | 6.00 ENT↑ | Im $b_{12}$ |
| 3.00 ENT↑ | Re $a_{11}$ | 5.00 ENT↑ | Re $b_{12}$ |
| 11.00 GSBA | ij | 12.00 GSBB | ij |
| 5.00 ENT↑ | Im $a_{12}$ | 7.00 ENT↑ | Im $b_{21}$ |
| 4.00 ENT↑ | Re $a_{12}$ | 6.00 ENT↑ | Re $b_{21}$ |
| 12.00 GSBA | ij | 21.00 GSBB | ij |
| 6.00 ENT↑ | Im $a_{21}$ | 8.00 ENT↑ | Im $b_{22}$ |
| 5.00 ENT↑ | Re $a_{21}$ | 7.00 ENT↑ | Re $b_{22}$ |
| 21.00 GSBA | ij | 22.00 GSBB | ij |
| 4.00 ENT↑ | Im $a_{22}$ | 5.00 ENT↑ | Im $b_{11}$ |
| 2.00 ENT↑ | Re $a_{22}$ | 4.00 ENT↑ | Re $b_{11}$ |
| 22.00 GSBA | ij | 11.00 GSBB | ij |
| | | WDTA | record data card |

**HP-97 PRINTOUT FOR EXAMPLE 4-4.1 OUTPUT**

```
      GSBa  print A matrix
4.00   ***  Im a11
3.00   ***  Re a11

5.00   ***  Im a12
4.00   ***  Re a12

6.00   ***  Im a21
5.00   ***  Re a21

4.00   ***  Im a22
2.00   ***  Re a22
- - - - - - - - - - - - - -
      GSBb  print B matrix
5.00   ***  Im b11
4.00   ***  Re b11

6.00   ***  Im b12
5.00   ***  Re b12

7.00   ***  Im b21
6.00   ***  Re b21

8.00   ***  Im b22
7.00   ***  Re b22
```

```
        GSBC  execute matrix addition

        GSBa  print resultant matrix
  9.00   ***  Im r11
  7.00   ***  Re r11

 11.00   ***  Im r12    Note that
  9.00   ***  Re r12    the R matrix
                        has replaced
 13.00   ***  Im r21    the A matrix
 11.00   ***  Re r21    in storage.

 12.00   ***  Im r22
  9.00   ***  Re r22
- - - - - - - - - - - - - -
              Reload A and B matrices
              by reading data card.

        GSBD  execute mat subtraction

        GSBa  print resultant matrix
 -1.00   ***  Im r11
 -1.00   ***  Re r11

 -1.00   ***  Im r12
 -1.00   ***  Re r12

 -1.00   ***  Im r21
 -1.00   ***  Re r21

 -4.00   ***  Im r22
 -5.00   ***  Re r22
- - - - - - - - - - - - - -
              Reload A and B matrices
              by reading data card.

        GSBE  exec mat multiplication

        GSBa  print resultant matrix
 89.00   ***  Im r11
-19.00   ***  Re r11

105.00   ***  Im r12
-21.00   ***  Re r12

 87.00   ***  Im r21
-26.00   ***  Re r21

104.00   ***  Im r22
-29.00   ***  Re r22
```

Example 4-4.2

Because the resultant matrix replaces the A matrix in storage, operations may be chained. This example demonstrates that chaining ability starting with the A and B matrices given in Example 4-4.1.

| | | |
|---|---|---|
| | GSBE | execute matrix multiplication: $A \times B \rightarrow A$ |
| | GSBC | execute matrix addition: $AB + B \rightarrow A$ |
| | GSBd | execute matrix interchange: $AB + B \rightleftarrows B$ |
| | GSBE | execute matrix multiplication: $B(AB + B) \rightarrow A$ |
| | GSBa | print resultant A matrix |
| 651.00 | *** | Im $a_{11}$ |
| -1194.00 | *** | Re $a_{11}$ |
| 792.00 | *** | Im $a_{12}$ |
| -1401.00 | *** | Re $a_{12}$ |
| 957.00 | *** | Im $a_{21}$ |
| -1640.00 | *** | Re $a_{21}$ |
| 1162.00 | *** | Im $a_{22}$ |
| -1923.00 | *** | Re $a_{22}$ |

The same data can be outputted (printed) in polar format using the polar-rectangular toggle under label "c" to bring a 1 to the display.

| | | |
|---|---|---|
| | GSBc<br>GSBc | } use polar-rectangular selection toggle |
| | GSBa | print A matrix in polar format |
| 151.40 | *** | $\angle a_{11}$ |
| 1359.94 | *** | $\|a_{11}\|$ |
| 150.52 | *** | $\angle a_{12}$ |
| 1609.37 | *** | $\|a_{12}\|$ |
| 149.73 | *** | $\angle a_{21}$ |
| 1898.80 | *** | $\|a_{21}\|$ |
| 148.86 | *** | $\angle a_{22}$ |
| 2246.81 | *** | $\|a_{22}\|$ |

# Program Listing I

| | | |
|---|---|---|
| 001 | *LBLA | LOAD MATRIX A |
| 002 | SF2 | indicate matrix A |
| 003 | *LBLB | LOAD MATRIX B |
| 004 | 1 | |
| 005 | 2 | |
| 006 | - | |
| 007 | X>0? | calculate storage register |
| 008 | 8 | location from subscript |
| 009 | X>0? | |
| 010 | - | |
| 011 | ENT↑ | |
| 012 | + | |
| 013 | 3 | |
| 014 | + | |
| 015 | EEX | |
| 016 | F2? | |
| 017 | CLX | |
| 018 | + | |
| 019 | R↓ | if polar data, convert |
| 020 | F1? | to rectangular format |
| 021 | →R | |
| 022 | R↑ | recover storage index |
| 023 | GSB8 | store matrix element |
| 024 | GTO1 | goto space and return |
| 025 | *LBLa | PRINT MATRIX A |
| 026 | EEX | initialize index register |
| 027 | STOI | for matrix A |
| 028 | GTOe | jump |
| 029 | *LBLb | PRINT MATRIX B |
| 030 | 2 | initialize index register |
| 031 | STOI | for matrix B |
| 032 | *LBLe | matrix print subroutine |
| 033 | GSB4 | recall matrix element |
| 034 | F1? | convert to polar format |
| 035 | →P | if flag 1 is set |
| 036 | X≷Y | print matrix element |
| 037 | PRTX | as complex quantity |
| 038 | X≷Y | |
| 039 | PRTX | (may be R/S statements |
| 040 | SPC | if desired) |
| 041 | ISZI | increment index by 2 |
| 042 | ISZI | |
| 043 | 8 | |
| 044 | RCLI | |
| 045 | X≤Y? | test for loop exit |
| 046 | GTOe | |
| 047 | GTO1 | goto space and return |
| 048 | *LBLC | ADD A AND B MATRICES |
| 049 | CF0 | indicate matrix addition |
| 050 | GTOC | jump |
| 051 | *LBLD | SUBTRACT A AND B MATRICES |
| 052 | SF0 | indicate matrix subtraction |
| 053 | *LBLC | |
| 054 | 8 | initialize index register |
| 055 | STOI | |

| | | |
|---|---|---|
| 056 | *LBL0 | matrix add/subtract subr |
| 057 | GSB4 | recall matrix B element |
| 058 | F0? | |
| 059 | CHS | change sign of element |
| 060 | X≷Y | parts if subtraction |
| 061 | F0? | is indicated |
| 062 | CHS | |
| 063 | X≷Y | |
| 064 | DSZI | decrement index |
| 065 | GSB4 | recall matrix A element |
| 066 | GSB2 | perform complex addition |
| 067 | GSB5 | store result as matrix A |
| 068 | DSZI | decrement index and |
| 069 | GTO0 | test for loop exit |
| 070 | GTO1 | goto space and return |
| 071 | *LBLE | MATRIX MULTIPLICATION |
| 072 | 1 | |
| 073 | 2 | calculate and |
| 074 | SF2 | temporarily store: |
| 075 | GSB7 | |
| 076 | 3 | |
| 077 | 6 | |
| 078 | GSB7 | $a_{11} \cdot b_{11} + a_{12} \cdot b_{21} = r_{11}$ |
| 079 | 9 | |
| 080 | GSB8 | |
| 081 | 1 | |
| 082 | 4 | calculate and |
| 083 | SF2 | temporarily store: |
| 084 | GSB7 | |
| 085 | 3 | |
| 086 | 8 | |
| 087 | GSB7 | $a_{11} \cdot b_{12} + a_{12} \cdot b_{22} = r_{12}$ |
| 088 | STOA | |
| 089 | X≷Y | |
| 090 | STOB | |
| 091 | 2 | |
| 092 | 5 | calculate and |
| 093 | SF2 | temporarily store: |
| 094 | GSB7 | |
| 095 | 7 | |
| 096 | 6 | |
| 097 | GSB7 | $a_{21} \cdot b_{11} + a_{22} \cdot b_{21} = r_{21}$ |
| 098 | STOC | |
| 099 | X≷Y | |
| 100 | STOD | |
| 101 | 4 | |
| 102 | 5 | calculate and store: |
| 103 | SF2 | |
| 104 | GSB7 | |
| 105 | 7 | |
| 106 | 8 | |
| 107 | GSB7 | $a_{21} \cdot b_{12} + a_{22} \cdot b_{22} = r_{22}$ |
| 108 | 7 | |
| 109 | GSB8 | |

## REGISTERS

| 0 scratch | 1 Re $a_{11}$ | 2 Re $b_{11}$ | 3 Re $a_{12}$ | 4 Re $b_{12}$ | 5 Re $a_{21}$ | 6 Re $b_{21}$ | 7 Re $a_{22}$ | 8 Re $b_{22}$ | 9 temp Re $r_{11}$ |
|---|---|---|---|---|---|---|---|---|---|
| S0 scratch | S1 Im $a_{11}$ | S2 Im $b_{11}$ | S3 Im $a_{12}$ | S4 Im $b_{12}$ | S5 Im $a_{21}$ | S6 Im $b_{21}$ | S7 Im $a_{22}$ | S8 Im $b_{22}$ | S9 temp Im $r_{11}$ |
| A temporary Re $r_{12}$ | | B temporary Im $r_{12}$ | | C temporary Re $r_{21}$ | | D temporary Im $R_{21}$ | | E scratchpad | I index |

# Program Listing II

| | | |
|---|---|---|
| 110 | 9 | |
| 111 | GSB9 | $r_{11} \to a_{11}$ |
| 112 | EEX | |
| 113 | GSB8 | |
| 114 | RCLB | |
| 115 | RCLA | $r_{12} \to a_{12}$ |
| 116 | 3 | |
| 117 | GSB8 | |
| 118 | RCLD | |
| 119 | RCLC | $r_{21} \to a_{21}$ |
| 120 | 5 | |
| 121 | GSB8 | |
| 122 | *LBL1 | space and return subroutine |
| 123 | SPC | |
| 124 | RTN | |
| 125 | *LBL7 | matrix multiply subroutine |
| 126 | EEX | |
| 127 | 1 | recall first matrix element |
| 128 | ÷ | |
| 129 | GSB9 | |
| 130 | RCLI | |
| 131 | FRC | |
| 132 | EEX | recall second matrix element |
| 133 | 1 | |
| 134 | x | |
| 135 | GSB9 | |
| 136 | STOE | complex multiplication |
| 137 | R↓ | |
| 138 | STOI | |
| 139 | R↓ | |
| 140 | ENT↑ | |
| 141 | R↑ | |
| 142 | x | |
| 143 | R↑ | |
| 144 | RCLI | |
| 145 | X⇄Y | |
| 146 | x | |
| 147 | LSTX | |
| 148 | R↓ | |
| 149 | − | |
| 150 | R↑ | |
| 151 | RCLE | |
| 152 | x | |
| 153 | R↑ | |
| 154 | RCLI | |
| 155 | x | |
| 156 | + | |
| 157 | X⇄Y | |
| 158 | F2? | jump if first product |
| 159 | GT07 | |
| 160 | 0 | recall first product |
| 161 | GSB9 | from scratchpad storage |

| | | |
|---|---|---|
| 162 | *LBL2 | complex add subroutine |
| 163 | X⇄Y | |
| 164 | R↓ | |
| 165 | + | |
| 166 | R↓ | |
| 167 | + | |
| 168 | R↑ | |
| 169 | RTN | |
| 170 | *LBL7 | setup scratchpad index |
| 171 | 0 | |
| 172 | *LBL8 | store storage index subr |
| 173 | STOI | |
| 174 | R↓ | |
| 175 | *LBL5 | complex storage subroutine |
| 176 | STOi | |
| 177 | X⇄Y | |
| 178 | P⇄S | |
| 179 | STOi | |
| 180 | P⇄S | |
| 181 | RTN | |
| 182 | *LBL9 | store recall index subr |
| 183 | STOI | |
| 184 | R↓ | |
| 185 | *LBL4 | complex recall subroutine |
| 186 | P⇄S | |
| 187 | RCLi | |
| 188 | P⇄S | |
| 189 | RCLi | |
| 190 | RTN | |
| 191 | *LBLc | POLAR/RECTANGULAR TOGGLE |
| 192 | CF1 | clear flag 1 to indicate |
| 193 | CLX | rectangular format and |
| 194 | RTN | place a zero in the display |
| 195 | *LBLc | |
| 196 | SF1 | set flag 1 to indicate |
| 197 | EEX | polar format and place a |
| 198 | RTN | one in the display |
| 199 | *LBLd | MATRIX INTERCHANGE |
| 200 | 8 | initialize index |
| 201 | STOI | |
| 202 | *LBL6 | |
| 203 | GSB4 | |
| 204 | DSZI | recall corresponding |
| 205 | GSB4 | matrix elements |
| 206 | ISZI | |
| 207 | GSB5 | |
| 208 | DSZI | interchange and store |
| 209 | R↓ | corresponding elements |
| 210 | R↓ | |
| 211 | GSB5 | |
| 212 | DSZI | decrement index and |
| 213 | GT06 | test for loop exit |
| 214 | GT01 | goto space and return |

| LABELS | | | | |
|---|---|---|---|---|
| A load A | B load B | C A+B→A | D A−B→A | E A×B→A |
| a print A | b print B | c polar/rect 1/0 | d A⇄B | e print loop start |
| 0 matrix add/subtract | 1 space & rtn | 2 complex addition | 3 | 4 complex recall |
| 5 complex store | 6 A⇄B subroutine | 7 matrix multiplication | 8 store index & complex sto | 9 store index & complex rcl |

| FLAGS |
|---|
| 0 subtract |
| 1 polar |
| 2 don't continue summation |
| 3 |

| SET STATUS | | |
|---|---|---|
| FLAGS ON OFF | TRIG | DISP |
| 0 ■ | DEG | FIX |
| 1 ■ | GRAD | SCI |
| 2 ■ | RAD | ENG ■ |
| 3 | | n 3 |

## PROGRAM 4-5 COMPLEX 2x2 MATRIX OPERATIONS — PART 2.

Program Description and Equations Used

This program is the second of two programs to manipulate complex 2x2 matrices. This program will perform matrix inverse ($A^{-1} \rightarrow A$), matrix transpose ($A^T \rightarrow A$), matrix complex conjugate ($A^* \rightarrow A$), and matrix interchange ($A \rightleftarrows B$). Because the resultant matrix from the matrix operation replaces the A matrix, chaining of matrix operations without data re-entry is easily done.

This program shares common register storage with Program 4-4, hence, matrix operations that require concatenation of routines contained in two different programs can be done without reloading any previous data.

The user may elect to work in either the polar or the rectangular co-ordinate systems, however, all data is stored in rectangular format. If flag 1 is set, the input data is converted from polar to rectangular, and vice-versa for output.

The algorithms used are:

Matrix inverse:

$$A^{-1} = \frac{1}{|A|}\begin{bmatrix} a_{22} & -a_{12} \\ -a_{21} & a_{11} \end{bmatrix} \qquad (4\text{-}5.1)$$

where $|A|$ is the determinant of A,

$$|A| = a_{11} \cdot a_{22} - a_{21} \cdot a_{12} \qquad (4\text{-}5.2)$$

Matrix transpose:

$$A^T = \begin{bmatrix} a_{11} & a_{21} \\ a_{12} & a_{22} \end{bmatrix} \qquad (4\text{-}5.3)$$

Matrix complex conjugate:

$$A^* = \begin{bmatrix} a_{11}^* & a_{12}^* \\ a_{21}^* & a_{22}^* \end{bmatrix}$$

Matrix interchange, see Eq. (4-4.3).

# User Instructions

| COMPLEX 2x2 MATRIX OPERATIONS – PART 2 | | | | |
|---|---|---|---|---|
| print A | print B | polar/rect 1/0 | A ⇄ B | calculate \|A\| |
| load A | load B | $A^{-1} \to A$ | $A^T \to A$ | $A^* \to A$ |

| STEP | INSTRUCTIONS | INPUT DATA/UNITS | KEYS | OUTPUT DATA/UNITS |
|---|---|---|---|---|
| 1 | Load both sides of the program card | | | |
| 2 | Select polar or rectangluar format | | [f] [C] | 0 (rect) |
| | | | [f] [C] | 1 (polar) |
| | | | [f] [C] | 0 (rect) |
| | | | | ⋮ |
| 3 | Load matrix A in selected format (rect shown) | | | |
| | a) load imaginary part of matrix element | Im $a_{ij}$ | [ENT↑] | |
| | b) load real part of matrix element | Re $a_{ij}$ | [ENT↑] | |
| | c) load subscript of matrix element | ij | [A] | |
| | Repeat this step for ij 11, 12, 21, 22 in any order. | | | |
| 4 | Load matrix B in selected format (polar used) | | | |
| | a) load angle of matrix element | $\measuredangle b_{ij}$ | [ENT↑] | |
| | b) load magnitude of matrix element | $\|b_{ij}\|$ | [ENT↑] | |
| | c) load subscript of matrix element | ij | [B] | |
| | Repeat this step for ij 11, 12, 21, 22 in any order. | | | |
| 5 | To print matrices in chosen format (say polar) | | | |
| | a) A matrix -- use f A | | [f] [*] | $\measuredangle_{11}$ |
| | b) B matrix -- use f B | | | $\| \|_{11}$ |
| | | | | $\measuredangle_{12}$ |
| | | | | $\| \|_{12}$ |
| | | | | $\measuredangle_{21}$ |
| | | | | $\| \|_{21}$ |
| | | | | $\measuredangle_{22}$ |
| | | | | $\| \|_{22}$ |

# User Instructions

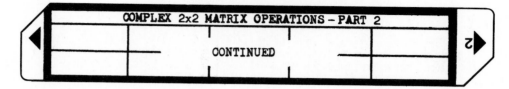

COMPLEX 2x2 MATRIX OPERATIONS - PART 2

CONTINUED

2

| STEP | INSTRUCTIONS | INPUT DATA/UNITS | KEYS | OUTPUT DATA/UNITS |
|---|---|---|---|---|
| 6 | To calculate matrix A inverse<br>(use step 5 to print out resultant A matrix) | | [C] | |
| 7 | To calculate matrix A transpose<br>(use step 5 to print out resultant A matrix) | | [D] | |
| 8 | To calculate matrix A complex conjugate<br>(use step 5 to print out resultant A matrix) | | [E] | |
| 9 | To calculate the determinant of the A matrix | | [f] [E] | Im \|A\|<br>Re \|A\| |
| 10 | To interchange matrices A and B in storage<br>(use step 5 to print matrices) | | [f] [D] | |

<u>Example 4-5.1</u>

Given the A and B matrices of Example 4-4.1, calculate $B^{-1}AB$. The loading of the A and B matrices is shown in Example 4-4.1, and is omitted here for brevity (they were actually loaded from the magnetic data card from Program 4-4).

Load Program 4-4, and load A and B matrices

GSBE form AB $\rightarrow$ A

Load this program (Program 4-5)

GSBa interchange AB and B

GSBC form $B^{-1} \rightarrow A$

Reload Program 4-4

GSBE form $B^{-1}AB \rightarrow A$

GSBa print result

```
-48.25  ***   Im a11
-46.00  ***   Re a11

-54.50  ***   Im a12
-55.25  ***   Re a12

 49.50  ***   Im a21
 45.75  ***   Re a21

 56.25  ***   Im a22
 53.00  ***   Re a22
```

# Program Listing I

|  |  |
|---|---|
| *LBLA | **LOAD MATRIX A** |
| SF2 | indicate matrix A |
| *LBLB | **LOAD MATRIX B** |
| 1 | |
| 2 | |
| - | |
| X>0? | |
| 8 | |
| X>0? | calculate storage register |
| - | location from subscript |
| ENT↑ | |
| + | |
| 3 | |
| + | |
| EEX | |
| F2? | |
| CLX | |
| + | |
| R↓ | if polar data, convert |
| F1? | to rectangular format |
| →R | |
| R↑ | recover storage index |
| GSB8 | store matrix element |
| GTO1 | goto space and return subr |
| *LBLa | **PRINT MATRIX A** |
| EEX | initialize index register |
| STOI | for matrix A |
| GTO7 | jump |
| *LBLb | **PRINT MATRIX B** |
| 2 | initialize index register |
| STOI | for matrix B |
| *LBL7 | matrix print subroutine |
| GSB4 | recall matrix element |
| GSB0 | print matrix element |
| ISZI | increment index by 2 |
| ISZI | |
| 8 | |
| RCLI | test for loop exit |
| X≤Y? | |
| GTO7 | |
| GTO1 | goto space and return subr |
| *LBLe | **CALCULATE DETERMINANT OF A** |
| SF2 | indicate determinant calc |
| *LBLC | **CALCULATE A MATRIX INVERSE** |
| EEX | |
| GSB9 | calculate and scratchpad |
| 7 | store $a_{11} \cdot a_{22}$ |
| GSB9 | |
| GSB3 | |
| 9 | |
| GSB8 | |
| 3 | |
| GSB9 | calculate $a_{21} \cdot a_{12}$ and |
| 5 | subtract from $a_{11} \cdot a_{22}$ which |
| GSBe | is stored |

|  |  |
|---|---|
| 9 | |
| GSB9 | |
| GSB2 | |
| F2? | if determinant calculation |
| GTO0 | goto print routine |
| →P | |
| 1/X | calculate and store $\frac{1}{\lvert A \rvert}$ |
| X⇄Y | |
| CHS | |
| X⇄Y | |
| →R | |
| 9 | |
| GSB8 | |
| 3 | |
| GSB9 | calculate and store: |
| 9 | |
| GSBe | $-\frac{a_{12}}{\lvert A \rvert} \rightarrow a_{12}$ |
| 3 | |
| GSB8 | |
| 5 | |
| GSB9 | calculate and store; |
| 9 | |
| GSBe | $-\frac{a_{21}}{\lvert A \rvert} \rightarrow a_{12}$ |
| 5 | |
| GSB8 | |
| EEX | |
| GSB9 | calculate and store: |
| STOA | |
| X⇄Y | |
| STOB | |
| 7 | |
| GSB9 | |
| 9 | $\frac{a_{22}}{\lvert A \rvert} \rightarrow a_{11}$ |
| GSB9 | |
| GSB3 | |
| EEX | |
| GSB8 | |
| RCLB | calculate and store: |
| RCLA | |
| 9 | |
| GSB9 | |
| GSB3 | $\frac{a_{11}}{\lvert A \rvert} \rightarrow a_{22}$ |
| 7 | |
| GSB8 | |
| GTO1 | |
| *LBLe | multiply and change sign subroutine |
| GSB9 | |
| GSB3 | |
| CHS | |
| X⇄Y | |
| CHS | |
| X⇄Y | |
| RTN | |

**REGISTERS**

| 0 | 1 | 2 | 3 | 4 | 5 | 6 | 7 | 8 | 9 |
|---|---|---|---|---|---|---|---|---|---|
| scratchpad | Re $a_{11}$ | Re $b_{11}$ | Re $a_{12}$ | Re $b_{12}$ | Re $a_{21}$ | Re $b_{21}$ | Re $a_{22}$ | Re $b_{22}$ | Re $\frac{1}{\lvert A \rvert}$ |

| S0 | S1 | S2 | S3 | S4 | S5 | S6 | S7 | S8 | S9 |
|---|---|---|---|---|---|---|---|---|---|
| scratchpad | Im $a_{11}$ | Im $b_{11}$ | Im $a_{12}$ | Im $b_{12}$ | Im $a_{21}$ | Im $b_{21}$ | Im $a_{22}$ | Im $b_{22}$ | Im $\frac{1}{\lvert A \rvert}$ |

| A | B | C | D | E | I |
|---|---|---|---|---|---|
| scratchpad | scratchpad | | | scratchpad | index / scratch |

# Program Listing II

```
109  *LBL0   common output subroutine
110  F1?     convert to polar if required
111  →P
112  X⇄Y     print both parts of a
113  PRTX    complex number
114  X⇄Y     (may be R/S statements
115  PRTX     if desired)
116  GTO1    goto space and return subr
117  *LBL2   complex add subroutine
118  X⇄Y
119  R↓
120  +
121  R↓
122  +
123  R↑
124  RTN
125  *LBL3   complex multiply subroutine
126  STOE
127  R↓
128  STOI
129  R↓
130  ENT↑
131  R↑
132  ×
133  R↑
134  RCLI
135  X⇄Y
136  ×
137  LSTX
138  R↓
139  -
140  R↑
141  RCLE
142  ×
143  R↑
144  RCLI
145  ×
146  +
147  X⇄Y
148  RTN
149  *LBLc   POLAR/RECTANGULAR TOGGLE
150  CF1     indicate rectangular format
151  CLX     and place a zero in display
152  RTN     return to keyboard control
153  *LBLc
154  SF1     indicate polar format and
155  EEX     place a one in the display
156  RTN     return to keyboard control
157  *LBLd   MATRIX INTERCHANGE
158  8       initialize index
159  STOI
160  *LBL6   loop start
161  GSB4    recall corresponding
162  DSZI    matrix elements
163  GSB4
164  ISZI
165  GSB5
166  DSZI    interchange and store
167  R↓      corresponding matrix
168  R↓      elements
169  GSB5
170  DSZI    decrement index and
171  GTO6    test for loop exit
172  GTO1    goto space and return subr
173  *LBLD   CALCULATE MATRIX A TRANSPOSE
174  3       recall and scratchpad store
175  GSB9    a12
176  STOA
177  X⇄Y
178  STOB
179  5       recall a21 and store in
180  GSB9    a12 location
181  3
182  GSB8
183  RCLB    recall a12 from scratchpad
184  RCLA    and store in a21 location
185  5
186  GSB8
187  GTO1    goto space and return subr
188  *LBL9   store recall index subr
189  STOI
190  R↓
191  *LBL4   complex recall subroutine
192  P⇄S
193  RCLi
194  P⇄S
195  RCLi
196  RTN
197  *LBL8   store storage index subr
198  STOI
199  R↓
200  *LBL5   complex storage subroutine
201  STOi
202  X⇄Y
203  P⇄S
204  STOi
205  P⇄S
206  RTN
207  *LBLE   CALCULATE MAT A COMPLEX CONJ
208  P⇄S     reverse the sign of the
209  1       imaginary parts of the
210  CHS     matrix elements
211  ST×7
212  ST×5
213  ST×3
214  ST×1
215  P⇄S
216  *LBL1   space and return subroutine
217  SPC
218  RTN
```

**LABELS**

| | | | | |
|---|---|---|---|---|
| A load A | B load B | C $A^{-1} \rightarrow A$ | D $A^T \rightarrow A$ | E $A^* \rightarrow A$ |
| a print A | b print B | c polar/rect | d A⇄B | e calc \|A\| |
| 0 complex print | 1 space & return | 2 complex add | 3 complex multiply | 4 complex recall |
| 5 complex store | 6 A⇄B subroutine | 7 common print routine | 8 sto index & cmplx store | 9 store index & cmplx rcl |

**FLAGS**

| | |
|---|---|
| 0 | |
| 1 | polar |
| 2 | used with \|A\| |
| 3 | |

**SET STATUS**

| FLAGS | ON | OFF | TRIG | DISP |
|---|---|---|---|---|
| | | | users choice | |
| 0 | | | DEG | FIX |
| 1 | | ■ | GRAD | SCI |
| 2 | | ■ | RAD | ENG |
| 3 | | | | n_____ |

# Part 5
# ENGINEERING MATHEMATICS

## PROGRAM 5-1 ELLIPTIC INTEGRALS AND FUNCTIONS.

Program Description and Equations Used

This program calculates complete elliptic integrals of the first kind and the following elliptic functions: elliptic sine (sn(u,k)), ellipic cosine (cn(u,k)), elliptic delta (dn(u,k)), and elliptic amplitude (am(u,k)).

The elliptic integral of the first kind is defined by Eq. (5-1.1), and the complete elliptic integral of the first kind is defined by Eq. (5-1.2), which can be evaluated using the infinite product shown in Eqs. (5-1.3) through (5-1.6). The product is terminated when $k_m$ becomes smaller than $10^{-10}$. Generally this condition is achieved after the 3rd term of the series, hence, the series converges rapidly. As the modulus, k, approaches 1, more iterations are required, e.g., K(.9) = 2.280549137 requires 4 iterations and K(.999) = 4.495596396 requires 5 iterations.

$$u(\phi,k) = \int_0^{\phi} (1 - k^2 \sin^2 x)^{-\frac{1}{2}} dx \qquad (5\text{-}1.1)$$

$$K(k) = u(\tfrac{\pi}{2}, k) \qquad (5\text{-}1.2)$$

$$K(k) = \frac{\pi}{2} \prod_{m=0}^{\infty} (1 + k_{m+1}) \qquad (5\text{-}1.3)$$

$$k_{m+1} = (1 - k_m')/(1 + k_m') \qquad (5\text{-}1.4)$$

$$k_m' = \sqrt{1 - k_m^{\,2}} \qquad (5\text{-}1.5)$$

$$k_0 \equiv k \qquad (5\text{-}1.6)$$

The elliptic modulus, k, is commonly expressed three different ways, which leads to some degree of confusion. In the Abramowitz and Stegun tables of elliptic functions [ 1 ], the parameters m and Θ are used where $m = k^2$, and $\Theta = \sin^{-1} k$. The parameter Θ is called the modular angle.

The elliptic sine is an elliptic function, and is defined in a somewhat reverse manner from the elliptic integral. Referring to Eq. 5-1.1, given the input $u(\phi,k)$, the limit of integration, $\phi$ must be found to satisfy the equality, then $\mathrm{sn}(u,k) = \sin\phi$. Likewise, the elliptic cosine is defined; $\mathrm{cn}(u,k) = \cos\phi$. Notice that when $k = 0$, the elliptic sine equals the trigonometric sine and likewise for the respective cosines.

The descending Landen transformation [12], [46] is used to calculate the elliptic sine. Starting with an initial value for $\mathrm{sn}(u_r, k_r)$ as given by Eq. (5-1.7), Eq. (5-1.8) is recursively used to find $\mathrm{sn}(u_0, k_0)$ which is the answer.

$$\mathrm{sn}(u_{m+1}, k_{m+1}) = \sin\left(\frac{\pi u_0}{2K(k)}\right) \tag{5-1.7}$$

$$\mathrm{sn}(u_{r-1}, k_{r-1}) = \frac{(1 + k_r)\,\mathrm{sn}(u_r,k_r)}{1 + k_r\,\mathrm{sn}^2(u_r,k_r)} \tag{5-1.8}$$

where

$$r = m+1,\ m,\ \ldots.,\ 1$$

and $k_r$ is obtained from storage, and was calculated from Eq. (5-1.4) during the complete elliptic integral calculation.

The descending Landen transformation is also the basis for Darlington's elliptic filter algorithms (Program 2-15).

The other elliptic functions are calculated from the elliptic sine as follows:

$$\mathrm{cn}(u,k) = (1 - \mathrm{sn}^2(u,k))^{\frac{1}{2}} \tag{5-1.9}$$

$$\mathrm{dn}(u,k) = (1 - k^2\cdot\mathrm{sn}^2(u,k))^{\frac{1}{2}} \tag{5-1.10}$$

$$\mathrm{am}(u,k) = \sin^{-1}\mathrm{sn}(u,k) = \phi \tag{5-1.11}$$

# User Instructions

| ELLIPTIC INTEGRALS AND FUNCTIONS | | | | |
|---|---|---|---|---|
| complete elliptic integral, K(k) | elliptic sine sn(u,k), u ↑ k | elliptic cosine cn(u,k), u ↑ k | elliptic delta dn(u,k), u ↑ k | print ? / elliptic amplitude am(u,k), u↑k |

| STEP | INSTRUCTIONS | INPUT DATA/UNITS | KEYS | OUTPUT DATA/UNITS |
|---|---|---|---|---|
| 1 | Load both sides of program card | | | |
| 2 | Select print/no-print option | | f E | 0 (R/S) |
| | | | f E | 1 (print) |
| | | | f E | 0 (R/S) |
| | | | | ⋮ |
| 3 | For complete elliptic integral, K(k) | k | A | K(k) |
| 4 | For elliptic sine, sn(u,k) | u | ENT↑ | |
| | | k | B | sn(u,k) |
| 5 | For elliptic cosine, cn(u,k) | u | ENT↑ | |
| | | k | C | cn(u,k) |
| 6 | For elliptic delta, dn(u,k) | u | ENT↑ | |
| | | k | D | dn(u,k) |
| 7 | For elliptic amplitude, am(u,k) | u | ENT↑ | |
| | | k | E | am(u,k) |

## Example 5-1.1

Evaluate the following elliptic functions and compare with Abramowitz and Stegun [ 1 ] Tables 17.1 and 17.5.

$$K(k);\ k = \sqrt{0.9}$$

$$\mathrm{sn}(3.09448898,\ \sin 88°)$$

HP-97 printout

```
             .9    √X
 9.486832981-01   ***   calculate k
                 GSBA
 2.578092113+00   ***   K(k)


     3.09448898 ENT↑    load u
            88.   DEG
                  SIN   calculate k = sin 88°
 9.993908270-01   ***   sin 88°
                 GSBB
 9.961946981-01   ***   sn(3.09448898, sin 88°)

                  DEG
                 SIN⁻¹  calculate and print Ø = sin⁻¹sn(u,k)
 8.500000001+01   ***
```

From Table 17.1 (p. 608 of [ 1]), K(m) for m = 0.9 is:

$$K(m) = 2.57809211334173$$

Rounded to ten significant figures, this figure agrees identically with the program output.

From Table 17.5 (p. 615 of [ 1]), the elliptic integral of the first kind for $\alpha = 88°$, $\emptyset = 85°$ is 3.09448898. The program output differs by 1 part in $8.5 \times 10^9$, which exceeds the precision of the input.

5-1

# Program Listing I

| Step | Key | Comment |
|---|---|---|
| 001 | *LBLA | COMPUTE COMPLETE ELLIPTIC INT |
| 002 | GSB2 | calculate K(k) |
| 003 | GTO9 | goto output routine |
| 004 | *LBL2 | K(k) calculation subroutine |
| 005 | STO0 | store k |
| 006 | Pi | calculate and store: |
| 007 | 2 | |
| 008 | ÷ | $\frac{\pi}{2} \rightarrow R1$ |
| 009 | STO1 | |
| 010 | EEX | |
| 011 | 1 | $10 \rightarrow R8$ |
| 012 | STO8 | |
| 013 | STOI | |
| 014 | EEX | |
| 015 | CHS | $10^{-10} \rightarrow R9$ |
| 016 | 1 | |
| 017 | 0 | |
| 018 | STO9 | |
| 019 | *LBL0 | K(k) loop start |
| 020 | EEX | calculate and store: |
| 021 | RCL0 | |
| 022 | X² | $k_m' = (1 - k_m^2)^{1/2}$ |
| 023 | - | |
| 024 | √X | |
| 025 | STO7 | |
| 026 | CHS | calculate and store: |
| 027 | EEX | |
| 028 | + | |
| 029 | RCL7 | $k_{m+1} = \frac{1 - k_m'}{1 + k_m'}$ |
| 030 | EEX | |
| 031 | + | |
| 032 | ÷ | |
| 033 | STO0 | |
| 034 | STOi | store $k_r$ for descending |
| 035 | ISZI | Landen transformation |
| 036 | EEX | |
| 037 | + | form $\prod (1 + k_{m+1})$ |
| 038 | ST×1 | |
| 039 | RCL9 | |
| 040 | RCL0 | test for loop exit |
| 041 | X>Y? | |
| 042 | GTO0 | |
| 043 | RCL1 | recall K(k) |
| 044 | RTN | return to main program |

| Step | Key | Comment |
|---|---|---|
| 045 | *LBLB | CALCULATE ELLIPTIC SINE |
| 046 | GSB3 | calculate sn(u,k) |
| 047 | GTO9 | goto output routine |
| 048 | *LBL3 | sn(u,k) calculation subr |
| 049 | STO2 | store k |
| 050 | R↓ | recover and store u |
| 051 | STO3 | |
| 052 | RCL2 | calculate K(k) |
| 053 | GSB2 | |
| 054 | DSZI | setup for sn(u,k) calc. |
| 055 | RAD | |
| 056 | RCL3 | form and store initial |
| 057 | Pi | sn value for descending |
| 058 | × | Landen transformation: |
| 059 | RCL1 | |
| 060 | ENT↑ | $sn(u_{m+1}, k_{m+1}) = \sin\left\{\frac{\pi u_0}{2K(k)}\right\}$ |
| 061 | + | |
| 062 | ÷ | |
| 063 | SIN | |
| 064 | STO4 | |
| 065 | *LBL1 | transformation loop start |
| 066 | RCLi | recursively use descending |
| 067 | EEX | Landen transformation to |
| 068 | + | find $sn(u_0, k_0)$: |
| 069 | RCL4 | |
| 070 | × | |
| 071 | RCLi | $sn(u_{r-1}, k_{r-1}) = \frac{(1+k_r) sn(u_r, k_r)}{1 + sn^2(u_r, k_r)}$ |
| 072 | RCL4 | |
| 073 | X² | |
| 074 | × | |
| 075 | EEX | |
| 076 | + | |
| 077 | ÷ | |
| 078 | STO4 | |
| 079 | DSZI | |
| 080 | RCLI | |
| 081 | RCL8 | test for loop exit |
| 082 | X≤Y? | |
| 083 | GTO1 | |
| 084 | RCL4 | recall sn(u, k) |
| 085 | RTN | return to main program |

**REGISTERS**

| 0 | 1 | 2 | 3 | 4 | 5 | 6 | 7 | 8 | 9 |
|---|---|---|---|---|---|---|---|---|---|
| $k_i$ | K(k) | $k_0$ | $u_0$ | sn(u, k) | | | scratch | 10 | $10^{-10}$ |

| S0 | S1 | S2 | S3 | S4 | S5 | S6 | S7 | S8 | S9 |
|---|---|---|---|---|---|---|---|---|---|
| $k_1$ | $k_2$ | $k_3$ | $k_4$ | $k_5$ | $k_6$ | | | | |

| A | B | C | D | E | I |
|---|---|---|---|---|---|
| | | | | | |

# Program Listing II

```
*LBLC   CALCULATE ELLIPTIC COSINE
GSB3    calculate sn(u,k)
GTO6    convert to cn(u,k) & output
*LBLD   CALCULATE ELLIPTIC DELTA
GSB3    calculate sn(u,k)
RCL2    form k•sn(u,k) and convert
×       to dn(u,k) then output
*LBL6
X²      routine to calculate:
CHS
EEX         (1 - (•)²)^½
+
√X
GTO9    goto output routine
*LBLE   CALCULATE ELLIPTIC AMPLITUDE
GSB3    calculate sn(u,k)
SIN⁻¹   convert to am(u,k)
*LBL9   output subroutine
F0?
PRTX    print and space if
F0?     flag 0 is set
SPC
RTN     return to main program
*LBL7   R/S lockup routine
R/S
GTO7
*LBLe   PRINT - R/S TOGGLE
F0?     jump if flag 0 is set
GTO8
SF0     set flag 0 and place a 1
EEX     in the display
GTO7    goto R/S lockup routine
*LBL8
CF0     clear flag 0 and place a
CLX     0 in the display
RTN     return control to keyboard
```

Flag 0 should be set (cleared) prior to magnetic card recording depending whether the user normally wants the program in the print (R/S) mode.

| LABELS | | | | | FLAGS |
|---|---|---|---|---|---|
| A K(k) | B sn(u,k) | C cn(u,k) | D dn(u,k) | E am(u,k) | 0 print |
| a | b | c | d | e print toggle | 1 |
| 0 K(k) loop | 1 sn loop | 2 K(k) | 3 sn(u,k) | 4 | 2 |
| 5 | 6 $\sqrt{1-x^2}$ | 7 R/S lock | 8 print toggle | 9 print or R/S | 3 |

| SET STATUS | | |
|---|---|---|
| FLAGS (ON OFF) | TRIG | DISP |
| 0 ☐ ☐ | DEG | FIX ■ |
| 1 | GRAD | SCI |
| 2 | RAD ■ | ENG |
| 3 | | n 9 |

## PROGRAM 5-2 BESSEL FUNCTIONS AND FM OR PHASE MODULATION SPECTRA.

Program Description and Equations Used

This program will calculate the magnitude of the spectral lines arising from a frequency of phase sine-wave modulation process. In addition, the power in the higher sidebands is calculated which can be used to help define the bandwidths necessary for a communication channel carrying frequency division multiplexed data with either frequency modulation (FM), or phase modulation (PM) on the individual subcarriers. Phase modulation is often used to transmit digital data with preconditioning such as Manchester biphase coding, or doublet modulation.

The spectra of both frequency modulated and phase modulated signals are the same when expressed as a function of the modulation index, m. The modulation index for the FM case is:

$$m_f = \frac{\text{peak carrier deviation from nominal frequency}}{\text{modulation frequency}}$$

Notice that the FM modulation index is modulation frequency dependent. The modulation index for the PM case is:

$$m_p = \left\{ \begin{array}{l} \text{carrier phase shift in radians produced by the} \\ \text{modulating frequency.} \end{array} \right.$$

Also notice that the PM modulation index is modulation frequency independent.

The carrier and carrier sideband levels are described in terms of Bessel functions with the modulation index as the argument. The spacing of the sidebands is equal to the modulating frequency. For example, with a modulation index of 5 and a modulation frequency of 15 kHz, the FM or PM spectra is:

| | |
|---|---|
| carrier amplitude | $J_0(5)$, |
| first sideband pair | $J_1(5)$, |
| second sideband pair | $J_2(5)$, |
| ⋮ | |
| n-th sideband pair | $J_n(5)$. |

Figure 5-2.1 shows the above concept graphically.

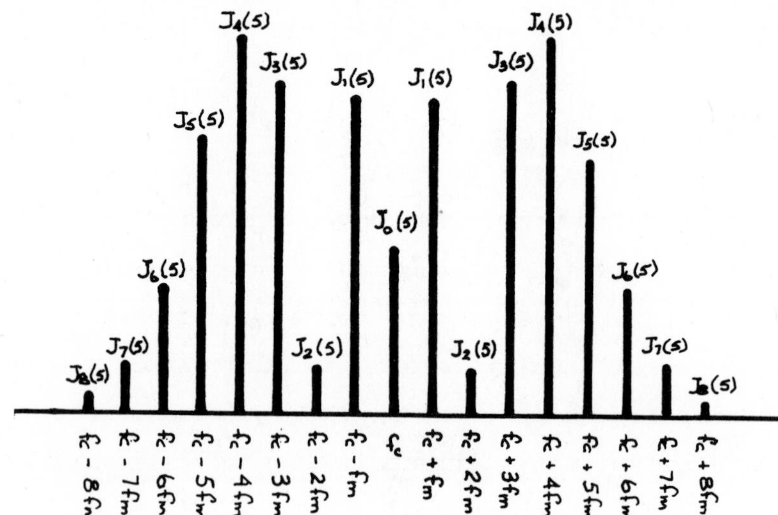


Figure 5-2.1 FM or PM modulation spectra.

A Bessel function identity allows the power remaining in the higher sidebands to be calculated. With FM or PM, all the sidebands carry modulation information in somewhat redundant form. If the higher order sidebands are removed by filtering, the modulation information can still be recovered, but the effective power will be reduced hence, the signal-to-noise ratio decreased; some distortion will also be introduced.

The Bessel function identity is:

$$J_0^{\,2}(m) + 2\sum_{i=1}^{\infty} J_i^{\,2}(m) = 1 \tag{5-2.1}$$

The summation is broken into 2 parts and the equation rearranged:

$$\sum_{i=n+1}^{\infty} J_i^{\,2}(m) = \tfrac{1}{2}(1 - J_0^{\,2}(m)) - \sum_{i=1}^{n} J_i^{\,2}(m) \tag{5-2.2}$$

Therefore, if the magnitudes of the first n sidebands are known, then the power in the higher sidebands may be calculated since power is proportional to magnitude squared.

When the modulating signal contains 2 sinewaves of different frequencies and amplitudes superposition does not hold, since the resulting spectra is represented by the products of the Bessel functions of the individual spectra. Let $m_1$ be the modulation index for modulation frequency $f_1$, and likewise, $m_2$ for $f_2$, then the combined modulation spectral components will be as shown in Table 5-2.1.

Table 5-2.1 Spectra for combined modulation

| Spectral Component | frequency of component | amplitude of component |
|---|---|---|
| Carrier | $f_c$ | $J_0(m_1) \cdot J_0(m_2)$ |
| Simple sidebands of | $f_c \pm f_1$ | $J_1(m_1) \cdot J_0(m_2)$ |
| | $f_c \pm f_2$ | $J_0(m_1) \cdot J_1(m_2)$ |
| | $f_c \pm 2f_1$ | $J_2(m_1) \cdot J_0(m_2)$ |
| | $f_c \pm 2f_2$ | $J_0(m_1) \cdot J_2(m_2)$ |
| | $\vdots$ | $\vdots$ |
| Intermodulation | $f_c \pm f_1 \pm f_2$ | $J_1(m_1) \cdot J_1(m_2)$ |
| | $f_c \pm f_1 \pm 2f_2$ | $J_1(m_1) \cdot J_2(m_2)$ |
| | $f_c \pm 2f_1 \pm f_2$ | $J_2(m_1) \cdot J_1(m_2)$ |
| | $\vdots$ | $\vdots$ |

The Bessel function of the first kind is easily evaluated using the summation of an infinite series; however, for values of m larger than 10, computational difficulties arise because of small differences between big numbers, i.e., using Eq. (5-2.3), Table 5-2.2 shows the individual terms for $n = 0$ and $m = 20$.

$$J_n(m) = \left(\frac{m}{2}\right)^n \sum_{i=0}^{\infty} \frac{\left(-\frac{m^2}{4}\right)^i}{i! \cdot (i+n)!} = \left(\frac{m}{2}\right)^n \sum_{i=0}^{\infty} T_j \qquad (5\text{-}2.3)$$

Table 5-2.2
Infinite series terms.

|  |  |
|---|---|
| 1.000000000 | $T_0$ |
| -100.0000000 | $T_1$ |
| 2500.000000 | |
| -27777.77778 | |
| 173611.1111 | |
| -694444.4444 | $T_5$ |
| 1929012.346 | |
| -3936759.889 | |
| 6151187.327 | |
| -7594058.428 | |
| 7594058.428 | $T_{10}$ |
| -6276081.347 | |
| 4358389.823 | |
| -2578928.890 | |
| 1315780.046 | |
| -584791.1313 | $T_{15}$ |
| 228434.0357 | |
| -79042.91893 | |
| 24395.96263 | |
| -6757.884387 | |
| 1689.471097 | $T_{20}$ |
| -383.1000219 | |
| 79.15289702 | |
| -14.96274047 | |
| 2.597697998 | |
| -0.415631680 | $T_{25}$ |
| 0.061483976 | |
| -0.008434016 | |
| 0.001075767 | |
| -0.000127915 | |
| 0.000014213 | $T_{30}$ |
| -0.000001479 | |
| 0.000000144 | |
| -0.000000013 | |
| 0.000000001 | |

The computed $J_o(20)$ by this method is 0.166021646. Because the range of the numbers exceed $10^{10}$, the least significant figures have been lost. Even though the summation was carried out until $T_i < 10^{-9}$, the answer is only accurate to 2 significant figures. The correct answer to $J_0(20)$ is 0.1670246646, which is computed by a slower, less direct method shown next.

Equation (5-2.4) is the recursion relationship for Bessel functions of the first kind.

$$J_n(m) = \frac{2}{m}(n-1)\cdot J_{n-1}(m) - J_{n-2}(m) \qquad (5\text{-}2.4)$$

All Bessel functions approach zero as the order becomes large. This characteristic can be used to compute Bessel functions. If $T_{n+2}(m) = 0$ and $T_{n+1}(m) = 10^{-9}$, the recursion relationship can be run backwards to arrive at a result that is proportional to $J_0(m)$. Abramowitz and Stegun [ 1 ] has the relations for the minimum starting index and the constant of proportionality for $J_0(m)$, i.e., given

$$T_i(m) = \frac{2}{m}(i+1)\cdot T_{i+1}(m) - T_{i+2}(m) \tag{5-2.5}$$

then, the minimum starting index is

$$i_{min} = 2.\mathrm{INT}\left(\frac{6 + \max(n,z) + (9z/(z+2))}{2}\right) \tag{5-2.6}$$

which for $n = 0$ may be reduced to

$$i_{min} = 2\cdot\mathrm{INT}\left(\frac{z^2 + 17\cdot z + 12}{2(z + 2)}\right) \tag{5-2.7}$$

where

$$z = 3m/2 \tag{5-2.8}$$

and "INT" means the integral part of the expression. The constant of proportionality is given by Eq. (5-2.9)

$$k = T_0(m) + 2\sum_{j=1}^{\frac{i_{min}}{2}} T_{2j}(m) \tag{5-2.9}$$

The first two Bessel functions are then:

$$J_0(m) = \frac{T_0(m)}{k} \tag{5-2.10}$$

$$J_1(m) = \frac{T_1(m)}{k} \tag{5-2.11}$$

With $J_o(m)$ and $J_1(m)$ and the recursion relationship given by Eq. (5-2.4), all the higher order Bessel functions may be evaluated.

# User Instructions

| | | | |
|---|---|---|---|
| BESSEL FUNCTIONS AND FM OR PM MODULATION SPECTRA | | | Output Format: 0: $J_0(m)$, $(1-J_0^2)/2$; 1: $J_1(m)$, $10\log\sum_2^\infty J_i^2$; 2 ...: $J_2(m)$..., $10\log\sum_3^\infty J_i^2$... |
| load m & start | print ? | | |

| STEP | INSTRUCTIONS | INPUT DATA/UNITS | KEYS | OUTPUT DATA/UNITS |
|---|---|---|---|---|
| 1 | Load both sides of program card | | | |
| 2 | Select print/no-print (R/S) option | | [B] | 0 (R/S) |
| | | | [B] | 1 (print) |
| | | | [B] | 0 (R/S) |
| | | | | ⋮ |
| 3 | Load modulation index and start | m | [A] | 0 |
| | | | | $J_0(m)$ |
| | | | | $(1-J_0^2)/2$ |
| | | | | 1 |
| | | | | $J_1(m)$ |
| | remaining power in higher sidebands in dB → | | | $10\log\sum_2^\infty J_i^2(m)$ |
| | | | | 2 |
| | | | | $J_2(m)$ |
| | | | | $10\log\sum_3^\infty J_i^2(m)$ |
| 4 | To stop analysis (print mode selected) | | [R/S] | |

Example 5-2.1

The 400 MHz carrier from a navigation satellite is phase modulated with a 400 Hz sinewave causing 60 degrees peak modulation. What is the modulation index, and what are the amplitudes of the PM sidebands?

The modulation index is the peak modulation expressed in radians:

$$m_p = 2\pi(60/360) = 1.0472 \text{ radians} \tag{5-2.12}$$

**HP-97 PRINTOUT FOR EXAMPLE 5-2.1**

```
      60.  D→R
           GSBA   load modulation index and start

       0.  ***    carrier
 0.744072  ***    Jo(m)
 0.223176  ***    (1 - Jo^2(m))/2

       1.  ***    first sideband, fc ± fm
 0.455031  ***    J1(m)
    -11.4  ***    relative power in higher sidebands in dB

       2.  ***    second sideband, fc ± 2fm
 0.124972  ***    J2(m)
    -26.4  ***

       3.  ***
 0.022329  ***    J3(m)
    -44.0  ***

       4.  ***
 0.002964  ***    J4(m)
    -63.5  ***

       5.  ***
 0.000313  ***    J5(m)
    -84.5  ***
```

Notice that 99% of the power is contained in the carrier and the first two sidebands (-26.4 dB = 0.23% remaining power in higher sidebands).

Example 5-2.2

Calculate the sideband structure of a commercial FM station transmitting a 15 kHz signal with 75 kHz peak carrier deviation. The modulation index is:

$$m_f = 75000/15000 = 5 \tag{5-2.13}$$

**HP-97 PRINTOUT FOR EXAMPLE 5-2.2**

| Printout | | Comment |
|---|---|---|
| 5. | GSBA | load $m_f$ & start |
| 0. | *** | carrier |
| -0.177597 | *** | $J_0(m)$ |
| 0.484230 | *** | $(1 - J_0^2(m))/2$ |
| 1. | *** | first sidebands |
| -0.327579 | *** | $J_1(m)$ |
| -1.1 | *** | power (dB) outside |
| 2. | *** | 2nd sideband pair |
| 0.046565 | *** | $J_2(m)$ |
| -1.1 | *** | |
| 3. | *** | |
| 0.364831 | *** | $J_3(m)$ |
| -3.0 | *** | |
| 4. | *** | |
| 0.391232 | *** | $J_4(m)$ |
| -7.4 | *** | |
| 5. | *** | |
| 0.261141 | *** | $J_5(m)$ |
| -13.6 | *** | |
| 6. | *** | |
| 0.131049 | *** | $J_6(m)$ |
| -21.8 | *** | |
| 7. | *** | |
| 0.053376 | *** | $J_7(m)$ |
| -31.2 | *** | |
| 8. | *** | |
| 0.018405 | *** | $J_8(m)$ |
| -41.7 | *** | |
| 9. | *** | |
| 0.005520 | *** | $J_9(m)$ |
| -53.3 | *** | |
| 10. | *** | $J_{10}(m)$ |
| 0.001468 | *** | |
| -65.7 | *** | |

Notice that one-half the power is contained in the first 3 sidebands and 99% of the power is contained in the first 6 sidebands.

The sideband structure for this example is shown in Fig. 5-2.1.

# Program Listing I

| | | |
|---|---|---|
| 001 | *LBLA | LOAD m AND START |
| 002 | STO0 | store m |
| 003 | F0? | |
| 004 | SPC | double space if flag 0 set |
| 005 | F0? | |
| 006 | SPC | |
| 007 | 1 | calculate minimum starting index plus two |
| 008 | . | |
| 009 | 5 | |
| 010 | x | |
| 011 | ENT↑ | |
| 012 | ENT↑ | |
| 013 | ENT↑ | |
| 014 | 1 | |
| 015 | 7 | |
| 016 | + | |
| 017 | x | |
| 018 | 2 | |
| 019 | ÷ | |
| 020 | 6 | |
| 021 | + | |
| 022 | X⇄Y | |
| 023 | 2 | |
| 024 | + | |
| 025 | ÷ | |
| 026 | INT | |
| 027 | ENT↑ | |
| 028 | + | |
| 029 | 2 | |
| 030 | + | |
| 031 | STOI | |
| 032 | 2 | |
| 033 | RCL0 | calculate and store 2/m |
| 034 | ÷ | |
| 035 | STOB | |
| 036 | CLX | initialize $T_{i+2}$ and $\Sigma\, T_{2j}(m)$ |
| 037 | STOE | |
| 038 | ST09 | |
| 039 | EEX | initialize $T_{i+1}$ |
| 040 | CHS | |
| 041 | 9 | |
| 042 | STOD | |

$$i_{min} = 2 \cdot int\left\{\frac{Z^2 + 17Z + 12}{2(Z+2)}\right\}$$

| | | |
|---|---|---|
| 043 | *LBL0 | calculate $T_1$ and $T_0$ |
| 044 | GSB1 | calculate and store $\Sigma\, T_{2j}$ |
| 045 | ST+9 | |
| 046 | CF2 | execute recursion formula |
| 047 | GSB1 | |
| 048 | F2? | test for loop exit |
| 049 | GT00 | |
| 050 | CLX | initialize i |
| 051 | STOI | |
| 052 | GSB7 | print i |
| 053 | RCLE | calculate and print $J_0(m)$: |
| 054 | RCL9 | |
| 055 | ENT↑ | |
| 056 | + | |
| 057 | RCLE | |
| 058 | - | |
| 059 | ST02 | |
| 060 | ÷ | |
| 061 | ST01 | |
| 062 | GSB6 | |
| 063 | X² | calculate, store and print: |
| 064 | CHS | |
| 065 | EEX | |
| 066 | + | |
| 067 | 2 | |
| 068 | ÷ | |
| 069 | ST05 | |
| 070 | GSB9 | |
| 071 | ISZI | increment and print i |
| 072 | GSB7 | |
| 073 | RCLD | calculate, store, and print $J_1(m)$: |
| 074 | CHS | |
| 075 | RCL2 | |
| 076 | ÷ | |
| 077 | ST02 | |
| 078 | GSB6 | |
| 079 | X² | calculate and print power in higher sidebands using Eq. (5-2.2) |
| 080 | CHS | |
| 081 | ST06 | |
| 082 | RCL5 | |
| 083 | + | |
| 084 | GSB8 | |

$$J_0(m) = \frac{T_0(m)}{k}$$

$$\frac{1 - J_0^2}{2}$$

$$J_1(m) = \frac{T_1(m)}{k}$$

## REGISTERS

| 0 | 1 | 2 | 3 | 4 | 5 | 6 | 7 | 8 | 9 |
|---|---|---|---|---|---|---|---|---|---|
| $m$ | $J_0(m), J_{n-1}(m)$ | $k,$ $J_1(m), J_n(m)$ | | | $(1-J_0^2)/2$ | $\sum_{i=1}^{n} J_i^2(m)$ | | | $\Sigma\, T_{2j}(m)$ |
| S0 | S1 | S2 | S3 | S4 | S5 | S6 | S7 | S8 | S9 |
| A $n$ | | B $2/m$ | | C | | D $T_i, T_{i+1}$ | | E $T_{i+1}, T_{i+2}$ | I $i, n$ |

# Program Listing II

| | | |
|---|---|---|
| 085 | *LBL2 | loop to calc Bessel function |
| 086 | RCL1 | $J_{n-2}$ |
| 087 | CHS | |
| 088 | RCL2 | $J_{n-1}$ |
| 089 | STO1 | |
| 090 | RCLB | $2/m$ |
| 091 | x | |
| 092 | RCLI | $n-1$ |
| 093 | x | |
| 094 | + | |
| 095 | STO2 | $J_n$ |
| 096 | ISZI | increment n |
| 097 | GSB7 | |
| 098 | RCL2 | recall and print $J_n(m)$ |
| 099 | GSB6 | |
| 100 | X² | calculate and print power |
| 101 | ST-6 | in higher sidebands |
| 102 | RCL6 | |
| 103 | RCL5 | |
| 104 | + | |
| 105 | GSB8 | |
| 106 | GTO2 | |

$$J_n(m) = \frac{2}{m}(n-1)J_{n-1}(m) - J_{n-2}(m)$$

| | | |
|---|---|---|
| 107 | *LBL1 | $T_1(m)$ recursion subroutine |
| 108 | DSZI | |
| 109 | SF2 | |
| 110 | RCLE | $T_{i+2}$ |
| 111 | CHS | |
| 112 | RCLI | $i+1$ |
| 113 | RCLB | $2/m$ |
| 114 | x | |
| 115 | RCLD | $T_{i+1}$ |
| 116 | STOE | |
| 117 | x | |
| 118 | + | |
| 119 | STOD | $T_i$ |
| 120 | RTN | |

$$T_i(m) = \frac{2}{m}(i-1)T_{i+1}(m) - T_{i+2}(m)$$

| | | |
|---|---|---|
| 121 | *LBL6 | print in dsp 6 subroutine |
| 122 | DSP6 | |
| 123 | GTO6 | |
| 124 | *LBL7 | print index in dsp 0 subr |
| 125 | DSP0 | |
| 126 | RCLI | |
| 127 | *LBL6 | |
| 128 | F0? | print and return if flag 0 |
| 129 | PRTX | is set, otherwise stop |
| 130 | F0? | |
| 131 | RTN | |
| 132 | R/S | stop and await R/S command |
| 133 | RTN | |

| | | |
|---|---|---|
| 134 | *LBL8 | calculate & prt 10·log subr |
| 135 | RCL5 | |
| 136 | ÷ | |
| 137 | LOG | |
| 138 | EEX | |
| 139 | 1 | |
| 140 | x | |
| 141 | DSP1 | set display format |
| 142 | RND | |
| 143 | *LBL9 | print and space if flag 0 |
| 144 | F0? | is set, otherwise stop |
| 145 | PRTX | |
| 146 | F0? | |
| 147 | SFC | |
| 148 | F0? | |
| 149 | RTN | |
| 150 | R/S | stop and await R/S |
| 151 | RTN | |
| 152 | GTO4 | program block |
| 153 | *LBLE | PRINT-R/S TOGGLE |
| 154 | F0? | jump if flag 0 is set |
| 155 | GTO3 | |
| 156 | SF0 | set flag 0 and place |
| 157 | EEX | a one in the display |
| 158 | GTO4 | goto R/S lockup routine |
| 159 | *LBL3 | |
| 160 | CF0 | clear flag 0 and place a |
| 161 | CLX | zero in the display |
| 162 | *LBL4 | R/S lockup routine |
| 163 | R/S | |
| 164 | GTO4 | |

Note:

Flag 0 should be set or reset prior to magnetic card recording to cause the program to initially be in the print or R/S mode respectively as users desire.

| LABELS | | | | |
|---|---|---|---|---|
| A load m and start | B R/S - pnnt toggle | C | D | E |
| a | b | c | d | e |
| 0 Jo & J1 calc loop | 1 Jo & J1 calc loop | 2 output calc loop | 3 R/S - print toggle | 4 R/S lockup |
| 5 | 6 dsp6, pnnt | 7 dsp0, prt I | 8 10log, dsp1 | 9 print & space |

| FLAGS | SET STATUS | | |
|---|---|---|---|
| 0 print | FLAGS | TRIG | DISP |
| 1 | ON OFF 0 □ □ | DEG | FIX ■ |
| 2 loop exit | 1 | GRAD | SCI |
| 3 | 2 ■ | RAD | ENG |
| | 3 | | n O |

## PROGRAM 5-3 CURVE FITTING BY THE CUBIC SPLINE METHOD.

Program Description and Equations Used

This program will fit a cubic spline interpolating curve through 2 to 9 equally spaced points [31]. The cubic spline represents the shape of the curve that would be generated if a clock spring were threaded through the data points. This technique is often used by draftsmen to draw a smooth curve through given points. The shape of such a curve looks natural, and is generally the shape one would attempt to draw by hand.

Let the ordinates, $y_i$, be given at $x_i = x_1 + (i-1)\cdot h$, where $i = 1,2, \ldots, n$, and h is the point spacing. Furthermore, let y(x) be the interpolating curve that is fitted to these points, and let $y_i'$ and $y_i''$ represent the first and second derivatives of y(x) evaluated at $x = x_i$. y(x) may be represented piecewise where the function and its first and second derivatives are matched at the boundaries. The first and last segments of the interpolating curve may have their first and second derivatives specified by the user. The individual cubic interpolating polynomial $f_i(x)$ can be expressed in terms of the ordinates $y_i$ and $y_{i+1}$, and either their first or second derivatives. Both forms will provide the same y(x), but the second derivative form requires simpler calculations.

Assume the third derivative, $y'''(x)$, is constant in each interval, h. This assumption implies that $y''(x)$ is linear in x, i.e.,

$$f_i''(x) = y_i'' \left\{1 - \frac{x - x_i}{h}\right\} + y_{i+1}''\left\{\frac{x - x_i}{h}\right\} \qquad (5\text{-}3.1)$$

Equation (5-3.1) is integrated twice with respect to x, and the constants of integration chosen so the boundary conditions are met to the extent that $f_i(x_i) = y_i$ $(i = 1,2,\ldots,n-1)$, and $f_{i-1}(x_i) - y_i$ $(i = 2,3, \ldots,n)$. The results of this integration yield:

$$f_i(x) = y_i(1 - (x-x_i)/h) + y_{i+1}(x-x_i)/h$$
$$- (h^2/6)(y_i'')\left[1 - (x-x_i)/h - (1 - (x-x_i)/h)^3\right]$$
$$- (h^2/6)(y_{i+1}'')\left[(x-x_i)/h - ((x-x_i)/h)^3\right] \qquad (5\text{-}3.2)$$

Since the first and second derivatives of the function must also match at the boundaries, Eq. (5-3.2) is differentiated with respect to x and evaluated at $x_i$:

$$f_i'(x_i) = (y_{i+1} - y_i)/h - (h/6)(2y_i'' + y_{i-1}'') \qquad (5\text{-}3.3)$$

and

$$f_{i-1}'(x_i) = (y_i - y_{i-1})/h + (h/6)(y_{i-1}'' + 2y_i'') \qquad (5\text{-}3.4)$$

Equating Eqs. (5-3.3) and (5-3.4) implying boundary match yields:

$$h \cdot y_{i-1}'' = 4h \cdot y_i'' + h \cdot y_{i-1}'' = (6/h)(y_{i-1} - 2y_i + y_{i+1}) \qquad (5\text{-}3.5)$$

where

$$i = 2, 3, \ldots, n-1.$$

This equation set represents n-2 equations in n unknowns. If the starting and ending second derivatives are specified ($y_1''$ and $y_n''$), then the number of unknowns is reduced by 2, and a solution exists to the equation set. This equation set may be expressed in matrix notation:

$$\begin{bmatrix} 4 & 1 & 0 & 0 & \cdots & 0 \\ 1 & 4 & 1 & 0 & \cdots & 0 \\ 0 & 1 & 4 & 1 & 0 \cdots & 0 \\ \cdot & & & & & \cdot \\ \cdot & & & & & \cdot \\ 0 & \cdots & 0 & 1 & 4 & 1 \\ 0 & 0 \cdots & 0 & 0 & 1 & 4 \end{bmatrix} \cdot \begin{bmatrix} y_2'' \\ y_3'' \\ \cdot \\ \cdot \\ \cdot \\ y_{n-2}'' \\ y_{n-1}'' \end{bmatrix} = \begin{bmatrix} (6/h^2)(y_1-2y_2+y_3) - y_1'' \\ (6/h^2)(y_2-2y_3+y_4) \\ (6/h^2)(y_3-2y_4+y_5) \\ \cdot \\ \cdot \\ \cdot \\ (6/h^2)(y_{n-2}-2y_{n-1}+y_n) - y_n'' \end{bmatrix} \qquad (5\text{-}3.6)$$

Because of the tridiagonal characteristic of Eq. (5-3.6), a Gauss reduction is an effective method for finding the values of the various second derivatives. Let,

$$d_i = (6/h^2)(y_{i-1} - 2y_i + y_{i+1}) \qquad (5\text{-}3.7)$$

and select $y_1'' = y_n'' = 0$ (another common selection is $y_1'' = y_2''/2$ and $y_n'' = y_{n-1}''/2$). If a recursion relationship is defined thus:

$$ {}_i4 = 1/(4 - {}_{i-1}4) \text{ for } i = \quad, 1, \ldots, n-1 \tag{5-3.8}$$

i.e.,

$$ {}_04 = 1/4 = 0.25 $$

$$ {}_14\ (1/3.75 = 0.266\bar{6} $$

$$ {}_24 = 1/(4 - {}_14) = .267857143 $$

$$\vdots$$

then the Gauss reduced matrix becomes:

$$
\begin{bmatrix}
(1/{}_04) & 1 & 0 & \cdots & 0 \\
0 & (1/{}_14) & 1 & \cdots & 0 \\
0 & 0 & (1/{}_24) & \cdots & 0 \\
\vdots & & & & \vdots \\
0 & \cdots & 0 & 0 & (1/{}_{n-3}4)
\end{bmatrix}
\cdot
\begin{bmatrix}
y_2'' \\ \vdots \\ \vdots \\ \vdots \\ y_{n-1}''
\end{bmatrix}
=
\begin{bmatrix}
d_2 \\
d_3 - {}_04 \cdot d_2 \\
d_4 - {}_14(d_3 - {}_04 \cdot d_2) \\
\vdots \\
\vdots
\end{bmatrix}
\tag{5-3.9}
$$

Equation (5-3.9) is evaluated by the program as shown by the flowchart in Fig. 5-3.1.

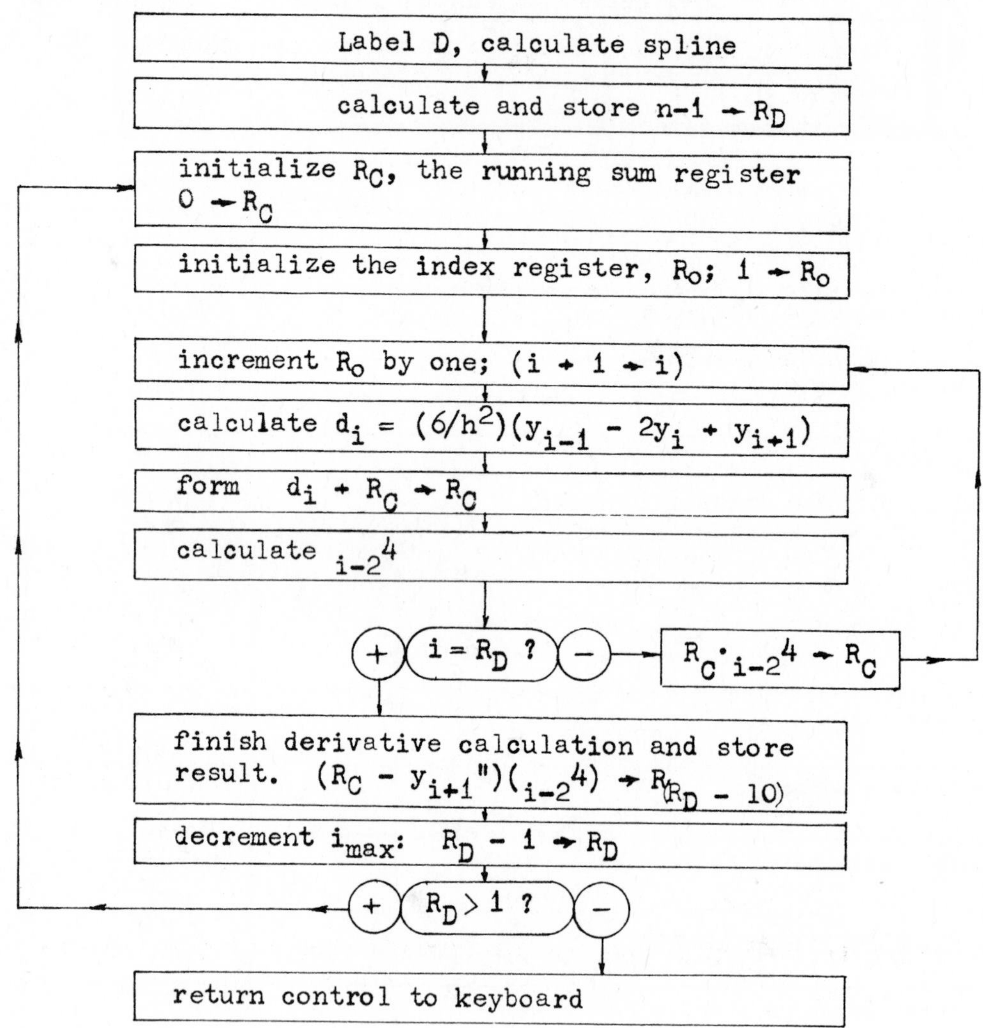


Figure 5-3.1 Flowchart of Gauss reduction algorithm.

# User Instructions

| CURVE FITTING BY THE CUBIC SPLINE METHOD | | | | |
|---|---|---|---|---|
| $\Delta x$ | start sweep | | | $x_1$ |
| number of points | load h | load data, $y_i$ | calculate spline | $x \rightarrow \hat{y}$ |

| STEP | INSTRUCTIONS | INPUT DATA/UNITS | KEYS | OUTPUT DATA/UNITS |
|---|---|---|---|---|
| 1 | Load both sides of magnetic card | | | |
| 2 | Load the number of data points | n | [A] | |
| 3 | Load h, the x interval | h | [B] | |
| 4 | Load y data | $y_1$ | [C] | 2 |
| | | $y_2$ | [C] | 3 |
| | | ⋮ | | |
| | | $y_{n-1}$ | [C] | n |
| | | $y_n$ | [C] | |
| 5 | Calculate spline | | [D] | |
| 6 | Load first x point | $x_1$ | [f] [E] | |
| 7 | Execute single point interpolation | x | [E] | $\hat{y}$ |
| | Step 7 may be used any number of times | | | |
| 8 | For linear sweep in x and corresponding interpolation of y: | | | |
| | a) Load sweep point spacing | $\Delta x$ | [f] [A] | |
| | b) Start sweep | | [f] [B] | $x_1$ |
| | | | | $\hat{y}_1$ |
| | | | | $x_1 + \Delta x$ |
| | | | | $\hat{y}$ |
| | | | | $x_1 + 2\Delta x$ |
| | | | | $\hat{y}$ |
| | | | | ⋮ |
| | | | | $x_1 + (n-1)\Delta x$ |
| | | | | $\hat{y}$ |

Example 5-3.1

Fit a cubic spline interpolating curve to the data given in Table 5-3.1. Provide the output sweep with x increments of 0.1.

Table 5-3.1 Data for cubic spline interpolation.

| x | 1 | 2 | 3 | 4 | 5 | 6 | 7 | 8 | 9 |
|---|---|---|---|---|---|---|---|---|---|
| y | 0 | 5 | 9 | 7 | 4 | 3 | 5 | 8 | 9 |

The HP-97 printer output is shown on the next page, and the interpolated output is plated in Fig. 5-3.2. The bold points represent the given data.

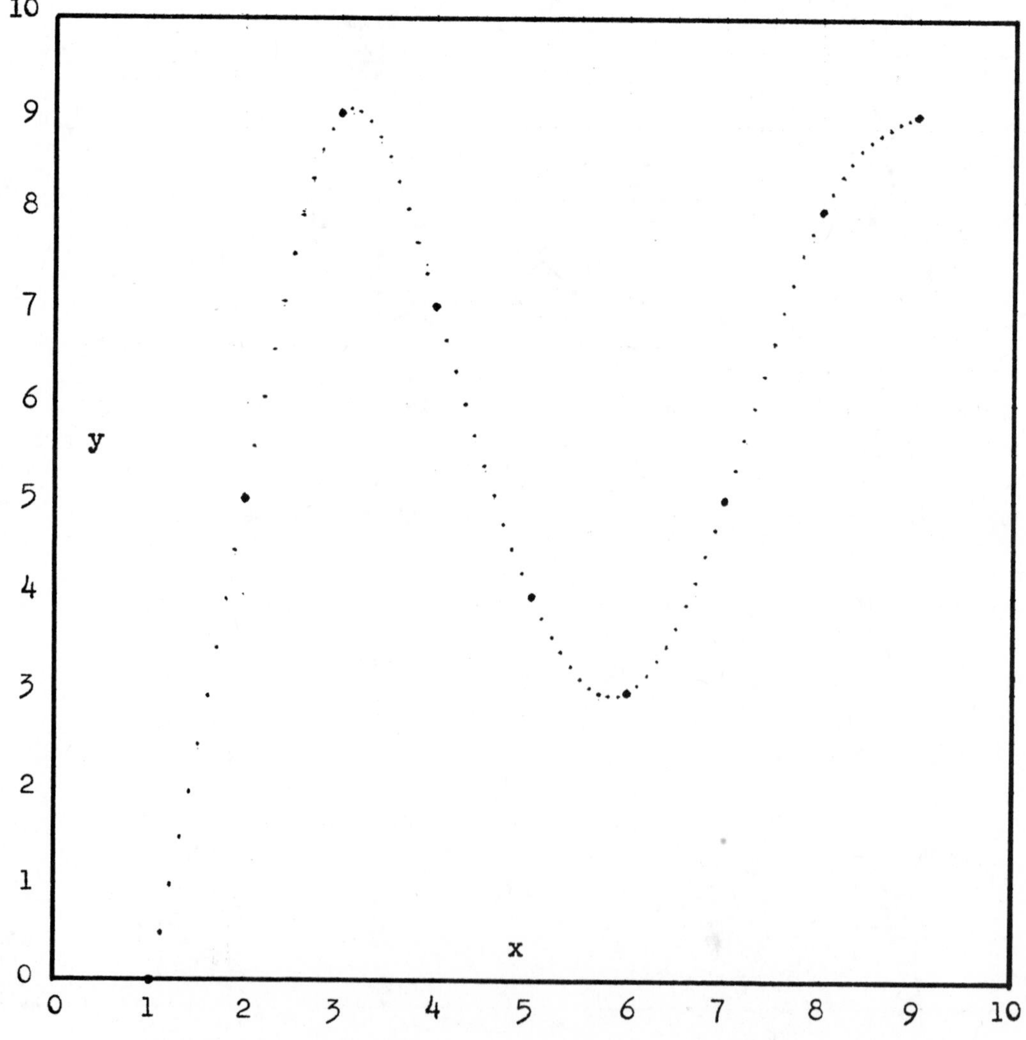


Figure 5-3.2 Cubic spline interpolation of given data.

## HP-97 PRINTOUT FOR EXAMPLE 5-3.1

### PROGRAM INPUT

```
9.000 GSBA   load number of data points

1.000 GSBB   load h, the x interval
             load y data points
0.000 GSBC   y1
5.000 GSBC   y2
9.000 GSBC   y3
7.000 GSBC   y4
4.000 GSBC   y5
3.000 GSBC   y6
5.000 GSBC   y7
8.000 GSBC   y8
9.000 GSBC   y9

      GSBD   execute spline calculation

1.000 GSBe   load x1, the first x point
 .100 GSBa   load  x interval for output sweep
      GSBb   start sweep
```

### PROGRAM OUTPUT

```
1.000  2.000  3.000  4.000  5.000  6.000  7.000  8.000    9.000
0.000  5.000  9.000  7.000  4.000  3.000  5.000  8.000    9.000

1.100  2.100  3.100  4.100  5.100  6.100  7.100  8.100 x
0.486  5.530  9.059  6.658  3.783  3.073  5.315  8.196 y

1.200  2.200  3.200  4.200  5.200  6.200  7.200  8.200
0.974  6.058  9.035  6.320  3.587  3.180  5.639  8.361

1.300  2.300  3.300  4.300  5.300  6.300  7.300  8.300
1.463  6.574  8.938  5.990  3.415  3.318  5.968  8.500

1.400  2.400  3.400  4.400  5.400  6.400  7.400  8.400
1.954  7.067  8.776  5.667  3.267  3.487  6.297  8.615

1.500  2.500  3.500  4.500  5.500  6.500  7.500  8.500
2.449  7.529  8.560  5.354  3.147  3.683  6.621  8.710

1.600  2.600  3.600  4.600  5.600  6.600  7.600  8.600
2.947  7.948  8.300  5.053  3.054  3.905  6.935  8.788

1.700  2.700  3.700  4.700  5.700  6.700  7.700  8.700
3.451  8.315  8.004  4.766  2.992  4.149  7.235  8.853

1.800  2.800  3.800  4.800  5.800  6.800  7.800  8.800
3.961  8.619  7.682  4.493  2.961  4.415  7.515  8.907

1.900  2.900  3.900  4.900  5.900  6.900  7.900  8.900
4.477  8.851  7.344  4.237  2.963  4.699  7.772  8.955
```

# Program Listing I

| | | |
|---|---|---|
| 001 | *LBLA | LOAD # OF DATA POINTS |
| 002 | STOA | store number of data points |
| 003 | EEX | set $y_n''$ to zero |
| 004 | 1 | |
| 005 | + | |
| 006 | STOI | |
| 007 | CLX | |
| 008 | STOi | |
| 009 | EEX | initialize index register |
| 010 | STOI | |
| 011 | RTN | |
| 012 | *LBLB | LOAD h, THE x POINT |
| 013 | STOB | SEPARATION |
| 014 | RTN | |
| 015 | *LBLC | LOAD y DATA |
| 016 | STOi | store y data |
| 017 | ISZI | increment storage index |
| 018 | RCLI | recall index to display |
| 019 | RTN | return control to keyboard |
| 020 | *LBLD | CALCULATE SPLINE |
| 021 | RCLA | calculate and store n-1 |
| 022 | EEX | |
| 023 | 1 | |
| 024 | STOD | |
| 025 | *LBL0 | spline outer loop |
| 026 | CLX | initialize running sum |
| 027 | STOC | |
| 028 | EEX | initialize index register |
| 029 | STO0 | |
| 030 | *LBL1 | spline inner loop |
| 031 | EEX | increment and store index |
| 032 | ST+0 | |
| 033 | RCL0 | |
| 034 | EEX | |
| 035 | + | |
| 036 | STOI | |
| 037 | RCLi | calculate $d_i$ |
| 038 | DSZI | |
| 039 | RCLi | |
| 040 | ENT↑ | |
| 041 | + | |
| 042 | – | |
| 043 | DSZI | |
| 044 | RCLi | |
| 045 | + | $d_i = \frac{6}{h^2}(y_{i-1} - 2y_i + y_{i+1})$ |
| 046 | 6 | |
| 047 | x | |
| 048 | RCLB | |
| 049 | X² | |
| 050 | ÷ | |
| 051 | RCLC | |
| 052 | – | $d_i - R_C \rightarrow R_C$ |
| 053 | STOC | |
| 054 | RCL0 | |
| 055 | 2 | |

| | | |
|---|---|---|
| 056 | – | jump if i-2 is zero |
| 057 | X=0? | |
| 058 | GTO2 | |
| 059 | STOI | initialize I |
| 060 | 4 | |
| 061 | *LBL3 | calculate $(_{i-2}4)^{-1}$ |
| 062 | 1/X | |
| 063 | CHS | |
| 064 | 4 | |
| 065 | + | |
| 066 | DSZI | |
| 067 | GTO3 | |
| 068 | GTO4 | |
| 069 | *LBL2 | initialize $(_{i-2}4)^{-1}$ |
| 070 | 4 | |
| 071 | *LBL4 | store $_{i-2}4$ |
| 072 | 1/X | |
| 073 | STOE | |
| 074 | RCL0 | |
| 075 | RCLD | |
| 076 | X=Y? | test for loop exit |
| 077 | GTO2 | |
| 078 | RCLC | |
| 079 | RCLE | |
| 080 | x | $R_C \cdot {}_{i-2}4 \rightarrow R_C$ |
| 081 | STOC | |
| 082 | GTO1 | goto inner loop start |
| 083 | *LBL2 | finish derivative calc |
| 084 | RCL0 | |
| 085 | 1 | calculate and store n+10 |
| 086 | 1 | as storage index for |
| 087 | + | derivative |
| 088 | STOI | |
| 089 | RCLC | |
| 090 | RCLi | calculate and store |
| 091 | – | second derivative, $y_1''$ |
| 092 | RCLE | |
| 093 | x | |
| 094 | RCLD | |
| 095 | EEX | |
| 096 | 1 | |
| 097 | + | $(R_C - y_{i+1}'')({}_{i-2}4) \rightarrow R_{R_D+10}$ |
| 098 | STOI | |
| 099 | R↓ | |
| 100 | STOi | |
| 101 | EEX | |
| 102 | RCLD | decrement $i_{max}$ |
| 103 | EEX | |
| 104 | – | |
| 105 | STOD | |
| 106 | X>Y? | test for loop exit |
| 107 | GTO0 | |
| 108 | SPC | |
| 109 | GTO8 | |

## REGISTERS

| 0 Δx for sweep & scratchpad | 1 $Y_1$ | 2 $Y_2$ | 3 $Y_3$ | 4 $Y_4$ | 5 $Y_5$ | 6 $Y_6$ | 7 $Y_7$ | 8 $Y_8$ | 9 $Y_9$ |
|---|---|---|---|---|---|---|---|---|---|
| S0 $X_1$ | S1 current x for sweep | S2 $Y_2'$ | S3 $Y_3''$ | S4 $Y_4''$ | S5 $Y_5'$ | S6 $Y_6''$ | S7 $Y_7''$ | S8 $Y_8''$ | S9 $Y_9'' = 0$ |
| A n | B h | C scratchpad | D index | E scratchpad | I index | | | | |

# Program Listing II

| Step | Key | Comment |
|---|---|---|
| 110 | *LBLe | LOAD FIRST x POINT ($x_1$ value) |
| 111 | P⇄S | store data |
| 112 | STO0 | |
| 113 | P⇄S | |
| 114 | GTO8 | |
| 115 | *LBLE | CALCULATE y ESTIMATE, $x \to \hat{y}$ |
| 116 | P⇄S | |
| 117 | RCL0 | $x - x_1$ |
| 118 | P⇄S | |
| 119 | - | |
| 120 | RCLB | $\frac{x - x_1}{h} \to R_C$ |
| 121 | ÷ | |
| 122 | STOC | |
| 123 | INT | $1 + \mathrm{INT}\left(\frac{x - x_1}{h}\right) \to R_I$ |
| 124 | EEX | |
| 125 | + | |
| 126 | STOI | |
| 127 | RCLC | $\frac{x_{i+1} - x}{h} \to R_D$ |
| 128 | - | |
| 129 | STOD | |
| 130 | RCLi | $\frac{x_{i+1} - x}{h} y_i$ |
| 131 | × | |
| 132 | RCLC | $\frac{x - x_i}{h} \to R_E$ |
| 133 | RCLI | |
| 134 | EEX | |
| 135 | - | |
| 136 | - | |
| 137 | STOE | |
| 138 | ISZI | $(y_{i+1}) \frac{x - x_i}{h} + (y_i) \frac{x_{i+1} - x}{h} \to R_C$ |
| 139 | RCLi | |
| 140 | × | |
| 141 | + | |
| 142 | STOC | |
| 143 | RCLE | $\frac{x - x_i}{h} - \left\{\frac{x - x_i}{h}\right\}^3$ |
| 144 | RCLE | |
| 145 | 3 | |
| 146 | $Y^x$ | |
| 147 | - | |
| 148 | RCLI | $(y''_{i+1}) \left\{ \frac{x - x_i}{h} - \left(\frac{x - x_i}{h}\right)^3 \right\}$ |
| 149 | EEX | |
| 150 | 1 | |
| 151 | + | |
| 152 | STOI | |
| 153 | R↓ | |
| 154 | RCLi | |
| 155 | × | |
| 156 | RCLD | $\frac{x_{i+1} - x}{h} - \left(\frac{x_{i+1} - x}{h}\right)^3$ |
| 157 | RCLD | |
| 158 | 3 | |
| 159 | $Y^x$ | |
| 160 | - | |
| 161 | DSZI | $(y''_i) \left\{ \frac{x_{i+1} - x}{h} - \left(\frac{x_{i+1} - x}{h}\right)^3 \right\}$ |
| 162 | RCLi | |
| 163 | × | |
| 164 | RCLI | |
| 165 | 1 | generate 0 if first interval otherwise generate 1 (frees up one register) |
| 166 | 1 | |
| 167 | - | |
| 168 | ENT↑ | |
| 169 | X≠0? | |
| 170 | ÷ | |
| 171 | X=0? | |
| 172 | R↓ | |
| 173 | × | compute running sum |
| 174 | + | |
| 175 | 6 | calculate $\frac{h^2}{6}$ |
| 176 | ÷ | |
| 177 | RCLB | |
| 178 | $X^2$ | |
| 179 | × | |
| 180 | CHS | finish running sum calc |
| 181 | RCLC | |
| 182 | + | |
| 183 | PRTX | print y estimate (may be R/S statement) |
| 184 | SPC | |
| 185 | GTO8 | goto R/S lockup |
| 186 | *LBLa | LOAD x FOR SWEEP |
| 187 | STO0 | |
| 188 | GTO8 | goto R/S lockup |
| 189 | *LBLb | START LINEAR SWEEP |
| 190 | SPC | |
| 191 | RCL0 | initialize registers |
| 192 | CHS | |
| 193 | P⇄S | |
| 194 | RCL0 | |
| 195 | + | |
| 196 | STO1 | |
| 197 | P⇄S | |
| 198 | *LBL9 | increment x value |
| 199 | RCL0 | |
| 200 | P⇄S | |
| 201 | ST+1 | |
| 202 | RCL1 | calculate largest x value |
| 203 | RCL0 | |
| 204 | P⇄S | |
| 205 | RCLA | |
| 206 | EEX | |
| 207 | - | |
| 208 | RCLB | |
| 209 | × | |
| 210 | + | |
| 211 | X⇄Y | test for loop exit |
| 212 | X>Y? | |
| 213 | GTO8 | (may be R/S statement) |
| 214 | PRTX | print current x value |
| 215 | GSBE | calc and print y estimate |
| 216 | GTO9 | |
| 217 | *LBL8 | R/S lockup subroutine |
| 218 | RTN | |
| 219 | GTO8 | |

**LABELS**

| | | | | |
|---|---|---|---|---|
| A load nbr of data points | B load h, the x interval | C load y data | D calculate spline | E $x \to \hat{y}$ |
| a load Δx for sweep | b start sweep | c | d | e load first x point |
| 0 loop destination | 1 loop destination | 2 initialize ;4 & scratch | 3 calculate ;4 | 4 gauss reduction |
| 5 | 6 | 7 | 8 | 9 loop destination |

**FLAGS**

| |
|---|
| 0 |
| 1 |
| 2 |
| 3 |

**SET STATUS**

| FLAGS (ON OFF) | TRIG | DISP |
|---|---|---|
| | USERS CHOICE | |
| 0 | DEG | FIX |
| 1 | GRAD | SCI |
| 2 | RAD | ENG |
| 3 | | n_____ |

## PROGRAM 5-4 LEAST SQUARES CURVE-FIT TO AN EXPONENTIAL FUNCTION.

Program Description and Equations Used

Many processes both in electrical engineering and in physics have behavior that can be described by an exponential law, e.g., the voltage across a capacitor being charged through a series resistor asymptotically approaches the charging voltage in an exponential manner. When time constants are to be determined from oscilloscope photographs of these phenomena, only part of the entire waveform is available, and some error is introduced transferring the photograph data into numbers. If these errors are random, then a least squares fit can help remove them.

The equation form for the exponential function is given by:

$$x = a(1 - e^{-bt}) \tag{5-4.1}$$

Let $d_i$ represent the difference between the measured point, $x_i$, and the exponential curve as shown by Fig. 5-4.1 and Eq. (5-4.2).

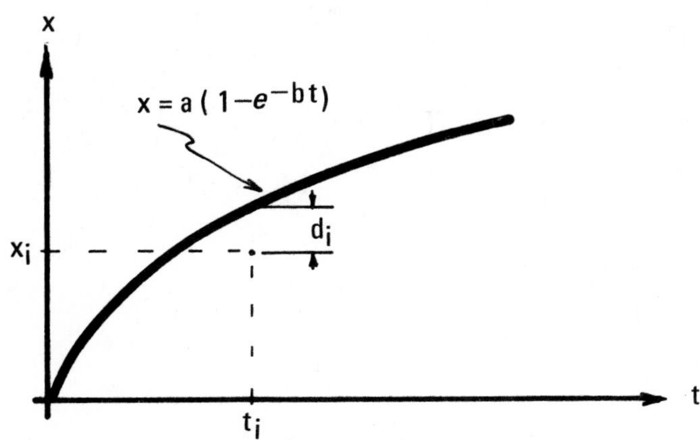


Figure 5-4.1 Exponential function.

$$d_i = x_i - a(1 - e^{-bt_i}) \tag{5-4.2}$$

The object of a least squares fit is to minimize the sum of the squares of the deviations as implied by Eq. (5-4.3).

$$S = \sum_i d_i^2 = \sum_i (x_i - a(1 - e^{-bt_i}))^2 \tag{5-4.3}$$

The minimum can be found by setting the derivatives of Eq. (5-4.3) to zero, i.e.:

$$\frac{\partial S}{\partial a} = 0 \quad , \quad \frac{\partial S}{\partial b} = 0$$

or

$$\frac{\partial S}{\partial a} = -2\sum_i \left\{ x_i - a(1 - e^{-bt_i}) \right\} \cdot (1 - e^{-bt_i}) = 0 \tag{5-4.4}$$

$$\frac{\partial S}{\partial b} = -2a\sum_i \left\{ x_i - a(1 - e^{-bt_i}) \right\} \cdot (t_i \cdot e^{-bt_i}) = 0 \tag{5-4.5}$$

Equations (5-4.4) and (5-4.5) represent 2 equations in 2 unknowns, a and b. Equation (5-4.4) is solved for a as shown in Eq. (5-4.6) and substituted into Eq. (5-4.5) to yield Eq. (5-4.7)

$$a = \frac{\sum_i x_i (1 - e^{-bt_i})}{\sum_i (1 - e^{-bt_i})^2} \tag{5-4.6}$$

$$g(b) \overset{\Delta}{\equiv} \sum_i x_i \cdot t_i e^{-bt_i} \sum_i (1 - e^{-bt_i})^2 -$$

$$\sum_i x_i (1 - e^{-bt_i}) \sum_i t_i \cdot e^{-bt_i}(1 - e^{-bt_i}) = 0 \tag{5-4.7}$$

To simplify things, the various sums in Eq. (5-4.7) are assigned numbers in the same respective order as they appear.

$$g(b) = \Sigma_1 \, \Sigma_2 - \Sigma_3 \, \Sigma_4 = 0 \tag{5-4.8}$$

The object is to find b so g(b) = 0. Since Eq. (5-4.7) is nonlinear, an iterative solution is employed to find b. Wegstein's method [29] is used and is flowcharted in Fig. 5-4.2. This method is chosen because no derivatives are required and the convergence is very rapid.

Basically Wegstein's method is Esperti's method where one curve is a straight line (see Program 2-9 for Esperti's method). Equation (5-4.8) will have to be modified as Wegstein's method finds the solution to f(b) = b, therefore, let f(b) be as shown in Eq. (5-4.9)

$$f(b) = \frac{\Sigma_3 \ \Sigma_4}{\Sigma_2} - \Sigma_1 + b \qquad (5.4\text{-}9)$$

The reason for this form is to try and avoid the small difference between big numbers problem. It is advisable to keep b between 0.1 and 10 for best accuracy. If the data is on a microsecond time scale, enter the time as though it were in seconds and denormalize b after it has been calculated. Likewise for millisecond data.

After b has been found by iteration, a is obtained by using Eq. (5-4.6), which can be expressed in terms of the numbered sums:

$$a = \frac{\Sigma_3}{\Sigma_2} \qquad (5.4\text{-}10)$$

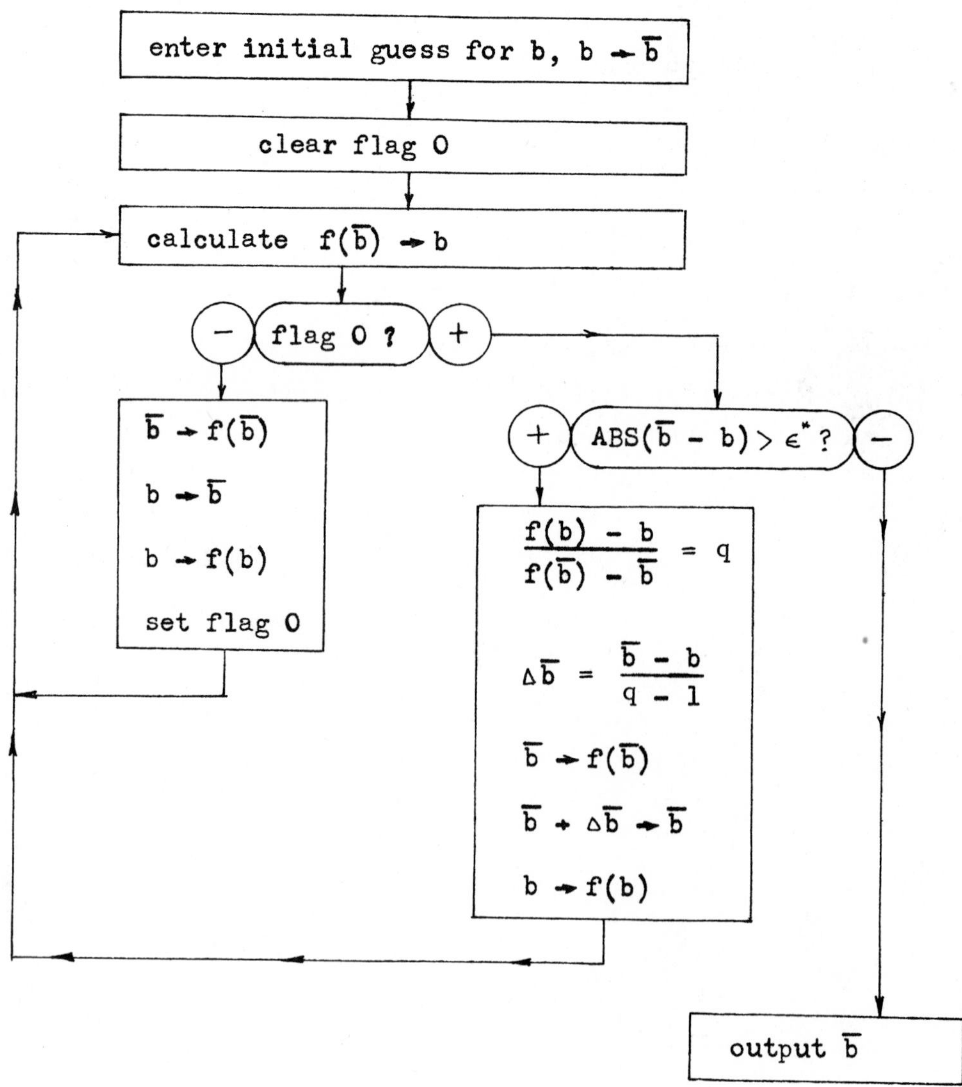


Figure 5-4.2 Flowchart for Wegstein's method.

---

* For this program, $\varepsilon$ is chosen at $10^{-6} \cdot \bar{b}$

# User Instructions

| LEAST SQUARES FIT TO AN EXPONENTIAL FUNCTION | | | | |
|---|---|---|---|---|
| compare input & least squares | | | print ? | clear input mode |
| $t_{start} \uparrow t_{stop} \uparrow \Delta t$ | data entry | estimate b | start least squares fit | $t \rightarrow \hat{x}$ |

| STEP | INSTRUCTIONS | INPUT DATA/UNITS | KEYS | OUTPUT DATA/UNITS |
|---|---|---|---|---|
| 1 | Load both sides of magnetic card | | | |
| 2 | Select print or R/S option (toggle) | | f D | 0 (R/S) |
| | | | f D | 1 (print) |
| | | | f D | 0 (R/S) |
| | | | | ⋮ |
| 3 | Load $t_{start}$, $t_{stop}$, and t | | | |
| | a) time of first data point | $t_{start}$ | ENT | |
| | b) time of last data point | $t_{stop}$ | ENT | |
| | c) data point spacing | $\Delta t$ | A | |
| 4 | Load data (10 points maximum) | | B | $t_{start}$ |
| | load x at $t_{start}$ | $x_1$ | B | $t_{start} + \Delta t$ |
| | load x at $t_{start} + \Delta t$ | $x_2$ | B | $t_{start} + 2\Delta t$ |
| | ⋮ | ⋮ | | ⋮ |
| | | | | $t_{stop}$ |
| | load last data point | $x_n$ | B | $t_{stop} + \Delta t$ |
| 5 | Load estimate for b $(0.1 \leq b \leq 10)$ | $b_{estimate}$ | C | |
| | To examine the currently stored value for b, key "C" without numeric entry. The input mode can be cleared with keys "f", "E". | | | |
| 6 | To clear input mode (used with step 5) | | f E | |
| 7 | Start least squared fit | | D | a |
| | | | | b |
| | | | | space |
| 8 | Optional; compare input data with least squares fit data | | f A | $t_{start}$ |
| | | | | $x_1$ |
| | | | | $\hat{x}_1$ |
| | | | | ⋮ |
| 9 | Calculate linear estimate for x given t | t | E | $\hat{x}$ |

Example 5-4.1

A constant voltage was suddenly connected to the field of a large dc traction motor, and an oscilloscope photograph taken of the current. The field time constant is needed to determine loop stability in the overall motor control loop. Table 5-4.1 shows the field current as read from the oscilloscope photo as a function of time.

Table 5-4.1 Motor field current vs. time.

| time, seconds | 0.1 | 0.2 | 0.3 | 0.4 | 0.5 | 0.6 | 0.7 |
|---|---|---|---|---|---|---|---|
| current, amps | 10 | 18 | 26 | 33 | 39 | 45 | 50 |

Assuming the field to be a simple series LR circuit, find the time constant and the asymptotic field current.

**HP-97 PRINTOUT FOR EXAMPLE 5-4.1**

```
 .100 ENT↑  load starting time
 .700 ENT↑  load stopping time
 .100 GSBA  load time increment

      GSBB  setup for data entry
10.000 GSBB load I(.1)
18.000 GSBB load I(.2)
26.000 GSBB load I(.3)
33.000 GSBB load I(.4)
39.000 GSBB load I(.5)
45.000 GSBB load I(.6)
50.000 GSBB load I(.7)

 1.000 GSBC load b estimate

      GSBD  start least sqrs fit

95.569 ***  a (asymptotic current)
 1.057 ***  b (1/τ, time constant)

τ = 1/1.057 = 0.9461 seconds
```

```
         GSBa  compare input & least squares
 0.100   ***   time
10.000   ***   I(t) input
 9.587   ***   I(t) from least sqs

 0.200   ***
18.000   ***
18.211   ***

 0.300   ***
26.000   ***
25.971   ***

 0.400   ***
33.000   ***
32.953   ***

 0.500   ***
39.000   ***
39.234   ***

 0.600   ***
45.000   ***
44.885   ***

 0.700   ***
50.000   ***
49.969   ***
```

# Program Listing I

| Step | Key | Comments |
|---|---|---|
| 001 | *LBLA | LOAD $t_{start}$, $t_{stop}$, $\Delta t$ |
| 002 | STO0 | store entries |
| 003 | R↓ | |
| 004 | STOD | |
| 005 | R↓ | |
| 006 | STOC | |
| 007 | GTOe | goto CF3 and R/S lockup subr |
| 008 | *LBLC | LOAD b ESTIMATE |
| 009 | F3? | if numeric input, store data |
| 010 | STOB | |
| 011 | RCLB | recall b estimate to display |
| 012 | GTO6 | goto R/S lockup subroutine |
| 013 | *LBLD | START LEAST SQUARES CALC |
| 014 | CF0 | indicate first time thru loop |
| 015 | *LBL9 | outer loop start |
| 016 | CLX | initialize sums: |
| 017 | STO1 | |
| 018 | STO2 | $0 \rightarrow \Sigma_1 \rightarrow \Sigma_2 \rightarrow \Sigma_3 \rightarrow \Sigma_4$ |
| 019 | STO3 | |
| 020 | STO4 | |
| 021 | 9 | initialize index |
| 022 | STOI | |
| 023 | RCLC | |
| 024 | RCL0 | initialize time register |
| 025 | - | |
| 026 | STO5 | |
| 027 | *LBL0 | summation loop start |
| 028 | ISZI | increment index |
| 029 | RCL0 | increment time |
| 030 | ST+5 | |
| 031 | RCLD | |
| 032 | RCL5 | test for loop exit |
| 033 | X>Y? | |
| 034 | GTO3 | |
| 035 | RCLB | |
| 036 | x | |
| 037 | CHS | $e^{-bt_i}$ |
| 038 | $e^x$ | |
| 039 | STO6 | |
| 040 | CHS | |
| 041 | EEX | $1 - e^{-bt_i}$ |
| 042 | + | |
| 043 | STO7 | |
| 044 | $X^2$ | $\Sigma_2 + (1-e^{-bt_i})^2 \rightarrow \Sigma_2$ |
| 045 | ST+2 | |
| 046 | RCLi | |
| 047 | RCL5 | |
| 048 | x | $\Sigma_1 + x_i \cdot t_i \cdot e^{-bt_i} \rightarrow \Sigma_1$ |
| 049 | RCL6 | |
| 050 | x | |
| 051 | ST+1 | |
| 052 | RCLi | |
| 053 | RCL7 | |
| 054 | x | $\Sigma_3 + x_i(1-e^{-bt_i}) \rightarrow \Sigma_3$ |
| 055 | ST+3 | |
| 056 | RCL5 | |
| 057 | RCL6 | |
| 058 | x | |
| 059 | RCL7 | $\Sigma_4 + t_i e^{-bt_i}(1-e^{-bt_i}) \rightarrow \Sigma_4$ |
| 060 | x | |
| 061 | ST+4 | |
| 062 | GTO0 | goto summation loop start |
| 063 | *LBL3 | start Wegstein solution |
| 064 | RCL3 | |
| 065 | RCL4 | |
| 066 | x | |
| 067 | RCL2 | $\frac{\Sigma_3 \cdot \Sigma_4}{\Sigma_2} - \Sigma_1$ |
| 068 | ÷ | |
| 069 | RCL1 | |
| 070 | - | |
| 071 | F0? | jump if not first time through loop |
| 072 | GTO1 | |
| 073 | RCLB | $\bar{b} \rightarrow f(\bar{b})$ |
| 074 | STOE | |
| 075 | + | |
| 076 | STO8 | $b \rightarrow \bar{b} \rightarrow f(b)$ |
| 077 | STOB | |
| 078 | STO9 | |
| 079 | SF0 | not first time thru loop |
| 080 | GTO9 | goto outer loop start |
| 081 | *LBL1 | jump destination |
| 082 | RCLB | |
| 083 | + | $f(\bar{b}) \rightarrow b$ |
| 084 | STO8 | |
| 085 | RCLB | |
| 086 | - | |
| 087 | RCLB | $\text{ABS}\left\{\frac{\bar{b} - b}{\bar{b}}\right\}$ |
| 088 | ÷ | |
| 089 | ABS | |
| 090 | EEX | |
| 091 | CHS | |
| 092 | 6 | test for loop exit |
| 093 | X>Y? | |
| 094 | GTO2 | |
| 095 | RCL9 | |
| 096 | RCL8 | |
| 097 | - | |
| 098 | RCLE | $q = \frac{f(b) - b}{f(\bar{b}) - \bar{b}}$ |
| 099 | RCLB | |
| 100 | - | |
| 101 | ÷ | |
| 102 | STOA | |
| 103 | RCLB | $\bar{b} \rightarrow f(\bar{b})$ |
| 104 | STOE | |
| 105 | RCL8 | |
| 106 | - | |
| 107 | RCLA | $\Delta\bar{b} = \frac{\bar{b} - b}{q - 1}$ |
| 108 | EEX | |
| 109 | - | |
| 110 | ÷ | |

**REGISTERS**

| 0 | 1 | 2 | 3 | 4 | 5 | 6 | 7 | 8 | 9 |
|---|---|---|---|---|---|---|---|---|---|
| $\Delta t$ | $\Sigma_1$ | $\Sigma_2$ | $\Sigma_3$ | $\Sigma_4$ | $t_i$ | $e^{-bt_i}$ | $1-e^{-bt_i}$ | b | f(b) |

| S0 | S1 | S2 | S3 | S4 | S5 | S6 | S7 | S8 | S9 |
|---|---|---|---|---|---|---|---|---|---|
| $x_0$ | $x_1$ | $x_2$ | $x_3$ | $x_4$ | $x_5$ | $x_6$ | $x_7$ | $x_8$ | $x_9$ |

| A | B | C | D | E | I |
|---|---|---|---|---|---|
| a, q | $\bar{b}$ | $t_{start}$ | $t_{stop}$ | $f(\bar{b})$ | index |

# Program Listing II

| Step | Key | Comments |
|---|---|---|
| 111 | RCLB | $\bar{b} + \Delta\bar{b} \rightarrow \bar{b}$ |
| 112 | + | |
| 113 | STOB | |
| 114 | RCL8 | $b \rightarrow f(b)$ |
| 115 | STO9 | |
| 116 | GTO9 | goto outer loop start |
| 117 | *LBL2 | Wegstein output |
| 118 | F1? | space if print mode set |
| 119 | SPC | |
| 120 | RCL3 | $a = \frac{\Sigma_3}{\Sigma_2}$ |
| 121 | RCL2 | |
| 122 | ÷ | |
| 123 | STOA | |
| 124 | GSB5 | gosub print or R/S subr |
| 125 | RCLB | recall b |
| 126 | GTO4 | goto print and space subr |
| 127 | *LBLc | COMPARE INPUT & LEAST SQRS |
| 128 | RCLC | setup time register and index register |
| 129 | RCL0 | |
| 130 | - | |
| 131 | STO5 | |
| 132 | 9 | |
| 133 | STOI | |
| 134 | *LBL7 | loop start |
| 135 | ISZI | increment register index |
| 136 | RCL0 | increment time index |
| 137 | ST+5 | |
| 138 | RCLI | test for loop exit |
| 139 | RCL5 | |
| 140 | X>Y? | |
| 141 | GTO6 | |
| 142 | GSB5 | output time |
| 143 | RCLi | recall and output input |
| 144 | GSB5 | |
| 145 | R↓ | calculate and output least squares estimate |
| 146 | GSBE | |
| 147 | GTO7 | goto loop start |
| 148 | *LBLE | LEAST SQUARES ESTIMATE |
| 149 | RCLB | calculate: $\hat{x} = a(1 - e^{-bt})$ |
| 150 | x | |
| 151 | CHS | |
| 152 | $e^x$ | |
| 153 | CHS | |
| 154 | 1 | |
| 155 | + | |
| 156 | RCLA | |
| 157 | x | |
| 158 | *LBL4 | print and space subroutine |
| 159 | GSB5 | gosub print or R/S subr |
| 160 | F1? | space if print mode set |
| 161 | SPC | |
| 162 | GTOe | goto CF3 and R/S lockup subr |

| Step | Key | Comments |
|---|---|---|
| 163 | *LBL5 | print or R/S subroutine |
| 164 | F1? | |
| 165 | PRTX | print and return if flag 1 is set, otherwise |
| 166 | F1? | |
| 167 | RTN | |
| 168 | R/S | stop and await R/S command |
| 169 | RTN | |
| 170 | *LBLB | LOAD DATA |
| 171 | 9 | initialize register index |
| 172 | STOI | |
| 173 | *LBL8 | data storage loop start |
| 174 | ISZI | increment register index |
| 175 | RCLI | calculate time for x(t) |
| 176 | EEX | |
| 177 | 1 | |
| 178 | - | |
| 179 | RCL0 | |
| 180 | x | |
| 181 | RCLC | |
| 182 | + | |
| 183 | R/S | display time & await entry |
| 184 | *LBLB | data storage |
| 185 | STOi | store data |
| 186 | GTO8 | goto loop start |
| 187 | *LBLe | CF3 and R/S lockup subr |
| 188 | CF3 | clear flag 3 |
| 189 | *LBL6 | R/S lockup subroutine |
| 190 | RTN | |
| 191 | GTO6 | |
| 192 | *LBLd | PRINT OR R/S TOGGLE |
| 193 | CF1 | clear flag 1 for R/S mode |
| 194 | CLX | and place a zero in display |
| 195 | RTN | return control to keyboard |
| 196 | *LBLd | toggle continued |
| 197 | SF1 | set flag 1 for print mode |
| 198 | EEX | and place a one in display |
| 199 | RTN | return control to keyboard |

Note:
Flag one should be set or reset prior to magnetic card recording depending whether the user wishes the program to normally come up in print or R/S mode after the card read. Step 2 can be skipped in this instance.

| LABELS | | | | | FLAGS |
|---|---|---|---|---|---|
| A load times | B load data | C load b estimate | D start least squares | E $t \rightarrow \hat{x}$ | 0 first time thru Wegstein |
| a output summary | b | c | d print toggle | e clear flag 3 | 1 print |
| 0 form sums | 1 Wegstein major loop | 2 Wegstein output | 3 Wegstein start | 4 print | 2 |
| 5 print or R/S | 6 R/S lock | 7 summary loop | 8 data input loop | 9 outer least squares loop | 3 |

| SET STATUS | | | | |
|---|---|---|---|---|
| FLAGS | ON | OFF | TRIG | DISP |
| | | | USERS CHOICE | |
| 0 | | ■ | DEG | FIX |
| 1 | □ | □ | GRAD | SCI |
| 2 | | | RAD | ENG |
| 3 | | | | n ____ |

# LIST OF ABBREVIATIONS

*LIST OF ABBREVIATIONS*

| | |
|---|---|
| alternative or alternate | alt |
| amplifier | amp |
| approximately | approx |
| arithmetic | arith |
| attenuation | atten |
| | |
| bandpass | BP |
| bandstop | BS |
| bandwidth | BW |
| branch | br |
| Butterworth | Buttr |
| | |
| calculation or calculate | calc |
| capacitor | cap |
| Chebyshev | Cheb |
| circuit | ckt |
| clear | clr |
| coaxial | coax |
| coefficient | coef |
| complex | cmplx |
| conductance | cond |
| conjugate | conj |
| conversion | conv |
| co-ordinates | co-ords |
| | |
| decibel | dB |
| decibel ripple | dBR |
| denominator | den |
| denormalization | denorm |
| density | dens |
| destination | dest |
| diameter | diam |
| display | dsp |
| distance | dist |
| | |
| electrical | elect |
| elements | elts |
| enter | ent |
| Equation(s) | Eq(s). |
| equivalent | equiv |
| evaluation | eval |
| even part of (·) | Ev(·) |
| execute | exec |
| | |
| feedback | fdbk |
| Figure | Fig. |
| format | fmt |
| frequency | freq |
| function | fcn |
| | |
| go substitute | go sub |
| go to | gto |
| | |
| henry | h |
| highpass | HP |
| | |
| imaginary | imag |
| increment | incr |
| initialize | init |
| input/output | I/O |
| integral | int |

| | |
|---|---|
| label | lbl |
| level | lvl |
| linear | lin |
| loop | lp |
| lowpass | LP |
| | |
| matrix | mat |
| minimum | min |
| multiplication | mult |
| | |
| negative | neg |
| numerator | num |
| | |
| odd part of(·) | Odd(·) |
| order | ord |
| | |
| page | pg, p |
| parameters | params |
| peak | pk |
| polynomial | poly |
| preamplifier | preamp |
| primary | pri |
| print | prt |
| program | pgm |
| | |
| recall | rcl |
| rectangular | rect |
| reflection | refl |
| register(s) | reg(s) |
| required | reqd |

| | |
|---|---|
| resistance | resist |
| return | rtn |
| review | revu |
| root sum square | RSS |
| root mean square | RMS |
| | |
| secondary | sec |
| section | sect |
| solution | soln |
| space | spc |
| specification(s) | spec(s) |
| square | sq |
| starting frequency | $f_{st}$ |
| stopping frequency | $f_{sp}$ |
| store | sto |
| subroutine | subr |
| sweep | swp |
| | |
| temporary | temp |
| terminating, terminal, or termination | term |
| through | thru |
| toggle | tog |
| total | tot |
| transform | xfm |
| transformer | xfmr |
| transistor | xstr |
| transmitter | xmit |
| transmission | xmsn |
| trigonometric | trig |

# BIBLIOGRAPHY

1 Abramowitz, M., and Stegun, I., Handbook of Mathematical Functions with Formulas, Graphs, and Mathematical Tables, AMS #55, Nat'l Bur. of Stds., Washington, D.C., 1972.

2 Amstutz, P., "Elliptic Approximation and Elliptic Filter Design on Small Computers," IEEE Trans. on Ckts. and Systems, vol CAS-25, Dec. 1978, pp. 1001-1011.

3 Antoniou, A., "Realization of Gyrators Using Operational Amplifiers and Their Use in RC Active Network Synthesis," Proc IRE (London), vol 116, Nov. 1969, pp. 1838-1850.

4 Bashkow, T.R., ch 26 in Mathematical Methods for Digital Computers, Eds. Ralston, A., and Wilf, H., Wiley, N.Y., 1960.

5 Belevitch, V., "Tchebycheff Filter and Amplifier Networks," Wireless Engineer, vol 29, April 1952, pp. 106-110.

6 Bell, W., Matrices for Scientists and Engineers, Van Nostrand Reinhold, N.Y., 1975.

7 Bennett, W.R., "Transmission Network," U.S. Pat 1,849,656, 15 March 1932.

8 Blinchikoff, H., and Zverev, A., Filtering in the Time and Frequency Domains, Wiley-Interscience, N.Y., 1976.

9 Bodway, G.E., "Circuit Design and Characterization of Transistors by Means of Three Port Scattering Parameters," Microwave Journal, vol 11, no. 15, May 1968.

10 Bruton, L., "Network Transfer Functions Using the Concept of Frequency Dependent Negative Resistance," IEEE Trans. on Ckt. Theory, vol CT-16, Aug. 1969, pp. 406-408.

11 Bunet, P., "On the Self Inductance of Circular Cylindrical Coils," Revue General de l'Electricite, Tome xliii, no. 4, Jan. 1938, p. 99.

12 Byrd, P., and Friedman, M., Handbook of Elliptic Integrals for Engineers and Physicists, Springer-Verlag, N.Y., 1954.

13 Callendar, M., "Q of Solenoid Coils," Wireless Engineer, vol 24, June 1947, p. 185.

14 Carnahan, B., Luther, H., Wilkes, J., Applied Numerical Methods, Wiley, N.Y., 1969.

15 Carson, R.S., High Frequency Amplifiers, Wiley-Interscience, N.Y., 1975.

16 Cohn, S., "Direct Coupled Resonator Filters," Proc. IRE, vol 40, Feb. 1957, pp. 186-196.

17 Daniels, R., Approximation Methods for Electronic Filter Design, McGraw-Hill, N.Y., 1974.

18 Darlington, S., "Simple Algorithms for Elliptic Filters and a Generalization Thereof," session 3 of IEEE Int. Symp. on Ckts. and Systems Proc., May 1978, pp. 35-39.

19 Daryanani, G., Principles of Active Network Synthesis and Design, Wiley, N.Y., 1976.

20 Deliyannis, T., "High-Q Factor Circuit with Reduced Sensitivity," Electronic Letters, vol 4, Dec. 1968, p. 577.

21 Dishal, M., "Design of Dissapative Band-Pass Filters Producing Exact Amplitude-Frequency Characteristics," Proc IRE, vol 37, Sept. 1949, pp. 1050-1069.

22 Doyle, W., "Lossless Butterworth Ladder Networks Operating Between Arbitrary Resistances," J. Math. Phys., vol 37, no. 1, April 1958, pp. 29-37.

23 Fano, R.M., "Theoretical Limitations on the Broadband Matching of Arbitrary Impedances," J. Franklin Inst., vol 249, Jan. 1950, pp. 57-83, and vol 249, Feb. 1950, pp. 139-154.

24 Froehner, W.H., "Quick Amplifier Design with Scattering Parameters," Electronics Magazine, 16 Oct. 1967.

25 Fortescue, Standard Handbook for Electrical Engineers, McGraw-Hill, N.Y., 1922 5th ed., p. 413.

26 Geffe, P.R., Designers Guide to Active Filters, Cahners Pub. Co., Boston, MA., 1974.

27 Geffe, P.R., "Microcomputer-Aided Filter Design," IEEE Ckts. and Systems Magazine, vol 1, no. 1, Jan. 1979, pp. 5-8.

28 Green, E., Amplitude-Frequency Characteristics of Ladder Networks, Marconi's Wireless Telegraph Co. Ltd., Essex, England, 1954.

29 Grove, W.E., Brief Numerical Methods, Prentice-Hall, Englewood Cliffs, N.J., 1966.

30 Grover, F.W., Inductance Calculations, Working Formulas and Tables, D. Van Nostrand, N.Y., 1946.

31 Hamming, R., Numerical Methods for Scientists and Engineers, second edition, McGraw-Hill, N.Y., 1973.

32 Hewlett-Packard Application note #95, "S parameters . . . . Circuit Analysis and Design," Hewlett-Packard Co., Sept. 1968.

33 Hewlett-Packard Journal, "S Parameters for Faster, More Accurate Network Design," vol 18, no. 6, Feb. 1967, p. 3-7.

34 Kawakami, M., "Nomographs for Butterworth and Chebyshev Filters," IEEE Trans. on Ckt. Theory, vol CT-10, June 1963, pp. 288-289.

35 Kerwin, W., and Heulsman, L., "Design of High Performance Active RC Band Pass Filters," 1966 IEEE Int. Conv. Rec., vol 14, part 10, pp. 74-80.

36 Lee, R., Electronic Transformers and Circuits, second ed., Wiley, N.Y., 1961.

37 Matthaei, G., "Synthesis of Tchebycheff Impedance-Matching Networks, Filters, and Interstages," IRE Trans. on Ckt. Theory, vol CT-3, Sept. 1956, pp. 163-172.

38 Moschytz, G., "Second-Order Pole-Zero Selection for n-th Order Minimum Sensitivity Networks," IEEE Trans. on Ckt. Theory, vol CT-17, Nov. 1970, pp. 527-534.

39 Norton, E.L., "Constant Resistance Networks with Applications to Filter Groups," BSTJ, vol 16, April 1937, pp. 178-193.

40 Orchard, H.J., "Formulae for Ladder Filters," Wireless Engineer, vol 30, Jan. 1953, pp. 3-5.

41 Orchard, H.J., "Computation of Elliptic Functions of Rational Fractions of a Quarter period," IRE Trans. on Ckt. Theory, vol CT-5, Dec. 1958, pp. 352-355.

42 Orchard, H.J., and Sheahan, D.F., "Inductorless Bandpass Filters," IEEE Jour. of Solid State Ckts., vol SC-5, June 1970, pp. 108-118.

43 Potter, J., and Fich, S., Theory of Networks and Lines, Prentice-Hall, Englewood Cliffs, N.J., 1963.

44 Reference Data for Electrical Engineers, Fourth Ed., ITT Corp., New York, N.Y., 1959.

45 Saal, R., and Ulbrich, E., "On the Design of Filters by Synthesis," IRE Trans. on Ckt. Theory, vol CT-5, Dec. 1958, pp. 284-327.

46 Skwirzynski, J., and Zdunek, J., "Note on Calculation of Ladder Coefficients for Symmetrical and Inverse Impedance Filters on a Digital Computer," IRE Trans. on Ckt. Theory, vol CT-5, Dec. 1958, pp. 328-332.

47 Still, A.F., Elements of Electrical Design, McGraw-Hill, N.Y., 1932.

48 Szentirmai, G., "Synthesis of Multiple Feedback Active Filters," BSTJ, vol 52, April 1973, pp. 527-555.

49 Temes, G., and La Patra, J., Circuit Synthesis and Design, McGraw-Hill, N.Y., 1977.

50 Temes, G., and Mitra, S., Eds., Modern Filter Theory and Design, Wiley-Interscience, N.Y., 1973.

51 Takahasi, H., "On the Ladder-Type Filter Network with Tchebycheff Response," J. Inst. Elec. Commun. Engrs., Japan, vol 34, Feb 1951, (In Japanese).

52 Terman, F.E., Radio Engineers Handbook, McGraw-Hill, N.Y., 1943.

53 Weinberg, L., Network Analysis and Synthesis, McGraw-Hill, N.Y., 1962.

54 Weinberg, L., and Slepian, P., "Takahasi's Results on Techbycheff and Butterworth Ladder Networks," IRE Trans. on Ckt. Theory, vol CT-7, June 1960, pp. 88-101.

55 Wheeler, H.A., "Simple Inductance Formulas for Radio Coils," Proc IRE, vol 16, no. 10, Oct 1928, p. 1398 and subsequent discussion in vol 17, no. 3, March 1929, p. 580.

56 White, D.R.J., A Handbook on Electrical Filters, Don White Consultants, Gainesville, VA., 1963.

57 Yengst, W.C., Procedures of Modern Network Synthesis, Macmillan, N.Y., 1964.

58 Zverev, A.I., Handbook of Filter Synthesis, Wiley, N.Y., 1967.

# INDEX

# INDEX